September 24–26, 2014
Paris, France

I0054881

Association for Computing Machinery

Advancing Computing as a Science & Profession

ICN'14
Proceedings of the First International Conference on Information-Centric Networking

Sponsored by:
ACM SIGCOMM

Supported by:
Ericsson, Verisign, Huawei, Cisco, PARC, Orange, & Panasonic

Association for Computing Machinery

Advancing Computing as a Science & Profession

The Association for Computing Machinery
2 Penn Plaza, Suite 701
New York, New York 10121-0701

Notice to Past Authors of ACM-Published Articles
ACM intends to create a complete electronic archive of all articles and/or other material previously published by ACM. If you have written a work that has been previously published by ACM in any journal or conference proceedings prior to 1978, or any SIG Newsletter at any time, and you do NOT want this work to appear in the ACM Digital Library, please inform permissions@acm.org, stating the title of the work, the author(s), and where and when published.

ISBN: 978-1-4503-3206-4

Additional copies may be ordered prepaid from:

ACM Order Department
PO Box 30777
New York, NY 10087-0777, USA

Phone: 1-800-342-6626 (USA and Canada)
+1-212-626-0500 (Global)
Fax: +1-212-944-1318
E-mail: acmhelp@acm.org
Hours of Operation: 8:30 am – 4:30 pm ET

Printed in the USA

General Chairs' Welcome Message

Welcome to ACM ICN 2014 in Paris!

This is the first event of hopefully a long series of successful conferences on Information-Centric Networking (ICN) that has fostered growing interest in the networking community. After a few workshops, notably at ACM SIGCOMM and IEEE INFOCOM in the past three years, the time has come for a dedicated venue to see the light. ICN'14 is organized as an intense three days event: the main conference is preceded by three tutorials.

Holding ICN 2014 in Paris was only made possible through the generous financial support from our many (industrial) supporters of the conference. We are particularly indebted to Ericsson and Verisign, whose extremely substantial financial contributions provided an early, solid basis for organizing a successful event. It would simply not have been possible to organize ICN in Paris without them. It is our privilege to acknowledge the generous support from Huawei (Gold sponsor), Cisco Systems and PARC (Silver sponsors), Orange and Panasonic (Bronze sponsors).

To encourage conference participation to this first event, the conference Organizing Committee has been working to provide as much travel support as possible. For this first year we have two kinds of travel support: the ACM SIGCOMM GeoDiversity travel grants and the ICN'14 student travel grants. The GeoDiversity grants are available for attendees in their early career from under-represented countries, based on need, distance to the conference venue, and impact of their attendance in increasing the diversity of conference participation. ICN'14 student travel grants are available for students for whom registration fees have been kept at the lowest possible level.

The organization of ICN has required the involvement and dedication of a large and enthusiastic group of volunteers. The conference would be impossible to organize without them. We want to highlight the commitment of our program committee chairs, Dirk Kutscher, Luca Muscariello and Lixia Zhang, who assembled an outstanding technical program committee that reviewed submitted papers and selected the final program. We are very grateful to the ICN steering committee led by George Polyzos: they devoted an enormous amount of time to make the overall organization a success. Huge thanks goes to all those who ensured specific roles such as the treasurer, Ignacio Solis, tutorial chair, Cedric Westphal, publication chair, Paulo Mendes, sponsorship chair, Börje Ohlman and publicity and registration chair, George Xylomenos. We also would like to thank Jörg Ott for sharing his experience about the organization of such event throughout all stages of preparation of the conference. We gratefully acknowledge the help of ACM and Sheridan Inc. with the preparation of the conference proceedings.

We hope that you will find ICN 2014 to be a stimulating and scientifically enriching experience. Any comment or proposal for improvement will be highly welcome and instrumental for the success of next events. We are sure that you will find the time to enjoy the intemporal and truly awing city of Paris you have the privilege to admire from its historical center.

ICN 2015 preparation is underway. ICN 2015 will be held in San Francisco, September 2015. You can find more information about the second edition of the ACM ICN conference at http://conferences.sigcomm.org/acm-icn/2015

Giovanna Carofiglio   **Luca Muscariello**

Bell Labs, Alcatel-Lucent   *Orange Labs, France*

Technical Program Committee Chairs' Welcome

Welcome to the first ACM Information Centric Networking (ICN) conference! After a successful series of ACM SIGCOMM ICN and IEEE INFOCOM NOMEN workshops showing a growing interest from the broader networking community, we initiated this new series of ACM conferences starting in 2014 and are very happy to welcome you to the first ACM ICN conference in Paris.

Nothing is as powerful as an idea whose time has come (Victor Hugo) and ICN with its concepts of providing access to named data as a first-order network service, of providing object- instead of connection-based security, and of enabling ubiquitous data replication and requestor anonymity is one of those ideas. Efforts in different international research projects have explored ICN benefits for different application areas such as mobile communications, video streaming and distribution, Internet of Things, and data-center communications. ICN is recognized as a major networking research area that relates to established networking research topics such as naming, network security, transport mechanisms, and caching, and has fueled relevant new research work in all of those areas.

Starting a new conference series is always associated with challenges. We are particularly happy to report that ICN'14 attracted 97 paper submissions, out of which the TPC selected 17 papers for oral presentation and 8 short papers for poster presentations. We are also delighted by the number of received demo proposals and accepted 10 demonstrations for the program. As the first conference in this new series, the program also includes a full day of tutorials to make the audience familiar with the fundamental concepts as well as the frontier of efforts in this new area. The program is completed by an industrial panel discussion with renowned experts from the networking community. We hope that ICN'14 will contribute to further advancing the state of the art in networking in general and in ICN in particular.

ICN'14 would not have been possible without the help from many individuals from the ICN community that supported us for setting up the conference. First, we would like to express our sincere gratitude to the members of the Technical Program Committee (TPC) whose efforts ensured the high quality of the program through a diligent review process. Every paper received three or more reviews, a considerable workload for the TPC given the number of submissions. In addition, we held an in-person TPC meeting to finalize the program and would especially thank everyone who was able attend. We would also like to thank Jeff Burke, Van Jacobson, Paul Mockapetris, Sara Oueslati and Paul Polakos for accepting our invitation to a panel discussion and Allison Mankin for organizing and chairing it. We hope that you will find the program and the discussions at the conference interesting and are looking forward to a successful series of future ICN conferences.

ICN 2015 preparation is underway. ICN 2015 will be held in San Francisco, September 2015. You can find more information about the second edition of the ACM ICN conference at http://conferences.sigcomm.org/acm-icn/2015

Dirk Kutscher
NEC Laboratories Europe

Luca Muscariello
Orange Labs, France

Lixia Zhang
UCLA, USA

Table of Contents

Demonstrations

ICN 2014 Conference Organization

General Chairs: Giovanna Carofiglio *(Alcatel-Lucent Bell Labs, France)*
Luca Muscariello *(Orange Labs, France)*

Program Chairs: Lixia Zhang *(UCLA, USA)*
Dirk Kutscher *(NEC Laboratories Europe, Germany)*
Luca Muscariello *(Orange Labs, France)*

Proceedings Chair: Paulo Mendes *(COPELABS / Lusófona University, Portugal)*

Sponsorship Chair: Börje Ohlman *(Ericsson Research, Sweden)*

Tutorial Chair: Cedric Westphal *(Huawei Innovation Center, USA)*

Publicity & Registration Chair: George Xylomenos *(AUEB, Greece)*

Treasurer Chair: Ignacio Solis *(PARC, USA)*

Steering Committee Chair: George C. Polyzos *(AUEB, Greece)*

Steering Committee: Giovanna Carofiglio *(Alcatel-Lucent Bell Labs, France)*
Van Jacobson *(Google, USA)*
Dirk Kutscher *(NEC Laboratories Europe, Germany)*
Giacomo Morabito *(University of Cantania, Italy)*
Luca Muscariello *(Orange Labs, France)*
Börje Ohlman *(Ericsson Research, Sweden)*
Jörg Ott *(Aalto University, Finland)*
Ignacio Solis *(PARC, USA)*
Lixia Zhang *(UCLA, USA)*
Bengt Alghren *(SICS, Sweden)*
Mayutan Arumaithurai *(Universität Göttingen, Germany)*

Program Committee: Tohru Asami *(University of Tokyo, Japan)*
Nicola Blefari-Melazzi *(University of Rome Tor Vergata)*
Jeff Burke *(UCLA, USA)*
Antonio Carzaniga *(University of Lugano, Switzerland)*
Patrick Crowley *(Washington University in St. Louis, USA)*
Lars Eggert *(NetApp, Germany)*
Christian Esteve Rothenberg *(University of Campinas, Brazil)*
Kevin Fall *(Carnegie Mellon University, USA)*
Stephen Farrell *(Trinity College Dublin, Ireland)*
Serge Fdida *(UPMC, France)*
Volker Hilt *(Bell Labs/Alcatel-Lucent, Germany)*
Myeong-Wuk Jang *(Samsung Electronics, Korea)*

Silver Supporters: CISCO parc A Xerox Company

Bronze Supporters: orange™ Panasonic

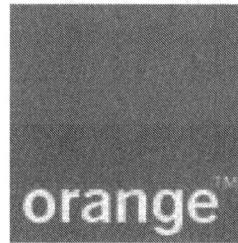

intel

An Introduction to NDN and its Software Architecture

Alexander Afanasyev
UCLA
alexander.afanasyev@ucla.edu

Jeff Burke
UCLA
jburke@remap.ucla.edu

Patrick Crowley
Washington University in St. Louis
pcrowley@wustl.edu

Steve DiBenedetto
Colorado State University
dibenede@cs.colostate.edu

Jeff Thompson
UCLA
jefft0@remap.ucla.edu

Beichuan Zhang
University of Arizona
bzhang@cs.arizona.edu

Lixia Zhang
UCLA
lixia@cs.ucla.edu

MOTIVATION

The NDN project investigates Jacobson's proposed evolution from today's host-centric network architecture (IP) to a data-centric network architecture (NDN). This conceptually simple shift has far-reaching implications in how we design, develop, deploy and use networks and applications. The NDN design and development has attracted significant attention from the networking community. To facilitate broader participation in addressing NDN research and development challenges, this tutorial will describe the vision of this new architecture and its basic components and operations.

Categories and Subject Descriptors

C.2 [Computer Systems Organization]: COMPUTER-COMMUNICATION NETWORKS; C.2.1 [Network Architecture and Design]: Packet-switching networks—Internet

Keywords

Network architecture; Named Data Networking

Tutorial Outline

- The NDN architecture and applications.

- Library support for application development.

- The NDN routing protocol and forwarding daemon (NFD).

- The NDN testbed: current operations, monitoring tools and procedures for participation.

- Open challenges in NDN design and development, to share with the community and invite efforts in addressing them.

- Illustrations of installation and use of the NDN platform and simulator, as well as HOWTOs to assist in further development.

ICN'14, September 24–26, 2014, Paris, France.
ACM 978-1-4503-3206-4/14/09.
http://dx.doi.org/10.1145/2660129.2666709

About the Speakers

Dr. Alexander Afanasyev is a postdoctoral scholar at the University of California, Los Angeles. His research interests include network systems and protocols, future Internet architectures such as Named Data Networking, and network security mobile systems, multimedia systems, and peer-to-peer environments.

Jeff Burke is a Co-PI and application team lead for the Named Data Networking research project. He is Asst. Dean for Technology and Innovation at the UCLA School of Theater, Film and Television (TFT), where he co-founded REMAP, a joint center of TFT and the Henry Samueli School of Engineering and Applied Science, which uses a mixture of research, artistic production, and community engagement to investigate the interrelationships among culture, community, and technology.

Patrick Crowley is an Associate Professor in the Department of Computer Science & Engineering at Washington University in St. Louis. He is also founder and CTO of Observable Networks, an early-stage network security company. His research interests are in computer and network systems architecture, with a current focus on information-centric networking, programmable network systems design, and the invention of superior network monitoring and security techniques.

Steve DiBenedetto is a PhD student at Colorado State University. His research interests include ICN security and inter-domain routing policies. Steve is a NDN Forwarding Daemon (NFD) developer and previously co-developed ANDaNA, a Tor-like onion routing application for CCNx.

Jeff Thompson has been a staff software engineer at UCLA REMAP for the Name Data Networking (NDN) project since 2013. As an undergraduate, he studied computer science and electrical engineering at MIT. His Masters work was in microrobotics and automation at the UC Berkeley Biomimetic Millisystems Lab.

Dr. Beichuan Zhang is an Associate Professor at the Computer Science Department, the University of Arizona. His research interest is in Internet routing architectures and protocols. He has been working on Named Data Networking, green networking, network topology, and overlay multicast.

Lixia Zhang is a professor in the Computer Science Department of UCLA. In the past she served on the Internet Architecture Board, the editorial board of the IEEE/ACM Transactions on Networking, vice chair of ACM SIGCOMM, and co-chair of the Routing Research Group under IRTF. Her research interests include the Internet architecture and protocol designs.

CCN 1.0

Nacho (Ignacio) Solis
Palo Alto Research Center
Ignacio.Solis@parc.com

Glenn Scott
Palo Alto Research Center
Glenn.Scott@parc.com

Glenn Edens
Palo Alto Research Center
Glenn.Edens@parc.com

MOTIVATION

CCN has become the groundwork of much of the ICN work in the past few years. Since the project started in 2007 and with the release of the CCNx distribution in 2009 there has been a growing interest in the CCN architecture. CCN has continued to advance as we've learned from simulation, research, experimentation and prototyping. CCN 1.0 is the evolution of CCN. This tutorial will cover the base networking protocol. It will go over the changes in the protocol and the reasons for the changes as well as a description of the new techniques and constructs used. Finally, as time permits we will go over the status of the current software suite.

Categories and Subject Descriptors

C.2.2 Network Protocols – Network Layer Protocols
C.2.m Computer Communication Networks - Miscellaneous

Keywords

CCN, Content-Centric Networking, Information Centric Networks, Content Based Networking, Named Data Networking

Tutorial Outline

➢ **Introduction to CCN 1.0.**

CCN Project update.

CCN 1.0 core protocol.

Procol changes since CCN 0.x.

CCN 1.0 auxiliary protocols and constructs.

Packet formats.

The CCNx 1.0 software suite.

➢ **PARC Utility Libraries.**

CCNx Forwarder.

CCNx Transport Stack and APIs.

Hello world.

About the Speakers

Nacho (Ignacio) Solis is a Principal Scientist at PARC where he works as a protocol architect for CCN. He has worked on ICN for the past 10 years in numerous environments including sensor networks, ad-hoc networks and disruptive environments. Nacho has led projects developing ICN network protocols as well as the ICN applications. He was been the PI and advisor on various DARPA programs where he incorporated ICN technologies to military networks. For the past 18 months Nacho has been working on the CCN 1.0 spec with the rest of the team.

Glenn Scott is a Principal Engineer at PARC where he acts as lead software architect for CCN. In his previous role as Senior Research Scientist at Sun (Oracle) Glenn led projects focused on iv distributed systems, filesystems and networking. He has a track record of moving computer science research into commercial product teams. Glenn is currently focusing on the implementation, design, testing, documentation and performance of the CCN 1.0 software suite.

Glenn Edens is Vice President at PARC, leading the Network and Distributed Systems group. He is in charge of CCN commercial efforts and industrial partnerships. In the past Glenn served CEO of Range Networks, SVP and Director of Sun Labs, Chief of Technology Strategy and Chief Scientist at HP; and President of AT&T Strategic Ventures. Glenn co-founded Grid Systems Corporation, the company that developed the first laptop computer.

ICN'14, September 24–26, 2014, Paris, France.
ACM 978-1-4503-3206-4/14/09.
http://dx.doi.org/10.1145/2660129.2666710

ICN Privacy and Name based Security

Nikos Fotiou
Mobile Multimedia Laboratory
Department of Informatics
School of Information Sciences and Technology
Athens University of Economics and Business
11362 Athens, Greece
fotiou@aueb.gr

George C. Polyzos
Mobile Multimedia Laboratory
Department of Informatics
School of Information Sciences and Technology
Athens University of Economics and Business
11362 Athens, Greece
polyzos@aueb.gr

MOTIVATION

The purpose of this tutorial is twofold: to discuss ICN privacy requirements and related solutions, as well as to acquaint participants with the latest advances in name-based security. ICN architectures are often criticized for exposing user preferences. Privacy issues in ICN cannot be investigated using traditional approaches since they differ significantly from the conventional end-to-end architectures. The tutorial will introduce a comprehensive threat model and it will present a methodology for evaluating privacy risks in ICN architectures. Moreover, it will detail related privacy preserving solutions.

Many ICN research efforts advocate that a departure from the traditional PKI model is desirable. To this end, they propose security solutions that are applied at the content level using the content name as a security primitive. Although (content) name-based security solutions can be built using traditional cryptographic solutions, recent advances in cryptography create opportunities for new, exciting applications. The tutorial will discuss the advantages of name-based security solutions and it will introduce Identity-Based cryptography and its applications in ICN.

Categories and Subject Descriptors
C.2.1 **[Computer-Communication Networks]**: Network Architecture and Design

Keywords
Homomorphic encryption; Identity-based encryption; Mix Networks

Tutorial Outline

Section 1: ICN Privacy

    a.   ICN Privacy requirements [4].

    b.   ICN Privacy solutions
        i. based on entropy [1]
        ii. based on mix-networks [2], and
        iii. based on homomorphic encryption [3].

    c.   Privacy analysis of ICN architectures [4].

Section 2: Name-based security

    d.   Self-certified names [5].

    e.   Identity-based encryption [6].

REFERENCES

[1]   S. Arianfar, T. Koponen, B. Raghavan, and S. Shenker. On preserving privacy in content-oriented networks. In *Proceedings of the ACM SIGCOMM workshop on Information-centric networking*, 2011.

[2]   S. DiBenedetto, P. Gasti, G. Tsudik, and E. Uzun. ANDaNA: Anonymous named data networking application. In *Proceedings of 19th Annual Network & Distributed System Security Symposium* (NDSS), 2012.

[3]   N. Fotiou, D. Trossen, G.F. Marias, A. Kostopoulos, and G.C. Polyzos. Enhancing information lookup privacy through homomorphic encryption. *Security and Communication Networks* (DOI: 10.1002/sec.910, published online on Nov. 15, 2013).

[4]   N. Fotiou, S. Arianfar, M. Särelä, and G.C. Polyzos. A Framework for Privacy Analysis of ICN Architectures. In *Privacy Technologies and Policy*, Springer Lecture Notes in Computer Science, 8450:117-132, 2014.

[5]   D.K. Smetters and V. Jacobson. Securing network content. PARC Technical Report, 2009.

[6]   X. Zhang, K. Chang, H. Xiong, Y. Wen, G. Shi, G. Wang, "Towards name-based trust and security for content-centric network. In *Proceedings of the 19th IEEE International Conference on Network Protocols* (ICNP), 2011.

About the Speakers

Nikos Fotiou is a post-doctoral researcher at the Mobile Multimedia Laboratory (MMlab), AUEB. He participated in the FP7 projects PSIRP and PURSUIT and the ESA-funded project φSAT. Dr. Fotiou received his Diploma in Information Systems Eng. from the University of the Aegean, Samos, Greece, his M.Sc.

ICN'14, September 24–26, 2014, Paris, France.
ACM 978-1-4503-3206-4/14/09.
http://dx.doi.org/10.1145/2660129.2666711

in Internetwokring from KTH, Stockholm, Sweden, and his Ph.D. in CS from AUEB, Athens, Greece. His Ph.D. dissertation investigated security requirements and solutions for ICN architectures. His paper "Access Control Enforcement Delegation for Information-Centric Networking Architectures," received the best paper award at the 2012 SIGCOMM ICN Workshop. He is co-author of a comprehensive survey article on ICN and he is a contributor to the Charm-Crypto, cryptographic library. His current research interests include security aspects of ICN, user privacy, access control delegation, and integrity and provenance verification mechanisms.

George C. Polyzos, Professor of Computer Science at AUEB, founded and is leading the Mobile Multimedia Laboratory (MMlab). Previously, he was Professor of Computer Science and Engineering at the University of California, San Diego, where he was co-director of the Computer Systems Laboratory, member of the Steering Committee of the Center for Wireless Communications, and Senior Fellow of the San Diego Supercomputer Center. Prof. Polyzos and the MMlab participated in the FP7 projects PSIRP and PURSUIT that developed the Information-Centric Networking (ICN) Publish-Subscribe Internet (PSI) architecture and the ESA-funded project φSAT, which investigated "The Role of Satellite in Future Internet Services," and co-authored a comprehensive survey article on ICN. Prof. Polyzos was also an organizer of the EIFFEL Think Tank, on the Steering Board of the Euro-NF Network of Excellence and head of its "Socio-Economic Aspects" and "Trust, Privacy and Security" joint research activities. He is the chair of the Steering Committee of the ACM SIGCOMM conference on Information-centric Networking and was TPC Co-Chair for the ACM SIGCOMM ICN 2013 workshop. Dr. Polyzos received his Diploma in EE from the National Technical University, Athens, Greece and his M.A.Sc. in EE and Ph.D. in CS from the University of Toronto. His current research interests include Internet architecture and protocols, ubiquitous computing, security and privacy, wireless networks, mobile multimedia communications, and performance evaluation of computer and communications systems.

Name-Based Content Routing in Information Centric Networks Using Distance Information

J.J. Garcia-Luna-Aceves

PARC, Palo Alto, CA 94304

Computer Engineering Department, University of California, Santa Cruz, CA 95064

jj@soe.ucsc.edu

ABSTRACT

The Distance-based Content Routing (DCR) protocol is introduced, which enables routers to maintain multiple loop-free routes to the nearest instances of a named data object or name prefix in an information centric network (ICN), and establish content delivery trees over which all or some instances of the same named data object or name prefix can be contacted. In contrast to all prior routing solutions for ICNs, DCR operates without requiring routers to establish overlays, knowing the network topology, using complete paths to content replicas, or knowing about all the sites storing replicas of named content. It is shown that DCR is correct and that is orders of magnitude more scalable than recent name-based routing approaches for ICNs, in terms of the time and signaling overhead needed to obtain correct routing to named content.

Categories and Subject Descriptors

C.2.2 [**Network Protocols**]: Routing protocols; C.2.6 [**Internetworking**]: Routers

General Terms

Theory, Design, Performance

Keywords

Information-centric networks; name-based content routing

1. INTRODUCTION

Several information centric network (ICN) architectures have been proposed [1, 4, 40] as alternatives to the current Internet architecture. They enable access to content and services by name, independently of their location, to improve system performance and end-user experience. At the core of all ICN architectures are name resolution and routing of content, and several approaches have been proposed. In many approaches, which date back to McQuillan's work on message addressing in the ARPANET [25], the names of data objects are mapped into addresses by means

ICN'14, September 24–26, 2014, Paris, France.

Copyright 2014 ACM 978-1-4503-3206-4/14/09 ...$15.00.

http://dx.doi.org/10.1145/2660129.2660141 .

of directory servers or overlays, and address-based routing is used for content delivery (e.g., [11, 20, 33]). By contrast, a number of ICN architectures use name-based routing of content, which integrates name resolution and content routing. With name-based routing, some of the routers (producers or caching sites) advertise local instances of named data objects (NDO) or name prefixes denoting a set of entities or content objects with names sharing a common prefix, and routes to them are established. The consumers of content issue content requests that are forwarded along the routes to the routers that issued the NDO or name prefix advertisements. This paper focuses on this type of routing in an ICN, and Section 2 summarizes the prior work in this area. Interestingly, no prior work has been reported using only distance information to the nearest copies of content.

We show that efficient name-based routing to the nearest instances of content can be attained using only distance information, without requiring routers to know the network topology, exchange path information, maintain routes to all network sites, or even know about all the instances of an NDO or name prefix. Section 3 presents DCR (*Distance-based Content Routing*), which is the first name-based content routing approach for ICNs based solely on distance information. DCR provides an integrated approach for routing to *any, some, or all* instances of the same NDO or name prefix in an ICN. This is important, because many applications of name-based content routing in ICNs may require the ability to route to some or all instances of a given NDO or name prefix. DCR builds a *multi-instantiated destination spanning tree* (MIDST) using signaling that is much more efficient than the signaling introduced in the past for shared multicast trees (e.g., [3, 21, 30]) or the spanning-tree approach for publish-subscribe signaling introduced for content-based networking (CBN) [6]. DCR is an example of routing to multi-instantiated destinations [12] in which a destination is an NDO or name prefix.

Section 4 shows that DCR provides multiple paths to NDOs or name prefixes without ever creating a routing-table loop, and that it converges to shortest paths to the nearest copies of content over which content requests and content can flow.

Section 5 discusses the signaling needed for a routing protocol based on DCR, and the importance of using signaling messages that do not require routers to ask for updates.

Section 6 compares the control-plane overhead incurred by DCR and routing approaches for ICNs based on DHTs, link-state routing, and distance-vector routing. DCR incurs far less signaling overhead and is much faster to converge to correct routing tables than prior approaches, because it does not require routers to know the network topology or all the instances of content replicas. Section 7 shows the results of a simple simulation experiment comparing DCR with a link-state approach similar to NLSR and OSPFN [22, 38]. The result of the experiment illustrates the fact that DCR is far more efficient than name-based content routing that relies on information about all replicas of content.

Section 8 shows that DCR also has performance benefits in the data plane compared to routing protocols like NLSR that do not enforce loop-free routes to content.

2. RELATED WORK

Many approaches have been proposed for routing over multiple paths to destinations that have a single instance in a network (e.g., [27, 28, 37, 41]). However, these solutions do not solve the problem of establishing valid routes to NDOs that can be replicated arbitrarily in a network. As we point out in [12], the approaches that have been advanced in the past to support name-based content routing adapt traditional routing algorithms (in which a destination corresponds to a single network node) in three ways: flooding the network with signaling packets that reach all destination instances, supporting routing information for all instances of a destination, or selecting a representative node of the set of destination instances. We summarize representative approaches in the rest of this section.

Directed Diffusion [15] was one of the first proposals for name-based routing of content. Requests for named content (called interests) are flooded throughout a sensor network, and data matching the interests are sent back to the issuers of interests. DIRECT [36] uses an approach similar to directed diffusion and provides named-based content routing in MANETs subject to connectivity disruption.

Gritter and Cheriton [13] proposed one of the earliest proposals for name-based routing of content; namely, a name-based routing protocol (NBRP) as an extension of BGP. Name-prefix reachability is advertised among content routers, and path information is used to avoid permanent loops.

Another early development on name-based routing of content was the CBCB (combined broadcast and content based) routing scheme for content-based networking [6]. CBCB consists of two components. A spanning tree of the network or multiple per-source trees based spanning the network are established, and publish-subscribe requests for content are sent between consumers and producers of content over the tree(s) established in the network.

DONA [18] uses flat names for content and either global or local IP addressing and routing to operate. If only local IP routing is used, content requests (FIND messages) gather autonomous-system (AS) path information as they are forwarded, and responses are sent back on the reverse paths traversed by requests. Within an AS, IP routing is used.

Content Centric Networking (CCN) [7] assumes the use of distributed routing protocols to build the routes over which content requests (Interest messages) are forwarded. A content request (called "Interest") may be sent over one or multiple routes to a name prefix. CCN originally advocated [16] the use of a link-state routing approach for intra-domain routing, such that routers describe their local connectivity and adjacent resources (content); and proposed adding content prefixes to BGP for inter-domain content routing. Several ICN projects have content routing modalities based

on the original CCN routing approach (e.g., [8, 9, 29, 34]). NLSR [22] and OSPFN [38] are two protocols for name-based routing of content based on this approach. Routers exchange topology information by flooding two types of link states advertisements (LSA). An LSA describes either the state of physical link or the presence of a local copy of a prefix. Routers flood LSAs just as it is done in traditional link-state routing protocols. A router running NLSR [22] computes multiple paths to an NDO or name prefix independently of other routers and no ordering of routes is enforced among routers. Using the information exchanged in LSAs, each router first computes a shortest path to an NDO or name prefix, deletes the adjacent link belonging to that path and computes a new path; the process continues until the router has considered all its adjacent links.

Routing in the Mobility First project [26] is similar to DONA and NBRP, in that it requires using either network addresses, source routing, or partial source routing.

A number of ICN projects (e.g., [31, 34]) have addressed content routing modalities based on distributed hash tables (DHT) running in overlays over the physical infrastructure to accomplish name-based routing.

We observe that prior content routing approaches use one or more of the following types of mechanisms: (a) maintaining paths to named content or using source routes to content; (b) flooding of information about the network topology and the location of replicas of content; (c) flooding of content requests; (d) establishing trees spanning the network over which name-based publish-subscribe signaling is performed; and (e) maintaining overlays for DHTs.

3. DCR

The operation of DCR assumes that: (a) each network node is assigned a name or identifier with a flat or hierarchical structure; (b) each piece of content is a *named data object* (NDO) that can be requested by name; (c) NDOs can be denoted using either flat or hierarchical naming, and the same naming convention is used for the entire system; and (d) routers cache content opportunistically. DCR provides multiple loop-free routes to the nearest replicas of prefixes using anchor names and the sequence numbers they create to establish a lexicographic ordering among routers. DCR extends prior sequence-numbering approaches used in protocols designed for routing to single-instance destinations (e.g., [5, 10, 24]). In addition, DCR establishes a MIDST (multi-instantiated destination spanning tree) for each NDO or prefix that requires routing to all or some of its replicas.

We denote the name of a specific NDO or a name prefix simply as *prefix*. A router that advertises having some or all the content corresponding to a prefix is called an *anchor* of the prefix. Each anchor of a prefix originates updates for the prefix periodically, and the update states the prefix, the name of the anchor, a distance to the prefix, and a sequence number that only the anchor is allowed to change.

We denote the lexicographic value of a name i by $|i|$, the set containing router i and its neighbor routers by N^i, and the set of next hops of router i for prefix j by S_j^i. The link from router i to router k is denoted by (i, k) and its cost is denoted by l_k^i. The cost of the link (i, k) is assumed to be a positive number that can be a function of administrative constraints and performance measurements made by router i for the link. The specific mechanism used to update l_k^i is outside the scope of this paper.

3.1 Information Stored and Exchanged

A router i running DCR maintains four tables: (a) a *link cost table* (LT^i) listing the cost of the link from router i to each of its neighbors; (b) a *neighbor table* (NT^i) stating routing information reported by each neighboring router for each prefix; (c) a *routing table* (RT^i) that stores routing information for each known prefix; and (d) a *multipoint routing table* (MRT^i) that stores routing information about routing trees created for those prefixes requiring multipoint communication support.

The entry in LT^i for link (i,k) consists of the name of neighbor k and the cost of the link to it (l_k^i).

The information stored in NT^i for each router $k \in N^i$ regarding prefix j is denoted by NT_{jk}^i, and consists of routing information for the nearest anchor and the root anchor of the prefix. The routing information for the nearest anchor reported by k consists of: the distance from neighbor k to j (d_{jk}^i); an anchor (a_{jk}^i) storing j; and the sequence number created by a_{jk}^i for j (sn_{jk}^i). The routing information for the root anchor of the prefix consists of: a root anchor (ra_{jk}^i); the distance from neighbor k to that anchor (rd_{jk}^i); and the sequence number created by ra_{jk}^i for j (rsn_{jk}^i). If prefix j is locally available at router i, then $a_{ji}^i = i$ and $d_{ji}^i = 0$. In this case router i is its own nearest anchor for prefix j, but need not be the root anchor for j.

The row for prefix j in RT^i specifies: (a) the name of the prefix (j); (b) the routing update information for prefix j (RUI_j^i); (c) the set of neighbors that are valid next hops (S_j^i); (d) a neighbor that offers the shortest distance to j ($s_j^i \in S_j^i$); and (e) an anchor list (A_j^i) that stores a tuple for each different valid anchor reported by any next-hop neighbor. Each tuple $[m, sn(m)] \in A_j^i$ states the name of an anchor m and the sequence number $sn(m)$ reported by that anchor.

RUI_j^i states: (a) a flag for each neighbor k denoting whether or not the information needs to be sent in an update to neighbor k (up_{jk}^i); (b) the current distance from i to j (d_j^i); (c) the anchor of j that has the smallest name among those that offer the shortest distance to j (a_j^i); and (d) the sequence number created by a_j^i for j (sn_j^i).

The entry for prefix j in MRT^i specifies: (a) the name of prefix j; (b) the multipoint update information for prefix j (MUI_j^i); and (c) the list of neighbor routers that have joined the MIDST for the prefix ($MIDST_j^i$). MUI_j^i states the root anchor of j (ra_j^i), the distance to the root anchor (rd_j^i), and the sequence number created by ra_j^i for prefix j (rsn_j^i).

An update message sent by router i to neighbor m consists of the name of router i; a message sequence number (msn^i) used to identify the message; and a list of updates, one for each prefix that needs updating. An update for prefix j sent by router i is denoted by U_j^i and states: the name of the prefix j; the distance to j (ud_j^i); an anchor (ua_j^i); and the sequence number created by ua_j^i for prefix j (usn_j^i).

The entry for prefix j in the update message received from neighbor k by router i is denoted by U_{jk}^i. It states the prefix name j, a distance to it (ud_{jk}^i), an anchor for the prefix (ua_{jk}^i), and the sequence number assigned to the prefix by the anchor (usn_{jk}^i).

Router i sends an update message periodically to each neighbor k containing updates made to RT^i since the last update message that i sent to neighbor k. Router i updates its distance table for $k \in N^i$ after any input event affecting the information stored in N_{jk}^i, including the local availability of prefix j at i. Router i stores new information reported by a neighbor k only when it includes an up-to-date sequence number; otherwise, router i does not trust the update, resets the information from that neighbor for the prefix, and schedules an update to correct the neighbor. Lastly, router i updates the entry for j in MRT^i based on updates received from its neighbors and signaling messages exchanged among routers to join the MIDST of j.

3.2 Routing to Nearest Copies of Prefixes

A router maintains the sequence numbers created by *all* the anchors reported by its neighbors. The information about a given anchor of a prefix is deleted after a finite time that is long enough to ensure that up-to-date information about valid anchors of the prefix is received, before anchor information is deleted.

A router can select neighbors as next hops to prefixes only if they report up-to-date information and offer shorter distances to the prefixes or the same distances but have lexicographically smaller names. Anchors send updates about their prefixes periodically and increment the sequence numbers they assign to prefixes. Let $sn(m)$ denote the sequence number associated with an anchor m in the set of anchors known to router i for prefix j (A_j^i). The following condition is sufficient to ensure that no routing-table loops are ever created when routers change their next hops.

Successor-Set Ordering Condition (SOC):
Neighbor $k \in N^i$ can become a member of S_j^i (i.e., be a next hop to prefix j) if the following two statements are true:

$$\forall [m, sn(m)] \in A_j^i \ (\ a_{jk}^i \neq m \lor sn_{jk}^i \geq sn(m)\ ) \tag{1}$$

$$(\ d_j^i < \infty \ \land \ [\ d_{jk}^i < d_j^i \lor (\ d_{jk}^i = d_j^i \ \land \ |k| < |i|\ )\ ]\ ) \lor \tag{2}$$
$$(\ d_j^i = \infty \ \land \ d_{jk}^i < d_j^i \ \land$$
$$\forall v \in N^i - \{k\} (\ [\ d_{jk}^i + l_k^i < d_{jv}^i + l_v^i\ ] \lor$$
$$[\ d_{jk}^i + l_k^i = d_{jv}^i + l_v^i \ \land |k| < |v|\ ]\ )$$

Only those neighbors reporting the most recent sequence numbers from the known anchors of prefix j can be considered as next hops (Eq. (1)), and they are ordered lexicographically based on their distances to prefix j and their names (Eq. (2)). If router i has a finite distance to prefix j, then it can select neighbor k as a next hop to j if either k is closer to the prefix than router i or is at the same distance to the prefix but $|k| < |i|$. If router i has no finite distance to prefix j, then it can have k as a next hop to j only if k reports the smallest *finite* distance to j among all neighbors, or it has the smallest identifier among those neighbors reporting the smallest finite distance to j.

Fig. 1 illustrates how DCR routes to the nearest replica of a prefix. The figure shows the routing information used for a single prefix when four routers (d, o, r, and u) serve as the anchors, and each link has unit cost. One ore more tuples are listed in lexicographic order next to each router, with each tuple stating a distance to an anchor of the prefix and the identifier of that anchor. The first tuple in the list states the smallest distance to the prefix and the anchor with the smallest name among all anchors at that same distance. Updates from each router state only the preferred anchor (e.g., the update from node e states r as the anchor and distance 1 to it). Each additional tuple next to a router, if any, states an alternate anchor for the prefix and the distance to it. All routers are assumed to have received the most-recent sequence numbers from any of the anchors of the prefix.

The updates generated by an anchor propagate only as long as they provide routers with shorter paths to prefixes. In Fig. 1, no routing update about the prefix propagates more than three hops, even though the network diameter is eight. In general, independently of how many anchors exist in a network for a given prefix, a router only has as many active anchors for a prefix as it has neighbors. This is the result of each router reporting only the best anchor it knows for each prefix. The arrowheads in the links between nodes indicate the router that is the next hop towards the prefix, and their shades indicate the anchor to which they point (e.g., the dark arrowheads point to d). Even in this small network of just 24 routers, most routers have multiple paths to the prefix, with at least one being a shortest path; all links can be used to forward requests for content; none of the routers know about all the four anchors of the prefix; and traversing any possible directed path in Fig. 1 necessarily terminates at d, o, r, or u, without traversing a loop.

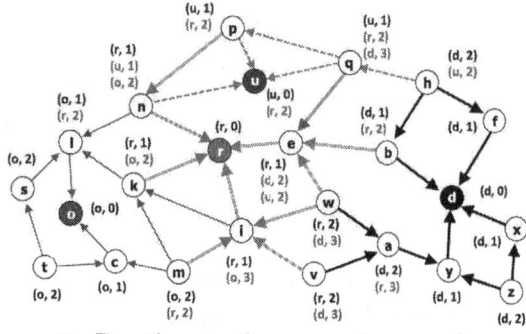

Figure 1: Routing to the nearest copy of a prefix

To illustrate how SOC prevents routing-table loops, assume that router o fails. In this case, routers l and c are unable to find neighbors that satisfy SOC and must send updates stating an infinite distance and a null anchor. After processing the update from routers l and c, routers s and t are unable to find neighbors satisfying SOC and must also send updates stating infinite distances and null anchors. However, after processing the updates from routers l and c, routers n, k and m are able to find neighbors that satisfy SOC and hence respond to l or c with updates stating the tuples $[d_j^n = 1, a_j^n = r]$; $[d_j^k = 1, a_j^k = r]$; and $[d_j^m = 2, a_j^m = r]$. In turn, these updates allow routers c, l, o, s and t to attain routes to prefix j using anchor r within a very short time. Section 4 proves that no routing-table loops are formed while routers change their routing tables in response to network changes or prefixes being replicated dynamically.

Algorithms 1 and 2 illustrate how a router can update its distance and routing tables according to SOC to support routing to the nearest instances of prefixes. It is assumed that, if needed, router i sends a scheduled update message after the two algorithms are executed.

Router i uses Algorithm 1 to update the information reported by its neighbor k regarding prefix j, and to determine whether k has reported valid routing information. The algorithm is executed after i receives an update from neighbor k regarding prefix j or any other input event affecting the information in N_{jk}^i. Router i stores the information reported by neighbor k if it includes an up-to-date sequence number from the reported anchor of prefix j; otherwise, it resets the

information from that neighbor for the prefix, and schedules an update to correct the neighbor.

Router i uses Algorithm 2 to determine which neighbors can be next hops for prefix j according to SOC. Using the information reported from these neighbors, it computes its minimum distance, anchor and sequence number for prefix j. The minimum distance to a prefix is computed using only those neighbors satisfying the constraints imposed by SOC for the cases in which $d_j^i < \infty$ and $d_j^i = \infty$.

Algorithm 1 Update NT_j^i

1: **INPUT:** A_j^i, NT_j^i, U_{jk}^i
2: $valid = 0$;
3: **for each** $[m, sn(m)] \in A_j^i$ **do**
4:    **if** $ua_{jk}^i \neq null \wedge (ua_{jk}^i \neq m \vee usn_{jk}^i \geq sn(m))$
5:    **then** $valid = 1$
6: **end for**
7: **if** $valid = 0$ **then**
8:    $up_{jk}^i = 1$ [schedule update U_j^i to neighbor k];
9:    $d_{jk}^i = \infty$; $a_{jk}^i = null$; $sn_{jk}^i = 0$
10: **else**
11:    $d_{jk}^i = ud_{jk}^i$; $a_{jk}^i = ua_{jk}^i$; $sn_{jk}^i = usn_{jk}^i$
12: **end if**
13: Execute Algorithm 2

Algorithm 2 Update RT_j^i

1: **INPUT:** N^i, NRT_j^i, RT_j^i;
2: $S_j^i = \emptyset$; $d_{min}(j) = \infty$;
3: **if** $d_j^i < \infty$ **then**
4:    **for each** $k \in N^i - \{i\}$ **do**
5:      **if** $d_{jk}^i < d_j^i \vee (d_{jk}^i = d_j^i \wedge |k| < |i|)$ **then**
6:        $S_j^i = S_j^i \cup \{k\}$;
7:        **if** $d_{jk}^i + l_k^i < d_{min}(j) \vee (d_{jk}^i + l_k^i = d_{min}(j) \wedge |a_{jk}^i| < |a_j^i|)$ **then**
8:          $d_{min}(j) = d_{jk}^i + l_k^i$;
9:          $s(j) = k$; $a(j) = a_{jk}^i$; $num(j) = sn_{jk}^i$
10:        **end if**
11:      **end if**
12:    **end for**
13: **else**
14:    **for each** $k \in N^i - \{i\}$ **do**
15:      **if** $d_{jk}^i + l_k^i < d_{min}(j)$ **then**
16:        $S_j^i = \{k\}$; $d_{min}(j) = d_{jk}^i + l_k^i$;
17:        $s(j) = k$; $a(j) = a_{jk}^i$; $num(j) = sn_{jk}^i$
18:      **end if**
19:    **end for**
20: **end if**
21: **if** $d_{min}(j) = \infty$ **then** $a(j) = null$; $num(j) = 0$; $s(j) = null$
22: **if** $(d_j^i \neq d_{min}(j) \vee a_j^i \neq a(j) \vee sn_j^i \neq num(j))$ **then**
23:    **for each** $k \in N^i - \{i\}$ **do** $up_{jk}^i = 1$ [schedule update U_j^i]
24: **end if**
25: $d_j^i = d_{min}(j)$; $s_j^i = s(j)$; $a_j^i = a(j)$; $sn_j^i = num(j)$

3.3 Routing to All or Some Copies of Prefixes

DCR supports routing to *all* or *some* anchors of the same prefix by means of *multi-instantiated destination spanning trees* (MIDST). All the anchors of a given prefix are connected with one another through the MIDST for the prefix, which is rooted at the anchor of the prefix with the smallest name, which we call the *root anchor* of the prefix. The MIDST is established using routing updates exchanged only by routers located between the root anchor and other anchors. To send data packets to all the anchors of a prefix, a router that is not part of the MIDST simply sends the packets towards the nearest anchor of the prefix; the first router in the MIDST that receives the data packets broadcasts them over the MIDST of the prefix.

The distance from router i to the root anchor ra_j^i is $rd_j^i = rd_{js}^i + l_s^i$, where $s \neq i$ is the next hop to ra_j^i selected by router i. If $i = ra_j^i$ then $rd_j^i = 0$. To build the MIDST for prefix j, routers select the root anchor of the prefix to be that anchor of the prefix that has the lexicographically smallest name; therefore, at each router i and for any neighbor $k \in N^i$, $|ra_j^i| \leq |ra_{jk}^i|$ and $|ra_j^i| \leq |a_{jk}^i|$.

The MIDST is established in a distributed manner using the distance updates exchanged among routers. A router that knows about multiple anchors for a prefix other than the anchor it considers to be the root anchor sends updates about the root anchor along the preferred path to each of the other anchors it knows. Routers that receive updates about the root anchor send their own updates to their preferred next hops to each other anchor they know. This way, distance updates about the root anchor propagate to all other anchors of the same prefix. Updates about the root anchor propagate only to those routers in preferred paths between the root anchor and other anchors. If router i changes its routing information for the root anchor of prefix j, it schedules an update about its root anchor to each neighbor that satisfies the following condition.

Root-Anchor Notification Condition (RNC):
Router i sends an update with the tuple $[ra_j^i, rd_j^i, rsn_j^i]$ to each router $k \in N^i - \{i\}$ for whom the following statements are true:

$$|a_{jk}^i| > |ra_j^i| \ \lor \ |ra_{jk}^i| > |ra_j^i| \tag{3}$$

$$\forall v \in N^i (a_{jv}^i = i) \ \lor \ \forall v \in N^i - \{k\}(a_{jk}^i \neq a_{jv}^i \ \lor \tag{4}$$

$$(d_{jk}^i + l_k^i < d_{jv}^i + l_v^i \ \lor \ [\ d_{jk}^i + l_k^i = d_{jv}^i + l_v^i \land |k| < |v|\ ]\ )\ )$$

Eq. (3) states that k has not reported as its anchor or root anchor the same root anchor adopted by i. Eq. (4) states that i forwards the update about the root anchor to k if either i is an anchor and all its neighbors report i as their chosen anchor, or k is the lexicographically smallest next hop to an anchor that is not the root anchor.

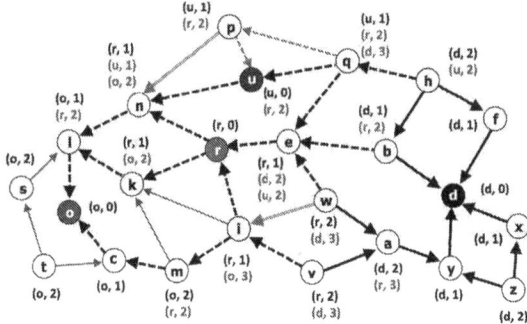

Figure 2: Propagating root anchor information

Fig. 2 shows how information about the root anchor of a prefix is propagated. In the example, router d has the smallest name among all the anchors of the prefix. The dark dashed arrowheads indicate those routers that propagate updates about d being the root anchor to some of their neighbors. For example, router b propagates a root anchor update to e because that neighbor is its best choice towards anchor r; and router g propagates a root anchor update to u because it is the best choice for u itself. Router r propagates an update stating that d is the root anchor to n and k because all its neighbors report r as their anchor, and e and i have already reported d as the root anchor.

Because of RNC, updates about the root anchor of a prefix reach all the other anchors of the prefix [12]. However, we observe in Fig. 2 that many routers (e.g., o, p, s, t) do not participate in the propagation of updates about d being the root anchor of prefix j, and some (i.e., p, s, and t) do not even receive updates about d being the root anchor of prefix j. Only those routers along shortest paths between two different anchors of the prefix may participate in the signaling. This is much more efficient than the traditional approach to building shared multicast trees [3, 21, 30], in which all routers have to have routes to the root d, which needs to be pre-defined.

To allow anchors and relay routers to join the MIDST of a prefix, routers use the following condition to select their next hops towards the root anchor, and forward their requests to those neighbors. Eq. (5) states that the root anchor reported by k has the smallest name among all anchors of j known to i, and also reports an up-to-date sequence number from such an anchor. Eq. (6) states that k must offer the shortest distance to the root anchor among all neighbors. Eq. (7) orders router i with its selected next hop to the root anchor based on the distance to the anchor and the sequence number created by the anchor.

Root-Anchor Ordering Condition (ROC):
Router i can select neighbor $k \in N^i$ as its next hop to its root anchor for prefix j if the following statements are true:

$$|ra_{jk}^i| \leq |ra_j^i| \ \land \ rsn_{jk}^i \geq rsn_j^i \tag{5}$$

$$\forall m \in N^i \ (\ rd_{jk}^i + l_k^i \leq rd_{jm}^i + l_m^i\ ) \tag{6}$$

$$rsn_j^i < rsn_{jk}^i \ \lor \ [\ rsn_j^i = rsn_{jk}^i \ \land \ rd_{jk}^i < rd_j^i\ ] \tag{7}$$

Each anchor of a prefix originates a join request and sends it to its its lexicographically smallest next hop to the root anchor. The join request can be identified by the prefix, the prefix and a nonce, or the anchor name and the prefix. Each router receiving and forwarding a join request stores an entry for the request denoting the neighbor from which it was received for a finite period of time. The join request traverses the path towards the root anchor of the prefix, until it reaches the root anchor or a router x that is already part of the MIDST of prefix j. The response to the request traverses the reverse path of the join request and makes each router processing the response become part of the MIDST.

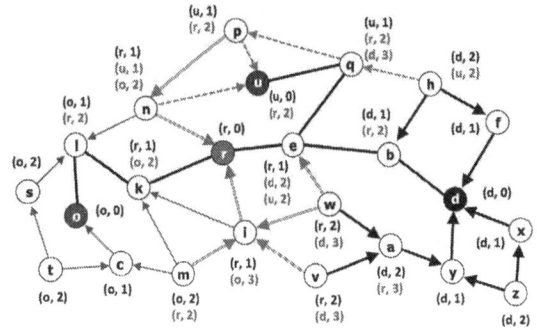

Figure 3: The MIDST of a prefix

Fig. 3 shows the resulting MIDST for the prefix in the same example of Fig. 2. Anchors u, r, and o send their join requests towards d to join the MIDST of the prefix. The links that constitute the MIDST are indicated by solid lines in the figure, and multipoint data traffic for the prefix can flow in both directions of those links.

To forward a content request to all anchors of a prefix, a router simply forwards the request to one of the nearest anchors of the prefix, and the request is then broadcast over the MIDST of the prefix as soon as it reaches the first router that has joined the MIDST. This approach is much the same as that used in shared-tree multicast routing.

Different approaches can be implemented to forward a content request to some of the anchors of a prefix. If enough nearest anchors are known, the request can be forwarded directly to them. Else, the request can be sent to a nearest anchor, who can then forward the request over the MIDST. Some of the anchors can be reached over the MIDST either by specifying a maximum number of hops that a request should traverse on the MIDST, or by means of a labeling scheme over the MIDST that denotes how many anchors can be reached through each branch of the MIDST at a given router in the MIDST(e.g., see [19]).

Specifying when a prefix requires routing to all its replicas, and hence the need for a MIDST, can be done in a number of ways. One approach is for the name of the prefix to denote the need for a MIDST; this is the equivalent of a multicast address for the case of traditional routing. An alternative approach is for a special signaling message to request the creation of a MIDST for a given prefix.

4. DCR CORRECTNESS

The following theorems prove that DCR guarantees that routing-table loops are never formed, even as the locations of content and the network topology change. Furthermore, routers running DCR attain the shortest distances to the nearest instances of each known prefix.

THEOREM 1. *No routing-table loops can be formed if SOC is used to select the next hops to prefixes at each router.* □

PROOF. The proof is by contradiction. Assume that a routing loop L_j for prefix j consisting of h hops is created at time t_L when the routers in L_j change successors according to SOC. Let $L_j = (n_1, n_2, ..., n_h)$, with $n_{i+1} \in S_j^{n_i}$ for $1 \leq i \leq h-1$ and $n_1 \in S_j^{n_h}$. According to SOC, each hop $n_i \in L_j$ ($1 \leq i \leq h$) can select its next hops (i.e., $S_j^{n_i}$) in only two ways, depending on whether or not $d_j^{n_i} < \infty$ when $n_i \in L_j$ selects its next hops before or at time t_L when L_j is formed.

Assume that there is a subset of hops $I_j \subset L_j$ such that $d_j^{n_m} = \infty$ when n_m joins L_j by adding n_{m+1} to $S_j^{n_m}$ for each $n_m \in I_j$. By assumption, router n_m uses Eq. (2) in SOC; therefore, $d_{jn_{m+1}}^{n_m} < \infty$ and router n_{m+1} must report to n_m either an anchor that router n_m did not know before, or a more recent sequence number created by an anchor known to n_m before the update from n_{m+1}. Furthermore, for all $q \in N^{n_m}$, it must be true that $d_{jq}^{n_m} > d_{jn_{m+1}}^{n_m}$ or $d_{jq}^{n_m} = d_{jn_{m+1}}^{n_m}$ and $|n_m| < |q|$. Therefore, the following relation must hold between $d_{jn_{m+1}}^{n_m}$ and $d_{jn_{m-1}}^{n_m}$ for any $n_m \in I_j$:

$$d_{jn_{m-1}}^{n_m} > d_{jn_{m+1}}^{n_m} \tag{8}$$
$$\vee \ (d_{jn_{m-1}}^{n_m} = d_{jn_{m+1}}^{n_m} \wedge |n_{m-1}| > |n_{m+1}|)$$

Consider a subset of hops $\{n_m, n_{m+1}, ..., n_{m+c}\} \in I_j$ that forms a contiguous chain in L_j, where $c \leq h$. It follows from Eq. (8) that

$$(d_{jn_{m-1}}^{n_m} = d_{jn_{m+c+1}}^{n_{m+c}} \wedge |n_{m-1}| > |n_{m+c}|) \tag{9}$$
$$\vee \ (d_{jn_{m-1}}^{n_m} > d_{jn_{m+c+1}}^{n_{m+c}}) \quad \text{for} \ h \geq c \geq 0.$$

On the other hand, by assumption, every hop $n_i \in L_j - I_j$ must have $d_j^{n_i} < \infty$ when it uses SOC to select its next hops and hence join L_j. Therefore, the following two equations must be satisfied for any $n_i \in L_j - I_j$:

$$d_{jn_i}^{n_i-1} \geq d_j^{n_i} \tag{10}$$
$$d_j^{n_i} > d_{jn_{i+1}}^{n_i} \geq d_j^{n_{i+1}} \tag{11}$$
$$\vee \ (d_j^{n_i} = d_{jn_{i+1}}^{n_i} \geq d_j^{n_{i+1}} \ \wedge \ |n_i| > |n_{i+1}|).$$

Consider a subset of hops $\{n_l, n_{l+1}, ..., n_{l+k}\} \in L_j - I_j$ that forms a chain in L_j, where $k \leq h$. Then either $d_j^{n_{l+i}} > d_{jn_{l+i+1}}^{n_{l+i}} \geq d_j^{n_{l+i}}$ for at least one hop n_{l+i} in the chain, or $d_j^{n_{l+i}} = d_{jn_{l+i+1}}^{n_{l+i}} \geq d_j^{n_{l+i}}$ and $|n_{l+i}| > |n_{l+i+1}|$ for each hop n_{l+i} in the chain. Accordingly, it follows from Eqs. (10) and (11) that

$$(d_{jn_{l+1}}^{n_l} = d_{jn_{l+k+1}}^{n_{l+k}} \ \wedge \ |n_l| > |n_{l+k}|) \tag{12}$$
$$\vee \ (d_{jn_{l+1}}^{n_l} > d_{jn_{l+k+1}}^{n_{l+k}}) \quad \text{for} \ h \geq k \geq 0.$$

It follows from Eqs. (9) and (12) that using SOC enforces the same lexicographical ordering among the hops of L_j for any given combination of chains of nodes in L_j that belong to I_j or $L_j - I_j$ and use SOC to select their next hops when they join L_j. Accordingly, it must be true that, if at least one hop in $n_i \in L_j$ is such that $d_{jn_{i+1}}^{n_i} > d_{jn_{k+1}}^{n_k}$, where $n_k \in L_j$ and $k > i$, then $d_{jn_{m+1}}^{n_m} > d_{jn_{m+1}}^{n_m}$ for any given $m \in \{1, 2, ..., h\}$, which is a contradiction. On the other hand, if $d_{jn_{i+1}}^{n_i} = d_{jn_{k+1}}^{n_k}$ for any n_i and n_k in L_j, then $|n_m| > |n_m|$ for any given $m \in \{1, 2, ..., h\}$, which is also a contradiction. Therefore, L_j cannot be formed when routers use SOC to select their next hops to prefix j. □

Assume that DCR is executed in a connected finite network G, that a router is able to detect within a finite time who its neighbor routers are, and that any signaling message sent over a working link between two routers is delivered correctly within a finite time. Further assume that topological changes and name prefix changes stop taking place after a given time t_T. The following theorem proves that DCR attains shortest paths to the nearest replicas of known prefixes within a finite time assuming for simplicity that the cost of any operational link is one unit.

THEOREM 2. *If DCR is used in network G, routes to prefixes converge to the shortest distances to the nearest anchors of the prefixes within a finite time after t_T.* □

PROOF. Without loss of generality, we focus on a specific prefix j. The proof is by simple induction on the number of hops (k) that routers are away from the nearest anchors of prefix j. Let the set of anchors in the network for prefix j be $A = \{\alpha_1, \alpha_2, ..., \alpha_r\}$, where r is at most equal to the number of routers in the network.

Basis case: For $k = 1$, consider an arbitrary neighbor n_1 of a given anchor α_i of prefix j, with $1 \leq i \leq r$. Given that the signaling between neighbors is reliable and no links fail after time t_T, router n_1 must receive an update $U_j^{\alpha_i}$ from α_i stating $d_j^{\alpha_i} = 0$, $a_j^{\alpha_i} = \alpha_i$, and $sn_j^{\alpha_i} = s(\alpha_i)$ (the most recent sequence number created by α_i) within a finite time after t_T; and it must update $d_j^{n_1} = 0$, $a_{j\alpha_i}^{n_1} = \alpha_i$, and $sn_{j\alpha_i}^{n_1} = s(\alpha_i)$.

Because $d_j^{n_1} = 0$ and $sn_{j\alpha_i}^{n_1} = s(\alpha_i)$ always satisfy SOC at router n_1 for prefix j, it must be the case that $\alpha_i \in S_j^{n_1}$. Furthermore, any other next hop in $S_j^{n_1}$ must also be an anchor, because the smallest link cost between neighbors equals 1 and hence the smallest value of $d_j^{n_1}$ equals 1. Router n_1 must set $d_j^{n_1} = 1$ and send and update stating that distance, together with the name of that anchor and the sequence number it created, after a finite time $t_1 > t_T$. Therefore, the basis case is true.

Inductive step: Assume that the theorem is true for an arbitrary router n_k that is k hops away from its nearest anchors of prefix j. It must then be true that $d_j^{n_k} = k$ after a finite time $t_k > t_1$. By assumption, the signaling between neighbors is reliable and no links fail after time $t_T < t_k$; therefore, each neighbor of n_k must receive updates from n_k a finite time after t_k stating $d_j^{n_k}$, $a_j^{n_k}$, and $sn_j^{n_k}$. Each neighbor $p \in N^{n_k}$ must update $d_{jn_k}^p = k$, $a_{jn_k}^p = a_j^{n_k}$, and $sn_{jn_k}^p = sn_j^{n_k}$ a finite time after t_k.

Let router $q \in N^{n_k}$ be more than k hops away from any anchor of prefix j. Because $d_j^{n_k} = k$ is the shortest distance from n_k to prefix j after time t_k, router q cannot have any neighbor reporting a distance to j smaller than k after time t_k. Therefore, $d_{jn_k}^q$ must satisfy Eqs. (1) or (2) of SOC within a finite time after t_k and router q must make n_k a next hop to prefix j a finite time after t_k. Furthermore, any neighbor of q in S_j^q must have also reported a distance of k hops to j. Router q selects the anchor in S_j^q with the smallest name, and sends an update within a finite time $t_{k+1} > t_k$ stating $d_j^q = k + 1$, together with the name of its chosen nearest anchor and the most recent sequence number created by that anchor. Therefore, router q and hence any router $k + 1$ hops away from the nearest anchors of prefix j must attain a shortest distance of $k + 1$ hops to prefix j within a finite time and the theorem is true. $\square$

It is shown in [12] that the proposed approach builds a MIDST for any destination prefix correctly and within a finite time.

5. NAME-BASED SIGNALING FOR DCR

DCR can be implemented using different name-based signaling approaches, depending on the ICN architecture in which it is used. The main decisions to be made are: (a) how to name routers, (b) the syntax of update messages, and (c) how to exchange such messages between neighboring routers. The naming of routers can be done using a hierarchical name space like the one proposed for NLSR [22]. With this naming scheme, the name of a router would be "/ $< network > / < site > / < router >$", and the name of the DCR daemon running in it would be "/ $< network > / < site > / < router > /DCR$."

The semantics of the update process in DCR consists of a router sending incremental routing-table updates to its neighbors. An update message is identified by the name of the router, the protocol (DCR), the type of message, and a sequence number incremented by the sending router. The update messages can be sent periodically and serve as an indication that the router is operational. The syntax of update messages and exactly how messages are exchanged between routers depend on the basic signaling defined in the ICN architecture in which DCR operates.

The signaling among routers can be receiver-initiated or sender-initiated. With receiver-initiated signaling, data follow an Interest stated by the receiver. The DCR process in a router using NDN or CCN must periodically send a "Routing Interest" (RI) to elicit routing updates from its neighbors. In contrast to NLSR, the state of each neighbor router is different and hence DCR signaling cannot be based on CCNx Sync as it is done in NLSR [22]. A router must send an RI stating "/ $< network > / < site > / < router > /DCR/update /seq\_no$" to each neighbor requesting routing information. A router receiving the RI responds with a content object corresponding to a "Routing Update" (RU) with the updates made to its routing table since the last RI.

Sender-initiated signaling consists of each router sending RUs to all its neighbors, without having to be asked explicitly by any one neighbor. Implementing this signaling approach is much more efficient but requires adding a "push" mechanism in the data plane of some ICN architectures (CCN and NDN) or changing the semantics of Interests. Hello messages stating the presence of a router can be sent as long-term RIs to which multiple RUs can be sent by the same router as needed. Alternatively, an RU can be sent as an Interest containing updates as a payload. The RIs or RUs sent from a router inform its neighbors that the router is alive.

If DCR were used in CCN or NDN, a DCR update would be digitally signed by the anchor that originates the update, and the update would state information that can be used in signature verification [16]. Hence, the problem of ensuring in DCR that an anchor of a prefix is valid is the same as the problem of ensuring in NLSR that an LSA regarding local content is valid. Security mechanisms similar to those proposed in NLSR [22] could be implemented in DCR. However, the design, verification, and performance of efficient security mechanisms for DCR and other name-based content routing protocols is outside the scope of this paper.

6. CONTROL-PLANE EFFICIENCY

To compare the performance of DCR with other name-based content routing approaches, we focus on the time, communication, and storage complexities of the approaches in the control plane. The number of routers in the network is denoted by N and E denotes the number of network links. The number of different name prefixes available in the network is denoted by C, the average number of replicas for a given name prefix is R, the average number of neighbors per router is l, and the network diameter is d.

We assume that a separate control message is sent for any given LSA or distance update. In practice, multiple LSAs and distance updates can be aggregated to conserve bandwidth. In fact, aggregating distance updates for multiple prefixes is easier than aggregating LSAs from multiple sources. However, given that the maximum size of a control message is a constant value independent of the growth of N or C, this aggregation does not change the order size of the overhead incurred by the routing protocols.

The communication complexity (CC) of a routing protocol is the number of messages that must be transmitted successfully for each router to have correct routing information about all the C prefixes. The time complexity (TC) of a routing protocol is the maximum time needed for all routers to have correct routing information for all prefixes when all messages are transmitted successfully. The storage complexity (SC) of a routing protocol is the maximum number of entries in the routing table of an arbitrary router. Given that the difference in the number of messages exchanged between neighbors with receiver-initiated or sender-initiated signaling is independent of N, C and R, our results apply to both types of signaling.

Link-State Routing (LSR):
This approach is used in NLSR and OSPFN. The LSA originated by a router regarding a link or a name prefix must be sent to all the other routers in the network, a router must transmit an LSA for each adjacent link and each prefix that is stored locally and each LSA must be flooded in the network, and each router must store a record for each link and prefix copy in the network. Accordingly, the time, communication, and storage complexities of LSR are:

$$TC_{LSR} = O(d); \quad CC_{LSR} = O(ERC + lEN); \quad (13)$$
$$SC_{LSR} = O(RC + E)$$

Distributed Hash Table (DHT):
The most efficient DHT scheme is a virtual DHT with one-hop routing [14], such that routers run the DHT locally and maintain routes to all routers in the network. The communication complexity associated with publishing a prefix in the DHT and associating r sites with the prefix (to support routing to any or all copies of the prefix) is $O(dRC)$ assuming no loops. The communication complexity of maintaining routes to all routers is $O(lNE)$, given that link-state routing is typically used. The fastest possible propagation of routes to all routers is order $O(d)$, and each router must store a record for as many prefixes as there are in the network. It follows that the complexity of the DHT approach is:

$$TC_{DHT} = O(d); \quad CC_{DHT} = O(dRC + lEN); \quad (14)$$
$$SC_{DHT} = O(C + E)$$

Traditional Distance-Vector Routing (DVR):
Because DVR signaling can traverse long paths, and long-term loops and "counting to infinity" can occur, the basic distance-vector approach is known to have $O(N)$ time complexity and $O(N^2)$ communication complexity [17]. Furthermore, each router must store and communicate distance information about all prefix replicas and destination nodes in the network. Accordingly, the complexity of DVR is:

$$TC_{DVR} = O(N); \quad CC_{DVR} = O(N^2RC); \quad (15)$$
$$SC_{DVR} = O(RC + N)$$

This is much worse than the previous two approaches and explains why name-based routing using distance vectors has not been considered in the past.

Distance-based Content Routing (DCR):
Independently of the number of anchors for a given prefix or routers in the network, the information a router stores and communicates for a given prefix in DCR is only its distance to the nearest anchor of the prefix, plus the anchor name and the latest sequence number created by that anchor. As the number of replicas increases, the distances from a router to the nearest replica of a prefix decreases, and it is always the case that the number of hops from any router to the nearest replica of a prefix (x) is at most d hops. Furthermore, DCR does not incur any routing-table loops. This means that: (a) any routing information propagates as fast as the shortest path between its origin and the recipient; and (b) the number of messages required for all routers to have a correct distance to a given prefix is $O(E)$, regardless of the number of times R the prefix is replicated. Given that there are C prefixes in the network, the complexity DCR is:

$$TC_{DCR} = O(x); \quad CC_{DCR} = O(EC); \quad SC_{DCR} = O(C) \quad (16)$$

It is clear from Eqs. 13 to 16 that DCR has far smaller storage complexity than LSR or DVR, because a router only stores one entry for a prefix, rather than entries for prefix replicas, and does not store any topology information. As R becomes $O(N)$, DCR requires orders of magnitude less storage overhead than LSR and DVR in large networks. DCR is also more efficient in terms of storage than the DHT approach in large networks, because a DHT requires routers to maintain network topology information. DVR allows routers to attain correct routing tables much faster than with DVR, LSR or DHT, because routers only exchange updates about nearest prefix copies, rather than all copies, and such updates need to traverse paths that become much shorter than the network diameter as content replicas proliferate.

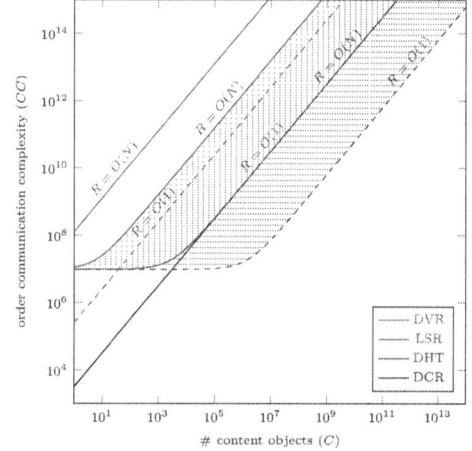

Figure 4: Impact of C and R on overhead

Fig. 4 illustrates the combined effect of the values of C and R on the communication complexity (signaling overhead) of DVR, LSR, DHT and DCR. To focus on the effect of C and R, we set $N = 500$, and assume that l and d are of order $O(log(N))$, which makes E order $O(Nlog(N))$. The number of replicas per objet is varied from order $O(1)$ to order $O(N)$. It is clear that the DVR and LSR approaches are orders of magnitude less efficient than the DHT and DCR approaches when content replicas proliferate. It is also worth noting that, as the number of content objects becomes far larger than the number of network nodes and the copies of such content objects proliferate, the signaling overhead of DCR and an ideal DHT approach are the same.

7. SIMULATION EXPERIMENT

A simple simulation experiment is used to contrast the signaling overhead incurred by DCR and the LSR approach exemplified by NLSR and OSPFN. QualNet [35] (version 5.0) is the discrete event simulator used. The implementation of DCR was based on modifications of the Distributed Bellman Ford implementation in Qualnet to support SOC, and the implementation of the LSR approach was based on the OSPF implementation by adding LSAs to advertise content the way NLSR and OSPFN do. In both cases RUs are sent without RIs that request them. LSR and DCR use the same time period to refresh their routing structures, and each simulation ran for 10 different seed values. We used static networks of 100 nodes, with nodes being uniformly distributed in the network to avoid disconnected nodes. The transmission of an update to all neighbors of a node is counted as a single transmission, and an update message in DCR and LSR carries all the updated distances or link states, respectively. The number of nodes requesting NDOs is increased from 10% to 40% of the 100 nodes of the network. Each node originally publishes two NDOs, and a node that caches an NDO that it requested advertises the NDO.

Table I shows the average number of control packets generated per node with DCR and LSR. As the rate of content requests increases and NDO replicas proliferate, the signaling incurred by LSR becomes excessive. On the other hand, with DCR, all updates fit in a single message and routers advertise only their distances to the nearest instances of NDOs. As a result, the signaling overhead of DCR remains constant independently of the number copies per NDO.

Table 1: Control-plane overhead

Approach	10%	20%	40%
DCR	100	100	100
LSR	699	1442	2269

8. DATA-PLANE EFFICIENCY

DCR operates independently of the data-plane mechanisms used for forwarding content and content requests in an ICN. However, the multipath loop-free routing provided by DCR has a major impact on the efficiency of the data plane in an ICN.

For example, in CCN [7] and more recently NDN [39, 29], each router maintains a forwarding table (FIB), a pending interest table (PIT), and a content store. The PIT has an entry for each Interest that has been forwarded and waiting for data to return. For a given Interest properly identified, the PIT states the "faces" (interfaces) over which the Interest has been received and the faces over which the interest has been forwarded. At each router, the FIB is populated from the routing table maintained by a routing protocol and states one or multiple next hops to a prefix. To obtain content in CCN and NDN, Interests are forwarded over the routes defined in the FIBs, and data packets are sent back along the reverse paths traversed by Interests.

It has been argued that, independently of the routing protocol used in the control plane, an Interest cannot loop if it is identified using the name of the content being requested and a nonce (e.g., see [39], Section 2.1). However, we show below that this need not be the case even if a nonce were to denote an Interest uniquely. Interest looping is a function of the way in which forwarding strategies for Interests interact with the FIB entries populated by the routing protocol.

Fig. 5 shows an example network of ten routers in which all links have unit cost and router d has advertised a given NDO j. For simplicity, the thickness of a link indicates its available bandwidth for data in both directions; hence, a thin link indicates that the link is perceived as congested. An arrowhead in the figure indicates the direction in which Interests can traverse a link based on the FIB entries in the routers induced by DCR and NLSR.

As Fig. 5(a) illustrates, the FIB entries obtained with DCR consist of next hops to prefix j that must belong to loop-free paths to the prefix, because routers coordinate their routing updates based on SOC. Interests flow over loop-free paths towards prefix j regardless of the forwarding strategy used in the data plane, the congestion state over links, forwarding decisions made at each router, and the length of time allowed for an Interest entry to be kept in the PIT.

With NLSR [22], each router uses the information it knows about the topology and the locations of a prefix to compute multiple paths to the prefix sequentially as described in Section 2. Fig. 5(b) shows the directions in which Interests can be forwarded when NLSR is used to build the FIBs. The FIB entries stored at routers need not define loop-free paths, because routers compute their paths to prefix j without any coordination with one another.

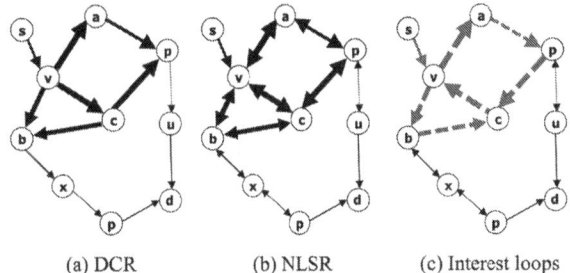

Figure 5: Multipaths in FIBs and Interest looping

Fig. 5(c) shows a scenario with router s issuing an Interest for j to router v. As a result of forwarding decisions made by b, p and c based on the perceived congestion to their neighbors, the Interest can traverse loop (v, b, c, v) or loop (v, a, p, c, v) as shown, or loop (v, a, p, c, b, v) not shown.

If v simply drops the Interest after receiving it again from c, which is the basic strategy in NDN, then router s must retransmit after a timeout expires or a negative acknowledgment is received. Because of looping, this may incur delays of order $O(N)$, where N is the number of network routers. On the other hand, if v attempts to reroute the Interest, there is no guarantee that the Interest will not loop again. The Interest from s may take eight or nine hops to be delivered after traversing one of the loops, or it may be dropped if its loop traversal leaves no rerouting alternatives. In general, rerouting of Interests in an ICN without loop-free routing in the control plane constitutes an on-demand depth-first search strategy in the data plane, which need not be successful and takes order $O(N)$ to deliver an Interest because of backtracking due to looping [2, 23].

If routing-table loops are allowed in the control plane, then Interest entries should be stored in the PITs long enough to ensure that no Interest that loops can be recirculated in the same loop. This means that Interest entries in the PITs must remain for time durations of order $O(N)$.

Interest flooding in the data plane can be used to ensure the delivery of Interests in order $O(d)$, where d is the network diameter and $d = O(log(N))$ (e.g., see [36]). However, this approach induces communication overhead larger than $O(EC)$, with E and C being the number of links and prefixes, respectively.

We have discussed Interest looping problems resulting from forwarding strategies in the data plane using stable FIBs populated with a routing protocol that is not loop-free. However, Interest looping can also occur with inconsistent FIBs that do not correspond to loop-free paths. Many approaches for loop-free multipath routing have been proposed [28, 37, 41] that work much better than single-path routing or equal-cost multipath routing. However, DCR is the first to augment the desired loop-free multipath routing functionality to the case of ICNs in which content can be replicated arbitrarily. DCR offers efficiency gains in the data plane that are inherent in using loop-free multipath routing, and does this while attaining high efficiency in the control plane.

Using DCR in the control plane reduces content-delivery delays by reducing the time that Interests take to reach routers that can answer them, and also allows PIT timers to be of order $O(d)$. This is the case even in the presence of topology changes or the relocation of prefixes in the network. Because DCR guarantees that routing tables and FIBs are always loop-free, routers can continue to forward Interests over remaining paths as stated in the FIBs while new routes are computed in the control plane. Furthermore, the time incurred by DCR to recompute loop-free paths to prefixes is $O(x)$, where $x \leq d$. This is much shorter than the time complexity of $O(N)$ that can be incurred in the rerouting of Interests in the data plane when FIB entries are not part of loop-free paths.

9. CONCLUSIONS

We introduced *Distance-based Content Routing* (DCR), the first approach for name-based content routing in ICNs based solely on distances to NDOs or name prefixes. DCR does not require any routing information about the physical topology of the network or information about all the replicas of the same content to provide multiple shortest paths to the nearest replica of content, as well as to all or some instances of an NDO or name prefix. DCR was shown to be loop-free at every instant and to converge to the shortest paths to the closets replicas of content.

DCR has smaller time complexity and orders of magnitude smaller communication and storage complexities than name-based routing approaches that require information about all content replicas. It has the same communication complexity of an ideal DHT approach when content replicas proliferate, and has smaller time and storage complexity than a DHT approach. A simulation experiment was used to illustrate the substantial savings in signaling overhead derived from having to communicate updates about the nearest copies of content, rather than all copies. In addition, DCR was shown to enable efficient and simple data planes, because it provides multiple loop-free paths over which content requests can propagate.

A detailed characterization of the performance of DCR and other name-based routing approaches is needed to address: the interaction of the control and data planes; the end-to-end delays incurred in obtaining NDOs; the impact of network size, number of NDOs, and naming hierarchy on the performance of the protocols; and the efficiency with which multi-point communication is supported.

Name-based routing approaches with communication and storage complexities smaller than order $O(EC)$ and $O(C)$ (with E and C being the number of links and name prefixes in the ICN, respectively) should be investigated.

10. REFERENCES

[1] B. Ahlgren et al., "A Survey of Information-centric Networking," *IEEE Commun. Magazine*, July 2012, pp. 26–36.

[2] B. Awerbuch, "A New Distributed Depth-First-Search Algorithm," *Information Processing Letters*, pp. 147?150, 1985.

[3] T. Ballardie, P. Francis, and J. Crowcroft, "Core Based Trees (CBT)," *Proc. ACM SIGCOMM 93*, Oct. 1993.

[4] M.F. Bari et al., "A Survey of Naming and Routing in Information-Centric Networks," *IEEE Commun. Magazine*, July 2012, pp. 44–53.

[5] J. Behrens and J.J. Garcia-Luna-Aceves, "Hierarchical Routing Using Link Vectors," *Proc. IEEE Infocom '98*, April 1998.

[6] A.Carzaniga et al., "A Routing Scheme for Content-Based Networking," *Proc. IEEE Infocom '04*, March 2004.

[7] Content Centric Networking Project (CCN) [online]. http://www.ccnx.org/releases/latest/doc/technical/

[8] Content Mediator Architecture for Content-aware Networks (COMET) Project [online]. http://www.comet-project.org/

[9] A. Detti et al., "CONET: A Content-Centric Inter-networking Architecture," *Proc. ACM ICN '12*, 2012.

[10] J.J. Garcia-Luna-Aceves and M. Spohn, "Scalable Link-State Internet Routing," *Proc. IEEE ICNP '98*, Oct. 1998.

[11] J.J. Garcia-Luna-Aceves, "System and Method for Discovering Information Objects and Information Object Repositories in Computer Networks," U.S. Patent 7,162,539, 2007.

[12] J.J. Garcia-Luna-Aceves, "Routing to Multi-Instantiated Destinations: Principles and Applications," *Proc. IEEE ICNP 2014*, Oct. 2014.

[13] M. Gritter and D. Cheriton, "An Architecture for Content Routing Support in The Internet," *Proc. USENIX Symposium on Internet Technologies and Systems*, Sept. 2001.

[14] A. Gupta, B. Liskov and R. Rodrigues, "Efficient Routing for Perr-to-Peer Overlays," *Proc. ACM NDSI '04*, March 2004.

[15] C. Intanagonwiwat, R. Govindan, and D. Estrin, "Directed Diffusion: A Scalable and Robust Communication Paradigm for Sensor Networks," *Proc. ACM MobiCom '00*, 2000.

[16] V. Jacobson et al., "Networking Named Content," *Proc. IEEE CoNEXT '09*, Dec. 2009.

[17] M.J. Johnson, "Updating Routing Tables after Resource Failure in a Distributed Computer Network," *Networks*, Vol. 14, No. 3, 1984.

[18] T. Koponen et al., "A Data Oriented (and Beyond) Network Architecture," *Proc. ACM SIGCOMM 07*, 2007.

[19] B.N. Levine and J.J. Garcia-Luna-Aceves, "Improving Internet Multicast Using Routing Labels," *Proc. IEEE ICNP '97*,1997.

[20] Q. Li and J.J. Garcia-Luna-Aceves, "Efficient Content Routing in MANETs Using Distances to Directories," *Proc. 2014 IEEE INFOCOM Workshop on Name-Oriented Mobility*, May 2 2014.

[21] E.L. Madruga and J.J. Garcia-Luna-Aceves, "Core Assisted Mesh Protocol for Multicast Routing in Ad-Hoc Networks," U.S. Patent 6,917,985, 12 July 2005.

[22] A.K.M. Mahmudul-Hoque et al., "NSLR: Named-Data Link State Routing Protocol," *Proc. ACM ICN '13*, 2013.

[23] S. Makki and G. Havas, "Distributed Algorithms for Constructing a Depth First Search Tree," *Proc. ICPP '94*, Aug. 1994.

[24] M. Marina and S. Das, "On-Demand Multipath Distance Vector Routing in Ad Hoc Networks," *Proc. IEEE ICNP '01*, 2001.

[25] J.M. McQuillan, "Enhanced Message Addressing Capabilities for Computer Networks", *Proceedings of the IEEE* , Nov. 1978.

[26] Mobility First project [online]. http://mobilityfirst.winlab.rutgers.edu/

[27] M. Mosko and J.J. Garcia-Luna-Aceves, "Multipath Routing in Wireless Mesh Networks," *Proc. IEEE WiMesh '05*, Sept. 2005.

[28] S. Murthy and J.J. Garcia-Luna-Aceves, "Congestion-Oriented Shortest Multipath Routing," *IEEE Infocom '96*, March 1996.

[29] NDN Project [online]. http://www.named-data.net/

[30] M. Parsa and J.J. Garcia-Luna-Aceves, "A Protocol for Scalable Loop-free Multicast Routing," *IEEE JSAC*, April 1997.

[31] Publish Subscribe Internet Technology (PURSUIT) Project [online]. http://www.fp7-pursuit.eu/PursuitWeb/

[32] J. Rajahalme et al., "On Name-Based Inter-Domain Routing," *Computer Networks*, pp. 975-985, 2011.

[33] J. Raju, J.J. Garcia-Luna-Aceves and B. Smith, "System and Method for Information Object Routing in Computer Networks," U.S. Patent 7,552,233, June 23, 2009

[34] Scalable and Adaptive Internet Solutions (SAIL) Project [online]. http://www.sail-project.eu/

[35] Scalable Network Technologies, *Qualnet*, http://web.scalable-networks.com/content/qualnet.

[36] I. Solis and J.J. Garcia-Luna-Aceves, "Robust Content Dissemination in Disrupted Environments," *Proc. ACM CHANTS 08*, Sept. 2008.

[37] S. Vutukury and J.J. Garcia-Luna-Aceves, "A Simple Approximation to Minimum-Delay Routing," *Proc. ACM SIGCOMM '99*, Aug. 1999.

[38] L. Wang et al., "OSPFN: An OSPF Based Routing Protocol for Named Data Networking," Technical Report NDN-0003, 2012.

[39] C. Yi et al., "Adaptive Forwarding in Named Data Networking," *ACM CCR*, Vol. 42, No. 3, July 2012.

[40] G. Xylomenos et al., "A Survey of Information-centric Networking Research," *IEEE Communication Surveys and Tutorials*, July 2013.

[41] W. Zaumen and J.J. Garcia-Luna-Aceves, "System for Maintaining Multiple Loop Free Paths between Source Node and Destination Node in Computer Network," US Patent 5881243, 1999.

Scalable Routing for
Tag-Based Information-Centric Networking

Michele Papalini, Antonio Carzaniga, Koorosh Khazaei
University of Lugano
Lugano, Switzerland

Alexander L. Wolf
Imperial College London
London, United Kingdom

ABSTRACT

Routing in information-centric networking remains an open problem. The main issue is scalability. Traditional IP routing can be used with name prefixes, but it is believed that the number of prefixes will grow too large. A related problem is the use of per-packet in-network state (to cut loops and return data to consumers). We develop a routing scheme that solves these problems. The service model of our information-centric network supports information pull and push using tag sets as information descriptors. Within this service model, we propose a routing scheme that supports forwarding along multiple loop-free paths, aggregates addresses for scalability, does not require per-packet network state, and leads to near-optimal paths on average. We evaluate the scalability of our routing scheme, both in terms of memory and computational complexity, on the full Internet AS-level topology and on the internal networks of representative ASes using realistic distributions of content and users extrapolated from traces of popular applications. For example, a population of 500 million users requires a routing information base of 3.8GB with an almost flat growth and, in this case, a routing update (one content descriptor) can be processed in 2ms on commodity hardware. We conclude that information-centric networking is feasible, even with (or perhaps thanks to) addresses consisting of expressive content descriptors.

Categories and Subject Descriptors

C.2.2 [**Computer-Communication Networks**]: Network Protocols—*Routing protocols*

Keywords

ICN, push/pull, tag-based routing, multi-tree routing

1. INTRODUCTION

A fundamental problem remains open in information-centric networking: there is yet no demonstrably scalable

ICN'14, September 24–26, 2014, Paris, France.
ACM 978-1-4503-3206-4/14/09.
http://dx.doi.org/10.1145/2660129.2660155.

scheme that supports true routing, that is, *packet switching* with multiple sources and destinations, as opposed to a per-flow or per-object lookup followed by a traditional host-based (i.e., location-based) data transfer. In fact, largely because of this gap, the validity and utility of a content-centric network layer has been rightly called into question [6].

The primary approach to routing and forwarding in ICN (as typified by CCN/NDN [10], but also in the earlier work on TRIAD [7]) is to adapt IP routing to use name prefixes instead of IP prefixes. While this approach has the great advantage of reusing much of the current network infrastructure, it also has fundamental limitations. First, since it is based on traditional *unicast* routing, it cannot reliably support multiple sources or destinations for the same information. A router may list multiple next hops for the same prefix, but the routing scheme provides no indication of how to forward consistently across routers so as to follow one *path* to a destination (or multiple paths to multiple destinations). Moreover, multiple next hops may lead to loops. In fact, the main approach is not to avoid loops, but merely to detect them, tracing each packet throughout the network with per-packet state, thereby increasing the overall cost of forwarding. For analogous reasons, unicast routing/forwarding cannot directly support "push" ICN communication [4]. Here again, the already vast and growing content space is believed to pose a fundamental scalability limitation to traditional routing.

We develop a different approach to routing, one based on *trees* in which edges are annotated with *content descriptors*. This new routing scheme has the following novel and important properties:

- It immediately supports both request/reply ("pull") and publish/subscribe ("push") ICN communication.

- It is compatible with in-network caching, as well as the full range of existing ICN addressing schemes, from content identifiers [12] to structured names [10] to tag sets [3]. We choose tag sets, since they are strictly the most expressive form of descriptor and yet admit to an intuitive and effective aggregation that is fundamentally superior to the aggregation of, say, name prefixes.

- It provides loop-free paths to multiple destinations, meaning that communication can be dynamically assigned an arbitrary fan out, from anycast (forward to any one of many destinations) to m-anycast (any m destinations) to multicast (all destinations).

- It provides extremely compact and efficient *locators* that can be used to achieve the throughput of current networks within the content-centric service interface.

- It does not require the presence of per-packet soft state within the network, unlike previous designs.

Clearly, a single tree may not use the most direct paths and would be more vulnerable to congestion and network partitioning. We therefore use *multiple trees* so as to reduce path lenghts on average, reduce congestion, and improve reliability. We develop a hierarchical multi-tree routing scheme that allows for the creation of sets of trees with specific properties at different levels (e.g., shortest-paths trees within an AS along with policy-specific inter-AS trees).

In principle, however, multiple trees also require larger routing tables, which leads us back to the fundamental question of scalability. We address the issue of scalability through the aggressive aggregation of content descriptors. Beyond the natural aggregation of tag sets, we develop a routing table based on PATRICIA tries that aggregate content descriptors *across all trees*. We also develop the necessary algorithms to maintain such routing tables incrementally, which is essential in the presence of dynamic, user-defined addresses.

We evaluate the memory complexity of the routing scheme and its implementation at the global network scale. We emulate the scheme over the full AS-level topology of the current Internet and within a number of representative ASes. In order to test the scheme under realistic current and potential future application demands, we extrapolate from traces of some characteristic content-driven applications [3]. These extrapolations give us various workloads of content descriptors that correspond to several hundred million users. We then use such workloads to assess the concrete memory requirements of the scheme on routers at the local (intra-AS) and global (inter-AS) levels.

Our analysis shows that content descriptors indeed aggregate effectively and, therefore, the routing information base remains contained in size even with a growing population of users and, consequently, more and more content descriptors. For example, for a number of representative applications, a population of 500 million users using a total of nearly 10 billion content descriptors would require a routing information base of 3.8GB, with an almost flat growth for additional users enabled by effective aggregation. We also show that this same aggregated routing information can be updated dynamically at a reasonably high frequency (500 updates per second) even on inexpensive, commodity PC hardware.

This work is based on a previously published ICN routing scheme [3], which we extend as follows: we introduce locators and content identifiers, we detail the scheme over a hierarchy of domains, and we develop concrete data structures to represent and aggregate routing information for which we also develop incremental update and maintenance algorithms. We also conduct an extensive and in-depth analysis of the scalability of the scheme.

2. NETWORK ARCHITECTURE

We begin by describing the service model, addressing scheme, and architecture of our information-centric network. The service model extends our prior ICN design [3, 4] and is also a significant superset of other, related models [10, 12]. We review the basic model here for clarity and completeness. We also introduce two extensions to the network architecture not previously described, namely *locators* and *identifiers*.

We propose a network characterized by two types of communication services: a request/reply ("pull") service and a publish/subscribe ("push") service. Both services in essence transmit information of interest from producers to consumers, and both use content *descriptors* (detailed below) to identify what information is offered by which producer and what information is of interest to which consumer.

The request/reply service consists of three primitive network functions:

Offer: A producer registers one or more descriptors that identify the data that the producer are willing and able to provide.

Request: A consumer requests data by issuing a request packet carrying a content descriptor or a content locator (detailed below). The network then delivers the request packet to one or more producers that are willing and able to satisfy the consumer's request.

Reply: A producer (or a caching router) responds to a request packet by returning a reply packet carrying the requested data.

The publish/subscribe service consists of two primitives:

Subscription: A consumer registers one or more descriptors that specify the data that the consumer wishes to receive.

Notification: A producer publishes a data packet carrying a descriptor that identifies the data.

Both request/reply and publish/subscribe services define and use routing information consisting of *content descriptors*. In request/reply, producers define routing information that attracts request packets towards them, while in publish/subscribe it is consumers that define routing information to attract notifications. Thus, routing for the two services differ only in the sources of routing information, but is otherwise conceptually identical. We therefore propose a network interface with a single *register* function to define routing information.

The semantics of descriptors is also identical for requests and notifications, which means that the matching algorithm used for forwarding requests and notifications is the same. However, the treatment of the two packets differ in other ways. A request is ideally an anycast packet, while notifications are multicast. Also, a request is expected to generate a corresponding reply, while a notification is a one-way message. Furthermore, the caching semantics are different. A request that can be satisfied by cached content will not be forwarded downstream toward the original producer, while a notification must be forwarded all the way to interested consumers (although notifications might also be cached for reliability purposes). Figure 1 summarizes the network architecture we propose.

The network also defines opaque host *locators*. Locators are attached to requests so that the corresponding replies can be forwarded back to the requesting application. In addition to replies, we propose to use locators to forward requests. In particular, a data reply can also carry the locator

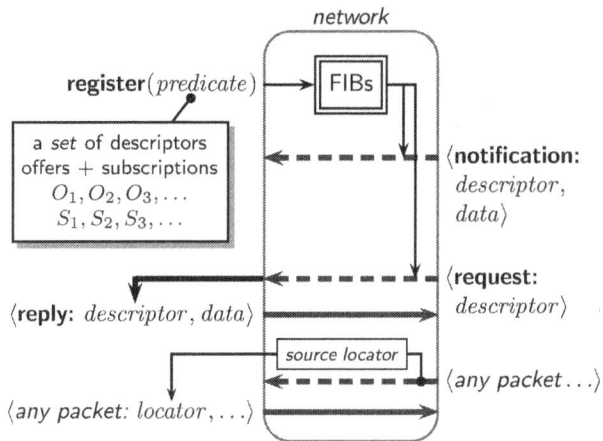

Figure 1: High-Level Network Architecture

of the producer so that the consumer can address follow-up requests (e.g., for the next data blocks) directly to that producer. Locators may be implemented with stable unicast addresses (e.g., IP addresses) or they may be based on transient state (e.g., a nonce that identifies a trail of pending interests in CCN). In Section 3.2 we detail an extremely efficient form of locators usable within our routing scheme.

2.1 Content Descriptors

Descriptors play a central role analogous to IP prefixes. The semantics of descriptors define the semantics of the network service, and in particular they define how data replies match requests, how offers match requests (and, therefore, how offers describe the data available from a producer), and how notifications match subscriptions. As discussed so far, descriptors are abstract and generic. Indeed, much of what we propose is conceptually independent of their specific form and semantics. However, in order to develop a concrete service and a corresponding concrete routing scheme, we must define descriptors. For this purpose we adopt "tags".

A descriptor consists of a set of string tags, with the matching relations corresponding to the subset relations between sets of tags: a descriptor R in a request would match a descriptor O in an offer when the request contains all the tags of the offer ($R \supseteq O$). Consistently, a descriptor N in a notification would match a descriptor S in a subscription when the notification contains all the tags of the subscription ($N \supseteq S$). For example, an offer for $\{icn14, paper\}$ would match a request $\{paper, routing, icn14\}$ or a request $\{icn14, paper, pdf, n32\}$.

Notice, however, that tag sets are strictly more expressive than name prefixes. A name prefix can be represented as a single tag set. For example, */org/gnu/software/* can be written as tag set $\{1{:}org, 2{:}gnu, 3{:}software\}$, and would match descriptor $\{1{:}org, 2{:}gnu, 3{:}software, 4{:}emacs\}$. Conversely, the semantics of a tag set would require exponentially many prefixes (all permutations) to express the same descriptor.

Tag sets aggregate analogously to prefixes. In particular, a descriptor X subsumes all other descriptors Y that contain X. For example, any descriptor matching $\{music, jazz\}$ would also match its subset $\{music\}$, so a router might combine the two by storing only the more general tag set $\{music\}$. We discuss more about aggregation in Section 3.5.

Tag sets differ from IP prefixes in a crucial way. While IP prefixes are assigned by network designers and administrators, descriptors are assigned by applications. This is also true of other forms of addressing in ICN, including names in a hierarchical name space or flat identifiers. In fact, application-defined addressing is arguably the most important defining property of ICN. Allowing applications to define network addresses empowers applications but at the same time leaves the network and applications themselves vulnerable to conflicts and also abuses in the use of the address space. With tag sets, as for name prefixes, this problem can be greatly reduced through conventions, for example by defining reserved tags and mandatory scoping tags equivalent to host names in URLs.

2.1.1 Content Identifiers

A content descriptor (a tag set) may contain a unique identifier, such as a cryptographic hash of the content, or an object identifier plus a version number and a block number. In this way, a descriptor can identify a data block uniquely. More generally, tag sets can encode meta-data and higher-level protocol information. However, we believe that information that has a specific function at the network or transport level should be represented with specific headers. In particular, at the network level we propose to use cache-control headers, as well as a *content identifier* to refer to a specific data block. The form of such identifiers is defined at higher levels, for example to allow a transport protocol to refer to the next sequence of blocks within a stream.

This separation between descriptors, identifiers, and other headers is consistent with the design of a protocol such as HTTP, where the URI does not identify a piece of immutable content, but other headers can be used for that purpose (e.g., ETags, Modified-Since) and yet other headers can specify additional properties of requests and replies, such as cache controls. This design also allows us to represent descriptors using a compressed, fixed-width header that hides individual tags. We describe this compressed representation next.

2.1.2 Representation of Tag Sets

Conceptually, a descriptor is a set of tags. Concretely, we represent descriptors as Bloom filters, and we develop our routing scheme around this representation. So, packets and routing messages carry Bloom filters, and the aggregation of routing information applies equivalently to them. Matching two descriptors amounts to checking the inclusion relation (bitwise) between two Bloom filters, while matching a descriptor against a predicate (i.e., a set of descriptors) amounts to finding one or more Bloom filters in the predicate that are subsets (bitwise) of the input Bloom filter.

In order to choose good Bloom filter parameters, which must be global properties of the routing scheme, we conservatively estimate here that tag sets would most likely contain no more than 15 tags. We therefore use Bloom filters with $k = 7$ hash functions and $m = 192$ bits, which ensures that a subset test $S_1 \subseteq S_2$ would be accurate up to a false-positive probability of $(1 - e^{-k|S_2|/m})^{k|S_1 \setminus S_2|}$. For example, for a descriptor of $|S_2| = 10$ tags, a test $S_1 \subseteq S_2$ with another descriptor S_1 that differs by $|S_1 \setminus S_2| = 3$ tags would evaluate to true (a false positive, since $|S_1 \setminus S_2| > 0$) with probability 10^{-11}. Of course, these are network configuration parameters that can be set as appropriate.

3. ROUTING SCHEME

We introduce a routing scheme based on multiple trees. At the core of the scheme is content-based routing on a spanning tree. We enhance this basic scheme with locators and with multiple trees within routing domains and over a hierarchy of domains (intra/inter-AS).

3.1 ICN Routing on One Tree

Consider a network spanned by a tree T. For now consider a router-level network. T is identified within each notification and request packet so that each router v can determine the set adj_v^T of its neighbors that are also adjacent to v in T. This can be done by adding an identifier for T in the packet and storing the adjacency set adj_v^T at each router v.

The forwarding information base (FIB) of router v associates each neighbor w in adj_v^T with the union $P_{T,w}$ of the predicates registered by all the hosts reachable through neighbor w on T, including w. Figure 2 shows an example.

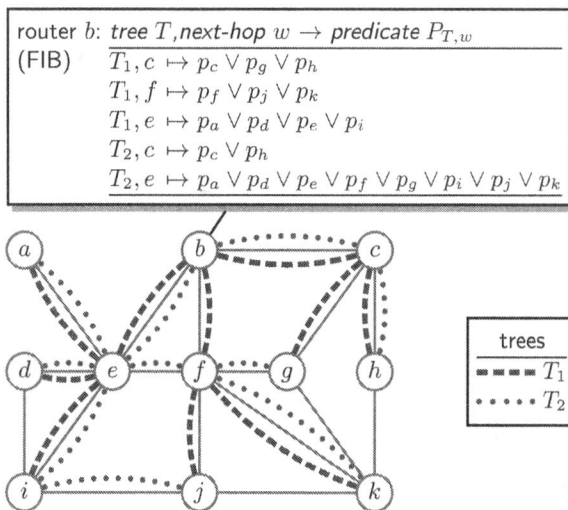

Figure 2: Multi-Tree Routing Scheme

With a FIB representing $P_{T,w}$ for all neighbor routers w in adj_v^T, forwarding proceeds as follows: Router v forwards a packet (notification or request) with descriptor X received from neighbor u on tree T to all neighbors $w \neq u$ in adj_v^T whose associated predicate $P_{T,w}$ matches X. We say that a predicate P matches a descriptor X if one of the descriptors in P matches X.

Since we use trees, we can control the global fan-out of a packet with local decisions. A packet starts with its global fan-out limit k set by the sender. A limit of $k = 1$, which is the default for requests, corresponds to an *anycast* delivery (the network delivers one copy of the packet), while a limit $k = \infty$, which is the default for notifications, corresponds to a *multicast* forwarding (the network delivers as many copies as there are interested receivers). A limit $1 < k < \infty$ can be also used and requires only minimal additional local processing: the router selects at most k matching neighbors and then partitions the fan-out limit over the selected neighbors.

3.2 Unicast Routing on Trees

We combine a locator-based unicast routing service with descriptor-based routing. To realize tree routing, we adapt a theoretical scheme for trees developed by Thorup and

Zwick [19]. Within a tree, each router is assigned a short label, which we refer to as a TZ-label, such that given the TZ-label of the destination plus its own TZ-label, a router can compute the next-hop towards the destination.

This scheme is extremely efficient both in space and time. In terms of space, a router needs to store its own TZ-label, which is at most $(1 + o(1)) \log_2 n$-bit long for a network of n nodes. In practice, we found that 46-bits are sufficient to cover the Internet at the AS-level. Thus, a router spends 46 bits for each tree. In terms of time, a forwarding decision requires a few basic operations on two TZ-labels, corresponding to an average of 10 CPU cycles and a throughput of 250M packets per second on a general-purpose, commodity CPU.[1]

The scheme can also be built efficiently. A tree can be labeled with a two-step distributed algorithm. In the first step, which could be combined with the construction of the tree, a converge-cast algorithm calculates the size of descendants of each node on the tree, while the second step consists of a depth-first-search numbering of nodes on the tree.

3.3 Locators and the Request/Reply Service

As discussed in Section 2, the network forwards packets using either an explicit destination locator or a content descriptor if no locator is given. Locators are network-defined quantities that may or may not have permanent validity (like IP addresses).

In our routing scheme we use TZ-labels to implement node locators. A node locator consists of a tree identifier plus the TZ-label of the destination on that tree. We now sketch a simple request/reply protocol that combines locators and descriptors, and that can be the basis for a full transport protocol for ICN.

The general idea is to use descriptors to find an object—that is, to forward a request towards a producer capable of satisfying the request—and then to use the more efficient locators to return the data block back to the consumer and also to request other data blocks from the same producer. To implement this idea, a request packet must carry the locator S of the source application (the consumer). When a request reaches a producer capable of satisfying the request or a router with a valid cached copy of the data, the producer or caching router sends back a data reply with destination locator S, which the network forwards back to the requesting application.

The advantage of locators within our scheme is that requests, unlike interest packets in CCN [10] which create a trail of pending interests, do not require any per-packet in-network state. Without per-router pending-interests tables, our scheme does not support the aggregation of simultaneous identical requests. However, identical requests that are not exactly simultaneous can still be effectively aggregated by caching data along the forwarding path.

A data reply may also specify one or more locators of the producer as its origin, as well as the identifiers of one or more follow-up data blocks. Specifically for our scheme, the multiple locators can be obtained using multiple trees, an approach that we detail below. A consumer receiving a data reply with an origin locator may then use that locator to send follow-up requests directly towards the same origin.

---

[1] These results are highlights of an extensive experimental evaluation, not reported here, of all-pairs traffic forwarded using TZ-labels on multiple trees at the AS level.

This, in particular, can substantially reduce the overhead of transferring large files.

Locators built on TZ-labels are relatively stable, since they change only when trees are rebuilt, for example in response to a topology change. Still, locators may also change within a flow if producers or consumers move within the network. A transport protocol that intends to support such mobility must correctly switch locators as applications move.

Lastly, a limitation of TZ-labels is that they may reveal the identity of consumers. If anonymity is required, then locators should be based on an appropriate anonymity-preserving routing scheme, such as onion routing [8].

3.4 Using Multiple Trees

Routing on a tree has two disadvantages. First, paths might be "stretched", meaning the distance between two nodes on the tree might be longer than on the full graph. Second, traffic would flow only on the tree, reducing the overall network throughput. It is well known that these problems can be alleviated by using multiple trees, and therefore we extend our routing scheme to use multiple trees. A notification or request is committed to, and thereafter routed using, one of those trees. Therefore, the forwarding process is identical to that over a single tree for an individual request or notification, but traffic is more evenly distributed and path lengths shortened on average. However, two aspects of the multiple-tree scheme are non-trivial: how to build and then select trees, and then how to combine multiple trees at different levels in hierarchical routing.

3.4.1 Building and Selecting Trees

The key to increasing throughput and reducing path lengths is in the choice of trees: first, the routing process must produce a good set of trees; second, when a request or a notification enters a routing domain, the access router must assign the request or notification to a tree in that domain. The choice of trees, the way they are built and then assigned by routers, could also be used to implement various routing strategies and policies.

The problem of covering a network with trees so as to achieve specific design objectives has been studied extensively from a theoretical perspective. For example, Räcke formulated a method to cover a network with trees to achieve the theoretically minimal congestion under unknown traffic [16]. However, such results are not applicable in practice, primarily because they can require an extremely high number of trees.

Our approach to building and selecting trees is therefore based on heuristics. To date we have studied two such heuristics for global trees, which are arguably the most crucial, and one for local trees.

H1: Latency Only (L): We choose a small number of root ASes and then build a shortest-paths (Dijkstra) tree for each root AS. This heuristic is intended to favor latency over any other routing objective. For the purpose of the analysis presented in this paper, we use a uniform-random choice over all ASes, which should give more conservative results. In practice, root ASes can be chosen in a number of ways using a distributed leader-election algorithm, perhaps favoring higher-tier ASes. Another and perhaps better way to select root ASes is to do it off line through a global administrative body, similar to the way top-level DNS servers and structures are configured today.

H2: Latency and Congestion (LC): We start with a first shortest-paths tree rooted at the AS with the lowest eccentricity representing the center of the network. We then increase the cost of each link used by the tree, and proceed iteratively to find another tree. The weight increase is by a fixed amount and, therefore, linear in the number of trees. At each iteration we select a new shortest-paths tree rooted at the AS with the lowest eccentricity. The new tree is computed with the current adjusted link weights and, therefore, it is likely to differ from all previous trees. These trees can be constructed using a slightly modified version of the fast distributed algorithm of Almeida et al. [2], which computes the eccentricity of node v in $diameter(G) + ecc(v) + 2$ rounds.

At the global level, trees are heavy in terms of memory because they store the aggregated predicates of the whole network. Therefore, we compute a relatively small number of global trees. Furthermore, we use shortest-paths trees that can be computed efficiently in a completely decentralized manner. Conversely, at the local level, trees are lighter and can be efficiently computed in a centralized manner. Since latency is crucial at the local level, the heuristic we use for local trees is also based on shortest-paths trees.

H3: Minimal Latency: We build shortest-paths trees rooted at every router within an AS.

To assign trees dynamically, routers select trees uniformly at random at the global level, while at the local level they always choose their own shortest-paths tree so as to obtain latency-minimal routes. In Section 4 we evaluate our scheme under the three heuristics.

3.4.2 Hierarchical Multi-Tree Routing

There can be multiple trees at different levels in the network, leading to a hierarchical routing scheme. We describe the case of two levels (intra- and inter-AS), although the scheme generalizes to more levels.

Routes are defined by global trees that span the AS-level network, and by local trees that span the internal network of each AS. Conceptually, each tree has a separate FIB, but concretely we aggregate predicates across trees so as to reduce space (Section 3.5). The FIB of a global tree contains the aggregate predicates of all the ASes. The FIB of a local tree contains the predicates of each internal host, possibly aggregated at the subnet level. An interior router needs to know only the local trees of its AS plus the TZ-labels of at least one gateway router for each global tree. A gateway router needs to know the local trees, the global trees, and the exterior connectivity of all the gateway routers of its AS, including their TZ-labels on the local trees. With this information, the network forwards packets either based on content descriptors or based on locators. We describe these two algorithms in turn.

Descriptor-Based Forwarding: A packet (request or notification) is first assigned to a local tree by its access router, and on that tree it is forwarded based on its content descriptor and fan-out limit as explained in Section 3.1. In addition to that, the packet is assigned to a global tree and sent to a gateway router that belongs to that tree using the TZ-label of that gateway on the local tree, which is known by the access router. On its global tree, a packet reaching a gateway router (or starting from that gateway) may have to cross the AS of that gateway to reach other gateways connected to the next-hop neighbor ASes on the global tree. This again is done on a local tree based on the TZ-labels of those gateways. And if the packet is entering that AS for the first time, then the local forwarding is performed via the content descriptor.

Locator-Based Forwarding: In our hierarchical routing scheme, a locator consists of a stack of node locators, each one consisting of a pair (T, ℓ) where T is a tree identifier and ℓ is the TZ-label of the destination node on T. With two levels, a destination locator contains the node locator (T_{AS}, ℓ_{AS}) of the destination AS on an AS-level tree T_{AS} plus the node locator (T_r, ℓ_r) of the destination router r on an inter-AS tree. Given a destination $(T_{AS}, \ell_{AS})/(T_r, \ell_r)$, forwarding proceeds as follows: If already in the destination AS, the access router pops the (T_{AS}, ℓ_{AS}) locator from the locator stack and forwards the packet on tree T_r using TZ-label ℓ_r. Otherwise, the router pushes a locator (T, ℓ_g) of a gateway router of its AS using any intra-AS tree T, and then forwards the packet accordingly. When a packet reaches the destination at the top of the stack, the router pops the locator and proceeds with what is left on the stack. If the top locator is at the AS level, then the gateway router might have to cross its AS to reach another gateway, in which case it would push a locator of that gateway onto the stack.

3.5 RIB Representation and Maintenance

We now describe a concrete implementation of the routing information base (RIB) for the multi-tree routing scheme. Conceptually, the RIB of a router v stores the following information for each tree T:

- adj_v^T is the adjacency list of T at v, meaning the subset of v's neighbors adjacent to v on T.

- ℓ_v^T is the TZ-label of router v on T.

- $P_v^T : w \to P_{T,w}$ is a map that associates each neighbor w in adj_v^T with a predicate $P_{T,w}$, where $P_{T,w}$ consists of a set of content descriptors (see Section 3.1 and, in particular, Figure 2).

Our primary goal is to obtain a compact representation of the RIB that also allows for efficient incremental updates. adj_v^T and ℓ_v^T require minimal space and standard data structures, and are also stable with trees. The P_v^T map changes with changing application preferences (content descriptors) and is also by far the heaviest component of the RIB. We therefore focus on the implementation of P_v^T.

With a naive implementation (depicted in Figure 2), multiple trees would have completely independent predicate maps P_v^T with only the basic aggregation of descriptors (described in Section 2.1). However, trees are likely to share many descriptors, simply because the descriptors represent offers or subscriptions that must be reachable from all trees. This suggests a representation of the predicate maps that further compresses the routing information across trees.

To exploit this form of aggregation, we develop a data structure in which routing information is not grouped by interface or tree, but rather by tag set. In practice, the RIB consists of a dictionary of tag sets, each associated with a set of tree/interface pairs. We use a PATRICIA trie to index the Bloom filters representing the tag sets, and we associate each tag set with a table of 16-bit entries representing tree/interface pairs. An example is shown in Figure 3.

PATRICIA tries have the advantage of requiring a minimal amount of memory, while also allowing for simple subset/superset checks implemented as tree walks. These checks

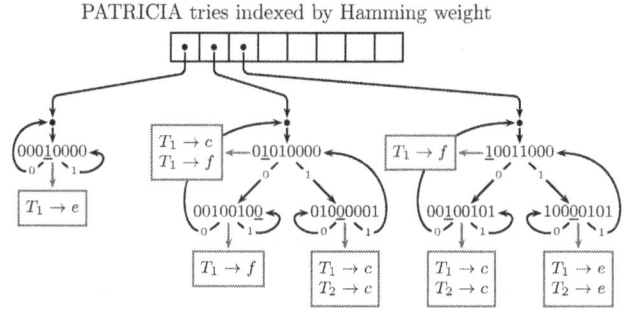

Figure 3: PATRICIA Trie Used for the RIB

are the essential building blocks for the maintenance of the RIB. The trie allows us to shortcut the search, much like a prefix search: if we are looking for subsets of an input filter f, and f contains a zero in a certain position identified by a node n, then we can skip the whole subtree of filters under n that contain a one in that position. In addition, we group filters by Hamming weight (in smaller tries). This allows us to skip entire tries containing filters that have too many elements to be subsets (or too few to be supersets) of the input filter. Since tries are independent of each other, subset/superset operations on different tries can also proceed in parallel.

Routing information propagates through update messages containing multiple descriptors, divided into an *addition delta*, a set of filters that we need to add in the RIB, and a *removal delta*, a set filters that we need to remove from the RIB. Figure 4 shows the main maintenance algorithm for the routing information. The main update function, *apply_delta*, processes an *update* message (of type delta) received from interface *ifx* that refers to a given *tree*.

```
void apply_delta (map<int,delta> & result,
                  delta update, int ifx, int tree) {
  for (filter f : update.removals)
    remove_filter(result, f, ifx, tree);
  for (filter f : update.additions)
    add_filter(result, f, ifx, tree); }

void add_filter (map<int,delta> & result,
                 filter f, int ifx, int tree) {
  if (!exists_subset_of(f, ifx, tree)) {
    add(f, ifx, tree);
    remove_supersets_of(f, ifx, tree);
    for (int i : interfaces[tree])
      if (i != ifx && no_subsets_on_other_ifx(f, i, tree))
        result[i].additions.add(f); } }

void remove_filter (map<int,delta> & result,
                    filter f, int ifx, int tree) {
  if (exists_filter(f, ifx, tree)) {
    remove(f, ifx, tree);
    for (i : interfaces[tree]) {
      if (i != ifx && no_subsets_on_other_ifx(f, i, tree)) {
        result[i].removals.add(f);
        result[i].additions.add(supersets_of(f, tree)); } } } }
```

Figure 4: Incremental Update Algorithm

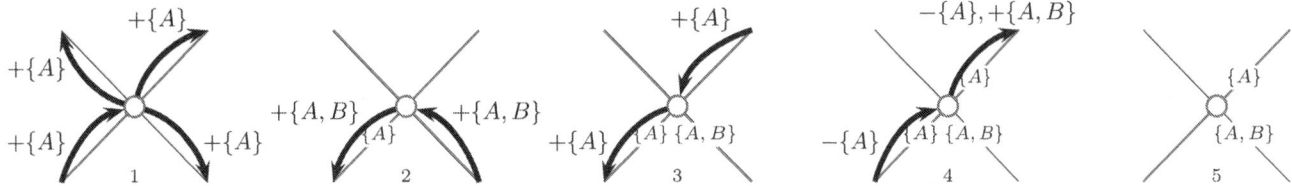

Figure 5: A Sequence of Incremental Updates

The update message may cause the router to update its own routing information base (shown in Figure 5 with tag sets attached to links) and may also trigger other update messages for the same tree (dark arrows). Such follow-up messages are returned in the *result* map. A tag set f is added in association with the incoming interface *ifx* only if f is not a superset of any existing tag set already associated with *ifx*. Also, when f is added, all supersets of f associated with *ifx* are removed. The router then propagates the addition of f to each interface i on the tree (other than *ifx*) when no subset of f is associated with any another interface. As an example, see the first three updates depicted in Figure 5.

Removals are similar to additions, except that removing a tag set f may also trigger the addition of supersets of f, as exemplified by the last updates depicted in Figure 5, where the removal of the tag set $\{A\}$ triggers the addition of tag set $\{A, B\}$. This maintenance algorithm ensures that routing tables remain minimal, in the sense that tag sets are aggregated as much as possible on a per-interface basis.

4. EVALUATION

We now present the results of an extensive experimental evaluation of our ICN routing scheme. We first assess the *effectiveness* of the scheme in routing information over the Internet using a few trees. We then study the *scalability* of the scheme both in terms of the memory requirements posed on routers, and also in terms of the cost of maintaining routing information for large numbers of content descriptors.

4.1 Effectiveness with k Trees

Here we consider the topological aspects of routing, and more specifically we evaluate the ability of our scheme to use the underlying network effectively. We conduct our analysis on the Internet AS-level topology, consisting of a graph of 42113 nodes and 118040 edges.[2] We use two measures of cost: *stretch* and *congestion*.

Stretch is the factor by which the distance between two nodes is extended by the routing scheme. Since our scheme routes each packet on a tree, this is the ratio between the distance on the tree and the distance on the full graph. Given a set of k trees, the stretch for the path between two nodes is the expected stretch; since we choose trees uniformly at random, it is simply the average stretch.

Congestion is the factor by which the usage of a link would grow using the routing scheme as compared to an optimal usage of the full network graph. The optimal usage here refers to the link usage with a distribution of traffic that achieves the best possible throughput. In practice, for each tree T, given a link (u, v) in T, we compute the cut defined by that link on T, meaning the partition of the nodes that

are on the two sides of the link on T. We then compute the number of links that cross the cut on the original graph, which is the total capacity of the network over that cut. Thus, we assume that, for the portion of traffic routed on T ($1/k$ of the total traffic for k trees), the link (u, v) would need to carry the traffic that could instead go over all the links that cross the cut. So, for a cut of size $s_{T,u,v}$ on a tree T out of k trees, link (u, v) is given a congestion of $s_{T,u,v}/k$, and the total congestion of that link is the sum of its congestion for all the k trees. Notice that this congestion factor is a very conservative measure, since it uses the globally optimal allocation of flow for all network cuts as a baseline.

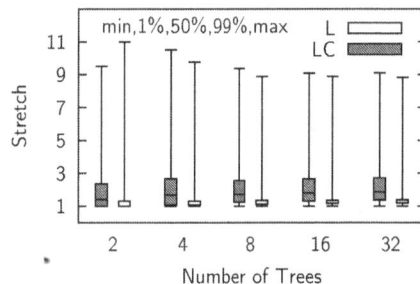

Figure 6: Path Stretch

In Figure 6 we show the expected stretch for various sets of global (AS-level) trees. We generate sets of 2, 4, 8, 16, and 32 trees using the heuristics H1 and H2 discussed in Section 3.4.1. The label L in the plots refers to the latency-only heuristic, H1, while LC refers to the latency-and-congestion heuristic, H2. Each box plot in the chart shows the minimum, the 1-percentile, the median, the 99-percentile, and the maximum. The plot shows that the maximum expected stretch decreases with more trees, while more trees lead to a minor increase of the median (expected) stretch. Despite the growth, we can see that the stretch is low: the median always remains under 2 and the 99-percentile under 3. There is also a clear difference between the two heuristics: heuristic L achieves better results than LC.

Our experimental analysis is consistent with another study on the approximability of the AS-level topology with trees. Krioukov et al. [13] studied two compact routing schemes that have a theoretical expected stretch of 3 [5, 19], and found that in practice, on the AS-level topology, their average stretch is instead close to 1. However, the two schemes require $O(n^{1/2}\log^{1/2}n)$ and $O(n^{2/3}\log^{4/3}n)$ trees, respectively. Our scheme also achieves an average stretch very close to 1, but under significantly smaller sets of trees.

Figure 7 shows the congestion for the same set of trees of Figure 6. This plot shows the 1-percentile, 5-percentile, median, 95-percentile, and 99-percentile of the distribution.

---

[2] http://irl.cs.ucla.edu/topology/ (retrieved 29/06/2012)

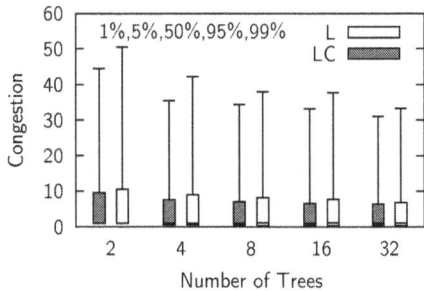

Figure 7: Link Congestion

The salient result is that most links experience no congestion penalty at all, experiencing a congestion factor of 1, and further that extreme levels of congestion are reduced when using more trees. As expected, the congestion factors for the L heuristic are higher as compared with the LC heuristic.

The analysis of stretch and congestion shows that different tree-building strategies may be used to achieve different design goals. More importantly, the general conclusion we can draw from this analysis is that even small sets of trees can cover the Internet at the AS-level topology quite well, with only minimal cost in terms of path-length stretch and link congestion.

4.2 Scalability: Memory and Maintenance

We now evaluate the memory requirements of our ICN routing scheme. For this assessment we develop a synthetic workload corresponding to the plausible behavior of users of different applications over a global-scale information-centric network [3]. We first analyze real traces from four classes of applications: active Web content and blog posts ("push"); video ("pull"); short messages and micro-blogging ("push"); and large BitTorrent downloads ("pull"). We then synthetically expand the resulting workload to 25 other languages that have a meaningful influence on Internet traffic, while preserving the semantic correlation between tags. The full description of these workloads, the methods used to normalize and expand them, and the way we associate users with different applications is detailed in a technical report [15].

4.2.1 Memory Requirements for Inter-AS RIBs

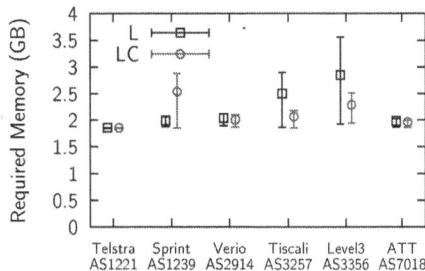

Figure 8: Sizes of Inter-AS RIBs

In Figure 8 we show the memory used by the RIBs of the gateway routers of different ASes. This analysis is based on simulations of the routing scheme with 8 trees and under a workload generated for 50 million users. However, since the exact connectivity between the ASes at the level of their gateway routers is not publicly available, we cannot determine how many trees would actually need to be known by each gateway. We therefore simulate all the possible cases and derive the distribution of the memory requirement for every case. The plot shows the minimum, the average, and the maximum amount of memory that would be needed to store the routing information for between 1 and 8 trees. We show the data for the two sets of heuristically derived trees labeled L and LC, as above. The variation is due to the different degree and location of the ASes on different trees. Usually an AS with many neighbors experiences less compression. Notice, however, that the absolute values are relatively low: the most demanding case, which is Level3 with the L heuristic, is less then 3.6GB of memory. Furthermore, the memory required by 8 trees (maximum value), is always less than twice the memory required by a single tree (minimum value). This means that under our scheme, descriptors aggregate well across trees.

4.2.2 Memory Requirements for Intra-AS RIBs

For each AS we also analyze the memory requirements at the intra-AS level. We use the internal AS topologies available from the Rocketfuel project [18]. The data are presented in Figure 9. The N and E labels in the graph

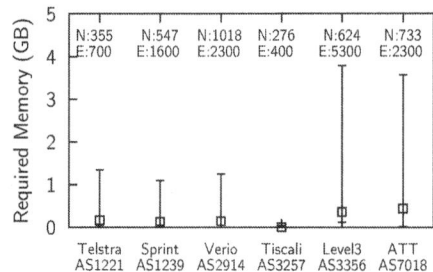

Figure 9: Sizes of Intra-AS RIBs

represent the number of nodes and edges in each AS, respectively. We plot the minimum, average, and maximum sizes of the RIBs used to store local trees. Recall that for the local (intra-AS) trees we store all the shortest-paths rooted at every node (heuristic H3). The number of users inside each AS depends on the distribution of the 50 million users over the AS-level topology. Considering the largest results, namely Level3 and AT&T, we can see that even using a large number of trees (since both have hundreds of routers) we still obtain good levels of aggregation and good results in absolute terms, with a maximum memory requirement of less than 4GB.

4.2.3 Scalability Analysis

The results discussed so far are limited to a relatively low number of users compared to the current population of Internet users. In order to better demonstrate the scalability of our routing scheme, we focus on a particular tier 1 AS (3257) and on a shortest-paths tree derived using heuristic H1 to study the memory requirement under a workload of almost 10 billion content descriptors corresponding to 500 million users. Figure 10 shows the memory required for a gateway

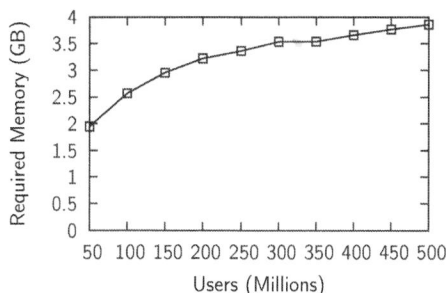

Figure 10: RIB Scalability

router for increasingly larger user populations. We can see that the growth of the memory requirement is relatively high initially, but steadily flattens, reaching 3.8GB for 500 million users. This is due directly to the aggregation of tags under our scheme: even with high numbers of users, the memory required to store all the routing information is likely to remain practically constant, since most of the new descriptors will be aggregated at no additional cost.

4.2.4 *RIB Incremental Updates*

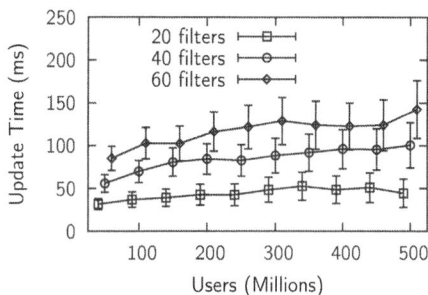

Figure 11: Scalability of the Maintenance Times

In Figure 11 we show the time needed to update the RIB using the algorithm described in Section 3.5. In this analysis we start from the RIBs computed for the experiment of Figure 10 and then apply updates of 20, 40, and 60 Bloom filters. The plot shows mean and standard deviation of the update time computed over 1000 updates. (The data points on the three lines are for the same values of the x-axis, but for purposes of readability have been slightly shifted to avoid obscuring each other.) The update time does not increase significantly with the size of the RIBs and is almost constant for each Bloom filter: 2.04ms on average. Our algorithm can handle 500 updates per second on large RIBs, even when run on a commodity PC (Intel Xeon with two quad core 2.53GHz CPUs and 16GB of RAM).

5. RELATED WORK

Although routing is one of the crucial aspects for the development of the notion of an information centric network, there is surprisingly little work on this topic. The NDN project proposes NLSR [9], a link-state routing protocol for NDN. NLSR is a traditional link-state protocol that uses NDN itself to transport routing information. NLSR realizes only a traditional unicast routing scheme that can support multiple paths with multiple runs of the Dijkstra algorithm.

Another interesting work is presented by Papadopoulos et al. [14] who developed two greedy forwarding algorithms in a hyperbolic space. This approach seems promising for routing in ICN and particularly with NDN naming. However, in order to work well in practice, the name space must be hyperbolic, and right now there is no evidence that that is the case. Another problem with this scheme is the relation between the name space and the network topology, meaning how names are distributed over the network. In fact, if names do not follow the same distribution (within the hyperbolic space) then paths can be stretched significantly. Finally, it is not clear how to compute the hyperbolic coordinates of routers and content using only local information.

A number of ICN proposals do not implement a routing scheme based on content names or identifiers, but instead map names or identifiers to network-level addresses. The PURSUIT project[3] uses flat names to identify each object together with a topology/resolution service to obtain a form of network-level unicast or multicast address used for the actual packet switching [11]. DONA [12] also uses flat names and uses a network of special "resolution handlers" to locate the content at the IP network level. NetInf[4] provides a name resolution scheme in combination with a name-based routing scheme similar to CCN/NDN. However, this name-based routing remains localized, so that *global* reachability is only supported through the name resolution scheme [1].

6. CONCLUSION AND FUTURE WORK

We have examined the fundamental problem of routing in an information-centric network, and the essential question of the scalability of routing state. We presented and evaluated a concrete scheme based on trees that supports a rich service model, including "push" communication and expressive content descriptors consisting of tag sets. Our evaluation confirms two intuitions: first, that the Internet can be approximated effectively with trees and, second, that tag-based content descriptors, which are more expressive than name prefixes, aggregate well under our scheme.

A crucial open question regarding routing is whether a multi-tree scheme, and in particular one that uses a few trees at the global level, can effectively support routing policies. We plan to explore this question by developing heuristic algorithms to build sets of trees that satisfy a given set of routing policies.

Another crucial problem that we only touched upon is tag-based forwarding. We reduce the overall complexity of forwarding with efficient locators. However, we are also working on highly parallel forwarding algorithms that combine hardware and software solutions to support high-speed forwarding with tables of hundreds of millions of tag sets. Related to the problem of forwarding, we plan to extend our evaluation, to cover forwarding but also to complement the workloads we used to evaluate the routing scheme. The workloads we used consist of content descriptors, extrapolated from traces of existing applications, that feed into the FIBs and RIBs. We will also consider other representative workloads, also extrapolated from real application traces, that are specifically intended to generate network traffic [17].

---

[3]http://www.fp7-pursuit.eu/
[4]http://www.sail-project.eu/

Acknowledgments

The work of M. Papalini was supported in part by the Swiss National Science Foundation under grant 200021-132565. The work of A.L. Wolf was partially sponsored by the U.S. Army Research Laboratory and the U.K. Ministry of Defence and was accomplished under Agreement Number W911NF-06-3-0001, and by the European Commission under grant number 318521 (Project HARNESS).

7. REFERENCES

[1] B. Ahlgren, C. Dannewitz, C. Imbrenda, D. Kutscher, and B. Ohlman. A survey of information-centric networking. *IEEE Communications Magazine*, 50(7):26–36, 2012.

[2] P. S. Almeida, C. Baquero, and A. Cunha. Fast distributed computation of distances in networks. In *51st IEEE Annual Conference on Decision and Control*, Dec. 2012.

[3] A. Carzaniga, K. Khazaei, M. Papalini, and A. L. Wolf. Is information-centric multi-tree routing feasible? In *Proceedings of the 3rd ACM SIGCOMM Workshop on Information-Centric Networking*, Aug. 2013.

[4] A. Carzaniga, M. Papalini, and A. L. Wolf. Content-based publish/subscribe networking and information-centric networking. In *Proceedings of the ACM SIGCOMM Workshop on Information-Centric Networking*, Aug. 2011.

[5] L. J. Cowen. Compact routing with minimum stretch. In *Proceedings of the Tenth Annual ACM-SIAM Symposium on Discrete Algorithms*, Jan. 1999.

[6] A. Ghodsi, S. Shenker, T. Koponen, A. Singla, B. Raghavan, and J. Wilcox. Information-centric networking: Seeing the forest for the trees. In *Proceedings of the 10th ACM Workshop on Hot Topics in Networks*, Nov. 2011.

[7] M. Gitter and D. R. Cheriton. An architecture for content routing support in the Internet. In *3rd USENIX Symposium on Internet Technologies and Systems*, Mar. 2001.

[8] D. Goldschlag, M. Reed, and P. Syverson. Onion routing. *Communications of the ACM*, 42(2):39–41, Feb. 1999.

[9] A. K. M. M. Hoque, S. O. Amin, A. Alyyan, B. Zhang, L. Zhang, and L. Wang. NLSR: Named-data link state routing protocol. In *Proceedings of the 3rd ACM SIGCOMM Workshop on Information-centric Networking*, Aug. 2013.

[10] V. Jacobson, D. K. Smetters, J. D. Thornton, M. F. Plass, N. H. Briggs, and R. L. Braynard. Networking named content. In *Proceedings of the 5th International Conference on Emerging Networking Experiments and Technologies*, Dec. 2009.

[11] P. Jokela, A. Zahemszky, C. Esteve Rothenberg, S. Arianfar, and P. Nikander. LIPSIN: Line speed publish/subscribe inter-networking. In *Proceedings of the ACM SIGCOMM Conference on Data Communication*, Aug. 2009.

[12] T. Koponen, M. Chawla, B.-G. Chun, A. Ermolinskiy, K. H. Kim, S. Shenker, and I. Stoica. A data-oriented (and beyond) network architecture. *SIGCOMM Computer Communications Review*, 37(4):181–192, Aug. 2007.

[13] D. Krioukov, K. C. Claffy, K. Fall, and A. Brady. On compact routing for the Internet. *SIGCOMM Computing Communications Review*, 37(3):41–52, July 2007.

[14] F. Papadopoulos, D. Krioukov, M. Boguñá, and A. Vahdat. Greedy forwarding in dynamic scale-free networks embedded in hyperbolic metric spaces. In *Proceedings of the IEEE Conference on Computer Communications (INFOCOM)*, Mar. 2010.

[15] M. Papalini, K. Khazaei, A. Carzaniga, and A. L. Wolf. Scalable routing for tag-based information-centric networking. Technical Report 2014/01, University of Lugano, Feb. 2014.

[16] H. Räcke. Optimal hierarchical decompositions for congestion minimization in networks. In *Proceedings of the 40th Annual ACM Symposium on Theory of Computing*, May 2008.

[17] W. So, A. Narayanan, and D. Oran. Named data networking on a router: Fast and dos-resistant forwarding with hash tables. In *Proceedings of the Ninth ACM/IEEE Symposium on Architectures for Networking and Communications Systems*, Oct. 2013.

[18] N. Spring, R. Mahajan, D. Wetherall, and T. Anderson. Measuring ISP topologies with Rocketfuel. *IEEE/ACM Transactions on Networking*, 12(1), Feb. 2004.

[19] M. Thorup and U. Zwick. Compact routing schemes. In *Proceedings of the 13th Annual ACM Symposium on Parallel Algorithms and Architectures*, July 2001.

On the Role of Routing in Named Data Networking*

Cheng Yi†
University of Arizona
yic@cs.arizona.edu

Jerald Abraham
University of Arizona
jeraldabraham@cs.arizona.edu

Alexander Afanasyev
UCLA
afanasev@cs.ucla.edu

Lan Wang
University of Memphis
lanwang@memphis.edu

Beichuan Zhang
University of Arizona
bzhang@arizona.edu

Lixia Zhang
UCLA
lixia@cs.ucla.edu

ABSTRACT

A unique feature of Named Data Networking (NDN) is that its forwarding plane can detect and recover from network faults on its own, enabling each NDN router to handle network failures locally without relying on global routing convergence. This new feature prompts us to re-examine the role of routing in an NDN network: does it still need a routing protocol? If so, what impact may an intelligent forwarding plane have on the design and operation of NDN routing protocols? Through analysis and extensive simulations, we show that routing protocols remain highly beneficial in an NDN network. Routing disseminates initial topology and policy information as well as long-term changes in them, and computes the routing table to guide the forwarding process. However, because the forwarding plane is capable of detecting and recovering from failures quickly, routing no longer needs to handle short-term churns in the network. Freeing routing protocols from short-term churns can greatly improve their scalability and stability, enabling NDN to use routing protocols that were previously viewed as unsuitable for real networks.

Categories and Subject Descriptors

C.2.2 [**Network Protocols**]: Routing protocols

General Terms

Analysis, Performance

Keywords

NDN; routing; routing scalability; adaptive forwarding

*This work was partially supported by the National Science Foundation (No. 1039615, 1040868, 1040036) and Cisco. Any opinions, findings, and conclusions or recommendations expressed in this material are those of the author(s) and do not necessarily reflect the views of the sponsors.
†Dr. Cheng Yi is currently with Google Inc.

1. INTRODUCTION

Named Data Networking (NDN) [13, 34] is a new network architecture that changes the basic network service semantics from "delivering packet to a given destination" to "retrieving data with a given name." NDN communication is receiver-driven: a data consumer sends *Interest* packets carrying the names of desired data; any node in the network can return *Data* packets that have matching names to satisfy the Interests. This two-way Interest-Data packet exchange takes the same network path but in opposite directions.

Symmetric Interest-Data exchange and in-network forwarding state enable a unique feature of NDN – *adaptive forwarding* ([32, 31]). More specifically, a node expects a Data packet to come back from the same interface where it forwarded the Interest within a reasonable time period (e.g., round-trip time), otherwise it should get a timeout or receive a NACK packet [31], which signals a failure of this attempt. Upon detection of a failure, the node can then send the Interest to other interfaces to explore alternate paths. This built-in failure detection and recovery capability works on the forwarding plane, with no intervention from the control plane. Our earlier work [31] shows that NDN's adaptive forwarding can handle link failures, prefix hijacking, and congestion control more effectively than IP networks.

Having an intelligent and adaptive forwarding plane raises new research questions. Today's IP networks put all intelligence into routing, which disseminates topology and policy information, computes routes, detects and recovers from failures while the data plane merely forwards packets according to the FIB. When the data plane has its own adaptability, are routing protocols still needed? If so, for what purpose and to what extent? If some of routing's tasks can be offloaded to forwarding, would that bring positive impact on routing protocols' design and operation, e.g., making routing more scalable and stable?

In this paper we investigate the role of routing in NDN networks. Through analysis, design, and extensive simulation, we find that a routing protocol is highly beneficial in bootstrapping the forwarding plane for effective data retrieval, and in efficient probing of new links or recovered links. However, *NDN routing does not need to converge fast following network changes*, which can be handled by adaptive forwarding more promptly. This enables one to significantly improve the scalability and stability of the routing system using larger keep-alive timer values that ignore short-term failures. Furthermore, routing algorithms that would not work well in today's IP networks may work fine in an

NDN network due to routing's reduced role in bootstrapping adaptive forwarding.

The rest of this paper is organized as follows. Section 2 reviews NDN with a focus on the adaptive forwarding plane. Section 3 discusses the role of routing in both IP and NDN. The coordination of NDN routing and forwarding is explained in Section 4. Section 5 evaluates the performance of the coordination. Section 6 discusses other possible routing schemes for NDN. Section 7 presents related work and Section 8 concludes the paper.

2. NDN FORWARDING OVERVIEW

Each NDN packet carries a *name* field that uniquely identifies a piece of data, e.g., /ndn/papers/routing.pdf/seg1. NDN routers forward Interests based on the names, and keep forwarding state for each pending Interest. When Data packets arrive, routers use names to match them to corresponding pending Interests and forward them accordingly. Each Interest also carries a *nonce* field that can be used to detect forwarding loops. In this section we briefly review NDN's forwarding process and how it handles link failures.

2.1 Forwarding Process

There are three key data structures in NDN's node model, i.e., *Forwarding Information Base* (FIB), *Pending Interest Table* (PIT) and *Content Store* (CS). FIB serves as the forwarding table. It is different from the FIB in IP routers in that it is indexed by name prefixes instead of IP prefixes, and each FIB entry may provide multiple interfaces instead of a single best interface for each name prefix. Unlike FIB, PIT and CS are unique to NDN. Both PIT and CS are indexed by names. A PIT entry records incoming and outgoing interface(s) of an Interest, and is used to guide Data forwarding. CS is a temporary cache of Data packets that can speed up the satisfaction of Interests.

In NDN, the forwarding process works as follows. When a router receives an Interest, it first checks the Interest name against the CS and returns the Data if there is a match. Otherwise, the router checks the Interest name against the PIT. If a PIT entry already exists, i.e., the Interest has already been forwarded but no Data has been returned yet, the router simply adds the incoming interface of the Interest to the PIT entry. If no PIT entry exists, the router adds a new PIT entry and further looks up the Interest name in the FIB using longest prefix match. If a matching FIB entry is found, the Interest is forwarded by a *forwarding strategy* module [13]. Otherwise, the router cannot satisfy the Interest and may send a NACK back to the incoming interface of the Interest [31]. When a router receives a Data packet, it checks the Data name against the PIT. If a PIT entry is found, the Data is stored in the CS and further forwarded to the incoming interfaces of the corresponding Interests, which have been recorded in the PIT. Otherwise, the Data is dropped since it is either unrequested or no longer wanted.

The forwarding strategy associated with the name space of an Interest determines whether and how to forward the Interest. It may take such information as ranking from the routing protocol, interface status, round-trip time (RTT) and congestion level into consideration. In this paper we adopt the forwarding strategy proposed in [31]. For each name prefix, each interface is assigned a color code depending on its current working status. It is *Green* for a working interface, *Red* if the interface is not working, and *Yellow*

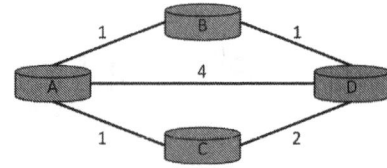

Figure 1: A simple network example.

if the status is uncertain. The forwarding strategy always prefers Green interfaces over Yellow ones, and never uses Red interfaces to forward Interests.

2.2 Failure Recovery

NDN's two-way symmetric traffic flow enables fast fault detection. Routers can calculate RTT for each Interest-Data exchange, which can be used as a prediction for future Interests. After forwarding an Interest, a router starts a timer based on the average of previous RTTs; potential network problems can be detected if no Data is received before the timer expires. With Interest NACKs [31], fault detection and notification is even faster. When network problems are detected, routers can explore alternative paths freely without worrying about loops, since loops can be detected by checking the nonce field carried in Interests. Fast fault detection and loop-free forwarding are the two unique features that make NDN's forwarding plane smart and adaptive – routers are able to handle network faults such as prefix hijacking, failures and congestion locally at the forwarding plane [31].

We use the simple example in Figure 1 to illustrate how NDN routers handle link failures. The cost of the links are marked in the figure; routers rank the interfaces using the cost of their best paths towards the destination. When there is no failure in the network, A uses B as its primary next hop for content provided by D. Interface A-B will be marked Green as long as Data continues to flow from B to A. When link B-D fails, A will keep sending Interests to B at first. However, B cannot satisfy the Interests due to the failure, so it will send NACKs back to A. Upon receiving a NACK, A will mark A-B Yellow and retry the next best interface, in this case A-C. Since there is no failure on this path, Data will flow back through path D-C-A. A will then mark interface A-C Green and start using C as the primary next hop.

3. ROLE OF ROUTING

Since NDN's forwarding model is a strict superset of the IP model, any routing scheme that works well for IP should also work well for NDN [13]. However, today's IP routing protocols suffer from issues such as slow convergence or poor scalability. On the other hand, NDN has a smart and powerful forwarding plane, which is able to take over part of routing's responsibility in IP. In this section, we first review IP routing, and then rethink the role of routing in NDN.

3.1 Routing in IP

IP's routing plane is intelligent and adaptive, but its forwarding plane is stateless and strictly follows routing. Therefore the routing plane is also regarded as the control plane. Routing is responsible for building the routing table and maintaining it in face of network changes, including both long-term topology and policy changes as well as short-term churns. When there is a change in the network, routers need to exchange routing updates with each other in order to reach new global consistency. The time period after a change happens and before all routers agree on the new routing state is called the *routing convergence period*. IP routing protocols need to converge fast in order to reduce packet loss and resume packet delivery after network changes.

However, fast routing convergence is challenging in large operational networks. The fundamental reason is that it conflicts with other design goals for routing protocols, i.e., routing stability and scalability. Routing stability ensures stable routing paths within the network. It is important for applications that suffer from RTT fluctuation; it also helps routers achieve traffic engineering goals. Routing scalability is essential for supporting a large number of nodes, links and prefixes[1] in the network. For link-state routing, each router knows the entire topology. These protocols can converge fast, but at the cost of poor stability and limited scalability. For distance/path-vector routing, routers do not have a full knowledge of the topology. They are able to achieve better scalability, but the convergence time may be as long as tens of minutes. Below we use link-state routing as an example to explain the issues with today's IP routing protocols.

The routing convergence period can be divided into four phases, i.e., *failure detection, update propagation, route computation* and *FIB update*. In link-state routing, routers periodically exchange HELLO messages to maintain connection: if no HELLO message is received within the DEAD interval, the link is considered down. Previous research ([7, 11]) recommended setting the HELLO interval to be on the order of milliseconds in order to detect failures quickly. However, this not only increases overhead but also affects routing stability, since a temporarily congested link may be mistakenly considered fluctuating down and up. After a link failure is detected, attached routers need to generate routing updates and propagate them to the rest of the network; when a router receives a routing update, it needs to recompute the routing table. To achieve fast routing convergence, all these steps should be done as quickly as possible. However, if the network is unstable (e.g., there is a flapping link), generating routing updates and recomputing routing table frequently will increase bandwidth and computation overhead as well as harm routing stability. At the same time, shortest path first (SPF) computation time increases with the size of the network; FIB update time depends on the number of prefixes. To achieve fast convergence, both the network size and the number of prefixes need to be limited, leading to poor scalability.

There are mechanisms to improve link-state routing stability and scalability. Dynamic timers improve routing stability by limiting the rate of update generation and SPF computation. However, these timers are increased exponentially each time, potentially increasing convergence time significantly when the network is unstable. Therefore, short initial timers have been suggested [11]. *Area* was introduced to improve routing scalability [22]. However, it leads to sub-optimal paths between areas and increases the complexity of configuration. Although inter-area routing can utilize

distance-vector or path-vector routing algorithms that may scale better, they converge much slower.

In summary, it is hard to achieve fast convergence, stability and scalability simultaneously in a routing protocol. If failures can be handled without global routing convergence, the requirement on fast convergence can be relaxed, making it possible to improve routing stability and scalability.

3.2 Routing in NDN

In NDN, the forwarding plane is the actual control plane since the forwarding strategy module makes forwarding decisions on its own. This fundamental change prompts us to rethink the role of routing in NDN. The first question is whether NDN still needs routing protocols. Conventionally, routing protocols are responsible for disseminating topology and policy information, computing routes and handling short-term network changes. For NDN to work without routing, routers need to be able to do the following things efficiently: 1) retrieve Data when the network is stable; 2) handle link failures; and 3) handle link recovery. Can NDN achieve these solely with the forwarding plane?

Another question that arises is if NDN does need routing protocols, how will they be different from today's existing routing protocols? With the intelligent and adaptive forwarding plane, can some of the routing plane's functionality be offloaded to the forwarding plane, and which? In addition, how will the design and operation of routing protocols benefit from this shift of functionality? In the next section we try to give answers to these questions.

4. ROUTING AND FORWARDING COORDINATION

In this section, we seek answers to the questions raised in 3.2. Previous research [31] shows that NDN routers are able to handle link failures effectively without routing. In this section we focus on whether NDN routers can retrieve Data and react to link recovery *efficiently* without routing. We show that NDN does need routing protocols to help bootstrap the forwarding process and handle link recovery. In addition, we specify how the routing plane coordinates with the forwarding plane, and present a simple method to improve routing stability and scalability in NDN.

4.1 Interface Ranking

The forwarding plane design presented in [31] assumes interfaces are ranked by routing preference. Can NDN routers retrieve Data efficiently without routing to rank the list of available interfaces? The answer is negative. In the extreme case, we can implement a forwarding strategy that floods every Interest to all available interfaces. This way we can always retrieve Data quickly through the best paths. However, it will also incur significantly high overhead. We can also implement forwarding strategies that randomly explore the interfaces or try them one-by-one in a round-robin fashion. Given enough time, routers should be able to find working paths since all possible paths will be explored. One big issue with this method is that path exploration may take extremely long time as shown in Section 5.3.

Consequently, NDN routers need good interface ranking to help bootstrap the forwarding process. The responsibility of providing interface ranking lies in the routing protocols. Existing routing algorithms such as link-state or

---

[1]Supporting large number of prefixes is particularly important in NDN since the number of name prefixes will be orders of magnitude larger than the number of IP prefixes in today's Internet.

Pseudocode 1 ProbingDue Algorithm
```
1: function PROBINGDUE(FibEntry, Intf)
2:     if Intf ≠ FibEntry.RoutingPreferredIntf then
3:         if FibEntry.LastProbingTime + M ≤ Now() or
4:             FibEntry.PacketsSinceLastProbing ≥ N then
5:             Return True
6:         end if
7:     end if
8:     Return False
9: end function
```

Pseudocode 2 Probing Algorithm
```
1: function PROBE(Interest, FibEntry, PitEntry)
2:     interface ← FibEntry.RoutingPreferredIntf
3:     if interface ∉ PitEntry.Outgoing and
4:         interface ∉ PitEntry.Incoming then
5:         if interface.Available then
6:             Interest.Nonce ← GenerateNonce()
7:             Transmit(interface, Interest)
8:             Add interface to PitEntry.Outgoing
9:             FibEntry.LastProbingTime ← Now()
10:            FibEntry.PacketsSinceLastProbing ← 0
11:        end if
12:    end if
13: end function
```

distance/path-vector routing can be used to rank the interfaces[2]. The details are explained as follows.

4.1.1 Link-State Routing

Link-state routing protocols store the entire network topology in the link-state database (LSDB), making it possible to compute optimal interface ranking. Suppose a node N has n interfaces $I_1 .. I_n$. For Data provided by node M, we rank these interfaces using $C_{N,k}^M$, which is the cost of the best path from N to M through interface I_k. One simple method to compute $C_{N,k}$ for all destinations through I_k is to remove all interfaces except I_k from N's LSDB, and run *Dijkstra's algorithm* to compute the shortest paths. This may not be the best method since it will end up calling Dijkstra's algorithm once for every interface. It is just used to illustrate how interface ranking can be done in link-state routing. Optimization of the algorithm is possible but out of the scope of this paper.

4.1.2 Distance/Path-Vector Routing

In distance-vector or path-vector routing, routers announce cost of the complete routing path towards each destination to their neighbors. When router N receives a routing announcement for Data provided by M from interface I_k, it simply adds the link cost of I_k to the received path cost to obtain its path cost $C_{N,k}^M$. The interfaces are then ranked by the path costs to M through them.

Note that a router may not receive routing announcement from all interfaces, since these routing protocols often incorporate split-horizon route announcement to prevent routing loops. If router N learns a route towards M through interface I_k, it will not advertise its route to M over I_k. Interfaces that do not receive routing announcement are assigned infinite cost to ensure they stay at the end of the ranked interface list. They will only be used as the last resort if all higher-ranked interfaces fail to retrieve Data.

These interfaces are useful in many situations. For example, in BGP if a provider P uses a customer C as the next hop, it will not make routing announcement to C. If C's best path fails, it will not have an alternative path until routing converges, in which case P will announce its alternative path to C. RBGP [14] is proposed to address this issue by allowing P to announce its alternative path to C even without failures. NDN, on the other hand, is able to achieve the same effect without changing the routing protocol.

4.2 Probing

It has been shown that NDN routers can handle link failures locally at the forwarding plane [31]. In this subsection we answer the question of whether the same applies to link recovery. Routers can detect link failures quickly by observing Interest-Data exchanges or Interest NACK. However, there is no explicit signal for link recovery from the forwarding plane. Again let's take Figure 1 as an example. After interface B-D recovers from a failure, interface A-B becomes the best interface for A to retrieve data from D. However, A will continue using interface A-C because the forwarding strategy prefers Green interfaces over Yellow ones. In this case, A needs to probe interface A-B by sending a copy of an Interest to it. If the probing Interest successfully brings Data back, interface A-B will be marked Green and be used to forward subsequent Interests to D.

There is a research question of when to perform probing. An Interest copy is used for probing so that regular Data retrieval will not be affected if probing is unsuccessful. However, this causes extra Interest and Data in the network. There is a trade-off between how fast a link recovery is detected and the amount of overhead caused by probing. In CCNx [2], a prototype implementation of NDN, routers probe alternative interfaces periodically in order to detect better paths. This enables routers to detect link recovery at the forwarding plane. Fast recovery detection is achievable through aggressive probing. However, it will incur significant overhead.

In fact, routing is able to help with the dilemma. If there is a routing protocol, it will be able to detect link recovery and converge to it by ranking the new best interface (Yellow) higher than the currently used one (Green). Thus we can take advantage of routing by only probing a Yellow interface if its ranking is higher than the Green interface(s). This way we can keep the probing overhead low, and switch back to the optimal paths as soon as routing converges. Routing convergence time is not a concern because the alternative paths found by the forwarding plane are of good quality [31]. Note that probing is also useful in failure handling if the alternative paths found by the forwarding strategy are not the optimal ones.

We propose a probing algorithm as presented in Pseudocode 1 and 2. After forwarding each Interest, the strategy module calls **ProbingDue** to check whether probing is needed. Two thresholds are introduced to further limit the probing overhead. For each FIB entry, M is the minimum time interval, and N is the minimum number of packets forwarded between two consecutive probings. The algorithm

---

[2]The case of BGP is more complex because it also takes routing policy into consideration. How to accommodate routing policy in interface ranking is part of our future work.

Table 1: Topologies Used in the Simulations.

Topology	Before Processing		After Processing	
	Node #	Link #	Node #	Link #
Abilene	12	30	11	28
AS1239-PoP	52	168	32	128
AS701-PoP	83	438	47	366
AS1239-Router	284	1882	N/A	N/A

returns true only if at least M time has elapsed or at least N packets have been forwarded since the last probing. The setting of M and N depends on the traffic load and the probing overhead network operators are willing tolerate. The probing algorithm (Pseudocode 2) sends a copy of the Interest to the routing preferred interface using a different nonce. The nonce is changed so that routers will not drop the probing Interest after seeing the original Interest.

4.3 Routing Stability and Scalability

Link-state routing protocols exhibit poor stability and scalability in IP due to the fast routing convergence requirement. However, there is a simple method to address these issues in NDN. Since NDN routers can handle network failures at the forwarding plane, short-lived failures can be masked from the routing protocols. Research shows that the duration of network failures follows a long-tailed distribution, and over 50% of failures last less than one minute ([20, 28]). Therefore, the number of routing events can be significantly reduced if routing protocols do not need to react to the short-lived failures. As a result, the bandwidth and CPU cycles consumed by routing updates can be reduced, and there will be less routing fluctuation. In addition, since there is no fast routing convergence requirement, larger networks and more name prefixes become affordable. In summary, both routing stability and scalability can be significantly improved.

For link-state routing, we can implement the idea by increasing the HELLO and DEAD interval. For example, if we set the DEAD interval to be one minute, over 50% of the link failures will be ignored by the routing protocol. Alternatively, we can increase the suppression timer for routing update generation and SPF computation to achieve the same effect. Although this idea looks simple, it can be applied to any existing IP routing protocol to improve its stability and scalability. We will evaluate the effectiveness of this method in the next section.

5. EVALUATION

In this section we use extensive simulations to show that NDN's packet forwarding performance under network failures is hardly affected by routing convergence time; by masking short-lived failures from routing protocols, one can effectively reduce routing overhead while maintaining high packet delivery performance in NDN networks.

5.1 Simulation Setup

Unless otherwise specified, we run experiments in the Qual-Net simulator [4] which provides complete implementations of OSPF and RIP routing protocols. We implement basic NDN operations and the forwarding strategy presented in [31] in the simulator. We also make necessary changes to the routing protocols as described in Section 4.1.

We use the Abilene topology [1] and selected Rocketfuel topologies [26] in the experiments. A summary of the topologies is presented in Table 1. We process the first three topologies to remove all single-homed nodes, because if the link of a single-homed node fails, the node will be disconnected from the network and thus cannot provide any insightful result. For OSPF, we use propagation delay as the cost of the links. Unless otherwise specified, we report results from the AS1239-PoP topology. Results for other topologies are similar and lead to the same conclusions. The AS1239-Router topology is only used to show the improvement of routing scalability [3].

We inject random link failures into the topologies. A shifted Pareto distribution is used to generate time-to-failure and time-to-recover values for each link independently. We use 120 seconds as the mean-time-to-recover, and 1000 seconds as the mean-time-to-fail; the scale parameter of the Pareto distribution is set to be 208 so that 50% of the failures last less than one minute [18, 20]. When a link fails, both directions of the link stop working. With this model, multiple network events (failures and recovery) can happen concurrently.

5.2 Failure Handling

In this set of experiments, we compare the packet delivery performance of NDN and IP in failure scenarios under different settings. We also evaluate the forwarding overhead of NDN when a prefix becomes unreachable due to failures.

5.2.1 Impact of Routing Convergence Time

In this experiment, we run OSPF as the routing protocol and study the impact of HELLO interval on packet delivery performance. We inject random link failures into the network as described in Section 5.1. In order to measure packet delivery performance in NDN and IP, we run simple applications among all pairs of nodes in the network. For NDN, each node announces a distinct name prefix and provides content under this prefix. Each node also acts as a consumer requesting data from all other nodes. A consumer sends one Interest towards each name prefix every second. If Data is not received, a consumer will retransmit the Interest every second up to twice. Different consumers request different pieces of Data from the same name prefix so that they do not affect each other. Caching is also disabled so that we can focus on routing and forwarding behaviors [4]. For IP, each node acts as both client and server. Each client sends one UDP request to each server every second [5]. The server responds with UDP packet carrying the content. Similar to NDN consumers, these clients also retransmit requests if replies are not received. The sizes of the UDP packets are the same as those in NDN.

Figure 2 and 3 present the packet delivery rate for each node pair in IP and NDN under different HELLO interval settings. Figure 2 shows that HELLO interval has a huge impact on the packet delivery performance in IP. The shorter HELLO interval, the faster packet delivery can be resumed.

---

[3] We do not run packet-level simulations on the topology due to performance limitations of the simulator.

[4] If consumers request the same content and caching is enabled, NDN would perform even better.

[5] The packet rate is much lower than real Internet traffic due to performance limitation of the simulator. In fact, the IP packet delivery performance will be worse if the packet rate is higher.

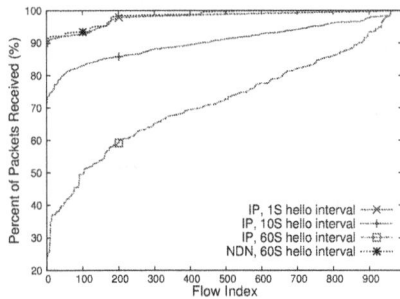

Figure 2: Packet delivery performance in IP under different HELLO interval.

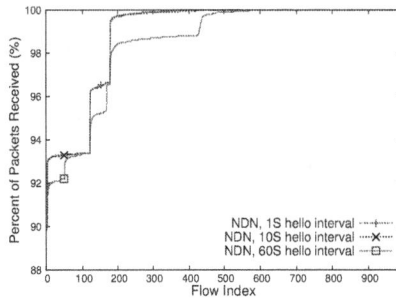

Figure 3: Packet delivery performance in NDN under different HELLO interval.

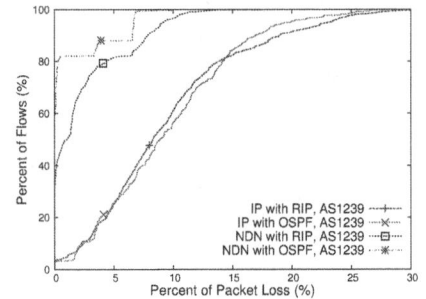

Figure 4: CDF of packet loss rate under different routing protocols.

The median packet delivery rate of IP is 99%, 91% and 72% when the HELLO interval is 1S, 10S and 60S respectively. Figure 2 also shows that NDN with 60S HELLO interval even works slightly better than IP with 1S HELLO interval.

Figure 3 shows the impact of HELLO interval on the packet delivery rate of NDN. When the HELLO interval increases from 1S to 10S, the performance degradation is negligible. When the HELLO interval increases from 10S to 60S, the packet delivery rate decreases slightly. This is because only two consumer retransmissions are allowed. The packet delivery performance can be further improved by allowing more consumer retransmissions. Overall, the HELLO interval has little impact on the packet delivery performance in NDN.

We also evaluate the packet delivery performance under different routing protocols. Figure 4 shows the CDF of packet loss rate of NDN and IP when OSPF and RIP are used. Although RIP is generally considered to have poor routing convergence properties, it performs quite well with NDN. NDN with RIP performs much better than IP with OSPF or RIP. The performance difference between OSPF and RIP in NDN is due to the difference in interface ranking. Recall that RIP may not provide cost for all interfaces, thus OSPF is able to provide better interface ranking.

5.2.2 Comparison with IPFRR

In the previous section we evaluate the packet deliver performance of plain IP, which relies on routing to handle network failures. However, IP networks may adopt solutions that handle network failures without routing convergence, e.g., IPFRR. In this experiment, we compare NDN against Loop-Free Alternate (LFA) [8], the only commercially available IPFRR solution. We implement LFA in a custom simulator, and repeat the link failure experiment in [31] without routing convergence. Only two consumer retransmissions are allowed for NDN. In each run of the experiment, we associate each link with a probability of failure, and randomly generate link failures. We run the experiments 1000 times for each link failure probability.

Figure 5(a) shows the average reachability of NDN and LFA with 95% confidence interval under different failure probability. We only consider the situations where the source and destination are not physically disconnected by the failures. The figure shows that NDN is always able to recover

from much more failure scenarios than LFA. Figure 5(b) shows the CDF of stretch of alternative paths found by NDN and LFA. The 98-percentile of path stretch for NDN and LFA is 1.06 and 1.13 respectively. In conclusion, NDN is able to cover more failure scenarios and find better alternative paths than LFA.

5.2.3 Prefix Unreachable

Previous experiments show that NDN performs well in handling link failures. When a node fails, however, the name prefix served by the node may become unreachable. In such cases, path exploration may lead to extra Interests all over the network. In this experiment we evaluate NDN's exploration overhead when a name prefix becomes unreachable. In each run of the experiment we fail one node and let all other nodes request content from this node before routing convergence[6]. Both NDN and IP applications will retransmit the same request twice. For each flow, we count the number of hops that each packet traverses in both NDN and IP, and compute the hop count ratio of NDN over IP. We run the experiment for every node failure scenario and present the CDF of the ratio in Figure 6.

In IP, retransmitted requests will be sent to the same paths, whereas in NDN, retransmitted Interests may trigger path exploration, leading to large overhead. Surprisingly, NDN incurs less overhead than IP in 26% of the cases. This is because retransmitted Interests do not always trigger path exploration in NDN. If a node has already explored all its interfaces, a further retransmission will only get a NACK back to the application without being further forwarded. In contrast, IP routers will always forward the packets before routing convergence. The ratio is smaller than 5 in 93% of the cases. Only in some rare cases does NDN cause excessively high exploration overhead.

The exploration overhead becomes significant when popular content becomes unreachable, as many consumers will be requesting the content and their Interests will trigger many attempts by routers to find working paths. But on the other hand, popular content is usually hosted and served by multiple servers placed at different locations. In addition, popular content is more likely to be cached by routers. Thus its

---

[6]After routing converges, routers will learn about the failure and stop forwarding the requests.

(a) Reachability.

(b) CDF of path stretch.

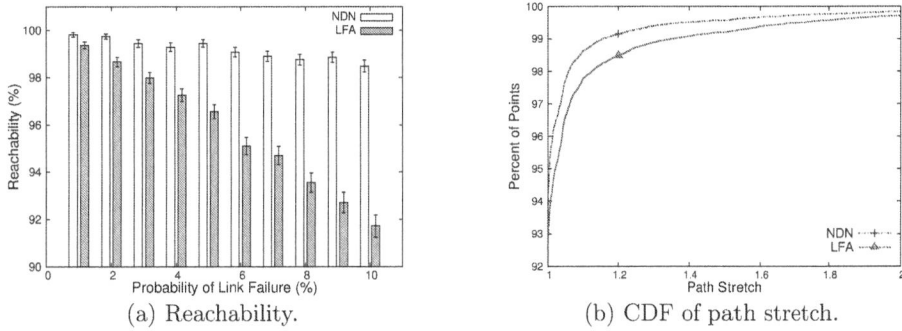

Figure 5: Comparison between NDN and IPFRR.

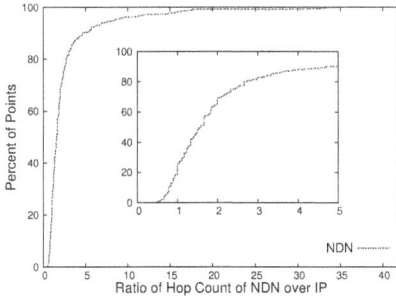

Figure 6: CDF of hop count ratio of NDN over IP when prefix is unreachable.

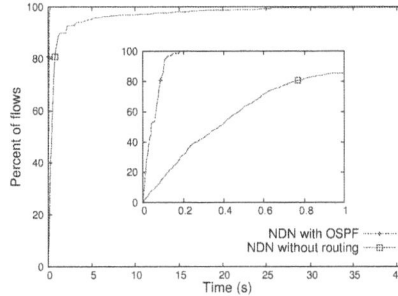

Figure 7: CDF of time to find working paths with and without routing.

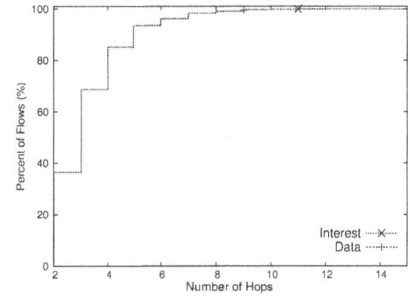

Figure 8: CDF of number of hops that probing Interests and Data traverse.

chance of becoming unreachable is slim. The overall impact in large scale networks needs further investigation.

5.3 Forwarding without Routing

In this experiment we show how NDN forwarding performs without routing. Since routers have no idea how to rank the interfaces without input from routing, we implement a forwarding strategy that prefers Green interfaces over Yellow ones, and randomly picks a Yellow interface if no Green interface exists. All interfaces are initialized to be Yellow. If Data is brought back from an interface, the interface will be marked Green and used to forward subsequent Interests.

In each experiment run, we pick one node as the consumer and another as the content provider. Assuming the consumer keeps retransmitting Interests until Data is received, we measure how long it takes to receive the data. We enumerate all combinations of consumers and providers and draw the CDF in Figure 7. In 89% of the cases, the consumer retrieves Data within one second. However, it can take up to 40 seconds to find a working path in some rare cases. The situation can get worse as the network becomes larger. In contrast, Data retrieval always follows the best paths when routing protocol can provide interface ranking. Therefore, although NDN has a powerful forwarding plane that is able to handle link failures on its own with only local information, the interface ranking provided by a routing protocol can make the local search more effective.

5.4 Routing and Forwarding Coordination

In this set of experiments we evaluate how NDN's routing and forwarding plane benefit from each other.

5.4.1 Probing Overhead

With the help of routing protocols, routers only need to perform probing when a better link is presented by routing. We evaluate probing overhead in this experiment. In each run of the experiment, we fail one link and run applications to let routers find working paths. Then we bring the link back up again, and run applications after routing convergence to measure the number of hops that probing Interests and Data traverse. Interest NACKs are counted as probing Interests. Applications are only run between node pairs whose traffic is affected by the failure. We run the experiment on all link failure scenarios and report the CDF in Figure 8. In 36% of the cases, probing Interests and Data only traverse 2 hops; they traverse no more than 6 hops in 94% of the cases. Probing Interests traverse more hops than Data in some rare cases, because a probing Interest does not necessarily bring Data back, and some of them may loop back to previously visited nodes and trigger NACKs. This experiment shows that by taking advantage of routing, probing only incurs very small overhead.

5.4.2 Routing Overhead

In this experiment, we evaluate the routing overhead of OSPF under different HELLO and DEAD interval settings. Specifically, we measure the number of HELLO messages, link-state (LS) updates and SPF computations for each node. HELLO and LS update messages constitute the majority of routing messages triggered by failures and recovery. We set the HELLO interval to be 1S, 10S and 60S; the DEAD interval is always four times the HELLO interval. Random

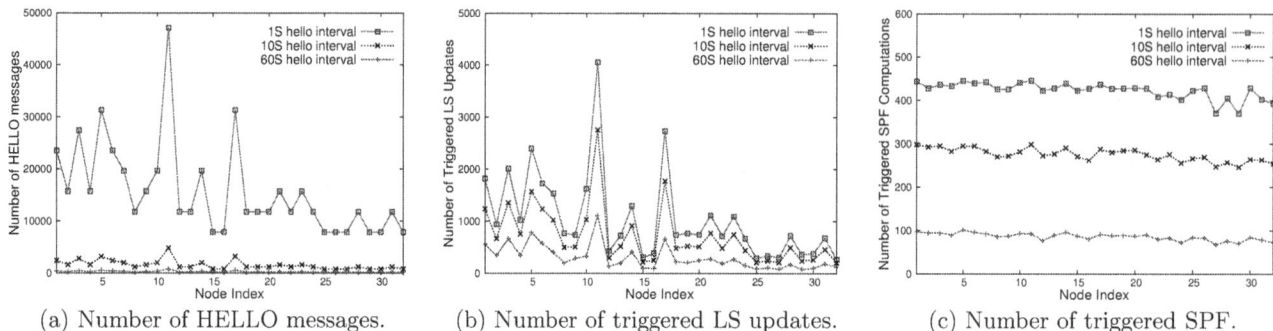

(a) Number of HELLO messages.

(b) Number of triggered LS updates.

(c) Number of triggered SPF.

Figure 9: Routing overhead under different HELLO intervals in AS1239 PoP-level topology.

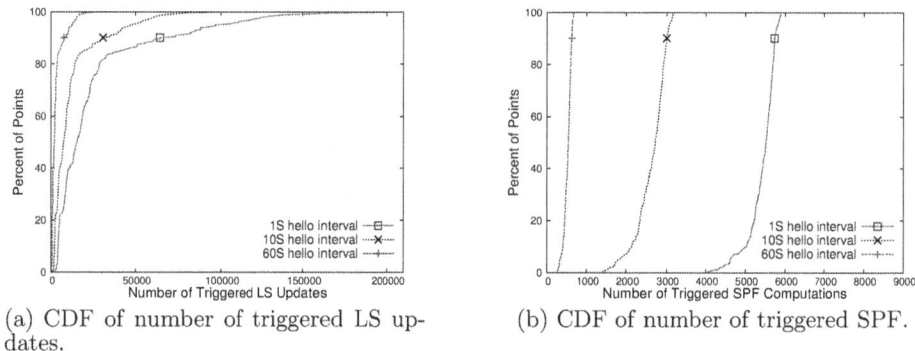

(a) CDF of number of triggered LS updates.

(b) CDF of number of triggered SPF.

Figure 10: Routing overhead under different HELLO intervals in AS1239 router-level topology.

link failures are injected into the network as described in Section 5.1, and each experiment is run for 3000 seconds. Only LS updates and SPF computations triggered by failures and recovery are counted[7]. The numbers obtained in this experiment are the same for both NDN and IP.

Figure 9(a) shows the number of HELLO messages sent by each node under different HELLO interval in AS1239-PoP topology. As the HELLO interval increases from 1 second to 60 seconds, the number of HELLO messages sent by each node is decreased by 98% as one would expect. Figure 9(b) and 9(c) present the number of triggered LS updates and SPF computations for each node. As the HELLO intervals increase, less failure events will be detected by OSPF. No routing update will be generated and propagated for the undetected failures, and thus no SPF computation will be performed. If we increase the HELLO interval from 1 second to 60 seconds, the number of LS updates is decreased by 52% to 80%, and the number of SPF computations is decreased by 77% to 82%. Therefore, we can effectively reduce the overhead caused by HELLO messages, LS updates and SPF computation by increasing the HELLO interval.

We run the same experiments in AS1239 router-level topology to illustrate how the method works in large ISP networks. The CDF of number of triggered LS updates and SPF computations are presented in Figure 10. The median numbers of LS updates and SPF computations are decreased by 87% and 90% when HELLO interval increases from 1 sec-

ond to 60 seconds. In conclusion, routing overhead can be significantly reduced by masking short-lived failures from the routing protocol. Since less LS updates are generated and propagated and less SPF computations are performed, routing becomes more stable and scalable.

6. DISCUSSION

Routing is a necessary subsystem for any large scale network. Like IP, NDN itself does not dictate what kinds of routing algorithms or protocols to use. However one can take advantage of NDN's adaptive forwarding plane to improve the stability and scalability of existing routing protocols, as well as enable routing protocols that are deemed difficult to adopt in IP networks.

Traditional Routing Protocols: With adaptive forwarding, routing in NDN only assumes a supporting role. It provides a reasonable starting point for forwarding which can then effectively explore different choices. The job of routing becomes more of disseminating topology and policy information than distributed computation of best paths. This new division of labor between routing and forwarding makes routing protocols simpler and more scalable. Traditional routing protocols such as OSPF, RIP, and BGP can benefit greatly from NDN's adaptive forwarding plane. They can be tuned for synchronizing among routers long-term topology and policy information without handling short-term churns.

Centralized Routing: Routing protocols have been designed to operate in a distributed manner to avoid single point of failure. With the increasing complexity in network management, however, Software-Defined Networking (SDN) has emerged to enable centralized management and control of

---

[7]Notice that OSPF also floods refresh link-state announcements periodically even in the absence of network event. These refresh updates are not counted since they are not affected by routing convergence behaviors.

networks, including logically centralized routing scheme. It is much easier to change the routing configurations on a central controller than on all participating routers, and to implement sophisticated traffic engineering schemes at the controller than on individual routers. Routing overhead can also be greatly reduced, since routing updates only need to be sent to the controller instead of being flooded to the entire network, and only the controller needs to perform SPF computations. However, one of the biggest concerns about centralized routing is the potentially prolonged convergence delay, which includes failure detection at local router, report to the controller, route recompilation at the controller, and dissemination of new routes to individual routers. NDN's adaptive forwarding removes the demands on convergence delay, making centralized routing feasible.

Coordinate-based Routing: In coordinate-based routing, instead of disseminate the network topology to routers, the coordinates of nodes are disseminated. The main characteristics of the network topology are embedded in the coordinates. Routers do greedy routing based on coordinates, i.e., forward packets to the neighbor whose distance (computed using coordinates) to the destination is the shortest among all neighbors. One example of such routing scheme is hyperbolic routing [23]. The advantages of this routing scheme include smaller routing tables (i.e., only need to know the destination's coordinates and neighbor routers' coordinates) and minimal routing updates (i.e., link failures and recovery do not affect a node's coordinates). However, in IP networks, this routing scheme is not guaranteed to be able to deliver packets. It is possible that the forwarding process runs into a local minimal, where all neighbors are farther to the destination than the current router. Path stretch may also get large. NDN's adaptive forwarding can fix these problems and make this routing scheme a possibility.

7. RELATED WORK

A massive amount of research has been conducted on how to gracefully accommodate routing changes with minimum impact on packet delivery in IP networks. One category of solutions rely on routing protocols to adapt to the changes. Francois et al. show that sub-second link-state routing convergence in large intra-domain networks is achievable by tuning various timers [11]. But this method incurs extra routing overhead and may also cause routing instability.

Fast reroute (FRR) mechanisms handle link failures by pre-computing alternative paths. MPLS FRR mechanisms provide backup paths in MPLS-enabled networks to protect specific links from failures [3]. Similarly, IPFRR mechanisms (e.g., [8]) provide temporary alternative paths before routing convergence in pure IP networks. However, it is hard for the FRR mechanisms to cover all possible failure scenarios; nor can they handle multiple link failures well.

Another category of solutions handle network failures via multipath forwarding. Path splicing [21] is an end-to-end multipath solution that provides link recovery controlled by end hosts. Each router provides multiple routing tables and let end hosts specify which one to use at each router. Path splicing may take a long time to find alternative paths, and sometimes may not be able to find them even if they exist [31]. MRC [16] provides multiple routing configurations to handle network failures. Different from path splicing, MRC lets routers switch configurations when failures are

detected. However, it may not handle multiple concurrent failures well due to the limited path choices.

There are also solutions that carry routing or forwarding information in the packet headers. Failure carrying packets (FCP) [17] puts failure information into the packet headers, and let routers recompute the routing tables on-the-fly upon receipt of FCP. However, the method increases computation overhead, and the sizes of FCP headers may become arbitrarily large. Liu et al. propose Data-Driven Connectivity (DDC) [19] to ensure forwarding connectivity at the data plane. DDC organizes the network as a destination-oriented directed acyclic graph (DAG) to avoid loops, and uses two bits in the packet header to notify link reversal. DDC has its own control plane algorithm, therefore cannot make use of existing routing protocols.

NDN keeps more states and does more processing at the forwarding plane than IP. However, these forwarding states also bring many benefits, such as native support of synchronous and asynchronous multicast, loop-free multipath data retrieval, efficient recovery from packet loss, flow balance and congestion control, which makes the forwarding plane more robust and efficient. The purpose of this paper is to assess how routing protocols can benefit from such a forwarding plane assuming it's already in place. There are a number of other work with promising results on how to build such an NDN forwarding plane that can operate at very fast speed [33, 25, 30]. On the other hand, the management and stability of the forwarding state on an Internet scale still need further improvement as argued in [29].

A considerable amount of research has been conducted on routing and forwarding in the context of NDN and ICN in general. Hoque et al. proposed NLSR [12], a link-state NDN routing protocol that runs on top of NDN. It is the first distributed routing protocol for NDN. INFORM [10] is a dynamic Interest forwarding mechanism based on Q-routing. It is able to discover cached Data copies in the network that are not announced through routing protocols. Tortelli et al. proposed COBRA [27], a bloom-filter based intra-domain routing algorithm for NDN. It is simple and efficient as no routing message is required between NDN nodes. Saino et al. applied cache-aware hash routing techniques to ICN and showed that inter-domain traffic can be reduced significantly with hash routing [24]. Carzaniga et al. investigated multi-tree routing in ICN [9]. Their proposed routing scheme supports both content delivery and event notification.

Routing scalability is also a critical issue for NDN to operate at Internet scale. Kutscher et al. discussed the routing scalability issue for Information Centric Networking (ICN) in general [15]. Afanasyev et al. [5] investigated the routing scalability issue specifically for NDN and proposed a solution based on map-n-encap. αRoute [6] is a novel name-based routing scheme for ICN. It utilizes distributed hash table to achieve scalable routing table size.

8. CONCLUSION

In this paper we study the role of routing in NDN. NDN's adaptive forwarding plane leads to a new division of labor between routing and forwarding planes. While the latter can detect and recover from link failures quickly independent from the former, the former helps bootstrap adaptive forwarding and handle link recovery. We specify how NDN routing coordinates with forwarding through interface ranking and probing mechanisms. Our analysis and simulations show that NDN routing protocols can benefit from the forwarding plane due to the relaxed requirement on timely detection of failures and convergence delay. Consequently NDN routing stability and scalability can be greatly improved. Moreover, the adaptive forwarding plane also enables new routing schemes that may not work well in IP to be used in an NDN network.

9. REFERENCES

[1] Abilene TM. http://www.cs.utexas.edu/~yzhang/research/AbileneTM/.

[2] CCNx. http://www.ccnx.org/.

[3] MPLS Traffic Engineering Fast Reroute – Link Protection. http://www.cisco.com/en/US/docs/ios/12_0st/12_0st10/feature/guide/fastrout.html.

[4] QualNet. http://web.scalable-networks.com/content/qualnet/.

[5] A. Afanasyev, C. Yi, L. Wang, B. Zhang, and L. Zhang. Scaling ndn routing: Old tale, new design. Technical Report NDN-0004, NDN, July 2013.

[6] R. Ahmed, M. Bari, S. Chowdhury, M. Rabbani, R. Boutaba, and B. Mathieu. αRoute: A name based routing scheme for Information Centric Networks. In *Proceedings of IEEE INFOCOM*, 2013.

[7] C. Alaettinoglu, V. Jacobson, and H. Yu. Towards Milli-Second IGP Convergence. Internet Draft draft-alaettinoglu-isis-convergence-00.txt, Nov. 2000.

[8] A. Atlas and A. Zinin. RFC 5286: Basic Specification for IP Fast Reroute: Loop-Free Alternates, 2008.

[9] A. Carzaniga, K. Khazaei, M. Papalini, and A. L. Wolf. Is information-centric multi-tree routing feasible? In *Proceedings of ACM SIGCOMM ICN Workshop*, 2013.

[10] R. Chiocchetti, D. Perino, G. Carofiglio, D. Rossi, and G. Rossini. Inform: A dynamic interest forwarding mechanism for information centric networking. In *Proceedings of ACM SIGCOMM ICN Workshop*, 2013.

[11] P. Francois, C. Filsfils, J. Evans, and O. Bonaventure. Achieving Sub-Second IGP Convergence in Large IP Networks. *ACM SIGCOMM CCR*, 35(3), July 2005.

[12] A. K. M. M. Hoque, S. O. Amin, A. Alyyan, B. Zhang, L. Zhang, and L. Wang. Nlsr: Named-data link state routing protocol. In *Proceedings of ACM SIGCOMM ICN Workshop*, 2013.

[13] V. Jacobson, D. K. Smetters, J. D. Thornton, M. F. Plass, N. H. Briggs, and R. L. Braynard. Networking Named Content. In *Proceedings of ACM CoNEXT*, 2009.

[14] N. Kushman, S. Kandula, D. Katabi, and B. Maggs. R-BGP: Staying Connected in a Connected World. In *Proceedings of USENIX NSDI*, 2007.

[15] D. Kutscher, S. Eum, K. Pentikousis, I. Psaras, D. Corujo, D. Saucez, T. C. Schmidt, and M. Wählisch. ICN Research Challenges. Internet draft, 2014.

[16] A. Kvalbein, A. Hansen, T. Cicic, S. Gjessing, and O. Lysne. Fast IP Network Recovery Using Multiple Routing Configurations. In *Proceedings of INFOCOM*, 2006.

[17] K. Lakshminarayanan, M. Caesar, M. Rangan, T. Anderson, S. Shenker, and I. Stoica. Achieving Convergence-Free Routing using Failure-Carrying Packets. In *Proceedings of ACM SIGCOMM*, 2007.

[18] S. Lee, Y. Yu, S. Nelakuditi, Z. li Zhang, and C. nee Chuah. Proactive vs Reactive Approaches to Failure Resilient Routing. In *Proceedings of IEEE INFOCOM*, 2004.

[19] J. Liu, A. Panda, A. Singla, B. Godfrey, M. Schapira, and S. Shenker. Ensuring Connectivity via Data Plane Mechanisms. In *Proceedings of USENIX NSDI*, 2013.

[20] A. Markopoulou, G. Iannaccone, S. Bhattacharyya, C.-N. Chuah, Y. Ganjali, and C. Diot. Characterization of Failures in an Operational IP Backbone Network. *IEEE/ACM Transactions on Networking*, 16(4):749–762, August 2008.

[21] M. Motiwala, M. Elmore, N. Feamster, and S. Vempala. Path Splicing. In *Proceedings of ACM SIGCOMM*, 2008.

[22] J. Moy. RFC 2328: OSPF Version 2, 1998. http://www.ietf.org/rfc/rfc2328.txt.

[23] F. Papadopoulos, D. Krioukov, M. Bogua, and A. Vahdat. Greedy Forwarding in Dynamic Scale-Free Networks Embedded in Hyperbolic Metric Spaces. In *Proceedings of IEEE INFOCOM*, 2010.

[24] L. Saino, I. Psaras, and G. Pavlou. Hash-routing schemes for information centric networking. In *Proceedings of ACM SIGCOMM ICN Workshop*, 2013.

[25] W. So, A. Narayanan, and D. Oran. Named Data Networking on a Router: Fast and Dos-resistant Forwarding with Hash Tables. In *Proceedings of ANCS*, 2013.

[26] N. Spring, R. Mahajan, D. Wetherall, and T. Anderson. Measuring ISP topologies with Rocketfuel. *IEEE/ACM Transactions on Networking*, 12(1):2–16, 2004.

[27] M. Tortelli, L. A. Grieco, G. Boggia, and K. Pentikousis. Cobra: Lean intra-domain routing in ndn. In *Proceedings of IEEE CCNC*, 2014.

[28] D. Turner, K. Levchenko, S. Savage, and A. C. Snoeren. A Comparison of Syslog and IS-IS for Network Failure Analysis. In *Proceedings of ACM IMC*, 2013.

[29] M. Wahlisch, T. Schmidt, and M. Vahlenkamp. Lessons from the past: Why data-driven states harm future information-centric networking. In *Proceedings of IFIP Networking*, 2013.

[30] Y. Wang, Y. Zu, T. Zhang, K. Peng, Q. Dong, B. Liu, W. Meng, H. Dai, X. Tian, Z. Xu, H. Wu, and D. Yang. Wire Speed Name Lookup: A GPU-based Approach. In *Proceedings of USENIX NSDI*, 2013.

[31] C. Yi, A. Afanasyev, I. Moiseenko, L. Wang, B. Zhang, and L. Zhang. A Case for Stateful Forwarding Plane. *Computer Communications: ICN Special Issue*, 36(7):779–791, April 2013.

[32] C. Yi, A. Afanasyev, L. Wang, B. Zhang, and L. Zhang. Adaptive Forwarding in Named Data Networking. *ACM SIGCOMM CCR*, 42(3), 2012.

[33] H. Yuan, T. Song, and P. Crowley. Scalable NDN forwarding: Concepts, issues, and principles. In *Proc. of IEEE ICCCN*, 2012.

[34] L. Zhang et al. Named Data Networking (NDN) Project. Technical Report NDN-0001, October 2010.

Congestion-Aware Caching and Search in Information-Centric Networks*

Mikhail Badov
University of Massachusetts
Amherst
mbadov@cs.umass.edu

Anand Seetharam
California State University
Monterey Bay
aseetharam@csumb.edu

Jim Kurose
University of Massachusetts
Amherst
kurose@cs.umass.edu

Victor Firoiu
BAE Systems
victor.firoiu@baesystems.com

Soumendra Nanda
BAE Systems
soumendra.nanda@baesystems.com

ABSTRACT

The performance of in-network caching in information-centric networks, and of cache networks more generally, is typically characterized by network-centric performance metrics such as hit rate and hop count, with approaches to locating and caching content evaluated and optimized for these metrics. We believe that user-centric performance metrics, in particular the delay from when a content request is made by the user to the time at which the requested content has been completely downloaded, are also important. For such metrics, performance is often determined by link capacity constraints and network congestion. We investigate network cache management and search policies that account for path-level (content-server to content-requestor) congestion and file popularity in order to directly minimize user-centric, content-download delay. Through simulation, we find that our policies yield significantly better download delay performance than existing policies, even though these existing policies provide better performance according to traditional metrics such as cache hit rate and hop count.

Categories and Subject Descriptors

C.2.1 [**Computer-Communication Networks**]: Network Architecture and Design - Distributed networks

General Terms

Performance, Design

*This work was funded in part by the DARPA Fixed Wireless program under contract FA8750-13-C-0169 and by the National Science Foundation under grant CNS-1117764. The views expressed are those of the authors and do not reflect the official policy or position of the Department of Defense, the National Science Foundation or the U.S. Government.

Keywords

Information-Centric Networking, Caching, Congestion

1. INTRODUCTION

A key component of many information-centric network (ICN) designs is the use of in-network caching at storage-enabled routers lying between content custodians (origin servers) and content requesters [3]. The key advantage of serving content to the requester from an in-network cache (particularly a cache enroute to the custodian) is that content will be returned to the user faster than if the content had been served by the content custodian. When designing and evaluating the effectiveness of cache management and content location schemes for such networks, one of the primary performance metrics has been cache hit probability — the fraction of content requests passing through a cache node that find the content stored in that node, — a performance metric used since the earliest analyses of standalone caches more than 40 years ago. More recently, when analyzing networks of caches, the number of hops between the requester and the in-network cache or custodian returning content, has been used as an additional performance metrics of interest, e.g., [1].

Cache hit rates and hop counts are *network-centric* performance metrics. Since a network exists to provide service to its users, *user-centric* performance metrics are also of great importance. For the case of content retrieval, the content download delay — the time from when a user first issues a request to the time when the content has been completely received by the user — is a natural performance metric of interest. Here, the capacity of the links on the download path between the requester and the in-network cache or custodian returning content, and the number of ongoing content flows using those links will influence the content download delay. Given the differences between traditional network-centric metrics and the user-centric metric of download delay, one might expect (and indeed we will see in this paper) that cache management and content-request routing approaches developed for network-centric metrics do not necessarily perform well when evaluated using download delay as the performance metric of interest, and that new approaches designed with congestion-sensitive download delay in mind can achieve better performance.

In this paper, we propose and evaluate new cache management (content replacement) and content-request routing

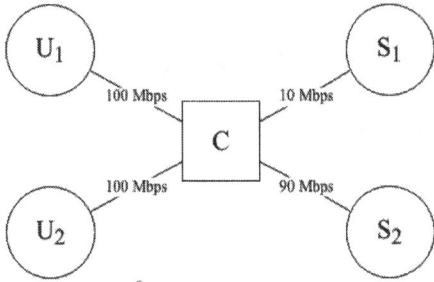

Figure 1: A cache-enabled content network

	Content Request Ratios					
Cached Content	F_1:0.50, F_2:0.50		F_1:0.10, F_2:0.90		F_1:0.01, F_2:0.99	
	Hit Rate	Delay	Hit Rate	Delay	Hit Rate	Delay
F_1	0.5	0.106	0.10	0.110	0.01	0.111
F_2	0.5	0.550	0.90	0.190	0.99	0.109

Table 1: Hit rate and average delay, under a static caching policy, for content of size 10 Mb with various content request ratios

schemes using a user-centric performance metric of content-download delay. We first consider the case of fixed routing of requests towards a custodian and present a congestion-aware cache management policy that considers the relative costs of downloading various content. The intuition behind our approach is that rather than optimizing hit rates, one should use space in the local cache to avoid using the most congested links to download requested content. We then consider the complementary challenge of content-request routing, investigating an approach in which the requester adopts a congestion-aware search for content, before routing the request to the custodian. Through simulation, we find that our policies yield significantly better download delay performance than existing policies, even though these existing policies provide better performance according to traditional metrics such as cache hit rate and hop count.

The remainder of this paper is structured as follows. Section 2 provides a simple, motivating example that provides intuition and insight into why cache management and content-routing policies that provide a high hit rate or low content-download hop count may perform poorly when download delay is the performance metric of interest. In Section 3, we describe our network model. We present our congestion-aware caching and search policies in Sections 4 and 5, respectively. These policies incorporate not only the popularity of a given piece of content, but also the estimated download delay in the presence of network congestion, as a basis for deciding what to cache, what to evict, and from where to download content. In Section 6, we evaluate our policies through simulation across a variety of topologies (including a grid, a scale-free network, a hybrid MANET, and ISP backbones based on Rocketfuel), finding that our policies yield the lowest average download delay in all studied networks. We discuss these findings in Section 7 and discuss related work in Section 8. Finally, Section 9 concludes the paper and outlines future work.

2. A MOTIVATING EXAMPLE

We begin with a simple example, shown in Figure 1, to provide intuition and insight into why cache management policies that optimize the network-centric goal of maximizing hit rate need not lead to good performance for a user's point of view, where content download delay is the metric of interest. Figure 1 shows two users, U_1 and U_2, and two servers, S_1 and S_2. A cache-enabled router C, with the ability to store exactly one piece of content, connects all nodes. The content universe consists of two equally sized pieces, F_1 and F_2, residing in S_1 and S_2, respectively. We assume that the users request a single piece of content at a time

(i.e., each user issues their next content request only after completely downloading the previous content). The links U_1-C and U_2-C both have a capacity of 100 Mbps, while the links C-S_1 and C-S_2 have a capacity 10 Mbps and 90 Mbps, respectively.

In this paper, we will assume the existence of some mechanism (e.g., TCP-like) that fairly shares link-bandwidth among multiple download flows traversing a common bottleneck link, although this assumption is not needed for this simple example. A flow's bottleneck link determines that flow's overall download rate along the path from content sender to content requester. Temporarily ignoring the cache, the end-to-end throughput between the users and the two servers, S_1 and S_2, would be 10 Mbps and 90 Mbps, respectively, due to the links C-S_1 and C-S_2 acting as bottlenecks. However, if a requester finds its content cached at C, that content can be downloaded at a rate of 100 Mbps.

Let us first consider the case that the request rates for F_1 and F_2 are equal. In this case, if F_1 is cached at C, the average download delay is 0.106 secs - F_1 requests are downloaded at 100 Mbps to U_1 with a delay of .1 secs from C, and F_2 requests are downloaded to U_2 from S_2 at a bottleneck rate of 90 Mbs, with a delay of .112 sec. If F_2 is cached at C, the average download delay increases to 0.555 secs, since F_1 requests are downloaded to U_1 from S_1 at a bottleneck rate of only 10 Mbps (requiring 1 sec to download), while F_2 requests are downloaded from C with a delay of .1 sec. *This example suggests that caching on the downstream end of a low-capacity or congested link can make most effective use of cache space.*

Suppose next that the request rates for F_1 and F_2 are 0.1 and 0.9 respectively (the middle column in Table 1). In this case, if F_1 is cached at C, the average download delay is 0.110 but the hit rate is only 0.1. Now suppose that F_2 (which receives 90% of the requests) is cached at C. The hit rate here increases to 0.9 but the delay *increases* to .19 secs. This increase in delay results from the fact that F_1 (which is only receiving 10% of the requests) must now be downloaded from S_1 over the slow 10 Mbps path. In this example, the policy of caching F_1 at C has the *best* performance from a user-centric point of view (minimizing download delay) but the *worst* performance from a network-centric point of view (maximizing hit rate). Similarly, the policy of caching F_2 at C has the *best* performance from a network-centric point of view but the *worst* performance from a user-centric point of view. *This example suggests that a caching policy that provides the best network-centric performance may provide very poor user-centric performance, and that caching policies designed for network centric performance metrics such as hit rate may not be well-suited for scenarios when user-centric performance metrics are of primary interest.*

Last, suppose the asymmetry in the F_1 and F_2 request rates increases further to 0.01 and 0.99, respectively. In this case, caching F_2 (which is receiving 99% of the requests) at C provides both a higher hit rate *and* a lower average delay, making this policy the winner from both a user-centric and a network-centric point of view. *This example suggests that content popularity, although not always the deciding factor, can play a role in determining the preferred cache management policy.*

We these insights, we can now consider cache management policies whose goals are to decrease the user-centric measure of average download delay.

3. NETWORK MODEL

We consider a typical ICN model with named content, but the cache management and content-request routing policies, insights, and results apply more generally to networks of caches. Our content universe consists of a finite set of distinct, but equally sized, content. Each piece of content has a node responsible for its permanent storage, referred to as the custodian. We assume there is some baseline mechanism for forwarding content requests (e.g., along a shortest path) from content requester to content custodian. Requests arrive exogenously at every node, and nodes route every exogenous and endogenous content request to the respective custodian, e.g. via shortest-path routing. Content delivery follows the request path.

Nodes are cache-enabled; the size of a cache is given in terms of the number of pieces of content that can be stored within. If a content request, en-route to the custodian, reaches a node that contains the content in its cache, then the intermediate node directly services the request from its own cache. This is a technique commonly used in ICN literature [4, 10].

Our goal is to design cache management and content-request routing policies that minimize content download delay. To this end, we factor congestion (resulting from simultaneous downloads using a link) into caching and routing decisions. We adopt a fluid model to capture the effects of congestion and heterogeneous link capacity on download throughput. Specifically, we assume there is some mechanism (e.g., TCP-like) that fairly shares link-bandwidth among multiple download flows that are bottlenecked at a link. If there are N flow crossing a link, each flow is guaranteed to receive a fair share of at least $1/N$ of the link bandwidth. The throughput of a content-download flow is limited by the most congested link on its path. Note that a flow may not use the fair share of bandwidth allocated to it across a link due to a bottleneck elsewhere along the path. In such a scenario, the capacity freed up by the congested flow may be fairly divided among other flows sharing that link.

4. CONGESTION-AWARE CACHING

In the section, we present a novel congestion-aware cache management policy that determines whether a piece of content passing through the router should be cached, and if so, what piece of content currently in the cache must be evicted to make room for this to-be-cached content. The effectiveness of our policy lies in the metrics used in its design — our policy considers the link congestion experienced along the path from content sender to content requester during content retrieval, combined with content popularity, in the caching and eviction process. Our intuition is that caches should preferentially retain content that has been forwarded over congested links, and evict content forwarded over uncongested links. We use a utility function to approximate the value of caching a given content item. We first describe the construction of our utility function, followed by the design of our management policy.

We design a utility function that operates at each node and estimates the download delay saved by caching a piece of content (that is currently being forwarded through that node) at that node. The download delay savings is defined as the difference between the time it takes for a requester to download content from this cache, and the time it would take the requester to download from the transmitting source (either the upstream cache or the custodian). We will use a fluid model to estimate download delay, with the flow's bottleneck link along the path determining flow throughput, and flow throughput, in turn, determining download time, as in our simple example in Section 2.

Content popularity will also play a role. The intuition here is that caching content that is costly (i.e., has a high download delay from where it is currently being served), but is also unpopular, will not provide significant benefit to the system as a whole. Similarly, caching a popular piece of content on a relatively uncongested path will also not provide significant benefit. Consequently, it is best to cache content that is both popular and costly, relative to the location of the source, the location of the cache, and the level of congestion experienced along the path between them.

Estimating Local Congestion: Each node keeps a count of the number of flows (active downloads) currently passing over each of its interfaces. The bandwidth B_l of link l available to a download flow is estimated by dividing the link capacity, C_l, by the number of flows passing through it, F_l:

$$B_l = \frac{C_l}{F_l}$$

Note that this is an underestimate of the bandwidth actually available to the flow on this link, since (as described above), any of the flows passing over a link may use less bandwidth than is allocated, due to bottlenecks elsewhere along the flow's path.

Estimating Popularity: The popularity of a piece of content f, denoted as P_f, is defined as the number of requests for the content divided by the number of total interest requests for all content. These requests may be counted during a moving window, updated according to an exponentially weighted moving average over the windows, or simply counted since the last time such counts were zeroed; we will assume the latter in our evaluation below, assuming that counts are zeroed when a router starts up. At a given cache, denote the number of times a piece of content has been requested at that cache by N_f. The set F is the set of all content that has been requested at the cache. We define P_f as:

$$P_f = \frac{N_f}{\sum_{f'}^{F} N_{f'}}$$

Considering End-to-End Throughput: A content download flow may be bottlenecked either in the source-to-cache (upstream) path segment or the cache-to-requester (downstream) path segment. Downstream congestion can limit the gain of caching content at the cache, especially if the effective cache-to-requester throughput is significantly lower than the source-to-cache throughput. Certainly, caching the content would still yield some gains, because other flows would not have to share the upstream link capacity. However, if the downstream links are the more congested, the upstream links are (by definition) less congested and therefore flow using the upstream links are less likely to benefit significantly from caching a piece of content at the cache (and thereby obviating the need for future requests for that content to use those upstream links). It would appear as though it is not beneficial to cache content if the requester has a path with low available bandwidth to the specified cache — it appears to neither decrease the download time for the next request for the content, nor significantly impact other flows sharing the upstream links. For this reason, considering downstream throughput is important in making caching decisions.

Putting it All Together: Let us define L_U as the set of links connecting the *upstream* source (the custodian, or another upstream cache) to the cache, and L_D as the set of links connecting the cache to the *downstream* requester. For every link l in either L_U or L_D, let B_l denote the available bandwidth for that link, in the presence of the congestion resulting from simultaneous downloads. Define the set B_{LU} as the set of available capacities of the links in L_U, and the set B_{LD} as the set of available capacities of the links in L_D. Using the fluid model, the cache-to-requester throughput is then $min(B_{LD})$. For the same reason, $min(B_{LD} \cup B_{LU})$ is the throughput of the end-to-end path. The estimated delay saved by caching the content for future requests is then $S/min(B_{LD} \cup B_{LU}) - S/min(B_{LD})$, where S is the content unit size.

Recalling the insights gained through our simple example in Section 2, we also want to take content popularity (as seen at a given cache) into account when defining the overall utility of caching file f at that given cache. The utility of caching f, given the set of bandwidth available at each link B_L at node N is thus the delay savings weighted by content popularity:

$$U_{f,N} = \left(\frac{S}{min(B_{LD} \cup B_{LU})} - \frac{S}{min(B_{LD})} \right) * P_f \quad (1)$$

We also consider a policy that takes only the upstream congestion level into account. This can be seen as absolute instead of relative savings. Such a policy could be relevant in the case of a hop-by-hop [14] congestion control mechanism (where there is no notion of end-to-end throughput). The utility value of the alternate policy is defined as:

$$U_{f,N} = \frac{S}{min(B_{LU})} * P_f \quad (2)$$

The various pieces of information needed to compute the utility value in Equations 1 and 2 can be obtained by piggybacking additional information in content-request and content-download packets already present in many ICN architectures. Specifically, an interest request for content that is being forwarded upstream towards the custodian contains the running minimum of B_l for all links that it has traversed and is (potentially) updated after passing through each link. Similarly, a running minimum of B_l is passed downstream with the content. In this manner, each cache obtains the values of B_{LU} and B_{LD} with each request. The other values

needed in Equations 1 and 2 are all locally-available pieces of information.

Eviction and Management: Given our utility function, cache management and eviction are simple. When new content enters a router, its utility is computed. If the computed utility value is lower than the lowest existing utility in the cache, the content is forwarded, without caching. Otherwise, the content with the lowest utility is evicted and the new content is cached. When deciding to cache a piece of content, a cache resets the running downstream B_l value, so that the utility computed at downstream caches will be computed with respect this cache, rather than the original source. This prevents all caches downstream of a congested link from caching the content.

5. CONGESTION-AWARE SEARCH

Typically, ICN proposals have advised using the strategy layer to route to the nearest replica [4]. However, the nearest replica is not guaranteed to be the one to which the requester has the highest throughput path or equivalently the smallest download delay. In this section, we thus describe a simple scoped-flooding protocol that locates requested cached content with minimum download delay. If cached content is not found with the scope of the flood, the content-requesting node routes a standard interest request for content towards the custodian, as described earlier. In our evaluation in the following section, we will compare content-aware search with a simple nearest-cache policy.

Our search policy operates as follows. Content requester R begins by flooding an interest request to all surrounding neighbors. These neighbors, in turn, flood the packet, so on, until a boundary, in terms of number of hops, or link weight, is reached. The weight of link l might correspond to the inverse of B_l, in which case the scoped flood would stop when a link of sufficiently low available bandwidth is encountered. A link may be assigned a high initial weight, preventing any queries from being sent over it. In this sense, the search is scoped, because it does not flood the entire network.

Any node, N, containing the requested file sends an interest reply message that is forwarded back to the requester along the reverse path, accumulating the minimum value of B_l of all links on the path back to R, in a manner similar to that discussed in the previous section. R then receives all replies, and selects the source to which it has the best connection (i.e., the maximum of the minimum throughputs). In this fashion, a user may retrieve content from a node that is further away in terms of hop count, but to which a better connection exists. Formally, if B_L is the set of effective capacities of the links lying on the path between R and N, then $min(B_L)$ is the effective throughput between R and N. The node N_B to which the requester has the best throughput, and thus the one selected to serve the content, is defined as:

$$N_B = max_N(min_l(B_L))$$

Caching Policy Interactions: Interesting interactions arise from combining a congestion-aware caching policy with a congestion-aware search policy. Most notably, the policies complement each other in two ways:

1. Cached content with high utility values would be discoverable even if the cache was not on the shortest path from the requester to the custodian; with search, con-

tent that ordinarily could only be downloaded slowly over congested network links, from a distant custodian, could now be quickly obtained.

2. If content is found via search and is delivered over an uncongested path, then the congestion-aware policy would likely not cache the content anywhere along the path, due to the low computed utility value. This would leave space for other, higher utility content to be cached, that could not be found nearby via search.

Together, these two properties provide a form of implicit coordination among nearby caches, preventing redundant caching not just along a path, but also across a group of nearby nodes.

6. PERFORMANCE EVALUATION

To evaluate the different caching and routing policies, we built a discrete-event simulator. An event is any action that has the potential of changing the throughput of existing flows. For example, a flow entering due to an exogenous interest-request arrival or exiting the network when requested content has been downloaded can impact the fair-share throughput of other flows, and introduce or remove bottlenecks. Additionally, changes in the routing (which will occur in the hybrid MANET scenarios we consider) can also change flow throughput. Before every new event, all existing flows are drained based on the time passed since the last event and the previously-calculated flow rate. Then, the rate of every flow is recomputed in the simulator based on the new network state. The key notion here is that flow rate is discretized, and does not change in between events. Our flow rate estimation is described in Algorithm 1.

We evaluate our caching and routing policies on simple network topologies such as grid and scale-free as well as real network topologies (Rocketfuel). We also perform simulations on a hybrid network consisting of a MANET and a cellular infrastructure to demonstrate the broad applicability of our cache management and request-routing policies across a variety of scenarios.

We assume that exogenous requests arrive at every node in the network according to a Poisson process with rate λ. Unless otherwise stated, we assume that content popularity follows a Zipfian distribution with rate $\alpha = 0.8$ and cache size $C = 500$. We consider a content universe of size $F = 10000$. Custodians are placed randomly throughout the network for each trial. Content unit size varies from 0.5 Mb to 3.0 Mb. We assume that shortest path routes are computed using Dijkstra's shortest-path (lowest-weight) algorithm. Error bars in our results correspond to 90% confidence intervals.

We evaluate the following set of cache management policies:

- **TERC+LRU**: Transparent en-route caching (TERC) is a common caching mechanism used in the ICN literature [4]. This policy caches everywhere along the path, and uses LRU as the cache eviction algorithm.
- **BTW+LRU**: The policy described in [1], using betweenness centrality to cache at the most central node along the download path, and LRU as the cache eviction algorithm.
- **CAC-E2E**: Our congestion-aware caching policy, considering the end-to-end path congestion.

- **CAC-UP**: Our congestion-aware caching policy, considering only upstream throughput.

We will also evaluate our cache management policies both with, and without, the following search policies.

- **SEARCH-CNG**: Congestion-based search, as described in Section 4.
- **SEARCH-HOP**: This policy finds the closest cache containing the content with respect to hop count. The search is also scoped (as described in Section 4)

Algorithm 1 Download Flow Rate Calculation

1: Determine the set of active flows, and mark each as unfinalized.
2: Determine the set of all links being utilized by those flows.
3: Create a list of effective link capacities, initialized to the set of maximum link capacities.
4: Find the bottleneck link - the utilized link with the lowest value of effective link capacity divided by number of unfinalized flows at that link (i.e., the link with the lowest fair share throughput for remaining flows.)
5: Find all unfinalized flows traversing the bottleneck link, and set the throughput of each of these flows to be the effective capacity of the bottleneck link.
6: Mark those flows as finalized.
7: For every link being traversed by any of those flows, reduce its effective capacity by that of the bottleneck link; this effectively allows all finalized flows to receive their fair share bandwidth.
8: Repeat Steps 4-8 until all flows have been finalized. At this point, the download throughputs of all flows have been determined.

6.1 Grid Topology

We begin by examining our caching policy in the context of a 10x10 grid topology. Two kinds of links that exist in the network: high capacity at 10 Mbps, denoted by solid lines, and low capacity at 2 Mbps, denoted by dotted lines in Figure 2. The grid is essentially split into two poorly-connected halves. Figure 2 shows the fraction of cached content across the entire topology whose custodian resides in the bottom-left cluster C, encompassed by the grey box.

Figure 3 shows the average download delay, average hop count, and average hit rate vs. arrival rate for content across all nodes. The higher the arrival rate, the more congested links become; the more flows in the system, the more they must complete for bandwidth. This is especially true in the case of links with a low initial capacity. Figure 2 shows TERC+LRU caches the files in C relatively uniformly throughout the network, with slightly higher concentrations in the cluster itself. This is due to the cache everywhere approach. Our congestion-aware caching scheme demonstrates an interesting property. The nodes on the top half of the grid with low-capacity links all tend to cache a high percentage of content originating from C. On the contrary, nodes on the bottom half of the grid, connected to the weak links cache little relatively from C. This is a direct consequence of our caching scheme; it is congestion-aware. Our policy assigns a high utility value to content traversing highly congested, low-capacity links. Likewise, it assigns a relatively low value

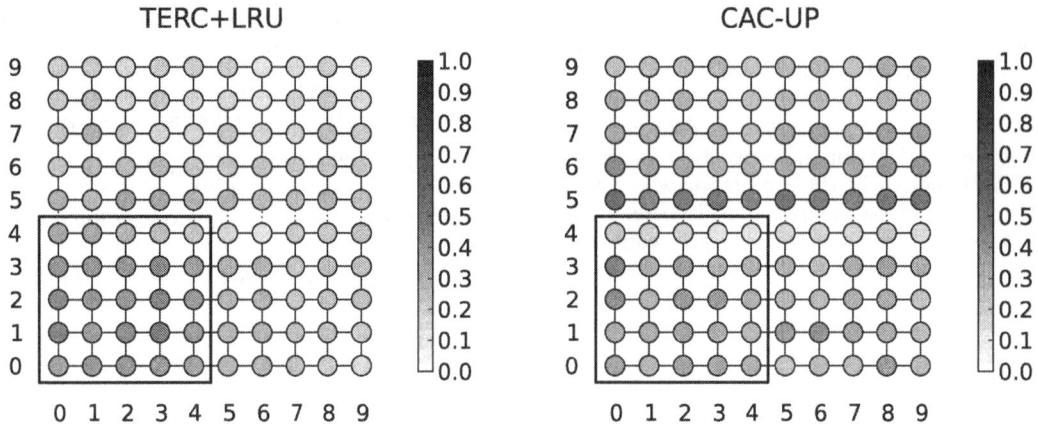

TERC+LRU   **CAC-UP**

Figure 2: A heatmap of percentage of content cached per node belonging to the custodians located within the grey box. The dotted links denote the poor connectivity between the top and bottom half of the grid.

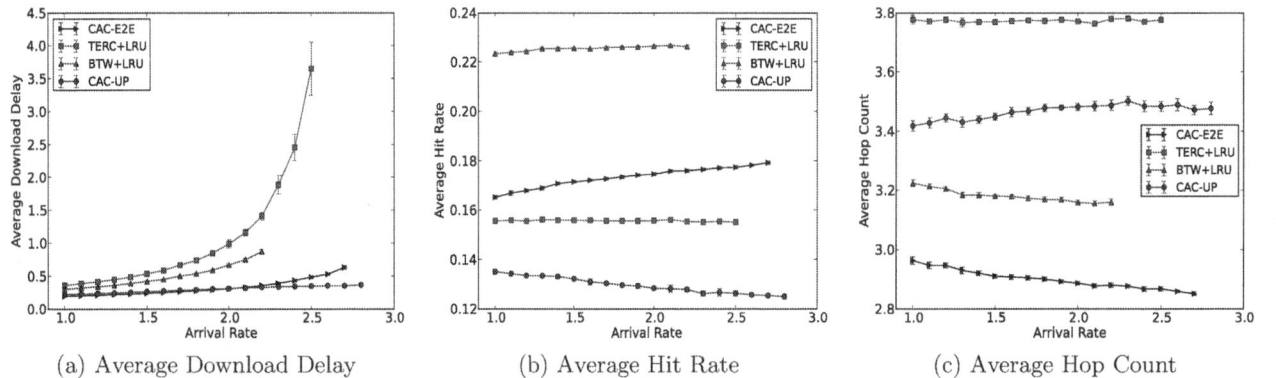

(a) Average Download Delay   (b) Average Hit Rate   (c) Average Hop Count

Figure 3: Grid network performance with increasing λ

to content that is obtained over uncongested, high-capacity links, making such content easy to evict. Together, these two properties work to not only cache, but to also retain, content that takes a long time to download from the custodian.

Figure 3 presents the average download delay, hit rate, and hop count for varying λ. As λ increases, the links in the network become more congested. As seen in Figure 3(a), the delay for TERC+LRU increases at the fastest rate. CAC-E2E and CAC-UP perform well even for higher arrival rates. It is also very instructive to note results in Figures 3(b) and 3(c). Note BTW+LRU has the *highest* average hit rate, but not the lowest delay — as in the case of our simple example in Section 2, *a higher hit rate does not necessarily translate to better download delay performance*. Although topology-aware, BTW+LRU does not consider network state, and thus makes no effort to cache content with respect to congested links. CAC-E2E and CAC-UP cache with respect to available link bandwidth, resulting in fewer flows traversing the low-capacity links and a consequently lower average delay.

6.2 Scale-free Network

We consider a scale-free network, such as the one considered in [1]. Here, there are 100 nodes, each link has a capacity of 10 Mbps, and the content unit size is 1 Mb. Even in

the case of homogeneous link capacity, effective throughput can vary greatly across links. A more central link will naturally have more flows traversing it. Within the Internet, central links are often provisioned with higher capacity to account for this. However, in a wireless or mesh network, all links may have identical capacity regardless of position. In this case, more central links become more congested, and are best avoided. Therefore, a congestion-aware caching policy can still provide gains even in the case of homogeneous link capacity. Figure 4 presents delay and hit rate as λ increases. As in the grid case, BTW+LRU provide the highest hit rate, but CAC-E2E and CAC-UP provide the lowest content-download delay.

6.3 Rocketfuel Topologies

Borrowing from the methodology of [2], we use topologies generated by Rocketfuel [6] (Sprint and Tiscali) to measure performance on a realistic, Internet-scale backbone network. The Rocketfuel topologies provide latencies and link weights inferred from measurement. We use the inverse of the link weights to estimate the relative link capacities, as network operators often use the inverse of link capacity to set link weight. Links in the two networks range from 10 Mbps to 100 Mbps. Here we set the content size to 3 Mb. In Figures 5 and 6, we vary λ. We can see that for realistic backbone topologies, the trend holds; BTW+LRU and TERC+LRU

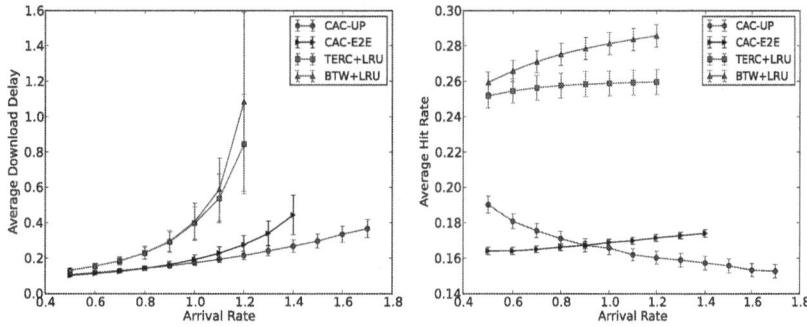

Figure 4: Scale-free download delay and hit rate with increasing λ

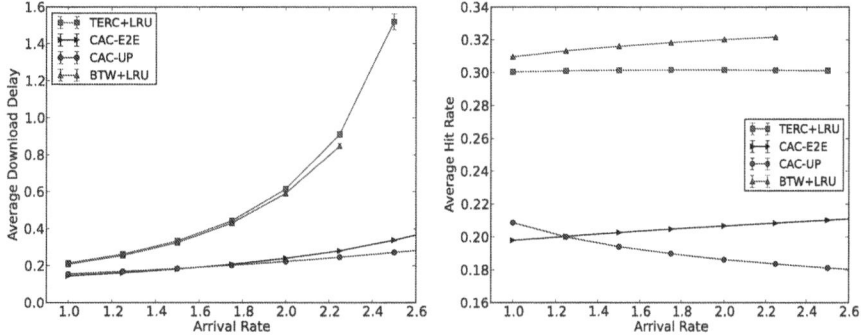

Figure 5: Sprint (US) topology download delay and hit rate with increasing λ

have high hit rates, but the average delay for both CAC policies is significantly lower. In Figures 7 and 8 we vary C and α, and set $\lambda = 1.0$. Across a variety of cache sizes, ranging from 0.1% to 1.0% of the content universe size, we see that the results remain the same; congestion-aware schemes yield lower delay. As α gets larger, we see the policies converge; as popularity becomes more skewed, it becomes more important to user-centric performance. We observed this in Section 2. We suspect that at higher arrival rates, as congestion plays a larger role, the policies again diverge.

Figures 9 and 10 show the performance of our proposed search policies (both scoped to two hops) as λ increases. Note that for both TERC+LRU and CAC-UP, using SEARCH-HOP results in a lower hop count. However, using SEARCH-CNG yields a lower average delay for both policies. Note that CAC-UP, using either search policy, outperforms TERC+LRU. We attribute this to the coordination described in Section 5. TERC+LRU, augmented with a search policy, would not necessarily have the same coordinative properties; although search would allow requesters to find content nearby, the caching would not be coordinated. Content that could be downloaded quickly would be cached everywhere along the path, creating unnecessary redundancy.

6.4 Hybrid Network

We simulate a Hybrid network, that is, a MANET where all nodes are connected to a base station. Nodes are grouped into clusters, and each cluster is either stationary or mobile over the course of the entire scenario. We use a random-waypoint mobility model to simulate cluster movement. Therefore, clusters merge and separate over time. In the

worst case, a cluster may become completely disconnected from all others, and must rely solely on the base station for connectivity. In this scenario, there are 100 nodes total, grouped into 10 clusters, 5 of which are mobile. Here, the content size is 0.5 Mb. The capacity of MANET links is 10 Mbps, while the capacity of the wireless base station links is 2 Mbps. For this reason, the base station, while allowing for connectivity where there would otherwise be none, is not a desirable resource; the base station weight is set to be 5x higher than that of the MANET links. Due to the scoped aspect of the search policies, neither sends search queries over the base station (although it is still used if the content is not found via search, and shortest-path routing so dictates).

Again, CAC-E2E and CAC-UP perform better than TERC+LRU and BTW+LRU, as our congestion-aware policies tend to cache content received over lower capacity links. Naturally, there is higher in variation in delay due to node mobility. As was true for the Rocketfuel evaluation, both congestion-aware policies perform better than both TERC policies when search is added. Here, the search policies perform fairly similarly; this is because inter-cluster congestion is low, and there is not a large difference between selecting the closest node, or the one to which the throughput is greatest.

7. DISCUSSION

Our initial exploration has demonstrated the benefits of designing caching and search policies based on congestion, but a number of open research questions remain.

In the design of our cache management policy we have considered the available capacity of the bottleneck link on an end-to-end path to decide whether content should be cached.

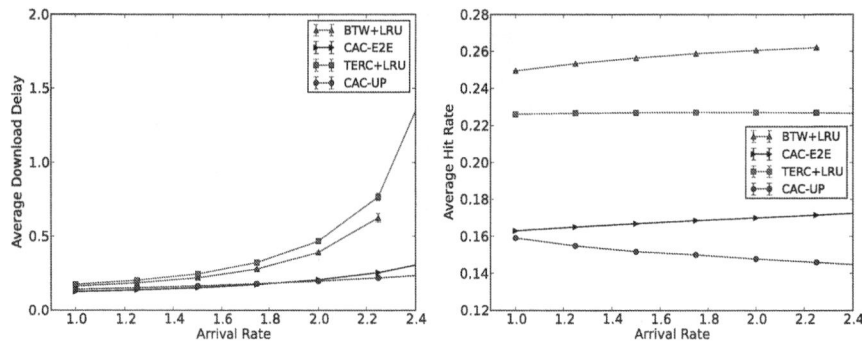

Figure 6: Tiscali (EU) topology download delay and hit rate with increasing λ

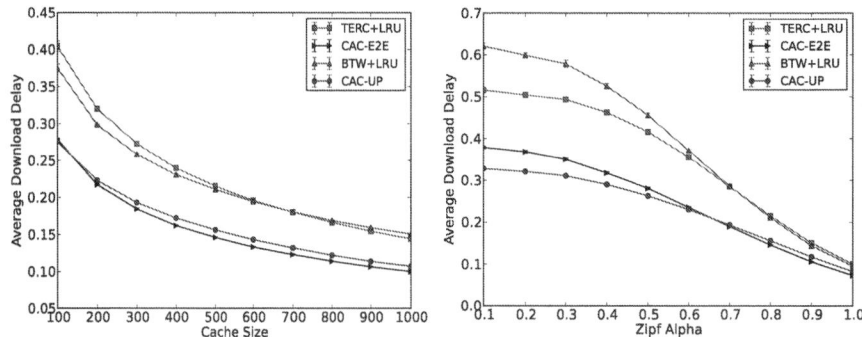

Figure 7: Sprint (US) topology download delay with increasing C and α.

We also experimented by only considering congestion on the upstream path from a node and observed that it provides very similar performance to the scheme that considers end-to-end path congestion. Though this observation needs to be validated through additional experimentation, we conjecture that this is due to cross streams; what is downstream for one node may be upstream for another, and in that manner, the congestion of links in all parts of the network is still factored into utility values of the upstream-only policy.

In our current model, the utility of a cached content does not vary over time. Therefore, a previously hard to obtain content may never be evicted from a cache, regardless of how easy to obtain it becomes in the future. This situation is more likely to arise in a mobile scenario where groups of nodes merge and split over time. Therefore, as part of our future work we plan to incorporate a notion of aging content periodically in the design of our cache policy. We have observed that a naive approach of decreasing the utility of cached content by a constant factor periodically does not perform well in our simulations.

One lesson we have learnt from this work is that congestion and caching are closely coupled; one directly influences the other. Though our long term objective is to design jointly optimal caching and routing policies for ICN, as a first attempt we aim to adopt a fixed point approximation approach. The approximation can start with an initial caching policy, determine the congestion, and then utilize the congestion to update the caching policy. The iterative process converges once the average congestion falls below a threshold.

8. RELATED WORK

Previous works have proposed caching schemes for ICN, leveraging various network properties to increase performance. In [1], the authors use betweenness centrality to make caching decisions, placing content at the point where they expect it to receive the most cache hits. In [9], the authors estimate the caching capacity of a path to fair-share cache space appropriately. The authors of [7] describe a policy which uses a coordinated age parameter to evict content. While not a caching scheme, [11] examines the impact of heterogenous cache sizes in ICN. In [8], the authors model bandwidth and cache sharing, and then use their model to estimate download delay.

Routing is another challenge of ICN. In [10], the authors propose a best-effort content location scheme that uses previous requests to estimate where content may reside. In [12], the authors develop a coordinated scheme to directly route users to replicated content.

Web proxy caching is similar in nature to ICN, and two works have examined non-traditional metrics as a basis for caching. In [13], the authors demonstrate that considering delay, and not just hit rate, is important to caching policies. In [15], the authors create a policy that estimates delay, and bases caching decisions on their estimation.

Several works propose caching policies that exploit topological and popularity factors in their caching decision. While [7] and [2] evaluate ICNs with respect to delay and congestion, to the best of our knowledge, no prior works have directly examined the relationship between hit rate, hop count, and end-user delay. The authors of [13] and [15] propose factoring delay into caching decisions. In [5],

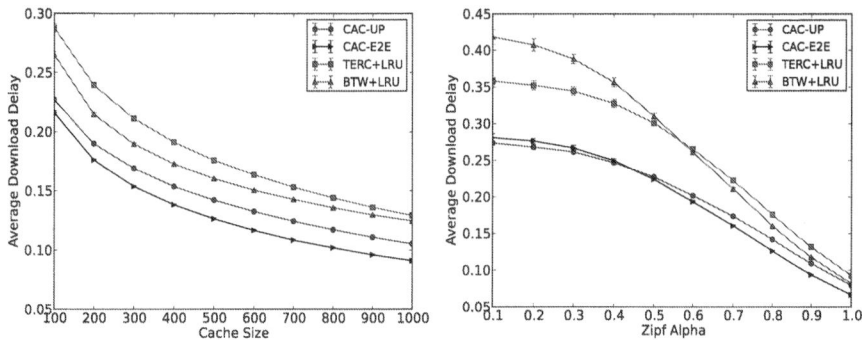

Figure 8: Tiscali (EU) topology download delay with increasing C and α.

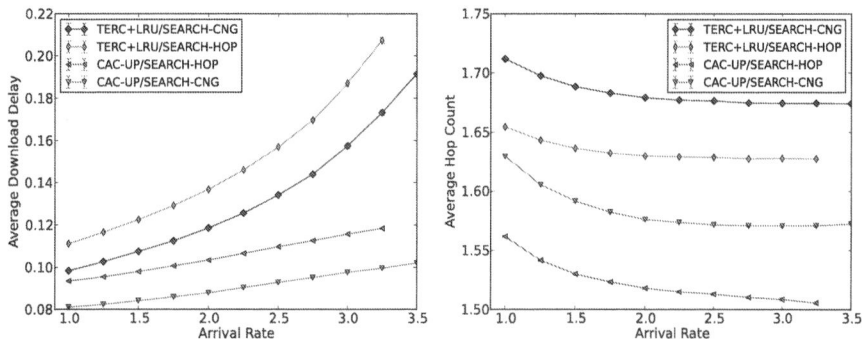

Figure 9: Sprint (US) topology download delay and hop count with increasing λ (using search)

the authors propose a caching algorithm factoring in overall popularity, and not just temporal locality, in caching decisions. However, no policies have been proposed to cache and route based on end-to-end congestion measurements.

9. CONCLUSION

In this paper, we have investigated network cache management and content-request routing policies that account for path-level (content-server to content-requestor) congestion and file popularity in order to directly minimize user-centric, content-download delay. Through simulation of several congestion aware congestion-aware cache management and content-request routing policies, and for a number of different network topologies, we showed that these content-aware policies yield significantly better download delay performance than existing policies, even though these existing policies provide better performance according to traditional metrics such as cache hit rate and hop count. Our finding that existing policies that provide superior performance according to network-centric performance metrics do *not* do so for user-centric metrics, makes a compelling case for considering user-centric performance metrics in designing and evaluating future ICN and other network protocols. Our future work includes investigating a more explicit coupling between local search and custodian-targeted routing of content requests, and an evaluation of our approaches in the presence of temporally-correlated content requests.

10. REFERENCES

[1] W. K. Chai, D. He, I. Psaras, and G. Pavlou. Cache "less for more" in information-centric networks.

IFIP'12, pages 27–40, Berlin, Heidelberg, 2012. Springer-Verlag.

[2] S. K. Fayazbakhsh, Y. Lin, A. Tootoonchian, A. Ghodsi, T. Koponen, B. Maggs, K. Ng, V. Sekar, and S. Shenker. Less pain, most of the gain: Incrementally deployable icn. SIGCOMM '13, pages 147–158, New York, NY, USA, 2013. ACM.

[3] A. Ghodsi, S. Shenker, T. Koponen, A. Singla, B. Raghavan, and J. Wilcox. Information-centric networking: Seeing the forest for the trees. HotNets-X, pages 1:1–1:6, New York, NY, USA, 2011. ACM.

[4] V. Jacobson, D. K. Smetters, J. D. Thornton, M. F. Plass, N. H. Briggs, and R. L. Braynard. Networking named content. CoNEXT '09, pages 1–12, New York, NY, USA, 2009. ACM.

[5] S. Jin and A. Bestavros. Popularity-aware greedy dual-size web proxy caching algorithms. ICDCS '00, pages 254–, Washington, DC, USA, 2000. IEEE Computer Society.

[6] R. Mahajan, N. Spring, D. Wetherall, and T. Anderson. Inferring link weights using end-to-end measurements. IMW '02, pages 231–236, New York, NY, USA, 2002. ACM.

[7] Z. Ming, M. Xu, and D. Wang. Age-based cooperative caching in information-centric networks. In *Computer Communications Workshops (INFOCOM WKSHPS), 2012 IEEE Conference on*, pages 268–273, March 2012.

[8] L. Muscariello, G. Carofiglio, and M. Gallo. Bandwidth and storage sharing performance in

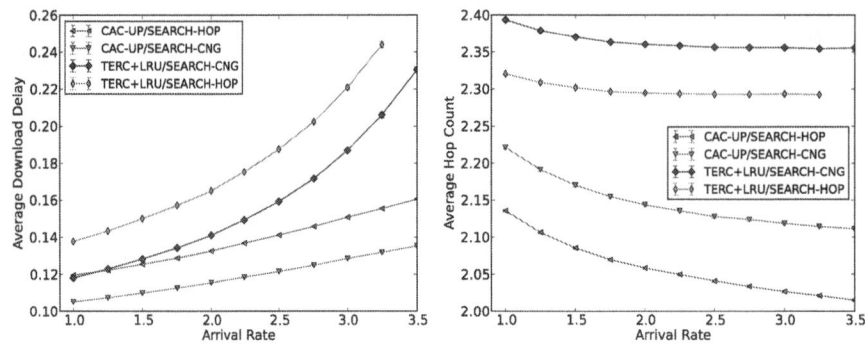

Figure 10: Tiscali (EU) topology download delay and hop count with increasing λ (using search)

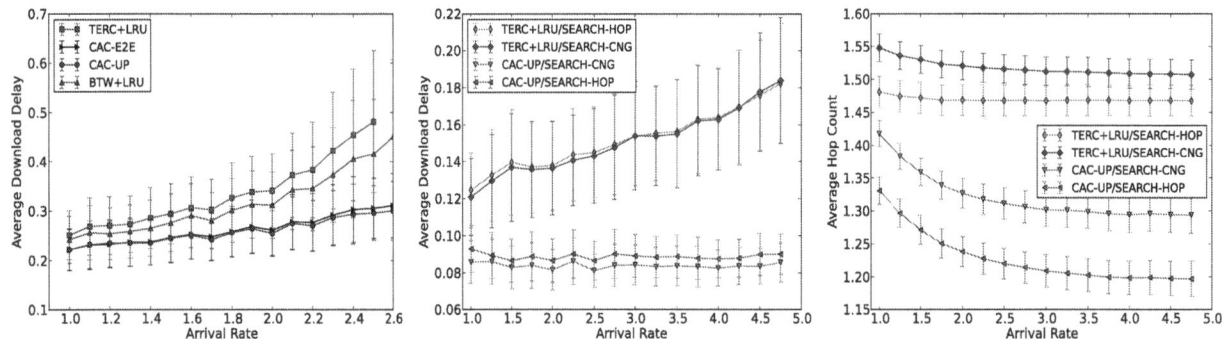

Figure 11: Hybrid MANET download delay (with and without search) and hop count with increasing λ

information centric networking. ICN '11, pages 26–31, New York, NY, USA, 2011. ACM.

[9] I. Psaras, W. K. Chai, and G. Pavlou. Probabilistic in-network caching for information-centric networks. ICN '12, pages 55–60, New York, NY, USA, 2012. ACM.

[10] E. J. Rosensweig and J. Kurose. Breadcrumbs: Efficient, best-effort content location in cache networks. In *INFOCOM*, pages 2631–2635. IEEE, 2009.

[11] D. Rossi and G. Rossini. On sizing ccn content stores by exploiting topological information. In *Computer Communications Workshops (INFOCOM WKSHPS), 2012 IEEE Conference on*, pages 280–285, March 2012.

[12] L. Saino, I. Psaras, and G. Pavlou. Hash-routing schemes for information centric networking. ICN '13, pages 27–32, New York, NY, USA, 2013. ACM.

[13] P. Scheuermann, J. Shim, and R. Vingralek. A case for delay-conscious caching of web documents. *Comput. Netw. ISDN Syst.*, 29(8-13):997–1005, Sept. 1997.

[14] Y. Wang, N. Rozhnova, A. Narayanan, D. Oran, and I. Rhee. An improved hop-by-hop interest shaper for congestion control in named data networking. *Computer Communication Review*, 43(4):55–60, 2013.

[15] R. P. Wooster and M. Abrams. Proxy caching that estimates page load delays. *Comput. Netw. ISDN Syst.*, 29(8-13):977–986, Sept. 1997.

Understanding Optimal Caching and Opportunistic Caching at "The Edge" of Information-Centric Networks

Ali Dabirmoghaddam[1]   Maziar Mirzazad-Barijough[1]   J. J. Garcia-Luna-Aceves[1,2]

[1]Computer Engineering Department, University of California, Santa Cruz, CA 95064
[2]PARC, Palo Alto, CA 94304
{alid,maziar,jj}@soe.ucsc.edu

ABSTRACT

A formal framework is presented for the characterization of cache allocation models in Information-Centric Networks (ICN). The framework is used to compare the performance of optimal caching everywhere in an ICN with opportunistic caching of content only near its consumers. This comparison is made using the independent reference model adopted in all prior studies, as well as a new model that captures non-stationary reference locality in space and time. The results obtained analytically and from simulations show that optimal caching throughout an ICN and opportunistic caching at the edge routers of an ICN perform comparably the same. In addition, caching content opportunistically only near its consumers is shown to outperform the traditional on-path caching approach assumed in most ICN architectures in an unstructured network with arbitrary topology represented as a random geometric graph.

Categories and Subject Descriptors

C.2 [**Computer Communication Networks**]: Network Architecture and Design; H.3 [**Information Storage and Retrieval**]: Systems and Software—*Information networks*

General Terms

Design,Theory

Keywords

information-centric networks; cache networks; network optimization; spatiotemporal locality of reference

1. INTRODUCTION

Several Information-Centric Networking (ICN) architectures [2,21] have been developed in an attempt to address the shift in the Internet communication paradigm from the conventional host-centric model towards a more flexible data-oriented design. As a result, ICN architectures seek to provide the necessary foundations for scalable and cost-efficient content distribution. A key design principle of many such architectures is the *universal in-network caching* of named data objects opportunistically. The *universality* of such opportunistic caching implies that it should be done *everywhere* and for *everything* in the network. The former requires all ICN routers to equally contribute in the network-wide process of caching, while the latter necessitates the ICN routers to cache all kinds of traffic they handle, irrespective of the popularity of the content or its geographical relevance. This approach is used to attain such performance benefits as reduced response time, efficient content distribution, and improved disruption tolerance.

As the review of prior work in Section 2 points out, even though universal in-network caching is assumed in many ICN architectures, there has been no quantitative analysis justifying this choice compared to opportunistic caching of content near its consumers. The main contribution of this paper is to provide a formal framework for the characterization of the performance of optimal in-network caching in ICNs, as well as opportunistic in-network caching at the edge of ICNs—*i.e.*, close to the end-users.

Section 3 uses the *Independent Reference Model* (IRM), which assumes that object references occur independently, to study the benefits of using universal caching compared to a simple policy of caching only at the edge of the network assuming a simple hierarchical caching structure. Our results, supported by extensive event-driven simulations over a wide range of configurations, indicate that the optimal caching approach based on universal caching provides only marginal benefits over the simple policy of caching only at the edge routers of the ICN. Although empirical studies [13] in the past have shown similar results, we present the first mathematical framework explaining this finding.

Section 4 addresses the impact of *locality of references* (*i.e.*, content requests) on the performance of caching in an ICN. Our work is inspired in part by the results delineated by Traverso *et al.* [31] on temporal locality of content references. We introduce a novel view of reference locality that captures both spatial and temporal aspects. The reference locality refers to the fact that a request to an object is likely to trigger subsequent requests from the same geographical neighborhood (*i.e.*, spatial locality) in the near future (*i.e.*, temporal locality). In other words, object references are localized in both space and time. Most prior work (*e.g.*, [4,15,26,28]) neglects the existence of such dependencies by assuming the IRM model.

Exploiting the notion of cluster point processes [9], we present a general method to synthesize traces of object references while maintaining their locality properties. The procedure we use for generating such non-stationary traces complies with the intuitive perception of spread of epidemics on today's social networks. An information object first attracts attention in a specific geographical region. People start sharing the content with their social contacts. A subpopulation of their contacts who find the content interesting re-share it and this process is repeated so long as the content retains its informational value in the network. We leverage the fact that this process closely matches that of a self-exciting Hawkes process [19] and present a new algorithm to produce a synthetic trace in which, while the collective popularity profile of objects follows the commonly observed Zipf distribution [3, 18], the occurrences of object-specific references over time and space are locally clustered when observed on a smaller scale. Based on this, we introduce a convenient measure to quantify the clustering degree of references on a scale from 0 to 1. We call this measure the *localization factor*, which can be used to cover the entire spectrum of reference patterns, from IRM (when it equals 0) to highly localized (when it goes to 1).

Armed with these new tools, we extend the comparison of universal in-network caching with simple caching at the edge of an ICN for traces not necessarily conforming to the IRM assumption. The results from our model in conjunction with event-driven simulations show that, while the optimal caching naturally drifts towards the edge as the caching budget increases, higher degrees of reference locality can further accelerate this transition. According to our findings, a 35% difference between edge- vs. optimal caching under the IRM assumption decreases to only 8% with a locality factor of 0.9.

Section 5 addresses the problem of caching in an unstructured ICN modeled using a random geometric graph. Given that optimal universal in-network caching is not possible to attain in this case, ICN architectures have adopted caching of content along the paths taken by content objects from producers or caches to consumers, which has recently been called Transparent En-Route Caching (TERC) [21]. The results from our simulations using ndnSIM [1] demonstrate that opportunistic caching at the edge of an ICN outperforms TERC in virtually all circumstances. While this result may be surprising at first, it can be explained with the insight gained by our modeling. TERC forces routers to store excessive amounts of content that induces much more content replacement along paths, while edge-caching tends to store more what is of interest to consumers near the routers.

Our work does not advocate specific mechanisms or ICN architectures. However, it provides new tools (e.g., the generation of meaningful synthetic traces) to analyze novel caching approaches in the future, and insight that has been missing to date on the caching schemes adopted in ICN architectures. In particular, given that universal in-network caching is not needed to attain efficiency, and given that edge-caching performs so well, new approaches should be developed that better integrate content routing and congestion control with content caching near consumers. Architecturally, our results indicate that deploying different types of routers in ICNs—some without any caching—would be far more cost effective. In the words of Fayazbakhsh et al. [13], content caching "at the edge" of ICNs indeed renders "less pain, most of the gain."

2. RELATED WORK

2.1 Caching

Although isolated caches have been studied extensively in the past (*e.g.*, [10, 20]), many aspects of interconnected networks of caches are not yet fully understood. Cache networks first became a subject of interest as a means to improve the performance of the Web [7, 27], and work on ICN architectures has renewed interest in this topic [4, 6, 16, 22–26, 33].

Understanding the full dimensions of networks of caches is naturally much more complicated than that of individual caches when operating in isolation. Many existing methods developed for analyzing the performance of isolated caches are based on algorithms that themselves are computationally expensive. For simplicity, these methods often introduce certain approximations that come at the inevitable cost of inaccuracy. Despite being negligible in the analysis of individual caches, these errors can aggregate and propagate through the system and produce a cascading effect when used in analysis of a tandem of caches.

A highly accurate approximation of least recently used (LRU) caching was introduced by Che *et al.* [7]. This analysis was recently revived in a seminal work by Fricker *et al.* [15] and shown to be applicable to a much wider range of scenarios beyond the specific conditions that Che *et al.* had initially anticipated. In the following, we briefly review this method which we shall refer to as "CHE-APRX"— abbreviated form of Che-approximation—hereinafter.

Consider a system comprising a total of N information objects and a LRU cache with capacity C. The requests for an object n come at the cache forming a Poisson process with rate $q(n)$. In fact, $q(n)$ signifies the popularity of object n in the system—*i.e.*, the proportion of total requests that belongs to n. The more popular an object n, the higher $q(n)$ as compared with other objects.

Che *et al.* define the *characteristic time* of a cache of size C, denoted by t_C, as the time it takes the cache to be filled with unique objects subject to the request rates $q(\cdot)$ under the IRM assumption, and show that t_C is indeed the unique root that solves the following equation for t:

$$C = \sum_{i=1}^{N} \left(1 - e^{-q(i)\, t}\right). \quad (1)$$

Knowing t_C, the miss probability $m(n)$ for an object n, according to CHE-APRX, is derived as:

$$m(n) \approx e^{-q(n)\, t_C}. \quad (2)$$

As mentioned earlier, the CHE-APRX has been proven to be very accurate and highly versatile. However, there are two important restrictions in this approximation.

1) Equal-sized objects. All information objects in CHE-APRX are of equal size—more precisely, unit-size such that the cache is able to store at most C objects. This assumption might seem far from reality at first, though becomes more plausible if objects are assumed to be segmented into equal-sized chunks, as required by many existing ICN proposals. It has also been shown [15] that CHE-APRX can readily be extended to also account for variable-sized objects. This, however, makes the derivations more unwieldy with little, if any, extra benefit to the purpose of our analysis. Hence, we choose to keep this assumption in place.

2) Independent object references. CHE-APRX assumes that the requests for information objects—a.k.a. references—arrive at the cache according to an i.i.d. process, independent of the past history of the requests and following a distribution determined by $q(\cdot)$ function. This assumption—generally referred to as the *Independent Reference Model* (IRM)—is fairly standard to many similar analyses for tractability and in order to calculate stationary hit/miss rates.

Although the IRM assumption is convenient, it is too simplistic in the context of cache networks, where object references exhibit strong correlation in both space and time domains. Consider for example a new song, while listed among the top hits of the month, may be highly popular for a certain period, but gradually gets faded out as newer hits are released. Furthermore, if the song is in a specific language, it may be well-received in certain regions of the world where that language is widely spoken, while attracting little attention in many other regions. The first example reflects the *temporal locality* of references, in contrast to the *spatial locality* highlighted by the second example. The IRM assumption disregards such localities in space and time by assuming that content popularity is stationary.

2.2 Architectures and Systems

In-network caching of named content is a cornerstone of many ICN architectures [2, 17, 21]. This consideration is so pervasive that many research papers (*e.g.*, [16, 21, 23, 29, 33]) use the notion of "cache network" as an abstraction to describe "content-centric networks".

The caching approach used in the vast majority of existing ICN proposals is the Transparent En-Route Caching (TERC) [21] by which *all* ICN routers in the network participate in the process of content caching in conjunction with their primitive function of relaying the information objects downstream. This naïve method of caching, however, has been subject of many controversies and criticisms [6, 13, 33]. To reduce caching redundancy, more complex varieties of this paradigm, such as probabilistic in-network caching (ProbCache) [24] and opportunistic caching using reinforced counters [12] have recently been introduced.

A handful of attempts in the past few years have been made to investigate most efficient methods of caching in ICN, both empirically [13, 31, 32] and analytically [4, 6, 24]. The results from some of these studies, however, are somewhat inconsistent and indecisive. For instance, the authors of [11] argue that caching at the *core* of the network can be more effective, as opposed to [13, 25] who advocate caching closer to the network *edge*.

Amidst this flurry of research, some researchers [6, 33] believe that the best cache placement strategy is greatly influenced by factors such as network topology; hence, there does not exist a unified strategy to be generally adopted. In contrast, other work [30] reports that the impact of topology on the performance of caching is limited.

Many notable analytical works [4, 15, 16, 26, 28, 33] focusing on the characterization of caching generally suffer from the limitations imposed by the IRM assumption. This assumption is so tightly coupled with the existing models of caching that Kurose writes [21]: "[The IRM] assumption is as fundamental for cache modeling as the memoryless assumption of exponential packet/circuit interarrival times ... are for modeling packet- and circuit-switched networks ..." This is indeed the case; however, just as exponential interarrival

times, the IRM assumption is only a simplifying assumption to make problems tractable; there is no evidence showing that real-world traffic adheres to the IRM model [8, 14].

Recently, Traverso *et al.* [31] have addressed the importance of temporal locality of references in the performance of today's caching networks. Their work leverages the concept of Poisson shot noise processes as a convenient mathematical tool to model and analyze temporal reference locality. They further show that adopting the IRM assumption results in an overly pessimistic view of caching performance.

3. HIERARCHICAL CACHING MODEL

Given a hierarchical network of caches, we ask the question: How much should each layer of the hierarchy of caches contribute in the caching process in order to get the most out of a constrained total caching budget? We frame this question as an optimization problem and present solutions based on non-linear integer programming.

Consider a hierarchy of LRU caches in the form of a tree with its root acting as the content source. We assume that the source stores permanent copies of all the information objects in the system. Alternatively, the source can be considered as a collection of all possible content hosts that are logically collapsed into one single entity as the root of the tree in our model.

The tree comprises $L + 2$ levels. The content subscribers (*i.e.*, users or information requesters) are at the 0th level, while the content source is at level $L + 1$. Subsequently, there exist L levels of nodes with caching capabilities between users and the content source which are sequentially labeled from bottom (level 1) to the top (level L).

The caching paradigm we seek to optimize is called "on-path caching" which works as follows. When a request for an object is raised at level 0, it is forwarded along the (unique) path of intermediate caches towards the root until a cache hit occurs. If all cache accesses are missed along the path, the request will be fulfilled by fetching a copy of the object directly from the source (root). Once located, the object is transferred on the reverse path back to the requester and a local copy is also stored on each and every cache along.

For simplicity, in the following analysis we assume that the hierarchy is a complete k-ary tree. Under the IRM assumption and given that the cache states are independent[1], the rate at which requests for an object n arrive at a particular cache at level ℓ can recursively be formalized as:

$$q_\ell(n) = \begin{cases} q(n) & \ell = 0, \\ k\, q_{\ell-1}(n)\, m_{\ell-1}(n) & 0 < \ell \le L, \end{cases} \quad (3)$$

where $m_{\ell-1}(n)$ is the miss probability of object n at a cache of level $\ell - 1$, which can itself be calculated directly using CHE-APRX (*i.e.*, Equations (1) and (2)).

3.1 The Expected Time To Access Content

A parameter of interest is the *expected time to access* (ETTA) an object n, which we denote by $\tau(n)$. This is defined as the expected duration between the time a user sends a request for an object n until a copy is located in the system (either at an intermediate cache or finally at the original source). We measure this duration in terms of the number of hops between the user and the closest replica of the content

---

[1]This assumption is reasonable when k is not very small.

along the path to the source. The following theorem gives a closed-form for calculating Etta in terms of the miss rates of the intermediate caches.

Theorem 1. *Consider a tree structure with $L + 2$ levels where the users are at level 0 and the content source at level $L + 1$. Employing an on-path caching strategy as described before, the expected time to access an object n is obtained as:*

$$\tau(n) = 1 + \sum_{i=1}^{L} \prod_{j=1}^{i} m_j(n), \qquad (4)$$

where $m_j(n)$ is the miss probability of content n at a cache of level j on the path from the user towards the root of the tree.

Proof. For an object n, the problem can be modeled by a discrete-time Markov chain whose states are the levels of the caching hierarchy plus an additional state of H denoting a cache hit (See Figure 1). Every state ℓ, $0 < \ell < L+1$ transits into either the following state $\ell + 1$ or H with probabilities $m_\ell(n)$ and $h_\ell(n) = 1 - m_\ell(n)$, respectively. States $L+1$ and H transit into state H with probability 1.

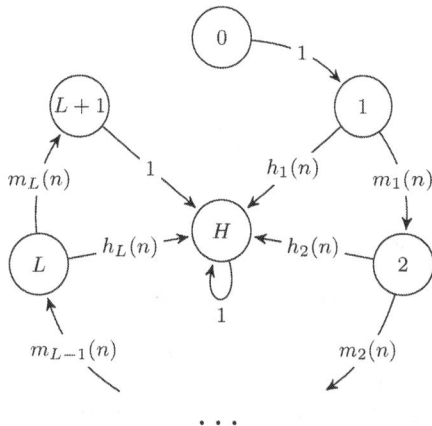

Figure 1: The Markov chain representing the process of locating an object on a cache tree. State 0 is where the users' requests are generated. State H denotes the state of a cache hit and other states correspond to the levels in the hierarchy from bottom to the top. State $L + 1$ is the root of the tree where the content source is located. $m_i(n)$ and $h_i(n) = 1 - m_i(n)$ are the miss and hit probabilities at a cache of level i.

Define $T_H \triangleq \inf\{t \geq 1 : X_t = H\}$ as the stopping time denoting when state H is visited for the first time. Also, the expected time to visit H as $\tau_0(n) \triangleq \mathbb{E}[T_H \mid X_0 = 0]$, where X_0 is a random variable denoting the initial state. We note that $\tau_0(n)$ counts the expected number of transitions to visit state H which can be expressed recursively as:

$$\tau_0(n) = 1 + \tau_1(n)$$
$$= 1 + 1 + m_1(n)\,\tau_2(n) + \big(1 - m_1(n)\big)\,\tau_H(n).$$

Also, it is clear that $\tau_H(n) = 0$ for every object n, since visiting state H implies that the content is already located. Similarly, $\tau_2(n) = 1 + m_2(n)\,\tau_3(n)$. By induction on the index i of $\tau_i(n)$, it is easy to verify that

$$\tau_0(n) = 2 + \sum_{i=1}^{L} \prod_{j=1}^{i} m_j(n).$$

In essence, $\tau_0(n)$ serves to count the expected number of steps it takes to locate the object in the hierarchy of caches. However, due to the presence of the additional state H, the real number of steps is always off by one from what $\tau_0(n)$ counts. Representing the actual expected value by $\tau(n)$, therefore, $\tau(n) = \tau_0(n) - 1$ and Equation (4) follows. □

A slightly modified version of the foregoing result has also been used in [5] as a measure of "virtual round-trip time" to access contents of various popularity classes.

3.2 Optimal Cache Allocation in Tree Structure

Definition 1. (The optimal cache allocation problem) *Given a fixed total cache budget C, find the optimal breakdown of the caching budget across different levels of the tree that minimizes the overall expected time to access subject to a given content popularity profile $q(\cdot)$.*

Under the IRM assumption, for a k-ary tree with L cache levels, we formulate this problem as a non-linear integer programming as follows:

$$\boldsymbol{c}^* = \operatorname*{argmin}_{\boldsymbol{c}} \sum_{n=1}^{N} q(n)\,\tau(n; \boldsymbol{c})$$

$$\text{s.t.} \quad \sum_{\ell=1}^{L} c(\ell)\,k^{(L-\ell)} = C, \quad \text{and}$$

$$c(\ell) \geq 0 \text{ and integer } \forall \ell \in \{1, \ldots, L\}, \qquad (5)$$

where $\boldsymbol{c}^* \in \mathbb{N}^L$ is the vector of optimal cache sizes on the tree in which $c^*(\ell)$ denotes the optimal capacity of an *individual* cache at the ℓth level.

3.3 Numerical Results

We collected some numerical results on the problem described above utilizing the active-set algorithm of the optimization toolbox in MATLAB. As the underlying topology, we considered k-ary tree structures of depth 7. The requesters are the leaves (*i.e.*, level 0) and the source (storing a permanent copy of all objects) is at the root (*i.e.*, level 6). The 5 intermediate levels—which we call ℓ_1 to ℓ_5 caches—are cache routers with LRU replacement policy.

All named objects in the system are ranked based on their global popularity—*i.e.*, the overall frequency of requests for that object throughout the system. For these simulations, we used 1 million data objects of all the same size whose popularities follow a Zipf distribution with exponent 1. References to these objects are Poisson distributed with rates proportional to their popularities. For the time being, we make sure that the references conform to the IRM assumption and that identical objects have the same popularity among all users. We shall later explain how the IRM assumption can be relaxed by focusing on more general classes of traffic with non-stationary behavior in time and space.

Figure 2 demonstrates the optimal breakdown of the caching budget across various levels of the tree hierarchy for complete trees of degree 2 to 5. Bars show what fraction of the caching budget is allocated to various levels for any given total budget. The darker the color, the lower the cache level in the hierarchy. As seen, there is a drift towards the edge as the caching budget increases. This is trivially expected when Etta is the objective criterion for the optimization problem. For trees with lower degrees, this behavior is more

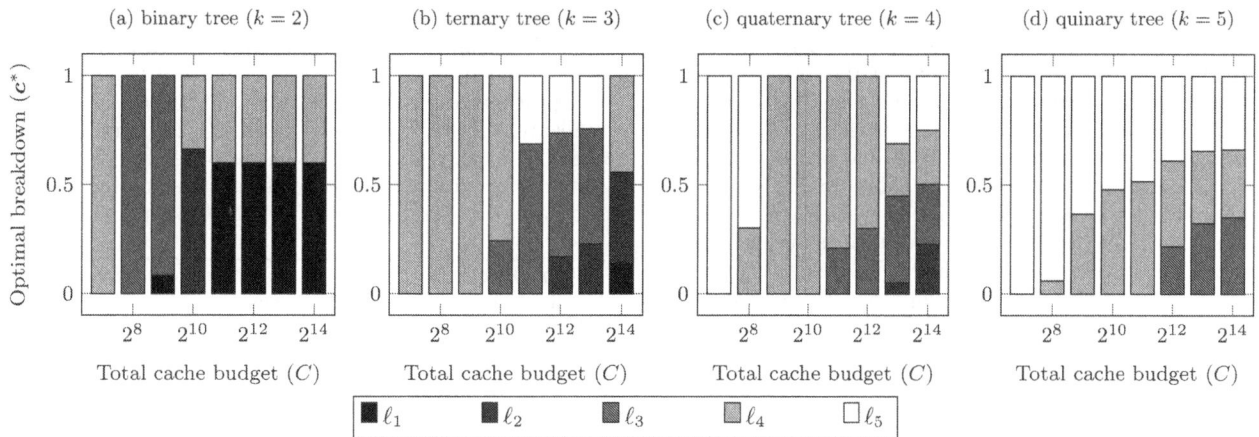

Figure 2: Optimal breakdown of caching budget across various levels of the tree for the given total cache budgets

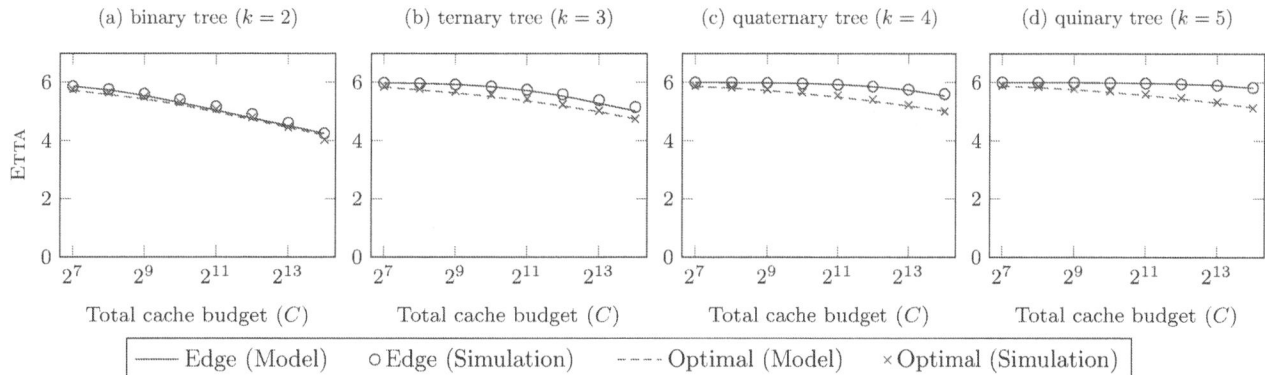

Figure 3: The overall expected time to access (ETTA) with respect to the total caching budget for optimal- vs. edge-caching

evident, because for the same total budget, edge caches in lower degree trees can receive larger shares, making edge-caching even more effective.

When the caching budget is large, edge-caching is clearly the optimal strategy. At the limit, a budget of $N \times k^L$ can be broken up evenly across all ℓ_1 caches giving each of them enough capacity to store a copy of all objects in the system. This results in an ETTA of close to 1 in the long run. The available budget, nonetheless, is usually much less than this in practice. Figure 3 serves to shed some light on the question of how different optimal caching performs in general as compared with pure edge-caching by comparing the overall ETTA for edge- with optimal caching.

The solid lines in Figure 3 represent edge-caching, where all the caching budget is evenly split across ℓ_1 caches. The dashed lines illustrate the optimal caching with a budget breakdown specified in the corresponding part of Figure 2. To verify the accuracy of these results, we also designed a discrete-event simulation based on ndnSIM [1], a NS-3 module implementing Named Data Networking. As seen, results from discrete-event simulations demonstrate almost perfect agreement with the proposed model.

Interestingly, Figure 3 suggests that edge-caching can perform comparably close to the optimal caching in practice. According to our results, the maximum difference observed between the two schemes is around 10%. The difference is seen to increase slightly with the degree of the tree. How-

ever, as Figure 2 also illustrates, the optimal breakdown tends towards the edge with an increased caching budget. This essentially means that the difference between the edge- and optimal caching is reduced with further increasing the budget. On the other hand, when the available budget is small, both edge- and optimal caching strategies appear to be equally ineffective. Thus, the maximum observed gap applies only to the cases where the available budget is modest—that is, neither so large to make edge-caching effectively optimal, nor so small to undermine the effectiveness of caching altogether.

Implementing edge-caching is practically more convenient, in that it only requires deploying ℓ_1 caches at the AS-level without any need to manipulate central routers deep in the core of the network. Although the effectiveness of edge-caching has previously been shown through extensive empirical studies [13], our work, to the best of our knowledge, presents the first formal framework as a basis to compare the two paradigms in more depth.

4. CAPTURING REFERENCE LOCALITY

To obtain useful insights out of the foregoing analysis, it is imperative to evaluate the model under realistic conditions. As discussed, the IRM assumption overlooks the correlation present among subsequent object references occurring over a certain period of time (i.e., temporal locality) and/or a specific region in space (i.e., spatial locality). We introduce a convenient model to generate object references while preserving their spatio-temporal locality properties. Before proceeding, let us have a closer look at the intuitive interpretation of the concepts of spatial and temporal locality.

Spatial locality of reference captures the impact that the geographical diversity of the users has on the observed trace of requested objects by them. More precisely, the requests coming from a specific region in space are more likely to be similar than those collected over regions far apart. For example, a certain news object might be of special interest in a certain area, while its global impact in the geography of interest remains limited. On the other hand, globally popular objects are seen to be requested from a wider range of geographical regions.

Temporal locality of reference captures the effect that, if an object is requested at a certain point in time, more likely it will be requested again in near future. In fact, nor are the object references scattered randomly and independently over time; rather, an object might be of particular interest at a certain time interval, while its popularity gradually fades out.

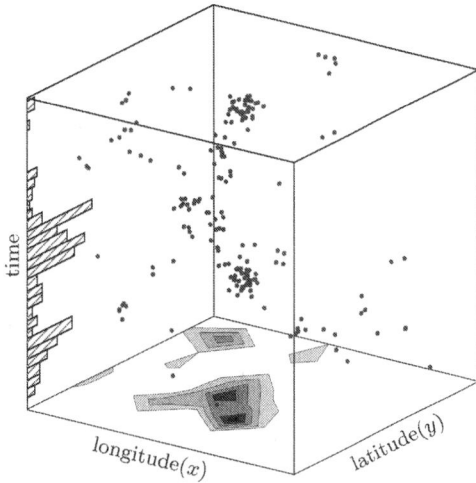

Figure 4: A cluster process representing references to a specific object file. The projection of points over X-Y plane represents the spatial density of requests, whereas the projection along the time axis reflects the temporal distribution.

4.1 Using Cluster Point Processes

In the light of the above discussion, an intuitive approach for simulating the spatio-temporal locality of object references is using "cluster point processes" [9]. A generic method for producing one such process works as follows. First, a point process Π generates "centers" of the process. Next, a point process X_p for each $p \in \Pi$ produces the off-springs. The combination of these points $X = \cup_{p \in \Pi} X_p$ constitutes a cluster process. Particularly, X is called a "Poisson cluster process" if Π is a Poisson process.

A specific example of the Poisson cluster process is "Hawkes process" [19] that is generated as follows. First, a Poisson process on $\mathbb{R}^d$ with intensity function $\rho(\cdot)$ creates the cluster centers Π. Then, for each cluster center $p \in \Pi$, the first-generation off-springs are generated as a Poisson process of intensity $\varphi(x - p)$, where $\varphi(\cdot)$ is a positive function on $\mathbb{R}^d$. This process continues repeatedly such that for every first-generation off-spring p_1, a Poisson process of intensity

$\varphi(x - p_1)$ generates the second generation off-springs and so on. The mean number of off-springs for each center point is determined as $\beta = \int \varphi(x)\,dx$. A natural requirement for this process to stop demands $\beta < 1$. Figure 4 illustrates one realization of the Hawkes process in $\mathbb{R}^3$. The contour plot on the X-Y plane represents the spatial density of the requests for a certain object, while the histogram along the time axis shows the temporal evolution of the object popularity.

Algorithm 1 Method for generating object references with localization in a d-dimensional space

---

Input: Number of objects (N), Zipf parameter (α) and localization factor (β)
Output: An aggregate Poisson cluster process X
Ensure: X is Zipf distributed with parameter α
1: **procedure** Generate-Trace(N, α, β)
2:     $X \leftarrow \varnothing$
3:     **for** n from 1 to N **do**
4:         $q_n \leftarrow M \times n^{-\alpha}$ $\triangleright$ M is some constant multiplier
5:         $\Pi_n \leftarrow$ Hawkes-Process(q_n, β)
6:         $X \leftarrow X \cup \Pi_n$
7:     **end for**
8:     **return** X
9: **end procedure**

Input: Intensity of cluster centers (ρ) and the expected number of off-springs (β)
Output: A Poisson cluster process Π
Require: $\rho \geq 0$ and $0 \leq \beta < 1$
10: **procedure** Hawkes-Process(ρ, β)
11:     $n_t \leftarrow$ Poisson(ρ)
12:     **for** i from 1 to n_t **do**
13:         $\Pi(i) \leftarrow$ Uniform(0,1)
14:     **end for**
15:     $idx \leftarrow 1, \quad end \leftarrow n_t$
16:     **while** $idx < n_t$ **do**
17:         $n_c \leftarrow$ Poisson(β)
18:         **for** j from 1 to n_c **do**
19:             $\Pi(++end) \leftarrow \Pi(idx) +$ Normal(0,σ)
20:         **end for**
21:         $n_t \leftarrow n_t + n_c, \quad idx++$
22:     **end while**
23:     **return** Π
24: **end procedure**

This procedure can be repeated for the number of objects in the system to generate a collective trace of all references. The procedure Generate-Trace in Algorithm 1 shows the pseudocode for this with inputs N denoting the total number of objects, α as the parameter of the Zipf distribution for object popularity, and β specifying the localization factor. For an object n, Line 4 calculates the intensity q_n at which the references to that object should be generated. To ensure that the global object popularity profile follows the desired Zipf distribution, we choose this rate to be directly proportional to the global popularity of the object in the system. Consequently, references to more popular objects will be placed over a wider geography and a longer course of time, as opposed to the less popular items which may only be requested from a specific region and a certain period. The multiplier M in Line 4 is a positive constant which can be interpreted as the maximum intensity—*i.e.*, the desired intensity for the most popular (first rank) object. Depending on the choice of N and α, one may need to set the value of this multiplier sufficiently large to ensure that the lower rank objects at the tail of the popularity distribution will also have a reasonable chance to appear in the trace.

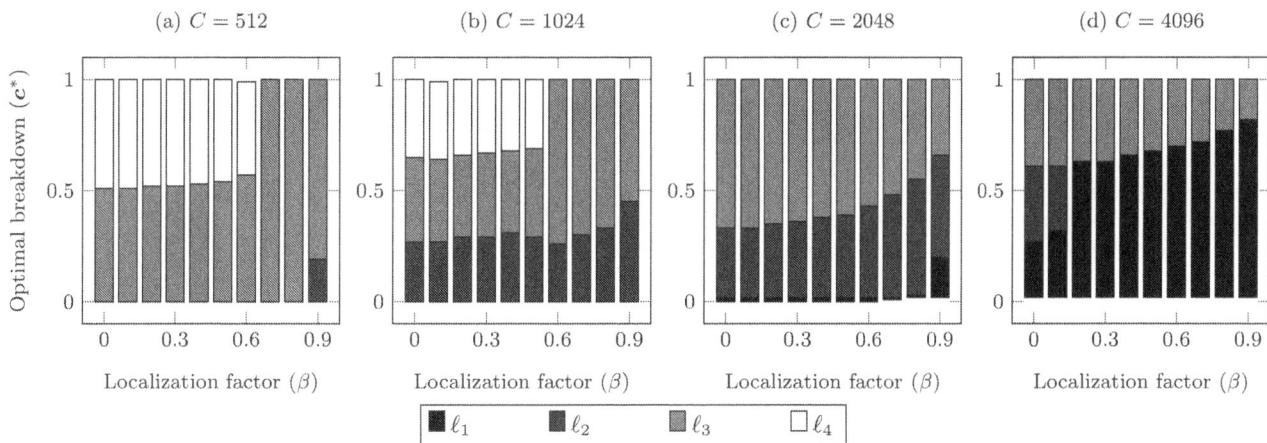

Figure 5: Optimal breakdown of caching budget across various levels of the tree for various localization factors

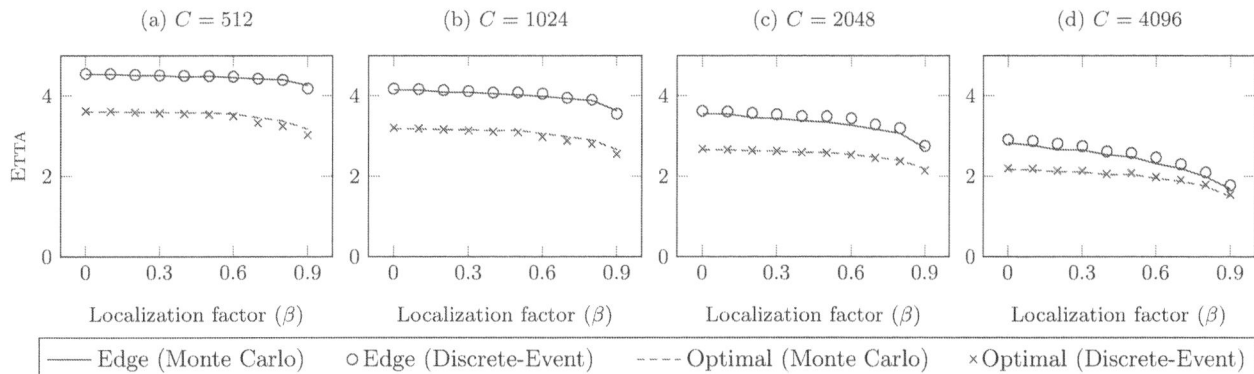

Figure 6: The overall expected time to access (ETTA) with respect to the localization factor for optimal- vs. edge-caching

Once the reference intensity is determined, a call to procedure HAWKES-PROCESS is made at Line 10 to produce the actual trace of references. The parameters ρ and β respectively determine the intensity of the centers and the expected number of next-generation off-springs in the underlying cluster process. The centers are uniformly scattered throughout the region, and for each center, the off-springs are normally distributed around it. The procedures UNIFORM and NORMAL are assumed to return coordinates in d-dimensional space with corresponding distributions and the parameters specified.

4.2 Caching under Non-stationary References

With a non-stationary stream of references, the popularity profile of objects in the system varies over both space and time. Consequently, the model discussed in Section 3 can no longer be used to analyze the behavior of the caching system. A useful insight which can help remedy this limitation is that while, in the big picture, the underlying process of object references is dynamic, when studied at a finer granularity, it can be well-approximated as a "piece-wise" stationary process. In other words, if we look at the process of references through a sufficiently small window in the time-space domain, the subprocess observed exhibits a rather stationary behavior.

Let $q_u(n, t)$ be the popularity of the nth object observed by a cache node u around a particular time t. As a gener-

alization of Equation (3), we can compute this quantity as follows:

$$
q_u(n, t) = \begin{cases} \lim_{\Delta t \to 0} \dfrac{\mathbb{E}[N_u(n, t + \Delta t]}{\Delta t} & u \in \{\ell_1\}, \\ \sum_{c \in \mathcal{C}_u} q_c(n, t)\, m_c(n, t) & u \notin \{\ell_1\}. \end{cases} \tag{6}
$$

Here, $\{\ell_1\}$ denotes the set of ℓ_1 caches; $N_u(n, t + \Delta t)$ denotes the number of references to object n coming at node u during interval $(t, t + \Delta t)$; and $\mathcal{C}_u$ represents the set of caches which have u as their upstream node. In other words, the aggregate miss streams of nodes in $\mathcal{C}_u$ form the input stream of u.

In most scenarios, it is neither practical nor necessary to work with the infinitesimal limit given in Equation (6). Rather, the input stream of a ℓ_1 cache could be partitioned into a number of smaller time bins over which the input process is assumed to be stationary. The size of the time bins does indeed depend on the degree of reference locality. The more localized the input stream, the more clustered are the occurrences of the references over time; hence, smaller time bins will be required to mitigate the approximation error.

This treatment can be used in conjunction with CHE-APRX when dealing with non-stationary streams of references. The miss rates and the corresponding ETTA's can be computed separately for individual intervals. The overall ETTA, subsequently, can be calculated as the time-average of individually computed ETTA's over specific intervals.

To evaluate the accuracy of this method, we conduct some Monte Carlo simulations backed by a series of discrete-event simulations we perform in ndnSIM [1]. The underlying topology we consider is a complete tree of degree 4 and depth 6 with 4 layers of intermediate caches. Our object catalogue contains 100 files with a Zipf popularity profile of parameter 1. Algorithm 1 is used to generate a 2-D trace of object references with various degrees of localization. Leaves of the tree span across one dimension and object references are directed at their L_1-closest cache. The other dimension captures the temporal distribution of references as discussed before.

Figure 5 demonstrates the optimal breakdown of cache budget across levels of the tree for various degrees of reference locality. Again, a drift towards the edge can be observed as the available caching budget increases. This transition is further accelerated with a larger localization factor. Figure 5(d) reflects this phenomenon more vividly. In particular, we observe that an increased localization factor from 0.0 to 0.9 has almost the same impact on the performance of the caching hierarchy as doubling the caching budget does.

Figure 6 compares the overall expected time to access for edge- vs. optimal caching with the same configurations as plots in Figure 5. As discussed earlier, for numerical analysis, we split the time into smaller non-overlapping intervals (bins). With zero localization, references are generated independently. The generated trace, therefore, conforms to the IRM assumption and hence, one single time bin is considered. With a localization factor of 0.9, we found that 5 time bins yield a good approximation with a maximum error of 6% over a wide range of configurations. For other cases in between, the number of bins are chosen proportionally. At this stage, we do not know how the number of bins should be chosen optimally to minimize the approximation error. Answering this question requires a deeper understanding of the behavior of the underlying point process, and we leave this as a subject for future research.

Figure 6 also captures how fast optimal on-path caching converges towards the edge as both the caching budget and localization factor increase. In the examples depicted, the maximum difference between the two schemes is around 35%. This is reduced to 8% on the far right of Figure 6(d) where every ℓ_1 cache gets enough capacity to store 16 objects.

The main focus of our study so far was primarily on a well-defined hierarchy of caches. In what follows, we broaden the scope of our findings by considering a more arbitrary topology of caches.

5. CACHING ON RANDOM NETWORKS

Let Π_0 be a point process on d-dimensional space representing a random deployment of cache nodes. We define the local cache of a sub-region in the space of interest as follows.

Definition 2. *A node $x \in \Pi_0$ is said to be the local cache for the region $\mathcal{C}_x$ defined as:*

$$\mathcal{C}_x = \left\{ y \in \mathbb{R}^d : \|y - x\| \leq \inf_{x' \in \Pi_0, x' \neq x} \|y - x'\| \right\}.$$

In fact, $\mathcal{C}_x$ comprises the closed set of points that are geographically closer to x than any other point in Π_0. In this sense, the process Π_0 forms a Voronoi tessellation of the space similar to the construction depicted in Figure 7. The solid dots are the points generated by Π_0 and the polygons

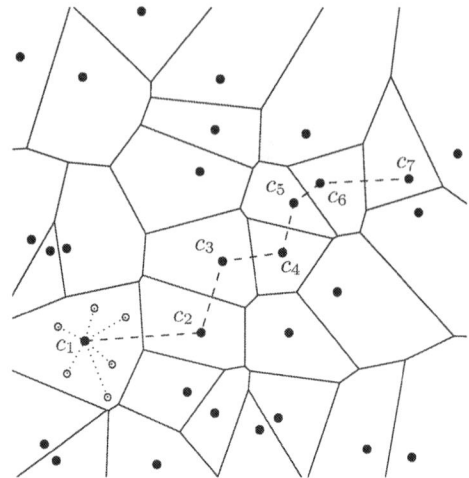

Figure 7: A Voronoi tessellation of the terrain via randomly deployed cache nodes. Solid dots are local caches to the cells they belong to, and empty dots indicate requests directed to them (shown only for one cell for clarity). The dashed line represents a path from cell 1 to cell 7. Cache node c_7 is the original source of the content to be routed to c_1, the initial requesting cell. On this way, if the content is cached at every cache node $c_i, i = 1, \ldots, 6$, it is called on-path caching. If the content is cached only at c_1, we call it edge-caching.

where they reside are the Voronoi cells. We shall refer to $\mathcal{C}_x$ as the cell of node x, hereinafter.

Each cache node is equipped with two types of storage. One part is the permanent storage used for publishing content. The other part is used for caching content from other nodes while the cache node serves to route the content towards some end-user/subscriber.

Subscription requests (generated by Algorithm 1), form a second point process. A request originating from cell $\mathcal{C}_x$ is first forwarded to x, the local cache of that cell. If x happens to have a copy of the requested object, it serves the request locally. Otherwise, it forwards the request towards the original owner of the content in a multi-hop fashion.

The connectivity among cache nodes is defined based on Euclidean distance such that every $x_i, x_j \in \Pi_0$ are connected through a bidirectional link iff $\|x_i - x_j\| \leq r$ for some constant $r > 0$. Such a paradigm is often adopted for modeling of wireless ad hoc networks and might not well represent a typical wired topology. Still, we believe it is interesting to study the performance of various caching schemes on a more general and irregular type of topology such as that of a random geometric graph.

5.1 The Routing and Caching Process

The routing is performed along the shortest path connecting source-destination pairs. For simplicity, we choose the critical radius r large enough to ensure that the network is connected. Hence, there always exists at least one path connecting each subscribing cell to the publishing source. Such paths typically cross through several cells and the traffic carried along them may be cached at the local caches of the cells where they intersect.

On the way towards the source, if a valid replica of the requested object is located at any of the intermediate caches along the path, the request will be handled locally and it will not be forwarded beyond that point. However, if no cache hit occurs along the path, the request will be served by the original source and the requested object will be routed back towards the requester on the reverse path.

For a well-structured tree topology, we observed suggestive evidence that edge-caching can perform comparably close to optimal caching in certain situations. Implementing optimal caching on a random configuration, nevertheless, is challenging if not impossible at all. This is perhaps why many existing ICN proposals adopt a simplified version of on-path caching in which all routers blindly cache every piece of information they relay.

Implementing edge-caching, in contrast, is not much of a burden on a random network so long as a clear definition of "edge" is given. Since object requests are scattered all over the network, there is no physical boundary to separate edge from the rest of the network. Instead, we give a logical definition of the edge. In fact, we say edge-caching takes place if caching is only performed at the local cache of the last cell where the traffic is being served,—i.e., the destination cell. According to this definition, a cache router is an edge cache for the cell it resides in and a non-edge cache for the traffic it relays to all other cells. An interesting aspect to investigate is a performance comparison of the simplified on-path caching—which for brevity we shall refer to as "on-path"—versus edge-caching in the above described configuration.

Although appearing different, the system we just described has many characteristics in common with the hierarchical topology we discussed in the previous section. In particular, for any given object, the original publisher (source) serves as the root of a tree. The object requesters (i.e., destinations) are the leaves, which can be from anywhere within the network. Of course, the induced tree structures differ for various object files. Consequently, a cache node can be part of several such logical trees and at different levels.

5.2 Simulation Results

We perform event-driven simulations on ndnSIM [1] to compare the performance of caching at the edge versus the standard on-path caching on a random geometric topology. The network consists of 200 cache nodes distributed uniformly and at random over a region of 100×100 square units. Nodes' radio range is set to 12 units giving each node an average degree of 8.93. We use a total of 1000 content objects with a Zipf popularity distribution of parameter 1. The objects are also uniformly distributed among nodes which act as original publishers of the designated objects. Hence, some nodes may publish more than one data object while some others none. With the foregoing settings, the following measurements are performed in the steady-state of the system when all caches are full.

Figure 8 shows how the average hop-count decreases with an increased locality factor when each node has a caching storage of size 10. In this case, edge-caching outperforms the standard on-path caching even under the IRM assumption (i.e., $\beta = 0$). This behavior is rather surprising because when the references are generated independently, there should seemingly exist no difference between the two schemes in terms of cache hits. However, a subtle observation is that replacements generally take place at a higher rate with on-path caching than with the edge-caching. This is due to the replacements that a cache incurs while relaying traffic to other cells. These replacements do not take place when caching is only done for the edge traffic.

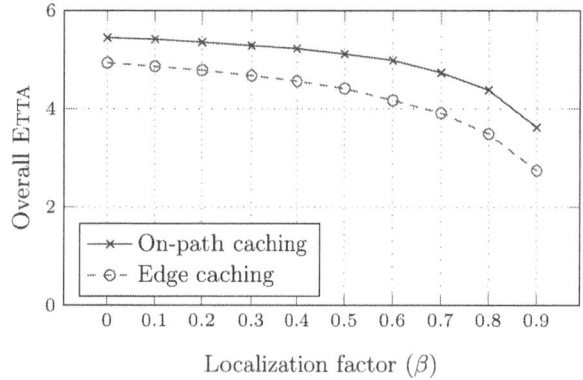

Figure 8: Overall expected time to access an object in a random geometric topology for various degrees of reference locality (from IRM ($\beta = 0$) to highly localized ($\beta = 0.9$))

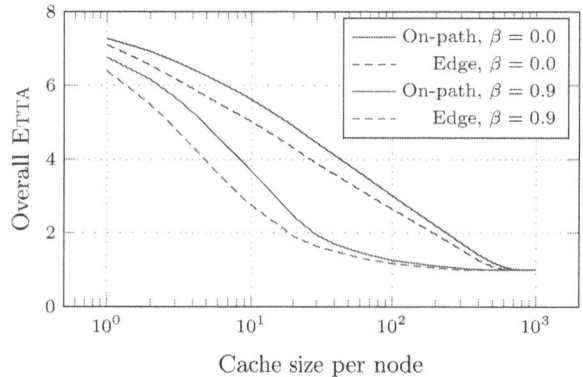

Figure 9: The impact of increasing the cache size on the caching gain for various degrees of reference locality. Edge-caching outperforms on-path caching in almost all scenarios.

Not all such replacements are useful. In fact, with a Zipf-like distribution, a vast majority of objects at the tail are individually unpopular and very unlikely to be requested. Yet, in the big picture, it is much more likely to see *some* object from this whole population of less popular items being referenced by *some* node throughout the network. With on-path caching, all such references result in replacements along the entire path serving the traffic to the destination cell. Once referenced, however, because the object is of little global interest, the odds are small that any of these affected caches serve any subsequent reference to the same object in near future. The replaced item takes up a space that could have otherwise been dedicated to a more popular item and thereby, diminishes the caching gain.

With edge-caching, such useless replacements occur at a lower rate and the caching capacity is utilized more efficiently. The same arguments hold in case of higher degrees of locality resulting in an even sharper contrast.

Figure 9 illustrates the impact of increasing the caching budget on the average hop-count. As seen, edge-caching outperforms on-path caching for all cache sizes and over various degrees of locality. The enhancements attained through increasing the budget size become more pronounced with a higher degree of reference locality. Another observation is that a localization factor of 0.9 requires roughly 6 times less caching budget to yield the same overall ETTA than it does under the independent reference model.

6. CONCLUSIONS AND FUTURE WORK

A computational framework was presented to compare the performance of in-network caching mechanisms in ICN. In particular, we compared optimal on-path caching against the simple strategy of caching only at routers near the consumers of an ICN in terms of their overall expected time to accessing content objects. The results using the commonly-used independent reference model showed that while the optimal breakdown of caching budget is markedly influenced by factors such as topology and caching budget, optimal caching provides only marginal benefits over edge-caching in most scenarios. We investigated the impact of locality of reference on the performance of ICNs, and introduced a tool to synthesize traces of object requests that preserves their spatial and temporal locality properties. The results using this model demonstrate that, while optimal caching naturally tends towards the edge with an increased caching budget, higher degrees of reference locality further accelerate this transition. This suggests that the difference between edge- and optimal on-path caching is far less than what the existing models based on the IRM assumption predict.

We also compared the on-path caching approach assumed in most ICN architectures today against edge-caching using random geometric graphs to model ICNs of irregular arbitrary topologies. The results of simulations in ndnSIM [1] confirm the result in our models, and in fact show that edge-caching outperforms on-path caching.

The results of this work open up new avenues for research in ICN. New ICN architectures should be investigated that exploit content routing with edge-caching. It is important to broaden the scope of this study by considering more realistic types of topologies than we have used, and the locality model we introduced should be fit against real-world traces to examine how localized content requests are in actual networks.

Acknowledgments

The authors gratefully thank the anonymous reviewers for their constructive comments on an earlier version of this manuscript. This research was sponsored in part by the Jack Baskin Chair of Computer Engineering at UCSC.

7. REFERENCES

[1] A. Afanasyev, I. Moiseenko, and L. Zhang. ndnSIM: NDN simulator for NS-3. Technical Report NDN-0005, NDN, 2012.

[2] B. Ahlgren, C. Dannewitz, C. Imbrenda, D. Kutscher, and B. Ohlman. A Survey of Information-Centric Networking. *IEEE Commun. Mag.*, 50(7):26–36, 2012.

[3] L. Breslau, P. Cao, L. Fan, G. Phillips, and S. Shenker. Web Caching and Zipf-like Distributions: Evidence and Implications. In *Proc. IEEE INFOCOM*, pages 126–134, 1999.

[4] G. Carofiglio, M. Gallo, and L. Muscariello. Bandwidth and Storage Sharing Performance in Information Centric Networking. In *Proc. ACM SIGCOMM Workshop on ICN*, pages 26–31, 2011.

[5] G. Carofiglio, M. Gallo, L. Muscariello, and D. Perino. Modeling Data Transfer in Content-Centric Networking. In *Proc. ITC*, pages 111–118, 2011.

[6] W. Chai, D. He, I. Psaras, and G. Pavlou. Cache "Less for More" in Information-Centric Networks (Extended Version). *Comput. Commun.*, 36(7):758–770, 2013.

[7] H. Che, Y. Tung, and Z. Wang. Hierarchical Web Caching Systems: Modeling, Design and Experimental Results. *IEEE J. Sel. Areas Commun.*, 20(7):1305–1314, 2002.

[8] L. Cherkasova and M. Gupta. Analysis of Enterprise Media Server Workloads: Access Patterns, Locality, Content Evolution, and Rates of Change. *IEEE/ACM Trans. Netw.*, 12(5):781–794, 2004.

[9] D. Daley and D. Vere-Jones. *An Introduction to the Theory of Point Processes*, volume I: Elementary Theory and Methods. Springer, New York, NY, USA, second edition, 2003.

[10] A. Dan and D. Towsley. An Approximate Analysis of the LRU and FIFO Buffer Replacement Schemes. *ACM SIGMETRICS Perform. Eval. Rev.*, 18(1):143–152, 1990.

[11] P. Danzig, R. Hall, and M. Schwartz. A Case for Caching File Objects Inside Internetworks. *SIGCOMM Comput. Commun. Rev.*, 23(4):239–248, 1993.

[12] G. Domingues, E. Silva, R. Leão, and D. Menasché. Enabling Information Centric Networks through Opportunistic Search, Routing and Caching. arXiv:1310.8258 [cs.NI], 2013.

[13] S. Fayazbakhsh, Y. Lin, A. Tootoonchian, A. Ghodsi, T. Koponen, B. Maggs, K. Ng, V. Sekar, and S. Shenker. Less Pain, Most of the Gain: Incrementally Deployable ICN. *ACM SIGCOMM Comput. Commun. Rev.*, pages 147–158, 2013.

[14] R. Fonseca, V. Almeida, M. Crovella, and B. Abrahao. On the Intrinsic Locality Properties of Web Reference Streams. In *Proc. IEEE INFOCOM*, pages 448–458, 2003.

[15] C. Fricker, P. Robert, and J. Roberts. A Versatile and Accurate Approximation for LRU Cache Performance. In *Proc. ITC*, pages 1–8, 2012.

[16] M. Gallo, B. Kauffmann, L. Muscariello, A. Simonian, and C. Tanguy. Performance Evaluation of the Random Replacement Policy for Networks of Caches. *Perform. Evaluation*, 72(0):16–36, 2014.

[17] A. Ghodsi, S. Shenker, T. Koponen, A. Singla, B. Raghavan, and J. Wilcox. Information-Centric Networking: Seeing the Forest for the Trees. In *Proc. ACM HotNets*, pages 1–6, 2011.

[18] P. Gill, M. Arlitt, Z. Li, and A. Mahanti. Youtube Traffic Characterization: A View from the Edge. In *Proc. ACM IMC*, pages 15–28, 2007.

[19] A. Hawkes. Spectra of Some Self-Exciting and Mutually Exciting Point Processes. *Biometrika*, 58(1):83–90, 1971.

[20] P. Jelenković and A. Radovanović. Least-Recently-Used Caching with Dependent Requests. *Theor. Comput. Sci.*, 326(1):293–327, 2004.

[21] J. Kurose. Information-Centric Networking: The Evolution from Circuits to Packets to Content. *Comput. Netw.*, 66(0):112–120, 2014.

[22] V. Martina, M. Garetto, and E. Leonardi. A Unified Approach to the Performance Analysis of Caching Systems. In *Proc. IEEE INFOCOM*, 2014.

[23] N. Melazzi, G. Bianchi, A. Caponi, and A. Detti. A General, Tractable and Accurate Model for a Cascade of LRU Caches. *IEEE Commun. Lett.*, 18(5):877–880, 2014.

[24] I. Psaras, W. K. Chai, and G. Pavlou. Probabilistic In-Network Caching for Information-Centric Networks. In *Proc. ACM SIGCOMM Workshop on ICN*, pages 55–60, 2012.

[25] I. Psaras, R. Clegg, R. Landa, W. Chai, and G. Pavlou. Modelling and Evaluation of CCN-Caching Trees. In *IFIP Networking*, pages 78–91. Springer, 2011.

[26] J. Roberts and N. Sbihi. Exploring the Memory-Bandwidth Tradeoff in an Information-Centric Network. In *Proc. ITC*, pages 1–9, 2013.

[27] P. Rodriguez, C. Spanner, and E. Biersack. Analysis of Web Caching Architectures: Hierarchical and Distributed Caching. *IEEE/ACM Trans. Netw.*, 9(4):404–418, 2001.

[28] E. Rosensweig, J. Kurose, and D. Towsley. Approximate Models for General Cache Networks. In *Proc. IEEE INFOCOM*, pages 1–9, 2010.

[29] E. Rosensweig, D. Menasche, and J. Kurose. On the Steady-State of Cache Networks. In *Proc. IEEE INFOCOM*, pages 863–871, 2013.

[30] D. Rossi and G. Rossini. Caching Performance of Content Centric Networks Under Multi-Path Routing (and More). Technical report, Telecom ParisTech, 2011.

[31] S. Traverso, M. Ahmed, M. Garetto, P. Giaccone, E. Leonardi, and S. Niccolini. Temporal Locality in Today's Content Caching: Why It Matters and How to Model It. *ACM SIGCOMM Comput. Commun. Rev.*, 43(5):5–12, 2013.

[32] G. Tyson, S. Kaune, S. Miles, Y. El-khatib, A. Mauthe, and A. Taweel. A Trace-Driven Analysis of Caching in Content-Centric Networks. In *Proc. ICCCN*, pages 1–7, 2012.

[33] Y. Wang, Z. Li, G. Tyson, S. Uhlig, and G. Xie. Optimal Cache Allocation for Content-Centric Networking. In *Proc. IEEE ICNP*, pages 1–10, 2013.

Analyzing Cacheable Traffic in ISP Access Networks for Micro CDN Applications via Content-Centric Networking

Claudio Imbrenda
Orange Labs
38-40, rue du general Leclerc
92130 Issy Les Moulineaux,
France
claudio.imbrenda@orange.com

Luca Muscariello
Orange Labs
38-40, rue du general Leclerc
92130 Issy Les Moulineaux,
France
luca.muscariello@orange.com

Dario Rossi
Telecom ParisTech
23, Avenue d'Italie
75013 Paris 13, France
dario.rossi@enst.fr

ABSTRACT

Web content coming from outside the ISP is today skyrocketing, causing significant additional infrastructure costs to network operators. The reduced marginal revenues left to ISPs, whose business is almost entirely based on declining flat rate subscriptions, call for significant innovation within the network infrastructure, to support new service delivery.

In this paper, we suggest the use of micro CDNs in ISP access and back-haul networks to reduce redundant web traffic within the ISP infrastructure while improving user's QoS. With micro CDN we refer to a content delivery system composed of (i) a high speed caching substrate, (ii) a content based routing protocol and (iii) a set of data transfer mechanisms made available by content-centric networking.

The contribution of this paper is twofold. First, we extensively analyze more than one month of web traffic via continuous monitoring between the access and back-haul network of Orange in France. Second, we characterize key properties of monitored traffic, such as content popularity and request cacheability, to infer potential traffic reduction enabled by the introduction of micro CDNs. Based on these findings, we then perform micro CDN dimensioning in terms of memory requirements and provide guidelines on design choices.

Categories and Subject Descriptors

C.2.1 [**Computer-Communication Networks**]: Network Architecture and Design—*Network communications*

Keywords

Information-Centric Networking; Network Traffic Measurements; Web caching; Content-Delivery Networks; Telco CDN

General Terms

Performance; Measurement

1. INTRODUCTION

In recent years, we have assisted to significant deployments of web-based content delivery solutions within ISP networks, with the aim to deliver a range of services directly managed by the ISP itself. Some examples are video on demand (VoD) and subscriber VoD (SVoD). Broadcast TV, traditionally delivered across IP multicast channels, has also been made available through web-based portals supported by various kinds of CDN technologies. The spread of web-based content delivery solutions has multiple root causes, e.g. enhanced flexibility and ease of access from a vast set of user terminals, mostly mobile.

In particular, today SVoD consumers expect to the able to access video from any device inside and outside the home (TV, HDTV, smart-phones, tablets, media players), and also ask for high levels of QoS. Traditional IP multicast fails to satisfy such a large set of requirements, leading ISPs to build their own video services on top of CDN systems. Further, CDNs usage has been fostered by the skyrocketing growth of Internet traffic volumes, mainly driven by video services. In fact, traffic volumes are no more carrying preeminently P2P file sharing applications, but video-based services with significant QoS requirements and often based on a third-party (e.g. Netflix) monthly subscription.

Today model, relying on third-parties to provide web services, whose quality depends on someone else network infrastructure (one or multiple ISPs), present various business weaknesses. Indeed, applications like file sharing or VoIP (e.g. Skype) respectively generate elastic flows with soft QoS constraints or negligible traffic, not creating additional network costs.

For video-centric services, the relation between investments and revenues tends to be unbalanced when third-party content providers do not recognize any additional revenue to the ISPs which, instead, shoulder investment and operational costs to deliver additional traffic shares at no incremental revenue. The end customer is not eager to pay more to solve the dispute among the two parties if this requires to loose Internet access flat rate. The dispute involving Netflix and Comcast, Verizon and AT&T in the USA is one good example displaying the difficulties and frictions in this market [26]. In terms of network resource utilization, IP multicast, nowadays considered as obsolete, offers a valuable advantage over web based systems for TV broadcasting. In fact, IP multicast operates within the network while web based systems are today installed in the PoP (point of presence) and assume to reach the end user via a fully transparent high capacity network that ISPs have low business incentive to guarantee.

In this paper, we propose a novel approach for ISP content delivery, referred to as *micro CDN* (μCDN), combining the service flexibility of web based CDNs with efficient redundant traffic reduction of IP multicast. A μCDN makes use of small storage that can work at high speed as can take advantage of fast memories. A few technologies suitable to achieve this goal already exist, i.e. JetStream [24], AltoBridge [5] and also Open Connect [27]. However, they suffer from the following limitations: (i) they provide no standardized architecture, (ii) do not interoperate and (iii) do not support all kinds of web content.

We believe that a promising candidate to satisfy the aforementioned goals is the content-centric networking (CCN) architecture (a.k.a. NDN) [21]. Indeed, by embedding a service agnostic content caching into the network architecture, CCN may provide a common underlying network substrate for the deployment of next generation CDN systems.

The remainder of the paper is organized as follows. Sec.2 surveys related work. In Sec.3, we introduce the network setup, the dataset and the monitoring tool, HACkSAw, developed to analyze web data traffic. In Sec.4, we provide an extensive analysis of the dataset and a thorough statistical characterization of the key performance indicators required to guide μCDN system design. In Sec.5, we gather a number of trace driven simulations of different caching systems, while Sec.6 presents the general network design, including feasibility considerations tailored to CCN. Finally, Sec.7 concludes the paper.

2. RELATED WORK

In the last few years, a significant body of work has tried to measure the relation between the amount of resources and efforts (pain) to achieve the gains promised by CCN[18, 14]. Most of these works are based on network simulations in some very specific scenarios, none of them taking into account the ISP infrastructure, but focusing on content placement and caching performance no deeper than the PoP.

Other recent works, based on network experimentation, have shown [8] the significant gains of CCN in some relatively downsized network settings. The drawbacks of computer simulation and network experimentation are that, while being valuable, they do not allow to generalize the results for realistic workloads, difficult to model and to synthesize in general scenarios. Analytical models of such systems [7, 9] allow to quickly evaluate the relation between QoS, network capacity and users' demand; however, current models either fail to provide reliable performance predictions or must be tuned, a posteriori, using a data sample [28],[34].

A common assumption to the evaluation of caching systems performance is to assume that content requests are generated under the IRM (Independent Reference Model), with a request distribution following a Zipf law. Considerable measurement efforts have been devoted to provide input to this workload in static settings, while very few consider the catalog dynamics over time. Characterization of video catalogs has especially attracted significant attention, from YouTube crawling [19], to measurement at a campus [38] or ISP [28, 34], just to cite a few. Focusing on YouTube traffic, [28], [34] show that IRM assumption may yield to a significant underestimation of the achievable caching gains. However, the main focus of [34] is to propose a fine grained characterization of the data, rather than assessing the impact on the expected CCN gain (even a lower bound), as we do in this work.

In this paper, we propose a different approach based on network measurements: we install a live web probe on some links between the access and back-haul network serving fiber customers in the Orange network in France. Then, we evaluate the amount of redundant traffic flowing through the back-haul and the required memory to install within customer premise equipments (CPEs) and edge router line cards.

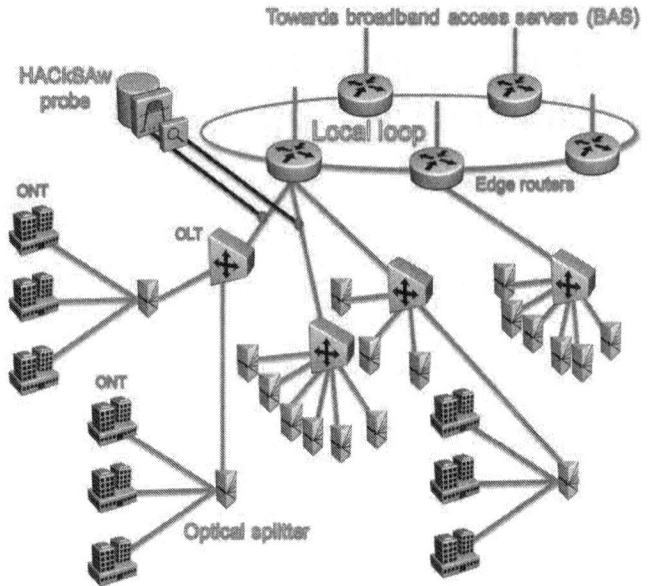

Figure 1: ISP network fiber access and back-haul.

Other work have measured cache performance for video applications [1], [2] but none of the previous work have considered also web content size which has, however, a significant impact on the amount of required storage to install in the network. Web content size is often neglected in previous work as which are based on the analysis on HTTP requests only, neglecting all HTTP replies. The most notable exceptions are [32] and [36] which use a measurement methodology similar to ours and analyze either HTTP request and replies.

3. WEB TRAFFIC MONITORING

This section introduces our traffic monitoring infrastructure, deployed within Orange France ISP network, the dataset under study and HACkSAw, our monitoring tool.

Our methodology is based on deep packet inspection (DPI) of the HTTP protocol and does not apply to HTTPs, where all bytes transferred across a TCP connection are encrypted. In our data set we observed 15% of all traffic on HTTPs and this statistic is expected to grow in the future as HTTP 2.0 specifies encryption by default. Considering the highly predominant usage of HTTP over HTTPs in our dataset the results presented in this paper are valuable to draw significant conclusion about cache performance at the network edge.

3.1 The monitoring infrastructure

Along the path between a PoP and the end customer, the monitoring probe can be placed at different network segments, ranging from the PoP or the broadband access server (BAS), where one observes the largest user fan-out, to the access network, where traffic is captured at a finer granularity. Our initial choice has been to perform monitoring of web traffic over the network segment between access and back-haul for fiber to the home users served by a GPON (Gigabit Passive Optical Network).

The promising findings over such dataset captured between the access and the back-haul have convinced us to permanently install the probe therein. As shown in Fig.1, each GPON consists of an OLT (optical line terminal), installed within a CO (central office) and accommodating, for instance, 16 line cards in a high density non blocking chassis. Line cards usually have a line rate of 1Gbps to 10Gbps and each one typically serves up to 64 users connected to a single optical line by a X64 optical splitter terminated by an ONT (optical network terminal) in the home. Each OLT has a back-haul link towards the local loop consisting of a given number of IP edge routers. Our probe (described in Sec.3.3) is installed at two such back-haul links in Paris, arriving at the same edge router as depicted in Fig.1.

3.2 The dataset

The probe captures every packet flowing on the wire and makes L3, L4 and L7 processing to collect a wide set of statistics at the different layers. In the paper we focus on L7, namely HTTP traffic, to obtain the relevant part of the paper's dataset: all HTTP requests and corresponding replies.

	Total	Daily Average
Distinct users	1478	1218
HTTP requests	369 238 000	8 586 000
HTTP data volume	37TB	881GB
Distinct objects	174 283 000	4 956 000

Table 1: Dataset summary: April 18 to May 30 2014.

Each detected HTTP request/reply transaction is recorded with a number of fields and associated statistics; namely time-stamp, user ID, object ID, Content-Length[15], and actual transaction length over the wire. We collect 42 days of data, from midnight April 18 to midnight May 30, 2014. Tab.1 reports a summary of such dataset. Details about the methodology used to process captured traffic and to obtain relevant statistics are provided hereafter.

Ref	Duration	Clients	Requests	Distinct objects	HTTP traffic
our dataset	42 days	1500	369M	174M	37TB
[2]	14 days	20k	–	–	40TB
[33]	14 days	20k	–	–	42TB
[16]	1 day	200k	48M	7M	0.7TB
[36]	8 days	1.8M	7.7G	–	256TB
[32]	1 day		42M	–	12TB
[14]	1 day	–	6M	–	–

Table 2: Overview of the dataset in this and related work.

Dataset of work inherent to caching or workload characterization, can either be request logs from servers, [37, 4, 14], gathered via active crawling techniques of popular portals [19, 11] or via passive measurement methodology [32, 36] as we do in this work. A comparison of some basic information about the dataset considered in this and related work is given in Tab.3.2, where it can be seen that our dataset has a significant span in terms of time, requests and distinct objects seen.

3.3 HACkSAw: the monitoring tool

We describe here HACkSAw, the continuous monitoring tool we have developed to collect our dataset and to process it in order to derive the statistics presented in next sections.

We recall that the measurement probe is installed at back-haul links with line cards ranging from 1Gbps to 10Gbps. Packets on the wire must be, then, captured and timestamped accurately at any of such mentioned line rates to prevent malfunctioning of the processing of the different protocol layers: IP, TCP/UDP, HTTP. The probe also requires to be installed in a network location guaranteeing symmetric routing, to carefully capture both directions of a

Tool	Detected Requests	CPU [sec]	Memory [GB]	0-length replies
Tstat2.4	2 531 210	445	0.3	1 128 109
Tstat2.3	1 348 642	345	0.4	N.A.
bro	2 559 056	8033	4.2	424 355
HACkSAw	2 426 391	368	5.8	328 465

Table 3: Performance of bro, Tstat and HACkSAw.

TCP connection and requests and replies of an HTTP transaction (possibly pipelined in a single TCP connection, i.e. HTTP/1.1).

Recent work on web caching within the radio mobile backhaul in New York metropolitan area [32] and in South Korea [36] have used proprietary tools satisfying the mentioned requirements. Unfortunately, none of these tools is publicly available.

Conversely, popular open source tools like *bro* [29] and *Tstat* [25] do not satisfy all necessary requirements. Indeed, *bro*, conceived as an intrusion detection system, is not suitable for high speed monitoring because it applies regular expressions on each packet to detect signatures of known threats, and therefore results to be very slow. *Tstat*, instead, is faster and accurate in analyzing TCP connections, but inaccurate in analyzing HTTP transactions. Consequently, both tools turn out to be not satisfactory for our needs.

For this reason, the analysis presented in this paper is based on a novel tool, called HACkSAw and that we developed to accurately and continuously monitor web traffic in a modern operational ISP network, at any line rate, for any workload.

A comparison of the performance of the different tools is reported in Tab.3, using the same one hour trace as benchmark. We experiment with two version of Tstat, since its last version (released May 6th, 2014) addresses some (though not all) shortcomings related to HTTP traffic analysis. *bro* detects about twice as much HTTP requests with respect to *Tstat* (v2.3), using 10 times more memory and running over 20 times slower, whereas HACkSAw manages to be almost as accurate as *bro*, and almost as fast as *Tstat*. *Tstat* (v2.4) catches most of the transactions, though it still fails to match the requests with the reply, and is hence unusable to reports the size of the object (at least when the Content-Length header is not within the first IP packet of the reply, which happens more than 30% of the cases in our benchmark). As such, if *Tstat* (v2.4) addresses shortcomings in terms of HTTP transactions recall, it still fails to provide a reliable measure of object size.

HACkSAw implements L3 packet collection (and reordering, when needed) and L4 flow matching and reconstruction, so that a TCP connection is properly tracked and analyzed. Scalability is achieved via efficient non-blocking multithreaded design, available in none of previous tools, enabling deployment of the probe in any access or back-haul link. At flow termination (after a TCP half close or an inactivity timeout), the payload stream is handed to one of the several consumer threads that are in charge of HTTP transactions analysis.

Accuracy is, thus, achieved via full payload analysis and full stream reconstructions (so that memory usage is close to that of *bro*). In the network setup previously described, HACkSAw runs on an IBM server with 2 quad-core Intel Xeon CPU E5-2643 at 3.30GHz with 48GB of RAM each, for a total of 96GB of RAM memory. The server is equipped with a Endace DAG7.5G4 card, allowing to capture packets from 4 Gigabit links simultaneously, allowing us to monitor 2 full-duplex Gigabit links. HACkSAw logs several information for each HTTP transaction namely:

- **request timestamp**, accurately given by the Endace DAG card;

- **user identifier**, computed as the obfuscated MAC address of their home router;

- **object identifier**, calculated as a hash of the full URL concatenated with the ETAG[15], when present;

- **reported object size**, from the HTTP Content-Length header, when present or computed from the chunk sub-headers in case of chunked transfer-encoding;

- **actual object size**, computed as the actual amount of unique (i.e., excluding TCP retransmissions) bytes on the wire, that may be lower than the reported object size in case of aborted transfer.

4. WEB TRAFFIC CHARACTERIZATION

Traffic characterization is an essential prerequisite of traffic engineering: network dimensioning and upgrading lie upon the knowledge of the relation between three entities: traffic demand, network capacity and quality of service. What makes traffic characterization a difficult task is the stochastic nature of Internet traffic, complex to synthesize via simple models.

In literature, a wide range of models exist, varying model abstraction and related complexity according to a more microscopic or macroscopic analysis of network dynamics. In this paper, we avoid a detailed representation of a network of caches, which turns out to be analytically intractable even for a simple tandem cache and simple workloads [17]. We rather prefer a simple characterization of web traffic, based on key system properties and applicable to general in-network caching systems. Such model abstraction, assuming an independent reference model (IRM), might be leveraged for the dimensioning of a micro CDN. The key factors impacting the performance of an in-network caching system and that our model takes into account are:

- the timescale at which content popularity may be approximated by an independent reference model (IRM) (Sec.4.1);

- the content popularity at the given timescale (Sec.4.2).

From their characterization, we later infer in Sec.5.1 the minimum useful amount of memory to embed in the home network and in edge routers in the Micro CDN architecture.

4.1 Timescale analysis

First, we define some statistics that will be used throughout the section: catalog, cacheability, traffic reduction. The *catalog* is the set of distinct objects requested in a given time interval. As introduced in [2], the *cacheability* is a statistic indicating the fraction of requests for objects requested more than once in a given time interval. The first request of an object is not considered cacheable, whereas all its subsequent requests in the same time interval are. The resulting definition of cacheability is

$$\frac{N_r - N_o}{N_r} = 1 - \frac{N_o}{N_r} \qquad (1)$$

where N_r is the number of requests observed in the given time interval, and N_o is the number of unique distinct objects observed (the cardinality of the catalog).

We also define the *traffic reduction*, a statistic measuring the maximum amount of traffic that can be potentially saved across a link over a given time interval as a consequence of content cacheability. Traffic reduction is defined as

$$\frac{R - R_u}{R} = 1 - \frac{R_u}{R} \qquad (2)$$

where R is the total traffic, and R_u is the uncacheable traffic, both measured in bytes. Before presenting observations from the network probe, we use a simple explanatory model to show that measuring content popularity at a timescale (as an example, over a large time window), where the IRM assumption does not hold, may lead to wrong predictions in terms of memory requirements.

We divide the time axis in windows of size $T > 0$, $W_i = [iT, iT + T)$, and assume that, in each time window W_i, objects in content catalog A_i are requested following a Poisson process of rate λ, with $A_i \cap A_j = \emptyset$ for all $i, j : i \neq j$. The average object size is σ bytes. A_i is Zipf distributed with parameters α, N, i.e. a content item of rank k is requested with probability $q_k = ck^{-\alpha}$, $k \in \{1, \ldots, N\}$, $|A_i| = N$.

By using the modeling framework developed in [7] for an LRU cache of size x in bytes, we know that if $T >> x^{\alpha}g$, with $1/g = \lambda c\sigma^{\alpha}\Gamma(1 - 1/\alpha)^{\alpha}$ the cache miss probability for an object of rank k tends to $\exp\{-\lambda q_k gx^{\alpha}\}$.

However, if one estimates the content popularity as the time average across m contiguous time windows, the estimated miss probability would be $\exp\{-\lambda q_k g(x/m)^{\alpha}\}$. Indeed, the right cache performance measured across m contiguous time windows of size T is still $\exp\{-\lambda q_k gx^{\alpha}\}$ resulting in an overestimation factor m of the required memory, for the same miss ratio.

In this section we estimate the timescale over which the IRM model can be used to estimate cache performance without using complex measurement-based models, e.g. [28],[34].

OBSERVATION 4.1. *In order to exploit a IRM cache network model for system dimensioning, one needs to estimate the smallest timescale, referred to as "cutoff" timescale at which the IRM assumption holds. As a consequence, above the cutoff timescale, every new content request gives a negligible contribution to catalog inference.*

In Fig.2(a),(b) we plot cacheability and traffic reduction as computed over our dataset at different time windows: from one hour to an entire contiguous week at incremental steps of one hour. The statistics are also computed starting at different time instants, delayed by one hour each. We observe that the two statistics have a cutoff scale above which they reach a plateau. In Fig.2(c), we report the time required for the cacheability to attain percentiles (namely, the 75%, 90%, 95% and 99%) of the long term value: it can be seen that 90% of the traffic reduction are attained in less than 24 hours, irrespectively of the start time.

OBSERVATION 4.2. *The cutoff scale is hard to be measured as it changes on a daily basis as a function of many factors that cannot be rigorously quantified. However, we observe that for practical purposes aggregate web traffic would benefit for caching no more than a daily content catalog.*

In Fig.2(a),(b) we also observe that the cacheability stabilizes at about 47% while traffic reduction amounts to almost 37%. These values provide a first rough estimation of the opportunities to cache data currently available within the ISP network at relatively low user fan-out. While statistics just presented provide insights on the potential gains achievable by caching a daily content catalog, we now investigate temporal evolution of the catalog.

To this aim, we introduce a measure of auto similarity based on the *Jaccard coefficient*, that indicates the proportion of objects in

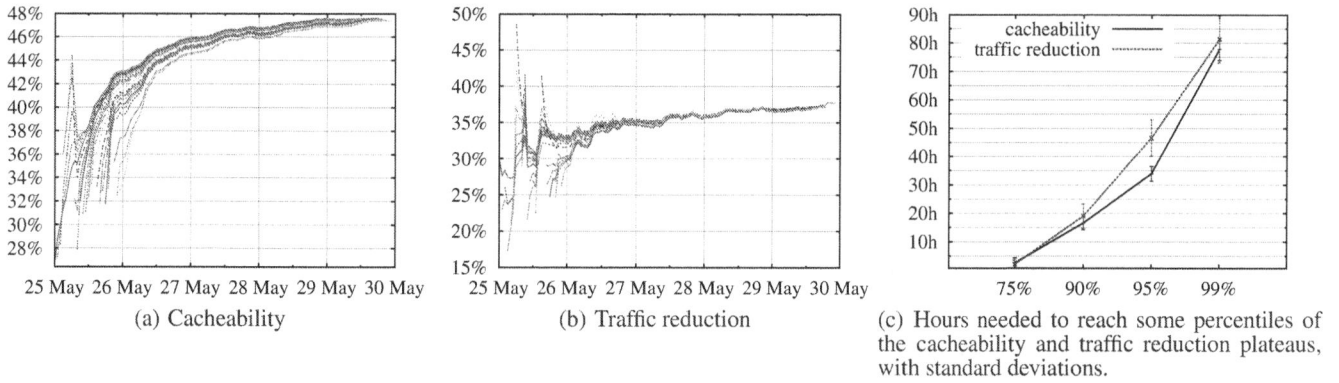

(a) Cacheability

(b) Traffic reduction

(c) Hours needed to reach some percentiles of the cacheability and traffic reduction plateaus, with standard deviations.

Figure 2: Cumulative cacheability and traffic reduction, starting from different hours and for various timespans.

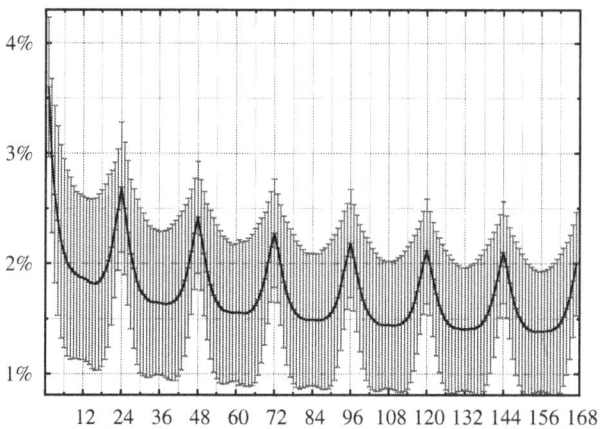

Figure 3: Jaccard auto correlation function $\mathcal{R}_{\Delta T}(k)$.

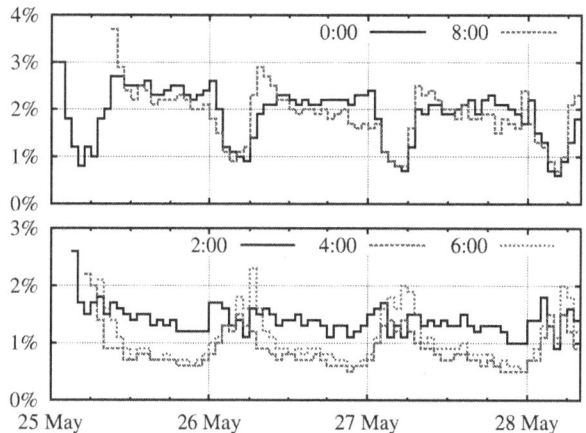

Figure 4: Jaccard coefficient, $J(C_{k_0 \Delta T}, C_{(k_0+k)\Delta T})$, $k_0 = 0, 2, 4, 6, 8.$

common between two given sets: $J(A, B) = \frac{|A \cap B|}{|A \cup B|}$ (If $A = B = \emptyset$ then $J(A, B) \triangleq 1$. Clearly, $0 \leq J(A, B) \leq 1$. We then define the Jaccard auto correlation function as

$$\mathcal{R}_{\Delta T}(k) = \frac{1}{n} \sum_{i,j:|i-j|=k}^{n} J(C_{i\Delta T}, C_{j\Delta T}) \qquad (3)$$

being $C_{i\Delta T}$ the content catalog measured over the time window $i\Delta T$. Fig.3 shows $\mathcal{R}_{\Delta T}(k)$ for $k = \{0, \ldots, 168\}$, $\Delta T = 1$hour, during one working week in May 2014 (showing standard deviation as error bars). An interesting conclusion can be drawn.

OBSERVATION 4.3. *The catalog is weakly auto-correlated, as $\mathcal{R}_{\Delta T}(k)$ falls from 100% to less than 5% and it completely regenerates asymptotically, as $\mathcal{R}_{\Delta T}(k) \to 0$ when $k \to \infty$. A periodic component with period of about 24 hours is also present as a result of users' daily routine.*

Finally, we show that catalog show a night/day effect in Fig.4, that reports $J(C_{k_0 \Delta T}, C_{(k_0+k)\Delta T})$, with $\Delta T = 1$hour and $k_0 < k \leq 72$, for multiple $k_0 = \{0, 2, 4, 6, 8\}$. The figure shows that the catalog has different properties during off peak hours ($k_0 = \{0, 2, 4\}$) than peak hours ($k_0 = \{6, 8\}$). Off-peak hours are characterized by content items that unlikely appears again in the future, while on-peak content items show periodic components of 24 hours.

4.2 Content popularity estimation

Hereafter, we present a model of content popularity estimated over 24 hours. According to the observations reported above, the timescale of interest turns out to be approximately defined by removing the night period, i.e. the off peak phase. This may be a complex task as the off peak phase changes on a daily basis. Nevertheless, we observe that the off peak phase has statistically weak impact on the overall distribution as it carries samples in the tail of the popularity distribution at low rate, so that 24 hours can be used as timescale. We test the empirical popularity against various models and find the discrete Weibull to be the best fit with shape around 0.24 (long tailed). In Fig.5, we report the empirical popularity distribution with corresponding 95% confidence bands (see [20] for similar analysis). We also plot, in red, the model fit to the available sample with 95% confidence bands. By means of extensive tests on this model we assess accuracy over all 24 hours samples on our data set. It follows that:

- for the *tail* of the distribution, a simple discrete Weibull passes a χ^2 goodness of fit test [12], with p-values exceeding 5% significance level, while

- the good model for the *entire distribution* turns out to be trimodal with three components: a discrete Weibull for the *head* of the distribution, a Zipf for the *waist* and, a Weibull

61

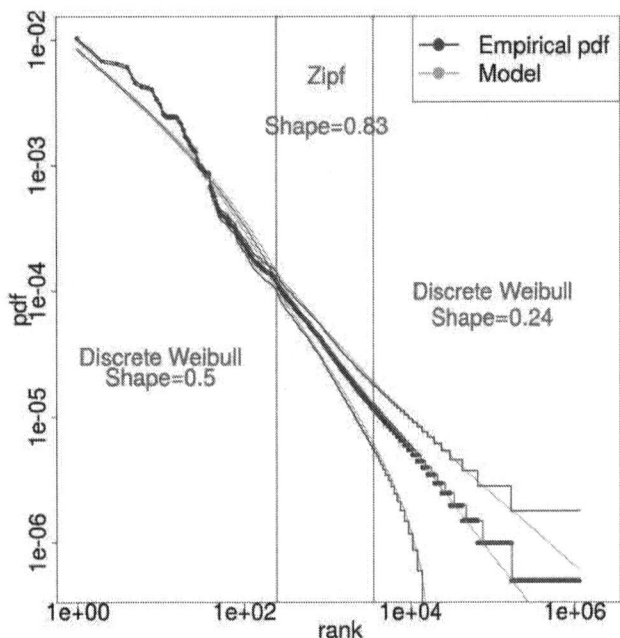

Figure 5: Empirical web content popularity and model fitting with corresponding confidence bands.

again for the *tail*, i.e. $f(k) =$

$$\begin{cases} \phi_1 \dfrac{\beta_1}{\lambda_1} \left(\dfrac{k}{\lambda_1} \right)^{\beta_1-1} e^{-(k/\lambda_1)^{\beta_1}} & k < k_1 \\[2ex] \dfrac{\phi_2}{k^{\alpha_2}} & k \in [k_1, k_2] \\[2ex] \phi_3 \dfrac{\beta_3}{\lambda_3} \left(\dfrac{k}{\lambda_3} \right)^{\beta_3-1} e^{-(k/\lambda_3)^{\beta_3}} & k > k_2 \end{cases}$$

with parameters $\lambda_1, \beta_1, \alpha_2, \lambda_3, \beta_3, \phi_1, \phi_2, \phi_3 \in \mathbb{R}^+; k_1, k_2 \in \mathbb{N}$. The parameters have been estimated by using standard maximum likelihood (ML) applied to the piecewise function $f(k)$. The set of parameters of each piece of $f(k)$ is estimated independently to the others in order to fix the shapes exponents $\beta_1, \alpha_2, \beta_3$ and the scale factors λ_1, λ_3. An ML estimator is not available for the entire distribution and we therefore use the method of moments to determine ϕ_1, ϕ_2, ϕ_3. The procedure can be iterated to obtain a better estimation by running ML first and MM afterwards. In our samples, after few iterations (e.g. four) the parameters stabilize to stationary values that we have reported for one day in Fig.5 where $\beta_1 = 0.5, \alpha_2 = 0.83, \beta_3 = 0.24$.

Interesting conclusions can be drawn from our popularity characterization. In literature, the majority of analytical models assume a Zipf distribution with shape $\alpha < 1$ for the entire distribution. Remark that, if the same Zipf law characterizing the waist is prolonged all over the support of the distribution, a finite support, corresponding to a content catalog estimation, must be imposed. Indeed, the miss probability of a cache (LRU or LFU) under Zipf requests with $\alpha < 1$ is a function of the ratio between the cache and catalog sizes, e.g. for LFU it is $1 - (x/N)^{1-\alpha}$ ([22]).

Cache performance would then depend on the ratio between cache and content catalog size, while it is a function of cache size only

under the more precise Weibull tail fit that we made. More, the cardinality of the catalog, N, is estimated with unbounded confidence intervals (see Fig.5), whereas all Weibull's parameters can be estimated with arbitrary low error, by increasing the size of the sample. As a consequence, an overestimation of the catalog size by a given factor under the all-Zipf model would lead to memory over-sizing of the same factor for a given target miss ratio.

Conversely, the miss ratio under Weibull requests ([23]), e.g. of an LRU cache, can be estimated with arbitrary precision by increasing the size of the sample to estimate the popularity law. Hence, we derive that

OBSERVATION 4.4. *Accurate content popularity characterization is fundamental to drive a correct cache system dimensioning. Approximate models based on (i) all-Zipf assumption, (ii) possibly fit over long time scales, coupled to (iii) IRM model assumptions, may lead to excessively conservative results, and ultimately to misguided system design choices.*

5. TRACE DRIVEN SIMULATIONS

In the following, we present some realistic simulations driven by our dataset. The goal is to evaluate the amount of memory required within the back-haul to absorb cacheable traffic and to assess the accuracy of the model introduced in previous section for the dimensioning of a micro CDN system.

5.1 Single LRU cache at edge router

The first set of simulations is based on an LRU cache installed at the probe and driven by real users' requests. We simulate a LRU cache with different sizes and measure (i) the average hit ratio, (ii) the potential traffic savings over two timescales (1 hour and 1 day). The LRU cache simulates a transparent cache: a web object is stored in chunks, so that in case of a cache miss, only the missing chunk is requested. A following request for a bigger part of an object partially present in cache generates another miss, but only for the missing part of the object.

We consider sizes of 1GB, 10GB, 100GB and 1TB, and never explicitly flush cache content. Performance metrics are reported in Fig.6(a),(d) and compared with two additional systems obtained by shuffling all the requests on a hourly and daily basis, reported in Fig.6(b),(e) and Fig.6(c),(f) respectively. Request shuffling is useful to remove time correlation, which has huge impact on cache performance as already discussed in Sec.4 (i.e., shuffling produces a workload closer to that of IRM model).

From the simulations we see that if the cache is big enough (1TB), time correlations has not impact on performance. For medium or small caches instead, time correlation affects significantly performance as hit ratios and saved traffic, twice as much in presence of temporal locality of requests.

We now assess memory requirements, showing statistics that are gathered in an online fashion by our probe. We introduce an additional metric, the *virtual cache size*, defined as the sum of the total observed sizes of the cacheable objects. Such additional metric, not accounted for by models, allows to quantify the effect of incomplete downloads (e.g. as an effect of user impatience). Since many objects, especially the largest ones, are not always entirely requested, we define the size of an object as the largest size observed on-wire for the given object.

Fig.7 plots cacheability (top row), traffic reduction (middle row) and virtual cache size (bottom row), over more than one month in 2014, over hourly and daily timescales. Different system configurations are arranged by columns: namely, we either assume that a single cache is installed within at the OLT level (left column),

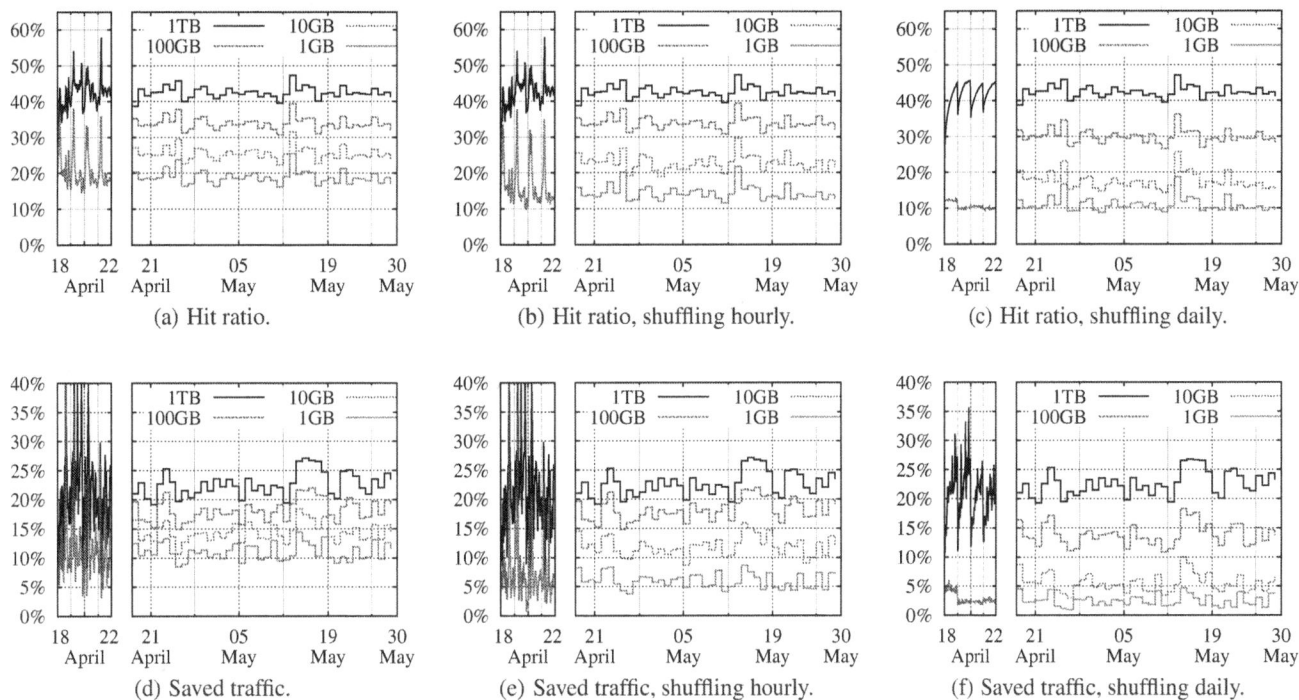

(a) Hit ratio.   (b) Hit ratio, shuffling hourly.   (c) Hit ratio, shuffling daily.

(d) Saved traffic.   (e) Saved traffic, shuffling hourly.   (f) Saved traffic, shuffling daily.

Figure 6: LRU cache simulations: behavior with one hour averages (left side) and the general view of the whole dataset with daily averages (right side).

or that caches are deployed only within ONT in the home of each user (middle column), or that caches are deployed at both ONT and OLT levels (right column). The OLT-caching scenario in the left column of Fig.7(a),(d),(g) is striking: with a little more than 100GB of memory, 35% of average traffic can be saved for a user fan-out equal to 2048. In the ONT-caching scenario, only duplicated requests coming from the same users are filtered by the cache: in this case, an average memory size of about 100MB (per user, totalizing 200GB given the user fan-out) reduces user traffic by 25%, corresponding to a same level of load reduction in the GPON access. Finally, the last column of figures, Fig.7(c),(f),(i), shows that employing caches at both OLT and ONT level, the ISP network would benefit from 25% load reduction in the GPON and 35% on back-haul links, while improving the latency for all users.

6. μCDN DESIGN CHOICES

The above results confirms the potential caching benefits arising from the deployment of limited additional memories. In this section, we comment on implications of the above findings in terms of the architectural design that is best suited to actually leverage this caching potential.

6.1 CCN as uniform CDN substrate

Transparent caching is today a very useful technique to reduce redundant traffic while, at the same time, providing higher levels of QoS to the users. All the different existing solutions cited [3, 30, 5, 27], are based on a common set of principles. They leverage DPI (Deep Packet Inspection) to identify and reconstruct content on-line. Once the content is identified, it is split into identifiable data chunks, corresponding to proper networking datagrams, that are cached and routed across the cache infrastructure. Most of these technologies are proprietary and their design and implemen-

tation details may only be obtained partially through non disclosure agreements. The challenge of integrating and inter-operate various CDN technologies into one inter-operable infrastructure has led to the creation of the standardization working CDNi at IETF [35]). However, such standardization activity struggles with attracting the main CDN players, so raising concerns about the success of the integration process. By embedding a service agnostic content caching into the network architecture, Information Centric approaches appear to be more promising candidates to provide a common underlying network substrate for the deployment of next generation CDN systems.

6.2 CCN communication model

Going one step further in terms of architectural details, the key characteristics of the communication model of today CDNs are put in perspective with evolutionary aspects of CCN in [10]. The main CDN components are (i) DNS and content based routing, (ii) HTTP and chunk-based data transfer (iii) in-network caching. Note that a commercial CDN also includes a large set of analytics to log service quality and monitor the CDN performance.

If we replace the data plane of a CDN system with CCN, the main innovation introduced is to overcome the current misuse of HTTP as a content-centric transport protocol and to integrate a chunk-based connectionless receiver driven transport coping with in-network caching.

Let us describe CCN communication model more in detail ([21]). The founding principle of CCN is to enrich network layer primitives with content awareness so that routing, forwarding, caching and data transfer functions are performed on content names rather than on location identifiers (IP addresses). Content items are divided into a sequence of chunks uniquely identified by a name and a permanent copy is stored in one or more repositories. The nam-

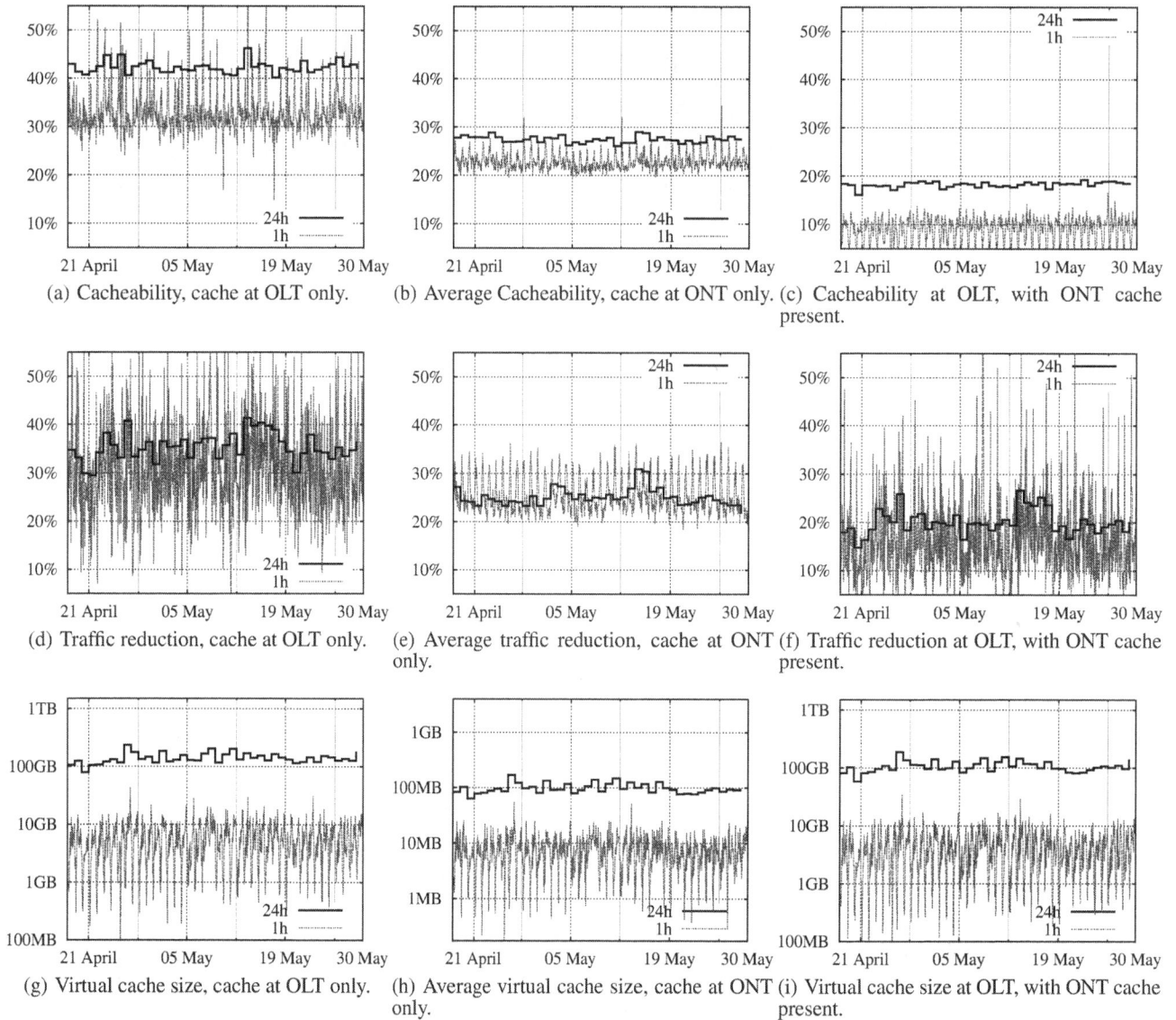

Figure 7: Time evolution of hourly and daily statistics; by rows cacheability, traffic reduction and virtual cache size are reported respectively in the three cases: (i) cache at OLT only, (ii) cache at ONT only and (iii) cache at OLT and ONT.

ing convention is not specified, only a hierarchical structure like the one already adopted by HTTP is required for entries aggregation in name-based routing tables.

Naming data chunks allows the network to directly interpret and treat content according to its semantic with no need for DPI (Deep Packet Inspection) as for transparent caching. The content delivery process is then driven by three basic communication mechanisms:

- Name based request routing. CCN forwarding engine is based on a name-based routing table storing one or more potential next hops towards a set of content items and on a Pending Interest Table (PIT) keeping track of ongoing requests in order to route data packets back to the user along the reverse request path (breadcrumb routing).

- Receiver-based connectionless transport. Differently from current sender-based transport model, CCN data transfer is triggered and controlled by user requests (Interests) in a pull-based fashion. Rate and congestion control is performed at the end user by means of a connectionless, yet stateful transport protocol with the follow-

ing characteristics: (i) no connection instantiation for the support for user/content mobility; (ii) support for retrieval from multiple sources, a priori unknown at the user (e.g. intermediate caches); (iii) support for multipath communication (to improve user performance and traffic load balancing).

-In-network caching. The content-awareness provided by names to network nodes enables a different use of routers' buffers, not only to absorb input/output rate unbalance but also for temporary in-network caching and processing (i.e. data transcoding) of in-transit Data packets. Even without additional storage capabilities in routers, the information access by name of CCN allows new uses of in-network wire speed storage. Indeed, network nodes temporarily store content items/chunks in order to serve future requests for the same content (reuse) and to recover from potential packet losses (repair). Upon reception of a chunk request, a CCN node first checks if the requested chunk is present in the local cache. If it is the case, the content is returned back to the user. Otherwise, the request is forwarded to the next hop by the ICN request routing.

CCN data plane can be easily implemented in hardware in CPEs (ONT or home gateways) and router line cards. The necessary processing of content requests and replies (that many proprietary products already do for transparent caching applications) results feasible at high speed and simplified w.r.t. transparent caching solution (as it does not involve complex DPI operations). For the adoption of CCN communication model, we believe that a required step may be the standardization of the main building blocks: packet formats, processing and API specifications.

6.3 Transparent web caching and encryption

As mentioned in Sec.3, the usage of encryption instead of plain text in the Internet is growing and is also considered a desirable feature to deploy increasingly as much as possible. HTTP 2.0 draft [6] currently under discussion in the HTTPbis IETF working group specifies encryption by default by using TLS 1.2 [13]. TLS provides communications security for client/server applications and encrypts everything included in the TCP byte stream. The encryption service provided by TLS is not compatible with proxy or transparent caching which is however a very important service successfully deployed to reduce bandwidth consumption in many network locations. Caching non encrypted web traffic in proxies or transparent appliances is today implemented and optimized by using HTTP almost as a transport layer. An HTTP datagram has also been proposed in [31] to effectively implement almost all the functionalities CCN provides, with the exception of data encryption and security in general. It is clear that encrypted web traffic, using TLS, can be cached only in the end points, i.e. the client web browser, or application, and in content provider appliances. Of course this latter end point can be distributed in a CDN which manages the encryption on behalf of the content provider. Therefore caching encrypted web traffic cannot be implemented as a transparent network primitive because it would always require the sender to delegate encryption to a third-party, e.g. a CDN. A minimum level of cooperation is required to guarantee inter-networking of communications primitives which are based on delegation. Datagram based packet-switched networks make use of delegation for data forwarding and routing but other services like name resolution, as provided by the DNS, do require delegation as well. We believe that in-network data caching is an additional transparent network primitive that cannot be implemented without guaranteeing the required level of security and interoperability that TLS cannot provide.

TLS tunnels can be bypassed in principle, at a certain extent, but not in a fully transparent way to the end users. A web proxy between the content provider and the user can terminate a TLS tunnel by issuing on the fly a fake certificate to the user and create a new TLS tunnel between the proxy and the user. In this way all traffic would not be encrypted anymore at the proxy. Caching would then be possible again. Such system is however a workaround and does not constitute a solution for many reasons: (i) the user is supposed to accept a certificate signed by a non trusted authority, (ii) the client adds the proxy as a trusted certification authority which can then issue trusted keys; (iii) the client accepts self certified certificates. This technique has the drawbacks to expose the user to higher level of vulnerability to external attackers. To the best of our knowledge, CCN is the only network architecture addressing data security by design instead of tunnel security, which is a feature that HTTP does not provide yet.

6.4 Technical feasibility

Previous sections have shown that significant benefits in terms of traffic reduction can be achieved at the cost of very limited additional memory. Indeed, a single ONT installed in a user's home

would only need to host approximately 100MB of additional memory. Such memory, currently not available in the optical device, is available in the home gateway, that are equipped with enough CPU resources to easily manage 100MB of RAM at 1Gbps. Upstream to the OLT, 100GB memory in a router line card would be enough to provide the early shown gains and it seems feasible in current hardware. Hence, the deployment of a μCDN technology in the home would only require to implement the content-centric forwarding engine in the home gateway firmware – which again seems feasible due to the current development effort on several CCN/NDN prototypes.

7. DISCUSSION AND CONCLUSION

In this paper, we provide evidence of the potential gains associated to the deployment of micro CDN technologies in ISP networks. Our analysis is grounded on a large dataset collected via the on-line monitoring of links between the access and the back-haul network of Orange France. Leveraging one month and a half of continuous traffic monitoring, we are able to support our design by an accurate characterization of content dynamics.

The large data set we have used allowed fine grained statistical analysis of content popularity dynamics, whose value goes beyond the primal objective of this paper. Indeed, the analysis demonstrates the inadequacy of traditional models, like simplistic Zipfs workloads, and their failure for prediction and dimensioning. The gains are striking: with a negligible amount of memory of 100MB on CPEs, the load in the access network (GPON) can be reduced by 25%, while embedding a 100GB of dynamic memory in edge IP router line cards can also reduce back-haul links load of about 35%.

The significant potential gains we have measured in today traffic does no apply to encrypted web application (15% in our dataset) which cannot be transparently cached. Caching TLS encrypted traffic is however going to be a significant issue for ISPs as it would require some form of interaction with the content provider, or the CDN on its behalf. Transparent caching of encrypted traffic might also be achieved by TLS tunnels interception which implies some form of increased vulnerability at the user's client. We suggest instead to use CCN as the best fit technology to address all the drawbacks of currently available workarounds and providing caching as a transparent network primitive. We additionally assess technical feasibility in nowadays hardware, and argue that such a small amount of additional memory can be supported at high speed on current technologies. We finally identify steps for micro-CDN implementation, outlining arguments to support a CCN-based deployment as basic building block. Our analysis suggests that CCN-based solutions are close enough to be deployed in real ISP networks – its realization is part of our ongoing work.

Acknowledgments

This research work has been partially funded by the Technological Research Institute SystemX, within the project "Network Architectures" hosted at LINCS and has been partially funded by the European Union under the FP7 Grant Agreement n. 318627 (Integrated Project "mPlane"). We thank Giovanna Carofiglio for the fruitful discussions and the anonymous reviewers who helped improving the manuscript.

8. REFERENCES

[1] H. Abrahamsson and M. Nordmark. Program popularity and viewer behaviour in a large tv-on-demand system. In *ACM IMC*, 2012.

[2] B. Ager, F. Schneider, J. Kim, and A. Feldmann. Revisiting cacheability in times of user generated content. In *INFOCOM IEEE Conference on Computer Communications Workshops , 2010*, pages 1–6, March 2010.

[3] Akamai Aura Lumen. Licensed suite of operator cdn solutions. http://www.akamai.com/html/solutions/aura_lumen_cdn.html.

[4] M. S. Allen, B. Y. Zhao, and R. Wolski. Deploying Video-on-Demand Services on Cable Networks. In *Proc. of the ICDCS*, Washington, DC, USA, 2007.

[5] Altobridge. Data-at-the-edge ®. http://www.altobridge.com/data-at-the-edge%E2%84%A2/architecture/.

[6] M. Belshe, R. Peon, and M. Thomson. Hypertext transfer protocol version 2, 2014.

[7] G. Carofiglio, M. Gallo, and L. Muscariello. Bandwidth and Storage Sharing Performance in Information Centric Networking. *Elsevier Science, Computer Networks Journal, Vol.57, Issue 17*, 2013.

[8] G. Carofiglio, M. Gallo, L. Muscariello, M. Papalini, and S. Wang. Optimal Multipath Congestion Control and Request Forwarding in Information-Centric Networks. In *Proc. of IEEE ICNP*, 2013.

[9] G. Carofiglio, M. Gallo, L. Muscariello, and D. Perino. Modeling Data Transfer in Content-Centric Networking. In *Proc. of ITC23*, 2011.

[10] G. Carofiglio, G. Morabito, L. Muscariello, I. Solis, and M. Varvello. From Content Delivery Today to Information-Centric Networking. *Elsevier Science, Commputer Networks Journal*, 2013.

[11] M. Cha, H. Kwak, P. Rodriguez, Y.-Y. Ahn, and S. Moon. Analyzing the Video Popularity Characteristics of Large-Scale User Generated Content Systems. *IEEE/ACM Transactions on Networking*, 2009.

[12] R. B. D'Agostino and M. A. Stephens, editors. *Goodness-of-fit Techniques*. Marcel Dekker, Inc., New York, NY, USA, 1986.

[13] T. Dierks and E. Rescorla. The Transport Layer Security (TLS) Protocol Version 1.2. RFC 5246 (Proposed Standard), Aug. 2008. Updated by RFCs 5746, 5878, 6176.

[14] S. K. Fayazbakhsh, Y. Lin, A. Tootoonchian, A. Ghodsi, T. Koponen, B. Maggs, K. Ng, V. Sekar, and S. Shenker. Less Pain, Most of the Gain: Incrementally Deployable ICN. In *Proc. of ACM SIGCOMM*, 2013.

[15] R. Fielding, J. Gettys, J. Mogul, H. Frystyk, L. Masinter, P. Leach, and T. Berners-Lee. Rfc 2616, hypertext transfer protocol – http/1.1, 1999.

[16] A. Finamore, M. Mellia, Z. Gilani, K. Papagiannaki, V. Erramilli, and Y. Grunenberger. Is There a Case for Mobile Phone Content Pre-staging? In *Proc. of ACM CoNEXT*, 2013.

[17] M. Gallo, B. Kauffmann, L. Muscariello, A. Simonian, and C. Tanguy. Performance Evaluation of the Random Replacement Policy for Networks of Caches. *Elsevier Science, Performance Evaluation Journal*, 2014.

[18] A. Ghodsi, S. Shenker, T. Koponen, A. Singla, B. Raghavan, and J. Wilcox. Information-centric Networking: Seeing the Forest for the Trees. In *Proc. of ACM HotNets-X*, 2011.

[19] P. Gill, M. Arlitt, Z. Li, and A. Mahanti. Youtube Traffic Characterization: a View From the Edge. In *Proc. of the ACM SIGCOMM IMC*, 2007.

[20] W. Gong, Y. Liu, V. Misra, and D. Towsley. On the Tails of Web File Size Distributions. In *Proc. of Allerton Conference on Communication, Control, and Computing*, 2001.

[21] V. Jacobson, D. Smetters, J. Thornton, and al. Networking Named Content. In *Proc. of ACM CoNEXT*, 2009.

[22] P. Jelenkovic, X. Kang, and A. Radovanovic. Near Optimality of the Discrete Persistent Access Caching Algorithm. In *Proc. of International Conference on Analysis of Algorithms (DMTCS)*, 2005.

[23] P. R. Jelenković. Asymptotic approximation of the move-to-front search cost distribution and least-recently-used caching fault probabilities. *The Annals of Applied Probability*, 9(2):430–464, 1999.

[24] Jet-Stream. Technology overview. http://www.jet-stream.com/technology-overview/.

[25] M. Mellia and al. http://tstat.tlc.polito.it.

[26] Netflix. The case against isp tolls, april 24, 2014. http://blog.netflix.com/2014/04/the-case-against-isp-tolls.html.

[27] Netflix. Open connect content delivery network. https://www.netflix.com/openconnect.

[28] F. Olmos, B. Kauffmann, A. Simonian, and Y. Carlinet. Catalog dynamics: Impact of content publishing and perishing on the performance of a lru cache. In *Proc. of ITC26*, 2014.

[29] V. Paxson. http://www.bro.org.

[30] PeerApp. Transparent caching in dsl operator networks. http://www.peerapp.com/Solutions/dsl.aspx.

[31] L. Popa, A. Ghodsi, and I. Stoica. HTTP as the narrow waist of the future Internet. In *ACM SIGCOMM Workshop on Hot Topics in Networks (HotNets'X)*, 2010.

[32] B. Ramanan, L. Drabeck, M. Haner, N. Nithi, T. Klein, and C. Sawkar. Cacheability analysis of HTTP traffic in an operational LTE network. In *In Proc. of WTS*, 2013.

[33] F. Schneider, B. Ager, G. Maier, A. Feldmann, and S. Uhlig. Pitfalls in HTTP Traffic Measurements and Analysis. In *Proc. of PAM*, 2012.

[34] S. Traverso, M. Ahmed, M. Garetto, P. Giaccone, E. Leonardi, and S. Niccolini. Temporal locality in today's content caching: why it matters and how to model it. *ACM SIGCOMM Computer Communication Review*, 43(5):5–12, 2013.

[35] R. van Brandenburg, O. van Deventer, F. L. Faucheur, and K. Leung. Models for HTTP-Adaptive-Streaming-Aware Content Distribution Network Interconnection (CDNI). RFC 6983 (Informational), July 2013.

[36] S. Woo, E. Jeong, S. Park, J. Lee, S. Ihm, and K. Park. Comparison of caching strategies in modern cellular backhaul networks. In *Proc. of ACM MobiSys*, 2013.

[37] H. Yu, D. Zheng, B. Y. Zhao, and W. Zheng. Understanding user behavior in large-scale video-on-demand systems. In *Proc. of the ACM SIGOPS/EuroSys*, New York, NY, USA, 2006.

[38] M. Zink, K. Suh, Y. Gu, and J. Kurose. Characteristics of YouTube network traffic at a campus network - Measurements, models, and implications. *Comput. Netw.*, 53(4):501–514, Mar. 2009.

Multi-Source Data Retrieval in IoT via Named Data Networking

Marica Amadeo
University "Mediterranea"
DIIES Department
Reggio Calabria, Italy
marica.amadeo@unirc.it

Claudia Campolo
University "Mediterranea"
DIIES Department
Reggio Calabria, Italy
claudia.campolo@unirc.it

Antonella Molinaro
University "Mediterranea"
DIIES Department
Reggio Calabria, Italy
antonella.molinaro@unirc.it

ABSTRACT

The new era of *Internet of Things* (IoT) is driving the revolution in computing and communication technologies spanning every aspect of our lives. Thanks to its innovative concepts, such as named content, name-based routing and in-network caching, *Named Data Networking* (NDN) appears as a key enabling paradigm for IoT. Despite its potential, the support of IoT applications often requires some modifications in the NDN engine for a more efficient and effective exchange of packets.

In this paper, we propose a baseline NDN framework for the support of *reliable* retrieval of data *from different wireless producers* which can answer to the *same Interest* packet (e.g., a monitoring application collecting environmental data from sensors in a target area). The solution is evaluated through simulations in ndnSIM and achieved results show that, by leveraging the concept of EXCLUDE field and ad hoc defined schemes for Data suppression and collision avoidance, it leads to improved performance in terms of data collection time and network overhead.

Categories and Subject Descriptors

C.2.1 [**Network Architecture and Design**]: Wireless communication

General Terms

Design; Performance

Keywords

Named Data Networking; Internet of Things; data retrieval; naming; transport

1. INTRODUCTION

The advent of low-cost, low-profile electronic devices along with the advancement in communication technologies is enabling more objects around us to gain intelligence and ability

to interact with one another, with the surrounding environment, with humans, and with remote systems via the Internet, hence bringing the Internet of Things (IoT) vision to life [1].

Thanks to its simple, connectionless communication model decoupling content from location, Named Data Networking (NDN) [2], one of the most noticeable information-centric networking architecture, appears as a promising solution for IoT [3]. Indeed, NDN systems give a *name* to the information instead of addressing a specific host/server, so consumers of data specify *what* they search for and not *where* they expect it to be provided. The consumer simply transmits an *Interest* packet to trigger the transmission of a *Data* packet from a potential producer; each received Data *consumes* the pending Interest in the forwarding nodes (*1-to-1* Interest and Data matching) so unsolicited and duplicated Data are avoided.

This shift from the IP-based host-centric paradigm of the traditional Internet to content-centric networking suits the IoT deployment (for example, many IoT applications request a *data item* regardless from the specific identifier of the producer; e.g., a temperature measurement in a given area), while promising simplicity and scalability in the application design, robustness and energy efficiency in massive data access [3].

A typical IoT traffic pattern that is not natively matched by the NDN paradigm is what we refer to as *multi-source data retrieval*, which is the focus of this paper. In this case, a consumer is interested in retrieving *different data items* of the same type from *different sources* at the same time. Data can be related to a particular event or collected from a given geographic area, with the consumer that is aware of or oblivious to the *number* and *identity of producers*. For instance, respectively, a monitoring system (consumer) asks for the energy consumption measurements of *all appliances* (producers) in a home; or a traffic control center is interested in retrieving accurate and reliable traffic information from vehicles in a specific road segment.

The *1-to-1* Interest-Data matching of vanilla NDN would require issuing an Interest packet to retrieve *each Data item*, and may be inefficient in terms of network and device resources. A more efficient solution would rather be the transmission of *a single Interest* to retrieve *many data items at once*. The requested changes to the NDN forwarding fabric would be small and the advantages manifold. First, *multi-source data retrieval* could leverage the expressiveness of the hierarchical Universal Resource Identifier (URI)-like NDN naming scheme to manage the multiple answers. Second, issuing a single Interest would avoid the redundancy of Interest packets circulating into the network, hence saving bandwidth.

Despite the intuitive convenience of such a solution, releasing the *1-to-1* matching between Interest and Data, conceived to ensure flow control and reduce the amount of unwanted data, would pose some issues that could be exacerbated in a wireless environment. For example, multiple nodes that store or generate Data matching the Interest (providing the same type/piece of information) risk colliding when attempting to reply to the same Interest, with consequent Data packet losses that would undermine reliability.

The forwarding fabric and retransmission routines at the NDN *Strategy* layer need to be re-engineered to improve *diversity* and *reliability* in data retrieval while ensuring *efficiency*. In such a context, the contributions of the paper are as follows:

- we clearly identify some representative IoT use cases where NDN multi-source data retrieval can be beneficially exploited and we debate issues that may arise;

- we design the overhauling of the vanilla NDN forwarding engine in order to support IoT multi-source data retrieval, with focus on producers deployed in a wireless environment;

- we implement *(i) distributed consumer-aided collision avoidance* and *Data suppression* mechanisms, enforced at the producer-side, to improve content retrieval from multiple sources; and *(ii)* a *retransmission routine* to counteract Data losses that relies on the NDN built-in EXCLUDE field in Interest packets, adequately rethought to allow selective Data retransmissions.

The remainder of the paper is organized as follows.

Section 2 introduces the fundamentals of NDN and debates the potential of this paradigm in IoT environments. Section 3 discusses multi-source data retrieval and representative IoT use cases with relevant open design issues. Details of our proposal are provided in Section 4, while Section 5 analyses the simulation results. Conclusive remarks are wrapped up in Section 6.

2. NDN FOR IOT

2.1 NDN in a nutshell

The NDN architecture is based on the *Content Centric Networking* (CCN) proposal, presented by Van Jacobson *et al.* in [4]. Communication is based on hierarchical, application-specific content names and two packet types: the *Interest*, used to ask for a content, and the *Data*, used to answer the Interest by carrying the content itself. Content integrity and authenticity are ensured by piggybacking the data publisher's signature and other authentication information in each Data.

In addition to the name of the requested content, an Interest can include several optional fields, including the following ones, which are relevant in the context of this paper: *(i)* EXCLUDE, which specifies the components that should not appear in the name of content returned in response; *(ii)* ANSWERORIGINKIND, which specifies if the requested content could be obtained from intermediate node or must be generated by the producer; *(iii)* SCOPE, which limits the

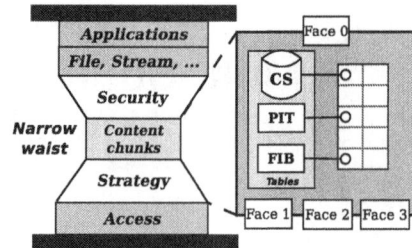

Figure 1: NDN hourglass model.

number of hops an Interest can propagate, e.g., Scope 2 limits its propagation to the first-hop node.

NDN also defines a specific node architecture and a set of basic packet processing rules.

Node model. As shown in Figure 1, each NDN node maintains three data structures: *(i)* a Content Store (CS) for temporary caching of incoming Data packets depending on local constrains and policies; *(ii)* a routing table named Forwarding Information Base (FIB) used to guide the Interests towards Data; and *(iii)* a Pending Interest Table (PIT), which keeps track of the forwarded Interest(s) that are not yet satisfied with a returned Data packet.

Depending on the application requirements and the access network interface(s), the *Strategy* layer permits to specify different transport and forwarding services, e.g., transmission (and retransmission) of Interests over a single or multiple interfaces simultaneously, management of different Interest priorities.

Forwarding fabric. When a NDN node receives an Interest, the following forwarding fabric is run. First, it searches for a name prefix longest-match in its CS. If a match is found, then the node sends the Data back to the incoming interface of the processed Interest. Otherwise, if there is a matching PIT entry, the Interest is discarded because an equal request has been already forwarded. Otherwise, a new PIT entry is created and the Interest is further forwarded to the interface stored in the FIB, and other actions can be taken according to the devised Strategy.

The Data packet follows the chain of PIT entries back to the requester(s): at the Data reception, every PIT entry is cancelled. If a match is not found in the PIT, then the Data packet is immediately dropped. As a consequence, traffic is *pull-based*: no contents flow unless a consumer has explicitly asked for them and there is a *1-to-1 matching* between Interest and Data. This significantly reduces the amount of unwanted data transfers (e.g., spam) and facilitates the deployment of accountability and control mechanisms on the content routers that manage Interest signaling (e.g., aggregation mechanisms for massive data access, congestion control).

2.2 Related work

NDN is a promising architecture for a general purpose future Internet, including the Internet of Things. Preliminary works in [3] and [5] outline the benefits that a content-centric approach could bring to IoT, including easy data retrieval, the support of mobility, multicast, scalability and security. However, NDN requires some adjustments and customizations to achieve efficient application and traffic performance in IoT, as argued in [6], where the initial design of a high-level NDN-based architecture for IoT has been proposed.

IoT systems are challenging due to *(i)* multifaceted network environments that may include wired and wireless segments; *(ii)* particular application patterns (e.g., one-to-many, many-to-many) and scope (e.g., locally-relevant data collection in home or on the road); *(iii)* highly heterogeneous device ecosystem where constrained devices coexist with more powerful devices.

Some early works on NDN have investigated peculiar IoT application domains or general optimization strategies for IoT traffic.

Smart building automation has been considered in [7] where the concept of *authenticated Interests* is introduced to allow only authorized applications to control the fixtures.

In [8], the secure configuration of a building management system is presented, while in [9] the initial design of a content-centric homenet is presented and the aspects of naming, node and service discovery are discussed. A secure named data home energy management system is proposed in [10], based on a publish-subscribe layer built on top of NDN to manage groups of fixtures and applications.

In [11] the issue of information freshness in IoT and its impact over NDN caching mechanisms are discussed. The consumer can specify the freshness requirements, and this information is used by the CS to determine if the cached information is suitable or not to satisfy the request.

A traffic optimization strategy to push contents at different granularities is presented in [12]. The authors consider one-way Interests that directly embed small data generated by sensors and are forwarded using the FIB and without creating a PIT entry, because no Data will be sent back. In addition, consumers send a subscription that specifies a sampling period, which is included in the FIB. By doing so, an intermediate node forwards the generated content only if it is compliant with the advertised period.

This paper focuses on a different and still largely unexplored topic: the NDN support of reliable and effective data retrieval from multiple producers in the IoT. This case deserves special attention and opens new issues that need to be managed at the *Strategy* layer of the NDN forwarding fabric, as deeply discussed in the next Sections.

3. THE CASE OF NDN MULTI-SOURCE DATA RETRIEVAL IN IOT

Asking for data from different producers is a common traffic and application pattern in IoT. Consumers may be interested in data items related to a particular event or a geographic area at a certain instant in time without being concerned with *which nodes* produce them. Indeed, in many scenarios:

- the precise *number* and *identity* of producers is not known in advance, e.g., because of the dynamicity and density of the network;

- data are not pre-stored but are *generated on demand* by nodes that host the capability of doing that (e.g., highly volatile data collected in dynamic scenarios);

- multiple different data are requested regardless of their origin to improve the accuracy of the application (e.g., monitoring applications take advantages from data diversity).

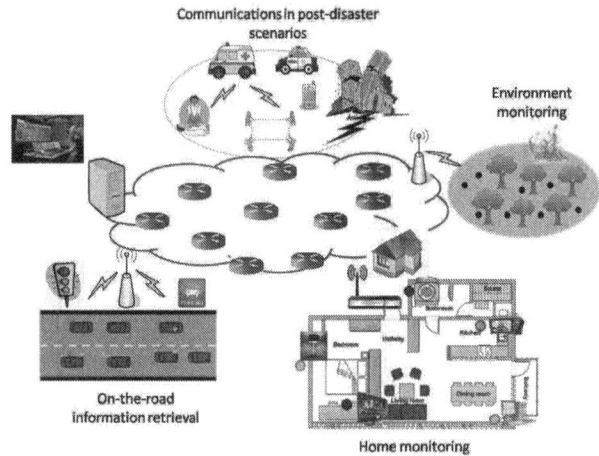

Figure 2: IoT use cases for multi-source data retrieval.

3.1 Use cases

The following use cases, also graphically sketched in Figure 2, clarify how transmitting *a single Interest* to retrieve multiple Data can be beneficially applied either as an efficient alternative to 1-to-1 Interest/Data exchange, when the producers are known, or as the only effective retrieval solution otherwise.

Home monitoring. In a home environment, a unique Home Server (HS) communicates typically wirelessly with a set of end devices (EDs), which may be resource-constrained sensors and actuators embedded in home appliances. EDs act as producers, while the HS is the principal consumer of Data, e.g., it monitors the energy consumption of devices, or the rooms temperature. In alternative, data requests may come from a remote consumer over the Internet, e.g., a utility company monitoring the energy usage of its subscribers. Both consumer and producers are static nodes exchanging small amounts of data (e.g., a measurement accounts for a couple of bytes).

The presence of any ED is known to the HS through a registration procedure where the HS assigns to each ED an identity, an application-specific namespace (e.g., */monitor/temperature* and */monitor/energy* for temperature sensors and devices measuring the energy consumption, respectively), and information for security configuration.

Issuing a single Interest to query a subset of sensors at once, instead of polling them separately, is an efficient solution in order to save network bandwidth.

Environmental monitoring. Wireless sensor networks are typically used for environmental monitoring. To this purpose, a huge number of tiny sensor nodes may be randomly and densely deployed to increase resilience in data collection from a monitored area (e.g., a forest). Sensor nodes take samples (e.g., air quality, relative humidity) over fixed or variable time periods and send them to a local or remote sink (consumer). Both consumer and producers are typically static nodes, unless to consider animals as mobile biological sensors.

The sink may send a single Interest, irrespective of the identifiers and placement of sensors (often unknown, since they are not individually placed), by only specifying the attributes of Data to be retrieved. Received data from different sources can feed the monitoring application for real-time and long-term analytics.

Shortening the data collection time would be particular helpful to promptly infer dangerous conditions, and along with the decrease of the generated traffic load contribute in saving the battery of sensors, which are left unattended for months and even years and may be either unrechargeable or equipped with power scavenging methods, such as solar cells.

Communication in post-disaster scenarios. After a natural disaster crucial information from the incident area has to be collected. Since the infrastructure might be out of action, patrol vehicles may send queries about latest state at various locations towards nodes that crowd-sense the scenario and survey local damage with their mobile devices, e.g., rescue volunteers, private citizens.

Multi-source data retrieval is the only viable solution to collect data from unknown nodes in this highly dynamic environment.

On-the-road information retrieval. Wi-Fi Access Points (APs) city-wide deployed or Road-side Units (RSUs) collect data from passing by vehicles. A remote server may specify the topological scope for relevant data collection. For instance, retrieved data may be road congestion information, pollution measurements from sensors embedded in vehicles, or even photos or videos from the area under surveillance.

An Interest broadcasted by an AP/RSU can request data from vehicles in radio range, without targeting a specific vehicle. Interests may be hop-by-hop relayed by vehicles in a given area of relevance that is wider than the RSU coverage. For instance, an Interest that conveys a name like */traffic/Road101/south/40,41/* requests traffic information about a specified region of Road 101 (southbound, kilometres 40-41). Several vehicles may reply and the larger the number of Data received in a pre-defined (typically short) time interval, the higher the accuracy of the surveillance application (e.g., for inferring traffic jam and promptly give rerouting suggestions to drivers).

Also vehicles may request road traffic information directly to other vehicles instead of relying on a remote server. By doing so, information can be retrieved in a shorter time. As shown in [13] the NDN's request/reply exchange model seems ideally suited to V2V local data exchange.

In summary, issuing a request per multiple Data is the simplest and more natural way to support the aforementioned use cases. The single-Interest solution would decrease the network bandwidth usage and shorten the data retrieval time, by also reducing the energy demands on resource-constrained wireless devices and enabling sleep modes more easily. However, changes at a macroscopic scale in the NDN engine and care in the design of meaningful naming schemes are necessary. Also specific routines should be devised at the *Strategy* layer to tackle the problems uniquely arising over the wireless segment that characterizes all the identified usage scenarios. The main design issues are discussed in the following.

3.2 Open Design Issues

Name diversity. To trigger more Data at once, the Interest should carry a name able to match the content of distinct producers. At the same time, the consumer must distinguish the retrieved Data. Thanks to the fact that the hierarchical URI-like NDN namespace is highly expressive and customizable, a proper naming scheme can be designed to accommodate such a feature.

PIT entries deletion. To support multi-source data retrieval with a single Interest, the PIT management should be rethought. The pending PIT entry should not be deleted upon the first Data arrival, and successive Data packets matching the same Interest should not be discarded.

Data collision. Due to the shared nature of the wireless medium, several producers are expected to reply to the received Interest and likely collide by simultaneously transmitting Data packets. A *distributed collision avoidance scheme* should be devised to reduce the amount of collisions.

Channel unreliability. Due to the inherent unreliability of the wireless channel, Interests and Data are subject to loss and corruption. Hence, *Interest retransmission routines* should be foreseen if the application asks for reliable Data retrieval. The collection of Data from multiple sources implies the definition of new workarounds to manage retransmission timeouts and to recover specific losses.

Data redundancy. A high number of producers could answer the same Interest (e.g., hundreds of sensors with similar collected data could simultaneously reply). A *Data suppression* mechanism is needed to cope with such situations accounting for the demands of the application and the potential constraints of the producers.

4. THE PROPOSAL IN DETAIL

The need for changes in the vanilla NDN implementation in order to support multi-source scenarios such as wireless sensor networks was preliminarily introduced in [14] and [15].

The work in [16] focuses on data collection from vehicles, however the proposal targets the retrieval of a single Data packet per Interest, originated from a vehicle passing nearby the RSU. Therefore, it does not tackle multi-source data retrieval as we defined in this paper.

In [17] a prefix hopping (PH) algorithm is proposed to support multi-source data retrieval in large scale peer-to-peer applications with frequent content updates. PH allows producers to generate multiple content names sharing a generic prefix in a fully distributed manner and it is an alternative solution to the standard NDN EXCLUDE filter, which instead we use in this paper.

In this work, we target *reliable NDN multi-source data retrieval* for IoT systems and focus on *single-hop* wireless scenarios. Such a choice is to dissect the complexity of the design at this first stage of research and then, in a future work, extend the analysis to multi-hop by using a divide and conquer approach. In multihop scenarios data redundancy and network congestion are unavoidably exacerbated. Proper countermeasures should be designed in this case, such as data aggregation at intermediate nodes, clustering schemes that elect multiple collection points inside the network, and so on.

In the following subsections, our proposal is described, by addressing the cases in which data are *(i)* locally processed by the one-hop far consumer, and *(ii)* requested by an application running over a remote host.

The main features of our proposal are summarized in Table 1.

Table 1: Main features of our proposal for reliable multi-source data retrieval

Issue	Solution
Name diversity	A *common name prefix* is included in the name field of a particular Interest, called *msINT*. Replied Data packets include an additional *producer-specific* name component
PIT entries deletion	The PIT entry for a *msINT* is kept until its lifetime expires; multiple Data packets are accepted
Data collision	Defer times are used to space-out Data transmissions from multiple sources
Channel unreliability	The *msINT* is retransmitted as its lifetime expires with an Exclude field indicating producers that already replied
Data redundancy	Overhearing is enforced at the producer-side to cancel Data transmissions

4.1 Local consumer scenario

In the reference *single-hop wireless scenario* a collection point (CP) is interested in the retrieval of N different Data packets from different producers. The number N:

- can be known by the consumer in advance and related to a specific set of producers; e.g., in a home environment the HS knows the number and the type of active data sources;

- can be a value set according to the accuracy demands of the application without a previous knowledge on the number or identity of potential producers, e.g., an RSU looks for data from different cars passing by.

In both cases, to retrieve the N Data items, the CP transmits a particular Interest, in the following referred to as multi-source Interest (*msINT*). The Interest can be simultaneously received by different nodes, some of which can be content producers that answer with a Data packet. To limit the Interest processing to single hop producers, the Interest's SCOPE field is set to 2 while the ANSWERORIGINKIND field specifies that only the original source can answer the request; hence, if a node is not a producer of the requested content, it simply discards the received Interest.

4.1.1 Naming and PIT management

Naming. Since the consumer must distinguish between different Data satisfying the same *msINT*, we assume that contents are associated with a *common name prefix* followed by a *producer-specific* part. Precisely, the first component(s) of the name are the same as those included in the *msINT*, while the last component(s) are related to the producer.

Depending on the application and network scenario, different producer-specific components can be devised, like logical names, random nonces, temporal/geographical information. For instance, in a home monitoring application, the CP sends the Interest */monitor/temperature* to collect data from a set of temperature sensors deployed in the house. The sensor in the kitchen answers with data */monitor/temperature/kitchen*, while the sensor in the bathroom answers with data */monitor/temperature/bathroom*. Vice versa, in case of a monitored environment where devices are not configured with logical names, a random nonce could be used, e.g., */monitor/temperature/0983*.

PIT management. The consumer does not delete the *msINT* at reception of the first Data packet, but simply caches the received content while maintaining the Interest in the PIT to accept successive Data. Consequently, the Interest lifetime T_{msINT} must be adequately set to accommodate the reception of multiple packets.

When a subsequent Data arrives, the consumer first checks the PIT. If the *msINT* is not expired, it looks at the Content Store to search for possible duplications. Although the producer-specific name component makes unique the Data of different producers, it is possible that the same producer answers with the same Data (or a fresher version) to subsequent *msINT*. If a CS match is found, cached Data is replaced only if the newly received Data is fresher than the previous one, otherwise the packet is discarded.

4.1.2 Collision Avoidance and Data Suppression

Depending on the expected number of producers, the Data characteristics and the interfering traffic in the scenario, different collision avoidance and suppression schemes can be devised, respectively, to reduce collisions among simultaneously transmitting nodes and to control Data redundancy.

We propose a distributed *consumer-aided* technique that allows the consumer to specify a set of rules for both the collision avoidance and the Data suppression decision to be enforced at the producer-side. Rules are specified in new optional field(s) in the Interest.

Collision avoidance. The collision avoidance scheme simply uses *defer times* to space-out Data transmissions from multiple sources. After receiving the *msINT*, each producer P computes its own collision avoidance timer, τ_{ca}, and waits. At the end of the waiting period, if the Data is still valid (no suppression rule has been executed), P sends the packet.

The simplest collision avoidance scheme is based on a purely *random* computation. The consumer advertises in *msINT* a *maximum NDN contention window* NCW_{max} and a slot time value V_{slot}.

Each producer extracts a random NCW_r value from a uniform distribution in the range $[0, NCW_{max} - 1]$ and then sets its defer time as $\tau_{ca} = V_{slot} * NCW_r$. Intuitively, the higher the number of potential producers the larger should be NCW_{max}. The consumer may also *dynamically* adjust the NCW_{max} when transmitting subsequent *msINTs*. More details about the *adaptive* NCW_{max} setting will be presented in Section 5.

In addition to a purely random scheme, other (optional) content's attributes could be taken into account for finer tuning of the collision avoidance timer, in order to give higher access priority to those Data that better match the request. For instance, if the consumer specifies a *freshness* parameter, intended as the time a certain packet will be allowed to be held by nodes, then the producers with fresher Data should probabilistically transmit before the others. In such a case, NCW_{max} will be set inversely proportional to the difference between the freshness advertised by the consumer, as conceived in [11], and the actual Data freshness.

Suppression rules. Optional content's attributes can be used to limit the number of producers answering the $msINT$. For instance, battery-powered producers could decide whether to transmit or not based on their residual charge.

Data suppression can also be decided during the collision avoidance waiting time, if some events occur on the channel while the producer is overhearing. For instance, if the consumer specifies the number N of expected Data packets and the producer overhears N Data transmitted by others nodes, then it can abort its own transmission.

4.1.3 Reliability

In order to collect N Data, the consumer CP waits for a specific time interval, which is equal to the $msINT$ lifetime, T_{msINT}. If the lifetime expires and the consumer has not received the expected N Data packets, it retransmits the $msINT$ up to a maximum number of times, n_{msINT}[1]. Specifically, if no content has been received, the consumer retransmits the same $msINT$; otherwise, if M Data packets have been received (with $M < N$), then CP transmits a $msINT$ with an active EXCLUDE field (EF).

In our design, the field contains the list of already received producer-specific components of the content name, e.g., *[kitchen;bathroom]* if we consider the home monitoring example. Therefore, only the producers whose specific name component do not appear in the list will answer the newly issued $msINT$, e,g, in the home example, the originator of the data named */monitor/temperature/bedroom*.

According to the official CCN implementation, *CCNx* [18], a consumer can simply enumerate the elements of the exclusion set, if that is sufficiently compact, or use Bloom filters to reduce the overhead. Therefore, how to actually implement the EXCLUDE field depends on the namespace design and the payload's constraints.

We also observe that the rationale behind the usage of the EXCLUDE field is the same as the one conceived in the legacy NDN architecture, but there is a fundamental difference in the Data retrieval scheme. Traditionally, the EXCLUDE field is set to improve the Interest propagation in the network, by keeping the assumption that *one Interest is consumed by one Data*. As described in [19], more Interests with a proper EXCLUDE field can be transmitted to discover more data of the same type. For instance, in Figure 3, after the consumer receives Data */name/n10*, it will send a new Interest, with the same name prefix but with "n10" in the EXCLUDE field, in order to retrieve more Data items if any exists.

Figures 4 instead summarize the behaviour of our multi-source retrieval algorithm, by considering the case when no retransmission occurs (a) and when the consumer retransmits the Interest with EXCLUDE field (b).

4.1.4 msINT lifetime setting

The $msINT$ lifetime depends on the time required to collect N Data and must be set to accommodate transmissions by the producers even in the worst-case, i.e., when considering the highest values of the collision avoidance timer, $\tau_{ca,max}$, and of the channel access delay, $maxAccessWait-Time$.

---

[1]Parameter n_{msINT} can be set to reflect the time-to-live (TTL) of the Data, so that $(n_{msINT} \cdot T_{msINT}) \leq$ TTL.

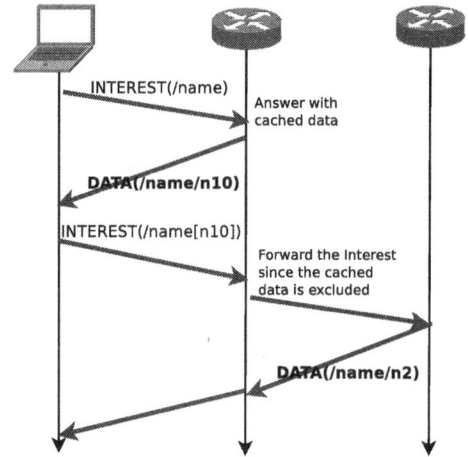

Figure 3: Traditional NDN data retrieval with the EXCLUDE **field.**

T_{msINT} is set as follows: $\tau_{ca,max} + maxAccessWaitTime$. The $maxAccessWaitTime$ parameter depends on the specific MAC layer technology and can be somehow inferred by the consumer[2].

4.2 Remote consumer scenario

The local scenario can be generalised to the case of a remote consumer (RC) that asks for Data to the collection point (CP), which then interacts with the wireless producers. The RC sends the so-called Long-Lived-Interest (LLI). Initially conceived in [19] and [20], the LLI is an Interest with a long lifetime in order to retrieve more Data with the same name in different time instants. The LLI acts as a subscription that avoids continuous Interest refresh and reduces the signalling overhead.

After receiving the LLI, the CP can decide to immediately answer with cached Data packets if any or it can build a $msINT$ that is broadcasted to collect the Data as described in the previous section. The CP may autonomously decide how many times the $msINT$ is retransmitted to retrieve all Data, without involving the RC.

Depending on the size, Data packets retrieved in the wireless segment can be *aggregated* in a single packet that does not exceed the path Maximum Transfer Unit (MTU) and sent back to the RC, or they can be individually transmitted. Moreover, if the application does not need individual reports, the CP can also perform filtering operations and/or compute local statistics and then send only the resulting Data back to the CR.

We use distinct names for $msINT$ and LLI for two main reasons:

1. the LLI usually refers to the retrieval of *multiple Data* from *the same content source* at different time instants, while $msINT$ is intended for retrieval from *different sources* more or less simultaneously;

---

[2]For the 802.11 access technology, $maxAccessWaitTime$ can be set to $W * (\sigma + T_{maxPkt})$, where W is the MAC-layer contention window size for broadcast transmissions, σ is the time slot duration, and T_{maxPkt} the time to transmit a packet of the largest size at the basic rate.

(a)

(b)

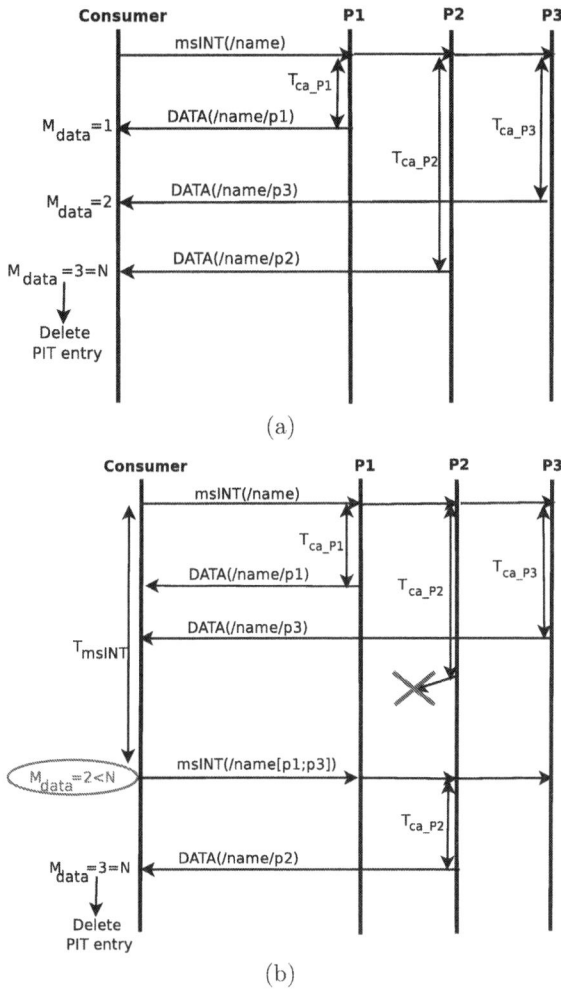

Figure 4: Flow chart of exchanged packets without retransmissions (a) and with retransmission and Ex-CLUDE Field (b).

2. the *LLI* lifetime is longer than the *msINT* lifetime: it must accommodate the overall Data collection time plus the round-trip-delay between the RC and CP.

5. PERFORMANCE EVALUATION

To assess the performance of the proposed multi-source data retrieval framework, we used the Network Simulator 3 (ns-3) and the open-source ndnSIM [21] module, specifically designed to support NDN. We properly overhauled ndnSIM to implement the conceived routines.

We consider two distinct cases for performance evaluation: *(i)* a Home scenario, where the CP is also the local consumer and it queries producers under its control; *(ii)* a Vehicular scenario where a remote consumer asks the CP to gather information from nearby sources, whose identity and number is not a priori known.

The main parameters settings are summarized in Table 2. Simulation results, averaged over 10 independent runs, are reported with the 95% confidence intervals.

Table 2: Simulation settings

Scenario	Parameter	Setting(s)
Home Monitoring	Collection pattern	periodical
	Total monitoring time	3 hours
	Monitoring interval	5 minutes
	Data Payload	128 byte
	Producers (N)	4-16
	Interfering traffic	CBR (20 Interest/s)
	Access technology	IEEE 802.11g
	Propagation model	Rayleigh
	Coverage radius	≈ 150 m
Vehicular Traffic Control	Collection pattern	occasional
	msINT retransmissions	0-3
	Data payload	1024 byte
	Vehicles (N_v)	40;80
	Interfering traffic	None
	Access technology	IEEE 802.11p
	Propagation model	Nakagami
	Coverage radius	≈ 300 m

5.1 Home scenario

The first set of results has been collected when considering a home network with an area size of $100m^2$. The CP is the home server that periodically (every 5 minutes) queries sensors to retrieve temperature measurements so to regulate air conditioning/heating in each room in a differentiated way.

We assume that a variable number of devices, N, ranging from 4 to 16, acts as producers by generating 128 bytes-long Data. Since the CP knows the identity and number of devices under its control, it will retransmit the *msINT* until the collection process is complete at every period.

For realistic evaluation, we consider the Rayleigh signal propagation and we model the interfering traffic as a constant bit rate (CBR) application with 20 Interests per second and Data packets of 1024 bytes. Therefore, packets could be lost due to collisions and adverse propagation effects.

As key performance indicators (KPI), we consider: *(i)* the *Interest overhead*, defined as the average ratio between the number of Interest sent by the CP and the received Data packets, at every collection round; *(ii)* the *collection time*, defined as the average time to complete the collection of N Data packets at every collection round; and *(iii)* the *Interest/Data number*, which is the overall number of Interests/Data transmitted/received by the CP during the entire monitoring time.

In Figure 5, we evaluate the performance of the collision avoidance routine of our multi-source data retrieval framework, in the following referred to as single Interest-multiple Data (SIMD), by varying the NCW_{max} parameter. The SIMD slot time V_{slot} is set equal to the IEEE 802.11g DIFS parameter.

Results are highly sensitive to the NCW_{max} setting.

The Interest overhead gets significantly lower (about halved) when NCW_{max} passes from 32 to 512 and the number of producers increases, since larger NCW_{max} are more effective to counteract more likely collisions. Interestingly, as the number of producers increases, the Interest overhead decreases; this is an intrinsic property of the SIMD scheme.

However, the bandwidth saved with a larger NCW_{max} is paid in terms of a longer collection time, that increases as the number of producers increases since more retransmissions should be performed to recover losses from a higher number of nodes. Recovery operations are slowed, since T_{msINT} gets longer as NCW_{max} increases.

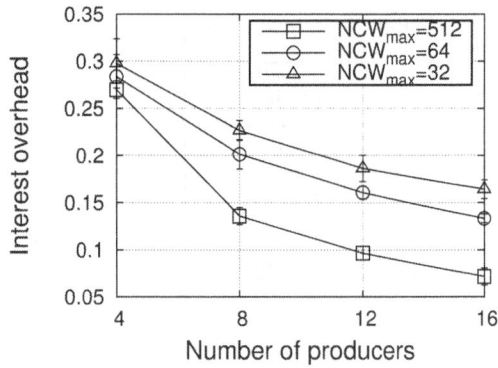

(a) Interest overhead

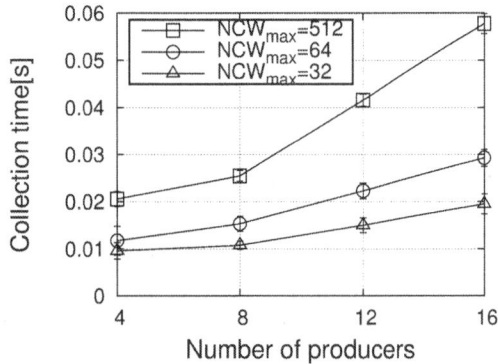

(b) Collection Time

Figure 5: Home scenario: metrics vs. the number of producers when varying the size of the NDN contention window for the SIMD scheme.

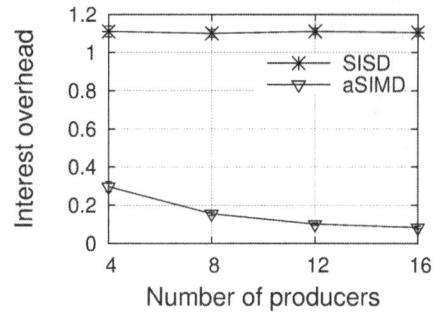

(a) Interest overhead

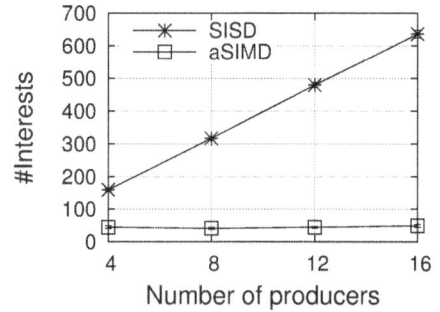

(b) Number of Interest packets

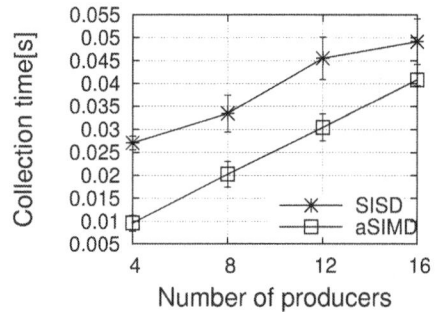

(c) Collection Time

Figure 6: Home scenario: metrics vs. the number of producers when comparing the SISD scheme against the adaptive SIMD (aSIMD) scheme.

In the considered scenario, since the CP knows how many nodes (N) are expected to reply to the issued $msINT$, a smarter solution would be to *adaptively* set the NCW_{max} parameter and advertise it in the Interest, so not to waste time and to limit collisions. Intuitively, a larger NCW_{max}, i.e., 512, is used when the number of nodes is higher; on the contrary, shorter values, i.e., 32, 64, are preferred in subsequent Interest retransmissions as the residual number of producers meant to reply is reduced.

In Figure 6, the performance of the adaptive SIMD is compared against the native NDN Single Interest-Single Data (SISD) retrieval scheme. In SISD, the Interest overhead is almost constant as the number of producers increases, nearly equal to 1.1, and heavily higher than the value experienced by adaptive SIMD (around 0.05-0.3), Figure 6(a). In particular, for 16 consumers, the overhead decreases by one order of magnitude.

The claimed efficiency of SIMD compared to SISD can be also observed in Figure 6(b): the number of Interest is extremely low and almost unsensitive to the number of producers. In addition, regardless of the number of producers, adaptive SIMD outperforms SISD also in terms of collection time, reduced of nearly 10ms.

5.2 Vehicular scenario

The second set of results considers a traffic congestion control application. The collection point is an RSU located in the central reservation of the highway "A1", consisting of a dual carriageway with three traffic lanes per each direction. A remote control center (RCC) is interested in the retrieval of the average vehicles speed in the north carriageway at kilometres 20-21 in order to estimate the overall conditions of the traffic. Each vehicle is equipped with a global positioning system (GPS) device and an IEEE 802.11p transceiver, and is able to store its kinematics (speed, acceleration) and position parameters (location, direction, and route number along with a timestamp).

The retrieval process is initiated by the RCC, which sends an LLI with name */traffic/speed/highwayA1/North/{20,21}*. At the reception of the LLI, the RSU broadcasts a $msINT$ to collect the kinematics parameters of as much as possible vehicles passing by. On receiving the $msINT$, vehicles in the North carriageway will schedule Data transmission by following the designed collision avoidance strategy. Once a consistent number of speed samples has been collected, the

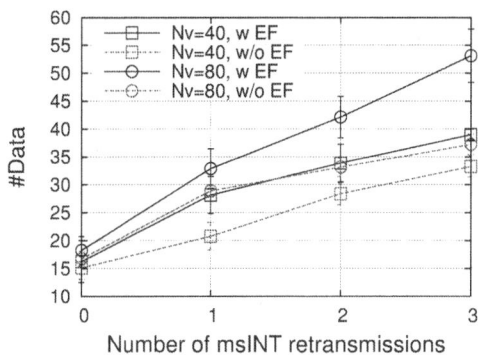

(a) Number of collected (distinct) Data packets

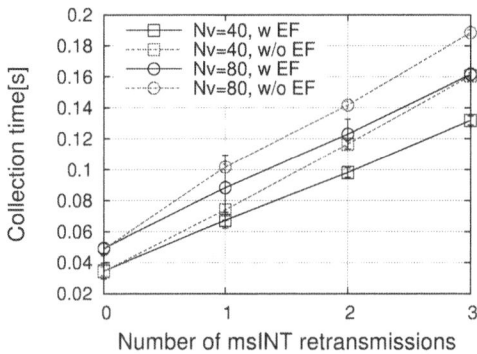

(b) Collection Time

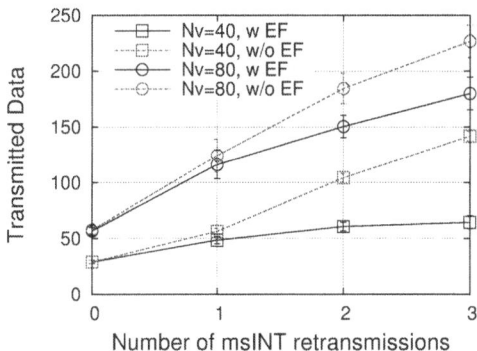

(c) Total number of transmitted Data packets

Figure 7: Vehicular scenario: metrics vs. the number of msINT retransmissions when varying the number of producers Nv for the SIMD scheme with and without the EXCLUDE field, NCW_{max}= 127, V_{slot} =IEEE 802.11p DIFS.

RSU calculates the average vehicle speed and sends a Data packet to the RCC. The RSU is oblivious to the number and the identity of vehicles in its transmission range. Therefore, it can retransmit the $msINT$ for a predefined number of times to maximize the number of collected Data.

As KPI, we consider the *number of Data collected by the RSU* and the correspondent *collection time*.

In the simulation, we vary the number of $msINT$ retransmissions (from zero - no retransmission occurs - to three), and we consider two distinct number of producer vehicles, 40 and 80.

In Figure 7 a simplified SIMD scheme (curves are labeled as *w/o EF*) is used as a benchmarking solution. An Interest is issued to retrieve Data at once and it does not foresee the use of the EXCLUDE field in retransmitted Interest. As a consequence, at every retransmission the same producers may attempt to reply and likely collide. For both schemes, as expected, the higher the number of $msINT$ retransmissions the higher the number of collected Data. Results clearly show that the retransmissions of the $msINT$ with the EXCLUDE field carrying the number of already received Data packets lead to the following benefits. The consumer can increase the number of different Data packets collected in a shorter time because a lower number of nodes is authorized to reply to subsequent retransmitted $msINT$. As a matter of fact, in presence of 40 producers, SIMD with the EXCLUDE field lets the RSU retrieve the same number of Data that is retrieved with 80 producers when the scheme without EF is considered, hence confirming the adequacy of the proposed solution to maximize data diversity.

The overall number of Data packets transmitted by producers is also reduced (Figure 7(c)), with a consequent benefit in terms of network bandwidth and device resources saving. It is worth noticing that the latter aspect may be especially advantageous for constrained devices, which can go back to a sleeping state once receiving the $msINT$ carrying their producer component in the EXCLUDE field, and hence acting as an implicit acknowledgement.

As a further notice, the Interest size may increase when the EXCLUDE field is conveyed. However, Bloom filters can be used to keep the incurred overhead under control[3].

6. CONCLUSION

In this paper we have investigated a common IoT traffic pattern, multi-source data retrieval, supported through named data networking. After scanning related IoT scenarios and identifying their peculiarities, the study pinpointed the potential benefits of NDN and open design issues, mainly involving the naming scheme design and some re-engineering in the forwarding fabric and retransmission routines.

The work designs a comprehensive framework for *reliable data retrieval* from *multiple wireless sources* from *local and remote consumers*. It tackles identified problems, through *(i)* a distributed consumer-aided collision avoidance scheme, *(ii)* a Data suppression mechanism to reduce packet redundancy, *(iii)* and the EXCLUDE field added in Interest packets to manage selective retransmissions. Simulation results in ndnSIM confirm the benefits of the conceived solution, that save bandwidth, while maximizing data diversity and shortening the collection time.

The conducted study would also provide some hints for future research. Indeed, the conceived solution is a *baseline framework* on top of which further modules may be designed for collision avoidance, suppression and retransmission to be customized according to the requirements of different applications, networks and devices. As a future work, we plan to extend the study to multi-hop wireless scenarios, where issues may be exacerbated and additional workarounds need to be devised.

---

[3]In [22] it is shown that for less than 100 components, with a filter length of 128 bytes, the false positive probability is below 1%.

7. ACKNOWLEDGEMENT

This work has been carried out within the national research project PON03PE_00050 DOMUS "Home automation systems for a cooperative energy brokerage service".

8. REFERENCES

[1] L. Atzori, A. Iera, and G. Morabito, "The Internet of Things: a survey," *Computer networks*, vol. 54, no. 15, pp. 2787–2805, 2010.

[2] L. Zhang *et al.*, "Named Data Networking (NDN) Project," PARC, Tech. Rep. NDN-0001, October 2010.

[3] Z. Sheng, S. Yang, Y. Yu, A. V. Vasilakos, J. A. McCann, and K. K. Leung, "A Survey on the IETF Protocol Suite for the Internet of Things: Standards, Challenges, and Opportunities," *IEEE Wireless Communications Magazine*, vol. 20, no. 6, pp. 91–98, 2013.

[4] V. Jacobson *et al.*, "Networking Named Content," in *ACM CoNEXT*, 2009.

[5] Y. Zhang, D. Raychadhuri, R. Ravindran, and G.-Q. Wang, "ICN based Architecture for IoT," in *Internet-Draft*, June 2014.

[6] M. Amadeo, C. Campolo, A. Iera, and A. Molinaro, "Named Data Networking for IoT: an Architectural Perspective," in *European Conference on Networks and Communications (EuCNC)*, Bologna, Italy, 2014.

[7] J. Burke, P. Gasti, N. Nathan, and G. Tsudik, "Securing Instrumented Environments over Content-Centric Networking: the Case of Lighting Control and NDN," in *IEEE INFOCOM NOMEN Workshop*, 2013.

[8] W. Shang, Q. Ding, A. Mariantoni, J. Burke, and L. Zhang, "Securing Building Management Systems Using Named Data Networking," *IEEE Network*, vol. 28, no. 3, pp. 50–56, 2014.

[9] R. Ravindran, T. Biswas, X. Zhang, A. Chakraborti, and G. Wang, "Information-Centric Networking Based Homenet," in *IFIP/IEEE ManFI Workshop*, 2013.

[10] J. Zhang, Q. Li, and E. M. Schooler, "iHEMS: an information-centric approach to secure home energy management," in *IEEE SmartGridComm*, 2012.

[11] J. Quevedo, D. Corujo, and R. Aguiar, "Consumer Driven Information Freshness Approach for Content Centric Networking," in *IEEE INFOCOM NOM Workshop*, Toronto, Canada, 2014.

[12] J. François, T. Cholez, and T. Engel, "CCN Traffic Optimization for IoT," in *The 4th International Conf. on Network of the Future (NoF)*, 2013.

[13] L. Wang, A. Afanasyev, R. Kunts, R. Vuyyuru, R. Wakikawa, and L. Zhang, "Rapid Traffic Information Dissemination Using Named Data," in *ACM NoM Workshop*, 2012.

[14] N.-T. Dinh and Y. Kim, "Potential of Information-Centric Wireless Sensor and Actor Networking," in *IEEE International Conference on Computing, Management and Telecommunications (ComManTel)*, 2013.

[15] J. P. Meijers, M. Amadeo, C. Campolo, A. Molinaro, S. Paratore, G. Ruggeri, and M. Booysen, "A Two-Tier Content-Centric Architecture for Wireless Sensor Networks," in *IEEE ICNP*, Gottingen, Germany, 2013.

[16] J. Wang, R. Wakikawa, and L. Zhang, "DMND: collecting data from mobiles using named data," in *IEEE Vehicular Networking Conference (VNC)*, 2010, pp. 49–56.

[17] F. Angius, C. Westphal, J. Wei, M. Gerla, and G. Pau, "Prefix Hopping: Efficient Many-To-Many Communication Support in Information Centric Networks," in *IEEE INFOCOM NOMEN Workshop*, 2013.

[18] "CCNx Project, http://www.ccnx.org."

[19] Z. Zhu, S. Wang, X. Yang, V. Jacobson, and L. Zhang, "ACT: audio conference tool over named data networking," in *ACM SIGCOMM workshop on Information-centric networking (ICN)*, 2011.

[20] A. Carzaniga, M. Papalini, and A. L. Wolf, "Content-Based Publish/Subscribe Networking and Information-Centric Networking," in *ACM SIGCOMM workshop on Information-centric networking (ICN)*, 2011.

[21] A. Afanasyev, I. Moiseenko, and L. Zhang, "ndnSIM: NDN simulator for NS-3," NDN Project, Tech. Rep. NDN-0005, July 2012.

[22] S. Tarkoma, C. E. Rothenberg, and E. Lagerspetz, "Theory and practice of Bloom filters for distributed systems," *IEEE Communications Surveys and Tutorials*, vol. 14, no. 1, pp. 131–155, 2012.

Information Centric Networking in the IoT: Experiments with NDN in the Wild

Emmanuel Baccelli
INRIA
emmanual.baccelli@inria.fr

Christian Mehlis
Freie Universität Berlin
mehlis@inf.fu-berlin.de

Oliver Hahm
INRIA
oliver.hahm@inria.fr

Thomas C. Schmidt
HAW Hamburg
t.schmidt@ieee.org

Matthias Wählisch
Freie Universität Berlin
m.waehlisch@fu-berlin.de

ABSTRACT

This paper explores the feasibility, advantages, and challenges of an ICN-based approach in the Internet of Things. We report on the first NDN experiments in a life-size IoT deployment, spread over tens of rooms on several floors of a building. Based on the insights gained with these experiments, the paper analyses the shortcomings of CCN applied to IoT. Several interoperable CCN enhancements are then proposed and evaluated. We significantly decreased control traffic (i.e., interest messages) and leverage data path and caching to match IoT requirements in terms of energy and bandwidth constraints. Our optimizations increase content availability in case of IoT nodes with intermittent activity. This paper also provides the first experimental comparison of CCN with the common IoT standards 6LoWPAN/RPL/UDP.

Categories and Subject Descriptors

C.2.1 [**Computer-Comm. Networks**]: Network Architecture and Design; C.2.2 [**Computer-Comm. Networks**]: Network Protocols; C.2.6 [**Computer-Comm. Networks**]: Internetworking; C.3 [**Special-purpose and application-based systems**]:

Keywords

CCN; NDN; ICN; IoT; Performance; Deployment

1. INTRODUCTION

The Internet is currently evolving in several directions. One path leads beyond end-to-end streams with Peer-to-Peer, CDNs and now ICN [1]. Endpoints in these information access models try to access named content, without direct mapping to a transport layer session at the (single) origin. The other evolves beyond traditional user terminal vs. router dichotomy: machine-to-machine (M2M) communications do not involve human source or destination, and

interconnected machines include billions of cheap tiny communicating objects which play both the roles of host and router in spontaneous (wireless) networks, i.e., the Internet of Things [2]. In this dual context, this paper explores the feasibility, advantages and challenges of an ICN-based approach in the Internet of Things.

1.1 The Next Billion of Connected Machines

The next billions of interconnected machines are expected to consist in a variety of heterogeneous devices, ranging from wireless sensors to actuators, wearables, Radio-Frequency IDentification (RFID) tags, smart home appliances and many other types of machines that were typically not internetworked so far. Connecting these devices to the global realm has been coined the Internet of Things (IoT). It is expected to profoundly transform our environment.

Most IoT devices will be very limited in terms of memory, CPU, or power capacities (from small batteries). The term *constrained devices* [3] was recently introduced to define a category of connected devices that are resource-challenged compared to PCs, smartphones or laptops. Constraints include (i) orders of magnitude less power consumption measured in mWatt instead of Watt, (ii) orders of magnitude less computational power measured in MegaFLOPS instead of GigaFLOPS, and (iii) orders of magnitude less memory measured in Kilobytes instead of Gigabytes. For cost reasons, and due to the specific nature of the envisioned (massive) deployments of IoT devices, such constraints are expected to remain the norm in this domain, in the foreseeable future [4].

The sheer numbers and a lack of user interfaces make interconnecting IoT devices a challenge. Different approaches have been designed which leverage both traditional, infrastructure-based network paradigms, and spontaneous wireless network paradigms [5]. They allow for device autoconfiguration and dynamic self-organization to relay data towards destination – even without the help of infrastructure and pre-provisioned access points. Current approaches fall into two categories: silo approaches such as Zigbee [6], and approaches based on open standards, protocol stacks, such as IPv6 with 6LoW-PAN [7] and RPL [8]. In the long run, one can expect that for the same reasons that led TCP/IP to prevail, an approach based on open standards and on a layered protocol stack will establish in the IoT. In the following, we will consider 6LoWPAN/IPv6/RPL as the reference networking solution for constrained devices in the IoT, with which ICN should measure up.

1.2 Why ICN for the Internet of Things?

Data in information-centric networking is delocalized and need not be retrieved via an end-to-end transport stream. Instead, hop-wise replication and in-network caching facilitate information dissemination in the IoT, and relax the demand for continued connectivity. Such perspectives, based on ICN, were recently mentioned as a potential alternative networking solution for the IoT [9].

More specifically, common communication patterns of the IoT such as content retrieval 'upon request' and 'scheduled' content updates are easily accommodated by ICN and may noticeably benefit from cache-assisted, hop-by-hop replication. The prevalent task of data fusion in the IoT may be implemented by augmented replication logic in a lightweight fashion. The combination of these mechanisms may save energy and radio resources, increase availability, and well reduce complexity. Most strikingly, ICN does reduce network layers and – in an optimized version – may subsume network, transport, and elementary application logic. Thus an ICN approach in the IoT might (i) offer opportunities to efficiently factorize functionalities e.g., caching and buffering for error control (ii) drastically reduce the complexity of autoconfiguration mechanisms compared to an approach based on a layered protocol stack, and (iii) achieve a smaller memory footprint compared to 6LoWPAN/IPv6/RPL.

However, a number of challenges should also be noted. Often, sensor data require freshness that conflicts with caching. Furthermore, there is also the demand for unscheduled traffic in the IoT e.g., the control of actuators, which is much easier to achieve in an end-to-end access model. Finally, in many ICN approaches, routing and forwarding significantly increases the burden over IP. In effect, state and cached content may blow up memory requirements of constrained nodes.

At the conceptual level, it remains fairly open whether benefits outweigh the shortcomings of ICN in the IoT, or not. It is the objective of the present paper to explore the basic feasibility and tradeoffs in an experimentally driven approach.

1.3 Related Work

While several ICN approaches have been developed, including NDN [10], PSIRP [11], Netinf [12], DONA [13], a number of key aspects remain challenges for ICN [14]. One example of such challenge is the design of routing schemes enabling automatic, efficient, and scalable forwarding information configuration on each ICN device. Related work proposed routing approaches based on proactive, link-state mechanisms [15], [16]. However, such approaches may not be directly applicable in the IoT, where constrained devices impose different requirements in terms of memory and power capacities. For instance, requirements for home, industrial and building automation [17] led to the design of the RPL [8] routing protocol, which can be more energy and memory efficient than standard link-state approaches. It does not require periodic flooding and allows partial topology knowledge.

Recent work has thus started to study ICN paradigms in IoT scenarios or similar contexts (e.g. mobile ad hoc networks). In [18], authors reports on early efforts to provide constrained devices with a CCN communication layer in practice. This implementation is however not interoperable with the full-blown, reference CCN implementation. This initial implementation was used in [19] to showcase a health monitoring application prototype in the context of a small home network. Several architecture design proposals emerged recently for ICN in the Internet of Things, such as [20] which proposes an overlay ICN architecture designed over the M2M ETSI standard, or [21] which identifies high-level requirements of ICN for IoT and proposes a network architecture for IoT based on ICN. Other efforts have proposed enhancements to tackle various issues with ICN in wireless scenarios. For instance, [22] focuses on MANETs scenarios and mobile nodes using ICN and proposes a mechanism reducing the overhead of NDN packet forwarding. On the other hand, [23] focuses on sensor networks and data collection from a data sink, and proposes in this context an NDN extension for directed diffusion with new packet types and neighbor distinction. This implementation is however not interoperable with the reference CCN implementation. In [24] authors propose a push mechanism for CCN, targeting sensor networks. In [25] a gossip mechanism for CCN is introduced, targeting wireless ad hoc networks. Another category of efforts have focused on tackling security and naming issues with ICN in the IoT, such as [26] which studies such issues with CCN in the context of lighting systems and building automation.

However, the above prior work only studied ICN approaches via theoretical analysis and simulations. In [19] and [18], preliminary tests are reported on small, toy networks. But to the best of our knowledge, there are no reports to date on larger scale deployments on IoT hardware, in environments matching requirements described by the industry, e.g., in [17]. Furthermore, prior work in this domain has either (i) focused on MANET, where machines are not constrained devices, or (ii) focused on wireless sensor networks and sink-centric data traffic (i.e., sensor-to-sink or sink-to-sensor) which is not representative of the whole IoT, where other types of devices participate, and other types of data traffic are significant, such as sensor-to-sensor traffic which is substantial in building automation scenarios (e.g., for lighting systems).

1.4 Contributions of this Paper

In this paper, we report on the first CCN experiments in a life-size IoT deployment, spread over tens of offices on several floors of a building, matching characteristics and requirements from building automation as specified in [17]. Based on the insights gained with these experiments, the paper analyses the shortcomings of NDN applied to IoT. Several interoperable CCN enhancements are then proposed and evaluated, which decrease interest traffic and focus data path and caching to match IoT requirements in terms of energy and bandwidth constraints, and increase content availability in case of IoT nodes with intermittent activity. This paper also provide the first experimental comparison of CCN with the alternative dominant approach in IoT based on 6LoWPAN/RPL/UDP. In addition to our real-world experiments, we discuss ICN in the context of IoT, based on an extensive literature survey.

The remainder of this paper is organized as follows. First, in § 2 we will compare IoT requirements with basic ICN characteristics to identify mismatches and challenges one faces with ICN in the Internet of Things. Then, in § 3 we will describe our ICN implementation for the IoT and our deployment setup in a building automation context. Based on insights gained from our experiments with the CCN implementation in this deployment, we will propose and evaluate in § 4 several interoperable enhancements for CCN operation in the Internet of Things. We will then present lessons learned in § 5. Finally, we will conclude and discuss future steps in § 6.

2. A PRIORI CHALLENGE OF ICN IN IOT: LIMITED MEMORY

Limited memory resources are fundamental in IoT scenarios. Before an ICN solution can be deployed and experimented with, it needs to be aligned with these constraints. In this section, we discuss memory requirements introduced by ICN and how we overcome this basic challenge. We separately discuss aspects concerning caching, protocol stack architecture, and routing schemes. For challenges we derived based on our experiments, we refer to Section 5.

2.1 Implications on Caching Capabilities

One of the fundamental aspects of ICN is in-network caching, which requires memory dedicated to content cache on nodes in the network. On constrained devices, available RAM is very limited and usually in the order of 10 kBytes [3]. This memory is shared by all processes running on the device, including the operating system, the full network stack, the application(s). Considering typical sizes of these software components in the IoT, the remaining cache size for content on constrained devices is at most in the order of 1 kByte. This is extremely small compared to cache sizes expected on types of devices initially targeted by ICN [27, 28]. As readings of sensor values are ephemeral information by nature – sensor data are continuously replaced by new data – one might argue to disable caching altogether. However, as we will show below, caching is not only doable, but also beneficial in the IoT (even with such limited resources).

First, a significant part of the data is expected to consist in small size content. The size of a common implementation of temperature values is 12 bytes, which allows to store ≈85 sensor values in a single cache. For medium-sized content (i.e., of size in the order of n kBytes, where n is the number of nodes in the network), distributed caching strategies could coordinate multiple devices to leverage in-network caching of all chunks. Typical medium-size content examples include accumulated, periodically-generated data, or software update binaries.

Second, beyond simple sensor scenarios with a single sink, the IoT envisions multiple consumers for the same content. For example, a temperature sensor asynchronously accessed by the air-conditioning system, the automated blinds, and windows of a room, each of which may react independently upon temperature evolution. For more powerful devices crowd computing [29] is an interesting application field. Similarly, caching ephemeral content within the network may significantly increase content availability because (i) nodes can then sleep as often as possible to save energy, and (ii) lossy multi-hop wireless paths towards content producers are shortened. We will study the effect of caching in Section 4.

2.2 Implications on Overlay Applicability

Deploying only the IP stack on constrained devices is already a challenge in terms of RAM and ROM. ICN approaches that work on top of IP might be impossible due to the additive memory requirements of both the ICN stack and the IP stack. Consequently, ICN implementations should work directly on top of the link layer. Note that for heterogeneous deployment border gateways can bridge between IP and ICN. For the experiments reported in this paper, we have thus used an ICN approach running directly above the MAC layer (see Sections 3 and 4).

2.3 Implications on Routing Approaches

Reduced memory of constrained devices also limits applicability of ICN routing approaches. Current proposals usually route either directly on names or indirectly via name resolution. Based on our previous observations, name resolution on top of IP is not viable. However, even some pure name-based routing schemes, such as [15] and [16] rely on an ICN overlay requiring an IP network, or use proactive link state algorithms. Link state routing results in both (i) a significant amount of control traffic, whether or not there is data traffic to carry in the network, and (ii) a significant amount of memory, typically in $O(n)$, where n is the number of nodes in the network. These characteristics do not match the memory and energy resources of constrained devices.

Routing protocols running on IoT devices should aim for $O(1)$ routing state and minimal control traffic – ideally none, especially when there is no data traffic to carry [30]. In Section 4, we introduce ICN routing with these properties.

3. STEPS TO ENABLE ICN IN THE IOT

In order to gain a full understanding of how ICN operates in the Internet of Things, it is inevitable to conduct experiments in real-world deployments or testbeds that reflect properties of such deployments. Testbeds help to avoid topologies and densities that are too artificial, too regular, or too isolated compared with the real word. They naturally include external interferences resulting from other radio networks, electrical devices, or simple human activity. The first step towards such experiments is implementing ICN code that runs on IoT hardware.

3.1 Porting CCN-Lite to RIOT

We have ported CCN-Lite [31], a bare-bone Linux open source implementation of NDN, to RIOT [32], an operating system for constrained devices. Among ICN approaches, we have chosen NDN because it can easily operate directly above the link layer – a requirement we identified in Section 2. We chose to base ourselves on CCN-Lite because this implementation is compliant with the reference NDN implementation (CCNx) while being very compact: less than 1,000 lines of C code and low memory footprint. And we chose RIOT as operating system to run on constrained devices because it is open source and fits IoT devices memory requirements, while allowing plain C code with all the standard headers, based on a (multi-)threading model comparable to POSIX. These characteristics guaranteed that porting Linux code to RIOT is straightforward, and a fair comparison with the non-IoT world. We also leveraged RIOT support for popular debugging tools such as Valgrind, Wireshark, gdb, and nativenet. Our implementation is open source and available online in GitHub [33].

Table 1 compares the ROM and RAM sizes of the binaries compiled for NDN network stacks and for 6LoWPAN/RPL network stacks, built upon state-of-the-art IoT operating systems (RIOT and Contiki), for state-of-the-art IoT hardware (Redbee Econotag board and MSB-A2 board). We observe that an ICN approach can significantly outperform common

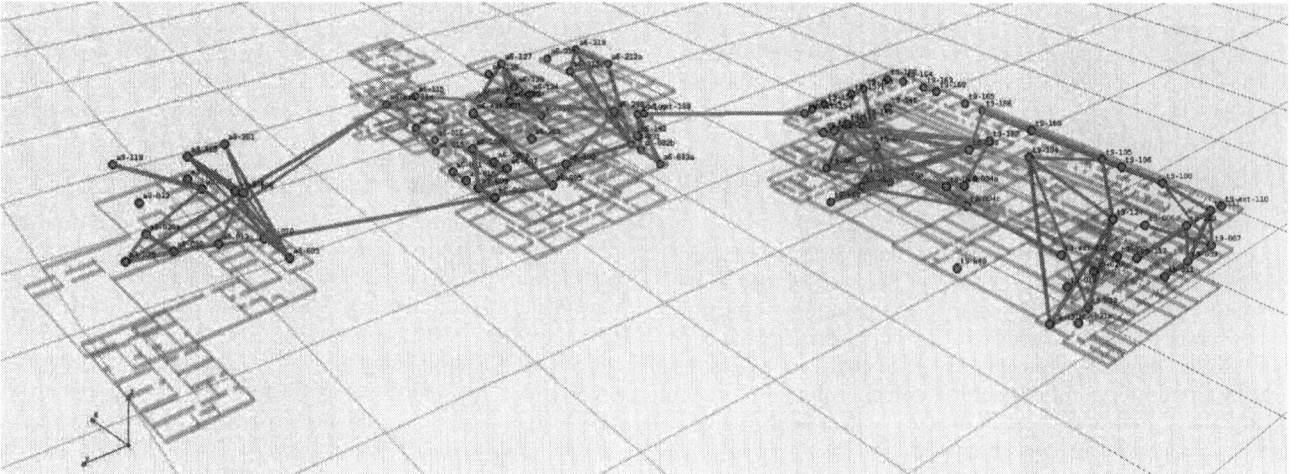

Figure 1: 3D visualization of the topology of the deployment, consisting in 60 nodes that interconnect via wireless communications (sub-GHz) and that are physically distributed in multiple rooms, multiple floors, and multiple buildings.

(a) RIOT on MSBA2

Module	ROM	RAM
RPL + 6LoWPAN	53412 bytes	27739 bytes
CCN-Lite	16628 bytes	5112 bytes

(b) Contiki on Redbee-Econotag

Module	ROM	RAM
RPL + 6LoWPAN	52131 bytes	21057 bytes
CCNx	13005 bytes	5769 bytes

Table 1: Comparing memory resources for common IoT operating systems and hardware.

IoT protocols in terms of ROM size (down to 60% less) and RAM size (down to 80% less).

3.2 Configuring NDN Deployment

In order to obtain a fully functional NDN network stack for the IoT, a FIB autoconfiguration mechanism is needed: in IoT scenarios, even less than in other scenarios, one cannot expect humans in the loop, so manual configuration is not part of the deployment. In particular, predefined location-based naming and simple routing schemes based on the structure of such names may thus not be possible in general. Furthermore, as mentioned in Section 2, existing ICN routing approaches are not appropriate for constrained devices in the IoT: alternative routing mechanisms must be used in this context, which require drastically less state.

In the context of ICN, the naming scheme is crucial. NDN uses a hierarchical name space, which allows for aggregation in routing. The amount of content items that can be expressed depends on the character set and name length. MTUs of common IoT link layer technologies range between ≈30 bytes and ≈100 bytes. To the best of our knowledge fragmentation within ICN is not addressed, hence naming and chunk size need to be aligned with the packet size to prevent fragmentation (not supported by the link layer).

4. NDN EXPERIMENTS AND OPTIMIZATIONS FOR IOT DEPLOYMENT

In the following, we will describe and evaluate several routing alternatives, as well as other aspects of NDN in the wild, such as the effect of caching in IoT.

4.1 Large-scale Deployment Setup

Typical IoT application scenarios, include building and home automation [34, 17], smart metering (e.g., [35]), or environment monitoring (e.g., [36]). These scenarios usually require a multi-hop wireless network. For the NDN experiments, we deployed our ICN IoT implementation on the campus testbed of *Freie Universität Berlin*, consisting in 60 nodes distributed in various rooms, on several floors, and in several buildings, as shown in Figure 1. This deployment matches the typical device density (several meters between nodes), distribution (one node per room), and environment (e.g., co-located wireless networks) described in [17] for building automation, e.g., HVAC devices, lighting devices, or fire-detection devices. Each node is equipped with a CC1100 radio chip operating at 868MHz, and sensors that can measure various parameters including room temperature, humidity etc. For more details we refer to [37]. Most of the nodes are deployed inside rooms, while a few nodes are deployed outdoor to better interconnect nodes in different buildings. Nodes interconnect via their wireless interface, which offers a maximum link layer frame size of 64 Bytes.

In order to monitor closely energy consumption, verify individual node behavior, and manage experiments on this deployment (e.g., flash nodes, gather results) each node is furthermore connected to its own docking station. Docking stations are interconnected via an Ethernet backbone. However, these docking stations are used only to monitor and manage the nodes. Nodes operate autonomously, i.e., each node can only use its own CPU, its own memory, and its own wireless interface to communicate with other nodes.

Basic Configuration of Experiments The following experiments use 400 ms interest timeout (stop-and-go, giving up after 5 tries), and 900 ms nonce timeouts. The content is named in a hierarchical fashion typical for NDN, without

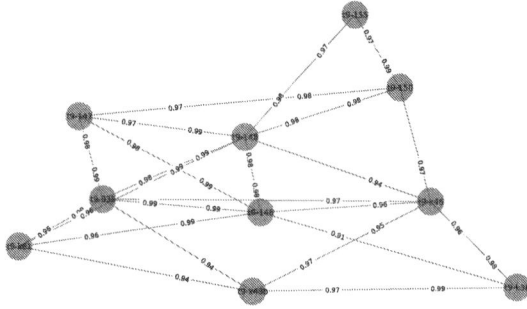

(a) 10 nodes are involved when a single consumer (t9-k38) requests content published by t9-155.

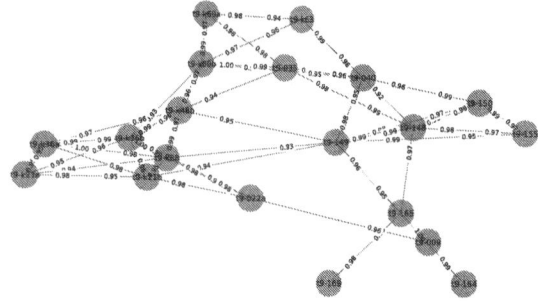

(b) 20 nodes are involved when multiple consumers (t9-149, t9-148, and t9-150) request content published by t9-k36a

Figure 2: Snapshot of the link-layer network topologies used in the experiments for single and multi consumer scenarios. Each topology spans over 3 floors in the right-most building shown in Figure 1. Link weights describe % of received packets, per link, per direction.

any encryption. Considering the maximum link layer frame size of 64 bytes in our deployment, we decide for a medium sized name length of 12 bytes including the chunk identifier (the exact names of the content chunks are */riot/text/a*, */riot/text/b* etc.). Note that with these names, the size of headers and names fit in a single link layer frame, both with CCN (16+12 = 28 bytes) and with 6LoWPAN/RPL/UDP (15+12 = 27 bytes), and still allow to carry realistic application data. Also note that the sizes of minimal CCN header (16 bytes, eliding optional fields) and of 6LoWPAN/RPL/UDP headers (15 bytes) are similar, and thus represent not a decisive factor in the differences observed in the following experiments. The length of content names is however a factor, as discussed in Section 5.1.

In the experiments, we consider a single content producer and one or multiple consumers. Due to the volatile nature of the wireless medium [38], the resulting link layer topologies based on our 60 node network might change on a per-transmission basis (cf., Figure 2). Note that IoT scenarios in home and building automation networks are typically multi-hop, but less than 5 hops in diameter [39]. Consequently, in our experiments, we placed content producer and consumers at least 2 hops apart.

To analyze the effects of NDN for typical radio packets payload in the IoT, we align the chunk size such that each chunk can be transmitted without fragmentation. In our case, MTU is 64 bytes, chunks are set to be 58 bytes long, of which 30 bytes of content. Since typical sensor content production is of the order of 200 bytes per minute [17], we set the basic configuration for consumers to periodically fetch 10 such chunks. However, other popular IoT radio technologies provide MTUs that are twice bigger (e.g. IEEE 802.15.4), or half smaller (e.g. Bluetooth LE). So we also check cases with 5 and 20 chunks per content item.

4.2 Vanilla Interest Flooding (VIF)

The simplest routing approach that requires minimal states is *interest flooding*, whereby each node in the network repeats an interest, upon first reception. In the following, we will call this simple mechanism Vanilla Interest Flooding (VIF). Using VIF, a consumer with an empty FIB can nevertheless disseminate its interest in content, and the flooded interest

will reach the producer which can then send the content on the reverse path. VIF fits the constraints of IoT devices because (i) it does not rely on any additional control traffic to maintain the FIB, (ii) it requires minimal state, i.e., only temporary pending interests on the reverse path of content that is sought after.

Figure 3(a) shows the results of an experiment using NDN with VIF for a single consumer scenario. In this experiment, the consumer periodically accesses content of size 5, 10, or 20 chunks of data, all of which were produced by another constrained node in the network shown in Figure 2(a).

While the experiment is successful in that NDN was demonstrated to operate on IoT hardware (meeting memory requirements), and the consumer could fetch the content, Figure 3(a) shows that, compared to its size, many packets were transmitted to fetch the content. This is due to the fact that each chunk triggers an interest, which requires network-wide flooding. In general, in a network of n nodes, and for k chunks of content, the number of transmissions for a single content item is $k \cdot ((n - 1) + \sqrt{n})$, assuming the average path length approximation $\sqrt{n}$. We observe that while VIF is simple and works in the scenario we tested, it does not scale well in terms of number radio transmissions when the network or the content grows in size. Radio transmission and reception are however very costly in terms of energy for battery-powered IoT devices. In the following, we have thus designed and tested enhancements reducing the number of radio transmissions and receptions in IoT environment.

4.3 Reactive Optimistic Name-based Routing (RONR)

In order to reduce the number of radio transmissions compared to basic interest flooding, we introduce Reactive Optimistic Name-based Routing (RONR), which automatically configures a temporary FIB entry on the reverse path taken by the first content chunk. That way, in case the FIB is empty (e.g., after booting) or if no FIB entry matches the name/prefix of the content in which the consumer is interested, only a single initial interest flooding is needed, while subsequent interests for chunks of that content can be unicast using the FIB entries thus auto-configured along the path. For example, in our experiments, after flooding an interest

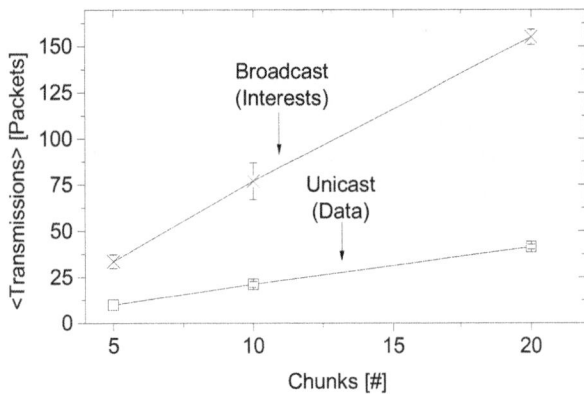

(a) Vanilla Interest Flooding

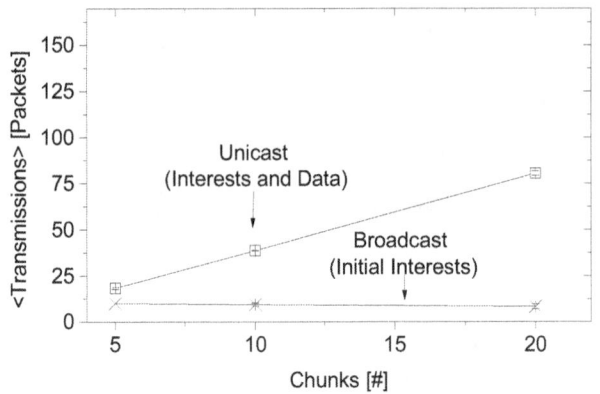

(b) Reactive Optimistic Name-based Routing

Figure 3: Single-consumer scenario. NDN performance for different routing schemes. Average number of packets transmitted in a network of 10 nodes to fetch content of various size.

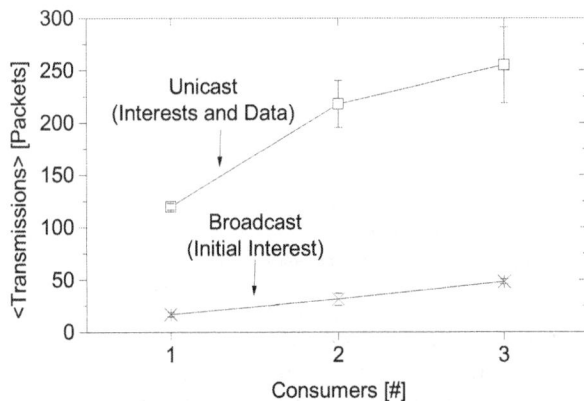

(a) Without caching

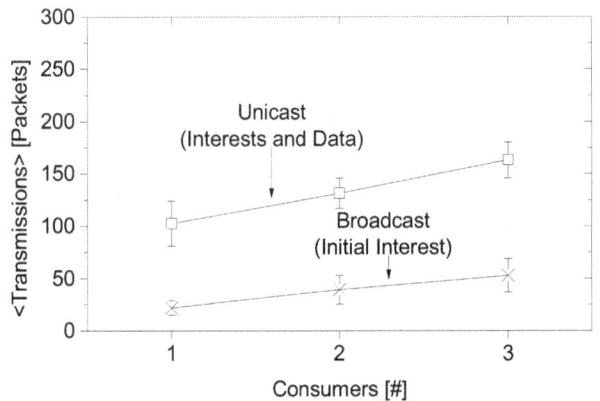

(b) With caching

Figure 4: Multi-consumer scenario. NDN performance for RONR and different content cache schemes. Average number of packets transmitted in a network of 20 nodes with a variable number of consumers.

for chunk /riot/text/a, nodes on the reverse path of that chunk store a temporary FIB entry for /riot/text/*, thus subsequent interests for chunks /riot/text/b, /riot/text/c can be unicast using the established path, instead of flooded.

RONR is optimistic because it first assumes that the whole content is stored on a single node (a cached replica or the original producer), which may not be the case in general. However, this assumption is reasonable in the IoT because typical content size is in the order of a few hundred bytes [17]. Furthermore, FIB entries timeout ensure that if the configured FIB entries do not lead to a node with the full content, the consumer will eventually revert to interest flooding, through which it can discover another node with the rest of the content, install new temporary FIB entries etc. This timeout strategy is common for reactive routing in multi-hop wireless scenarios [40].

In Figure 3(b), we show the results of an experiment using NDN with RONR, for the exact same topology and scenario as for Figure 3(a). We observe that the number of radio transmissions decrease about 50% compared to NDN with VIF. In particular the number of broadcast transmissions is drastically reduced because, with RONR, only the first

interest packet of a content item is flooded, while subsequent interests are unicast, using temporary FIB entries established by RONR. A quick back-of-the-envelope analysis shows that in a network of n nodes, and for k chunks of content, the number of transmissions is $(n - 1) + 2(k - \frac{1}{2})\sqrt{n}$, assuming again the average path length approximation $\sqrt{n}$. Therefore, RONR scales much better than VIF when network size or content size grows. RONR thus better fits IoT devices energy requirements compared to VIF, while still fitting other requirements of constrained devices by (i) not relying on any control traffic, and (ii) requiring minimal state, i.e., only temporary FIB entries on the reverse path of content that is sought after (not counting PIT state, of course).

An enhancement of RONR could be even more optimistic and tentatively aggregate prefixes in the following manner. If a FIB entry is pointing to an interface for content with prefix /riot/text/* and an interest for /riot/temp/c is answered by a chunk of content through the same interface (after the initial interest flooding phase), the enhancement would optimistically aggregate the prefixes and create a FIB entry for /riot/* pointing to this interface. In the best case, this will indeed lead to all the requested content matching this prefix, via unicast only. In the worst case, after unicast transmission and time-out, the consumer will eventually revert to interest flooding, through which it can discover another node with the rest of the content, install new temporary FIB entries etc. For this paper, however, we have only tested RONR without this enhancement, and leave its analysis for future work.

4.4 Multiple Consumers & Impact of Caching

In this section, we evaluate experimentally the impact of ICN caching. The same content (20 chunks) is accessed alternatively by one, two, or three consumers that are topologically close to one another (pairwise, maximum hop distance is 1). In order to accommodate for more consumers while keeping them apart from the producer with at least 2 hops, a larger topology shown in Figure 2(b) was used for the following experiments. To reduce signaling overhead, we use RONR as routing scheme for NDN interest packets.

In Figure 4(a) we show the results of our experiment with a disabled content cache. We observe that, as expected, the number of radio transmissions scales almost linearly with the number of consumers. In a network of n nodes, and for k chunks of content and m consumers within radio reach, the number of transmissions is $m \cdot ((n-1) + 2(k - \frac{1}{2})\sqrt{n})$, still assuming the average path length approximation $\sqrt{n}$.

Next, we enable cache capacity of 20 chunks on all nodes, which corresponds to RAM usage of 2 kBytes (2 % of 96 kbytes overall RAM). Figure 4(b) shows the results we obtained for the exact same topology and scenario as for Figure 4(a), except the caching. We observe that the number of radio transmissions needed to retrieve the content is drastically reduced, by up to 50% in this scenario. In detail, the number of broadcast transmissions is almost similar, while the number of unicast packets decreases substantially. This is consistent with the facts that the initial interest flooding (broadcasted) is not modified, while cached content chunk shorten unicast paths, thus reducing the number of unicast transmissions. In the best case, if the initial flood for subsequent consumers can be reduced to a local broadcast because only neighbors with cached content receive the interest, the number of transmissions becomes $2(k - \frac{1}{2})(\sqrt{n} + n - 1) + n + m - 2$.

4.5 Comparison with 6LoWPAN/RPL/UDP

In this section, we compare NDN with 6LoW-PAN/RPL/UDP, a common protocol suite for the current IoT. For fair comparison, we use the following setup. On the ICN side, we deploy RONR with a cache size of 2 kBytes, as this leads to the best performance results in our previous analysis. On the RPL side, we first let the network converge until the RPL root and the routing entries are installed in nodes, before we start the experiment (i.e., we factor out the control traffic transmissions necessary to bootstrap the network).

In Figure 5, we show the results we obtained for the exact same topology and scenario as for Figure 4(b), except the network stack used was 6LoWPAN/RPL/UDP with default settings instead of NDN. We observe that the 6LoW-PAN/RPL/UDP network stack yields much more transmissions compared to NDN (cf., Figure 4(b)), approximately three times more. This is due to two main factors. On one hand, the amount of control traffic generated by the *proactive* 6LoWPAN/RPL/UDP network stack is a big penalty

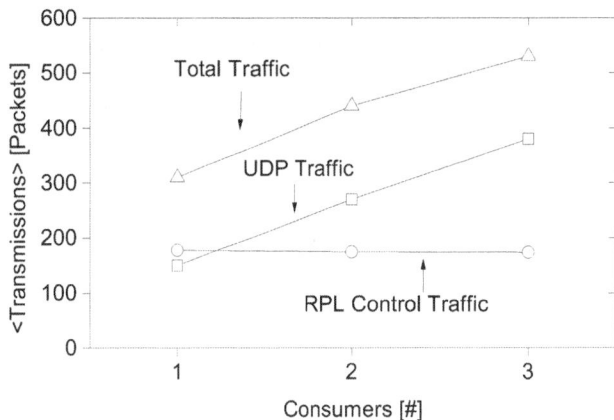

Figure 5: Multi-consumer scenario with 6LoW-PAN/RPL/UDP. Average number of packets transmitted in a network of 20 nodes.

compared to the *reactive* CCN approach we tested. On the other hand, compared to our CCN approach, the unicast paths created by the 6LoWPAN/RPL/UDP network stack do not benefit from *caching* and are thus always maximum length, which can in some cases be even longer than the shortest topological paths, as shown in [41]. Note that we have not used RPL extensions such as [39], which could reduce the length of unicast paths. Furthermore, as discussed in Section 4.1, we observed that the naming scheme and the header sizes were not a decisive factor explaining the performance gap between the CCN stack and the 6LoW-PAN/RPL/UDP in the experiments we conducted. All in all, we can conclude that NDN may be a potential alternative to 6LoWPAN/RPL/UDP, which should be studied more in the context of IoT in future work.

5. A POSTERIORI CHALLENGES: WHAT ARE THE LESSONS LEARNED

In this section, we gathered further considerations and observations concerning ICN in the Internet of Things, based on our practical experience with NDN implementation and deployment. In the following, we distinguish energy consumption aspects, wireless connectivity aspects, and communication model aspects.

5.1 Energy Consumption

Energy consumption is mainly impacted by network transmissions, which are affected by content naming, content caching, network flooding, and local wireless broadcast.

5.1.1 Impact of Names

Routing information about names and prefixes should dynamically be auto-configured in IoT devices. The resulting overhead not only depends on the routing protocol but also on the size of names to be processed in ICN packets. In our experiments, we deployed VIF, a very basic approach based on *flooding*, whereby each node in the network repeats (on all interfaces) each flooded packet upon first reception (on any interface).

Flooding is used (i) to disseminate an interest message when no forwarding information is available, or (ii) to disseminate names and topology information, e.g., with link state routing approaches [15], [16]. However, flooding is costly in terms of energy since each flood requires O(n) packet transmissions and O(nm) packet receptions, where n is the number of nodes in the network and m is the average node degree. Each packet received will not only be costly in terms of pure packet reception but will also trigger its processing, which includes CPU-expensive string comparisons with variable lengths, trying to match received names with names stored locally. Furthermore, recent work [42] identifies ICN packet processing as a CPU bottleneck, serious enough to provide DOS attack opportunities. This processing is even more costly on constrained devices since their CPU typically does not benefit from advanced functionalities such as prefetching or super scalar instruction set, and thus needs one cycle per byte compared. Table 2 shows a benchmark for the number of required CPU cycles per CCNlite operation for our implementation in RIOT. The top 3 functions, which represent 85% of the CPU cycles, involve string comparison and name matching.

These observations thus call for (i) the least possible recourse to flooding and (ii) the shortest possible names. Note that short names also ensure that packet fragmentation is avoided at the link layer: long names that do not fit in the MTU of the link layer split interest packets in several transmissions which is inefficient in terms of energy. Shorter names should however not sacrifice prefix aggregability, so that scalability remains in terms of number of nodes in the network vs. routing state. In our experiments, we have demonstrated the use of small, hierarchical names of 12 bytes and the minimal CCN header all of which carried by link layer packets with very constrained MTU (64 bytes). In practice, it still allowed about 30 bytes of content payload, which is appropriate for IoT scenarios, where content generated by sensors is in the order of a few hundred bytes per minute [17]. Even with slightly longer names implementing a typically deeper hierarchy as described in [17], there is still enough space for payload. For instance, with names such as *$/zone1/room2/dev7/temp/a$*, there is about 20 bytes for content payload with the link layer we used in our experiments.

Note however that human-readable names may not be required or useful in a context of machine-to-machine communication, whereby no humans are in the loop. More compact naming (e.g., a binary representation, or a more compact ASCII representation) may thus be applicable and would leave more space for content in packets constrained by small MTUs. Furthermore, the computations incurred by cryptographically-generated names (or parts of names) are expected to yield both substantial energy consumption penalty for constrained node in the IoT. In this paper, however, we do not consider security-related aspects for names – which are considerations that are orthogonal to the aspects studied here. Nevertheless, security mechanisms typically yield substantially longer headers. We can therefore also conclude that a standard CCN header compression scheme would be useful in the IoT.

5.1.2 Impact of Caching

The impact of in-network caching on energy aspects with ICN approaches has been studied by recent work such as [43], which indicates that energy consumption incurred by caching reduces energy efficiency. But on the other hand, studies such as [44] show that CCN can be more energy efficient than other content delivery approaches such as CDN and P2P by

# of instructions	Function
14,002,814	memcmp_ssse3
7,525,050	ccnl_nonce_find_or_append
4,062,659	ccnl_i_prefixof_c
1,462,304	dehead
956,238	ccnl_core_RX_i_or_c
895,590	ccnl_extract_prefix_nonce_ppkd
845,042	memcpy_ssse3

Table 2: CPU cycles per CCN function.

leveraging the most energy efficient devices in the network. It remains to be seen at large scale on the Internet which ICN approaches introduce low overhead in terms of energy consumption. In the IoT, to the best of our knowledge, there are no studies yet that focused on energy aspects of ICN due to the use of caching.

In Section 4, we demonstrated experimentally that savings in terms of energy consumption are possible thanks to (even small) in-network caching since (i) on-path or near-path caching can decrease the number of intermediate energy-challenged devices on the path to reach content in some scenarios, and (ii) content producers such as sensors could sleep more while their content could still be available in other caches in the network.

5.1.3 Impact of Local Wireless Broadcast

In case of multiple PIT hits, the NDN stack could use a single multicast transmission if all matching neighbors are reachable through the same wireless interface – which is the case in most IoT scenarios where nodes only have a single interface (omnidirectional radio). We have thus enhanced our NDN implementation with such a link-local multicast awareness mechanism called Content Forwarding Aggregation (CFA). In scenarios where multiple geographically close consumers are interested in the same content at approximately the same time, CFA leads to substantial gains in terms of number of radio transmissions necessary to deliver the content. With CFA, a content chunk may be forwarded as a single multicast to multiple nodes that have expressed interest in this content. Using link-local multicast, CFA reaches nodes within the same radio range without implementing explicitly location-awareness mechanisms.

Another opportunity to leverage the multicast nature of IoT devices' wireless interface concerns caching. Very often, a node will overhear unsolicited chunks of content that are being transmitted in its radio vicinity. In such case, instead of discarding this content, the node could cache this unsolicited chunk in its content store, if there is space left, with a lower priority than solicited content. We have thus enhanced our NDN implementation with such a mechanism, called Opportunistic Near-Path Caching (ONPC), which increases availability of the content and further reduces the number of radio transmissions in case of several consumers of the same content. However, due to lack of space, we do not show experimental results with CFA or ONPC in this paper.

5.2 Wireless Connectivity

Although ICN is applicable in wireless networks, several issues arise when applied to the wireless regime at work in IoT. In the following, we distinguish aspects concerning frame size, fragmentation, and bidirectional links.

5.2.1 Frame Size and Packet Fragmentation

Several link layer technologies are currently used in the IoT, and it is likely that multiple technologies will be used in the future, too. Currently, the dominant IoT link layer in the field of building automation and industrial automation is IEEE 802.15.4. The maximum frame size is very small (127 bytes or less). Other popular wireless link layers provide an even smaller maximum frame size, such as Bluetooth Low Energy [45] which typically allows a payload of ≈30 bytes. These frame sizes are more than ten to a hundred times smaller compared to traditional Ethernet or WiFi frames. Consequently, fragmentation and reassembly mechanisms are necessary. While Bluetooth provides its own, IEEE 802.15.4 does not. To bridge this gap, 6LoWPAN introduced (i) a standard header compression scheme, and a (ii) standard fragmentation and reassembly mechanism for IPv6 operation in the IoT, both on top of IEEE 802.15.4 link layer. It is worth noting that ICN cannot benefit from the same mechanisms for fragmentation and compression. Overlay architectures conflict with the memory constraints in the IoT (cf., Section 2.2) as well as with packet sizes of common IoT link layers.

In our real-world deployment, we demonstrated that NDN can be implemented directly on top of an IoT link layer, without compression/fragmentation mechanisms (see Sections 3 and 4). Omitting these optimizations is suitable for basic scenarios in which small enough names and small enough chunks can be used in the first place. Our results give confidence that we can already start with ICN in the IoT. However, in the future, ICN approaches for the IoT need an equivalent of what 6LoWPAN is providing for IPv6. For illustration, NDN will typically use up to 40 bytes for the header and data encoding, which is negligible in the common Internet (≈2% of the capacity of standard 1500 bytes MTU) but occupies ≈28% of the capacity of standard 802.15.4 frames. Neither can it be expected that all chunk sizes on all ICN networks will be defined by IEEE 802.15.4 frame size (which would be inefficient), nor can it be expected that names indicated in interest packets will always be short enough to fit in a single 802.15.4 frame of 127 bytes, for example. Note that fragmentation approaches need to take into account that altered chunks can break security and naming schemes.

5.2.2 Bidirectional links

Many ICN approaches assume bidirectional links. This is not true in general in spontaneous wireless networks [5], and thus this assumption does not hold in the IoT. In such context, a high proportion of links are asymmetric, e.g., 10% loss rate from A to B and 80% loss rate from B to A. In reality, a substantial fraction of the links are unidirectional, i.e., loss rate strictly below 100% in one direction, and 100% loss rate in the reverse direction. Last but not least, wireless link quality between two nodes A and B can vary significantly over time, even at small time scales [38] – a phenomenon we also experienced in our experiments.

The above wireless connectivity characteristics lead to the following observations. ICN routing protocols running on constrained devices need to satisfy conflicting requirements (i) negligible control traffic to reduce energy consumption and small state to fit memory constraints, while at the same time (ii) dynamic tracking of wireless link to avoid non-functional paths. The goal is to not forward an interest in the first place if reverse link is not "good enough". The overhead for failing is a reverse path taken by content which often fails and will lead to PIT time-outs, interest flooding, etc. Subsequently, this might lead to the same failing reverse path – and thus be very inefficient both in terms of energy and delay.

5.3 Different Communication Models

The ICN communication model is based on a *pull* paradigm: in a first phase, a node expresses interest in some content, and in a second phase, the node should receive this content. However, this communication model alone is not sufficient to accommodate typical traffic patterns in the IoT. Aside of pull, these patterns include for instance *push* paradigms (e.g., for actuators), and *observe* paradigms [46] whereby a node can register for updates from a given content producer (e.g., a sensor measuring the real-time evolution of a given parameter). Note that explicit acknowledgements are also typically used in this context, for example patterns such as push+ACK, or request+reply+ACK are the norm in this domain. Recent work has started to integrate these patterns in ICN, such as [24] which proposes a push mechanism for CCN on sensor networks.

Furthermore, the simplified communication model at the base of ICN was initially designed with the assumption that the number of consumers is much larger than the number of producers, targeting use cases that are comparable to the scenarios CDNs aim for. Such an assumption does not hold in general in the IoT, where consumers (e.g., a data sink) are often outnumbered by producers (e.g., sensors). In consequence, content caching strategies designed for scenarios similar to CDN will not be efficient in the IoT, and thus, alternative strategies should be designed for content replication and content cache replacement in the IoT with ICN.

6. CONCLUSION AND PERSPECTIVES

ICN has recently been identified as a potential alternative network paradigm for the Internet of Things. In this paper, we have carried out experiments with NDN on a real IoT deployment consisting in tens of constrained nodes in multiple rooms of multiple buildings. Based on this experience, we have shown that ICN is indeed applicable in the IoT, and that it can offer advantages over an approach based on 6LoWPAN/IPv6/RPL in terms of energy consumption, as well as in terms of RAM and ROM footprint. We have proposed several interoperable NDN enhancements to decrease energy consumption and routing state. Furthermore, we identified several areas where future work is needed. Topics include (i) an efficient header compression and fragmentation/reassembly adaptation layer below NDN to fit typically small frame sizes, (ii) IoT-specific content replication and cache replacement strategies, (iii) enhancements of the basic ICN communication model to accommodate IoT traffic patterns, (iv) further studies on the impact of caching on content availability in the context of sleeping nodes, and (v) short naming schemes optimized for constrained devices.

Acknowledgments We would like to thank the anonymous reviewers and our shepherd, Lan Wang, for their valuable comments. Furthermore, we would like to thank Lixia Zhang for first discussions about NDN support in RIOT. This work was partially supported by ANR and BMBF within the SAFEST and Peeroskop projects, and the DAAD within the guest lecture program.

7. REFERENCES

[1] B. Ahlgren *et al.*, "A survey of information-centric networking," *IEEE Communications Magazine*, vol. 50, no. 7, pp. 26–36, 2012.

[2] L. Atzori *et al.*, "The internet of things: A survey," *Computer Networks*, vol. 54, no. 15, pp. 2787–2805, 2010.

[3] C. Bormann *et al.*, "Terminology for Constrained-Node Networks," *RFC 7228*, 2014.

[4] L. Mirani, "Chip-makers are Betting that Moore's Law Won't Matter in the Internet of Things," 2014. [Online]. Available: http://qz.com/218514

[5] J. Cordero *et al.*, "Enabling Multihop Communication in Spontaneous Wireless Networks," in *ACM SIGCOMM eBook on "Recent Advances in Networking", Volume 1, Chapter 9, pp. 413-457*, 2013.

[6] ZigBee Alliance, "ZigBee Specifications," 2012.

[7] G. Montenegro *et al.*, "Transmission of IPv6 Packets over IEEE 802.15.4 Networks," *RFC 4944*, 2007.

[8] T. Winter and P. Thubert, "RPL: IPv6 Routing Protocol for Low-Power and Lossy Networks," *RFC 6550*, 2012.

[9] A. Ghodsi *et al.*, "Information-centric networking: Ready for the real world?" *Dagstuhl Reports (Seminar 12361)*, vol. 2, no. 9, pp. 1–14, 2012.

[10] V. Jacobson *et al.*, "Networking named content," in *Proc. of ACM CoNEXT*, 2009, pp. 1–12.

[11] N. Fotiou *et al.*, "Illustrating a publish-subscribe internet architecture," *Telecommunication Systems*, vol. 51, no. 4, pp. 233–245, 2012.

[12] C. Dannewitz *et al.*, "Network of information (netinf): An information-centric networking architecture," *Computer Comm.*, vol. 36, no. 7, pp. 721 – 735, 2013.

[13] T. Koponen *et al.*, "A data-oriented (and beyond) network architecture," *SIGCOMM Comput. Commun. Rev.*, vol. 37, no. 4, pp. 181–192, 2007.

[14] D. Kutscher *et al.*, "ICN Research Challenges," IRTF Internet Draft 02, 2014.

[15] M. Hoque *et al.*, "NLSR: Named-data Link State Routing Protocol," in *Proc. of ACM SIGCOMM WS on ICN*, 2013, pp. 15–20.

[16] L. Wang *et al.*, "Ospfn: An ospf based routing protocol for named data networking," 2012.

[17] J. Martocci *et al.*, "Building Automation Routing Requirements in Low-Power and Lossy Networks," *RFC 5867*, 2010.

[18] B. Saadallah *et al.*, "CCNx for Contiki: implementation details," in *Tech. Report RT-0432*. INRIA, 2012.

[19] T. Biswas *et al.*, "Contextualized information-centric home network," in *ACM SIGCOMM*, 2013.

[20] L. Grieco *et al.*, "Architecting information centric etsi-m2m systems," in *Proc. of PERCOM*, 2014.

[21] Y. Zhang *et al.*, "ICN based Architecture for IoT," in *IETF Internet Draft*, 2013.

[22] Y. Yu *et al.*, "Interest propagation in named data manets," in *Proc. of IEEE ICNC*, 2013, pp. 1118–1122.

[23] M. Amadeo *et al.*, "Named data networking: A natural design for data collection in wireless sensor networks," in *Proc. of IEEE/IFIP Wireless Days*, 2013, pp. 1–6.

[24] J. Francois *et al.*, "CCN Traffic Optimization for IoT," in *Proc. of NoF*, 2013.

[25] F. Angius *et al.*, "Bloogo: Bloom filter based gossip algorithm for wireless ndn," in *Proc. of ACM NoM Workshop*, 2012, pp. 25–30.

[26] J. Burke *et al.*, "Securing instrumented environments over content-centric networking: the case of lighting control," *arXiv preprint arXiv:1208.1336*, 2012.

[27] S. Arianfar *et al.*, "On Content-Centric Router Design and Implications," in *Proc. of ACM ReARCH*, 2010.

[28] D. Perino *et al.*, "A Reality Check for Content Centric Networking," in *Proc. of ACM ICN WS*, 2011.

[29] D. G. Murray *et al.*, "The Case for Crowd Computing," in *Proc. of ACM MobiHeld WS*, 2010, pp. 39–44.

[30] P. Levis *et al.*, "Overview of existing routing protocols for low power and lossy networks," *IETF Internet Draft*, 2009.

[31] "CCN Lite: Lightweight implementation of the Content Centric Networking protocol," 2014. [Online]. Available: http://ccn-lite.net

[32] E. Baccelli *et al.*, "RIOT OS: Towards an OS for the Internet of Things," in *IEEE INFOCOM*, 2013.

[33] "RIOT open source code on GitHub," 2014. [Online]. Available: https://github.com/RIOT-OS/RIOT

[34] A. Brandt, J. Buron, and G. Porcu, "Home Automation Routing Requirements in Low-Power and Lossy Networks," IETF, RFC 5826, 2010.

[35] Z. Fan *et al.*, "The new frontier of communications research: Smart grid and smart metering," in *Proc. of ACM e-Energy*, 2010, pp. 115–118.

[36] G. Wittenburg *et al.*, "Fence Monitoring - Experimental Evaluation of a Use Case for Wireless Sensor Networks," in *Proc. of EWSN*, 2007.

[37] M. Baar *et al.*, "The ScatterWeb MSB-A2 Platform for Wireless Sensor Networks," FU Berlin, TR, 2008.

[38] E. Baccelli and C. Perkins, "Multi-hop Ad Hoc Wireless Communication," *IETF Internet Draft*, 2014.

[39] M. Goyal *et al.*, "Reactive Discovery of Point-to-Point Routes in Low-Power and Lossy Networks," *RFC 6997*, 2013.

[40] C. Richard *et al.*, "Defining an Optimal Active Route Timeout for the AODV Routing Protocol," in *Proc. of IEEE SECON*, 2005, pp. 26–29.

[41] W. Xie *et al.*, "A Performance Analysis of Point-to-Point Routing along a Directed Acyclic Graph in Low Power and Lossy Networks," in *Proc. of IEEE NBiS*, 2010, pp. 111–116.

[42] M. Wählisch *et al.*, "Backscatter from the Data Plane – Threats to Stability and Security in Information-Centric Network Infrastructure," *Computer Networks*, vol. 57, no. 16, pp. 3192–3206, 2013.

[43] N. Choi *et al.*, "In-network caching effect on optimal energy consumption in content-centric networking," in *Proc. of IEEE ICC*, 2012, pp. 2889–2894.

[44] U. Lee *et al.*, "Greening the internet with content-centric networking," in *ACM e-Energy*, 2010.

[45] M. Isomaki *et al.*, "Transmission of IPv6 Packets over BLUETOOTH Low Energy," *IETF Internet Draft*, 2014.

[46] Z. Shelby *et al.*, "Constrained application protocol (coap)," *IETF Internet Draft*, 2014.

Communication Patterns for Web Interaction in Named Data Networking

Ilya Moiseenko
UCLA
iliamo@cs.ucla.edu

Mark Stapp
Cisco Systems
mjs@cisco.com

David Oran
Cisco Systems
oran@cisco.com

ABSTRACT

Named Data Networking (NDN) is an information-centric networking architecture that has recently attracted significant attention. At first glance NDN's pure pull-based communication model seems to match the request-reply mechanics of HTTP/Web interactions. In reality, modern Web communication patterns involve passing client-side information and/or application state in requests. As we attempt to apply these communication patterns to NDN, we find that it is not immediately clear how to use NDN effectively. In this paper, we examine multiple diverse approaches to running modern Web-like applications over the NDN communication architecture, discussing advantages and drawbacks of each of the proposed approaches. Our primary goal is to start a focused discussion of how NDN can support modern Web communication patterns effectively.

Categories and Subject Descriptors

C.2 [**COMPUTER-COMMUNICATION NETWORKS**]: Network Architecture and Design; Network Protocols; Distributed Systems

Keywords

NDN; REST; Web

1. INTRODUCTION

The Web today is a universal platform for many kinds of services, from familiar content browsing and media streaming to purpose-built applications hosted in browsers and in stand-alone agents. The backbone of the web is the HTTP protocol [1] [2], which is based on a request/response model running on top of a point-to-point connection to a server. A client sends a request in the form of a message containing a URI [3], request meta-information, and possible body content. The server responds with a message containing entity meta-information, and possible entity-body content.

Named Data Networking is a recently proposed general-purpose, information-centric network architecture [4] [5]. It uses a pull-based model: clients send requests into the network in order to retrieve data; no other unsolicited transmission is allowed. NDN

defines two types of network packets; the two possess highly asymmetric properties. Clients send Interest packets, which contain only a name and a minimal set of additional control fields. Servers respond with Data packets, which contain the data associated with the name in the corresponding Interest.

In this paper, we examine diverse approaches to matching the needs of an important category of modern applications to the capabilities of the NDN protocol architecture. Challenges present themselves when we attempt to support Web communication as it might take place over a future NDN internet. Our goal is to stimulate progress on this topic in the research community. We do not believe it is either desirable or straightforward to simply reproduce HTTP bit-for-bit within an NDN protocol envelope. Rather, we explore the approach of enabling NDN-based Web clients to pass the necessary meta-information and application state to Web server applications that use NDN. We start with the necessary abstract communication patterns and use those patterns to explore how they might be realized within NDN protocol mechanics.

In Section 2 we provide a brief overview of the NDN architecture. In Section 3 we describe the current state-of-the-art with Web applications over the IP Internet and explain some of the immediate problems that arise when IP is replaced with NDN. In Section 4 we introduce NDN communication patterns suitable for Web-like interaction and provide a high-level examination of their advantages and drawbacks. Section 5 describes an analytic model used to quantify the efficiency of the proposed NDN communication patterns. Section 6 contains a summary of our observations and a comparison chart of the communication patterns discussed in this paper.

2. NAMED DATA NETWORKING

Named Data Networking (NDN) proposes the replacement of IP's endpoint-to-endpoint communication model with one centered around named objects. NDN offers two distinct packet types: *Interest* and *Data*. Both types carry a *name*, which uniquely identifies an information object. Names in NDN are hierarchically structured, and contain distinct components. Large objects that cannot be carried in a single Data packet are *segmented* into multiple packets; the segment number is carried as a component at the end of the name. An example representation of an NDN name might be: `/com/example/data/object/1`. Applications are expected to design appropriate naming schemes for the kinds of communication they require.

To retrieve data, a consumer requests it by sending an Interest packet containing the name of the desired content. A router uses this name and its Forwarding Information Base (FIB) to forward the Interest closer to the location of the data. When an Interest reaches an entity who has a matching Data packet, the Data packet is returned to the consumer. Each router who forwards the Interest constructs an entry in a Pending Interest Table (PIT). Each PIT entry contains the Interest name, the ingress interface(s) where the Interest has arrived, and the egress interface(s) to which the Interest has been forwarded. Data packets are returned by following the reverse path of the Interest, using the per-Interest state kept in the PIT.

NDN routers can cache any passing Data packet in a data structure called a Content Store (CS). A cached Data packet can be used to satisfy an Interest. One of NDN's central tenets is that a consumer does not care whether a Data packet was served from a router cache or from the original producer: the trust in data is decoupled from the place and time the data was obtained, and any consumer can validate the integrity and provenance of the content using the Data packet's signature.

Crucially, one Interest packet returns at most one Data packet. A client retrieves a large, segmented object by sending multiple Interests naming each segment. In NDN, there are no unsolicited Data packets; the PIT mechanism in a router prevents unsolicited Data packets from being processed or forwarded. This symmetry between Interest and Data packets is often called *flow balance*.

3. WEB INTERACTION

Arguably, the most widespread and economically important of the Internet's application infrastructures is the modern Web, which uses HTTP/TCP/IP as its foundational protocol underpinnings. In addition to carrying content data, the HTTP protocol defines a wide range of meta-data for both requests and responses. The meta-data are carried in HTTP headers, part of the messaging protocol. The meta-data sent in client requests may be information about the client application itself, including information about acceptable content languages and data encodings.

A large fraction of these Web applications use a transactional paradigm known as Representational State Transfer (REST) [6]. REST improves scalability by distributing application state from servers to clients. A pure RESTful request is self-contained — it carries all the information necessary for a service to process the request. Without the client-side context, a RESTful service may be inefficient or impaired, or may not be able to function at all. The familiar HTTP cookie is a simple form of distributed context, where a service uses the HTTP protocol to convey tokens, often opaque, to its clients. The tokens are typically unique to each client; this allows the service to associate multiple requests from a given client together. The cookie may carry client-side state directly, or may be used as a reference to state held at the server.

The usability of these distributed applications depends on the latency between user action and the rendering of a result. Because the Web is composed of multiple highly distributed services, this issue of latency (round-trips within the transport or the application protocol) has considerable importance in the system design. Modern browsers and other applications have evolved to be ever more efficient in the way they use round-trips, by caching content locally, and by reusing DNS information and TCP connections. Some modern browsers even speculatively initiate DNS queries and TCP connection activity in order to improve perceived responsiveness [7].

As we view the current state of HTTP/RESTful communication, then, we see these key points:

- Clients have data to send in their requests, in the form of HTTP header meta-data and other application-specific RESTful state.
- Many client requests are intimately bound to the client context data associated with them; the context and the request are carried together in the HTTP communication protocol messages. The client-specific data tends to make each request

unique even when clients are accessing common resources or services.
- Latency and number of network round-trips are key factors in efficiency and perceived responsiveness.

Given our understanding of the existing NDN protocols, RESTful interactions encounter a number of challenges:

- All of the client-side context and meta-data associated with a request must be encoded in the Interest name field: no other field is present in the base NDN architecture.
- NDN Content objects are immutable, and the object names are bound to fixed data. Services are not able to return different results based on client-specific processing unless the clients use unique names in their requests.
- NDN's stateful forwarding supports clients (consumers) who do not have to have a globally-routable address (name). Web services that require bidirectional data flow cannot get their own requests to their clients unless the clients have routable names.
- Many web sites and RESTful applications depend on being able to identify (or at least count) the specific clients making requests. NDN mechanisms like Interest aggregation and pervasive caching prevent producers from seeing some Interest packets.

In the next section, we will examine a range of approaches to supporting RESTful and Web applications on NDN networks. Each approach addresses the challenges we have outlined above in a different way, adapting the basic NDN protocols in more or less significant ways.

4. NDN COMMUNICATION PATTERNS

In this section, we explore communication patterns suitable for running transactional and interactive REST- or Web-like applications over NDN. We focus on the key issue as we see it: how can servers obtain the client meta-data and context information that is associated with client requests? We start with an approach that relies solely on the existing design of NDN, but several important drawbacks compel us to try out alternative patterns which introduce various degrees of changes in NDN. The two types of NDN packets divide the discussion into two corresponding categories: approaches using clients' Interest packets alone, and approaches where the server is obliged to retrieve information from client-sourced Data packets.

We discuss benefits and disadvantages of each communication pattern as well as the effect each has on the network, considering several specific factors as we examine each approach:

- Interest name size: impact on routers
- Data name size: impact on Data packet efficiency
- Round-trips
- Client data segmentation and reliable delivery
- Potential security vulnerabilities: reflection, amplification, flooding, spoofing/poisoning

4.1 Name Component

In the basic NDN protocol design, an Interest packet carries little more than a Name field. In some previous work, Interest names have been used to pass commands to an NDN router [8], to pass authenticated requests to a lighting controller [9], and to convey the current state of a system to support distributed dataset synchronization [10].

Today's interactive Web applications need to pass meta-information and application-specific data with their requests, so we begin by examining the consequences of using the Interest's Name field to convey that information. An Interest packet is routed through the network via the name it carries. Application meta-information and client-side data required for a particular type of request could be carried by appending it using one or more trailing name components. This pattern is illustrated in Figure 1.

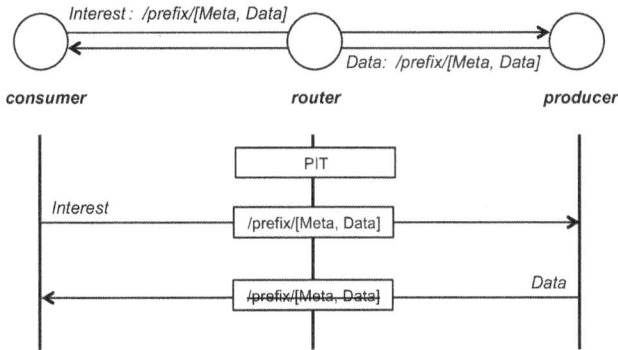

Figure 1: Interest name carries client-side information.

This communication pattern works with the current NDN architecture, and naively seems fairly natural. The client-side data is bound to each Interest packet directly, satisfying the server's expectation that the client-side context will be present along with each client request.

However, there are a number of significant drawbacks to this simple approach. The first concern is related to stateful packet forwarding in NDN. Contemporary HTTP requests that perform browsing often convey hundreds of bytes (or even kilobytes) of supplemental information in HTTP headers [11] [12]. If this meta-information and application-specific data is placed in the Interest name, there may be a significant additional overhead on intermediary NDN routers. Each router will have to process these large names, increasing the computational load, and the accumulated name state held in their PIT data structures will consume substantially more memory.

A second concern is decreased network throughput and increased nodal processing delays. The entire name must be echoed in each Data packet. Inside the NDN router, longer names may lead to more operations on name components, slowing down packet processing. The name-to-payload ratio can turn out to be far from optimal. Regardless of the eventual fragmentation scheme NDN proposes, large names will reduce available packet space, reducing space for the actual content. This leads to decreased goodput, and potentially more fragmentation and reassembly operations per Data packet.

A third concern is the possibility of cases where a single Interest name is not able to carry all required application data. While there is no clear consensus within the NDN community on the maximum allowed size of the name, there is a clear possibility that meta-information and application data (e.g. HTTP POST or a large cookie) may be larger than the maximum name length can accommodate. Within the constraints of the current NDN protocol, meta-information and application data would have to be subdivided into multiple Interests' names, transmitted as multiple Interest packets and reassembled by the producer. Figure 2 illustrates how NDN might accommodate transmitting arbitrary sized client-side data to the producer, and retrieving an arbitrary sized response from it.

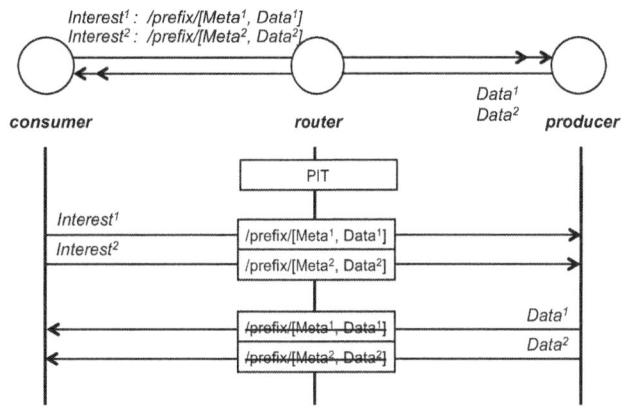

Figure 2: Client data carried in multiple Interests.

According to this pattern, the consumer sends no fewer Interests than needed to both accommodate client-side data in Interests and fetch all segments of the producer's reply. This pattern appears to take only a single round-trip to transmit the whole request and receive the whole reply. But once multiple related packet transmissions are introduced, we now need to consider some sort of reliable delivery of consumer-supplied information. That is, the client must re-transmit its Interests in the absence of any timely response or acknowledgement that they have been delivered. This complexity leads us to examine some alternative protocol approaches.

The conventional design of NDN interactions is that the producer acknowledges arrival of Interest packets in its Data packets, but the situation may be more nuanced. The completion time for Web and application requests requiring dynamic on-demand content can vary widely. As a result, it is not clear how the client should estimate waiting time between Interest retransmissions. One extreme is to use an Interest retransmission timer at the scale of network RTT. But this may result in many unnecessary retransmissions of Interests if the server processing time is significantly greater than RTT. The other extreme is to use a timer scaled to the tolerable application response delay. This in turn results in poor responsiveness in cases when network retransmission is indeed necessary. NDN protocol mechanics do not inherently distinguish network-level and application-level responsiveness, despite the substantially differing time scales.

One solution might be for the producer to use Data packets to acknowledge delivery of Interest packets containing meta-information and application data. The producer application would acknowledge each of these Interest packets prior to the execution of the actual content request, resulting in a two-phase operation. First, an initial set of Interest packets conveys the client-side data; Data packets from the producer acknowledge receipt of this information. Then a second round of Interest packets retrieves the actual producer-side content. This pattern is illustrated in Figure 3.

Note that this approach employs parallel Interest transmission to reduce overall latency. Separating the delivery of client data from the Interests used to retrieve producer content eliminates the need for all Interests in the exchange to use the same name, reducing the Interest size penalty. However, a significant problem with this approach is that the first round of 'acknowledgement' Data packets must be signed with the producer's private key in order to be considered valid. Signing a Data packet is computationally costly. If malicious clients flood Interests like these, this could lead to a denial of service (DoS) attack on the producer. In addition, the producer requires some means of associating the client-side data in

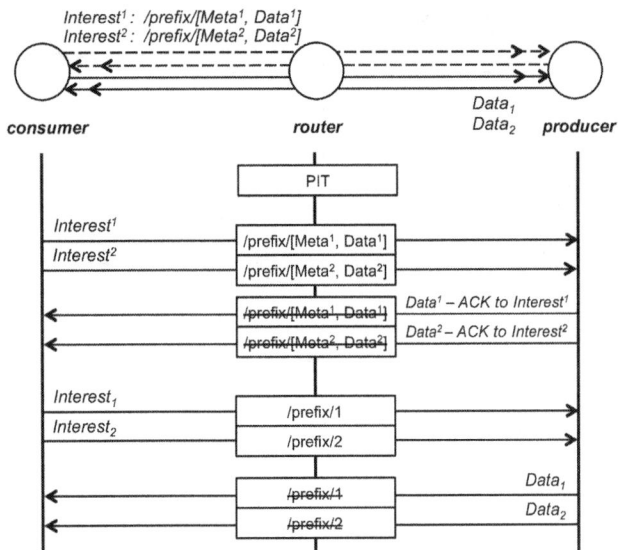

Figure 3: Two-phase Interest exchange.

the initial round of Interests with the subsequent Interests for the producer's content, resulting in more interaction state at the server.

4.2 Compressed name component

Including significant client-side data in Interest names raises concerns about memory scalability for the PITs of intermediary NDN routers, and decreased throughput due to the need to echo the entire name in each Data packet. These concerns can be partially addressed by compressing the client-side data into a constant size compact representation, and using this representation in the router PIT and in Data messages.

To achieve compression, a specialized Name component could be introduced to hold client meta-information and application data. An NDN router recognizing this specialized name component could then compute a hash of the component. This operation would effectively reduce the amount of state held in the PIT, compressing variable meta-information and application data into a constant size hash value. In order to forward Data packets back to the consumer, the producer application would replace the specialized name component with the corresponding hash value. As a result, Data packet names would continue to match the names in the PITs of intermediary routers, while occupying less space. This technique is illustrated in Figure 4.

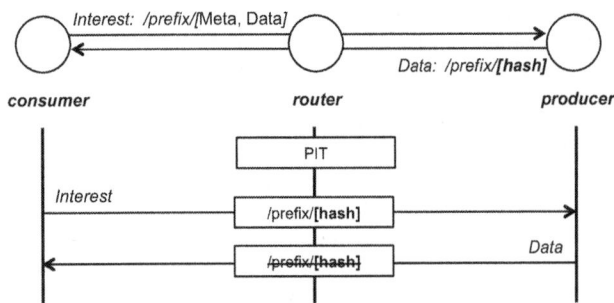

Figure 4: Consumer-supplied name-component is compressed to a hash.

4.3 Common Issues with Interest Names

Even with name component compression, all protocol approaches where meta-information and application data are pushed in Interest packet name components still have a number of common problems.

Exposure of meta-information and application data impairs confidentiality. If meta-information similar to HTTP cookies and HTTP headers such as Referer and User-agent are passed unencrypted in an Interest name component, the user can be easily tracked and deanonymized by a third-party observer. If security-sensitive data is held in these meta-information structures, the compromise could be even more substantial.

Signature generation must be performed on-the-fly for all Data packets that acknowledge the arrival of Interest packets with names carrying meta-information and application data. The per-client information creates names that are unpredictable, so the producer application must build and sign the corresponding Data packets dynamically. This introduces a potential vulnerability to a resource-exhaustion attack. NDN signature generation with public key cryptography is computationally expensive — significantly more expensive than, for example, SYN cookie generation.

Interest packet flooding in NDN networks can be a vector for Distributed Denial of Service (DDoS) attacks [13]. It has been shown that many Interest flooding attacks can be mitigated by exploiting stateful forwarding in NDN routers, such as by observing the rate with which Interests successfully retrieve Data packets on a per-prefix per-interface basis [14]. If meta-information and application data is pushed in Interests and if producer applications acknowledge every Interest with a Data packet, the per-prefix per-interface statistics may be distorted. An artificially high Interest satisfaction rate might jeopardize detection and mitigation of Interest flooding attacks.

4.4 Application Data field

We have examined some approaches to carrying client-side information in Interest names; now we'll explore sending request meta-data in the Interest packet, but outside the Interest name. In this approach, an Interest carries the additional application data in an *ApplicationData* field. This field would contain opaque data, and thereby not influence the operation of NDN routers or their processing in any way. The Interest name only requests the named content, and does not carry any client- or application-specific information. Figure 5 illustrates this approach.

The client includes an AppData field in its "base" Interest packet - the Interest for segment zero of a possibly segmented Data object. For Web-like interactions, the AppData field would carry meta-information about the client application, including stored cookies (i.e. what is found today in HTTP headers). In a standalone REST-ful application, the field would carry client-side application context data.

The AppData field is opaque to routers. No special name components are present, and no special name processing takes place at routers. If a client Interest packets name a cacheable object, intermediate routers can perform normal CS processing and return the cached data. If an application requires server-side processing, client Interests must use unique-ified names so that Interests from different clients avoid aggregation.

The client does not have to send the entire AppData in each Interest during a multi-segment exchange. In an ongoing exchange of packets to retrieve larger, segmented Data objects, the server may need to associate the correct client context with each individual Interest in order to respond properly. To accomplish this, the

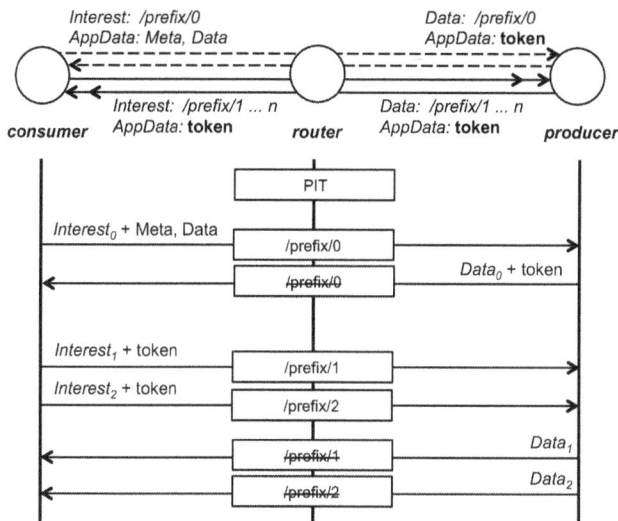

Figure 5: Interest carrying ApplicationData field.

server could generate a token — presumably shorter than the entire client context data — and return it to the client with the first Data packet. Subsequent Interests then would include this token in the AppData, allowing the server to properly associate the client meta-data with each individual Interest packet. If a series of exchanges required dynamic, frequently updated client context, obviously that context would have to be transferred between client and server as it changed.

Employing such a token mechanism requires that each Interest contain either the client context, or a corresponding server-generated token. This may affect a client's choice of initial Interest window size. If the initial Interest window size is just one, data fetching efficiency during the first round trip is reduced. If the initial Interest window is greater than one, the client has not been offered a server-side token, so it must transmit redundant application data in each Interest in this window. The choice of initial window size for Interests using a scheme like this may have delicate trade-offs.

The communication pattern with the Application Data field has the following benefits:

- The Interest name does not need any special processing. There is no need for complex name matching at the PIT or CS: exact-match for names is available.

- The application context information travels directly with the Interests; the client context, name, and returning data remain bound together.

- The application data can be transferred just once, with the initial Interest. Subsequent Interests can refer to the context if a server-generated token is returned in Data packets.

- No additional round-trips are needed.

Any scheme that "pushes" client data in Interest packets increases Interest packet size, possibly substantially. The NDN property of flow balance assumes that Interest packets will generally be small compared to the corresponding Data packets. Pushing 'unsolicited' data might compromise that property. To address this concern we might consider a limit on the size of Interest packets. A 4KB limit, for example, would be adequate for most current Web-like interactions [11]. However, this is still quite large — possibly large enough to make bandwidth accounting for Interests more important. A RESTful application that required a larger client payload would need to send multiple Interests, or use a different mechanism.

4.5 Data Locator field

The alternative to pushing client-side data with Interest packets is a communication pattern where the producer application pulls data it needs from the client. An essential piece of such protocols is a so called Interest-Interest exchange [15]. In this exchange, an initial Interest packet is expressed by the consumer application as usual. This initial Interest prompts the producer application to express one or more Interest packets in return. These requests from the producer retrieve client-specific information from the client; the producer then uses that information to satisfy the client's original Interests.

The Interest-Interest information could be placed in the initial client Interest name, but this approach would suffer from some of the same constraints as the examples in the previous sections — extremely long NDN names have drawbacks. Enclosing one name in another, for example, will not allow both names to approach their maximum lengths, which is inconvenient for application designers.

In our view, a better alternative would be to introduce an optional *DataLocator* field in the Interest packet. The presence of the DataLocator would serve as an indication for the producer that some supplemental information — meta-information, consumer-supplied data, etc. — is available to be fetched from the client before processing the initial request. The DataLocator would therefore contain a name the producer could use to express Interests that reach the client application. We discuss some variations of this mechanism below.

4.5.1 Routable name

This pattern requires the consumer application to provide a routable name at which it can be reached. The client must be prepared to package necessary meta information and application data in properly-formatted and signed Data packet(s). The consumer application might acquire a routable prefix from the point of presence (PoP) of the Internet Service Provider (ISP) that it is currently connected to, or through some other means.

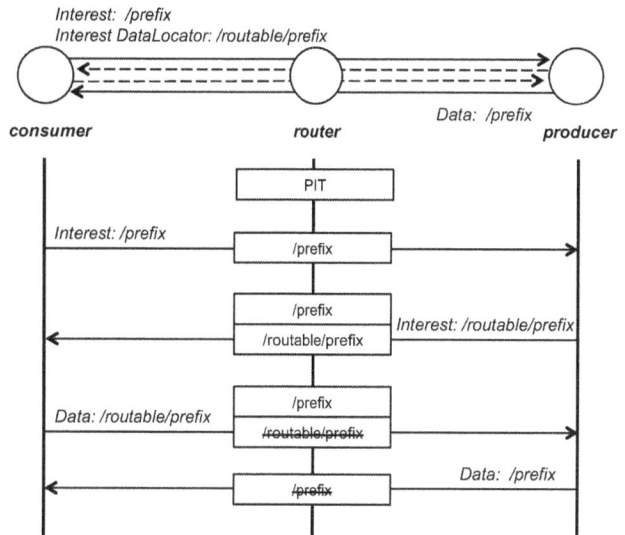

Figure 6: Interest-Interest exchange with routable name.

The consumer application sends an Interest packet containing the name for the producer to use in a DataLocator field. When the producer application receives the Interest, it transmits an Interest packet using the name specified in the DataLocator field to fetch meta-information and/or application data associated with the client's request. This communication pattern is illustrated in Figure 6.

The immediate advantage of this protocol is eliminating "pushed" data from client's Interests, which do not need to convey more than a single name. This restores the NDN flow balance property. A second important benefit is that the producer application is now in control of the data retrieval process. The producer is subject to standard NDN flow control and congestion control mechanisms as it retrieves Data from the client.

A third benefit is that some client-side data can benefit from NDN's natural on-path caching. Web cookies that represent the state of the server, kept on the client, may be stable for extended periods of time. Client data associated with related idempotent requests (e.g. HTTP GETs) can be cached in the intermediary routers that are located closer to the producer. Both the client and server therefore benefit from the NDN mechanisms that localize traffic and reduce latency.

However, the use of routable names for the server to fetch client data has several drawbacks. First, the client must acquire and convey a routable name prefix. A mobile consumer will either have to acquire a new prefix every time its connectivity changes, or use some sort of indirection service to map a stable name alias to its current routable prefix. This adds complexity, and introduces the possibility of traffic interruptions.

Second, the DataLocator mechanism's use of a routable name could be used to launch a reflection attack involving the producer. If an attacker specifies the name of a target third party, the producer will be induced to direct Interests to that third party. The reflection attack might be mitigated if the DataLocator is inspected when Interests enter the client's Internet Service Provider (ISP) network. The ISP ingress router could perform a check similar to an ingress filter in Reverse Path Forwarding (RPF) [16], accepting and forwarding Interest packets carrying DataLocators that will route to the source face. The router would drop any Interests with DataLocator names that would route elsewhere.

4.5.2 Non-routable transient name

The problems caused by the use of routable prefixes in the DataLocator field prompt us to explore the possibility of using non-routable prefixes for client-side data. This approach uses the per-packet router PIT state to construct an ephemeral path for Interests going back from the producer to the client in a manner somewhat like Kite [17]. As shown in (Figure 7), this introduces several changes in the forwarding mechanism of an NDN router:

1. The client constructs a unique name, preferably using a distinguished (by convention) non-routable prefix, and includes it in a DataLocator field.
2. When an Interest containing a DataLocator field arrives at a router, the DataLocator name is saved in the PIT along with the name in the Interest packet itself.
3. The producer responds with an Interest using the non-routable name taken from the DataLocator. As the producer's Interest moves through the network, each NDN router performs an exact match on the producer's Interest name using the extended PIT entries created as it forwarded the client's original Interest. If the router finds a match, it creates a new PIT entry for the non-routable name with the egress interface matching the ingress interface of the original Interest. The FIB is not consulted: the producer's Interest is forwarded on the inverse path of the consumer's original Interest packet using the PIT alone.

The DataLocator name is not independently routable. If the server (or anyone else) tries to access this information object outside the context of the enclosing Interest/Data exchange, the operation will fail. Further, since the names used cannot be forwarded outside the reverse path, reflection attacks are eliminated.

The fact that these non-routable Interests bypass the normal FIB does not prevent them from being satisfied by a Content Store. If a router's CS cache has a matching entry, this entry can be returned to the producer. However, the non-routable name can take any form, including self-certifying and other flat names, and therefore reverse forwarding cannot depend on longest prefix lookup.

When a mobile consumer changes its connectivity, the path for reverse Interest packets can be quickly rebuilt by client-side retransmission of its Interest packet, which will create necessary PIT state again.

If client meta information or application data is too large to fit in one Data packet, the consumer application segments it into multiple Data packets just as would be done for any large Data object. The producer application issues multiple interests to retrieve the entire information object. In order to accommodate this, the algorithm matching DataLocator names in the PIT ignores any segment number name component. Pipelining would allow a producer to fetch arbitrary size client data with minimal round trips.

5. ANALYTIC MODEL

In this section, we develop a simple analytic model and use it to characterize each communication pattern. We model bidirectional traffic between an HTTP/Web-like client (consumer) and an HTTP/Web-like server (producer); network traffic is an obvious, key metric applicable to all of the communication patterns we have considered.

The model applies NDN *segmentation* as data objects grow large. Segmentation is the operation where a content producer splits a large data object into smaller pieces, naming and signing each separately. NDN flow balance, the one-to-one correspondence between Interest and Data packets, assumes that Data packets have constant

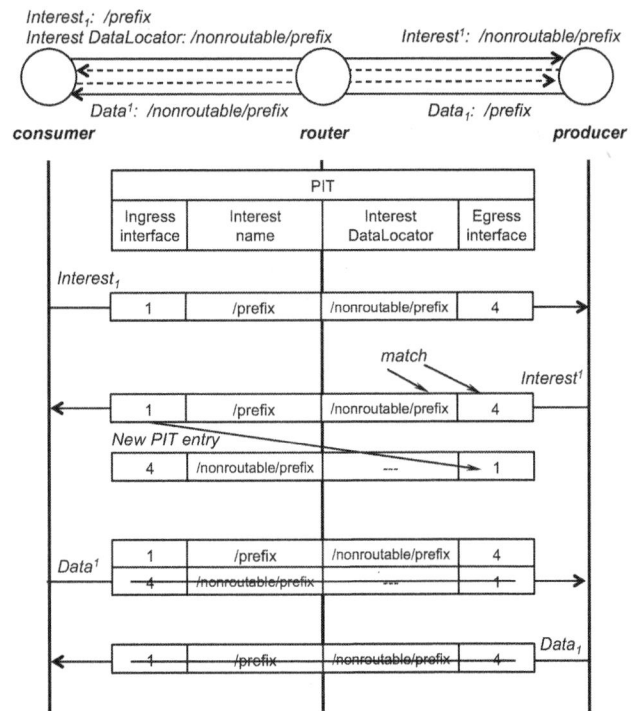

Figure 7: Interest-Interest exchange with non-routable name.

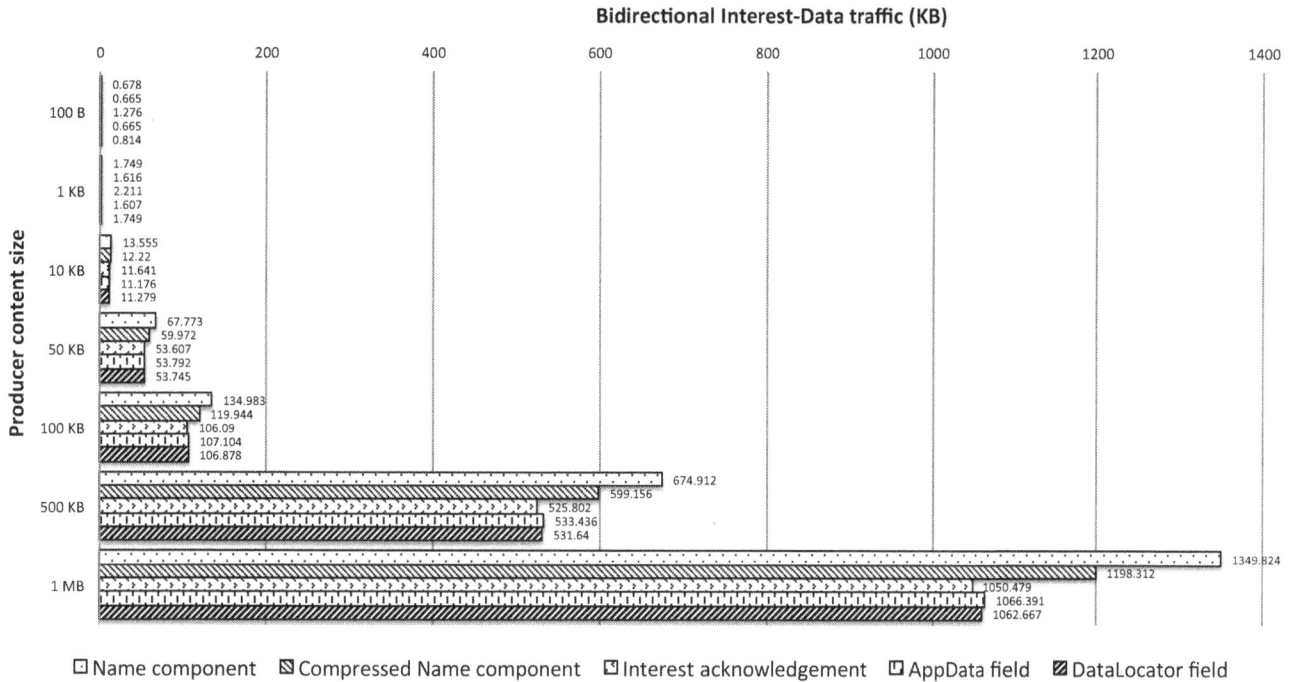

Figure 8: Bidirectional traffic model using 512 bytes of client data.

size for simplifying hop-by-hop flow- and congestion control. A large name field reduces the available space for the content payload in each fixed-size Data packet. A given content object requires more or fewer segments (packets) depending on the payload space made available in each pattern.

The model utilizes a base Interest name (prefix) that is 50 bytes long, with 512 bytes of client-side data. We do not argue that this is accurate or representative of actual traffic; rather that it is not unrealistic given the current web traffic patterns [11].

We use this simplified arithmetic equation to compute the number of segments (*NoS*):

$$Number\ of\ segments\ (NoS) = \frac{Producer\ content\ size}{Space\ for\ content}$$

The choice of the communication pattern affects the amount of space available for content in Data packets. In the name component pattern, all of the client data is appended to the base name prefix. In the compressed name component pattern, Data packet names have a large hash value (e.g. SHA-512) appended to the base name prefix. In the Interest acknowledgement pattern, client data is not echoed in the name of Data segments. In the application data pattern, producer generates and echoes back a token (e.g. SHA-256), carried in its Data segments. In the DataLocator pattern, client data is not echoed in the name of Data segments.

$$Space = Data\ size - \begin{cases} Prefix - Client\ data & (Name\ component) \\ Prefix - Hash & (Compressed\ name) \\ Prefix & (Interest\ ack.) \\ Prefix - Token & (Application\ data) \\ Prefix & (Data\ Locator) \end{cases}$$

Name component pattern carries client data in the Interest name. Each segment is fetched with an Interest carrying the relatively large name.

$$Interest\ traffic = NoS * (Prefix + Client\ data)$$

Large names force the producer to send more segments, increasing the amount of bidirectional traffic:

$$2way\ traffic = Interest\ traffic + NoS * Data\ size$$

Compressed name component pattern carries client data in each Interest name, but echoes back only the hash of the client data in each Data packet of the producer's response.

$$Interest\ traffic = NoS * (Prefix + Client\ data)$$

Total amount of bidirectional traffic:

$$2way\ traffic = Interest\ traffic + NoS * Data\ size$$

Interest acknowledgement pattern uses an initial series of Interests containing client data, acknowledged with signed Data packets. The producer's actual content is then fetched using the normal length Interest packets.

First round — acknowledged delivery of client data. A Data packet with Interest acknowledgement has a negligible payload, therefore:

$$1st\ round\ traffic = (Prefix + Client\ Data) * 2$$

Second round — fetching segmented content from the producer.

$$2nd\ round\ traffic = NoS * prefix + NoS * Data\ size$$

Total amount of bidirectional traffic:

$$2way\ traffic = 1st\ round\ traffic + 2nd\ round\ traffic$$

Application Data pattern carries client data in a single Interest, in a special Interest packet field. The producer generates and echoes back a token, carried in its Data segments. Subsequent Interests, if any, use the producer's token and do not have to convey the client data explicitly.

$$Interest\ traffic = (Prefix + Client\ data) + NoS * (Prefix + Token)$$

Total amount of bidirectional traffic:

$$2way\ traffic = Interest\ traffic + NoS * Data\ size$$

Pattern \\ Criteria	Name component	Compressed Name component	Interest acknowledgement	Application Data field	Routable DataLocator	Non-routable DataLocator
Impact on router memory	**Large**	Normal	**Large**	Normal	Normal	2 x Normal
Payload/Name ratio in Data packets	**Low**	Normal	**Low**	Normal	Normal	Normal
Round trips	1 round	1 round	**2 rounds**	1 round	**2 rounds**	**2 rounds**
Support of large client data	**No**	**No**	Multiple Interest packets	**No**	Multiple Data packets	Multiple Data packets
Retransmission of client data	**Slow, timescale of application RTT**	**Slow, timescale of application RTT**	Fast, timescale of network RTT	Fast, timescale of network RTT	Fast, timescale of network RTT	Fast, timescale of network RTT
Disruption scenarios	PIT inflation DoS on router's fragmentation & reassembly	DoS on router's hashing	DoS on producer's signing DDoS with Interest flooding		Client mobility Reflection attack	

Table 1: Comparison chart of communication patterns.

DataLocator pattern carries an additional name in a special field of each Interest packet. For the purposes of this arithmetic traffic model, the *routable* and *non-routable* locator names are identical. We use 50-byte name lengths for both the content name and the DataLocator name.

The client's Interest packets carry the content name and a DataLocator name. The producer responds with its own Interest(s) using the DataLocator name.

$$Interest\text{-}Interest\ traffic = 2 * Prefix * NoS + Prefix$$

The client provides its client data in Data object(s) using the DataLocator name, then retrieves the actual content from the producer.

$$Data\text{-}Data\ traffic = Data\ size + NoS * Data\ size$$

Total amount of bidirectional traffic.

$$2way\ traffic = Interest\text{-}Interest\ traffic + Data\text{-}Data\ traffic$$

Figure 8 summarizes the results of applying this arithmetic model. The canonical NDN Interest formulation proves to be noticibly less efficient than any other. Name field size has an obvious impact for any but the smallest contents; even the use of a compressed name component has a considerable though less-dramatic impact. The network bandwidth used by the other three protocol patterns is roughly equivalent. This particular metric does not distinguish among these other approaches particularly, though we highlight some key comparison points in Table 1 and discuss it in the next section.

6. CONCLUSION

In this paper we have explored the characteristics of HTTP or REST-like interactions using the NDN communication model. Active state transfer from the client to the server is one of the defining characteristics of these interactions. This state transfer from client (consumer) to server (producer) in NDN is challenging, for a number of reasons:

- Interest packets are lightweight: they do not have a "payload" field to carry ancillary parameters, and have no confidentiality protection mechanisms without additional protocol machinery.
- Interests create state on every NDN router, whose size is correlated with the size of the names carried.

- Interests are aggregated in order to reduce the router state and save upstream bandwidth. Additional name manipulation needs to be implemented in clients to guarantee Interest propagation all the way to the producer application where this is necessary.
- NDN clients (consumers) are not required to have a routable name, making it difficult for them to 'publish' data as NDN content objects.

We describe a number of communication patterns to enable NDN to handle RESTful transactions. All, in our view, have significant drawbacks or disadvantages, as summarized in Table 1.

The **Name component** pattern has an impact on all processing and message efficiency, due to name size expansion.

The **Compressed name component** pattern violates the NDN assumption that Interests and returning Data packets use identical names. Interests still carry potentially large names; there is no way to perform fast retransmission of Interest packets without additional protocol machinery.

The **Interest acknowledgement** pattern uses two phases: one set of Interests conveys client-side data, and a second retrieves the producer-side content. This helps by allowing retransmission of client data without waiting for a server timeout, but imposes a burden on producers. It also may frustrate Interest flooding mitigation techniques by skewing the network statistics they depend on.

The **Application Data field** pattern is efficient, but requires changes in the Interest packet format, and potentially challenges the inherent NDN assumption that Interest packets are small.

The **Routable DataLocator** pattern not only requires changes in the Interest packet format, but also depends on a client's obtaining a routable prefix to be able to respond to Interests sent by the producer. This pattern is awkward for mobile clients, and may make NDN services vulnerable to reflection attacks.

The **Non-routable DataLocator** pattern exploits stateful forwarding to instantiate a transient reverse path for Interests sent by the producer. Since no information in the FIB is being used for reverse forwarding, the DataLocator name can be non-routable. The consumer does not need to obtain a routable prefix, but the router's forwarding algorithm is more complicated.

Eventually, these Web-like/REST-like interactions in NDN may evolve in ways that make them significantly different from their current forms in the IP Internet. But some fundamental constraints or properties will continue to hold: technical feasibility (e.g. scalability, latency) that affect all distributed, REST-ful services, and business needs that drive the 'commercial' Web. In our opinion, REST-like applications are important, and therefore it is highly desirable that they be supported effectively. This deserves consideration in the ongoing discussion and design of the NDN architecture.

7. REFERENCES

[1] T. Berners-Lee, R. Fielding, and H. Frystyk, "RFC 1945: Hypertext Transfer Protocol–HTTP/1.0," *The Internet Society*, 1996.

[2] R. Fielding, J. Gettys, J. Mogul, H. Frystyk, L. Masinter, P. Leach, and T. Berners-Lee, "RFC 2616: Hypertext Transfer Protocol–HTTP/1.1," *The Internet Society*, 1999.

[3] T. Berners-Lee, R. Fielding, and L. Masinter, "RFC 3986: Uniform resource identifier (URI): Generic syntax," *The Internet Society*, 2005.

[4] V. Jacobson, D. K. Smetters, J. D. Thornton, M. F. Plass, N. H. Briggs, and R. L. Braynard, "Networking named content," in *Proc. of CoNEXT*, 2009.

[5] L. Zhang et al., "Named data networking (NDN) project," NDN Project, Tech. Rep. NDN-0001, October 2010.

[6] R. T. Fielding and R. N. Taylor, "Principled design of the modern Web architecture," *ACM TOIT*, vol. 2, no. 2, pp. 115–150, 2002.

[7] I. Grigorik. High performance networking in google chrome. [Online]. Available: http://www.igvita.com/posa/high-performance-networking-in-google-chrome/

[8] CCNX documentation. [Online]. Available: https://www.ccnx.org/releases/latest/doc/technical/Registration.html

[9] J. Burke, A. Horn, and A. Marianantoni, "Authenticated lighting control using Named Data Networking," *UCLA, NDN Technical Report NDN-0011*, 2012.

[10] Z. Zhu and A. Afanasyev, "Let's ChronoSync: Decentralized dataset state synchronization in Named Data Networking," in *ICNP*, 2013.

[11] B. Newton, K. Jeffay, and J. Aikat, "The Continued Evolution of Web Traffic," in *MASCOTS*. IEEE Computer Society, 2013, pp. 80–89.

[12] S. Ramachandran. Web metrics: Size and number of resources. [Online]. Available: https://developers.google.com/speed/articles/web-metrics

[13] P. Gasti, G. Tsudik, E. Uzun, and L. Zhang, "DoS and DDoS in Named Data Networking," in *ICCCN 2013*. IEEE, 2013, pp. 1–7.

[14] A. Afanasyev, P. Mahadevan, I. Moiseenko, E. Uzun, and L. Zhang, "Interest flooding attack and countermeasures in Named Data Networking," in *IFIP Networking Conference, 2013*. IEEE, 2013, pp. 1–9.

[15] J. Burke, P. Gasti, N. Nathan, and G. Tsudik, "Securing Instrumented Environments over Content-Centric Networking: the Case of Lighting Control," *arXiv preprint arXiv:1208.1336*, 2012.

[16] F. Baker and P. Savola, "RFC 3704: Ingress filtering for multihomed networks," Tech. Rep., 2004.

[17] Y. Zhang, H. Zhang, and L. Zhang, "Kite: A Mobility Support Scheme for NDN," NDN Project, Tech. Rep., 2014.

CCN-KRS: A Key Resolution Service for CCN

Priya Mahadevan[1]   Ersin Uzun[1]   Spencer Sevilla[2]   J. J. Garcia-Luna-Aceves[1,2]
[1]Palo Alto Research Center, Palo Alto, CA 94304
[2]Computer Engineering Department, University of California, Santa Cruz, CA 95064
{priya.mahadevan, ersin.uzun}@parc.com, {spencer, jj}@soe.ucsc.edu

ABSTRACT

A key feature of the Content Centric Networking (CCN) architecture is the requirement for each piece of content to be individually signed by its publisher. Thus, CCN should, in principle, be immune to distributing fake content. However, in practice, the network cannot easily detect and drop fake content as the trust context (i.e., the public keys that need to be trusted for verifying the content signature) is an application-dependent concept. CCN provides mechanisms for consumers to request a piece of content restricted by its signer's public key or the cryptographic digest of the content object to avoid receiving fake content. However, it does not provide any mechanisms to learn this critical information prior to requesting the content.

In this paper, we introduce a scalable Key Resolution Service (KRS) that can securely store and serve security information (e.g., public key certificates of publishers) for a namespace in CCN. We implement KRS as a service for CCN in ndnSIM, a ns-3 module, and discuss and evaluate such a distributed service. We demonstrate the feasibility and scalability of our design via simulations driven by real-traffic traces.

Categories and Subject Descriptors

C.2.0 [**General**]: Security and protection;
C.2.1 [**Network Architecture and Design**]: Network communications;
C.2.6 [**Network Protocols**]: Protocol architecture

General Terms

Security, Design, Performance

Keywords

Information-centric networking; security

1. INTRODUCTION AND MOTIVATION

The way in which users and applications use the Internet has changed dramatically since its early days. The shift from a few thousand people using it to access shared computing resources to billions of people world-wide running a wide range of applications has exposed several limitations of the current Internet design. A number of recent research efforts are focused on designing Information-Centric Networking (ICN) architectures [1] that emphasize efficient and scalable content distribution via named information (or content). Content Centric Networking (CCN) [2], is one of the ICN architectures that has been widely experimented with in the networking community.

One of the main tenets of CCN is to name content, instead of communication end-points. Users interested in a piece of content ask for it directly by name by sending an Interest packet. An Interest packet is forwarded by CCN nodes in the network towards a content source, until it reaches a node that can respond with a matching piece of content (called a Content Object) whose name matches the name stated in the Interest packet. The Content Object is sent back to the requesting user, and can optionally be cached by relay nodes between the node responding to the Interest packet and the consumer that requested it. Hence, a CCN router can respond to an Interest packet it receives with a matching cached Content Object. CCN requires every Content Object to be cryptographically signed by its publisher. Thus, globally addressable and routable content can be authenticated by anyone requesting the content. CCN entities that request content are called *consumers* and they always verify content signatures in order to assert:

- *Integrity* – A valid signature (computed over a content hash) guarantees that the signed content is intact.
- *Origin Authentication* – Anyone can verify whether content originates with its claimed publisher, because a signature is bound to the public key of the signer.
- *Correctness* – A consumer can determine whether delivered content corresponds to what was requested because a signature binds the content name to its payload.

A consumer, having its own trust context and policy, can easily differentiate a genuine piece of content from a fake one (i.e, content signed by unauthorized/untrusted keys) after verifying its signature (and potentially a chain of certificates to reach to a trust anchor). However, it is a challenge for an intermediary node in the network to differentiate a genuine piece of content from a fake one since applications (and the namespaces they operate on) are not likely to adhere to a uniform trust model. It is practically infeasible for a CCN router to maintain an up-to-date global knowledge of such mappings considering that applications themselves are constantly evolving and new applications are being developed everyday. In other words, CCN needs to operate efficiently even in the presence of fake content in router caches.

CCN provides two mechanisms to mitigate the above problem and enforce a consumer's trust preferences at the network layer. While requesting named content through Interest packets, consumers can optionally include which key is acceptable as the signer for the requested content or specify the cryptographic digest of the content [details in Section 2]. The immediate requirement for consumers to use these mechanisms is that they must either (1) have the publisher's public key before issuing an Interest for any Content Object from that publisher, or (2) know the digest of the Content Object before issuing an Interest for it. However, CCN does not provide any solution to this proverbial "chicken-and-egg" problem.

In this paper, we propose a Key Resolution Service (KRS) for CCN. KRS is a service that maps a CCN content name, such as "/parc/papers/krs.pdf", to a set of corresponding security information, such as the public key certificate of the authorized publisher for the namespace and/or the cryptographic digest of the Content Object. By querying KRS before issuing an Interest for a piece of content, consumers can acquire the necessary security context required to activate the trust enforcement mechanisms at the network layer. In other words, KRS allows consumers in CCN to learn and specify the public key of a publisher or the content digest they would trust in an Interest. As long as the routers in the network enforce such restrictions, this technique effectively guarantees delivery of trustworthy content regardless of the number of fake Content Objects carrying the same name that might be cached anywhere in the network.

Given that secure acquisition of keys prior to requesting content is required for CCN to be robust against content-poising attacks [3, 4], our KRS design (in combination with the proposal by Ghali [4] requiring either the publisher public key digest (PPKD) or the content-digest field be included in every Interest) constitutes the first practical solution to mitigate denial of service attacks via content poisoning/spoofing in CCN.

The rest of the paper is organized as follows: Section 2 gives an overview of the CCN architecture. Section 3 outlines the set of requirements that KRS must meet. Section 4 provides an overview of the KRS architecture and operation. Section 5 describes our implementation and evaluation methodology. Section 6 presents KRS performance results for several different scenarios. Section 7 concludes the paper.

2. CCN OVERVIEW

All communication in CCN is via two distinct types of packets: *Interests* and *Content Objects* (CO). Both of these packets carry a hierarchically structured name that uniquely identifies a piece of content. A consumer interested in a piece of content requests it by sending an Interest packet that carries the name of the desired piece of content. CCN routers use the name in the Interest to forward it towards likely sources of data by performing a longest prefix match on the name in their forwarding table. A CO whose name exactly matches that in the Interest is sent back to the requesting consumer. Only Interests are routed in CCN. COs take

the reverse of the path taken by the corresponding Interest packet. Any intermediate router can choose to cache any CO that it receives. If a router receives an Interest packet for a CO that it already has in its cache, it can respond with the matching cached CO. Since CCN consumers can receive content from any node, including from caches of intermediate nodes, it is imperative that they verify the authenticity of the CO they receive.

To verify the authenticity of a CO, a CO contains the following fields, in addition to the name of the content and the data:

- PublisherPublicKeyDigest (PPKD): The digest of the public key required to verify the signature. It is typically a SHA-256 digest.

- KeyLocator: The public key or certificate required to verify the signature.

- Content-digest: The cryptographic digest of the CO.

- Signature: A public-key signature generated by the publisher covering the entire content.

An Interest packet in CCN can also include a PPKD, thus allowing consumers to explicitly specify the publisher's public key digest. If this entry is present in an Interest, a matching CO must have the same digest in its PPKD field and a valid signature. CCN Interests can also include content-digest to request a unique CO. To make sure that a consumer only receives content that it would trust (i.e., prevent denial of service attacks by content/cache poisoning), it should issue all its Interests with at least one of the PPKD or content-digest restriction set. However, as long as a consumer device/application doesn't come preloaded with that information, it needs a mechanism to be able fetch this security context before sending an Interest for any content.

To solve the above need, we envision a global CCN Key Resolution Service (KRS) that allows consumers to resolve content names to publisher public key and/or the content digest. KRS is loosely analogous to DNS – just as the DNS today allows clients to resolve hostnames to IP addresses, KRS allows consumers to resolve content names to relevant security information.

3. KRS REQUIREMENTS

We envision KRS as a distributed key-value store service, where the key is the content name (or name prefix) and the value is the KRS record that contains the necessary security information required to verify content authenticity. We first describe the requirements that such a global service must satisfy:

Security: KRS itself must be secure. Only valid content publishers must be able to add, delete and modify entries. Consumers and publishers also need to securely obtain root public keys for KRS. When a consumer queries the KRS and receives a response back, the consumer must be able to independently verify the received KRS record.

Scalability: Studies [5, 6] estimated the number of unique webpages to be of the order of 10^{12} in 2011. This number is expected to grow significantly over the next few years. Since we envision KRS to be globally deployed and widely used, it should be able to support and resolve up to 10^{14} content names.

Response Time: KRS must exhibit similar performance as DNS and the response time of KRS to consumer requests should be similar to the response time of DNS.

Flexibility: KRS should be able to resolve a content name to one of: (i) content hash (ii) publisher public key certificate or (iii) public key certificate chain. It must be flexible enough to include any other information that might be deemed necessary in the future.

Seamless Application Support: KRS must operate transparently in a manner similar to DNS today. Rather than requiring CCN applications to programmatically interact with and manage KRS individually, applications should ideally integrate with consumer devices at the system level, similar to how DNS operates in the Internet today.

Discovery: KRS must be discoverable by client devices, just as local DNS servers are discoverable by devices today. For example, when a device joins a WiFi network at a coffee shop, the device has no *a priori* information regarding the network topology, but must still be able to discover the name of a nearby KRS server.

4. KRS DESIGN OVERVIEW

We designed KRS as a global service that runs over CCN to address the requirements described in Section 3. All communication among KRS servers is via CCN Interests and COs. Consumers send requests specifying the name of the content they would like to resolve in the form of an Interest to KRS, and the service returns the KRS record containing the security information for that content name in the form of a CO.

Our KRS design is influenced by that of DNS, given the similarities in requirements between KRS and DNS. We split KRS into two interacting components: *local* KRS servers that receive requests from CCN consumers, and *authoritative* KRS servers that store and manage KRS records. We illustrate the operation of KRS in Figure 1.

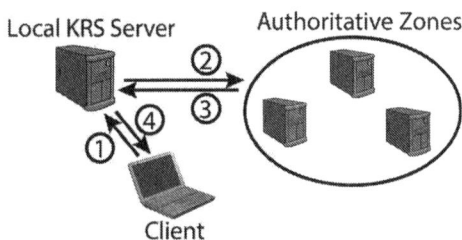

Figure 1: Client Querying KRS

As stated previously, CCN names are hierarchical. We exploit this hierarchy in content names to assign a KRS zone to manage a name prefix. A KRS zone, comprised of one or more authoritative servers, is responsible for storing all KRS records associated with that name prefix.

KRS organizes zones into a hierarchy similar to DNS. We achieve scalability by distributing the storage and management of all associated KRS records to individual KRS zones. An authoritative server in a KRS zone may recruit additional servers at any time to handle the storage and serving of KRS records for the name prefix that it is managing; it can also add a new zone to handle a new subprefix of the content name prefix that it is managing.

Local KRS servers are responsible for receiving and forwarding requests from CCN consumers to the appropriate KRS zone authoritative server. To this end, the main data structure at any KRS server is the "next-hop" table that stores the name and the public key of the KRS service that either stores the KRS record for that content name or knows the name of the next-hop service to whom the KRS request can be forwarded.

Local KRS servers might be discovered by clients either via a secure automatic configuration service (i.e., a CCN equivalent of DHCP with server authentication) or via a predictable (or predetermined) name prefix for the local KRS service such as "/krs." For the latter, CCN nodes in a given network would need to have appropriate entries to forward the Interests to the closest local KRS server.

For example, a client wishing to obtain the security information for the content name /parc/papers/krs.pdf can create a CCN Interest and ask for the KRS record for that name using its local KRS service's prefix (/krs in this case), resulting in the name /krs/q=/parc/papers/krs.pdf in the Interest.[1]

On receiving this Interest, the local KRS server performs a look-up in its next-hop table to determine the name of the KRS zone service that can handle the KRS query. In the absence of an entry corresponding to the zone service name, the local KRS server queries the root KRS service to obtain the globally routable name of the responsible KRS zone service (e.g., /parc-krs). The local KRS server uses this globally routable prefix to forward the query over to the service responsible for that KRS zone. Upon receipt of this Interest, the authoritative KRS zone service extracts the content name for which the KRS record has been requested and compares it against the records it stores to retrieve either (1) the final response to the query in the form of a KRS record, (2) the next zone service that the query should be forwarded to, or (3) the message that no such record exists.

In the case of (1) or (3) above, the authoritative server responds to the received Interest by encapsulating the appropriate KRS record as a CCN CO with the same name as in the received Interest. To handle case (2), the KRS server performs a lookup in its next-hop table and creates a query, in the form of an Interest for that KRS zone, which should know more about the namespace that is being queried. This process repeats until either case (1) or case (3) above is performed by an authoritative service. Although we described the process as interactive, we emphasize that all steps in the process can be completed with previous responses to the same query cached either at CCN nodes as COs at the network layer or cached KRS records for popular or recent queries in KRS servers at the application layer.

Once the local KRS server receives a CO encapsulating the requested KRS record, it first decapsulates the record and re-encapsulates it in a new CO that would satisfy the Interest received from the consumer.

Figure 2 depicts the various fields in a KRS record. The name in the KRS record is the name (or name prefix) that is being resolved, and the payload is the security information associated with that name (i.e., a content-hash or public key). Further, each KRS record is individually secured with

---

[1]Most recent CCNx specification (CCNx 1.0) allows Interests to have a payload. In future implementations, the query part of the name can be carried as payload for shorter names and better overall PIT usage efficiency.

a cryptographic signature and carries a public key certificate or certificate chain for the signing key. A consumer receiving a KRS record would only trust it if the signature on the record is valid and the certificate chain for the signing key anchors at a trusted entity (e.g., a global certificate authority). As stated previously, each KRS record is transmitted as a CCN CO, which includes a signature that can be used to authenticate the KRS service itself and a PPKD field that can be used to limit acceptable responses to an Interest carrying a KRS query to trusted KRS service instances only.

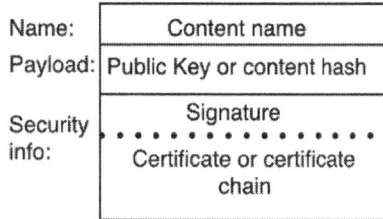

Name:	Content name
Payload:	Public Key or content hash
Security info:	Signature
	Certificate or certificate chain

Figure 2: KRS Record

Having provided an overview of the KRS architecture, we next address how we meet each of the requirements listed in Section 3.

4.1 Improving Scalability

Scalability in KRS is attained through the use of a longest-prefix-matching (LPM) algorithm used for lookups in the next-hop table and for retrieving the stored KRS record itself. Using LPM to look up entries in the next-hop table significantly cuts down on KRS recursive referrals, thereby improving KRS response time. LPM also enables the use of "default" records, thereby significantly reducing the burden on KRS to store records for every single content item published.

As an example, a publisher may have one public-private key pair which it uses to sign all content published with the prefix /parc/papers. Thus, rather than storing the same key as a separate KRS record for each piece of published content under the prefix /parc/papers, KRS simply stores the key once in the authoritative zone /parc, with the notation "*" that this record is the final response for any name including the prefix /parc/papers. LPM is enabled through the simple designation of a "*" record for a prefix, which indicates that there are no further KRS records below that prefix.

4.2 Improving KRS Performance with Caching

KRS records can be cached in two separate ways: nodes in the underlying CCN network may cache the COs (that encapsulate a KRS record) and return them for subsequently expressed Interests, and KRS servers may *also* themselves cache and return KRS records. To highlight the distinction between these two forms of caching, consider an example where a local KRS server receives a request to resolve the content name "/parc/csl/papers/krs.pdf". In the process of recursively resolving this request, the local KRS server may receive and cache the KRS record for the name prefix "/parc/csl/papers". Subsequently, the local KRS server

receives a request to resolve "/parc/csl/papers/paper2.pdf". Though these two requests share the prefix "/parc/csl/papers", CCN caching cannot provide any benefits, since CCN caches use exact matching on names to return a matching CO and the last component of the two prefixes are dissimilar[2]. Instead, KRS servers perform LPM on the requested content name "/parc/csl/papers/paper2.pdf" and respond with the cached KRS record for "/parc/csl/papers", thereby improving performance significantly.

4.3 KRS Forwarding Policies

So far, we have described a recursive forwarding policy employed by authoritative KRS servers, whereby they directly query the next-hop service in charge of the subprefix. An alternative to the recursive technique is the iterative forwarding technique. Here, the server simply responds to the Interest with a CO that contains the globally routable name and the public key of the next-hop service able to process the KRS request. When the requesting server receives this CO, it constructs a new KRS query for the newly learnt KRS service name. The requesting server can also optionally cache this globally routable name and the public key of this KRS service in its next-hop table.

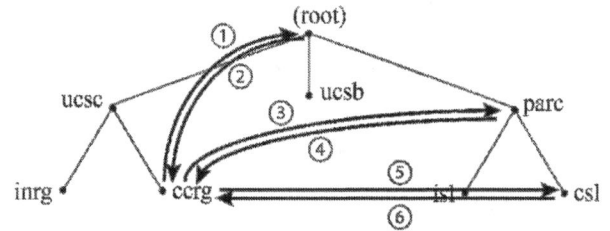

Figure 3: Top-Down Forwarding

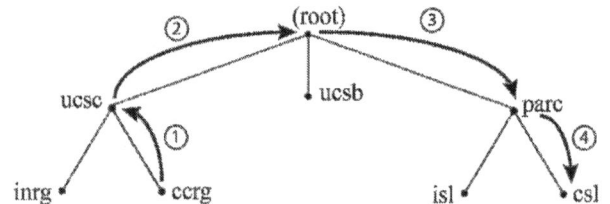

Figure 4: Bottom-Up Forwarding

In DNS, local resolvers come pre-loaded with the addresses of root and top level domain (TLD) servers. This technique bootstraps the resolution process and ensures that a resolver always has an address to send its first query to, even if it has no immediate forwarding information for the query. We refer to this model, illustrated in Figure 3, as *top-down* forwarding. We use an analogous technique in KRS to bootstrap the next-hop table entries at KRS servers. KRS may also employ *bottom-up* forwarding, wherein all local resolvers have a prefix name, and therefore a place in the prefix hierarchy. When a local resolver receives a query for which it

---

[2]Unlike previous CCN protocol specifications, the current specification CCNx 1.0 requires CCN caches to perform exact matching on names.

has no immediate forwarding information, instead of directly querying the root of the prefix tree, it sends the query to its parent, as illustrated in Figure 4. We examined the trade-offs between top-down and bottom-up forwarding in [7]. For example, bottom-up forwarding serves to keep local requests more local, yet can potentially result in more referrals, since it introduces more intermediate zones along the path. However, well-designed caching policies help to ameliorate these referrals while simultaneously reducing load on higher-level authoritative servers.

4.4 Bootstrapping and KRS Maintenence

In the previous section, we described how queries are forwarded through the KRS and answered by the authoritative zone. However, before a query is answered, the KRS must be populated with records, and these records must be kept up-to-date. Among the multiple ways of achieving this, we advocate a federated approach similar to the one deployed in DNS today to handle globally routable namespaces and corresponding key registrations. Like in DNS, this registration information can be maintained by the registries, which contract with registrars to provide registration services to the publishers. A publisher can select a designated registrar for the namespace it chooses to own. Unlike DNS, we expect most registrars in KRS to also act as certification authorities that can issue public key certificates to publishers for top level namespaces they own. As in DNS, only the designated registrar may modify or delete information about a KRS record for a namespace and we also envision a global entity, similar to ICANN, that will coordinate the namespace allocations and manage the KRS root servers.

One difference between today's DNS and KRS will be the number of top level zones in the root. We expect this number to be significantly larger for KRS and the contractual arrangements for zone file access may not scale. However, it is expected that DNS will experience the same problem in the near future as the number of global top-level domains increase. The ICANN Zone File Access Advisory Group has published a concept paper [8] with four new access models to alleviate this problem, all of which are equally applicable to the KRS system proposed here. We omit a discussion about these models due to space restrictions in this paper but refer interested readers to [8] for more details.

Similar to DNSSEC [9], each KRS record itself is cryptographically signed for security purposes. However, unlike DNSSEC, KRS records are signed by the publishers that owns the namespace to authenticate the KRS record at the consumer application. Additionally, KRS queries are always answered in the form of CCN COs, and independent from any KRS record they may be carrying, COs are signed by the KRS server that generated it and these signatures are used for authentication at the KRS protocol level.

5. KRS IMPLEMENTATION AND EVALUATION METHODOLOGY

We implemented KRS as an application level service running over ndnSIM [10], which is a ns-3 [11] module. We used simulations and trace-based analysis to evaluate the performance of KRS under a varying range of system parameters.

We first provide an overview of our evaluation methodology. In our ns-3 simulations, we input a realistic Internet topology as the underlying CCN topology with KRS running as an overlay application on this topology. We chose nodes in this topology to represent both local KRS servers and authoritative servers in KRS each zone. As part of the initialization process, KRS records are distributed across respective zones and handled by the designated authoritative server. These records are drawn from representative traffic traces. Client requests that need to be resolved are processed by local KRS servers and matching KRS records are fetched as discussed in Section 4.

At each local KRS server, we quantified the overhead as measured by the number of KRS messages that are required to fetch the matching KRS record. Each referral to the next zone results in two KRS messages – an Interest message and the returning record CO. We also measure the system latency at the local KRS servers as the time required for the local KRS server to obtain the record after it receives the resolution query.

For all the above evaluations, we experimented with a range of KRS specific parameters such as the forwarding scheme used and cache size. All reported KRS latency values represent network latency; we do not include the time required to perform the optional record authenticity verification operation at each KRS server. By default, we used recursive top-down forwarding in all our experiments, except when comparing the benefits of recursive versus iterative forwarding.

Similar to any global distributed system, KRS performance results are dependent on the system and network environment parameters, as well as the workload used to drive the performance evaluation. In the rest of this section, we describe our workload as well as results from our parameter sensitivity analysis that we used in our KRS simulation experiments.

5.1 Representative Workload

As CCN is an emerging network architecture, there are no representative traffic traces currently available. We chose the well-accepted technique of translating HTTP GET requests to CCN Interests [12], and thus ensured that the heirarchy in HTTP URLs directly mapped to the hierarchy in CCN names. Our workload serves two purposes: (i) it determines the records *stored* in KRS and the KRS zone hierarchy and (ii) it represents the set of content names that clients request to be resolved.

We used the IRC trace[3] [13] consisting of roughly five hundred thousand individual HTTP GETs.We removed requests to CDNs and shared hosting services as these URL structures did not translate well to CCN name hierarchies and our resulting trace consisted of approximately 350,000 HTTP GETs. We translated each HTTP GET to a corresponding CCN name by reversing the order of the hostname and replacing each "." with a "/". Thus, the HTTP object "mail.google.com/bob" corresponded to the CCN CO name "/com/google/mail/bob". We aggregated prefixes that span multiple ccTLDs as they all refer to the same CO. Thus, "/au/com/google", "/uk/co/google", and "/com/google" were aggregated to "/com/google".

We plot the distribution of client requests in our traces in Figure 5 and confirm that the requests follow the Zipf distribution, with $alpha = 0.9258$. This result is important

---

[3]collected at FIX-West over two days of 2009 at Ames Research Center in Mountain View, California

since it implies that a majority of the queries to KRS are for resolving the same content name.

Next, we examined the number of components in each name that needed to be resolved. We plot the distribution of the number of components in each name (black solid line) in Figure 6, with a mean of 7.36 and a standard deviation of 1.68. Since the distribution in Figure 6 is collected over the set of all *names*, it is implicitly weighted by the popularity of the requested COs. We filtered multiple resolution requests for the same CO to show the distribution of unique prefixes in Figure 6 (red solid line), with a mean of 7.48 and a standard deviation of 1.64. This distribution influences the depth of the KRS tree (zone) hierarchy and the number of referrals that need to be performed, thereby impacting KRS performance.

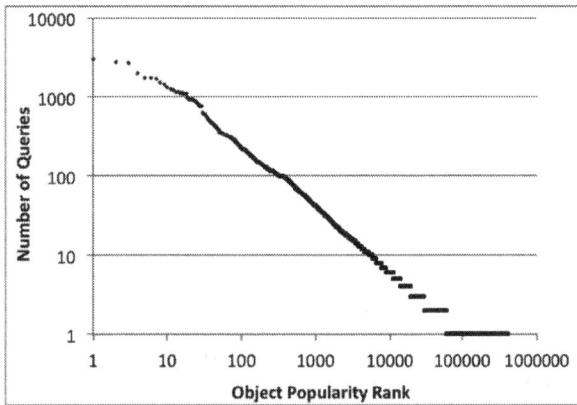

Figure 5: Popularity of COs

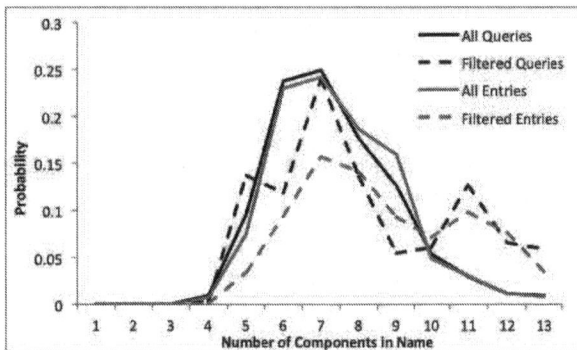

Figure 6: PDF of Name-Components in a Resolution Request

5.1.1 Domain-based Filtering

In our trace set, we observed 29932 unique second-level domains (e.g. "google", "yahoo", etc); Figure 7 illustrates the popularity distribution of these domains, with the Y-axis counting all requests for the domain. This distribution is *also* Zipf, with $alpha = 0.8640$ implying that a small number of domains are responsible for a significant portion of the total number of requests. Scalability considerations in the topology we used for running our simulations required us to narrow the request set to include a much reduced number of

second-level domains, but at the same time we ensured that the filtered set is still representative of the original requests. We reduced our request set down to the 5 most popular second-level domains ("google", "yahoo", "msn", "friendster", and "cnn"), which resulted in a total of 113,531 requests expressed for 34,834 different COs. This set of domains also provided a diverse spread that captured many different Web use-cases such as search, homepage, social, and news.

To show that this filtered set is still representative of the observed workload, we calculated the probability density function for both the weighted and unweighted name-components in our filtered set. We depict these by the black and red dashed lines respectively in Figure 6. These dashed lines roughly follow the distribution for the entire request set, with one primary difference: the "bump" at 11 components. This bump is explained by the prefix-set distribution of CNN, which employs a much deeper naming tree, both for its articles and the individual HTTP elements referenced within an article. Thus, as input for our KRS experiments, we used a final set of 113,531 requests for 34,834 unique COs.

5.2 Zone Distribution and Colocation

The distribution of zones in KRS is critical to its performance, since it determines the number of authoritative servers that will be needed to power KRS resolution. Note that the distribution of *prefixes* does not necessarily reflect the distribution of *zones*. For example, a query-set consisting of the single prefix

"/parc/csl/papers/krs.pdf" would still require 4 KRS zones: the root zone, "parc", "csl", and "papers".

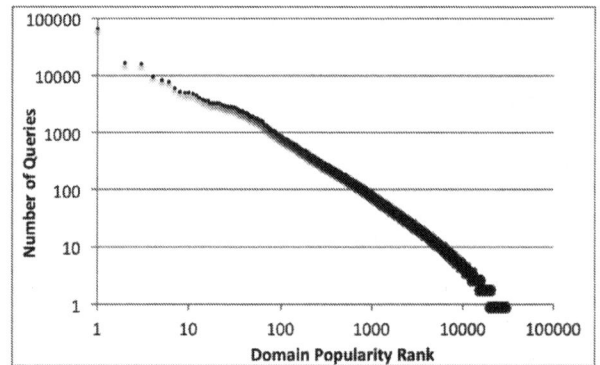

Figure 7: Popularity Of Second-Level Domains

From our filtered request set, we removed all leaf nodes and duplicates to create a set of 38,244 unique KRS zones. As before, we analyzed the number of components for each zone name in our set; we plot the cumulative density function (CDF) for all zones as well as for each second-level domain in Figure 8. While the CDF for Google, MSN, and Yahoo all roughly followed that of the mean CDF for all zones, the CDFs for both Friendster and CNN exhibited different behavior. CNN's CDF was essentially two components higher than the average, but this was consistent with the aforementioned behavior observed in Figures 6. For Friendster, the increase from 5 to 7 is explained by the Friendster name-prefix format, which followed the pattern "/com/friendster/blogs/{username}/{contentname}".

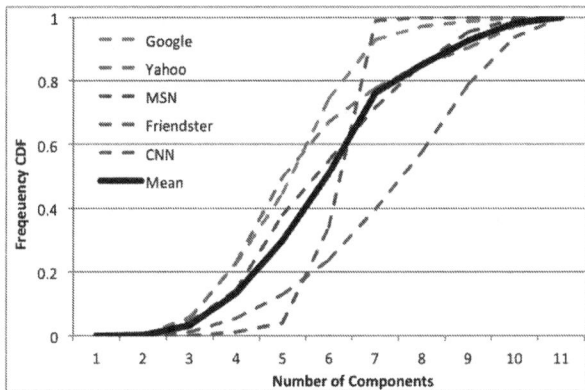

Figure 8: CDF of Name-Components In A Zone

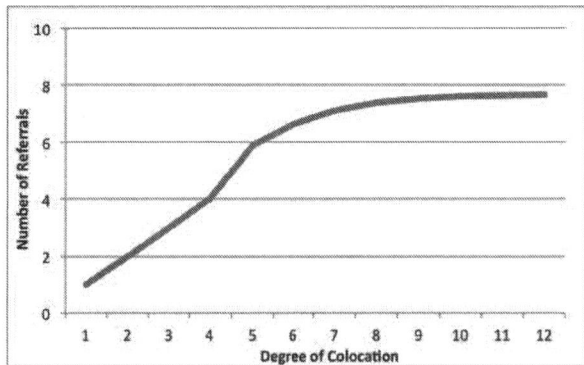

Figure 9: Expected Mean Number of Referrals With Colocation

We present the CDF since it illustrates the percent of zones containing up to a certain number of components. This parameter is important because though our filtered request set requires 38,244 different zones, it is unlikely that each zone will be hosted on a separate server. Rather, we expect that a single server may be responsible for a large number of zones, either through the use of default entries or simply by hosting multiple zone-files; we call this process *zone colocation*. While zone colocation for a domain is the responsibility of the organization owning the domain, it is still an important parameter to consider as it directly impacts the number of referrals that need to be performed as well as the response time to get back a KRS record.

To explore zone colocation, we started by defining a global *zone colocation number* Z which represents a "cap" on how long a zone's prefix may be. For example, when $Z = 3$, the zones "/parc", "/parc/papers", and "/parc/csl" may each be located on separate servers, but the zone "/parc/csl/lab3" may *not* have its own server: rather, it *must* be colocated with "/parc/csl". To analyze the system effects of varying Z, we calculated the number of referrals for our request set for different values of Z. For this calculation, we assumed that every zone that *may* have its own server, *does* have its own server. We explicitly assumed no caching. Thus, if a request has n components, it will result in exactly n referrals, unless $n > Z$, in which case the Zth referral definitively answers the query.

Figure 9 illustrates how we anticipate the mean number of referrals to vary with Z. At low values (e.g. $Z = 2$), the mean number of referrals is close to Z, since almost all requests have $> Z$ components. However, as Z increases, we observed a mean referral count of 7.11 at $Z = 8$ and 7.66 at $Z = 12$. This result highlights the fact that so few requests have a component-length of > 7 that even if colocation is not used, it will not significantly degrade KRS performance. Thus, we conclude that only Z values lower than 7 are useful for improving system performance via limiting referrals.

Building on this result and from Figure 8, we chose Z values for each domain based on the distribution of names. Thus, we chose a value of $Z = 5$ for Google, MSN, and Yahoo, and $Z = 6$ for Friendster and CNN. This roughly corresponded to a value of 0.3 in the CDF for each domain, and reduced our set of 38,244 unique zones down to a manageable 713. Thus, in our simulation topology we have 713

KRS authoritative servers, with each server handling one zone.

5.3 Underlying CCN Topology

To pick the underlying CCN topology for our KRS performance evaluation, we chose a modified version of Rocketfuel's "Verio US" topology [14] consisting of 921 nodes in one connected component. We classified 462 leaf nodes as "client" nodes that connected to 269 "gateway" nodes; the remaining 190 nodes were classified as "backbones". Each node employed a LRU cache eviction policy; we varied the cache size and report the results in Section 5.4. KRS servers run as a service over the nodes in this topology. To ensure that we are observing the performance of the underlying CCN topology itself, we disabled all KRS record caching, and employed a recursive forwarding scheme at every KRS server. For the sake of evaluating only KRS performance, we disregarded the presence of individual clients in our evaluation, and configured local KRS servers to directly request the prefixes from the workload described above.

We assumed that authoritative KRS servers are located at the edge of the network, either at client or gateway nodes. We distributed the 713 authoritative KRS servers across the combined total of 731 client and gateway nodes and assigned similar prefixes (e.g. /com/friendster/blogs and /com/frienster/www) to nodes that were close to each other in the topology.

5.4 CCN Caching

Our goal in this experiment was to determine the cache size to be set in CCN. We started by choosing one node in the above topology to represent a local KRS server that requested every Interest in the aforementioned request-set, with the time between requests randomly generated according to an exponential distribution with $\mu = 1.0$ request/sec. We repeated our experiments for various cache sizes (i.e. the number of elements cached), including cache size 0. We measured both the average KRS messages passed and average latency per request and plot them in Figure 10. With no caching, we observed an average number of 7.66 KRS messages passed (3.83 referrals) per request; this number correlated well with the expected results shown in Figure 9, given the degree of colocation. The mean latency of 1.02 seconds per request was roughly similar to values observed by collecting DNS traffic [15]. We note that a direct com-

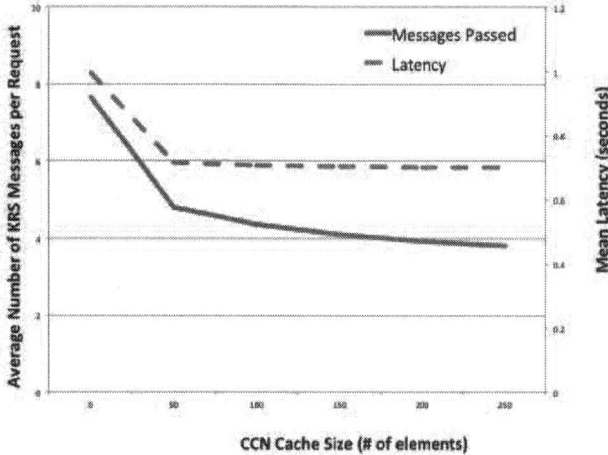

Figure 10: Average KRS messages per request vs CCN cache size

parison between KRS and DNS is not valid because: (1) our values are collected without caching, (2) KRS zone tree being much deeper than that of DNS, results in a much higher number of mean KRS referrals, and (3) the underlying network architecture is completely different. As expected, with caching enabled, we observed an immediate, sharp drop-off, both in latency and average number of KRS messages per request. In accordance with observations about the popularity distributions of COs and their effects on caching [16, 17, 18], we achieved a majority of these benefits even at low cache sizes. Thus, we set CCN cache size to be 100 in the rest of our KRS simulation experiments.

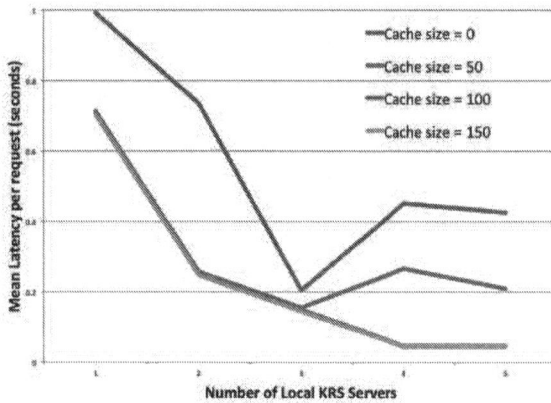

Figure 11: Latency And Number of Local KRS Servers

5.5 Local KRS Servers

Next, we evaluated whether the *number* of local KRS servers issuing KRS requests impacted the average number of KRS messages and latency per request. We repeated the same experiment as above while varying the number of local

KRS servers. To account for different topological locations, we ensured that local KRS servers were deployed only at client nodes. Whenever a local KRS server issued a request, it simply chose the first unrequested prefix from the request set. Since our evaluation topology consisted of one individual ISP in the United States, we did not consider client locality, as several studies [19, 20, 21, 22] have shown that client locality is only significant at a coarse-grained level, or where cultural/linguistic boundaries were crossed.

We observed that the average number of KRS messages per request remained unaffected by the number of local KRS servers making requests; this result was expected, since we explicitly disabled all KRS caching. However, we also observed a decrease in mean latency as we increased the number of local KRS servers; this decrease is illustrated for different CCN cache sizes in Figure 11. Notably, for all cache sizes the mean latency did not continue to decrease when we increased the number of local KRS servers beyond 4. We attribute this decrease in latency to two factors: better link-utilization and shorter average distance. However, these benefits are primarily attained with even a small number of local KRS servers, and this explains the lack of change in latency beyond 5 local KRS servers. Thus, for the purpose of our evaluation, we concluded that 4 or 5 is an acceptable value for setting the minimum number of local KRS servers.

6. KRS PERFORMANCE RESULTS

In the previous section, we described our workload and the impact of different system and configuration parameters as well as network characteristics on KRS performance. In this section we evaluated KRS itself, using the configuration parameters chosen in the previous section; we studied KRS behavior under varying KRS-specific parameters such as KRS cache size and forwarding scheme (iterative versus recursive) used.

6.1 KRS Recursion and Caching

Caching and forwarding are fundamentally intertwined and directly impact each other: if caching is disabled, then both the recursive and iterative forwarding schemes result in the same number of referrals and KRS messages. As cache size increases, the forwarding scheme used has growing importance, since it determines which intermediate KRS servers receive and cache entries. To evaluate the impact of these parameters, we enabled KRS caching and examined how KRS cache size impacted average number of KRS messages per request. As discussed previously, we set CCN cache size to 100 elements, and the number of local KRS servers to five (5).

We define a "recursion number" R, where zones with prefix-length $> R$ resolve prefixes recursively, and zones with prefix-length $\leq R$ do so iteratively. We designed this model by observing policies enacted by real-world DNS servers today, where authoritative servers higher in the hierarchy (e.g. root and TLD servers) generally disable recursive resolution [15] to address concerns about performance and security. In all our previous experiments, KRS used recursive forwarding, thus $R = 0$ for those experiments.

In Figure 12, we plot the average number of KRS messages per request as a function of varying KRS cache size (number of elements cached) for different values of R. We note that the *size* of the KRS cache does not have a very strong effect on average messages per request.

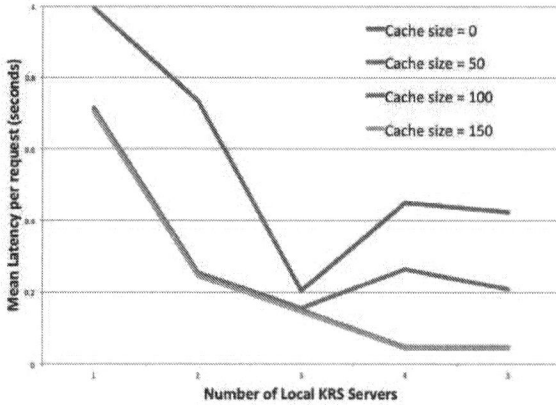

Figure 12: KRS Caching For Varying Values of R

The above result can be explained by considering the results observed in Figure 10, and recalling that this experiment was run with a *CCN* node cache size of 100. As seen from our request workload, KRS requests follow a Zipf distribution implying that a majority of KRS requests are satisfied from CCN's cache. Increasing KRS cache sizes thus does not have any further impact on reducing KRS messages. Furthermore, when $R = 0$, every server is responding recursively. Thus no querying server may learn the name of the second-hop KRS authoritative server and its public key to be cached for future use.

The true strength of longest prefix matching for looking up entries in the next-hop table is not realized and thus there is no reduction in the number of referrals. Effectively, the KRS cache is used only for exact-matching, and the observed performance as we increase the KRS cache size roughly mimics that of increasing the CCN cache size.

We note that increasing the value of R significantly reduces the average number of KRS messages per request as soon as KRS caching is enabled. The benefits are significant for a KRS cache size of 50. However, increasing KRS cache size further does not reduce the average KRS messages much more – the average KRS messages line flattens out with further increase in KRS cache size.

With KRS caching enabled, the true strength of *longest-prefix-matching* is realized and used to reduce intermediate referrals, as described in Section 4.

For example, when $R = 1$, the root server "/" responds iteratively, so local KRS servers may learn the name and the key of the authoritative server handling "/com." They cache this entry in their next-hop table. Thus, even for a small KRS cache size, we quickly see the majority of gained performance benefits, since increasing the KRS cache size further does not reduce any more intermediate referrals. Likewise for both $R = 2$ and $R = 3$: small cache sizes are sufficient to store the set of next-hop server names and their keys, and this caching is responsible for the majority of the performance benefits observed.

6.2 KRS Storage

In this subsection, we discuss the storage requirements for KRS records.

We expect a KRS record to be about 6 KB on average. As described in Section 4, a KRS record consists of the content name, the public key or content hash, the signature, and a certificate or a certificate chain. While CCN names can be arbitrarily long and can have an arbitrary number of components, for efficiency purposes, we expect content names to not exceed 1 KB [2]. Even for a strong 4096-bit signing key, the associated certificate size is about 1.5 KB. Thus, we expect an average KRS record to be approximately 6 KB.

For successful KRS resolution, authoritative zones *must* store the set of KRS entries for which they are responsible. From the colocation methodology described in Section 5, we ran tests on a set consisting of 34,834 unique KRS records. Assuming each record is on average 6 KB in size, storing 34,834 records require approximately 209 MB across the *entire system*. Since this system contains only the five most popular domains, and given that our evaluation shows that these domains do accurately reflect the hierarchy and distribution of name-prefixes, we expect that storing all the KRS records for an organizational domain would require approximately 40 MB on average.

From our experiments in Section 6.1, it is notable that we achieved a majority of KRS performance benefits from caches as small as 50. Even assuming that caches must be two orders of magnitude larger (5000 elements) in order to see these same benefits in a larger topology, storage requirements for caching KRS records at intermediate KRS servers is not a concern.

6.3 Creating, Updating, and Deleting Entries

KRS must also support creating, updating, and deleting records. However, evaluating the performance of such operations is challenging, for several reasons. Today's content delivery protocols and systems largely perform these operations off-line, and as a result it is challenging to find collected data-sets from which we can construct a realistic workload for evaluation, as we did in Section 5.1. We expect the set of create/update/delete entries to not be a significant performance overhead. This expectation comes from the observation that offline configuration (i.e. manually configuring a DNS or HTTP server) are acceptable *only* because such operations happen much more infrequently than content is read.

Additionally, KRS's longest prefix matching look-up algorithm for retrieving KRS records provides significant benefits. Through the use of default entries, KRS provides a powerful mechanism to mitigate the number of create, update, and delete operations. By simply storing the key used to sign every CO under a particular name prefix, no further KRS operations are needed, regardless of how frequently a publisher changes the COs below this prefix.

7. CONCLUSION

We proposed a Key Resolution Service (KRS) for CCN. KRS provides a system for the registration, storage and distribution of security information associated with namespaces in CCN. By taking advantage of the hierarchical naming scheme in CCN, KRS can securely and unambiguously map namespaces in CCN to public keys that are authorized to publish in those namespaces. Additionally, KRS supports a secure mapping between a content name and the cryptographic digest of the Content Object carrying that name.

By analyzing a set of collected real HTTP traces, we estimated the workload for a KRS system and designed realistic experiments to evaluate the scalability of our system under various conditions. Our experiments show that the proposed KRS design is scalable to a global deployment and that small cache sizes at different layers (i.e., at KRS and the CCN layer) significantly benefit KRS performance.

To the best of our knowledge, KRS is the first practical proposal that can fully eliminate the threat of content poisoning attacks in CCN (and its sibling architecture NDN) by enabling consumers to acquire the necessary security information to unambiguously request and receive trustworthy content —regardless of the existence of untrustworthy content in router caches that might share the same name.

8. ACKNOWLEDGMENTS

This research was supported in part by the NSF Future Internet Architecture (FIA) Program Award G015.3707.

9. REFERENCES

[1] Bengt Ahlgren, Christian Dannewitz, Claudio Imbrenda, Dirk Kutscher, and Börje Ohlman. A Survey of Information-Centric Networking. *IEEE Commun. Mag.*, 50(7):26–36, 2012.

[2] PARC. Content centric networking project (ccn). http://www.ccnx.org.

[3] Paolo Gasti, Gene Tsudik, Ersin Uzun, and Lixia Zhang. Dos and ddos in named data networking. In *Computer Communications and Networks (ICCCN), 2013 22nd International Conference on*, pages 1–7. IEEE, 2013.

[4] Cesar Ghali, Gene Tsudik, and Ersin Uzun. Elements of trust in named-data networking. *CoRR*, abs/1402.3332, 2014.

[5] Diego Perino and Matteo Varvello. A reality check for content centric networking. *In Proc. ACM SIGCOMM Workshop ICN*, 2011.

[6] We Knew The Web Was Big... http://googleblog.blogspot.com/2008/07/we-knew-web-was-big.html.

[7] Spencer Sevilla, Priya Mahadevan, and JJ Garcia-Luna-Aceves. FERN: A unifying framework for name resolution across heterogeneous architectures. *Proc. IFIP NETWORKING*, 2013.

[8] ICANN Zone File Access Advisory Group. gtld zone file access in the presence of large numbers of tlds. http://www.icann.org/en/topics/new-gtlds/zfa-concept-paper-18feb10-en.pdf, 2010.

[9] S. Weiler and D. Blacka. RFC 6840: Clarifications and Implementation Notes for DNS Security (DNSSEC). *IETF Standard*, 2013.

[10] Alexander Afanasyev, Ilya Moiseenko, and Lixia Zhang. ndnSIM: NDN simulator for NS-3. Technical Report NDN-0005, NDN, October 2012.

[11] ns-3 network simulator. http://www.nsnam.org/.

[12] Won So, Ashok Narayanan, and David Oran. Named data networking on a router: fast and dos-resistant forwarding with hash tables. In *Proceedings of the ninth ACM/IEEE symposium on Architectures for networking and communications systems*, pages 215–226. IEEE Press, 2013.

[13] IRCache traces. ftp://ircache.net.

[14] Neil Spring, Ratul Mahajan, and David Wetherall. Measuring isp topologies with rocketfuel. *ACM SIGCOMM Computer Communication Review*, 32(4):133–145, 2002.

[15] J. Jung, E. Sit, H Balakrishnan, and R Morris. DNS Performance and the Effectiveness of Caching. *Networking, IEEE/ACM Transactions on*, 10(5):589–603, 2002.

[16] Seyed Kaveh Fayazbakhsh, Yin Lin, Amin Tootoonchian, Ali Ghodsi, Teemu Koponen, Bruce M Maggs, K C Ng, Vyas Sekar, and Scott Shenker. Less Pain, Most of the Gain: Incrementally Deployable ICN. In *Proceedings of SIGCOMM 2013*, page 1. ACM, 2013.

[17] L Breslau, P. Cao, L Fan, G Phillips, and S. Shenker. Web caching and Zipf-like distributions: Evidence and implications. 1:126–134, 1999.

[18] Mark E Crovella and Azer Bestavros. Self-similarity in World Wide Web traffic: evidence and possible causes. *Networking, IEEE/ACM Transactions on*, 5(6):835–846, 1997.

[19] T Chung, J Han, H Lee, and J Kangasharju. Spatial and temporal locality of content in BitTorrent: A measurement study. *Proc. IFIP NETWORKING*, 2013.

[20] John S Otto, Mario A Sánchez, David R Choffnes, Fabián E Bustamante, and Georgos Siganos. On blind mice and the elephant: understanding the network impact of a large distributed system. In *ACM SIGCOMM Computer Communication Review*, volume 41, pages 110–121. ACM, 2011.

[21] Michal Kryczka, Ruben Cuevas, Carmen Guerrero, and Arturo Azcorra. Unrevealing the structure of live bittorrent swarms: methodology and analysis. In *Peer-to-Peer Computing (P2P), 2011 IEEE International Conference on*, pages 230–239. IEEE, 2011.

[22] Ruben Cuevas Rumin, Nikolaos Laoutaris, Xiaoyuan Yang, Georgos Siganos, and Pablo Rodriguez. Deep diving into bittorrent locality. In *INFOCOM, 2011 Proceedings IEEE*, pages 963–971. IEEE, 2011.

Exploiting ICN for Flexible Management of Software-Defined Networks

Mayutan Arumaithurai*, Jiachen Chen*, Edo Monticelli*, Xiaoming Fu* and K. K. Ramakrishnan‡
*Institute of Computer Science, University of Göttingen, Germany.
Email: {arumaithurai,jiachen,monticelli,fu}@cs.uni-goettingen.de
‡University of California, Riverside, CA, U.S.A. Email: kk@cs.ucr.edu

ABSTRACT

Networks are becoming increasingly complex and service providers incorporate additional functionality in the network to protect, manage and improve service performance. Software Defined Networking (SDN) seeks to manage the network with the help of a (logically) centralized control plane. We observe that current SDN solutions pre-translate policy (what) into forwarding rules at specific switches (where). We argue that this choice limits the dynamicity, flexibility and reliability that a software based network could provide. Information Centric Networking (ICN) shifts the focus of networks away from being predominantly location oriented communication environments. We believe ICN can significantly improve the flexibility for network management. In this paper, we focus on one of the problems of network management – service chaining – the steering of flows through the different network functions needed, before it is delivered to the destination. We propose Function-Centric Service Chaining (FCSC), a solution that exploits ICN to provide flexibility in managing networks that utilize virtualization to dynamically place functions in the network as required. We use a real-world topology to compare the performance of FCSC and a more "traditional" SDN solution. We show that FCSC reacts to failures with fewer packet drops, adapts to new middleboxes more quickly, and maintains less state in the network.

Categories and Subject Descriptors

C.2.3 [**Network Operations**]: Network Management

General Terms

Design; Management

Keywords

ICN; Service Chaining; Network Management; SDN; Network Function Virtualizaion; Middlebox

1. INTRODUCTION

Service provider networks (and networks in general) are becoming increasingly complex. Both network operators and users require various additional functionalities in the network for management and processing of data flows. Software Defined Networking (SDN) aims to manage the network and the functions provided by separating the control plane from the data plane. The SDN controller(s) possess a global view of the network and can therefore simplify the network management as compared to the traditional distributed architectures typical of the Internet. However, even in an SDN environment, management logic ("what") is intricately coupled with the node location ("where"). With the use of virtualization and the prevalence of mobility the location of a particular function in the network may no longer be fixed. We envision that the performance of SDN would be further improved by incorporating the ideas of information-centricity that decouple the location of a particular network function instance from the identity of the function it provides. In this work, we make a first attempt by incorporating Information Centric capabilities into a common and important problem of network management – Service Chaining.

The need to perform additional processing of packets of a data flow in the network before it is delivered to the destination has become an integral element of providing Internet services. These functions include the modification of the packet header (*e.g.*, NAT, proxy), discard packets (*e.g.*, firewall), collection of statistical information (*e.g.*, Deep Packet Inspection (DPI)) or even the modification of the payload (*e.g.*, optimization and compression). They are provided in the form of *Middleboxes* [9, 19, 40] for policy control, security and performance optimization. The middleboxes have to be resident on the path of a flow, which implies that the traffic has to be deviated from its "natural" IP shortest path and forced through the middleboxes. We use the term *Service Chaining* to describe the action of steering packets through these middleboxes. For example, a network operator might require flows that access dynamic web pages such as Facebook, Twitter, FourSquare, Google Instant, or MyYahoo to go through middleboxes like Content Delivery Network (CDN), Dynamic Site Accelerator (DSA [1]), TCP optimization over tunnel, *etc.*, in order to improve the perceived user experience [2].

The limited presence of middleboxes at specific locations in the network often results in sub-optimal routing and lower performance (*e.g.*, increased latency, lower throughput, *etc.*). This is especially true in environments like cellular networks [15, 16] where middlebox functions are restricted to be in the

"Network Data Center" and thus have a significant impact on latency. The recent introduction of Network Function Virtualization (NFV) [14, 20] promises to make it easier to dynamically and flexibly deploy middleboxes. NFV allows for middlebox functions to be virtualized and therefore be present in greater number and positioned on-demand. We envisage network service providers will increasingly adopt NFV to provide network resident functionality, not only for reducing CAPEX but also for offering more flexibility to customers who would like customized processing of their packets. However, managing such a network of dynamically placed functions can be much more complex. Current routing protocols deployed in IP networks constrain how packets can be deviated from well-defined path (e.g., shortest path) and thus cannot take full advantage of the great flexibility offered by NFV.

Recently proposed solutions for Service Chaining in Software Defined Networking (SDN) [22, 33, 45] attempt to perform Network Management by making use of a (logically) centralized controller that has the capability to setup flow-based forwarding rules on the switches [18, 27] of the desired path. Such solutions provide greater control over the network in order to steer packets of a flow more flexibly, without being constrained by traditional routing such as OSPF and BGP. But the controller has to keep track of the status of the middleboxes and the network.

We argue that the existing approaches have a common issue of unnecessarily coupling the routing with the policy. I.e., when an SDN controller decides the *functions* a flow needs, it also decides the *path* the flow has to go through and setup *state* on the intermediate switches. These solutions have limitations in *scalability*, *dynamicity* and *flexibility* and therefore have difficulty in adapting to the requirements of a large scale, dynamically changing middlebox set supported by NFV (see §3.3 for detailed descriptions).

Information-Centric Network (ICN [4,21,44]) is a new networking paradigm that introduces ContentNames to decouple the user interests from data location. Following this line of thinking, we present *Function-Centric Service Chaining* (FCSC), a novel approach that decouples the *functions* a flow needs from the *location* of network function instances (and thus routing) via a naming layer (see Fig. 1). Such a decoupling facilitates the dynamic modification of the functions needed by a flow on the controller or the middleboxes (e.g., DPI, load balancer). This also enables switches to dynamically detect the load (popularity) of a certain function and accordingly instantiate/dispose of network function instances (co-resident with the switch or on some other node). The enroute function-based routing allows more dynamic use of the newly created instances and faster recovery from node/link failures. FCSC intrinsically supports the presence of multiple instances for the same functionality and can perform network-layer load-balancing among these nodes at any time. By placing the flow state in the packet header, FCSC helps to reduce the amount of state stored in the network and results in much better scalability compared to the per-flow state solutions like SDN. FCSC is therefore able to provide a highly dynamic and adaptive Service Chaining capability and effectively exploit the promise of NFV in the software-based network of the future.

The key contributions of this work are:

- We exploit the combination of ICN with SDN to meet the dynamic requirements of service chaining. We pro-

pose FCSC, a scalable and flexible architecture, that clearly separates the policy (required functions) from the routing by introducing a light-weight (function) naming layer.

- With the help of varying number of flows and dynamic creation/deletion of virtual service instances on a synthetic and a real-world Rocketfuel topology, we show how FCSC compliments the current SDN solution in terms of network state amount, packet drop rate on node failure and overall latency.

The rest of the paper is organized as follows: §2 discusses previous work on service chaining and information-centric network; §3 provides detailed description on the service chaining scenario and the problems with the existing solutions. §4 describes the design rational of FCSC and §5 details upon the solution. §6 illustrates simulation results and conclusion is inferred in §7.

2. RELATED WORK

In this section, we briefly present existing work on service chaining, then present an overview of ICN and finally present existing work that involves both SDN and ICN.

2.1 Existing Solutions for Service Chaining

Existing Service Chaining solutions can be broadly classified into 3 classes: indirection-based, policy-based and SDN-based.

2.1.1 Indirection-based Service Chaining:

Several proposals for service chaining regard *indirection* as an indispensable element for achieving high flexibility to support various scenarios including node mobility, caching and anycast. Works in [6,40] propose an architectural modification to TCP/IP networks in order to allow further indirection than what is supported by DNS, allowing simple integration of middleboxes into the TCP/IP architecture. [6] highlights the problem of having an IP address – location-dependent element – as the identifier of end hosts, and proposes the introduction of several levels of indirection. Other similar works include [10, 17, 30, 31, 37, 39]. Unfortunately, these solutions rely on predetermined nodes that provide the service, thus becoming inflexible to react to node failure as well as new instances of middlebox functionality.

2.1.2 Policy-Based Routing (PBR):

Cisco's policy-based approach [13] allows the administrator to specify adjunctive rules for routing, that are selectively applied depending on the traffic characteristics (e.g., IP 5-tuple, rate, etc.). Since the rules must be manually configured on each PBR router, the solution scales poorly and cannot dynamically react to network condition changes.

2.1.3 SDN-based Service Chaining:

Several solutions have been presented that leverage SDN [22, 33, 45]. The general idea is to have a logically central controller that has a comprehensive view of the administered network portion and of the networking elements present. This controller can determine the best route for each flow that traverses the network and can take into consideration the potential need for this flow to go through one or more middleboxes. To make its decision effective, the controller must add forwarding rules to the involved switches, instructing them on the new next hop for each flow that deviate from its standard IP path.

2.2 Information Centric Networking

Information Centric Networking (ICN) has been actively studied in recent years [4, 5, 11, 12, 21, 24]. ICN shifts the focus of the network from node location (IP, MAC, *etc.*) to data names. Such design enables name-based routing which forwards the requests of a specific name towards a best source of the data in terms of latency, available bandwidth, source load and *etc.* Named-Data Networking NDN [4, 21] is one of the popular ICN solutions. NDN uses human-readable, hierarchical names such as `/thisroom/projector` or `/icn/papers/FCSC.pdf`. The forwarding engines perform the longest-prefix matching in the FIB to find the next-hop router closer to the data provider. FCSC adopts the idea of ICN since the naming layer focuses more on the name of the functions rather than the location of the function instances. It is implemented on a model similar to NDN (naming and routing) but with some changes (no Pending Interest Table or reverse-path forwarding).

2.3 Works that Combine ICN and SDN

There are several works that try to explore the potential for combining ICN and SDN [29, 34, 38]. But most of these works use SDN technology to enable incremental deployment of ICN. To the best of our knowledge, this is the first work that tries to improve the performance of SDN via information-centric concept (ICN).

3. SCENARIO DESCRIPTION AND PROBLEM STATEMENT

In this section, we describe the scenarios we envision of how network resident functionality of middleboxes could be utilized and point out the shortcomings of the state-of-art SDN solutions. We will use these as the basis to demonstrate the benefits of our proposed approach.

3.1 Service Chaining Scenario

An Autonomous System (AS), for example an IP network, data center or an information centric network, is typically composed of many edge routers and a set of core routers/switches. Packets from users enter this AS from one of the edge routers (Ingress). These packets categorized into flows (either by 5-tuple in IP or "Interest" prefix in ICN) need to go through a specified set of functions in the core in *a particular order*, as required by policy. The functions may include Deep Packet Inspection (DPI), policy, QoS, Network Address Translation (NAT), Dynamic Site Accelator (DSA), proxying, transparent caching, accounting and logging *etc.* It is also possible that a subset of these functions may in fact be provided by third parties, and possibly in a cloud-resident platform [35].

3.2 Detailed Requirements

With the growth of the middleboxes and the network traffic, we envision that an efficient service chaining network should meet the following requirements:

3.2.1 Flexibility:

The outcome of packet processing by a middlebox may change the set of function(s) to be applied on subsequent packets of the flow. *E.g.*, after a packet goes through DPI, the policy or algorithm may determine the need for additional network resident functions like intrusion detection, logging, *etc.*, to be applied on the flow. It is also possible that functions can reduce/replace the functions a flow needs to go through. *E.g.*, after observing a set of packets in a flow, the DPI can decide to remove the virus scan and even DPI itself from the function list. Therefore, even if a set of apriori service functions were specified, they might be changed during the lifetime of the flow. An efficient service chaining network should support such changes in a flexible way – the middleboxes should be able to determine the functions of a flow *themselves* and the changes should take effect *immediately*.

3.2.2 Dynamicity:

The advent of NFV allows for network resident middleboxes to dynamically incorporate (additional) functionality by spinning up additional virtual machines on demand. *E.g.*, if there are many more flows that require firewall functionality but fewer flows require DPI functionality, the network manager should be able to instantiate more firewall nodes and reduce the number of DPI nodes. Since more functions are running on virtualized platforms, these functions can potentially be placed anywhere in the network instead of on only a selected set of predefined nodes. This requires the network to be able to apply these changes as soon as possible while keeping the communication cost low. For the functions having multiple instances, the network should also be able to balance the load on these instances to optimize performance.

3.2.3 Scalability:

The scalability requirement comes in three dimensions: the number of functions, the number of flows and the size of the network. With more customized services provided to network users, it is envisioned that there would be an increase in the number of network functions available. For the networks that adopt NFV, the number of instances of network functions can also grow to be large. A scalable service chaining solution should not limit the number of users/flows, the number of functions a flow should traverse, or the size of the network due to the response latency or the number of states stored in the network.

3.2.4 Reliability:

A productive service chaining solution should also take reliability into consideration. The solution should be able to dynamically react to the node (middleboxes, switches or controllers) failures and the link failures within a threshold. As suggested by [32], the recovery time of a failure should be within 10s of milliseconds.

3.3 Limitations of Existing SDN Solutions

Current SDN solutions [22,33,45] perform better than policy based routing (PBR) and indirection based solutions. However, they are still not able to meet the requirements mentioned above, because:

Flexibility: When a middlebox like DPI needs to change the functions a flow requires, it has to rely on the controller to build a new path that goes through a certain instance of each of these functions. This results in extra control overhead in both communication and latency for every flow whenever the set of functions are changed. This is not desirable since the controller in SDN design is supposed to *generate* the rules but not be involved in the real-time handling of packets [43].

Dynamicity: It is difficult for SDN controllers to perform real-time decisions on the path of a flow to balance the load in the network and on the function instances. The problem will become more severe when the number of flows grows and NFV enables more dynamic instantiation/disposition of function instances.

Scalability: SDN solutions place rules for every flow on the switches. The number of rules stored in the network is proportional to the number of flows, the functions the flows require and the size of the network. It is very difficult to scale when the network has larger number of flows or the network itself grows larger.

Reliability: When a middlebox or a link fails, the switches in the existing SDN solutions have to rely on the central controller to build a new path for the flow. This increases the convergence time while dealing with such failures and might violate the typical 30-50ms convergence time target requirement typical in a large provider networks. Alternatively, the controller has to setup backup paths proportional to the number of hops for every flow to ensure quick convergence time. But this exacerbates the scalability problem.

4. FCSC OVERVIEW

In this section, we start by reasoning the design choices we have made and then describe the whole architecture based on the design choices. Design details will be provided in §5.

4.1 Design Rationale

To achieve the requirements of flexibility, dynamicity and reliability as described above, we propose to add a naming layer (similar to ICN) to the current SDN architecture. Moreover, to improve the scalability of the system, we choose to put flow-state in the packet header rather than in the switches. But our solution is still backwards compatible with existing SDN-based service chaining solutions.

4.1.1 Naming Layer

ICN provides flexibility to users – they only need to request the network with *what* they want rather than *where* that data might reside. Such a shift in the focus of the network also provides better dynamicity and reliability – a request can go to *any* of a set of possible data providers/caches in the network.

We find a strong similarity between the fundamental needs that drive service chaining and the capabilities offered by ICN. Middleboxes that need to change the function list of flow (*e.g.*, DPI) require flexibility – they only need to care about the *functions* the flow requires rather than asking the SDN controller to build a path to *where* the flow should go through. While forwarding a packet, the network can forward the packet to *any* of the instances that provides the same function. This allows the dynamic adoption of new function instances and can also help fast recovery when a function instance/link fails.

To achieve high performance (line-speed forwarding in the network), we primarily incorporate the hierarchical naming capabilities of an ICN environment like NDN, to represent the function list and the longest-prefix matching in the FIB to forward packets. The reverse-path forwarding (PIT) and

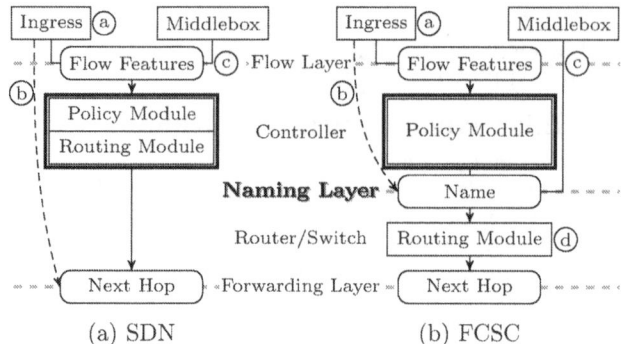

(a) SDN   (b) FCSC

Figure 1: Architectural design of FCSC *vs.* SDN.

caching (Content Store) capabilities that are used in an ICN for information distribution is not key to this solution. According to [36, 42], line-speed (hashed) name forwarding is achievable with existing hardware.

4.1.2 Flow State in the Packet Header

We note that the solutions of existing SDN-based service chaining incorporate flow state in the switches – the switches maintain state on how to forward a specific packet based on the 5-tuple (or other header features) of that packet. Such a design results in the number of rules in the network to be proportional to the number of flows and the number of functions these flows require. It does not scale well with the growth of clients (flows) and the adoption of new functions in the network.

Therefore, we choose to put the flow state – the functions the packet still need to traverse through – in the packet header. The function list of a packet (in the form of an ICN name) is tagged to the packet header when it enters the network. After traversing through a middlebox, the name of the applied function is removed from the header and the network will forward the packet to the next function it requires.

In our solution, the network only needs to maintain forwarding information on a per-function basis rather than a per-flow basis. The amount of state stored is therefore proportional to the functions in the network but not the flows, and thus our solution can scale much better than existing solutions.

4.1.3 Compatibility with existing SDN solutions

Network management, as exemplified by service chaining, needs SDN for flexible placement of functions and more powerful routing, and achieves this because it has a (logically) centralized view of the whole network. The purpose of our solution is not to replace these ideas in SDN solutions or to remove the existence of the (logically) central controllers, but to make them more flexible by the modifications proposed in our paper: namely the naming layer and the use of flow state in the packet header. Our solution can also be backwards compatible with the existing SDN solutions by naming all the intermediate switches (in the form of IP or MAC addresses) and setup a separate forwarding table on every switch in a hop-by hop manner. But that will result in the loss of the benefits mentioned above.

4.2 Architecture Description

Fig. 1 illustrates the logical separation of the architecture of FCSC compared to existing SDN solutions. As described above, we add a *Naming Layer* in the architecture that separates the *policy* module (the module that manages *what* functions should be applied to a flow) from the *routing* module (the module that manages *where* the function instances reside). The representation of the naming layer (the function list a packet should go through) resides in the packet header to scale the network better. To help understand the figure, we describe the differences between the two solutions in the following 4 scenarios (following the marking on the figure):

a. Flow initiation:

In SDN, on seeing a new flow, the ingress sends the flow feature (*e.g.*, 5-tuple) to the controller. In this case, the controller has the *function* module and *routing* module coupled. The controller determines the result, a set of forwarding rules (*e.g.*, 5-tuple↦NextHop) that are then incorporated on different switches on the path.

In FCSC, the controller determines which functions the flow needs and return the result only to the ingress. The ingress then tags the packets of the flow with the function list. On seeing the functions carried in the packet header, switches in the network will look into their FIB (in the form of Function↦NextHop) and decide the outgoing "face" of the packet. The FIB of the switches are controlled by the *Routing Module*. The *Routing Module* can either be distributed (*e.g.*, OSPFN [41], IS-IS [8]) or logically centralized (*e.g.*, SDN).

b. Proactive rules:

The controller can also setup wildcard proactive rules on every ingress. An SDN controller essentially has to build a path for every flow from each ingress. This increases complexity since almost every edge router can be an ingress and there might exist $O(N^2)$ *src-dst* paths where N is the number of edge routers even without considering different paths for a same *src-dst* pair.

In FCSC, the controller only needs to flood the wild card rules (FlowFeature↦FunctionList) to all the ingress. The core of the network does not have to keep any state on a per flow basis any more.

c. Policy change by middleboxes:

When certain middleboxes need to change the policy (function list) of a flow, in SDN the middleboxes have to request the controller to build a new path for the flow. This might result in even more state in the network and also higher latency, just like what we would experience at the beginning of a flow.

FCSC allows middleboxes to determine the new policy, without having to request the controller to change forwarding rules at specific switches. These middleboxes change the function list in the packet header and the network will forward it towards the next middlebox automatically. Additionally, they may notify the ingress to change the function list for the future packets of the flow. This solution therefore only requires a change in the state of the packet header and the ingress as opposed to every switch on the old and new path. Therefore, unlike existing solutions, it does not require additional set up time while a middlebox like DPI tries to modify the policy. It is thus able to quickly enforce the policy on the newly arriving packets.

d. Dynamic routing:

With existing SDN solutions, the functions a flow requires is represented by the path it follows. Whenever a middlebox

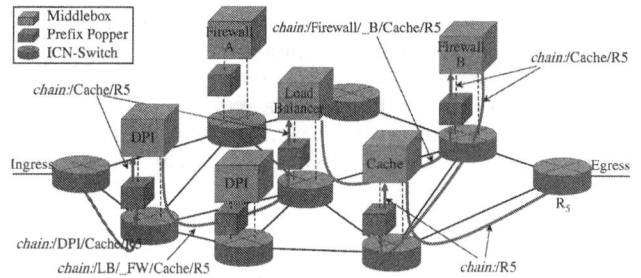

Figure 2: **Example of the name changing of a packet in FCSC.**

fails, the failure notification has to be reported to the controller before the new path that includes another instance of the function is built for the flow. Approach in [32] precomputes backup paths to shorten the recovery time on such failures, but this results in exponential complexity due to the permutations and function combinations. When a new instance of a function is adopted, it is also difficult to use it for existing flows for purposes of load balancing.

FCSC separates the routing of flows from the policy. The switches can decide (an alternate) outgoing face based on its own FIB. This shortens the response time for node/link failures and can make use of new instances of functions on the fly (as long as the FIB is updated based on the *Routing module*).

5. DESIGN DETAILS

In this section, we describe in detail how we design the architecture to ensure a highly efficient and scalable service delivery network.

5.1 Naming Strategy

We extend the ICN principle of *naming content* to *naming function*. Every instance that provides the same function is referred to by the same name, *e.g.*, `/DPI`, `/Firewall`, *etc.*

When the network policy requires a flow to go through a sequence of functions, the policy executor (the controller or the ingress) will encapsulate each packet of the flow with a header containing a name that represents the sequence of functions to be executed, in a FCFS manner. *E.g.*, a packet header with name *chain:*/`DPI/Cache/R5` implies that DPI and cache function must be applied to that packet before it exits the network from the egress R_5. Here, we use the scheme identifier (as per URI Generic Syntax [7]) "*chain*" to represent the packets for service chaining. We can use other identifies like "*monitor*", "*ctrl*", *etc.*, to represent packets meant for other purposes (*e.g.* monitoring and controlling, *etc.*)

The switch fronting a middlebox (SxFM) will pop the first part of name (prefix) in the packet header before it forwards the packet to a middlebox function associated with it. Some policy nodes can also change the name to redirect the packet towards other functions.

Prefix popping is a simple and stateless task. It can be separated from the switching and the middlebox functions. If necessary, we can include a designated hardware component for acceleration,or instantiate a virtual prefix popping function, on the SxFM (although we believe it is a simple task). Since it is a stateless task, the SxFM can also have multiple of these components (either hardware-based or software-based) that run in parallel to ensure line-speed forwarding is achieved on the SxFM.

Fig. 2 illustrates the lifetime of a packet in our network. The ingress encapsulates the incoming packet with a header *chain:*/DPI/Cache/R5 as desired by policy. The network forwards the packet to the SxFM of the "best" DPI function (in terms of relative location, latency or other criteria). The prefix /DPI is removed when passing through the prefix popping function (represented by a green box) before entering the DPI box. The DPI function decides the packet should also go through a firewall and since there is a load balancer for the two firewalls in the network, the DPI adds a prefix /LB/_FW to the header. The prefix is replaced with /Firewall/_B by the load balancer since it decides that the flow should go through Firewall B. The remaining prefixes are popped one by one when going through the Firewall B and Cache. On reaching R_5, the egress sees its own name and therefore it decapsulates the packet and forwards the original packet out of the network.

5.2 Routing Strategy

Middleboxes need to advertise their existence before they can be used by the flows. A middlebox offering a certain service (*e.g.*, Firewall) advertises the name of the service as prefix (*e.g.*, /Firewall). Packets whose names have the prefix /Firewall can be routed towards this middlebox as a consequence of the normal name based routing. A packet in FCSC is only forwarded to one middlebox even when multiple middleboxes exist for the same function (prefix). The intermediate switches can monitor the popularity of a function based on these prefixes, and they can create additional instances where needed with NFV support.

The decision of *which* exact instance of the function a packet should traverse is determined by the routing module. FCSC does not limit the routing module that can be adopted. To better support different routing strategies, we provide a simple standard interface for the routing module to control the forwarding decision. We add a "cost" field in the FIB and thus the data structure looks like Function↦{Next-Hop, Cost}. If multiple "NextHop"s exist for the same function, the switch will always forward the packet to the next hop with the lowest cost. The routing module can have different interpretations of the "cost", *e.g.*, link latency, policy, energy/work-load considerations, *etc.*

The choice of the routing scheme can affect the dynamicity and reliability of the whole solution. We discuss the benefits and issues of some possible routing solutions – generally categorized into centralized and distributed schemes. But, it should be noted that regardless of which routing scheme is used, FCSC is able to achieve better scalability since we only maintain function state.

Centralized/SDN solutions (*e.g.*, [33]) have better control over the node state including what is maintained at switches and middleboxes. They provide more flexible control in determining where middleboxes should be placed and monitoring node state. Routing based on names of function instances may offer better real-time load balancing capability, faster failure recovery and utilization of new function instances.

Distributed routing solutions (*e.g.*, [41]) allow every switch to have the intelligence to make routing decisions on its own. This would enable dynamicity in routing to a newly created instance or avoiding a failed link/middlebox. But these solutions might incur higher control overhead for synchronizing the network state on every switch, especially when automatic load balancing is required for different instances of the same function.

We realize that both the centralized and the distributed routing methods face the difficulty of achieving real-time load balancing similar to [3]. A compromise is for the network to incorporate a load balancer to dynamically distribute the load on the servers/middleboxes that have the same functionality. Our architecture can fully support such load balancers (see the example in §5.1).

5.3 Stateful Middleboxes

There might be some functions in the network that need to maintain state. In such a case, all the packets of a flow should go through the same instance, even though they may not care which actual instance they might use. This implies that the different instances for the same function cannot be treated equivalently. The two firewalls in Fig. 2 could be an example of this kind. FCSC adopts the hierarchical name in ICN to meet this requirement. Instead of using the same name, the multiple instances share a common prefix (function name), but they have function-level unique ID. *E.g.*, the firewalls in Fig. 2 are called /Firewall/_A and /Firewall/_B respectively.

While advertising the prefix, the middleboxes advertise the whole name instead of the function name itself. If a packet can go through any of the instances for a function, it just puts the function name in the header (*e.g.*, *chain:* /Firewall/Cache). Otherwise, it will use the full name (*e.g.*, *chain:*/Firewall/_A/Cache). This can be determined by the policy executor or on the fly. ICN switches perform the longest-prefix match, and therefore the packet can be forwarded to the required function instance, if specified. While popping the name from the packet header, we can also perform "longest-prefix popping" of the full instance name from the name list. To avoid ambiguity, this solution requires that the instance ID space should not overlap the function name space. *E.g.*, Firewall B pops both the /Firewall and /_B prefixes from the packet header in Fig. 2.

For the functions that require visibility of the bidirectional packets of a flow, the policy module can also specify the function instance via its full name and create a function (instance) list in the reverse order. *E.g.*, if say the firewall function (only) requires packets from both directions, the policy layer can create name *chain:*/DPI/Firewall/_A/Cache for one direction and *chain:*/Cache/Firewall/_A/DPI for the other.

5.4 Security

Security is another big concern in service chaining. The users of the network should not have any chance to infiltrate the network and steer the packets through paths that are not allowed by the policy.

FCSC encapsulates each packet at the point they enter the network and decapsulates them on egress. Therefore, the service provider network is essentially transparent to users. We do not provide any user interfaces to the clients and therefore there should be no way a user can interact with the encapsulation/decapsulation function or the other function modules in the network. No client of FCSC can violate this policy by altering the packet in some way.

6. EVALUATION

In this section, we evaluate on a custom simulator (widely used in previous works [12] [11]) the dynamicity, reliability and scalability of FCSC with a distributed routing module and compare it to a relatively simple (physically) centralized SDN solution that is conceptually similar to [33, 45]. These approaches use the basic OpenFlow protocol constructs that is a controller interacting with network forwarding elements [28].

We recognize that there are approaches for decentralized SDN solutions like [23, 43], but the results from [25] show that the inconsistent SDN control state can *significantly* degrade performance of logically centralized control applications that are agnostic of the underlying state distribution. In addition, the communication overhead for keeping all the controllers synchronized has to be addressed. Moreover, even if there exists multiple controllers, it is still fair to assume that each of these controllers is in charge of a set of routers (a portion of the network). Therefore, the centralized solution we use here can also be viewed as such a portion.

We first demonstrate the benefits of FCSC on a small synthetic topology (shown in Fig. 3a). Subsequently, we run a large-scale simulation on a real world topology to evaluate the scalability and the efficiency of our solution in a more realistic environment.

6.1 Study of FCSC Behavior

Fig. 3a shows a simple topology with multiple middleboxes. R_1-R_6 are FCSC capable switches. N_1-N_4 and DPI provide functions A and B and DPI as noted in the figure. Src and Dst are the source and destination of a flow of interest. $Ctrl$ is the central controller in an SDN solution. The link latency between switches is $2ms$ and the latency between switches and the end-systems (middlebox, src, dst, control) is $10ms$. The bandwidth on the link is $100Mbps$ (large enough to support the flow). The processing latency on all the middleboxes (including $Ctrl$) is $1ms$, or $1000pps$ (packets per second). The sending rate at src is also $1000pps$.

We use several scenarios to compare the behavior of FCSC with the simple SDN solution:

6.1.1 Proactive rules for flow initiation:

We first compare the initiation phase for both solutions. We compare FCSC with an SDN solution without proactive rules set up in the switches.

Fig. 3b shows the overall latency (the amount of time spent from Src to Dst in the network) of every packet in the initiation phase of a flow that requires DPI and B function. Because FCSC does not make a request to the central controller, it can achieve significantly lower latency for the first 30 packets of a flow compared to the SDN solution. This reduction may be critical for small flows that require timely processing of middlebox functions (*e.g.*, games).

We recognize that with proactive rules set up in the switches, SDN solutions can achieve lower latencies, as good as FCSC. However, we believe it still requires a lot more effort to pre-calculate the paths for different permutations as compared to our solution.

6.1.2 Dynamic Policy change on Middleboxes:

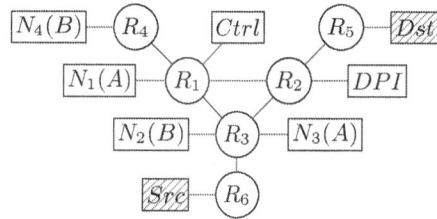

(a) Demo Topology

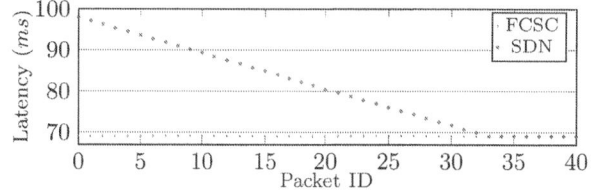

(b) Flow initiation using proactive rules

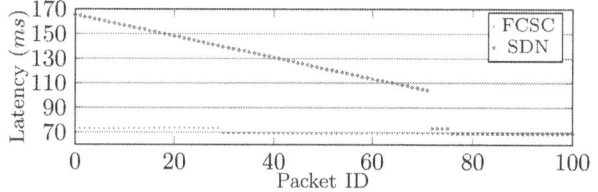

(c) Dynamic function modification by DPI

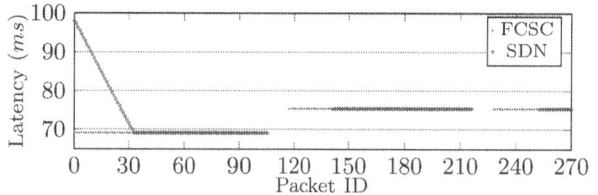

(d) Dynamic failure recovery

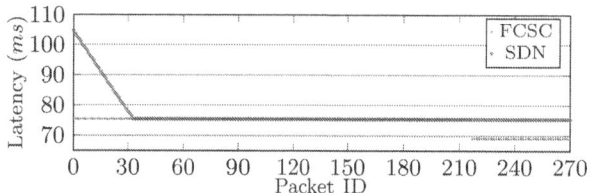

(e) Dynamic adaptation to new instances

Figure 3: Behavior of FCSC: Topology and Results.

In the second experiment, the default policy requires a flow to go through DPI and B functions (represented as a *chain:*/DPI/B). But the DPI then decides to add function A and also removes itself from the function list (the name then becomes *chain:*/A/B) after it examines the first packet of the flow (this is a typical dynamic function processing required in service provider networks for actions such as mobile video processing etc.). In the SDN solution, DPI requests $Ctrl$ to create a new path for the flow and block the packets from being forwarded before the new path is built. In contrast, with FCSC, DPI directly renames the packets that continue to arrive and notifies the ingress (R_6) to change the policy. There is no need to block the packets at the DPI.

Fig. 3c shows the latency of the first 90 packets in the flow. In FCSC, only the first 29 packets go through DPI with less than $75ms$ overall latency. However, in SDN, 73 packets flow into *DPI* before *Ctrl* can setup a new rule for the later packets. The overall latency of the first packet grows up to $165ms$. Another 4 packets experienced a loop since the rules are not setup atomically.

From the result, we see that FCSC responds faster to the dynamic policy changes, this results in lower packet latency and also lower DPI load (process & modify 29 headers *vs.* process & buffer 73 packets in this example).

6.1.3   Dynamic failure recovery:

In the third trace, the flow is required to go through functions A and B (represented as *chain:/*A/B). The initial shortest path routing in both SDN and FCSC choose to go through N_3 for A and N_2 for B. We dispose N_3 at $150s$ and N_2 at $240s$ and see the packet loss and recovery time in FCSC and SDN.

Fig. 3d shows the overall latency of the packets that reach *Dst*. The packets in the outgoing buffer of SxFM and on the link to a failed middlebox (~ 10 pkts) have to be dropped in both solutions. Since the intermediate switches can redirect the packets without going to the central controller, FCSC can have around 25 more successful deliveries every time a node fails. This value can increase when the network is becoming more complex or the controller is farther away from the failure.

6.1.4   Dynamic adaption to new instances:

The last trace has a flow that goes through functions A and B. At the beginning of the trace, only N_1 and N_4 are instantiated. N_3 is created at $150s$ and N_2 is created at $240s$.

Fig. 3e shows the overall latency of the packets in the flow. The SDN solution does not modify the path of the ongoing flows due to the complexity (the problem is similar to a warehouse location problem and is NP-complete). Therefore, the latency does not change even when the new instances are created for the functions. FCSC enables the middleboxes to advertise their function prefix to the network and the switches can redirect flows based on that information and therefore this solution can adapt to the new instances and the latency is lowered. Note that when N_3 is instantiated at $150s$, the flow is redirected to N_3 for the shorter distance from the ingress, but the overall latency is not changed because the same number of hops are traversed. However, adding N_2 reduces the latency in FCSC as the packets do not have to flow to N_4.

6.2   Large Scale Evaluation

We adopt a slightly modified Rocketfuel topology [26] (Exodus, AS-3967, see Fig. 5) to evaluate FCSC in a real world environment. The 18 cities present in this topology is used as the core network. The latency between every pair of these core switches is determined by the average of the latency on the links between the two cities. We eventually get 30 links with latency ranging from $2ms$ to $21ms$ and a mean value of $6.6ms$. The latency between the core switches and the end-hosts, middleboxes and the controller is set to $6ms$. Since the original topology only contains latency information, we assign $100Mbps$ bandwidth to all the links.

We assume that there exist 11 different functions in the network. One of them is unique in that the DPI-like function rewrites the function list as needed. The flows belong to one of the 100 different applications. Every application requires

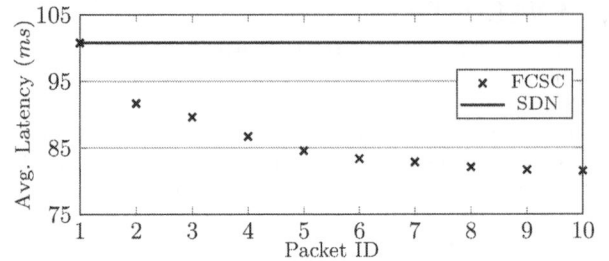

Figure 4: Benefit of increasing # of instances per function.

a range of different network functions varying in number from 1 to 4. DPI can dynamically change the functions a flow that needs.

6.2.1   Varying number of function instances

We first study the benefits of adopting FCSC in a network that dynamically creates virtual instances at random switches. We study 100 long-lasting ($5min$) flows starting at $0s$ with different sending rate (ranging from $120kbps$ to $1.05Mbps$).

At the beginning of the simulation, we have 1 instance for each function initialized. Then, we start a new randomly located instance for each function every half a minute until the maximum number of instances is reached (the maximum number of instances for each run is shown in the x-axis in Fig. 4). In the first run, only the initial middleboxes are used for the entire 5 minutes; in the second run, in addition to the initial functions, another one instance per available function is randomly placed on a switch in the network at time $30s$ and lasts until the end of the simulation. In the third run, a third instance is put into the network at time $60s$ and so on.

Fig. 4 shows the average latency vs. the number of instances eventually initiated for that simulation run. We see that FCSC can automatically adapt by making use of new instances that are closer, even for the ongoing flows and the average latency drops from $100.75ms$ to $91.66ms$ when adding a second instance. The latency is further reduced to around $85ms$ when we have 5 instances created. This is beneficial for long flows compared to the alternative SDN solution where the ongoing flows are unaffected by dynamic addition of functions in the network, unless the controller resets the rules.

The results illustrate that FCSC is able to seamlessly take advantage of new instances of virtual middleboxes that have the same functionality, even when the network is not overloaded. We can also observe that the higher the number of instances, the lower the incremental benefit. In our scenario consisting of 18 switches, more than 8 instances do not yield additional benefit. Ignoring the absolute numbers, since it is topology dependent, one can nevertheless envision that there is a tradeoff between user-experience and the cost of the deployment. Another way to reduce the latency is to pick an optimal location to instantiate the middlebox. This is an additional optimization that can complement our architectural proposal, and is part of our future work.

6.2.2   Varying number of flows & function instances

We now load the simulation with a varying number of flows (50, 100, 150, ..., 500). Each flow has its own arrival time (within the first $5min$), a sending rate in the range

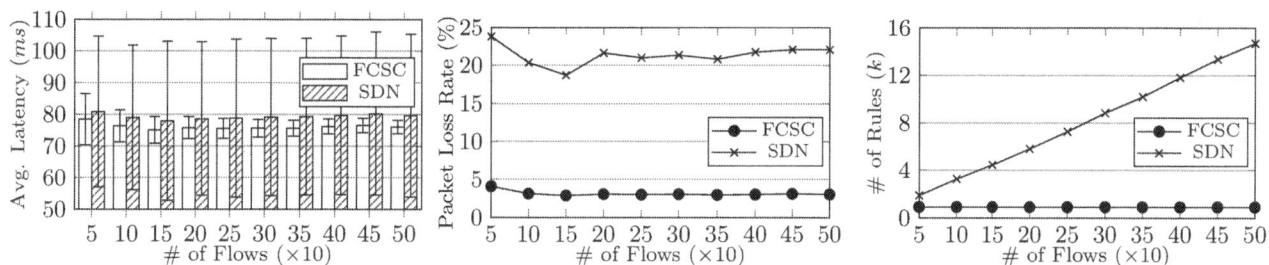

(a) Latency (and 95% CI) vs. # of flows (b) % of packets lost vs. # of flows (c) # of rules vs. # of flows

Figure 6: Results for varying-flow simulation.

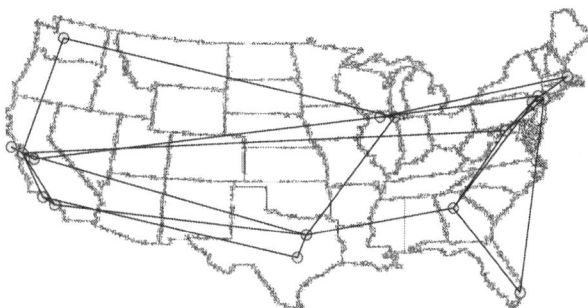

Figure 5: RocketFuel topology (Exodus, AS-3967).

($1.2Mbps$ - $11.9Mbps$) and duration ($0.05s$ to $91.24s$). We also randomly generated $1,151$ middlebox creation/failure events during the simulation period. We run the trace on both the FCSC and SDN solutions and compare the average latency for the flows, packet loss caused by middlebox failure, and the number of rules stored on the switches.

Fig. 6a shows the average latency along with 95% confidence interval (CI) for the different flows. FCSC provides lower average latency and less variability compared to the SDN solution, since the flows are able to take advantage of new instances that are closer.

The overall percent of packet lost in Fig. 6b shows that with the dynamic failure recovery, FCSC helps to deliver more packets to the destination. Lower loss rate usually means lower re-transmission rate and also lower overall network cost.

FCSC capable switches only maintain rules on a per available instance of a function, unlike the SDN solution that keeps rules for each flow type (defined by a n-tuple, potentially with wild-cards). Therefore, the number of rules do not change when we vary the number of flows (as shown in Fig. 6c). However the number of rules in SDN grows with the number of flows. We argue that our solution can be more scalable especially in a large network with millions of concurrent flows.

7. SUMMARY

Existing SDN-based network management solutions pre-translate the policy (what) into the forwarding rules at specific switches (where). Such a design choice limits the benefits that a truly software-based network could provide. By proposing FCSC, we explore the potential of using information-centric concepts within an SDN-based network management environment, especially focusing on service chaining. Using both synthetic and realistic topologies, we show that FCSC is able to provide policy makers simpler interfaces to control a flow (flexibility), is able to react to middlebox failures with fewer packet drops (reliability), is able to more quickly adapt to new instances of middlebox functionality (dynamicity), and requires less state to be maintained in the network (scalability). For our future work, we will explore better routing mechanisms that can fully exploit the benefits provided by FCSC.

8. ACKNOWLEDGMENTS

The research leading to these results has received funding from the EU-JAPAN initiative by the EC Seventh Framework Programme (FP7/2007-2013) Grant Agreement No. 608518 (GreenICN), NICT under Contract No. 167 and the Volkswagen Foundation Project "Simulation Science Center". The views and conclusions contained herein are those of the authors and should not be interpreted as necessarily representing the official policies or endorsements, either expressed or implied, of the GreenICN project, the Simulation Science Center project, the European Commission, or NICT.

9. REFERENCES

[1] http://blog.streamingmedia.com/2010/10/how-dynamic-site-acceleration-works-what-akamai-and-cotendo-offer.html.

[2] http://blog.streamingmedia.com/2011/12/its-official-akamai-to-acquire-content-good-for-akamai-bad-for-customers.html.

[3] J. Abley and K. E. Lindqvist. Operation of anycast services. In *IETF, RFC*, number 4786, 2006.

[4] B. Ahlgren, M. D'Ambrosio, M. Marchisio, I. Marsh, C. Dannewitz, B. Ohlman, K. Pentikousis, O. Strandberg, R. Rembarz, and V. Vercellone. Design considerations for a network of information. In *Conext*, 2008.

[5] S. Arianfar, P. Nikander, and J. Ott. On Content-centric Router Design and Implications. In *Re-Arch*, 2010.

[6] H. Balakrishnan, K. Lakshminarayanan, S. Ratnasamy, S. Shenker, I. Stoica, and M. Walfish. A layered naming architecture for the internet. In *SIGCOMM*, 2004.

[7] T. Berners-Lee, R. Fielding, and L. Masinter. Uniform Resource Identifier (URI): Generic Syntax . In *IETF, RFC*, number 3986, 2005.

[8] R. Callon. Use of OSI IS-IS for Routing in TCP/IP and Dual Environments. In *IETF, RFC*, number 1195, 1990.

[9] B. E. Carpenter and S. Brim. Middleboxes: Taxonomy and Issues. In *IETF, RFC*, number 3234, 2002.

[10] I. Castineyra and M. Steenstrup. The Nimrod routing architecture. In *IETF, RFC*, 1992.

[11] J. Chen, M. Arumaithurai, X. Fu, and K. K. Ramakrishnan. G-COPSS: A Content Centric Communication Infrastructure for Gaming Applications. In *ICDCS*, 2012.

[12] J. Chen, M. Arumaithurai, L. Jiao, X. Fu, and K. K. Ramakrishnan. COPSS: An Efficient Content Oriented Publish/Subscribe System. In *ANCS*, 2011.

[13] CISCO. Policy-based routing. Technical report.

[14] C. Cui, H. Deng, D. Telekom, U. Michel, H. Damker, I. Guardini, E. Demaria, R. Minerva, and A. Manzalini. Network Functions Virtualisation. In *SDN and OpenFlow World Congress*, 2012.

[15] J. Erman, A. Gerber, K. K. Ramakrishnan, S. Sen, and O. Spatscheck. Over the Top Video: The Gorilla in Cellular Networks. In *IMC*, 2011.

[16] J. Erman and K. Ramakrishnan. Understanding the Super-sized Traffic of the Super Bowl. In *IMC*, 2013.

[17] B. Ford. Unmanaged Internet Protocol: taming the edge network management crisis. *arXiv preprint*, 2006.

[18] B. Heller, R. Sherwood, and N. McKeown. The Controller Placement Problem. *SIGCOMM CCR*, pages 473–478, 2012.

[19] M. Honda, Y. Nishida, C. Raiciu, A. Greenhalgh, M. Handley, and H. Tokuda. Is it still possible to extend TCP? In *IMC*, 2011.

[20] J. Hwang, K. Ramakrishnan, and T. Wood. NetVM: high performance and flexible networking using virtualization on commodity platforms. In *NSDI*, 2014.

[21] V. Jacobson, D. K. Smetters, J. D. Thornton, M. F. Plass, N. H. Briggs, and R. L. Braynard. Networking Named Content. In *CoNEXT*, 2009.

[22] S. Jain, A. Kumar, S. Mandal, J. Ong, L. Poutievski, A. Singh, S. Venkata, J. Wanderer, J. Zhou, M. Zhu, J. Zolla, U. Hölzle, S. Stuart, and A. Vahdat. B4: experience with a globally-deployed software defined wan. In *SIGCOMM*, 2013.

[23] T. Koponen, M. Casado, N. Gude, J. Stribling, L. Poutievski, M. Zhu, R. Ramanathan, Y. Iwata, H. Inoue, T. Hama, et al. Onix: A Distributed Control Platform for Large-scale Production Networks. In *OSDI*, 2010.

[24] T. Koponen, M. Chawla, B.-G. Chun, A. Ermolinskiy, K. H. Kim, S. Shenker, and I. Stoica. A data-oriented (and beyond) network architecture. *SIGCOMM CCR*, pages 181–192, 2007.

[25] D. Levin, A. Wundsam, B. Heller, N. Handigol, and A. Feldmann. Logically centralized?: state distribution trade-offs in software defined networks. In *HotSDN*, 2012.

[26] R. Mahajan, N. Spring, D. Wetherall, and T. Anderson. Inferring link weights using end-to-end measurements. In *IMW*, 2002.

[27] N. McKeown, T. Anderson, H. Balakrishnan, G. Parulkar, L. Peterson, J. Rexford, S. Shenker, and J. Turner. OpenFlow: Enabling Innovation in Campus Networks. *SIGCOMM CCR*, pages 69–74, 2008.

[28] N. McKeown, T. Anderson, H. Balakrishnan, G. Parulkar, L. Peterson, J. Rexford, S. Shenker, and J. Turner. Openflow: enabling innovation in campus networks. *SIGCOMM CCR*, pages 69–74, 2008.

[29] N. B. Melazzi, A. Detti, G. Mazza, G. Morabito, S. Salsano, and L. Veltri. An openflow-based testbed for information centric networking. In *FutureNetw*, 2012.

[30] R. Moskowitz and P. Nikander. Host Identity Protocol (HIP) Architecture. In *IETF, RFC*, number 4423, 2006.

[31] A. Myles, D. B. Johnson, and C. Perkins. Mobile host protocol supporting route optimization and authentication. *JSAC*, pages 839–849, 1995.

[32] P. Pan, G. Swallow, A. Atlas, et al. Fast reroute extensions to RSVP-TE for LSP tunnels. In *IETF, RFC*, number 4090, 2005.

[33] Z. A. Qazi, C.-C. Tu, L. Chiang, R. Miao, V. Sekar, and M. Yu. SIMPLE-fying middlebox policy enforcement using SDN. In *SIGCOMM*, 2013.

[34] R. Ravindran, X. Liu, A. Chakraborti, X. Zhang, and G. Wang. Towards software defined ICN based edge-cloud services. In *CloudNet*, 2013.

[35] J. Sherry, S. Hasan, C. Scott, A. Krishnamurthy, S. Ratnasamy, and V. Sekar. Making middleboxes someone else's problem: network processing as a cloud service. In *SIGCOMM*, 2012.

[36] W. So, A. Narayanan, and D. Oran. Named data networking on a router: fast and dos-resistant forwarding with hash tables. In *ANCS*, 2013.

[37] Stoica, Adkins, Ratnasamy, Shenker, Surana, and Zhuang. Internet Indirection Infrastructure. In *SIGCOMM*, 2002.

[38] M. Vahlenkamp, F. Schneider, D. Kutscher, and J. Seedorf. Enabling Information Centric Networking in IP Networks Using SDN. In *SDN4FNS*, 2013.

[39] M. Walfish and H. Balakrishnan. Untangling the Web from DNS. In *NSDI*, 2004.

[40] M. Walfish, J. Stribling, M. N. Krohn, H. Balakrishnan, R. Morris, and S. Shenker. Middleboxes No Longer Considered Harmful. In *OSDI*, 2004.

[41] L. Wang, A. Hoque, C. Yi, A. Alyyan, and B. Zhang. Ospfn: An ospf based routing protocol for named data networking. *Tech. Rep*, 2012.

[42] Y. Wang, Y. Zu, T. Zhang, K. Peng, Q. Dong, B. Liu, W. Meng, H. Dai, X. Tian, Z. Xu, et al. Wire speed name lookup: A gpu-based approach. In *NSDI*, 2013.

[43] M. Yu, J. Rexford, M. J. Freedman, and J. Wang. Scalable Flow-based Networking with DIFANE. In *SIGCOMM*, 2010.

[44] L. Zhang, D. Estrin, J. Burke, V. Jacobson, J. D. Thornton, D. K. Smetters, B. Zhang, G. Tsudik, D. Massey, C. Papadopoulos, et al. Named data networking (ndn) project. *Relatório Técnico NDN-0001, Xerox Palo Alto Research Center-PARC*, 2010.

[45] Y. Zhang, N. Beheshti, L. Beliveau, G. Lefebvre, R. Manghirmalani, R. Mishra, R. Patney, R. Subrahmaniam, M. Shirazipour, C. Truchan, and M. Tatipamula. StEERING: A Software-Defined Networking for Inline Service Chaining. In *ICNP*, 2013.

VIP: A Framework for Joint Dynamic Forwarding and Caching in Named Data Networks

Edmund Yeh[*]
Northeastern University
Boston, MA, USA
eyeh@ece.neu.edu

Tracey Ho[†]
California Inst. of Technology
Pasadena, CA, USA
tho@caltech.edu

Ying Cui
MIT
Cambridge, MA, USA
yingcui@mit.edu

Michael Burd
California Inst. of Technology
Pasadena, CA, USA
burdmi@gmail.com

Ran Liu
Northeastern University
Boston, MA, USA
liu.ran1@husky.neu.edu

Derek Leong
Inst. for Infocomm Research
Singapore
dleong@i2r.a-star.edu.sg

ABSTRACT

Emerging information-centric networking architectures seek to optimally utilize both bandwidth and storage for efficient content distribution. This highlights the need for joint design of traffic engineering and caching strategies, in order to optimize network performance in view of both current traffic loads and future traffic demands. We present a systematic framework for joint dynamic interest request forwarding and dynamic cache placement and eviction, within the context of the Named Data Networking (NDN) architecture. The framework employs a virtual control plane which operates on the user demand rate for data objects in the network, and an actual plane which handles Interest Packets and Data Packets. We develop distributed algorithms within the virtual plane to achieve network load balancing through dynamic forwarding and caching, thereby maximizing the user demand rate that the NDN network can satisfy. Numerical experiments within a number of network settings demonstrate the superior performance of the resulting algorithms for the actual plane in terms of low user delay and high rate of cache hits.

Categories and Subject Descriptors

C.2.1 [**Computer-Communication Networks**]: Network Architecture and Design—network communications

[*]E. Yeh gratefully acknowledges support from the National Science Foundation Future Internet Architecture grant CNS-1205562 and a Cisco Systems research grant.

[†]T. Ho gratefully acknowledges support from the Air Force Office of Scientific Research grant FA9550-10-1-0166.

General Terms

Theory, Design, Management

Keywords

Named data networking; content centric networking; information centric networking; forwarding; caching; routing

1. INTRODUCTION

Emerging information-centric networking (ICN) architectures are currently changing the landscape of network research. In particular, Named data networking (NDN) [1], or content-centric networking (CCN)[2], is a proposed network architecture for the Internet that replaces the traditional client-server model of communications with one based on the identity of data or content. This abstraction more accurately reflects how the Internet is primarily used today: instead of being concerned about communicating with specific nodes, end users are mainly interested in obtaining the data they want. The NDN architecture offers a number of important advantages in decreasing network congestion and delays, and in enhancing network performance in dynamic, intermittent, and unreliable mobile wireless environments [1].

Content delivery in NDN is accomplished using two types of packets, and specific data structures in nodes. Communication is initiated by the data consumer or requester. To receive data, the requester sends out an *Interest Packet*, which carries the (hierarchically structured) name of the desired data (e.g. /northeastern/videos/WidgetA.mpg/1). The Interest Packet is forwarded by looking up the data name in the *Forwarding Information Base (FIB)* at each router the Interest Packet traverses, along routes determined by a name-based routing protocol. The FIB tells the router to which neighbor node(s) to transmit each Interest Packet. Each router maintains a *Pending Interest Table (PIT)*, which records all Interest Packets currently awaiting matching data. Each PIT entry contains the name of the interest and the set of node interfaces from which the Interest Packets for the same name arrived. When multiple interests for the same name are received, only the first is sent toward the data source. When a node receives an interest that it can fulfill with matching data, it creates a *Data Packet* containing the data name, the data content, together with a signature by the producer's key. The Data Packet follows in reverse the path taken by the corresponding Interest Packet, as recorded by the PIT state at each router traversed. When the Data Packet arrives at a router, the router locates the matching PIT entry, transmits the data on all interfaces listed in the PIT entry, and then removes the PIT entry. The router may optionally cache a copy of the received Data Packet in its local *Content Store*, in order to satisfy possible future requests. Consequently, a request for a data object can be fulfilled not only by the content source but also by any node with a copy of that object in its cache [1].

Assuming the prevalence of caches, the usual approaches for forwarding and caching may no longer be effective for ICN architectures such as NDN. Instead, these architectures seek to optimally utilize both bandwidth and storage for efficient content distribution. This highlights the need for joint design of traffic engineering and caching strategies, in order to optimize network performance in view of both current traffic loads and future traffic demands. Unlike many existing works on centralized algorithms for static caching, our goal is to develop distributed, dynamic algorithms that can address caching and forwarding under changing content, user demands, and network conditions.

To address this fundamental problem, we introduce the *VIP framework* for the design of high performing NDN networks. The VIP framework relies on the new metric of *Virtual Interest Packets* (VIPs), which captures the measured demand for the respective data objects in the network. The central idea of the VIP framework is to employ a *virtual* control plane which operates on VIPs, and an *actual* plane which handles Interest Packets and Data Packets. Within the virtual plane, we develop distributed control algorithms operating on VIPs, aimed at yielding desirable performance in terms of network metrics of concern. The flow rates and queue lengths of the VIPs resulting from the control algorithm in the virtual plane are then used to specify the forwarding and caching policies in the actual plane.

The general VIP framework allows for a large class of control and optimization algorithms operating on VIPs in the virtual plane, as well as a large class of mappings which use the VIP flow rates and queue lengths from the virtual plane to specify forwarding and caching in the actual plane. Thus, the VIP framework presents a powerful paradigm for designing efficient NDN-based networks with different properties and trade-offs. In order to illustrate the utility of the VIP framework, we present two particular instantiations of the framework. The first instantiation consists of a distributed forwarding and caching policy in the virtual plane which achieves effective load balancing and adaptively maximizes the throughput of VIPs, thereby maximizing the user demand rate for data objects satisfied by the NDN network. The second instantiation consists of distributed algorithms which achieves not only load balancing but also stable caching configurations. Experimental results show that the latter set of algorithms have superior performance in terms of low user delay and high rate of cache hits, relative to several baseline routing and caching policies.

We begin with a formal description of the network model in Section 2, and discuss the VIP framework in Section 3. We present two instantiations of the VIP framework in Sections 4 and 5. The performance of the proposed forwarding and caching policies is numerically evaluated in comparison with several baseline routing and caching policies using simulations in Section 5.3.

Although there is now a rapidly growing literature in information centric networking, the problem of optimal joint forwarding and caching for content-oriented networks remains open. In [3], a potential-based forwarding scheme with random caching is proposed for ICNs. A simple heuristically defined measure (called potential value) is introduced for each node. A content source or caching node has the lowest potential and the potential value of a node increases with its distance to the content source or caching node. Potential-based forwarding guides Interest Packets from the requester toward the corresponding content source or caching node. As the Data Packet travels on the reverse path, one node on the path is randomly selected as a new caching node. The results in [3] are heuristic in the sense that it remains unknown how to guarantee good performance by choosing proper potential values. In [4], the authors consider one-hop routing and caching in a content distribution network (CDN) setting. Throughput-optimal one-hop routing and caching are proposed to support the maximum number of requests. Given the simple switch topology, however, routing is reduced to cache node selection. Throughput-optimal caching and routing in multi-hop networks remains an open problem. In [5], the authors consider single-path routing and caching to minimize link utilization for a general multi-hop content-oriented network, using primal-dual decomposition within a flow model. Here, it is assumed that the path between any two nodes is predetermined. Thus, routing design reduces to cache node selection [5]. The benefits of selective caching based on the concept of betweenness centrality, relative to ubiquitous caching, are shown in [6]. Cooperative caching within ICNs has been investigated in [7], where an age-based caching scheme is proposed. These proposed cooperative caching schemes have been heuristically designed, and have not been jointly optimized with forwarding strategies. Finally, adaptive multipath forwarding in NDN has been examined in [8], but has not been jointly optimized with caching strategies.

2. NETWORK MODEL

Consider a connected multi-hop (wireline) network modeled by a directed graph $\mathcal{G} = (\mathcal{N}, \mathcal{L})$, where $\mathcal{N}$ and $\mathcal{L}$ denote the sets of N nodes and L directed links, respectively. Assume that $(b, a) \in \mathcal{L}$ whenever $(a, b) \in \mathcal{L}$. Let $C_{ab} > 0$ be the transmission capacity (in bits/second) of link $(a, b) \in \mathcal{L}$. Let L_n be the cache size (in bits) at node $n \in \mathcal{N}$ (L_n can be zero).

Assume that content in the network are identified as *data objects*, with the object identifiers determined by an appropriate level within the hierarchical naming structure. These identifiers may arise naturally from the application, and are determined in part by the amount of control state that the network is able to maintain. Each data object (e.g. `/northeastern/videos/WidgetA.mpg`) consists of a sequence of *data chunks* (e.g. `/northeastern/videos/WidgetA.mpg/1`). We assume that any data object is demarcated by a *starting chunk* and an *ending chunk*. Content delivery in NDN operates at the level of data chunks. That is, each Interest Packet requests a particular data chunk, and a matching Data Packet consists of the requested data chunk, the data chunk name, and a signature. A request for a data object consists of a sequence of Interest Packets which request al-

118

l the data chunks of the object, where the sequence starts with the Interest Packet requesting the starting chunk, and ends with the Interest Packet requesting the ending chunk.[1] In the VIP framework which we introduce below, distributed control algorithms are developed in a virtual control plane operating at the data object level, while forwarding of Interest Packets and caching of Data Packets in the actual plane operate at the data chunk level.

We will operate our forwarding and caching algorithms over a set $\mathcal{K}$ of K data objects in the network. As mentioned above, $\mathcal{K}$ may be determined by the amount of control state that the network is able to maintain. Since the data object popularity distribution evolves at a relatively slow time scale compared to the caching and forwarding, one approach is to let $\mathcal{K}$ include the set of the most popular data objects in the network, which is typically responsible for most of the network congestion.[2] For simplicity, we assume that all data objects have the same size z (in bits). The results in the paper can be extended to the more general case where object sizes differ. We consider the scenario where $L_n < Kz$ for all $n \in \mathcal{N}$. Thus, no node can cache all data objects.

For each data object $k \in \mathcal{K}$, assume that there is a unique node $src(k) \in \mathcal{N}$ which serves as the content source for the object. Interest Packets for chunks of a given data object can enter the network at any node, and exit the network upon being satisfied by a matching Data Packet at the content source for the object, or at the nodes which decide to cache the object. For convenience, we assume that the content sources are fixed, while the caching points may vary in time.

Assume that routing (topology discovery and data reachability) has already been accomplished in the network, so that the FIBs have been populated for the various data objects. Upon the arrival of an Interest Packet at an NDN node, the following sequence of events happen. First, the node checks its Content Store (CS) to see if the requested data object chunk is locally cached. If it is, then the Interest Packet is satisfied locally, and a Data Packet containing a copy of the data object chunk is sent on the reverse path. If not, the node checks its PIT to see if an Interest Packet requesting the same data object chunk has already been forwarded. If so, the new Interest Packet (interest, for short) is suppressed while the incoming interface associated with the new interest is added to the PIT. Otherwise, the node checks the FIB to see to what node(s) the interest can be forwarded, and chooses a subset of those nodes for forwarding the interest. Next, we focus on Data Packets. Upon receiving a Data Packet, a node needs to determine whether to make a copy of the Data Packet and cache the copy or not. Clearly, policies for the forwarding of Interest Packets and the caching of Data Packets are of central importance in the NDN architecture. Thus far, the design of the strategy layer for NDN remains largely unspecified. Moreover, in the current CCN implementation, a Data Packet is cached at every node on the reverse path. This, however, may not be possible or desirable when cache space is limited.

We shall focus on the problem of finding dynamic forwarding and caching policies which exhibit superior performance in terms of metrics such as the total number of data ob-

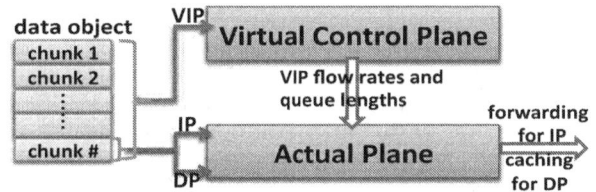

Figure 1: VIP framework. IP (DP) stands for Interest Packet (Data Packet).

ject requests satisfied (i.e., all corresponding Data Packets are received by the requesting node), the delay in satisfying Interest Packets, and cache hit rates. We propose a VIP framework to solve this problem, as described in the next section.

3. VIRTUAL INTEREST PACKETS AND THE VIP FRAMEWORK

The VIP framework for joint dynamic forwarding and caching relies on the essential new metric of *virtual interest packets* (VIPs), which are generated as follows. As illustrated in Figure 1, for each request for data object $k \in \mathcal{K}$ entering the network, a corresponding VIP for object $k \in \mathcal{K}$ is generated.[3] The VIPs capture the *measured demand* for the respective data objects in the network, and represent content popularity which is empirically measured, rather than being given a priori. Specifically, the VIP count for a data object in a given part of the network represents the *local* level of interest in the data object, as determined by network topology and user demand.

The VIP framework employs a *virtual* control plane which operates on VIPs *at the data object level*, and an *actual* plane which handles Interest Packets and Data Packets *at the data chunk level*. This design has two motivations. First, this approach reduces the implementation complexity of the VIP algorithm in the virtual plane considerably (as compared with operating on data chunks in the virtual plane). Second, as shown in Section 4.2 below, this approach leads to a desirable implementation which forwards all the Interest Packets for the same ongoing request for a data object on the same path, and which caches the entire data object (consisting of all data chunks) at a caching node (as opposed to caching different chunks of the same data object at different nodes). At the same time, the approach also allows Interest Packets for non-overlapping requests for the same data object to be forwarded on different paths, thus making multi-path forwarding of object requests possible.[4]

Within the virtual plane, we develop distributed control algorithms operating on VIPs, aimed at yielding desirable performance in terms of network metrics of concern. The

---

[1] The data chunks in between the starting and ending chunks can be requested in any order.

[2] The less popular data objects not in $\mathcal{K}$ may be distributed using simple techniques such as shortest-path forwarding with little or no caching.

[3] More generally, VIPs can be generated at a rate proportional to that of the corresponding data object requests, which can in some cases improve the convergence speed of the proposed algorithms.

[4] In principle, the VIP algorithm in the virtual plane can be applied at the chunk level (corresponding to the case where there is only one chunk in each data object). In this case, the virtual and actual planes operate at the same granularity. On the other hand, the complexity of implementing the algorithm in the virtual plane would be much larger. The

flow rates and queue lengths of the VIPs resulting from the control algorithm in the virtual plane are then used to specify the forwarding and caching policies in the actual plane (see Figure 1). A key insight here is that control algorithms operating in the virtual plane can take advantage of local information on network demand (as represented by the VIP counts), which is unavailable in the actual plane due to interest collapsing and suppression.

In order to illustrate the utility of the VIP framework, we present two particular instantiations of the framework in Sections 4 and 5. For both instantiations, the following hold. First, the VIP count is used as the common metric for enabling both the distributed forwarding and distributed caching algorithms in the virtual and actual control planes. Second, the forwarding strategy in the virtual plane achieves load balancing through the application of the backpressure algorithm [9] to the VIP queue state. Finally, one caching algorithm determines the caching locations and cache replacement policy for both the virtual and actual planes. The two instantiations differ in the manner in which they use the VIP count to determine caching actions.

3.1 VIP Dynamics

We now specify the dynamics of the VIPs within the virtual plane. Consider time slots of length 1 (without loss of generality) indexed by $t = 1, 2, \ldots$. Specifically, time slot t refers to the time interval $[t, t + 1)$. Within the virtual plane, each node $n \in \mathcal{N}$ maintains a separate VIP queue for each data object $k \in \mathcal{K}$. Note that no data is contained in these VIPs. Thus, the VIP queue size for each node n and data object k at the beginning of slot t (i.e., at time t) is represented by a *counter* $V_n^k(t)$.[5] Initially, all VIP counters are set to 0, i.e., $V_n^k(1) = 0$. As VIPs are created along with data object requests, the counters for the corresponding data object are incremented accordingly at the entry nodes. After being forwarded through the network (in the virtual plane), the VIPs for object k are removed at the content source $src(k)$, and at nodes that have cached object k. That is, the content source and the caching nodes are the *sinks* for the VIPs. Physically, the VIP count can be interpreted as a *potential*. For any data object, there is a downward "gradient" from entry points of the data object requests to the content source and caching nodes.

An exogenous request for data object k is considered to have arrived at node n if the Interest Packet requesting the starting chunk of data object k has arrived at node n. Let $A_n^k(t)$ be the number of exogenous data object request arrivals at node n for object k during slot t (i.e., over the time interval $[t, t + 1)$).[6] For every arriving request for data object k at node n, a corresponding VIP for object k is generated at n ($V_n^k(t)$ incremented by 1).[7] The long-term exogenous VIP arrival rate at node n for object k is $\lambda_n^k \triangleq \lim_{t \to \infty} \frac{1}{t} \sum_{\tau=1}^{t} A_n^k(\tau)$.

---

[5] We assume that VIPs can be quantified as a real number. This is reasonable when the VIP counts are large.

[6] We think of a node n as a point of aggregation which combines many network users. While a single user may request a given data object only once, an aggregation point is likely to submit many requests for a given data object over time.

[7] For the general case where object sizes differ, $V_n^k(t)$ is incremented by the object size z_k for every arriving request for object k.

Let $\mu_{ab}^k(t) \geq 0$ be the allocated transmission rate of VIPs for data object k over link (a, b) during time slot t. Note that at each time t and for each object k, a single message between node a and node b can summarize all the VIP transmissions during that time slot.

In the virtual plane, we assume that at each time t, each node $n \in \mathcal{N}$ can gain access to any data object $k \in \mathcal{K}$ for which there is interest at n, and potentially cache the object locally. Let $s_n^k(t) \in \{0, 1\}$ represent the caching state for object k at node n during slot t, where $s_n^k(t) = 1$ if object k is cached at node n during slot t, and $s_n^k(t) = 0$ otherwise. Now note that even if $s_n^k(t) = 1$, the content store at node n can satisfy only a limited number of VIPs during one time slot. This is because there is a maximum rate r_n (in objects per slot) at which node n can produce copies of cached object k.[8]

The time evolution of the VIP count at node n for object k is as follows:

$$V_n^k(t+1) \leq$$
$$\left(\left(V_n^k(t) - \sum_{b \in \mathcal{N}} \mu_{nb}^k(t) \right)^+ + A_n^k(t) + \sum_{a \in \mathcal{N}} \mu_{an}^k(t) - r_n s_n^k(t) \right)^+$$
(1)

where $(x)^+ \triangleq \max(x, 0)$. Furthermore, $V_n^k(t) = 0$ for all $t \geq 1$ if $n = src(k)$.

From (1), it can be seen that the VIPs for data object k at node n at the beginning of slot t are transmitted during slot t at the rate $\sum_{b \in \mathcal{N}} \mu_{nb}^k(t)$. The remaining VIPs $(V_n^k(t) - \sum_{b \in \mathcal{N}} \mu_{nb}^k(t))^+$, as well as the exogenous and endogenous VIP arrivals during slot t, are reduced by r_n at the end of slot t if object k is cached at node n in slot t ($s_n^k(t) = 1$). The VIPs still remaining are then transmitted during the next slot $t + 1$. Note that (1) is an inequality because the actual number of VIPs for object k arriving to node n during slot t may be less than $\sum_{a \in \mathcal{N}} \mu_{an}^k(t)$ if the neighboring nodes have little or no VIPs of object k to transmit.

4. THROUGHPUT OPTIMAL VIP CONTROL

In this section, we describe an instantiation of the VIP framework in which the VIP count is used as a common metric for enabling both the distributed forwarding and distributed caching algorithms in the virtual and actual control planes. The forwarding strategy within the virtual plane is given by the application of the backpressure algorithm [9] to the VIP queue state. Note that while the backpressure algorithm has been used for routing in conventional source-destination-based networks, its use for forwarding in ICNs appears for the first time in this paper. Furthermore, backpressure forwarding is being used in the virtual plane rather than in the actual plane, where interest collapsing and suppression make the application of the algorithm impractical.

The caching strategy is given by the solution of a max-weight problem involving the VIP queue length. The VIP flow rates and queue lengths are then used to specify forwarding and caching strategies in the actual plane, which handles Interest Packets and Data Packets. We show that

---

[8] The maximum rate r_n may reflect the I/O rate of the storage disk. Since it is assumed that all data objects have the same length, it is also assumed that the maximum rate r_n is the same for all data objects.

the joint distributed forwarding and caching strategy adaptively maximizes the throughput of VIPs, thereby maximizing the user demand rate for data objects satisfied by the network.

We now describe the joint forwarding and caching algorithm for VIPs in the virtual control plane.

ALGORITHM 1. *At the beginning of each time slot t, observe the VIP counts $(V_n^k(t))_{k \in \mathcal{K}, n \in \mathcal{N}}$ and perform forwarding and caching in the virtual plane as follows.*

Forwarding: *For each data object $k \in \mathcal{K}$ and each link $(a, b) \in \mathcal{L}^k$, choose*

$$\mu_{ab}^k(t) = \begin{cases} C_{ba}/z, & W_{ab}^*(t) > 0 \ and \ k = k_{ab}^*(t) \\ 0, & otherwise \end{cases} \quad (2)$$

where

$$W_{ab}^k(t) \triangleq V_a^k(t) - V_b^k(t), \quad (3)$$

$$k_{ab}^*(t) \triangleq \arg \max_{\{k:(a,b)\in\mathcal{L}^k\}} W_{ab}^k(t),$$

$$W_{ab}^*(t) \triangleq \left(W_{ab}^{k_{ab}^*(t)}(t) \right)^+.$$

Here, $\mathcal{L}^k$ is the set of links which are allowed to transmit the VIPs of object k, $W_{ab}^k(t)$ is the backpressure weight of object k on link (a, b) at time t, and $k_{ab}^*(t)$ is the data object which maximizes the backpressure weight on link (a, b) at time t.

Caching: *At each node $n \in \mathcal{N}$, choose $\{s_n^k(t)\}$ to*

$$maximize \sum_{k \in \mathcal{K}} V_n^k(t) s_n^k \quad subject \ to \sum_{k \in \mathcal{K}} s_n^k \le L_n/z \quad (4)$$

Based on the forwarding and caching in (2) and (4), the VIP count is updated according to (1).

At each time t and for each link (a, b), backpressure-based forwarding algorithm allocates the entire normalized "reverse" link capacity C_{ba}/z to transmit the VIPs for the data object $k_{ab}^*(t)$ which maximizes the VIP queue difference $W_{ab}^k(t)$ in (3). Backpressure forwarding maximally balances out the VIP counts, and therefore the demand for data objects in the network, thereby minimizing the probability of demand building up in any one part of the network and causing congestion.

The caching strategy is given by the optimal solution to the max-weight knapsack problem in (4), which can be solved optimally in a greedy manner as follows. For each $n \in \mathcal{N}$, let $(k_1, k_2, \ldots, k_K)$ be a permutation of $(1, 2, \ldots, K)$ such that $V_n^{k_1}(t) \ge V_n^{k_2}(t) \ge \cdots \ge V_n^{k_K}(t)$. Let $i_n = \lfloor L_n/z \rfloor$. Then for each $n \in \mathcal{N}$, choose

$$s_n^k(t) = \begin{cases} 1, & k \in \{k_1, \cdots, k_{i_n}\} \\ 0, & \text{otherwise} \end{cases} \quad (5)$$

Thus, the objects with the highest VIP counts (the highest local popularity) are cached.

It is important to note that both the backpressure-based forwarding algorithm and the max-weight caching algorithm are *distributed*. To implement the forwarding algorithm, each node must exchange its VIP queue state with only its neighbors. The implementation of the caching algorithm is local once the updated VIP queue state has been obtained.

To characterize the implementation complexity of Algorithm 1, we note that both the computational and communication complexity of the back pressure forwarding algorithm per time slot is $O(N^2K)$, where the bound can be

improved to $O(NDK)$ if D is the maximum node degree in the network. Assuming fixed cache sizes, the computational complexity of the caching algorithm per time slot can be found to be $O(NK)$.

In the following section, we show that the forwarding and caching strategy described in Algorithm 1 is *throughput optimal* within the virtual plane, in the sense of maximizing the throughput of VIPs in the network $\mathcal{G} = (\mathcal{N}, \mathcal{L})$ with appropriate transmission rate constraints.

4.1 Maximizing VIP Throughput

We now show that Algorithm 1 adaptively maximizes the throughput of VIPs in the network $\mathcal{G} = (\mathcal{N}, \mathcal{L})$ with appropriate transmission rate constraints. In the following, we assume that (i) the VIP arrival processes $\{A_n^k(t); t = 1, 2, \ldots\}$ are mutually independent with respect to n and k; (ii) for all $n \in \mathcal{N}$ and $k \in \mathcal{K}$, $\{A_n^k(t); t = 1, 2, \ldots\}$ are i.i.d. with respect to t; and (iii) for all n and k, $A_n^k(t) \le A_{n,\max}^k$ for all t.

To determine the constraints on the VIP transmission rates $\mu_{ab}^k(t)$, we note that Data Packets for the requested data object must travel on the reverse path taken by the Interest Packets. Thus, in determining the transmission of the VIPs, we take into account the link capacities on the reverse path as follows:

$$\sum_{k \in \mathcal{K}} \mu_{ab}^k(t) \le C_{ba}/z, \text{ for all } (a, b) \in \mathcal{L} \quad (6)$$

$$\mu_{ab}^k(t) = 0, \text{ for all } (a, b) \notin \mathcal{L}^k \quad (7)$$

where C_{ba} is the capacity of "reverse" link (b, a).

4.1.1 VIP Stability Region

To present the throughput optimality argument, we first define the VIP stability region. The VIP queue at node n is *stable* if

$$\limsup_{t \to \infty} \frac{1}{t} \sum_{\tau=1}^{t} 1_{[V_n^k(\tau) > \xi]} d\tau \to 0 \text{ as } \xi \to \infty,$$

where $1_{\{\cdot\}}$ is the indicator function. The *VIP network stability region* Λ is the closure of the set of all VIP arrival rates $(\lambda_n^k)_{k \in \mathcal{K}, n \in \mathcal{N}}$ for which there exists some feasible joint forwarding and caching policy which can guarantee that all VIP queues are stable. By feasible, we mean that at each time t, the policy specifies a forwarding rate vector $(\mu_{ab}^k(t))_{k \in \mathcal{K}, (a,b) \in \mathcal{L}}$ satisfying (6)-(7), and a caching vector $(s_n^k(t))_{k \in \mathcal{K}, n \in \mathcal{N}}$ satisfying the cache size limits $(L_n)_{n \in \mathcal{N}}$.

Theorem 2 in the Appendix precisely characterizes the VIP stability region in the virtual plane. To our knowledge, Theorem 2 is the first instance where the effect of caching has been fully incorporated into the stability region of a multi-hop network.

4.1.2 Throughput Optimality

By definition, if the VIP arrival rates $\boldsymbol{\lambda} = (\lambda_n^k)_{k \in \mathcal{K}, n \in \mathcal{N}} \in \text{int}(\Lambda)$, then all VIP queues can be stabilized. In general, however, this may require knowing the value of $\boldsymbol{\lambda}$. In reality, $\boldsymbol{\lambda}$ can be learned only over time, and may be time-varying. Moreover, stabilizing the network given an arbitrary VIP arrival rate in the interior of Λ may require (time sharing among) multiple forwarding and caching policies.

We now show that the joint forwarding and caching policy in Algorithm 1 adaptively stabilizes all VIP queues in the network for any $\boldsymbol{\lambda} \in \text{int}(\Lambda)$, without knowing $\boldsymbol{\lambda}$. Thus, the policy is *throughput optimal*, in the sense of adaptively maximizing the VIP throughput, and therefore the user demand rate satisfied by the network.

THEOREM 1 (THROUGHPUT OPTIMALITY). *If there exists* $\boldsymbol{\epsilon} = (\epsilon_n^k)_{n \in \mathcal{N}, k \in \mathcal{K}} \succ \mathbf{0}$ *such that* $\boldsymbol{\lambda} + \boldsymbol{\epsilon} \in \Lambda$, *then the network of VIP queues under Algorithm 1 satisfies*

$$\limsup_{t \to \infty} \frac{1}{t} \sum_{\tau=1}^{t} \sum_{n \in \mathcal{N}, k \in \mathcal{K}} \mathbb{E}[V_n^k(\tau)] \leq \frac{NB}{\epsilon} \qquad (8)$$

where $B \triangleq \frac{1}{2N} \sum_{n \in \mathcal{N}} \left((\mu_{n,\max}^{out})^2 + (A_{n,\max} + \mu_{n,\max}^{in} + r_{n,\max})^2 + 2\mu_{n,\max}^{out} r_{n,\max} \right)$, $\epsilon \triangleq \min_{n \in \mathcal{N}, k \in \mathcal{K}} \epsilon_n^k$, $\mu_{n,\max}^{in} \triangleq \sum_{a \in \mathcal{N}} C_{an}/z$, $\mu_{n,\max}^{out} \triangleq \sum_{b \in \mathcal{N}} C_{nb}/z$, $A_{n,\max} \triangleq \sum_{k \in \mathcal{K}} A_{n,\max}^k$, *and* $r_{n,\max} = Kr_n$.

PROOF. Please refer to [10]. □

The forwarding and caching policy in Algorithm 1 achieves throughput optimality in the virtual plane by exploiting both the bandwidth and storage resources of the network to maximally balance out the VIP load (or the demand for data objects in the network), thereby preventing the buildup of congestion. Equivalently, Algorithm 1 is throughput optimal in the actual plane when Interest Packets are not collapsed or suppressed. Note that Theorem 1 can be seen as the multi-hop generalization of the throughput optimal result in [4].

4.2 Forwarding and Caching in the Actual Plane

We now focus on the development of forwarding and caching policies for the actual plane, based on the throughput optimal policies of Algorithm 1 for the virtual plane. Forwarding and caching in the actual plane take advantage of the exploration in the virtual plane to forward Interest Packets on profitable routes and cache Data Packets at profitable node locations.

4.2.1 Forwarding of Interest Packets

The forwarding of Interest Packets in the actual plane follows the pattern established by the VIPs under Algorithm 1 in the virtual plane. For a given window size T, let

$$\bar{\nu}_{ab}^k(t) = \frac{1}{T} \sum_{t'=t-T+1}^{t} \nu_{ab}^k(t') \qquad (9)$$

be the average number of VIPs for object k *transmitted* over link (a, b) over a sliding window of size T under Algorithm 1 prior to time slot t.[9]

Forwarding: At any node $n \in \mathcal{N}$, Interest Packets for all data objects share one queue and are served on a First-Come-First-Serve basis. Suppose that the head-of-the-queue Interest Packet at node n at time t is an interest for the *starting chunk* of data object k. If (i) node n has not yet received a request for data object k, or if the last type-k data chunk in the last Data Packet received at node n prior to t is the *ending chunk* of object k, *and* if (ii) there is no

PIT entry at node n for any chunk of data object k, then forward the Interest Packet to node

$$b_n^k(t) \in \arg \max_{\{b:(n,b) \in \mathcal{L}^k\}} \bar{\nu}_{nb}^k(t). \qquad (10)$$

That is, the Interest Packet is forwarded on the link with the maximum average object-k VIP flow rate over a sliding window of size T prior to t, under Algorithm 1. This latter link is a "profitable" link for forwarding the Interest Packet at time slot t, from the standpoint of reducing delays and congestion. If either condition (i) or (ii) does not hold, then forward the Interest Packet on the link used by node n to forward the most recent Interest Packet for a chunk of object k.[10]

If the head-of-the-queue Interest Packet at node n at time t is an interest for a chunk of data object k which is not the starting chunk, then forward the Interest Packet on the link used by node n to forward the most recent Interest Packet for a chunk of object k.

The above forwarding algorithm ensures that a new request for data object k (which does not overlap with any ongoing request for object k) at time t is forwarded on the link with the maximum average object-k VIP flow rate over a sliding window of size T prior to t. At the same time, the algorithm ensures that an ongoing request for data object k keeps the same outgoing link from node n. This ensures that in the actual plane, all the Interest Packets for an ongoing request for data object k are forwarded on the same path toward a caching point or content source for data object k. As a direct result, the Data Packets for all chunks for the same ongoing request for data object k take the same reverse path through the network.

Note that the Interest Packets for non-overlapping requests for data object k can still be forwarded on different paths, since the quantity $b_n^k(t)$ can vary with t. Thus, the forwarding of data object requests is inherently *multi-path* in nature.

It can be seen that the computational complexity (per time slot) of both the averaging operation in (9) and the link selection operation in (10) is $O(N^2 K)$. Thus, the complexity of forwarding (per time slot) in the actual plane is $O(N^2 K)$.

4.2.2 Caching of Data Packets

As mentioned in Section 3, within the instantiations of the VIP framework we consider, the caching algorithm in the actual plane coincides with the caching algorithm in the virtual plane. Thus, in the current context, the caching algorithm for the actual plane is the same as that described in (5). Thus, at each time slot t, the data objects with the highest VIP counts (highest local popularity) are cached locally.[11]

---

[9] Note that the number $\nu_{ab}^k(t)$ of VIPs for object k transmitted over link (a, b) during time slot t may not be the same as the allocated transmission rate $\mu_{ab}^k(t)$. $\nu_{ab}^k(t)$ may be less than $\mu_{ab}^k(t)$ if there are few VIPs waiting to be transmitted.

[10] The router nodes need not know the names of the starting chunk and ending chunk beforehand. These names can be learned as the routers forward Interest Packets and receive Data Packets for the popular data objects. Before the names of the starting and ending chunks are learned, Interest Packets for the data object can be forwarded using a simple technique such as the shortest path algorithm.

[11] For practical implementation in the actual plane, we cannot assume that at each time, each node can gain access to the data object with the highest local popularity for caching. Instead, one can use a scheme similar to that discussed in Section 5.2, based on comparing the VIP count of the data object corresponding to a Data Packet received at a given

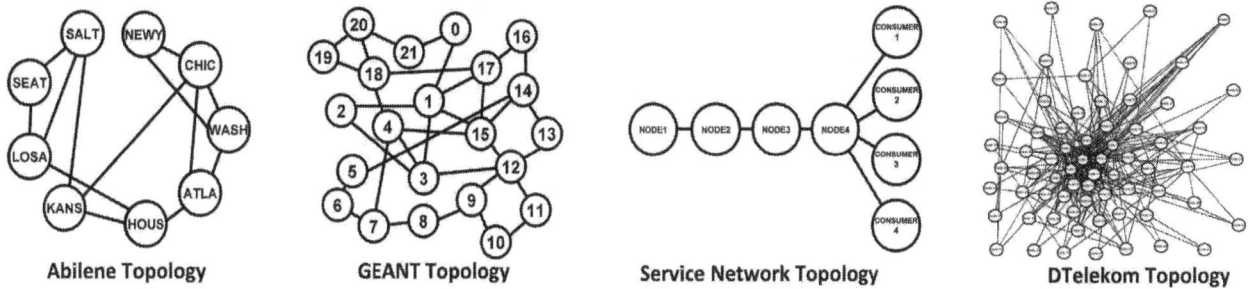

Figure 2: Network Topologies

In attempting to implement the caching algorithm in (5), however, we encounter a problem. Since the VIP count of a data object is decremented by r_n immediately after the caching of the object at node n, the strategy in (5) exhibits oscillatory caching behavior, whereby data objects which are cached are shortly after removed from the cache again due to the VIP counts of other data objects now being larger. Thus, even though Algorithm 1 is throughput optimal in the virtual plane, its mapping to the actual plane leads to policies which are difficult to implement in practice.

In the next section, we demonstrate another instantiation of the VIP framework yielding a forwarding and caching policy for the actual plane, which has more stable caching behavior.

5. STABLE CACHING VIP ALGORITHM

In this section, we describe a practical VIP algorithm, called Algorithm 2, that looks for a stable solution in which the cache contents do not cycle in steady-state. Although Algorithm 2 is not theoretically optimal in the virtual plane, we show that it leads to significant performance gains in simulation experiments.

5.1 Forwarding of Interest Packets

The forwarding algorithm in the virtual plane for Algorithm 2 coincides with the backpressure-based forwarding scheme described in (2)-(3) for Algorithm 1. The forwarding of Interest Packets in the actual plane for Algorithm 2 coincides with the forwarding scheme described in (10). That is, all the Interest Packets for a particular request for a given data object are forwarded on the link with the maximum average VIP flow rate over a sliding window of size T prior to the arrival time of the Interest Packet for the first chunk of the data object.

5.2 Caching of Data Packets

The caching decisions are based on the VIP flow in the virtual plane. Suppose that at time slot t, node n receives the Data Packet containing the first chunk of data object k_{new} which is not currently cached at node n. If there is sufficient unused space in the cache of node n to accommodate the Data Packets of all chunks of object k_{new}, then node n proceeds to cache the Data Packet containing the first chunk of data object k_{new} as well as the Data Packets containing

all subsequent chunks for data object k_{new} (which, by the forwarding algorithm in Section 4.2.1, all take the same reverse path through node n). That is, the entire data object k is cached at node n. Otherwise, the node compares the *cache scores* for k_{new} and the currently cached objects, as follows. For a given window size T, let the cache score for object k at node n at time t be

$$CS_n^k(t) = \frac{1}{T} \sum_{t'=t-T+1}^{t} \sum_{(a,n)\in\mathcal{L}^k} \nu_{an}^k(t') = \sum_{(a,n)\in\mathcal{L}^k} \bar{\nu}_{an}^k(t),$$
(11)

i.e., the average number of VIPs for object k *received* by node n over a sliding window of size T prior to time slot t. Let $\mathcal{K}_{n,old}$ be the set of objects that are currently cached at node n. Assuming that all data objects are of equal size, let $k_{min} \in \mathcal{K}_{n,old}$ be a current cached object with the smallest cache score. If k_{new} has a lower cache score than k_{min}, then object k_{min} (consisting of all chunks) is evicted and replaced with object k_{new}. Otherwise, the cache is unchanged. If objects have different sizes, the optimal set of objects is chosen to maximize the total cache score under the cache space constraint. This is a knapsack problem for which low complexity heuristics exist.

At each time t, the VIP count at node n for object k is decreased by $r_n s_n^k(t)$ due to the caching at node n. This has the effect of attracting the flow of VIPs for each object $k \in \mathcal{K}_{n,new}$, where $\mathcal{K}_{n,new}$ denotes the new set of cached objects, to node n.

The Data Packets for data objects evicted from the cache are potentially cached more efficiently elsewhere (where the demand for the evicted data object is relatively bigger). This is realized as follows: before the data object is evicted, VIPs and Interest Packets flow toward the caching point as it is a sink for the object. After eviction, the VIP count would begin building up since the VIPs would not exit at the caching point. As the VIPs build further, the backpressure load-balancing forwarding policy would divert them away from the current caching point to other parts of the network.

We now find the caching complexity for Algorithm 2. Note that the complexity of calculating the cache scores (per time slot) in (11) is $O(N^2 K)$. Due to link capacity constraints, the number of new data objects which arrive at a given node in a time slot is upper bounded by a constant. Thus, for fixed cache sizes, the total computational complexity for the cache replacement operation (per time slot) is $O(N)$. In sum, the caching complexity for Algorithm 2 per time slot is $O(N^2 K)$.

node to the VIP counts of the data objects currently cached at the node.

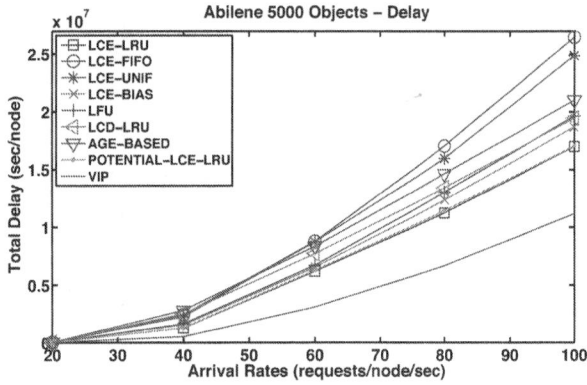

Figure 3: Abilene Network: Delay

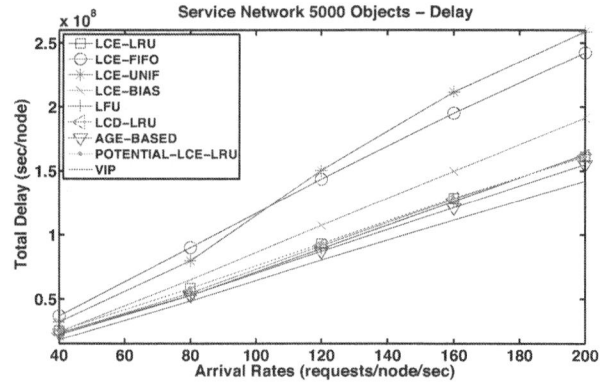

Figure 5: Service Network: Delay

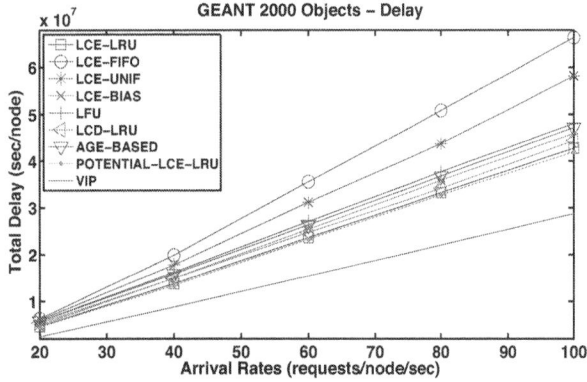

Figure 4: GEANT Network: Delay

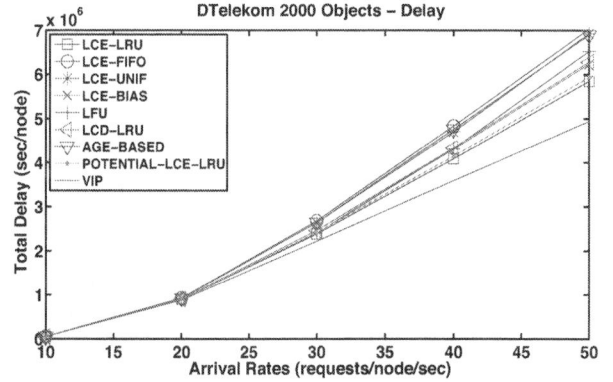

Figure 6: DTelekom Network: Delay

5.3 Experimental Evaluation

This section presents the experimental evaluation of the Stable Caching VIP Algorithm (Algorithm 2).[12] Experimental scenarios are carried on four network topologies: the Abilene Topology (9 nodes), the GEANT topology (22 nodes), the Service Network topology (8 nodes), and the DTelekom Topology (68 nodes) in Figure 2.

In the Service Network and Abilene topologies, all link capacities are chosen to be 500 Mb/s. In the GEANT and DTelekom topologies, all link capacities are chosen to be 200 Mb/s. The Interest Packet size is 125 B; the Data Packet size is 50 KB; the data object size is 5 MB. At each node requesting data, object requests arrive according to a Poisson process with an overall rate λ (in requests/node/sec). Each arriving request requests data object k (independently) with probability p_k, where $\{p_k\}$ follows a (normalized) Zipf distribution with parameter 0.75. In the GEANT and DTelekom topologies, a total of 2000 data objects are considered, while in the other topologies (Service Network and Abilene), 5000 data objects are considered. The buffers which hold the Interest and Data Packets at each node are assumed to have infinite size. We do not consider PIT expiration timers and interest retransmissions.

In the Abilene, GEANT, and DTelekom topologies, object requests can be generated by any node, and the content source for each data object is independently and uniformly distributed among all nodes. The cache sizes at all nodes are identical, and are chosen to be 5 GB (1000 data objects) in the Abilene topology and and 2 GB (400 data objects) in the GEANT and DTelekom topologies. In the Service Network topology, NODE 1 is the content source for all objects and requests can be generated only by the CONSUMER nodes. The cache sizes at NODE 2, NODE 3, NODE 4 and the CONSUMER nodes are 5 GB.

In the virtual plane, the slot length is 200 $msec$ in the GEANT and DTelekom topologies and 80 $msec$ in the other topologies. Forwarding uses the backpressure algorithm with a cost bias to help direct VIPs toward content sources.[13] The cost bias is calculated as the number of hops on the shortest path to the content source, and is added to the VIP queue differential. In the actual plane, the time step for forwarding and caching decisions is 5 μsec in the GEANT and DTelekom topologies and 2 μsec in the other topologies, i.e., the transmission time of one Interest Packet. The window size T is 5000 slots. Each simulation generates requests for 100 sec and terminates when all Interest Packets are fulfilled. Each curve in Figures 3-10 is obtained by averaging over 10 simulation runs.

Simulation experiments were carried out to compare the Stable Caching VIP Algorithm against a number of popular caching algorithms used in conjunction with shortest path forwarding and a potential-based forwarding algorithm. In shortest path forwarding, at any given node, an In-

---

[12]Our simulations are carried out on a computer with dual Intel E5 2650 CPU's (2.60GHz) and 128 GB RAM space.

[13]It can be shown that the cost-biased version is also throughput optimal in the virtual plane, as in Theorem 2.

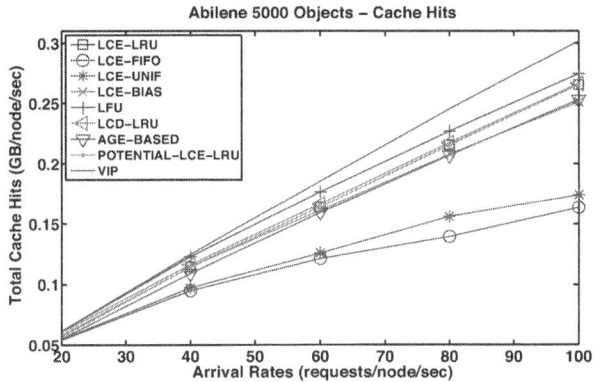

Figure 7: Abilene Network: Cache Hits

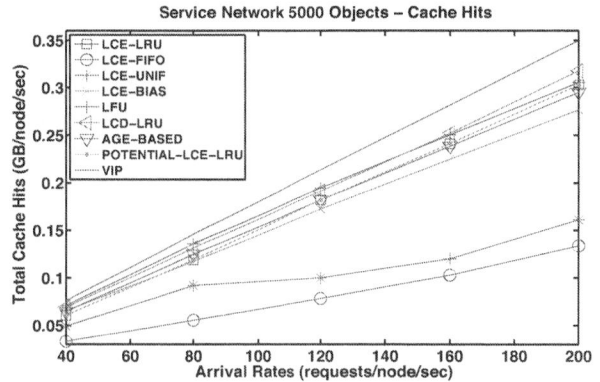

Figure 9: Service Network: Cache Hits

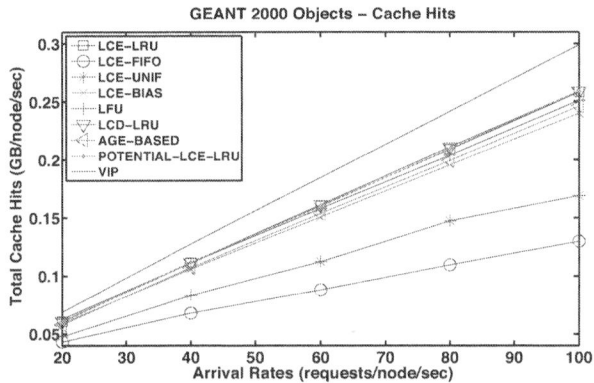

Figure 8: GEANT Network: Cache Hits

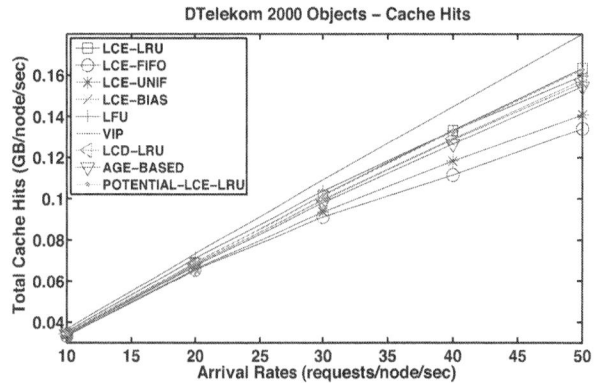

Figure 10: DTelekom Network: Cache Hits

terest Packet for data object k is forwarded on the shortest path to the content source for object k.[14] The Data Packet corresponding to the Interest Packet may be retrieved from a caching node along the shortest path. In potential-based forwarding, a potential value for each data object at each node is set as in [3]. At each time and for each node, an Interest Packet for object k is forwarded to the neighbor with the lowest current potential value for object k. Each caching algorithm consists of two parts: caching decision and caching replacement. Caching decision decides whether or not to cache a new data object when the first chunk of this object arrives and there is no remaining cache space. If a node decides to cache the new data object, then caching replacement decides which currently cached data object should be evicted to make room for the new data object. We considered the following caching decision policies: (i) Leave Copies Everywhere (LCE), which decides to cache all new data objects, and (ii) Leave a Copy Down (LCD)[11], where upon a cache hit for data object k at node n, object k is cached at the node which is one hop closer to the requesting node (while object k remains cached at node n). We considered the following caching replacement policies: (i) Least Recently Used (LRU), which replaces the least recently requested data object, (ii) First In First Out (FIFO), which replaces the data object which arrived first to the cache; (iii) UNIF, which chooses a currently cached data object for replacement, uniformly at random, and (iv) BIAS, which chooses

[14]We assume that all chunks of a data object are cached together.

two currently cached data objects uniformly at random, and then replaces the less frequently requested one. In addition, we considered Least Frequently Used (LFU) and age-based caching [7]. In LFU, the nodes record how often each data object has been requested and choose to cache the new data object if it is more frequently requested than the least frequently requested cached data object (which is replaced). In age-based caching [7], each cached object k at node n is assigned an age which depends on p_k, the (Zipf) popularity of object k, and the shortest-path distance between n and $src(k)$. The cache replacement policy replaces the cached object for which the age has been exhausted the longest.

We considered LCE-LRU, LCE-FIFO, LCE-UNIF, and LCE-BIAS combined with shortest path forwarding. We also considered (under shortest path forwarding) LCD combined with LRU, as well as LCE-LRU combined with potential-based forwarding.

The delay for an Interest Packet request is the difference between the fulfillment time (i.e., time of arrival of the requested Data Packet) and the creation time of the Interest Packet request. A cache hit for a data chunk is recorded when an Interest Packet reaches a node which is not a content source but which has the data chunk in its cache. When a cache hit occurs, the corresponding metric is incremented by the size of the chunk in cache.

Figures 3-6 show the delay performance of the algorithms. It is clear that the Stable Caching VIP Algorithm significantly outperforms all other algorithms tested. For instance, for the Abilene topology at $\lambda = 100$ requests/node/sec, the total delay for the VIP algorithm is only 55% of the delay for the closest competitor (LCE-LRU), and only about 36% of the delay for the worst performing algorithm (LCE-FIFO). Figures 7-10 show the cache hit performance for the algorithms. Again, the Stable Caching VIP Algorithm has significantly higher total cache hits than other algorithms. For the Service topology at $\lambda = 200$ requests/node/sec, the total number of cache hits for Algorithm 2 is about 10% higher than that for the closest competitor (LCD-LRU) and is more than two times the number of cache hits for the worst performing algorithm (LCE-FIFO).

In sum, the Stable Caching VIP Algorithm significantly outperforms all competing algorithms tested, in terms of user delay and rate of cache hits.

6. CONCLUSION

The joint design of traffic engineering and caching strategies is central to information-centric architectures such as NDN, which seek to optimally utilize both bandwidth and storage for efficient content distribution. In this work, we have introduced the VIP framework for the design of high performing NDN networks. In the virtual plane of the VIP framework, distributed control algorithms operating on virtual interest packets (VIPs) are developed to maximize user demand rate satisfied by the network. The flow rates and queue lengths of the VIPs are then used to specify the forwarding and caching algorithms in the actual plane, where Interest Packets and Data Packets are processed. Experimental results show that the latter set of algorithms have superior performance in terms of user delay and cache hit rates, relative to baseline routing and caching policies.

7. REFERENCES

[1] L. Zhang, D. Estrin, J. Burke, V. Jacobson, J. Thornton, D. K. Smetters, B. Zhang, G. Tsudik, kc claffy, D. Krioukov, D. Massey, C. Papadopoulos, T. Abdelzaher, L. Wang, P. Crowley, and E. Yeh. Named data networking (ndn) project. October 2010.

[2] V. Jacobson, D. K. Smetters, J. D. Thornton, M. F. Plass, N. H. Briggs, and R. L. Braynard. Networking named content. In *Proceedings of the 5th international conference on Emerging networking experiments and technologies*, CoNEXT '09, pages 1–12, New York, NY, USA, 2009. ACM.

[3] S. Eum, K. Nakauchi, M. Murata, Y. Shoji, and N. Nishinaga. Catt: Potential based routing with content caching for icn. In *Proceedings of SIGCOMM 2012 ICN*, pages 49–54, Helsinki, Finland, August 2012.

[4] M. Amble, P. Parag, S. Shakkottai, and L. Ying. Content-aware caching and traffic management in content distribution networks. In *Proceedings of IEEE INFOCOM 2011*, pages 2858–2866, Shanghai, China, April 2011.

[5] H. Xie, G. Shi, and P. Wang. Tecc: Towards collaborative in-network caching guided by traffic engineering. In *Proceedings of IEEE INFOCOM 2012:Mini-Conference*, pages 2546–2550, Orlando, Florida, USA, March 2012.

[6] W. Chai, D. He, L. Psaras, and G. Pavlou. Cache "less for more" in information-centric networks. In *Proceedings of the 11th International IFIP TC 6 Conference on Networking - Volume Part I*, IFIP'12, pages 27–40, Berlin, Heidelberg, 2012. Springer-Verlag.

[7] Z. Ming, M. Xu, and D. Wang. Age-based cooperative caching in information-centric networks. In *Computer Communications Workshops (INFOCOM WKSHPS), 2012 IEEE Conference on*, pages 268–273, March 2012.

[8] C. Yi, A. Afanasyev, L. Wang, B. Zhang, and L. Zhang. Adaptive forwarding in named data networking. *SIGCOMM Comput. Commun. Rev.*, 42(3):62–67, June 2012.

[9] L. Tassiulas and A. Ephremides. Stability properties of constrained queueing systems and scheduling for maximum throughput in multihop radio networks. 37(12):1936–1949, December 1992.

[10] E. M. Yeh, T. Ho, Y. Cui, M. Burd, R. Liu, and D. Leong. Vip: A framework for joint dynamic forwarding and caching in named data networks. http://www.ece.neu.edu/~eyeh/papers/vipicn.pdf. Technical report, 2014.

[11] N. Laoutaris, S. Syntila, and I. Stavrakakis. Meta algorithms for hierarchical web caches. In *Performance, Computing, and Communications, 2004 IEEE International Conference on*, pages 445–452, 2004.

APPENDIX

THEOREM 2 (VIP STABILITY REGION). *The VIP stability region of the network $\mathcal{G} = (\mathcal{N}, \mathcal{L})$ with link capacity constraints (6)-(7), and with VIP queue evolution (1), is the set Λ consisting of all VIP arrival rates $(\lambda_n^k)_{k \in \mathcal{K}, n \in \mathcal{N}}$ such that there exist flow variables $(f_{ab}^k)_{k \in \mathcal{K}, (a,b) \in \mathcal{L}}$ and storage variables $(\beta_{n,i,l})_{n \in \mathcal{N}; i=1,\cdots,\binom{K}{l}; l=0,\cdots,i_n \triangleq \lfloor L_n/z \rfloor}$ satisfying*

$$f_{ab}^k \geq 0, \; f_{nn}^k = 0, \; f_{src(k)n}^k = 0, \quad \forall a, b, n \in \mathcal{N}, \; k \in \mathcal{K} \tag{12}$$

$$f_{ab}^k = 0, \quad \forall a, b \in \mathcal{N}, \; k \in \mathcal{K}, \; (a,b) \notin \mathcal{L}^k \tag{13}$$

$$0 \leq \beta_{n,i,l} \leq 1, \; i = 1, \cdots, \binom{K}{l}, \; l = 0, \cdots, i_n, \; n \in \mathcal{N} \tag{14}$$

$$\lambda_n^k \leq \sum_{b \in \mathcal{N}} f_{nb}^k - \sum_{a \in \mathcal{N}} f_{an}^k + r_n \sum_{l=0}^{i_n} \sum_{i=1}^{\binom{K}{l}} \beta_{n,i,l} \mathbf{1}[k \in \mathcal{B}_{n,i,l}],$$
$$\forall n \in \mathcal{N}, \; k \in \mathcal{K}, n \neq src(k) \tag{15}$$

$$\sum_{k \in \mathcal{K}} f_{ab}^k \leq C_{ba}/z, \quad \forall (a,b) \in \mathcal{L} \tag{16}$$

$$\sum_{l=0}^{i_n} \sum_{i=1}^{\binom{K}{l}} \beta_{n,i,l} = 1, \quad \forall n \in \mathcal{N} \tag{17}$$

Here, $\mathcal{B}_{n,i,l}$ denotes the caching set consisting of the i-th combination of l data objects out of K data objects at node n, where $i = 1, \cdots, \binom{K}{l}$, $l = 0, \cdots, i_n \triangleq \lfloor L_n/z \rfloor$.

PROOF. Please refer to [10]. □

Coupling Caching and Forwarding: Benefits, Analysis, and Implementation

Giuseppe Rossini and Dario Rossi
Telecom ParisTech, Paris, France
first.last@telecom-paristech.fr

ABSTRACT

A recent debate revolves around the usefulness of pervasive caching, i.e., adding caching capabilities to possibly every router of the future Internet. Recent research argues against it, on the ground that it provides only very limited gain with respect to the current CDN scenario, where caching only happens at the network edge.

In this paper, we instead show that advantages of ubiquitous caching appear only when meta-caching (i.e., whether or not cache the incoming object) and forwarding (i.e., where to direct requests in case of cache miss) decisions are tightly coupled. Summarizing our contributions, we (i) show that gains can be obtained provided that ideal Nearest Replica Routing (iNRR) forwarding and Leave a Copy Down (LCD) meta-caching are jointly in use, (ii) model the iNRR forwarding policy, (iii) provide two alternative implementations that arbitrarily closely approximate iNRR behavior, and (iv) promote cross-comparison by making our code available to the community.

Categories and Subject Descriptors

C.2.1 [**Network Architecture and Design**]: Network communications, Packet-switching networks

General Terms

Algorithms; Performance; Design;

Keywords

Information Centric Networking; Caching; Forwarding

1. INTRODUCTION

With the advent of Information Centric Networking (ICN) [2], the network evolves from a simple interconnections of pipes and buffers, and rather becomes a network of caches. This induces a radical change in network operations: as opposite to IP networks, where routers transfer and discard IP

packets in the shortest possible time, ICN routers instead aim at storing content chunks for the longest useful time. In turn, new challenges arise for ICN performance evaluation, on both modeling [6–8, 10, 17, 23, 31] and algorithmic aspects [9, 11–13, 15, 24, 25, 29, 30, 35, 39].

At high level, a cache network can be modeled as a triple $\langle \mathcal{F}, \mathcal{D}, \mathcal{R} \rangle$, where: $\mathcal{F}$ represents the forwarding policy, determining the next hop for each content request, whereas content items travel back along breadcrumbs left by the requests [22, 30]; a meta-caching algorithm $\mathcal{D}$ lets node decide whether to store any new content item passing by; a replacement algorithm $\mathcal{R}$ selects, in case of positive decision in the previous step, which cache element should be evicted to make room for the new one.

Given the pervasiveness of caches in ICN, meta-caching is considered a crucial element to differentiate content of individual caches. Forwarding is instead essential to extend the reach beyond caches that lay on the path toward the repository, possibly reaching off path copies. Yet, while ICN performance are dependent on the triple $\langle \mathcal{F}, \mathcal{D}, \mathcal{R} \rangle$, with few exceptions research has so far limitedly considered a single of the above aspect in isolation – implicitly assuming either Shortest Path Routing (SPR) forwarding or Leave a Copy Everywhere (LCE) meta-caching.

Most importantly, a debate has been recently ignited around the usefulness of ubiquitous caching [16, 19]. While it is well understood that systematically caching the same object everywhere is not necessarily beneficial for system performance, however conclusive results have yet to emerge from the discussion. In particular, very recent work [16] shows that the most of the caching gain is attainable by simply (and painlessly) caching at the edge of the network. Yet, we argue that [16] misses a crucial point: i.e., that the interaction of the above policies concurs in determining the global ICN performance. While authors of [16] correctly select an ideal forwarding policy $\mathcal{F}$, that achieves (locally) optimal forwarding decisions, their (implicit) selection of the $\langle \mathcal{D}, \mathcal{R} \rangle$ pair (and especially of the LCE meta-caching policy $\mathcal{D}$ that, as we will see, plays a paramount role) yields to an underestimation of ICN performance.

In the reminder of this paper, we overview related work in Sec. 2, and especially highlight the simulation [16] and modeling [31] work we directly compare with. Sec. 3 then explores benefits of $\langle \mathcal{F}, \mathcal{D}, \mathcal{R} \rangle$, showing that significant gains can be obtained when ideal Nearest Replica Routing (iNRR) forwarding and Leave a Copy Down (LCD) meta-caching are jointly in use: indeed, LCE nullifies benefits of iNRR by forcing multiple synchronous evictions in spatially disjoint caches, while this can be avoided by LCD (or even simple probabilistic) meta-caching. Sec. 4 then carries on an extensive simulation comparison with edge caching techniques proposed in [16]: we gather that [16] underestimates ICN gain due to (i) a limited focus on $\mathcal{F}$ forwarding policy neglecting meta-caching $\mathcal{D}$, coupled to a (ii) oversimplified network scenario with poor path diversity, so that iNRR potential cannot be fully exploited. Sec. 5 introduces our iNRR model, that builds over [31]: while [31] only considers shortest path routing toward permanent content stored at some custodian (modeling on path caching with SPR), we extend it with the ability to look for nearby temporary content replicas (modeling off path caching with iNRR). Finally, we remark that iNRR is however an *ideal* forwarding strategy: therefore, we propose and evaluate two practical implementations that, trading off delay vs distance, achieve arbitrarily close performance to iNRR in Sec. 6. To promote cross-comparison, all our code is available to the scientific community at [1].

2. BACKGROUND

Taxonomy. Tab. 1 reports a taxonomy of related work addressing ICN evaluation. The table is split in two portions, meta-caching (top) and forwarding (bottom): it clearly emerges that $\mathcal{F}$ and $\mathcal{D}$ aspects have been so far studied separately. Work focusing on meta-caching [9, 13, 24, 25, 29] usually assumes Shortest Path Routing (SPR) as underlying request forwarding strategy. In this context, many policies have been proposed that are either deterministic (LCE, LCD [24, 25], Betweenness [9]) or probabilistic (Fix [5,25], ProbCache [29], WAVE [13]). These policies exploit different information (ranging from simple distance [25, 29] to more complex topological properties [9]) and possibly explicitly take into account ICN chunking [13].

Similarly, work focusing on forwarding policies [6–13, 15–17, 23–25, 29–31, 35, 39] usually assumes that new contents are always cached, which is commonly referred to as Leave a Copy Everywhere (LCE) in meta-caching terms. The interest of alternative strategies to SPR is that there may be closer cached copies laying *off path* between the requester and the custodian of the permanent copy, that thus SPR is unable to reach. To achieve this purpose, the ICN community has tested several forwarding approaches, ranging from multiple disjoint source routed paths [35], to dynamic approaches based on flooding [12], learning [11,39], or routing using potential [15]. Of particular interest, [16] considers an ideal Nearest Routing Replica (iNRR) scheme that allows to reach the closest, possibly off path, cached copy. While iNRR is not a practical scheme, as it requires instantaneous knowledge of the status of all caches in the network, however it provides an ideal upper-bound to $\mathcal{F}$ performance, and as such is worth considering. Additionally, we offer two distributed NRR implementations in Sec. 6, that can attain performance arbitrarily close to that of iNRR.

Modeling. Concerning modeling work, separation of $\mathcal{F}$, $\mathcal{D}$ and $\mathcal{R}$ is easily understood: due to the complexity in analysing caching networks, studies have tackled each aspect in isolation. In particular, considering simple topologies (e.g., cascades or trees), [24] models LCD meta-caching ($\mathcal{D}$ policy), while [17] addresses LRU and random replacement ($\mathcal{R}$ policies), and [7,8] explicitly account for the fact that objects are split in chunks. Considering instead more com-

Table 1: Taxonomy of related work: Meta-caching and forwarding have been, so far, separately studied.

Meta-caching $\mathcal{D}$	Type	Knob	Ref
LCE			[6–13, 15–17, 23–25, 29–31, 35, 39]
Fix	Prob.	p	[5, 25, 35]
ProbCache	Prob.	Distance	[29]
LCD	Det.	Distance	[24, 25, 35]
WAVE	Prob.	Distance	[13]
Btw	Det.	Centrality	[9]

Forwarding $\mathcal{F}$	Type	Knob	Ref
SPR			[6–13, 15–17, 23–25, 29–31, 35, 39]
Source routing	Prob.	-	[35]
Flooding	Prob.	*Distance*	[12]
INFORM	Prob.	*Delay*	[11]
CATT	Det.	*Distance*	[15]
NDN	Det.	*Dist, Delay*	[39]
iNRR	Det.	-	[6, 16]

plex networks, [31] models object-level cache hit of Shortest Path Routing (SPR) on arbitrary topologies, while in the context of wireless networks, an asymptotic analysis of SPR vs iNRR (under LCE) is provided in [6].

We point out that while ICN introduces a number of new challenges (e.g., chunk vs object level, pervasive caching, request routing over complex topologies, etc.), caching is not a new problem. As such, in terms of modeling techniques, the above work possibly extends to the ICN context previous seminal work. More precisely, [17,24] build over the Che [10] approximation, while model in [7,8] extend Jelenkovic's [23] to the case of multiple chunk and [31] extends the Dan and Towsley [14] LRU approximation from a single cache to a network of caches operating according to SPR forwarding. In Sec. 5 we extend [31] to model iNRR forwarding, in reason of its performance as we will see shortly.

Simulation. Separation of $\mathcal{F}$, $\mathcal{D}$ and $\mathcal{R}$ is instead less justified in simulative work. In part, this is due to the fact that a natural choice for $\mathcal{R}$ is the Latest Recently Used (LRU) policy, though it has been pointed out that random replacement (i) exhibits similar performance at a lower complexity [17, 18, 35] (ii) it may be preferable to LRU due to line rate constraint [5, 28]. We further point out that, while the joint impact of meta-caching $\mathcal{D}$ and replacement $\mathcal{R}$ policies has gained limited attention (among others, by our own work [35]), *to the best of our knowledge, the forwarding $\mathcal{F}$ and meta-caching $\mathcal{D}$ policies have not been jointly considered so far.* As the performance impact of the $\langle \cdot, \mathcal{D}, \mathcal{R} \rangle$ couplet is limited with respect to that of $\langle \mathcal{F}, \mathcal{D}, \cdot \rangle$, in this work we mostly focus on the latter. We start by showing this impact in Sec. 3. Then, in Sec. 4, we critically contrast recent results that (too) quickly dismiss ubiquitous caching [16].

3. COUPLING BENEFIT

We start by showing that, provided that forwarding and meta-caching decisions are jointly considered, sizeable gains appear. Simulation results are obtained with ccnSim [34], an highly scalable chunk-level[1] simulator that we have developed and optimized over the last few years. To give an idea of ccnSim scalability, the large-scale scenario reported

---

[1]To facilitate comparison with [16,31] that consider object-level caching, in this work we use ccnSim at object level.

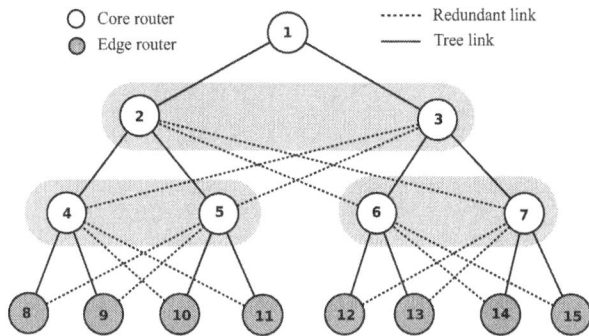

Figure 1: Redundant 4-level binary tree. Dashed links are present with probability μ. Shadowed blocks represent aggregate caches seen by lower level nodes in presence of redundancy ($\mu > 0$).

in Sec. 4, corresponding to one billion worth of object requests, out of a 100 million object catalog, with caches storing 100,000 objects, can be simulated by a common off-the-shelf PC equipped with 8GB of RAM memory in few hours [34]. For this work, we extended ccnSim to include a number of meta-caching (e.g., ProbCache [29], Btw [9]) and forwarding (e.g., iNRR [16]) algorithms, that we make available, along with the scenarios and scripts used to gather results in this paper, at [1].

3.1 Scenarios

To facilitate comparison with [16] in Sec. 4 and with [31] in Sec. 5, we consider network scenarios as similar as possible to those introduced there, namely access tree [16] and grid [31] topologies. We point out that [16] additionally considers access trees to be attached to PoP of realistic backbone networks (gathered with Rocketfuel as in our previous work [33,35]). Despite great effort is made in [16] to describe the scenario, however the lack of crucial parameters (e.g., repository placement, content redundancy and allocation to repositories, etc.), makes a 1-to-1 comparison difficult. As such, to promote cross-comparison, we make our scenarios available to the scientific community, under the form of configuration files for ccnSim, so that independent research can confirm (or disprove) our findings.

We argue that it would be possible to use *realistic topologies* and *workload*, to reinforce the realism of the evaluation. Yet, we also point out that considering realistic topologies would let the scenario significantly drift from [31], rendering the cross-comparison task harder. Additionally, while trace-driven evaluation [16,21,38] is tempting, we argue that it is not necessary for a *relative* performance comparison. Indeed, CDN request traces from Akamai [16] offer only an aggregated but partial view of the requests served by many ISPs, which can bias the results. Further, while [21,38] show that real workloads yield to caching results that are more favorable with respect to synthetic workloads where object popularity is stationary over the whole period (due to a temporal request correlation on short time scales [21] and of a finite object lifetime on a longer timescale [38]), at the same time we expect temporal correlation to be beneficial to any ICN strategy. Additionally, an advantage of synthetic workload is to ensure convergence of the results

shown in the following, that are thus technically sound, albeit possibly conservative as they neglect temporal request correlation.

Specifically, we consider a 10x10 grid (100 nodes) and a 6-level binary tree ($2^6 - 1 = 63$ nodes). Since networks are engineered adhering to fault tolerance and resilience principles, it is extremely unlikely for an access topology to have exactly a single physical link between any pair of parent and child nodes as in [16] – as otherwise, cutting a single link up in the hierarchy would cut a whole subtree. As such, we consider that a node may have an additional link to its aunt (i.e., the immediate sibling of its direct parent) that can be used for backup or load balancing. Each additional link, represented with dashed lines in the 4-level tree of Fig. 1, is present with i.i.d. probability $\mu \in [0, 1]$.

For simplicity, we consider topologies with uniform delay (1ms), as heterogeneity plays a minor role [33,35], and consider to operate below congestion (links have infinity capacity). As in [16], that offers fitting over global Akamai dataset, we consider object popularity to follow a Zipf distribution with $\alpha \approx 1$. We use homogeneous size caches, with a cache to catalog size ratio of 0.1% (much more conservative that 5% in [16]) instantiated in a small (large) scenario where caches are able to store 100 (100,000) objects out of a 100,000 (100,000,0000) objects catalog. Small vs. large scale scenarios allow us to respectively explore wide parameter settings vs. gather performance on a more realistic use case. Simulations start from empty caches, and statistics are gathered after the hit ratio reaches steady state. Results reported in the following are averaged over 20 runs.

3.2 Performance

As performance metric, we consider the average distance that the content has traveled in the ICN network. This metric has the advantage of being very insightful and compact at the same time, as it directly relates to user QoE (i.e., delay) as well as network QoS (i.e., load and cache hit). Moreover, while [16] additionally expresses cache hit and repository load, it however mostly reports relative error between iNRR and alternate strategies: as direct comparisons are de facto impossible, and to limit redundancy given space constraints, we hence avoid reporting additional metrics beyond the content distance.

In terms of $\mathcal{F}$, instead of being limited by implementation (and configuration) details of the numerous proposed ICN forwarding policies [11,12,15,35,39], we consider (i) iNRR [16] as upper-bound of the achievable performance for off-path caching, and (ii) SPR that can limitedly hit on-path copies. In terms of meta-caching $\mathcal{D}$, we instead implement (and make available in [1]) several of the proposals in Tab. 1: we prefer to include a relatively large list (to the risk of annoying the reader), as we believe a systematic investigation of coupled forwarding/meta-caching to be necessary (in reason of the previously shown gap in the current literature). We include LCE as a term of comparison, that we instead expect to provide a performance lower-bound as it provides poor cache diversity and forces high eviction rates over the whole network. Finally, in terms of replacement $\mathcal{R}$ we experiment with LRU and uniform probabilistic replacement [5] (though we mostly report results concerning the former due to secondary $\mathcal{R}$ impact).

Fig. 2 reports the average distance at which content is found in the ICN network as function of the meta-caching

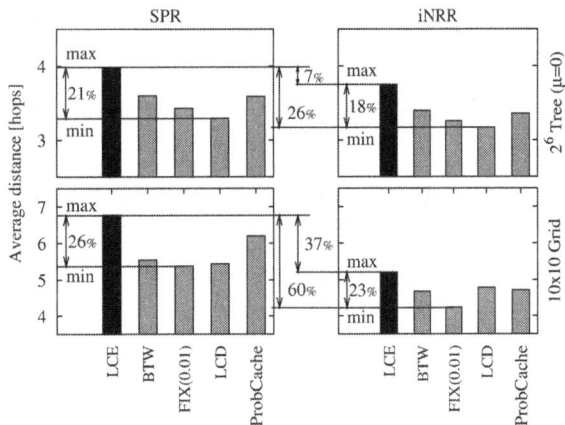

Figure 2: ⟨F,D⟩ performance at a glance: average content distance as a function of meta-caching policies, for SPR (left) and iNRR (right) forwarding, on tree (top) and grid (bottom) topologies.

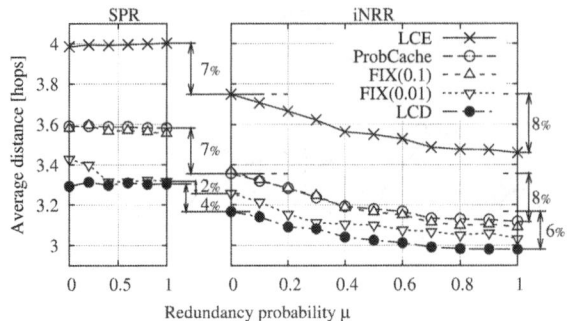

Figure 3: Sensitivity analysis of ⟨$\mathcal{F}$,$\mathcal{D}$⟩ when $\mathcal{R}$=LRU: 6-level binary tree topology, with varying redundancy probability μ.

policies, for SPR (left) and iNRR (right) forwarding, on tree (top, without additional links $\mu = 0$) and grid topologies (bottom). The plot is annotated with percentage gain that could be achieved by moving from the ⟨SPR,LCE⟩ worst-case to other, more sensible, ICN configurations.

First, recall that the top plots of Fig. 2 report the scenario of [16]: in this case, [16] correctly points out that the difference between ⟨SPR,LCE⟩ and ⟨iNRR,LCE⟩ is below 10%. Yet, as authors limitedly experiment with a naive LCE meta-caching, they ignore potential gain due to LCD (about 21% even considering SPR) or the joint use of LCD and iNRR (about 26%). Additionally, we point out that gains in this scenario are limited by the poor path diversity that the tree offers to iNRR. For instance, in the example provided in Fig. 1 for a 4-level tree, starting at node 15, on-path caching with SPR traverses 4 caches from the edge to the root (i.e., 15, 7, 3, 1): iNRR disposes of only 2 additional off-path nodes when $\mu = 0$ (i.e., 6, 14), but of 6 nodes when $\mu = 1$ (i.e., 4, 5, 6, 12, 13, 14).

Hence, gains of ⟨iNRR,LCD⟩ are potentially higher on more meshed topologies, that allow iNRR to explore a larger (and closer) neighborhood. This clearly reflects in the bottom plot of Fig. 2, obtained on a 10x10 grid: in this case, the difference between ⟨SPR,LCE⟩ and ⟨iNRR,LCE⟩ is about 37%. Additional gain could be attained by coupling iNRR forwarding to LCD or fixed probabilistic FIX decisions, for a reduction of the average distance of about 60%. Clearly, as content travels less than half the path in ⟨SPR,LCE⟩, the network load also divides by over a factor of two, and similarly happens for user latency. – shortly, as opposed to findings in [16], ubiquitous caching cannot be dismissed without a second look.

4. ⟨$\mathcal{F}$, $\mathcal{D}$, $\mathcal{R}$⟩ SIMULATION

4.1 Consistency of coupling gains

Fig. 3 reports a sensitivity analysis of the gains achievable by coupling meta-caching policies to forwarding policies such as iNRR, gathered via simulation over smoothly varying network redundancy $\mu \in [0, 1]$. The plot is annotated with gain

from ⟨SPR,·⟩ to ⟨iNRR,·⟩, as well as with gain due to the redundancy (from $\mu = 0$ to $\mu = 1$ for any given ⟨$\mathcal{F}$,$\mathcal{D}$⟩ setting). As it can be expected, redundancy plays a negligible role for SPR (though in case of multiple equivalent paths, SPR chooses between them at random, possibly traversing different caches). Unsurprisingly, deterministic LCD decisions consistently achieve best performance for trees [25], exhibiting furthermore a good interplay with iNRR. Next comes simple probabilistic decisions FIX($\frac{1}{100}$), while complex probabilistic strategies driven on either distance (Prob-Cache [29]) or topological properties (e.g., Btw [9]) achieve intermediate gain. In reason of the added complexity (as it is often pointed out, simpler solutions are preferable due to line rate constraints [5, 28]) and limited gain, we thus disregard the latter meta-caching policies, while we point out simple probabilistic decisions to be a good-enough candidate for ICN.

Overall, the average path length increases from slightly less than 3 hops for ⟨iNRR,LCD⟩ to about 4 hops for ⟨SPR,LCE⟩, i.e. a sizeable 33% increase (though gain may be larger for more meshed topologies). Finally, we experiment with different Zipf skews: while we do not report pictures for reason of space, we observe that gain increases for growing α.

4.2 Comparison with edge-caching

We perform an exhaustive comparison of ICN vs Content Distribution Network (CDN) strategies. In particular, we consider some of the edge-caching techniques that [16] offers as "good enough" replacement for ICN. We again focus on the access tree topology, to mimic scenario in [16], and additionally consider that networks are possibly engineered with fault tolerance (i.e., redundancy probability μ).

As far as CDN is concerned, we include the *Edge* strategy where only leaf nodes have caching space, corresponding to a naïve CDN scenario. We then implement *EdgeCoop*: as the terse description ("CDN routes can do a scoped lookup in sibling cache") in [16] does not allow to understand whether only caches having a common parent can cooperate, we opt for an approach that is as favorable as possible to Edge-Coop, to avoid any bias toward ICN. Our implementation of EdgeCoop allows caching only at leaf nodes, but exploits iNRR routing strategy: thus, any temporary copy that is cached at a distance shorter than or equal to that of the permanent copy stored at the custodian above the root of the tree is possibly accessed (in practice, only half of the leaf

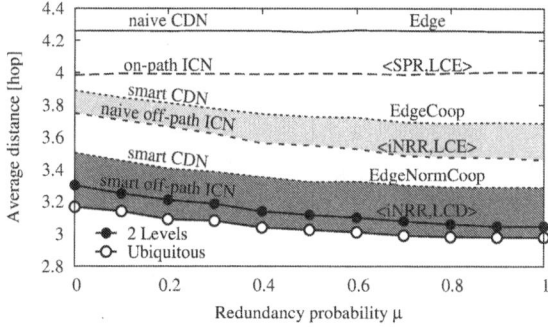

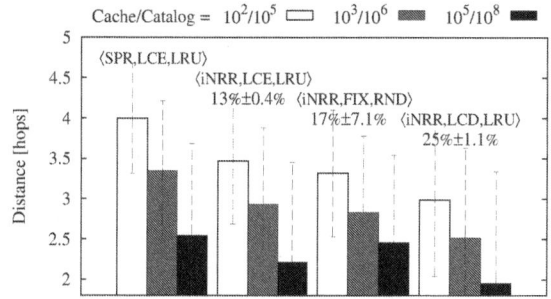

Figure 5: Small- vs medium- and large-scale scenarios. Relative gain ($\mu \pm \sigma$) over $\langle$**SPR,LCE,LRU**$\rangle$ remains similar over all scenarios.

μ	$\langle SPR, LCE\rangle$	Edge Coop	$\langle iNRR, LCE\rangle$	Edge Norm Coop	$\langle iNRR, LCD\rangle$ 2-Levels	$\langle iNRR, LCD\rangle$ Ubiquitous
0	2%	4%	8%	14%	19%	22%
1	2%	10%	15%	19%	25%	27%

Figure 4: Comparison of several ICN vs CDN [16] strategies: average distance $E[d_X]$ of strategy X, as a function of the redundancy probability μ. Additionally, the figure tabulates the gain of strategy X over Edge, measured as $\big(E[d_{\mathbf{Edge}}] - E[d_X]\big)/E[d_{\mathbf{Edge}}]$.

nodes are accessible when $\mu = 0$, while all leafs are accessible for $\mu = 1$). Under homogeneous cache size, as in CDN-like scenarios only leaf nodes are equipped with caches, it follows that Edge and EdgeCoop scenarios have about half the cache space of ICN scenarios. To perform a fair comparison, we thus consider as in [16] an *EdgeNormCoop* scenario where individual caches are twice as large as in the previous case, so that the overall cache space is the same as in ICN scenarios. Since distance is our main performance metric, and since EdgeNormCoom allocates all cache space as close as possible to users, we expect to get a conservative estimate of ICN benefits, if any, from our comparison.

As far as ICN is concerned, we first consider a naïve $\langle$SPR,LCE$\rangle$ strategy where caching is ubiquitous but, due to SPR forwarding, only on-path caches can be exploited. We further include $\langle$iNRR,LCE$\rangle$ that [16] identifies as ICN best-case, and finally include the $\langle$iNRR,LCD$\rangle$ configuration, representing an even better alternative. In particular, to assess at a more fine-grained the value of ubiquitous caching, in the $\langle$iNRR,LCD$\rangle$ case we further consider (i) an *Ubiquitous* case where the total cache budget is allocated evenly across caches of all 6-levels of the tree and (ii) a *2-Levels* case (also considered in [16]) where the total cache space is allocated evenly across the last two levels of the tree, while nodes up in the hierarchy are not equipped with caching functionalities.

Results of the comparison are shown in Fig. 4. To confirm that we do not aim at exaggerating ICN gains, consider the CDN EdgeNormCoop vs ICN $\langle$iNRR,LCE$\rangle$ strategies. While the comparison is favorable to ICN in [16] (in terms of latency, congestion and origin load performance), the reverse holds in our conservative settings (where thus distance is lower for CDN EdgeNormCoop than for ICN).

Next, to facilitate the ICN vs CDN comparison, two shaded regions are shown in the plot. On the basis of the light-gray region separating $\langle$iNRR,LCE$\rangle$ from EdgeCoop, [16] concludes that ICN does offer only minimal performance improvement over sensibly configured CDN scenarios, so that

(most of the) ICN gain is within reach of (less painful) CDN solutions. The dark-gray region between $\langle$iNRR,LCE$\rangle$ and $\langle$iNRR,LCD$\rangle$ instead represents the potential gain due to joint meta-caching and forwarding, missed so far by related work (including [16]), in reason of a narrow focus on specific aspects of the whole algorithmic space (recall Tab. 1).

Another interesting considerations can be made comparing the CDN-EdgeCoopNorm vs $\langle$iNRR,LCD$\rangle$ in the 2-Levels (black points) and Ubiquitous (white points) cases. Recall that these three strategies have the same cache space, but differ in the cache placement strategy. As we previously pointed out, CDN places all cache budget to the leaf, close to the users, which should be beneficial in terms of the distance to the hit. Yet, cooperation via scoped lookups with iNRR forces in this case to possibly longer paths up and down the tree. In the ICN case instead, paths to cached content can be shorter due to the statistical multiplexing gains that arise due to aggregation of requests coming from multiple leafs. At the same time, as it is still beneficial to cache the most popular content close to the users, these gain exhibit diminishing returns for an increasing number of levels of aggregation. From Fig. 4 we see indeed that *Ubiquitous* caching (6-level in this example) further reduces the distance with respect to *2-Levels*, albeit the gain reduces.

Finally, the figure tabulates gain of a strategy X over Edge, computed as $\big(E[d_{\mathbf{Edge}}] - E[d_X]\big)/E[d_{\mathbf{Edge}}]$ where $E[d_X]$ represents the average distance of strategy X. It can be seen that $\langle$iNRR,LCD$\rangle$ gain is sizeable, for both binary trees ($\mu = 0$) and trees with full redundancy ($\mu = 1$). Yet, we point out the ultimate goal for an ISP to deploy ICN is to ameliorate the service delivered to users, while possibly reducing the delivery costs [4]. Under this light, it is hard to assess whether the technical gains shown in this section translate into economic gains that are substantial enough to justifying ICN deployment – which is outside the scope of this paper and rather calls for technico-economic studies.

4.3 Small to large-scale scenarios

Small, medium (or large) scale scenarios allow us to respectively explore wide parameter settings, and gather performance on a more realistic (or extreme) use case. We fix $\alpha = 1$ and the cache to catalog size ratio C/N to a conservative 0.1%, and let the cache C and catalog sizes N vary. Precisely, we instantiate a small-scale scenario with $C/N = 10^2/10^5$, a medium-scale with $C/N = 10^3/10^6$ and a large-scale with $C/N = 10^5/10^8$. As video is preeminent, and given an average size of YouTube videos of 10MB [20], medium and large scale cache sizes vary from the feasible 10GB [5,28] to the challenging 10TB [36] range. Catalog size of the medium scenario is of the same order of magnitude as in [16], whereas the large-scale scenario models a more challenging YouTube scenario.

Average distances (and coefficient of variation) are reported in Fig. 5 for naïve on-path caching ⟨SPR,LCE,LRU⟩, naïve off-path caching ⟨iNRR,LCE,LRU⟩, simple probabilistic off-path meta-caching and replacement ⟨SPR,FIX,RND⟩, and the best off-path strategy ⟨SPR,LCD,LRU⟩. Each strategy is annotated with the average gain over ⟨SPR,LCE,LRU⟩ (± standard deviation across different scales).

We see that performance improve (i.e., distance decreases) for large catalogs. This can be explained considering that, for fixed Zipf $\alpha = 1$ and fixed cache to catalog ratio C/N, a larger cache C can accommodate a larger fraction of top content out of the entire catalog N. Formally, $\sum_i^C i^{-\alpha} / \sum_i^N i^{-\alpha}$ increases from small to large catalog, so that $C=100$ (100,000) most popular cached objects corresponds to the 43% (63%) of the whole requests for a $N=100,000$ (100,000,000) catalog.

Hence, we gather that small scale scenario (i) corresponds to conservative cache hit results and (ii) allows a reliable estimate of the relative gain of ubiquitous caching over on-path caching – as the relative gain over ⟨SPR,LCE,LRU⟩ is the same for all scenarios (except the simplistic ⟨SPR,FIX,RND⟩ case we disregard in the following).

5. MODELING iNRR

As shown in the previous section, iNRR achieves interesting performance with respect to SPR forwarding. Furthermore, iNRR benefits are especially apparent with topologies having redundant links. As such, it would be useful to have an approximate iNRR model valid for arbitrary network of caches. We tackle this challenge by extending the aNET model proposed in [31], that unlike other caching models is applicable to any topology but is limited to Shortest Path Routing. In this section, we first recall aNET (Sec. 5.1) and introduce the relevant notation, then present our iNRR extension (Sec. 5.2) before comparing their accuracy (Sec. 5.3).

5.1 aNET model and notation

According to our terminology, a ⟨SPR,LCE,LRU⟩ network is modeled by aNET [31]. aNET approximates network behavior by decomposing the problem and computing the LRU approximation [14] for each cache in the network. The network itself is represented as a graph $G = (V, E)$ with $v \in V$ a vertex node having a cache of size $|v|$ objects. We denote the content catalog with $\mathcal{N}$, with size $N = |\mathcal{N}|$. As ⟨SPR,LCE,LRU⟩ forwards the miss stream of each cache along the SPR toward the permanent replica, it follows that the incoming request stream at each cache accounts for both exogenous user request, as well as the miss stream of neighboring caches. aNET takes into account this incoming stream by iterating the solution of individual caches, and reevaluating the miss stream until the stabilization of the whole system. aNET iteratively solves the following set of equations reported in Fig. 6.

Incoming requests at node v for content $i \in \mathcal{N}$ are expressed in (1). The first term in (1) represents the exogenous arrival rate $\lambda_{i,v}$ for content i, and the second term accounts for the miss stream $m_{i,u}$ coming from neighboring nodes u having v as their next hop $R(u, \mathcal{S}(i))$ in the shortest path

$$r_{i,v} = \lambda_{i,v} + \sum_{u:R(u,\mathcal{S}(i))=v} m_{i,u} \qquad (1)$$

$$p_{i,v} = \frac{r_{i,v}}{\sum_{j=1}^{N} r_{jv}} \qquad (2)$$

$$\vec{\pi}_v = LRU(\vec{p}_v, |v|) \qquad (3)$$

$$m_{i,v} = r_{i,v}(1 - \pi_{i,v}) \qquad (4)$$

Figure 6: aNET model

toward the repository $\mathcal{S}(i)$ for content $i \in \mathcal{N}$. The local popularity $p_{i,v}$ is expressed by (2), representing the relative proportion of request of content i at node v. Given the steady state local request distribution over all contents $\vec{p}_v$ and a cache size $|v|$, each cache v applies in (3) the LRU algorithm [14] to determine the probability $\vec{\pi}_v$ that any given content $i \in \mathcal{N}$ is present in its cache. Finally, the miss stream $m_{i,v}$ is computed as in (4).

Two crucial points in the above set of equations are worth stressing. First, (4) was only proven to hold for an Independent Reference Model (IRM) [31]. Second, the approximate LRU algorithm (3) was designed only for IRM streams [14]. However, as the request stream also consists of miss stream of the neighbors as per (1), the aggregate request stream is not IRM: hence, steps (3)-(4) consist in an IRM violation, and are potential sources of error in the approximation.

5.2 iNRR model

We extend the set of aNET equations to model iNRR forwarding strategy. Under SPR forwarding, content can be possibly found only along the shortest path toward a custodian of permanent content replicas: hence, the miss stream (1) aggregates requests of shortest paths passing through v. The crucial difference from aNET is that, under iNRR forwarding, any *valid* path is possibly followed. By valid path, we imply that (i) paths are loop free, (ii) in case multiple copies are stored at several nodes along any given path, the closest copy is accessed. Additionally (iii) in case of multiple copies having equal distance over multiple paths, each copy is equally likely to be chosen.

To model the above observations (i)–(iii), we introduce the following notation. As in aNET, the SPR routing matrix for the network $R(v, u), v, u \in V$ indicates v's next hop to reach node u. Nodes are directly connected to v when $R(u, v) = v$, and we indicate with $N(v) = \{u : R(u, v) = v\}$ the set of v's neighbors. For convenience, $\mathcal{S} = \mathcal{S}(i), \forall i \in \mathcal{N}$ indicates the unique repository in the network (the model can be easily extended to the case of multiple repositories), so that $R(v, \mathcal{S})$ represents the FIB information used by SPR to reach it.

In addition to SPR FIB information (possibly hitting content cached on-path to $\mathcal{S}$ as in aNET), iNRR is able to find any off-path content that is not located further than the repository (so that caches as close as the repository, can offload the latter). To identify such content, we define $D(v, u)$ as the SPR distance between any two nodes $v, u \in V$. We next define $B(v, u)$ as the ball centered in v having ray $D(v, u)$, i.e., $B(v, u) = \{x \in V : D(v, x) \leq D(v, u)\}$. Thus, $B(v, u)$ represents the set of nodes that are not further away than u from v. For convenience, we also define the border and interior of $B(v, u)$ as $B_b(v, u) = \{x \in V : D(v, x) = D(v, u)\}$ and $B_i(v, u) = \{x \in V : D(v, x) < D(v, u)\}$ re-

$$r_{i,v} = \lambda_{i,v} + \sum_{u:u\in N(v)} m_{i,u,v} \qquad (5)$$

$$p_{i,v} = \frac{r_{i,v}}{\sum_{j=1}^{N} r_{jv}} \qquad (6)$$

$$\vec{\pi}_v = LRU(\vec{p}_v, |v|) \qquad (7)$$

$$m_{i,v} = r_{i,v}(1 - \pi_{i,v}) \qquad (8)$$

$$s_{i,v,u} = \sum_{\substack{x:R(v,x)=u \\ \wedge\, x\in B(v,\mathcal{S})}} \left[\prod_{y\in B_i(v,x)} (1-\pi_{i,y}) \right] \frac{\pi_{i,x}^2}{\sum_{z\in B_b(v,x)} \pi_{i,z}} \qquad (9)$$

$$m_{i,v,u} = \begin{cases} m_{i,v}s_{i,v,u} & u\neq R(v,\mathcal{S}) \\ m_{i,v}\left(1 - \sum_{w\neq u} s_{i,v,w}\right) & u = R(v,\mathcal{S}) \end{cases} \qquad (10)$$

Figure 7: iNRR model

spectively. For instance, $B_b(v,\mathcal{S})$ represents the set of nodes that are as far from v as the server $\mathcal{S}$, while $B_i(v,u)$ represents the set of nodes closer than u to v. Finally, we denote with $m_{i,u,v}$ the proportion of miss stream for content i coming from u to v. Then, our iNRR model iteratively solves $\forall i \in \mathcal{N}, v \in V$ the set of equations reported in Fig. 7. Shortly, while (6), (7) and (8) perform the same steps as in aNET, iNRR modifies (5) to account for a proportion of miss stream of neighboring nodes, and further adds equations (9) and (10) to quantify this proportion.

As per observation (iii), any node u will split its miss stream equally among its neighbors $N(u)$. This is modeled by (5), where all v's neighbors $N(v)$ contribute to request arrival at v, with $m_{i,u,v}$ the proportion of miss stream for content i coming from u. Observations (i) and (ii) are instead expressed through (9) and (10). More precisely, (9) defines the split ratio $s_{i,v,u}$ among neighboring nodes, and (10) applies the split ratio to the miss stream $m_{i,v}$, depending on whether u lays on the shortest path to the server $u = R(v,\mathcal{S})$ or not.

Especially, (9) bares additional discussion. The term $s_{i,v,u}$ represents the proportion of the miss stream of node v sent through v's immediate neighbor u to reach node x for content i. iNRR forwards such requests iff:

- Next hop for x from v passes through $u = R(v,x)$, and the distance $D(v,x)$ is shorter than or equal to the distance toward the server $R(v,\mathcal{S})$, i.e., x falls in the ball $B(v,\mathcal{S})$ (external sum).

- Any node y closer than x to v, i.e., laying in the interior ball $B_i(v,x)$, does not own the content i, which happens with probability $1 - \pi_{i,y}$ for each node (internal product).

- The selected node x owns the item i (with probability $\pi_{i,x}$), and it is chosen among all the nodes $z \in B_b(v,x)$ at the same distance from v (terms $\pi_{i,x}/\sum_z \pi_{i,z}$).

Finally, by means of (10), we differentiate the case in which the neighbor $u = R(v,\mathcal{S})$ is the immediate next hop toward the repository or not, giving preference to cached copies to offload the repository. Hence, the miss stream that finds objects in the ball $B(v,\mathcal{S})$ flows through off-path

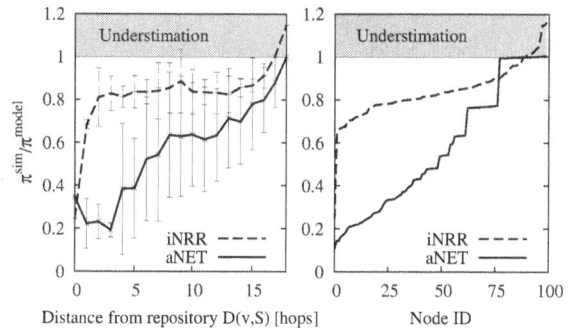

Figure 8: iNRR vs aNET hit rate π accuracy, on a 10x10 grid: per-node (left) and as function of the distance from the repository (right).

neighbors, whereas the rest of the miss stream flows through the next hop $u = R(v,\mathcal{S})$, thus on-path to $\mathcal{S}$. As in aNET, we iterate until convergence (average distance between two consecutive steps of (5) to be $< 10^{-5}$).

5.3 iNRR vs aNET accuracy

Our model inherits IRM assumption of aNET, hence it also inherits possible inaccuracy due to IRM violation. As aNET vs. iNRR model different ICN architecture, namely on-path vs. off-path caching, their result cannot be directly compared. Thus we evaluate their accuracy against simulation of $\langle SPR, LCE, LRU\rangle$ vs. $\langle iNRR, LCE, LRU\rangle$ respectively, and consider a 10x10 grid, where the iNRR gain over SPR is visible (recall Fig. 2). We compute accuracy with respect to simulation for (i) each node individually, as well as for (ii) all nodes having the same distance $\{x : D(x,\mathcal{S}) = d\}$ from the repository. More precisely, indicating the average hit probability for node v as $\bar{\pi}_v$, we evaluate accuracy in Fig. 8 as the ratio $\bar{\pi}_v^{sim}/\bar{\pi}_v^{model}$.

As for aNET, we know from [31] that the impact of IRM violation grows with the size of the network under study (or, equivalently, decreases with the density of repository in the network). This is because the IRM assumption does not hold especially for long paths, as miss stream prevails over the exogenous arrivals. Consequently, we expect aNET to be negatively affected by the large topology size, as the SPR distance to $\mathcal{S}$ can grow quite large. We instead expect iNRR forwarding to lessen the impact of IRM violation with respect to SPR. First, this is due to the fact that iNRR find closer copies (see Sec. III-A of [31]). Second, and most important, under iNRR nodes split their miss stream across each neighbor: as this mixes independent miss stream flows, it results in a more IRM-like miss flows with respect to SPR routing (similarly to what happens by increasing the k-arity of the SPR tree in Sec. III-A of [31]). Hence, we point out comparison on the same scenario to be unfair, as aNET and iNRR are neither operating on the same distance, nor on the same neighbor fanout. To partly compensate for this bias, we attach clients to each grid node, i.e., $\lambda_{i,v} > 0, \forall v$, so to reinforce the IRM component of the request arrival, in an attempt to make the comparison more favorable to aNET.

For the sake of readability, in the left plot of Fig. 8 nodes are ranked for increasing $\bar{\pi}_v^{sim}/\bar{\pi}_v^{model}$ ratios. In the right plot of Fig. 8, we complement the average ratio with standard deviation bars. First, results confirm that iNRR error

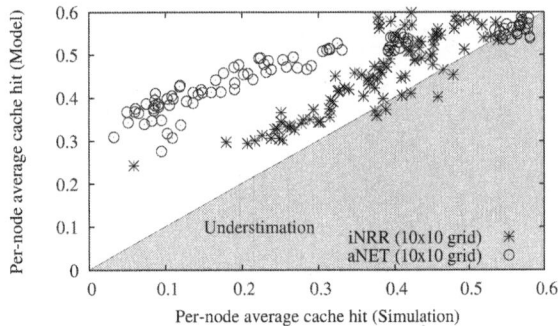

Figure 9: Scatter plot of the average cache hit per node $\bar{\pi}_v$ obtained via simulation vs model, for aNET and iNRR, on a 10x10 grid.

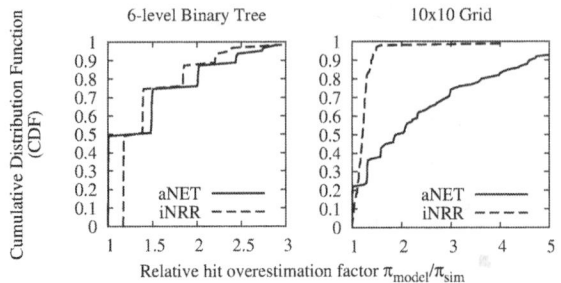

Figure 10: CDF of the cache hit overestimation for aNET vs iNRR model, on a 6-level binary tree (left) and a 10x10 grid (right).

is significantly lower than aNET. We can further observe that the iNRR error is less affected by the topological position (essentially, SPR distance) from the repository with respect to aNET. In the aNET case, the ratio becomes closer to 1 as the distance from the repository increases: notice the large plateau of about 20 nodes (i.e., leaves of the SPR distribution tree rooted at $\mathcal{S}$) having unity ratio in top of Fig. 8, that are aggregated at $d = 18$ in bottom of Fig. 8. We further show a scatter plot of the average cache hit per node $\bar{\pi}_v$ obtained via simulation vs model in Fig. 9, showing that under iNRR model overestimation reduces especially for nodes with low cache hit.

To further exacerbate difference between iNRR and aNET, we consider additional scenarios that reinforce the soundness of the above reasoning. Specifically, we contrast a 6-level binary tree scenario (where clients are attached only at leaf nodes) to the 10x10 grid in Fig. 10. The figure depicts CDFs of the cache hit overestimation (computed as $\bar{\pi}_v^{model}/\bar{\pi}_v^{sim}$, inverse w.r.t. metric shown in Fig. 8): as expected, performance are very close in the tree but very far apart in the grid, confirming our reasoning. Aside, notice the perfect match of LRU [14] for the SPR case in the tree topology, that no longer holds for iNRR, where leaf nodes also possibly receive a non-IRM miss-stream component of other nodes.

6. APPROXIMATE iNRR IMPLEMENTATION

6.1 Framework

It should be clear that iNRR is an ideal forwarding policy, requiring an oracle or, equivalently, the knowledge of the state of all caches to instantaneously propagate of in the whole network. We thus propose two practically viable implementations of Nearest Neighbor Routing (NRR). We cast these solutions on the ground of the general framework we develop in [12], that we briefly recall here.

We assume ICN nodes to be equipped with a FIB structure, proactively populated by a SPR routing protocol, containing information that allows to follow the shortest path toward a permanent copy of the repository. Requests forwarded along the FIB have thus the chance to find *on path* cached copies, and in case no cached copy is found, they ultimately access the permanent replica at the custodian.

Additionally, we require ICN nodes to be equipped with a Temporary FIB data structure (TFIB), reactively populated by an *off path* exploration of the ICN network, triggered by

user demand on a new request. We assume that the *exploration phase* is carried only for the first (or few) chunk(s) of a new content, and is aimed at dynamically constructing a path toward the closest cached replica. The path is then stored in the TFIB. In the subsequent *exploitation phase*, the forwarding process can use the new TFIB entry for the next chunks requests of the same content (overriding thus FIB entries). While it is outside the scope of this paper, we point out that TFIB is possibly managed as a LRU cache, so that TFIB entries span over subsequent requests of different users for the same content.

6.2 Design

In this section, we focus on the *exploration phase*, of which we provide two alternative implementations based on scoped flooding, namely NRR' and NRR", that respectively require one and two phases. Both NRR' and NRR" flood requests over the network, limiting the flooding scope via a TTL field. In modeling terms, NRR limits the radius ρ of the ball centered around v, i.e., $B_\rho(v) = \{u : D(v, u) \leq \rho\}$.

Differences from NRR' and NRR" arise in the way requests are treated during the exploration phase. NRR' floods *regular request* packets, so that it generates possibly multiple data chunks in return – one per each cached copy found in $B_\rho(v)$. Hence, NRR' possibly generates an overhead in terms of load and cache eviction rate, though the duration of the exploration phase is the minimum possible before the closest copy is hit. Conversely, NRR" floods *meta request* packets, with a flag set to indicate that only a binary reply concerning content availability, but not the whole content data, is requested in return[2]. Replies of this first phase populate the TFIB with a negligible load (no actual data is sent), avoiding cache pollution due to eviction (as only meta information about the chunk is sent), but introduces a delay (data downloaded in the second phase).

6.3 Evaluation

Before considering the tradeoff induced by NRR' vs NRR" in terms of load vs delay, let us first analyze their impact on cache eviction. We compare NRR' and NRR" to iNRR by measuring the number of additional hops needed on av-

---

[2]This technique is already commonly used, e.g., in HTTP GET vs HEAD request methods: in the former case, the HTTP response encapsulates the whole object data, in the latter case, only the headers concerning the object.

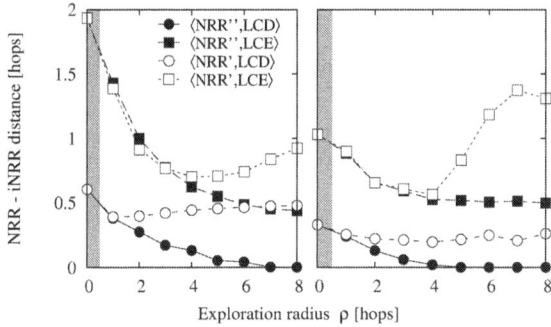

Figure 11: Additional distance of NRR implementations with respect to iNRR: NRR' vs NRR" policies, for LCE or LCD meta-caching, as a function of the exploration radius ρ. 10x10 grid (left) and 6-level $\mu=1$ tree (right).

erage to find the content. For completeness, we consider $\mathcal{D} \in \{\text{LCE,LCD}\}$ and $\mathcal{F} \in \{\text{NRR',NRR"}\}$ with respect to the ideal ICN strategy $\langle\text{iNRR,LCD,LRU}\rangle$. Fig. 11 depicts the number of additional hops as a function of the radius ρ for the grid (left) and tree (right) topologies. The picture reports all $\langle\mathcal{F},\mathcal{D}\rangle$ combinations of NRR" (black) vs NRR' (white) and LCD (circle) vs LCE (square) settings. For $\rho = 0$, NRR degenerates in SPR routing (shadowed region).

Several interesting insights are gathered from Fig. 11. First, performance of $\langle\text{iNRR,LCD,LRU}\rangle$ can be approximately arbitrarily close with $\langle\text{NRR",LCD,LRU}\rangle$, as the additional distance goes to zero for $\rho \geq 6$ on trees and grids. Second, cache eviction due to LCE implies an important performance penalty for both NRR' and NRR" (as expected due to results in previous section). Third, even under LCD, cache eviction due to flooding possibly translate into an important performance penalty as well: this is due to the use of regular request packets in NRR', generating data in return that possibly yields multiple cache evictions. Fourth, notice that additional distance decreases for growing ρ only in the case of NRR": this means that NRR" exploration is not only effective but also robust. Conversely, in the NRR' case, whenever ρ increases, eviction increases as well due to both higher chance to find the content on the one hand, and longer paths up to ρ on the other hand. This phenomenon is especially evident for the tree under LCE meta-caching: as soon as ρ becomes comparable with the distance to the repository, this allows a significantly larger portions of the tree to be explored, with consequent massive eviction[3]. We thus conclude that $\langle\text{NRR",LCD}\rangle$ with (arbitrarily large) ρ is able to (arbitrarily close) approximate iNRR.

We now comment on the load and delay induced by NRR' and NRR". As far as load is concerned, NRR" is clearly more lightweight than NRR'. Indeed, while the number of requests sent by NRR' and NRR" is the same, the amount of data chunks sent in return equals either (i) the number of cache hits for NRR', or (ii) the single closest hit for NRR". As chunks travel multiple links, NRR" significantly reduces the load not only because it sends a single chunk (major impact

---

[3]Intuitively, under LCE cache pollution extends to the other side of the tree. Under LCD, as popular content is pulled toward the edge of the network, requests do not explore the whole network, successfully limiting cache pollution.

on load), but also because it sends the closest among all cached chunks (second order impact).

As far as delay is concerned, NRR' is possibly faster than NRR" due to the fact that whenever the data is found, it is immediately sent back, whereas NRR" requires an additional phase. While at a first glance it may seem that delay under NRR" would be roughly double with respect to NRR', however this is not the case. Observe first that exploration delay only affects the first chunk, and not subsequent chunks that instead exploit readily available TFIB information. Hence, the delay penalty of the first chunk diminishes weighted over the whole content transmission. Additionally, Fig. 11 shows that content is closer in NRR" than in NRR': for instance, in the 10x10 grid, the median number of hops is $d'' = 2$ under NRR" and $d' = 3$ under NRR'. Denoting with δt the average link delay, the median duration of the two phases in NRR" takes $2(2d''\delta t)$: compared to a median duration of $2d'\delta t$ for single-phased NRR', this accounts for a modest 25% increase, that moreover applies to the first chunk only.

7. DISCUSSION AND CONCLUSION

This paper offers new arguments to the debate about gain vs pain of ubiquitous caching. Our contributions can be summarized as follows. First, we show that gains of ubiquitous caching only appear by jointly considering $\mathcal{F}$ forwarding and $\mathcal{D}$ meta-caching policies. Specifically, we show that, in both ideal and practical settings, meta-caching policies (such as LCD or even simple random policies) are necessary to enable potential gains offered by smart forwarding policies (such as iNRR and variants) – as otherwise these potential gains are completely offset by cache pollution dynamics.

Under this light, it appears that while [16] dismisses ubiquitous caching due to its limited gains, the comparison has however missed the actual best-case for ICN performance. Indeed, our results show that $\langle\text{iNRR,LCD},\cdot\rangle$ obtains significant gains beyond the $\langle\text{iNRR,LCE},\cdot\rangle$ strategy identified in [16] as the ICN optimum. Yet, this work is by no means complete, as gains are obtained over a limited set of synthetic topologies, with a temporally stationary and spatially uniform catalog. Since LCD has been designed for hierarchical topologies, alternative meta-caching policies, as 2-LRU [26], may be preferable in the general case. Similarly, the benefits of aggregation may be exacerbated by workload where requests are spatially correlated [33]. Finally, results need to be confirmed on realistic workload, such as real traces [16, 21] or synthetic workload fit on real traces [38].

Consequences of these findings can be discussed from multiple viewpoint. From a technical viewpoint, it follows that future ICN literature should not limitedly consider a naïve $\langle\text{SPR,LCE,LRU}\rangle$ strategy, as it offers a too weak candidate for comparison, but also consider $\langle\text{iNRR,LCD,LRU}\rangle$ or even better alternatives [37]. Comparison with optimal strategies [3] is still missing: gauging the distance from optimum would help in understanding the extent of gains that are still possible beyond $\langle\text{iNRR,LCD,LRU}\rangle$. From an economic viewpoint, business considerations will answer whether such gains are economically worth the deployment of ICN – yet, business considerations should be taken on the ground of all relevant technical information. On this regard, caching is likely to play an important role but surely not the only one. ICN are indeed appealing also to solve the curse of mobility, and additionally offer an appealing model where security is bound to content, as opposed to the channel used for its transmission. All these aspects are outside the scope of this work.

We then model performance of iNRR under arbitrary cache networks by extending aNET [31]. We observe that iNRR is far more accurate than aNET: this follows from the fact that, due to a reduced average distance with respect to SPR, as well as an increased mixing of miss streams typical of iNRR, the IRM model violations are less violent for iNRR than they are for aNET. Still, we notice that due to a systematic cache hit overestimation, there is room for improvement in iNRR, e.g., following the approach in [27]. Additionally, iNRR currently models an LCE policy: hence, extending the model to the LCD policy seems a logical next step.

Finally, we evaluate two practically viable implementations of NRR based on scoped flooding. We start by observing that the exploration approach proposed in [16] is a necessary ingredient to reach off-path content. To put our contribution in perspective, we may say that this work finds the remaining two necessary ingredients. Indeed, exploration has possible unwanted consequences: since popular content is possibly hit at multiple caches, data sent back in return may unnecessarily replicate at multiple caches of these paths [12]. We identify meta-caching as the second ingredient, necessary to limit the proliferation of the same content on routers along each of these return paths. We finally identify meta-interests [32] as the last ingredient, necessary to avoid proliferation over multiple paths. Meta-interests let NRR" attain (i) the shortest possible distance, as it achieves an arbitrarily close approximation of iNRR, (ii) the lowest possible data overhead, as it avoids multiple parallel requests for the same chunk, at the price of (iii) a tolerable increase for the delay of the first chunk.

Acknowledgements

This work has been carried out at http://www.lincs.fr. We thank our shepherd, Cedric Westphal, and the anonymous reviewers whose useful comments have contributed in significantly ameliorating the quality of this paper.

8. REFERENCES

[1] http://www.infres.enst.fr/~drossi/ccnSim.
[2] B. Ahlgren, C. Dannewitz, C. Imbrenda, D. Kutscher, and B. Ohlman. A survey of information-centric networking. *IEEE Communications Magazine*, 50(7), 2012.
[3] A. Araldo, M. Mangili, F. Martignon, and D. Rossi. Cost-aware caching: optimizing cache provisioning and object placement in icn. In *IEEE Globecom*, 2014.
[4] A. Araldo, D. Rossi, and F. Martignon. Design and evaluation of cost-aware information centric routers. In *ACM ICN*, 2014.
[5] S. Arianfar and P. Nikander. Packet-level Caching for Information-centric Networking. In *ACM SIGCOMM, ReArch Workshop*, 2010.
[6] B. Azimdoost, C. Westphal, and H. R. Sadjadpour. On the throughput capacity of Information-centric networks. In *ITC*, 2013.
[7] G. Carofiglio, M. Gallo, and L. Muscariello. Bandwidth and Storage Sharing Performance in Information Centric Networking. In *ACM SIGCOMM, ICN Workshop*, 2011.
[8] G. Carofiglio, M. Gallo, L. Muscariello, and D. Perino. Modeling Data Transfer in Content-Centric Networking. In *ITC*, 2011.
[9] W. Chai, D. He, I. Psaras, and G. Pavlou. Cache less for more in information-centric networks. In *IFIP Networking*. 2012.
[10] H. Che, Z. Wang, and Y. Tung. Analysis and design of hierarchical web caching systems. In *IEEE INFOCOM*, 2001.
[11] R. Chiocchetti, D. Perino, G. Carofiglio, D. Rossi, and G. Rossini. INFORM: a dynamic interest forwarding mechanism for information centric networking. In *ACM SIGCOMM, ICN Workshop*, 2013.
[12] R. Chiocchetti, D. Rossi, G. Rossini, G. Carofiglio, and D. Perino. Exploit the known or explore the unknown?: hamlet-like doubts in icn. In *ACM SIGCOMM, ICN Workshop*, 2012.
[13] K. Cho, M. Lee, K. Park, T. Kwon, Y. Choi, and S. Pack. WAVE: Popularity-based and collaborative in-network caching for content-oriented networks. In *IEEE INFOCOM, NOMEN Workshop*, 2012.
[14] A. Dan and D. Towsley. An approximate analysis of the lru and fifo buffer replacement schemes. *ACM SIGMETRICS*, 1990.
[15] S. Eum, K. Nakauchi, M. Murata, Y. Shoji, and N. Nishinaga. CATT: potential based routing with content caching for icn. In *ACM SIGCOMM, ICN Workshop*, 2012.
[16] S. K. Fayazbakhsh, Y. Lin, A. Tootoonchian, A. Ghodsi, T. Koponen, B. M. Maggs, K. Ng, V. Sekar, and S. Shenker. Less pain, most of the gain: Incrementally deployable. In *ACM SIGCOMM*, 2013.
[17] C. Fricker, P. Robert, and J. Roberts. A versatile and accurate approximation for lru cache performance. In *ITC*, 2012.
[18] M. Gallo, B. Kauffmann, L. Muscariello, A. Simonian, and C. Tanguy. Performance evaluation of the random replacement policy for networks of caches. In *ACM SIGMETRICS*, 2012.
[19] A. Ghodsi, S. Shenker, T. Koponen, A. Singla, B. Raghavan, and J. Wilcox. Information-centric networking: seeing the forest for the trees. In *ACM HotNets'X*, 2011.
[20] P. Gill, M. Arlitt, Z. Li, and A. Mahanti. Youtube traffic characterization: a view from the edge. In *ACM IMC*, 2007.
[21] C. Imbrenda, L. Muscariello, and D. Rossi. Analyzing cacheable traffic in ISP access networks for micro CDN applications via content-centric networking. In *ACM ICN*, 2014.
[22] V. Jacobson, D. K. Smetters, N. H. Briggs, J. D. Thornton, M. F. Plass, and R. L. Braynard. Networking Named Content. In *ACM CoNEXT*, 2009.
[23] P. R. Jelenković. Asymptotic approximation of the move-to-front search cost distribution and least-recently used caching fault probabilities. *Annals of App. Prob.*, 9(2), 1999.
[24] N. Laoutaris, H. Che, and I. Stavrakakis. The LCD interconnection of LRU caches and its analysis. *Performance Evaluation*, 63(7), 2006.
[25] N. Laoutaris, S. Syntila, and I. Stavrakakis. Meta Algorithms for Hierarchical Web Caches. In *IEEE ICPCC*, 2004.
[26] V. Martina, M. Garetto, and E. Leonardi. A unified approach to the performance analysis of caching systems. In *IEEE INFOCOM*, 2014.
[27] N. Melazzi, G. Bianchi, A. Caponi, and A. Detti. A General, Tractable and Accurate Model for a Cascade of LRU Caches. *Communications Letters, IEEE*, 18(5):877–880, May 2014.
[28] D. Perino and M. Varvello. A reality check for content centric networking. In *ACM SIGCOMM, ICN Workshop*, 2011.
[29] I. Psaras, W. K. Chai, and G. Pavlou. Probabilistic in-network caching for information-centric networks. In *ACM SIGCOMM, ICN Workshop*, 2012.
[30] E. J. Rosensweig and J. Kurose. Breadcrumbs: Efficient, Best-Effort Content Location in Cache Networks. *IEEE INFOCOM*, 2009.
[31] E. J. Rosensweig, J. Kurose, and D. Towsley. Approximate Models for General Cache Networks. *IEEE INFOCOM*, 2010.
[32] D. Rossi and G. Rossini. Method for managing packets in a network of information centric networking (ICN) nodes, Patent EPO14305866.7/2014.
[33] G. Rossini and D. Rossi. A dive into the caching performance of content centric networking. In *IEEE CAMAD*, 2012.
[34] G. Rossini and D. Rossi. ccnSim: an highly scalable ccn simulator. In *IEEE ICC*, 2013.
[35] G. Rossini and D. Rossi. Evaluating ccn multi-path interest forwarding strategies. *Computer Communications*, 36(7), 2013.
[36] G. Rossini, D. Rossi, M. Garetto, and E. Leonardi. Multi-Terabyte and Multi-Gbps Information Centric Routers. In *IEEE INFOCOM*, 2014.
[37] M. Tortelli, D. Rossi, G. Boggia, and L. A. Grieco. Pedestrian Crossing: The Long and Winding Road toward Fair Cross-comparison of ICN Quality. In *Q-ICN*, 2014.
[38] S. Traverso, M. Ahmed, M. Garetto, P. Giaccone, E. Leonardi, and S. Niccolini. Temporal locality in today's content caching: why it matters and how to model it. *ACM SIGCOMM CCR*, 43(5):5–12, 2013.
[39] C. Yi, A. Afanasyev, I. Moiseenko, L. Wang, B. Zhang, and L. Zhang. A case for stateful forwarding plane. *Computer Communications*, 36(7), 2013.

An Information Centric Network
for Computing the Distribution of Computations

Manolis Sifalakis
Dept of Mathematics and Computer Science
University of Basel
sifalakis.manos@unibas.ch

Basil Kohler
Dept of Mathematics and Computer Science
University of Basel
basil.kohler@unibas.ch

Christopher Scherb
Dept of Mathematics and Computer Science
University of Basel
christopher.scherb@unibas.ch

Christian Tschudin
Dept of Mathematics and Computer Science
University of Basel
christian.tschudin@unibas.ch

ABSTRACT

Named Function Networking (NFN) extends classic Information Centric Networking (ICN), such that in addition to resolving data access by name, it also supports the concept of function definition and application to data (or other functions) in the same resolution-by-name process. This empowers the network to select internally (optimal) places for fulfilling a potentially complex user expression. Forwarding optimization and routing policies become thereafter a basis of dynamic decisions for (re)-distributing computations, and retrieving results.

In this paper we describe the intrinsic operations and mechanisms of an instantiation of NFN based on untyped Lambda expressions and Scala procedures. Then, we demonstrate through a series of proof-of-concept experiments how they extend the capabilities of an information centric network (CCN), for orchestrating and distributing data computations, and re-using cached results from previous computations. In the end we report and discuss the main observations stemming from these experiments and highlight important insights that can impact the architecting of ICN protocols that focus on named-data.

Keywords

Network architectures; information centric networking; named data networking; named-function networking

1. INTRODUCTION

The architectural foundations and design "principles" of the early Internet made very simple to link networks and interconnect resources. The success of these foundations enabled unprecedent growth and innovations for services and applications on either side of the IP layer. Today ICN research focuses on architecting away the shortcomings of

ICN'14, September 24–26, 2014, Paris, France.
Copyright is held by the owner/author(s). Publication rights licensed to ACM.
ACM 978-1-4503-3206-4/14/09 ...$15.00.
http://dx.doi.org/10.1145/2660129.2660150 .

host-centricity in the original Internet, addressing aspects of node mobility, security, dynamics of content dissemination, and most important, factoring out location dependence from the interaction of the user with information. Two common design foundations in many ICN architectures [22] are the adoption of indirection semantics (by varying similarity to a publish-subscribe system [4]), and the use of names to address content without involving host references; as implied in the characterisation "Named Data Networking" [10]. This contributes to a perception and use of the network as a data repository, a global database of some sort, or in its simplest form as a (semantic) memory.

It is worth pondering to what extent these key design foundations of current ICN architectures simplify all possible aspects of *interconnecting information*, and what potential is thereby created for application/service innovation. On first sight, and amidst the cloud computing era, only connecting users to information seems a "halfway vision" for an information-centric Internet.

A broader vision called "Named Function Networking" (NFN) was introduced in [21] where information *access* (ala ICN) is complemented by information *processing* (as in Cloud computing). NFN essentially generalises the semantics of access names in ICN, such that they are treated as expressions. A name can thus interchangeably represent a mapping to an information object, a function capable of processing information objects, or an expression that combines the two (and involving multiple names).

By composing expressions involving named data as well as named functions the user can describe information transformations, and the network gets in-charge of finding if and *how* the result can be obtained or synthesised, by interlacing expression-resolution with name-based forwarding. In this process in-network caching is now extended to also involve caching of computation results.

Like in the case of removing locality-of-storage aspects from data names, NFN removes locality-of-execution: instead of inferring from a user request the location for the computation and expecting from the routing substrate to reinforce its reachability, the NFN network discovers or appoints alternative places for hosting computations.

In this paper we present the NFN concept in action. We report our first experiences on a small testbed, demonstrate though a series of experiments the added value, and finally discuss our observations and the challenges encountered.

The remaining of this paper is organised as follows. In Sec. 2 we provide an overview of the main concepts, design tenets and mechanisms of NFN, and we present the node architecture and the unified expression resolution/forwarding strategy. In Sec. 3 we present a number of concept-proofing experiments, and report the results. In Sec. 4 we discuss the main observations, the issues we encountered, and possible solutions alongside their implications on ICN architecting. Finally Sec. 6 concludes the paper.

2. NAMED FUNCTION NETWORKING (IN A NUTSHELL)

NFN blends the interpretation of a program's control-flow with network forwarding, and thereby dynamically distributes computation tasks across an ICN network; orchestrating in this way the interaction of code with data on user's behalf (and outside his explicit control). This orchestration is effected in one of three different ways, depicted in Fig. 1.

The first case is an attempt to locate results of computations that may have already taken place before, and so in case (a) a node handling a request avoids recomputing information which exists elsewhere in the net. Case (b) applies when information needs be generated, either because it never was computed before or is not timely available. Case (c) covers the situation when some function or data required to evaluate an expression, is "pinned down" (non retrievable) by policy or other reasons. In this case the name resolution (evaluation and possibly execution) is delegated (pushed) towards the pinning site.

To achieve these objectives, names in NFN *represent* functional programs in their simplest, most compact and archaic form: λ-calculus expressions. Their manipulation and evaluation (progressively) "interferes" with name-based forwarding in ICN, and thereby is subject to network conditions, load, and routing policies.

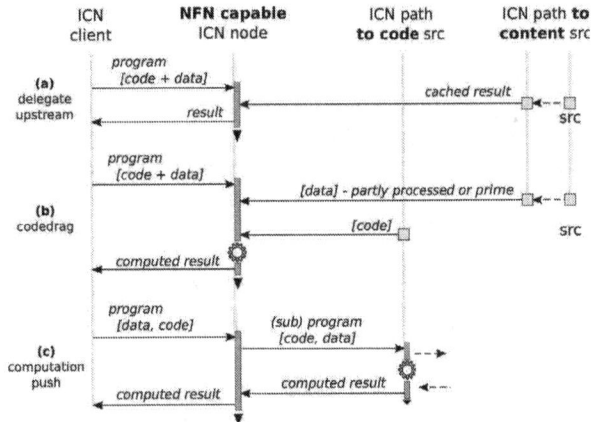

Figure 1: Three scenarios that NFN must handle: upstream fetch, separate code and data fetch, computation push

2.1 Lambda calculus & Expression evaluation

Church's Lambda (λ) Calculus, which is the basis of functional programming, defines recursively the form of terms that compose a valid expression, in one of three cases: variable lookup, function application and function abstraction

$$\texttt{expr ::= v | expr-l expr-r | } \lambda \texttt{x.expr}$$

The most basic form of a λ-term is just a variable name v (that may be resolved). The second valid form `expr-l expr-r`, the so called function application, is nothing else than a simple function call `expr-l(expr-r)` with one argument (`expr-r`). Notice that both the function and its argument are in turn λ-expressions and the only distinction of their roles is their relative left-vs-right placement. The third term form is called abstraction: $\lambda\texttt{x.expr}$ is a definition of a function with one argument. It consists of a λ-expression `expr`, in which all occurrences of the formal parameter x are the places where the actual parameter value (function argument) has to be substituted.

Invocations (applications) and definitions of function with more than one arguments are possible by a succession of single argument function invocations and definitions respectively. Parentheses may be used to make expressions more readable but strictly speaking are not needed.

Complex expressions are transformed (evaluated) and often reduced to simpler ones, by iteratively applying *beta-reduction* operations whenever a function application term is encountered (beta-reduction specifies the rules of transformation). For example, the following line succession of λ-expressions shows such a sequence of (simplifying) transformations between equivalent forms, through beta-reductions.

$(\lambda\texttt{p}.\lambda\texttt{q}.(\texttt{p q p})) \ (\lambda\texttt{x}.\lambda\texttt{y}.\texttt{x}) \ ((\lambda\texttt{z}.\lambda\texttt{s}.\texttt{z}) \ (\lambda\texttt{k}.\texttt{k})) \ \rightarrow$
$(\lambda\texttt{q}.((\lambda\texttt{x}.\lambda\texttt{y}.\texttt{x}) \ \texttt{q} \ (\lambda\texttt{x}.\lambda\texttt{y}.\texttt{x}))) \ ((\lambda\texttt{z}.\lambda\texttt{s}.\texttt{z}) \ (\lambda\texttt{k}.\texttt{k})) \ \rightarrow$
$(\lambda\texttt{x}.\lambda\texttt{y}.\texttt{x}) \ ((\lambda\texttt{z}.\lambda\texttt{s}.\texttt{z}) \ (\lambda\texttt{k}.\texttt{k})) \ (\lambda\texttt{x}.\lambda\texttt{y}.\texttt{x}) \ \rightarrow$
$(\lambda\texttt{y}.((\lambda\texttt{z}.\lambda\texttt{s}.\texttt{z}) \ (\lambda\texttt{k}.\texttt{k}))) \ (\lambda\texttt{x}.\lambda\texttt{y}.\texttt{x}) \ \rightarrow$
$(\lambda\texttt{z}.\lambda\texttt{s}.\texttt{z}) \ (\lambda\texttt{k}.\texttt{k}) \ \rightarrow$
$(\lambda\texttt{s}.\lambda\texttt{k}.\texttt{k})$

When starting the evaluation of an expression from a different term and following a different convention for selecting the next term to reduce (e.g. innermost/rightmost – $\lambda\texttt{z}.\lambda\texttt{s}.\texttt{z}$– as opposed to leftmost –$\lambda\texttt{p}.\lambda\texttt{q}.(\texttt{p q p})$), one may realise that different reduction paths emerge, all of which however lead to the same result (confluence theorem). This is a basis for alternative resolution strategies such as call-by-name/need/value/etc. *Call-by-name* resolution is particularly useful in the context of network computations because sub-expression resolution is delayed until their result "becomes essential"; implying in this way a potential saving of processing resources and reduction of the entailed amount of network traffic.

Although on first sight the untyped λ-calculus, presented above, seems nothing more than an elegant name-reshuffling machinery, it nevertheless allows us to express program logic of arbitrary complexity, very compactly encoded in ICN names, and limited only by the maximum allowed length of a name (i.e. packet size). On the other hand, actual binary data processing operations, cannot be efficiently handled at the name-manipulation level (although theoretically possible in reality it is impractical). For this reason NFN assumes two levels of program execution: One regards the name-manipulation and the orchestration of computation distribution; handled by the functional untyped λ-calculus. The other regards native code execution for actual data processing tasks at the identified execution site(s), which in our prototype is done in Java byte code for procedures written in the Scala language [18].

Overall the use of λ-calculus in NFN serves a role similar to a simple IDL[1] language, involving only two operations:

---

[1]Interactive Data Language, but also Intermediate Definition Language

(i) variable look-up –the name resolution ala ICN–, and (ii) term reduction, where a function is applied to its arguments and composes new terms from them.

2.2 NFN node architecture

In its current instantiation NFN extends the CCN/NDN [10] architecture[2], hereafter referred to as CCN, (i) by integrating a λ-*expression resolution engine* in a CCN relay, and (ii) by optionally hosting an application processing/execution environment. These two extensions correspond to the two levels of program execution discussed earlier.

The λ-expression resolution engine is situated within the CCN relay, and processes all Interests that have the *implicit* postfix name component /NFN (this is by analogy to the way the current CCN protocol implementation handles name checksum hashes). It embodies a Krivine *Abstract Machine* [12] (AM) that follows a call-by-name reduction strategy for "lazy evaluation" of λ-expressions. Call-by-name evaluation guarantees that Interests for the recursive evaluation of sub-expressions will be sent out in the network only if/when the result of the sub-expression is needed. To implement the required primitives (Table 1) we used the ZAM [13] instruction set of Caml, on a *Stack-Machine* with two stacks: One, for holding intermediate reduction state, and the other for resolving external invocations to native code data processing functions. This implementation is compact and lightweight in a typical CCNx relay, enabling controlled resource allocation for NFN-extended processing.

Primitive	λ-op	AM Instructions
RBN(v)	VAR	ACCESS(v);TAILAPPLY
RBN(\x body)	ABSTR	GRAB(x);RBN(body)
RBN(f g)	APPLY	CLOSURE(RBN(f));RBN(g)
ACCESS(var)	Lookup name *var* in environment E and push the corresponding closure to the argument stack A	
CLOSURE(code)	Create a new closure using E and term *code*, push it to the argument stack A.	
GRAB(x)	Replace E with a new environment which extends E with a binding between x and the closure found at the top of A.	
TAILAPPLY	Pop a closure from the argument stack A and replace the current configuration's E and T with those found in the closure.	

Table 1: Krivine Abstract Machine primitives using the ZAM instruction set.

The application processing environment is currently a Scala language[18] ComputeServer (practically a JVM), layered over CCN by being attached to a node-local Face. The CCN relay demuxes to it requests for data processing computations by usual longest prefix match against prefix /COMPUTE. The application processing environment is optional in the sense that there is no requirement for all NFN nodes to be capable of "number crunching" data processing operations

(NFN nodes that have a pure router/forwarder role, only need the AM for the distribution of computation tasks and caching of results).

On NFN nodes hosting a ComputeServer, a native code named function is registered in the NFN realm with a *publish* primitive. This, aside from populating the CCN node's FIB with a corresponding namespace entry, also inserts in the AM's dictionary a mapping to a 'call <num> <func>' statement (where <num> refers to the number of arguments required to invoke <func>). When processing a CCN name as a λ-expression, and <func> is encountered in the next term, it is replaced with the respective call mapping. This prepares the AM to interface with the ComputeServer by "mangling" enough additional terms for the external native function invocation. Furthermore, the call operation is a "game-changer" during the expression resolution, because it forces a switch in the evaluation strategy from call-by-name to call-by-value momentarily, for the completion of the external native code operation. This means that before the external call to <func> is made, each mangled term that will be used as a parameter must be a fully evaluated and resolved expression.

2.3 Distributing computations: Program translation & network forwarding

In NFN a name can hold an expression of the sort func(data), which imperates the application of func on data. Such an expression can be encoded equivalently in any of the λ-expressions that follow[3].

1. func data
2. (λzy.z y) func data
3. (λy.func y) data
4. (λz.z data) func

The equivalence of these expressions and the ability to convert any of them to any other is the essence of NFN.

As code and data are treated interchangeably by virtue of their names in the ICN network, both func and data can be independently addressable CCN names for content. For example if

```
func: /name/of/transcoder
data: /name/of/media
```
then the application of a transcoding function on the media content can be represented by means of these names in the following *named expression*, according to the 3rd form above.

λy.(/name/of/transcoder y) /name/of/media

NFN packages this named expression inside a CCN Interest as follows (in this symbolism of a CCN Interest, '|' delimits individual name components[4])

i_n[/name/of/media | (λy.(/name/of/transcoder y))]

The term inversion in CCN's wire format has to do with its longest prefix-match forwarding as we will see shortly. In general the term placement in a name composition relates to how the ICN architecture implements its resolution process based on the name's components. A more convenient representation that we will use hereafter to refer to the same Interest is

i_1{ (λy.(/name/of/transcoder y)) /name/of/media }

---

[2]Architecture compatibility with ver $\leq$ 0.8.1 of CCNx, and ver $\leq$ 0.2 of NDN.

[3]The possible forms are not limited to these four only of course.

[4]We use this convenience notation recursively, when a name component is itself a CCN name.

The underlined name component appears in the first (position 0) in the Interest packet encoding, influencing by rule of longest prefix match, the Interest forwarding.

To distribute computations in the network, NFN currently implements the following strategy (Fig. 2). Initially (phase 1) using Interest i_1, a cached copy of a transcoded version of media is sought for, en-path to /name/of/media. Having component /name/of/media in first position warrants that the Interest will travel in the direction of the data source. Representing "a transcoded version of media" as /name/of/media/name/of/transcoder is a perfectly plausible search also at the data source, even in a CCN-only node if such a naming convention has been adopted.

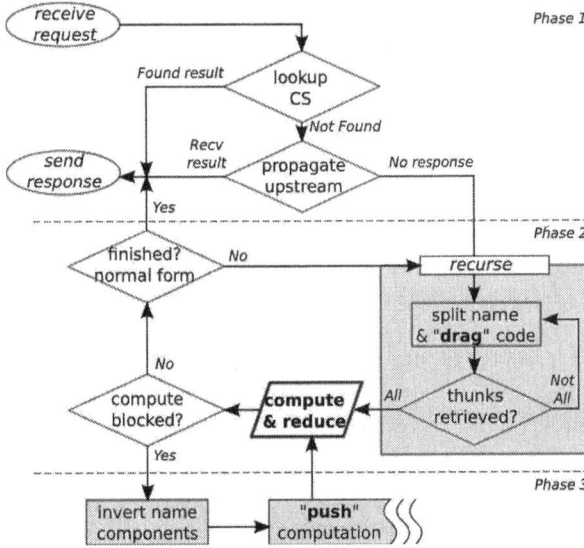

Figure 2: NFN forwarding strategy for CCN.

If this search does not yield results, then ideally one of the NFN nodes that has received the Interest en-path to the source of /name/of/media, may attempt to compute the result (subject to policies, and processing resource availability). This is made feasible at any NFN node, by extracting the CCN names from the λ-expression and forking separate individual Interests for /name/of/media and /name/of/transcoder. Each of those will hopefully retrieve the video data and the transcoder code respectively, enabling the node to compute and then cache the result ("code drag" case in Fig. 1). At the end of this 2nd phase the result will be cached still en-path and possibly close to the data source, increasing its re-use potential in other requests.

If any of the two Interests does not yield the content back for some reason, and before giving up, there is still the possibility to take the computation off-path (phase 3). The NFN node may become a computation-proxy directing the computation towards the code source by simply transforming the named expression in i_1 to an equivalent form as in a new Interest i_2

$i_2\{$ (λz.(z /name/of/media)) /name/of/transcoder $\}$
This equivalent form of the expression refers to the same computation, but has the /name/of/transcoder name component in the first position, which results in forwarding the Interest in the direction of the function ("computation push" in Fig. 1). Due to the symmetric routing in CCN, if the computation succeeds on-the-way to /name/of/transcoder, the

result will travel the same way back to the proxy point and satisfy the original Interest.

The Interest for /name/of/transcoder may yield no results in phase 2 if the code data does not exist, due to a "name pinning" policy for not distributing the code, etc. What is important, however is that: (a) Distribution of computation tasks in the network does not entail forwarding state or cache state alterations – ephemeral content may appear in a cache as a by-product, which in absence of popularity will be eventually erased. (b) Computations may or may not take place, leaving the computation placement and resource allocation decision entirely to the network (avoiding single point of failure, compensating for routing failures, and partly protecting against DoS attacks targeting a specific host or service).

Finally, in the whole process of evaluating a named expression, requests for intermediate results in nested terms can in fact retrieve only *thunks*. One can think of a thunk in NFN as a reference or contract for the feasibility of a computation, whose results can be retrieved later in time. Thunks allow the evaluation of a named expression to progress even when results are not available yet (enabling asynchronous and parallel computations as we will demonstrate in one of the experiments later on)[5].

3. EXPERIENCES WITH NFN

In this section we report and discuss our experiences with a proof-of-concept evaluation of NFN in a small testbed topology. The goals set out for this evaluation have been to

- Showcase the ability of NFN for dynamic distribution of computation tasks and interactions between static data and functions inside an ICN network (and involving the benefits of caching computation results).

- Test, and identify occasions where NFN empowers network side decisions and optimisations. Understand the nature of these optimising decisions, and develop insights of how to improve the effectiveness of NFN.

- Have a first indication of the comparative overhead of running NFN, in a CCN network.

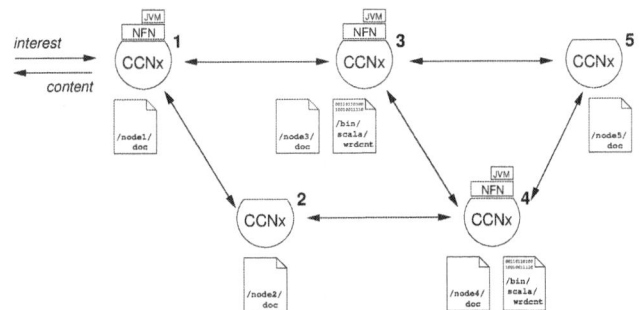

Figure 3: Testbed topology – two CCN & three NFN nodes.

---

[5] A thunk-ed name appearing in a CCN packet has 2 postfix components i_n [..|/NFN|/TH] for delivering to, and appropriately interpreting by, the NFN resolver

3.1 Experimental set-up

Our testbed is a hybrid topology including CCN-NFN as well as CCN-only nodes (Fig. 3). The topology and size of the testbed were kept simple enough for alpha-testing and ease of tracking the node interactions, and at the same time complex enough to serve our demonstration purposes of NFN's features. As shown in Fig. 3, it consists of five nodes, where two are pure CCN nodes and the other three are NFN nodes (AM extension to the CCN relay) hosting additionally the Scala [18] ComputeServer (JVM) execution environment; connections between nodes are bidirectional; client requests always arrive at Node1 first. Any deviations from this set-up is reported in the individual sections of the experiments.

The FIBs of the nodes are initialised manually (in absence of dynamic routing currently for CCN) and such that each node can reach every other node over the shortest path. When more than one paths are available, both are included.

In regard to content distribution, we have placed a different document at every node's content store with name /nodeX/doc. Additionally, the content stores of Node3 and Node4 contain bytecode of a word counting procedure, published with name /bin/scala/wrdcnt, and corresponding FIB entries are placed in all other nodes. This procedure takes as a single argument a document and computes the number of words in it. In our simulation it waits for 500 milliseconds to model a more compute-intensive function, before returning its result.

3.2 Six cases where the network is in charge of placing computations

Experiment 1 (code+content pull): The first experiment is a vanilla check of case (b) of Fig. 1 for carrying out locally computations by first retrieving code and data. It starts by a user requesting the word-counting of /node1/doc. Following our default mapping of λ-expressions to CCN messages, the argument /node1/doc becomes the first name component, which characterises Node1 as the recipient of the expression. When Node1 starts resolving the expression and the component /bin/scala/wrdcnt is encountered, it issues Interest i_2 to retrieve it, which is satisfied by Node3. When Node1 receives the bytecode of the procedure it applies it to the locally available document and returns the word count result in a content object to the client.

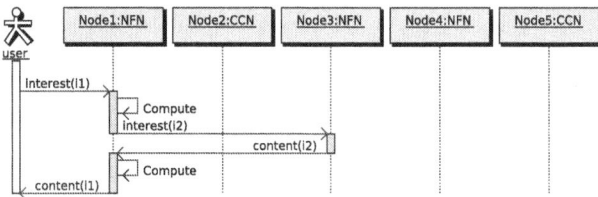

Figure 4: Experiment 1 – the network pulls code, applies it to locally available data
i_1{/bin/scala/wrdcnt (/node1/doc)}
i_2{/bin/scala/wrdcnt}

Experiment 2 (computation push): The second experiment demonstrates case (c) of Fig. 1 for delegating a computation, as a result of name manipulations in NFN that influence decision of the CCN forwarding fabric. The client

issues a word-counting request as in experiment 1, but this time for /node5/doc, which is located on Node5, a CCN-only node. As neither of the missing named objects is available locally on Node1, according to the strategy discussed in Sec. 2.3, Node1 places the name component /node5/doc at the first position and propagates the Interest i_2 towards Node5. However, at Node5 the Interest times out because it is a CCN-only node: the remaining name components cannot be matched exactly or the Interest cannot be propagated further based on longest prefix match.

Node1 then reverts to the next phase of the strategy from Sec. 2.3 and transforms the expression to an equivalent one that has the component /bin/scala/wrdcnt at the first position in the name. This new Interest i_3 is now forwarded by CCN to Node3. This node has a local copy of wrdcnt, which means it can start evaluating the expression and then separately request the content of /node5/doc in i_4. This time, the name can be matched exactly: Node3 receives the content, computes the result and returns it to Node1, who in turn satisfies the client request.

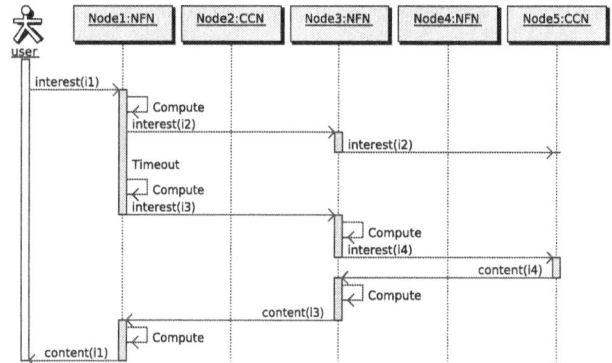

Figure 5: Experiment 2 – computation push (the network works around a CCN-only node)
i_1{/bin/scala/wrdcnt (/node5/doc)}
i_2{/bin/scala/wrdcnt (/node5/doc)}
i_3{(λx.(x /node5/doc)) (/bin/scala/wrdcnt)}
i_4{/node5/doc}

Experiment 3 (failover conditions): Assume the same query was issued as in experiment 2 and additionally that the connection between Node1 and Node3 failed: How should the network use the alternate path that exists between Node1 to Node5? Fig. 6 shows that interest i_2 (which carries the complete name expression) now travels to Node5 via Node2 and Node4. As before, this request times out. Then the transformed Interest i_3 is generated as before by Node1; it is sent to Node2, which is a CCN-only node, and upon reaching Node4, the computation completes there! Note that although there is an alternative (albeit longer) path to Node3, who may compute the expression, re-routing does not try to deliver the computation there. Instead, another (additional and closer) location is found for the computation, on Node4. Since the locality of computation is not part of the user request, if alternative computation-capable places are available, NFN might try to exploit them rather than forcing traffic to one only specific place!

Experiment 4 (recursive distribution): For this experiment another native (bytecode) procedure that accepts a

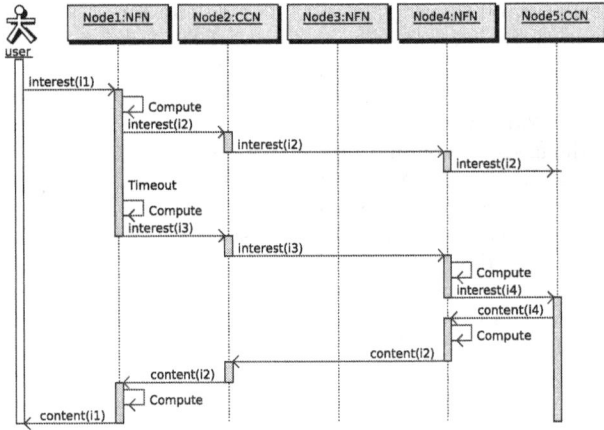

Figure 6: Experiment 3 – failover (the network discovers another suitable computing place)

i_1{/bin/scala/wrdcnt (/node5/doc)}
i_2{/bin/scala/wrdcnt (/node5/doc)}
i_3{(λx.(x /node5/doc)) (/bin/scala/wrdcnt)}
i_4{/node5/doc}

variable list of integer arguments and sums their values, is registered with name /bin/scala/sum at Node1.

In Fig. 7, a client sends a request for the sum of the word-counts of two documents in i_1. The word-counting of each document can take place independently and at different places. As shown this is orchestrated at Node1, where /bin/scala/sum (first name component of i_1) is found. The expression evaluation progresses by two reduction steps until the point that results from the word-counting sub-expressions are necessary for the sum to be computed. Each sub-expression is resolved *in turn* through a separate Interest: The first subexpression leads to Interest i_2, forwarded to Node3 and computed there. The second subexpression yields Interest i_3 which is computed at Node4. The partial results are collected at Node1 which can then use them to evaluate the sum and return the answer to the client.

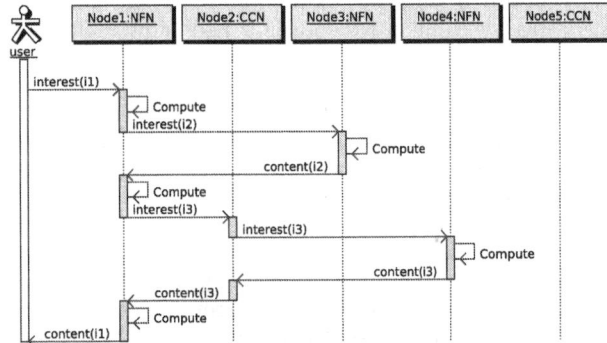

Figure 7: Experiment 4 – sequential evaluation of sub-expressions

i_1{(((λf.λg.(f (g /node3/doc) (g /node4/doc)))
            (/bin/scala/wrdcnt)) (/bin/scala/sum)}
i_2{/bin/scala/wrdcnt (/node3/doc)}
i_3{/bin/scala/wrdcnt (/node4/doc)}

This experiment 4 shows how more complex computations are recursively decomposed by NFN into a workflow of tasks with rather opportunistic coupling among them (compare this to the tight signalling coupling expected by components of most SoA architectures today). Later on, in Sec. 3.3, we show how through the use of *thunks* the same request is worked out in parallel, effectively providing an opportunistic Map-Reduce transport across an ICN network.

Experiment 5 (cached results prevent repeated computations): This experiment extends the previous one to show that if the result of a (presumably popular) computation can be cached, this will reduce the computational cost or delivery time of subsequent similar computations.

A word-count request for document (/node3/doc) is sent in Interest i_1, before the request for the sum of the two document word-counts as in experiment 4. Node1 passes the request in i_2 to Node3 (where both the data and code are available), which computes and returns the result; Node1 will cache this result. When the next request for summing up the two word-counts of /node3/doc3 and /node4/doc4 is received in i_3, Node1 already has the result of the first computation for /node3/doc. Hence, it issues only one Interest (i_4) for the sub-expression involving the word-count of /node4/doc. This time the request for i_3 completes much faster than in the previous example, as seen in Fig. 12 (comparing the times of $Exp4$ and $Exp5_2$).

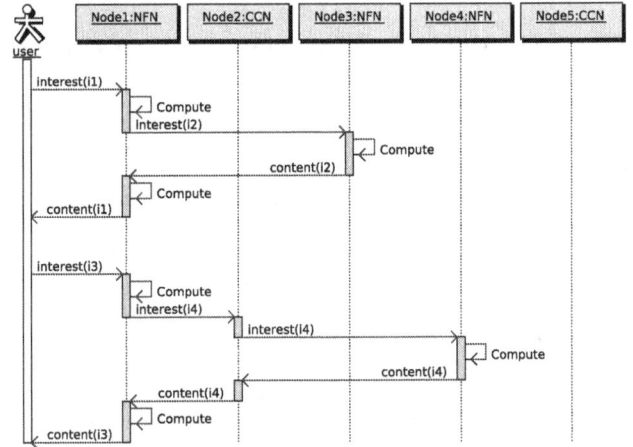

Figure 8: Experiment 5 – accessing cached results

i_1{/bin/scala/wrdcnt (/node3/doc)}
i_2{/bin/scala/wrdcnt (/node3/doc)}
i_3{((λf.λg.(f (g /node3/doc) (g /node4/doc)))
            (/bin/scala/wrdcnt)) (/bin/scala/sum)}
i_4{/bin/scala/wrdcnt (/node4/doc)}

Experiment 6 (Node loaded, pass it to the next): It can happen that some NFN node capable of data computations is overloaded, e.g. only because it happens to be closer to popular content or because it receives voluminous requests. The opportunistic location-decoupled nature of computations in NFN can enable implicit load-balancing in the ICN network.

In this experiment, Node3 is designated to be in *overloaded* state and the link between Node4 and Node5 was cut. The client sends a request i_1 for word-counting content object /node5/doc5, which is to be found on the CCN-only Node5.

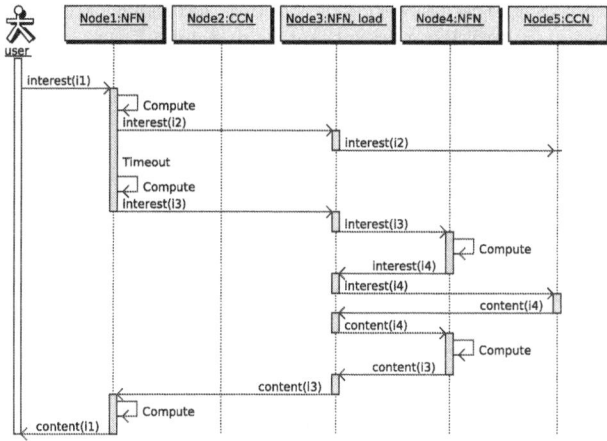

Figure 9: Experiment 6 – implicit load-balancing
i_1{/bin/scala/wrdcnt (/node5/doc)}
i_2{(λx./bin/scala/wrdcnt x) /node5/doc5}
i_3{(λx.(x /node5/doc)) (/bin/scala/wrdcnt)}
i_4{/node5/doc}

At first, the network reacts similarly to experiment 2: when the propagated whole request in i_2 arrives to Node5 it times out. Node1 re-admits the program modified (according to the strategy in Sec. 2.3) as Interest i_3. This time however, Node3 cannot assume the computation because it is marked overloaded, and instead forwards it towards Node4. Node4 computes the result by retrieving /node5/doc5 via Node3 and using the local copy of /bin/scala/wrdcnt. In the end, not only the client request was not rejected but a load-balancing action was taken implicitly by the network rather that being administratively configured.

3.3 Gratuitous parallelism with thunks

Experiment 7 is a modified version of Experiment 4 where two word-counting results are summed up. We have now enabled the use of thunks to allow asynchronous non-blocking dispatching of the two sub-expressions.

When Node3 receives the request i_2 for word-counting /node3/doc, it will immediately return a thunk (and start the actual work). A thunk response contains a temporary name that is routable back to the node that started the computation, along-side an optional completion time estimate. It is a "contract" that allows the requester (Node1) to continue work (e.g. proceed in the reduction of a blocked expression, and evaluation of other sub-terms) and ask for the thunk-ed result later. At the same time Node1 may adjust the PIT timer for the pending Interest from the client not to expire for as long time as the longest sub-computation will need (time estimate returned with the thunk) – so as to refresh the Interests on the thunks later on – and pass an equivalent thunk name response to the client. In case the PIT timer on Node1 expires without having successfully acquired the thunk-ed result, the client can either re-issue the request, or try and re-animate the partially completed computation by using the thunk name as a "reminder" to refer Node1 to possibly cached state of the sub-computation.

Meanwhile, Node3 and Node4 compute in parallel the results for the i_2 and i_3 and when the thunk-ed requests arrive anew from Node1, they respond with the actual results. This

second round of Interests sent from Node1, contain the thunk names and *not* the original names of the sub-expressions. This guarantees that the computation results will be retrieved from the correct (contracted) places.

The effect of thunks and the parallelism that they enable can be seen in the measurements of Fig. 12, where experiment 7 terminates in roughly half the time of experiment 4 although the client asks for the same computation result in both settings.

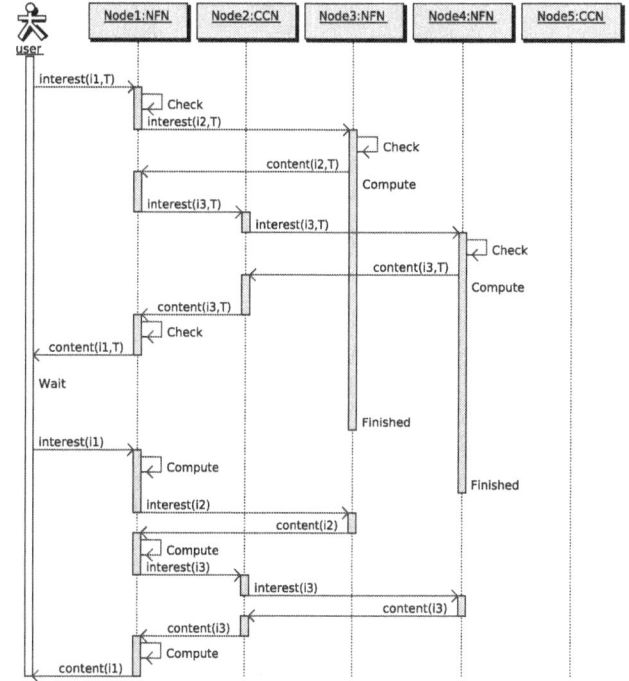

Figure 10: Experiment 7 – gratuitous parallelism
i_1{((λf.λg.(f (g /node3/doc) (g /node4/doc)))
        (/bin/scala/wrdcnt)) (/bin/scala/sum)}
i_2{(λx./bin/scala/wrdcnt x) (/node3/doc)}
i_3{(λx./bin/scala/wrdcnt x) (/node4/doc)}

3.4 Preferential opportunism in the distribution of computations

The previous experiments demonstrated the NFN network's ability to discover places where computations can take place. In this process it is also possible for clients to "give hints" to NFN for preferential placement of computations, through simple user-prepared abstraction transformations of the λ-expression or selected sub-terms, in the initial request. For example, as seen in **experiment 8** (Fig. 11), the following two equivalent expressions even though they produce the same result, they follow different resolution paths in the network:
i_1{/bin/scala/wrdcnt (/node3/doc)}
i_3{(λf.(f /node3/doc)) (/bin/scala/wrdcnt)}
Transforming i_1 before issuing the initial request, with a λ-abstraction to i_3, does nothing else than simply changing the argument name, which will comprise the first prefix component in the CCN name (shown underlined). In the first case the computation will be attempted first near /node3/doc, and in the latter near /bin/scala/wrdcnt. This trick can be

exploited *by the client* to format programs, such that preferences for the distribution of computations are expressed –but importantly, they cannot be enforced– for individual sub-expressions (in the program).

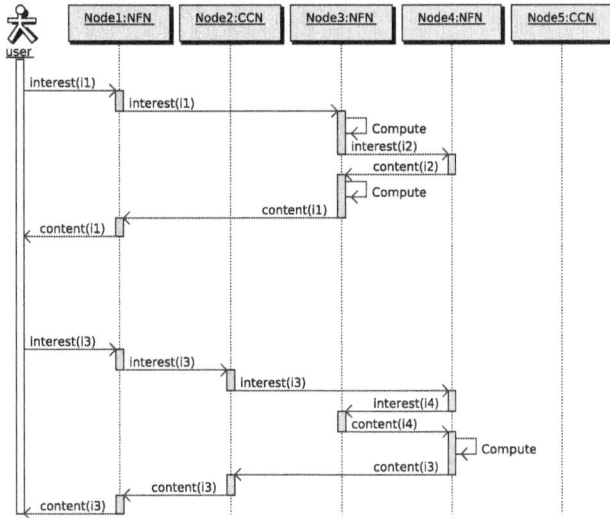

Figure 11: Experiment 8 – same result, but different preferences hinted at by the client
$i_1\{(\lambda d./bin/scala/wrdcnt\ d)\ \underline{/node3/doc3}\}$,
$i_2\{\underline{/bin/scala/wrdcnt}\}$,
$i_3\{(\lambda f.f\ /node3/doc3)\ \underline{/bin/scala/wrdcnt}\}$,
$i_4\{\underline{/node3/doc3}\}$

3.5 Performance overhead of NFN-over-CCN

Fig. 12 provides an indication of the completion times for the experiments we conducted, and for each of them the distribution of delay components across (*i*) native code execution at the ComputeServer/JVM, in blue, (*ii*) waiting time on Interest timeouts in the CCN network, in red, and (*iii*) NFN processing, in white. NFN processing includes expression evaluation at the abstract machine and communication with the ComputeServer.

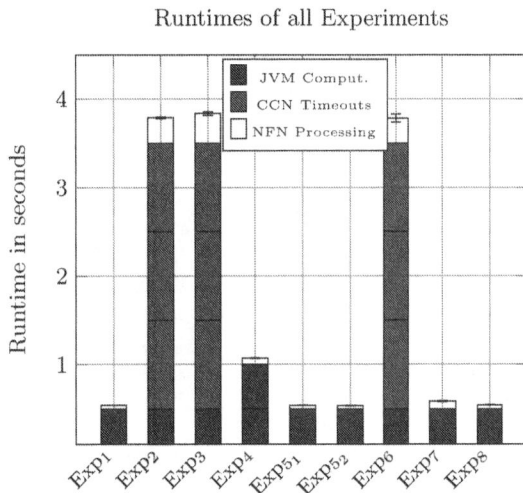

Figure 12: Per experiment runtimes

Although these experiments are only indicative (given the non-quantitative character of our experiments), nevertheless two standing out observations may be made. The first is that NFN processing is definitely affordable in the time scales of operation and decisions in CCN. Even with a very crude prototype implementation all NFN AM-related operations across up to 3-4 nodes take only a fraction of the typical CCN Interest timeout; and affirms the lightweight type of operation it adds to the ICN forwarding plane.

The second observation regards the overhead that the current CCN architecture inflicts on NFN, witnessed in the effects of timeouts (as an implicit feedback mechanism) on the total completion time of NFN client requests. The agility of NFN in making decisions is seriously limited by the absence of fast feedback; after probing for computations that are infeasible or for content/code that cannot be retrieved. The effect is more pronounced in NFN than in CCN only, since a typical NFN request entails several CCN level transactions.

4. DISCUSSION & KEY INSIGHTS

4.1 NACKs, explicit vs. implicit feedback

In most of the experiments presented as well as others that we have conducted, it is easy to realise that the role of deciding alternative courses of action as entailed in the *resolution-forwarding* strategy of Sec. 2.3, is almost always assumed by the first NFN node upstream from the client (Node1 here). This is because of the fact that in the interaction with the CCN substrate this is the first one to detect timeouts and react to them. If explicit notifications were available by the CCN protocol (such as ACKs/NACKs), to help detect faster infeasible computations or unavailable content, the role of selecting alternative actions would be assumed by NFN nodes "deeper" in the network, and lending to much wider distribution of tasks and computations. The time scale of decisions would also be much shorter (currently waiting for 1-3 timeouts), thus improving NFN's agility.

In current absence of explicit notifications in the CCN architecture, a number of alternative solutions deserve exploration. One of them is to regard thunks as a means of explicit notifications e.g. as in Map-Reduce type of operations. A thunk currently includes a time-to-compute estimate, which in practical reality it is challenging to qualify at different nodes in absence of a global clock. This time estimate is mostly useful therefore to differentiate unavailability from statistical plausibility (of acquiring a result), which is otherwise not discernible from timeouts. A NACK in this context is nothing more than a thunk with a timer to infinity. The problem with this "NFN-level" approach is that in a hybrid environment the semantics would only be understood by NFN nodes, making its effects partial or occasional.

Another partial solution[6], which would likely improve the problem, without architecting explicit notifications inside CCN, would be the creation of a decreasing timeout gradient as Interests travel away from the receiver. This would require that all CCN nodes have the same default PIT timer, and that an Interest travelling from hop to hop has a means to request its registration in the PIT with an increasing decrement from the default timer. The Interest will then have the possibility of expiring earlier the further away it has travelled from the source, and the respective NFN node

---

[6]Contributed by one of the reviewers of this paper

would be the one to seek alternative courses of action. This approach is quite fragile however and requires hard-wiring common defaults to all CCN nodes.

4.2 The right semantics for thunks

Following up the topic of thunks, so far we have used them to convey a notification of the sort: *"I start computing now, contact me later for the result"*. An alternative type of semantics, would be to convey the notification: *"I can compute, contact me when to start"*. The latter semantics have the benefit of allowing the client side of the computation to "collect offers" and choose among several candidate places where a computation can be completed, or delay a parallelized execution for later. Although this would have the cost of some additional communication work on the client side of the computation (e.g. Node1 in Experiment 4 and 7), it could however avoid triggering redundant computations in different places when the request is multicast by CCN in several directions. This exploration is the topic of future quantitative evaluation.

4.3 Security

Intuitively one may ponder on the security implications of having a possibility to spawn arbitrary computations from the middle of the network through "hand-grenade" programs masqueraded as normal requests (even by accident). Although we have not architected NFN or engineered its key functions with security as a prime concern, we have been however security-implications aware.

The tenets of caching and re-using computation results, and the removal of locality-of-execution, are two top-listed features of NFN, which can minimize the effectiveness of DoS attacks towards specific targets in the network (more than what is actually possible in today's Internet).

Call-by-name expression resolution warrants that a request for evaluating a sub-expression will be dispatched in the network only if the result of that sub-expression will actually be used, making the plausibility of an attack not deterministically discernible.

Thunks with the alternative semantics describe before have also the potential to protect against waste of computation resources: the orchestrating NFN node can ensure that thunked computations are spawned only if their enclosing expression is feasible and allowed.

All these features to start with, although not securing the network, they nevertheless, intend to limit or localise the effects of an attack, and make it difficult to plan against specific targets.

Additionally, access control to functions can be protected by similar means that it is today in SoA. Data cannot be altered in NFN, only new data can be generated from other data and while older fade-away from caches. Every entity that generates new data must sign them according to data authorship rules in CCN, and when source data are transformed by some function, chained signing can be used to assert and verify the function owner, its inputs and its outputs (independently always of location).

4.4 NFN in ICN architectures

Clearly (to us), NFN-type of functionality deserves to be a part of an ICN enabled Internet. The question is where should this functionality be fleshed out? Should it be *part of* the ICN forwarding plane or engineered *on top of* it?

The arguments that speak against its embedding in the ICN plane are those of execution performance overhead, and architectural simplicity (the internetworking layer "needs" to be super fast and simple). On the aspect of execution performance, our first indications (albeit admittedly very preliminary to support evidence) are that the overhead is easily sustainable considering the CCN protocol time scales of operation (decisions driven by timeouts). Moreover, as the typical NFN topology would sufficiently be a hybrid one, involving NFN as well as CCN-only nodes, scalability should not be a concern (although this also requires a quantitative validation to confirm).

The counter arguments that speak for its placement in the ICN plane are twofold: (*i*) Name manipulation by NFN's Abstract Machines influence the forwarding/routing semantics, which naturally belongs to the network's forwarding and routing layer, by analogy that NAT's IP address manipulation functions today are part of the IP and transport layers. On the other hand, the actual NFN's data processing execution environment and host of application logic, resides at CCN's application layer, mostly to be found near the network's edge. (*ii*) It is critical that routing and compute-placement decisions are made as close as possible where things (timeouts, unavailability of resources or capabilities) can be discovered, i.e. close to the root cause. Otherwise, if nodes somewhere at the edge have to discover what happened, one needs either to setup rich diagnostic feedback protocols and pay a price for that complexity and additional delay, or let the edge nodes timeout, which is catastrophic for performance.

Finally, if one accepts a de-facto role of NFN in ICN, the question arises about the feasibility of NFN with other architectures apart from NDN/CCN. We have seen that NFN names contain two types of components, one which is routable/resolvable in the ICN, and another which is glue for expressions, and which is not directly routable but manipulated by the AM in NFN. Interestingly, the latter also appears in most ICN architectures, often specialised as a "routing context" but which is nevertheless identified with simple manipulations: E.g. AS routing vector in DONA [11], *scope* in PSIRP/PURSUIT [8], *routing hints* in NetInf [6], *namespaces* in Convergence [16], and so on. On the other hand, a more challenging requirement in other ICN architectures is NFN's current reliance on symmetric paths for the implementation of the combined expression-resolution strategy (Sec. 2.3). This is a topic of follow up exploration.

5. RELATED WORK

Mostly related to the work presented in this paper is the research on Service Centric Networking (SCN) [2]. SCN envisions to create processing workflows inside an ICN network through a manipulated concatenation of names that identify network services in the network to be interfaced. Expressibility of distributed computations and workflow creation in SCN is much more basic when compared to NFN. On the other hand SCN creates workflows by means of interface specifications and service descriptions. This feature of SCN can provide an elegant approach of introducing SLAs in NFN, which can be the basis for an information centric Service-oriented-Architecture.

An inspiring work for our ideas is Borenstein's Atomic-Mail [1] from 1992, who proposed and developed a "programmable email system". Similarly inspiring has been the idea of a Turing Switch [5], which is a universal network interconnecting element on which all link-layer and network-layer functions are expressed through λ-calculus programs.

In seeing the network as a distributed database, work on declarative networking [14] pioneered interesting ideas, including a network query language (NDlog), that enabled access to distributed information and coordination of computations at disparate locations, without explicit reference of communication primitives. Although the core philosophy and methodology between declarative networking and NFN are different (e.g. declarative query language, versus imperative functional programs), there are important similarities and analogies that deserve further exploration and possible cross fertilisation of ideas.

In the general topic of in-network programmability, in the past, Active Networking (AN) research [3] envisioned users able to load programs [23, 19] in a network data path that supports programming primitives [7, 20], or programming language frameworks, eg. [9, 17]. A modern re-incarnation of parts of the AN vision is found today in the objectives of Software Define Networking [15]. Unlike AN and SDN, however, NFN's primary focus is not on explicitly programming a data path, but rather letting the network compose a data path that satisfies the needs of a high level user program, thus the main decision making lies with the network.

6. CONCLUSIONS AND FUTURE WORK

NFN captures an essential aspect of modern use of the Internet: multi-modality of information and multi-purpose use. With this goal it extends the ICN name semantics and proposes that a name generally stands for a function: a constant mapping (as in ICN today), but also a complex recipe involving many sub-operations. *Name resolution* in the current ICN-way is then only a special case of *expression resolution*.

We presented first experiences with NFN in action, and demonstrated through a series of experiments several scenarios where this functional extension leads easily to a generalization of "information access" in the network: static information look up complemented by dynamic computation on the fly. We have gained interesting insights to fuel follow up work and orient more extensive evaluations, but also which have the possibility to influence architectural work in CCN and ICN in general.

7. REFERENCES

[1] N. Borenstein. Computational mail as network infrastructure for computer-supported cooperative work. In *Int'l conference on Computer-Supported Cooperative Work*, 1992.

[2] T. Braun et al. Service-Centric Networking. In *Int'l IEEE Conference on Communications (ICC)*, pages 1–6, June 2011.

[3] A. Campbell et al. A survey of programmable networks. *SIGCOMM Comput. Commun. Rev.*, 29(2):7–23, Apr. 1999.

[4] M. Caporuscio et al. Design and evaluation of a support service for mobile, wireless publish/subscribe applications. *IEEE Trans. Softw. Eng.*, 29(12):1059–1071, December 2003.

[5] J. Crowcroft. Turing Switches: Turing machines for all-optical Internet routing. Technical Report UCAM-CL-TR-556, Cambridge University, Jan. 2003.

[6] C. Dannewitz et al. Network of Information (NetInf) - An information-centric networking architecture. *Comput. Commun.*, 36(7):721–735, Apr. 2013.

[7] D. Feldmeier et al. Protocol Boosters. *IEEE JSAC, Special Issue on Protocol Architectures for 21st Century Applications*, 16(3), April 1998.

[8] N. Fotiou et al. Developing Information Networking Further: From PSIRP to PURSUIT. In *International Conference on Broadband Communications, Networks, and Systems*, pages 1–13. Springer, 2010.

[9] M. Hicks et al. PLAN: A Packet Language for Active Networks. In *3rd ACM SIGPLAN Int'l conference on Functional Programming*, 1998.

[10] V. Jacobson et al. Networking Named Content. In *Int'l ACM conference on Emerging networking experiments and technologies (CoNEXT)*, 2009.

[11] T. Koponen et al. A data-oriented (and beyond) network architecture. *SIGCOMM Comput. Commun. Rev.*, 37(4):181–192, Aug. 2007.

[12] J.-L. Krivine. A call-by-name lambda-calculus machine. *Higher Order Symbol. Comput.*, 20(3):199–207, Sept. 2007.

[13] X. Leroy. The Zinc Experiment: An Economical Implementation of the ML Language. Technical Report TR 117, INRIA, 1990.

[14] B. T. Loo et al. Declarative networking: Language, execution and optimization. In *Int'l ACM SIGMOD Conference on Management of Data*. ACM, 2006.

[15] N. McKeown et al. Openflow: enabling innovation in campus networks. *SIGCOMM Comput. Commun. Rev.*, 38(2), Mar. 2008.

[16] N. B. Melazzi. Convergence: extending the media concept to include representations of real world objects. In *The Internet of Things*, pages 129–140. Springer, 2010.

[17] S. Merugu et al. Bowman and CANEs: Implementation of an Active Network. In *37th Allerton Conference on Communication, Control and Computing,*, Monticello, IL, September 1999.

[18] M. Odersky et al. An Overview of the Scala Programming Language. Technical Report IC/2004/64, EPFL Lausanne, 2004.

[19] S. Schmid et al. A highly flexible service composition framework for real-life networks. *Computer Networks, Special Issue on Active Networks*, 50:2488–2505, October 2006.

[20] C. Tschudin and R. Gold. Network Pointers. *ACM SIGCOMM Comput. Commun. Rev.*, 33(1):23–28, Jan. 2003.

[21] C. Tschudin and M. Sifalakis. Named functions and cached computations. In *Annual IEEE conference on Consumer Communications and Networking*, Jan. 2014.

[22] G. Xylomenos et al. A survey of information-centric networking research. *Communications Surveys Tutorials, IEEE*, 16(2):1024–1049, Feb. 2014.

[23] J. Zander and R. Forchheimer. Softnet - An approach to high level packet communication. In *2nd Amateur Radio Computer Networking Conference*, 1983.

Design and Evaluation of Cost-aware Information Centric Routers

Andrea Araldo
LRI-Paris-Sud University
91405 Orsay, France
araldo@lri.fr

Dario Rossi
Telecom ParisTech
75013 Paris, France
dario.rossi@enst.fr

Fabio Martignon
LRI-Paris-Sud University
91405 Orsay, France
fabio.martignon@lri.fr

ABSTRACT

Albeit an important goal of Information Centric Networking (ICNs) is traffic reduction, a perhaps even more important aspect follows from the above achievement: the reduction of ISP operational costs that comes as consequence of the reduced load on transit and provider links. Surprisingly, to date this crucial aspect has not been properly taken into account, neither in the architectural design, nor in the operation and management of ICN proposals.

In this work, we instead design a distributed cost-aware scheme that explicitly considers the cost heterogeneity among different links. We contrast our scheme with both traditional cost-blind schemes and optimal results. We further propose an architectural design to let multiple schemes be interoperable, and finally assess whether overlooking implementation details could hamper the practical relevance of our design. Numerical results show that our cost-aware scheme can yield significant cost savings, that are furthermore consistent over a wide range of scenarios.

Categories and Subject Descriptors

C.2.1 [**Network Architecture and Design**]: Network communications, Packet-switching networks

General Terms

Algorithms; Performance; Design;

Keywords

Information Centric Networking; Cost-Awareness

1. INTRODUCTION

Information Centric Networks (ICN) let end-users' applications directly access named content, as opposite to addressable entities as in the current TCP/IP Internet. One among the expected benefits of ICN consists in *traffic reduction* through transparent caching, as opposite to deploying

per-application "network accelerators" as typically happens nowadays.

Yet, benefits of ICN with respect to current technologies, such as caching at the network edge as in CDN, are so far unclear. On the one hand, recent research [12, 13] argues that benefits of ubiquitous ICN caching may, in reason of an unfavorable cache-to-catalog ratio, be neither sufficient[1], nor actually necessary[2]. On the other hand, before concluding that ICN has yet to convince, all the relevant factors need to be taken into account. These factors include, for instance: more optimistic ICN cache sizes due to algorithmic design [31] (rather than memory technology advances, which happen at a much lower pace), or the existence of a temporal correlation of the active catalog and requests [34] (that makes ICN caching more effective) or economic aspects [4] (since cost reduction is the ultimate goal of traffic reduction).

We argue that especially this latter aspect has yet to receive the attention it deserves in the ICN community. Namely, economic aspects [4] are perhaps the most important among ICN key performance indicators, and should be considered as a proxy of ICN success: capital expenditures for ICN deployment will be planned according to a direct measure of the expected operational ISP costs (and, especially, savings) under ICN. Yet, despite much research has focused on ICN performance *within* ISP boundaries, to date few works evaluate the effect of ICN on cost reduction *across* boundaries [24, 26, 17, 4].

In this work, we thus challenge the implicit simplifying assumption made in the literature that all inter-ISP links have equal cost, and address the *design and performance evaluation of cost-aware techniques*, whose main design goals are (i) flexibility to support multiple ICN architectures, (ii) interoperability with currently existing or future schemes, (iii) robust operation to ensure practical relevance of our proposal and, finally, (iv) simplicity to facilitate its adoption.

The rest of this work is organized as follows. In Sec. 2 we illustrate our system model, outline the guiding criteria of our design, and propose a simple distributed technique to achieve cost-effective ICN operations. We evaluate our proposal in Sec. 3, where we contrast it with traditional

---

[1]As [13] brilliantly points out, "changing the overall network architecture in order to tame the exponentially growing world of content with the logarithmic sword of caching seems a classical example of taking a knife to a gunfight: it may make for a great story, but it won't end well."

[2]In particular, [12] argues that most of the caching gain is attainable by simply (and painlessly) caching at the edge of the network, as in the current CDN model.

cost-blind schemes as well as the optimal solution, gathered in centralized settings, as a reference – showing that results are structurally similar, and performance very close, to that achieved by ideal policies. We then assess robustness of operation under implementation constraints, as well as over a wider range of scenarios, in Sec. 4. Finally, Sec. 5 places our proposal in the context of related effort, and Sec. 6 summarizes our main lessons.

2. SYSTEM MODEL AND DESIGN

In this section, we first introduce our model of economic interactions (Sec. 2.1). We then describe the principles (Sec. 2.2) that guide our design (Sec. 2.3). Finally, we introduce the terms of comparison, i.e., traditional cost-blind and optimal ICN strategies (Sec. 2.4).

2.1 Economic interactions

As shown in Fig.1, an ISP serves a rate λ_o of requests for a named object o belonging to the catalog $\mathcal{C}$. To serve these requests, the ISP possibly has to retrieve the object through one of its available *external links* (we denote them with the set $\mathcal{L}$), paying a related cost.

In case the ISP is operating caches, some of these requests can hence be served within the ISP network: in this case, the incoming demand λ_o is filtered by caches within the network, so that the demand crossing the ISP boundary for object o is $\lambda_o(1 - h_o)$, where h_o is the cache hit ratio for o. The demand for object o flows to a specific external link, according to the Forwarding Information Base (FIB). Indicating with $FIB(o)$ the result of the FIB lookup at the egress node for object o (i.e., lookup for content providers as in DONA [18], or for name prefix as in CCN [16]), the subset $\mathcal{C}_j$ of the original catalog $\mathcal{C}$ that is attainable through link j is thus $\mathcal{C}_j = \{o : FIB(o) = j\} \subseteq \mathcal{C}$. It follows that the load on the external link j will be (using unit object size for the sake of simplicity in the formulation):

$$\rho_j = \sum_{o \in \mathcal{C}_j} \lambda_o(1 - h_o). \tag{1}$$

In the current Internet, an ISP can retrieve content from other ISPs, CDNs or Content Providers (CPs) directly connected to the ISP network. As commonly done in the BGP literature [10, 15, 32], we abstract the different types of interactions by distinguishing three categories of links, based on the cost associated to the traffic flow:

(i) **Settlement-free peering links** (e.g., connection between ISPs of the same tier) do not imply any economic transaction between the connected ISPs;

(ii) **Provider links** (e.g., transit link to a higher-tier ISP) involve a cost for the ISP, that is typically proportional to some properties (e.g., 95th percentile) of the traffic volume;

(iii) **Customer links** (e.g., links toward lower tier ISP, or CPs in multihoming [15, 21] or CDNs nodes) imply a revenue[3] for the ISP.

The maximization of the cache hit ratio, irrespectively of the link through which the requests exit the ISP network, has usually been the objective of ICN research. In contrast, we argue that the primary goal of an ISP is to minimize the

[3]For correctness, it is worth specifying that usually CDNs pay ISPs to send them traffic only in case ISPs are sufficiently large. In the other cases, settlement-free agreements are established [19, 4].

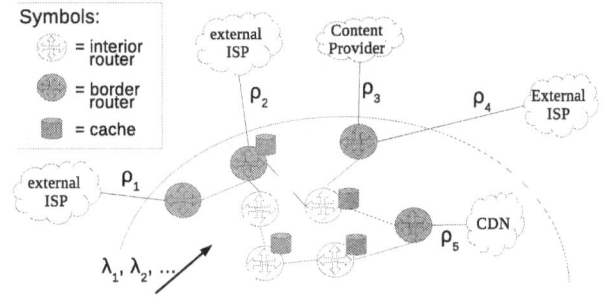

Figure 1: ISP model used throughout this work. The ISP is connected to third party networks through external links having prices π_j, and supporting a total traffic load of ρ_j.

cost associated to external links' utilization. In other words, by installing a limited amount of cache storage within its network, the ISP may not want to blindly maximize the hit ratio independently from the object cost: rather, the ISP aims at caching objects that lead to larger cost savings, i.e., objects that are accessible through the most expensive links.

Hence, unlike current literature that evaluates the cache vs bandwidth tradeoff within ISP boundaries [8], we instead assume as in [32] that these internal links have no cost. As commonly done in the literature and confirmed by very recent work [14] stating that the 95% charging model is still widely used, we consider that the cost incurred in retrieving objects is directly proportional to the traffic flowing on that link. Ultimately, the ISP operational cost jointly depends on the traffic load ρ_j crossing any given link j and the link price π_j:

$$\sum_{j \in \mathcal{L}} \pi_j \rho_j = \sum_{j \in \mathcal{L}} \pi_j \sum_{o \in \mathcal{C}_j} \lambda_o(1 - h_o). \tag{2}$$

Thus, we argue that ISPs are interested in minimizing the above overall cost (2), considering not only the popularity λ_o but also the link prices π_j, as opposite to maximizing the overall hit ratio $\mathbb{E}[h_o]$ in a cost-blind fashion. In an ongoing related effort [5], we show these to be contrasting objectives in an optimization framework. In this work, we instead focus on a complementary perspective: the design of a distributed cost-aware mechanism, whose performance approaches the one gathered by the solution of a centralized optimization problem.

2.2 Cost-aware ICN guidelines

Our design of a cost-aware ICN is guided by a number of principles, namely (i) **Flexibility**, (ii) **Simplicity**, (iii) **Interoperability** and (iv) **Robustness**: these principles ensure that the resulting cost-aware design (i) can be fit in any existing ICN architecture, (ii) is simple enough to be worth implementing, (iii) is backward and forward compatible with extensions of any specific architecture and (iv) its implementation does not degenerate, under adverse conditions, in suboptimal behavior. In this section, we follow the above rationales in the selection process of the ICN architectural components that are apt to expose cost-aware functionalities.

Following the taxonomy in [36], we namely consider the (i) **Naming**, (ii) **Routing**, (iii) **Forwarding** and (iv) **Caching** components: indeed, retrieval costs for named objects could (i) be embedded in the object name, and (ii) be possibly propagated via an ICN routing protocol; or (iii) be based on name resolution strategies, and consequently path or content-replica selection, which can be achieved in distributed settings by affecting forwarding decisions at each hop; or finally (iv) be embedded in caching-related components, by e.g., preferably storing the most costly objects.

2.2.1 Flexibility

Cost-aware ICN design should be general and flexible, so that it could be plugged as a component in any existing design, rather than requiring a complete redesign of the architecture. Since caching is a common point of most ICN architectures, a plausible option is to design cost-awareness around this component.

Conversely, exploiting peculiar naming schemes is not advisable, since this choice would break flexibility (as CCN-like prefix-based and DONA-like flat names are processed in different ways). Hence, it follows that exploiting the ICN routing component, as it is tightly coupled to naming, is not advisable either. Finally, exploiting the ICN forwarding component does not seem to be a good option, as this could reduce the degrees of freedom, and could compromise ICN efficiency: for instance, in terms of forwarding it would be advisable to exploit off-path cached copies via Nearest Replica Routing [12], which could be compromised by cost-aware solutions modifying the forwarding behavior.

2.2.2 Simplicity

Cost-awareness should be as simple as possible to implement, as simplicity is often a key ingredient to the success of an idea, and the KISS (Keep It Simple, Stupid!) is among one of the basic principles of computer science (and beyond [23]).

This guideline suggests that ICN components such as forwarding and routing are not ideal candidates. Indeed, forwarding operations already pose significant challenges to be performed at high-speed, and are matter of research per se [35, 37, 33]. Similarly, we can rule out routing as, other than still being under definition, it is significantly complex (as testified by much valuable research on BGP). The simplicity goal thus indicates the caching or naming component as the natural target for cost-awareness: e.g., the former could exploit price information encoded in the latter to realize cost savings.

2.2.3 Interoperability

To maximize interoperability, the architectural design should allow multiple algorithms to transparently integrate, without mutually affecting their respective behaviors. As previously outlined, introducing cost-awareness in the forwarding component could break other desirable properties. Similarly, while routing weights are used to affect load within the ISP network, they may impact forwarding, which is thus not advisable. Finally, exploiting peculiar naming schemes is not advisable, not only because it would compromise security (as cryptographic signatures of the content are generally associated to names, so that verifiability would be lost), but also because it could compromise interoperability (as it is not straightforward to stack multiple modifications, in a furthermore invertible manner).

To ensure interoperability in the remaining component (i.e., caching), what is required is a syntactically rich way to let multiple independent strategies to transparently interoperate. This means, in particular, accommodating multiple caching policies beyond the cost-aware we propose in this work, such as policies driven by popularity (LCD [20], Unif [6], TwoHit [22]) or based on distance [27] or topological properties [9, 28]: since each of the above policies exploits different practical aspects, their benefits are possibly worth integrating.

We argue that a simple way to let these policies interoperate is via a standard packet format: i.e., border routers could tag packets with cost-related information for further processing in the network. We additionally notice that, since price information is domain-specific, packets would be tagged by border routers upon entrance in a new domain, ensuring safety of operation (e.g., against cheating neighboring domains).

2.2.4 Robustness

Finally, it would be desirable that cost-awareness is not compromised in practice when deployed in different scenarios (e.g., different popularity or cost settings), unexpected operational points (e.g., interaction with untested algorithms), or external constraints (e.g., packet framing format). In all the above situations, the expected behavior should hopefully be maintained, and in any case it must not deteriorate or adversely impact the architecture performance.

For instance, consider the packet framing formats. While it is totally out of the scope of our work to propose a format, which is indeed a matter of discussion at IRTF [1], we outline two possibilities to represent cost-related information: (i) to use a simple but rigid syntax, using a fixed-size field of a standard packet header format versus (ii) using a more complex but flexible syntax as Type Length Value (TLV) encoding.

Both implementations have pros and cons: experience with TCP/IP tells that while fixed-size fields are simpler (thus, faster) to handle, they also scale badly over time, and tend to become critical resources (e.g., IP TOS field). Moreover, while mechanisms to circumvent these limits exist (e.g., IP options), however they happen to be rarely used in practice. Conversely, flexibility (e.g., of TLV) comes at a price of increased complexity: historically, following the principle of pushing complexity to the edge, fixed framing has been preferred for lower layers of the protocol stack, that need to be treated within the network core, relegating syntactically more expressive formats to the application layer.

For our purpose, both solutions are in principle possible. For the sake of simplicity, during the design and evaluation phase it would be preferable to consider that border routers can tag packets with arbitrary information. However, this may not be true in practice, as the information bits available to express price differences may be limited. It follows that the architectural design should be stress-tested against such imposed limitations: in case benefits disappear, this can either be symptomatic of ill architectural design (requiring a redesign of some component), or be more general and thus worth bringing up as matter of discussion in the standardization process [11].

2.3 Cost-aware ICN design

Summarizing, the above principles identify the most flexible, simple, interoperable and robust design as the one embedding cost-awareness in the *caching component*. However, the design space is still fairly large.

As Fig. 2 shows, at every arrival of a new object, a *decision* has to be taken: whether to cache the new object (aka meta-caching), in which case a *replacement* policy is triggered to select a previously cached object to be discarded. Both replacement and decision are possible candidates to exploit cost-related information. We now discuss practical tradeoffs of cost-aware caching, that lead to our proposal.

2.3.1 Meta-caching vs Replacement policies

Intuitively, to reduce costs, it would be desirable for an ICN not only to cache the most popular objects (which results in *caching efficiency*) but also and especially those that are obtained through the most expensive links (which results in *cost reduction*). Otherwise stated, the aim of cost-aware caching would be thus to bias the caching process toward more expensive objects. We argue this bias is better introduced in the cache decision (or meta-caching) policy, to avoid the proliferation of irrelevant content along multiple caches, which would happen in case any new content were systematically accepted in the cache (Leave a Copy Everywhere, LCE) and which would lead to an excessive number of repeated evictions. Therefore, deterministic [20, 22] or probabilistic [6, 22, 27, 9] meta-caching policies would be preferable. By extension, it would be better to bias the acceptance toward more expensive objects in the cache, than to bias the replacement process toward cheaper objects a posteriori.

Moreover, a cost-aware *replacement* process would require storing in the cache additional per-object metadata regarding the price of all objects, as their price needs to be accounted for to select the candidate for replacement. This is undesirable, since it increments complexity and costs. On the contrary, a cost-aware *decision* strategy is simpler to implement, as price-related information can be added within the packet header by the ISP border router once, and exploited independently by any router to take its meta-caching decision upon the reception of a new packet.

2.3.2 Cost-Aware (CoA) proposal

Overall, we design a cost-aware scheme based on modular meta-caching strategies (based on topological information, distance, popularity, cost, etc.). As exemplified in Fig. 2, composition can be simply achieved via product of functions, so that a meta-caching component driven by both cost and popularity will accept a new object with probability $\alpha(\cdot)\beta(\cdot)$, where $\alpha(\cdot)$ and $\beta(\cdot)$ jointly but independently weight popularity and price, respectively.

In practice, only *border routers* know the link through which objects enter the ISP domain, and can thus (i) compute a cost-related meta-caching probability $\beta(\cdot)$ and tag the packet accordingly; (ii) additionally, in case they are equipped with storage components, border routers take a caching decision according to $\alpha(\cdot)\beta(\cdot)$ prior to forwarding the packet. *Interior routers* along the path then (iii) take independent caching decisions based on the cost-related information tagged by border routers, and by any other information (e.g. centrality, distance), which possibly differs among routers.

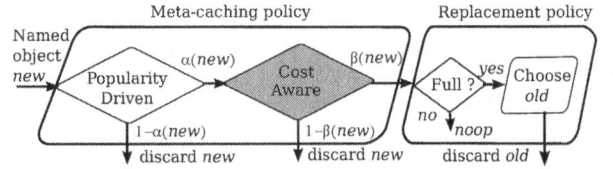

Figure 2: Cost-aware ICN design, plugged within the meta-caching decision policy of the caching component.

2.3.3 Popularity-driven vs Cost-aware decisions

It is not to be forgotten that, beyond the price of individual links, content popularity still plays a paramount role. Indeed, popularity and cost factors are independent and may even trade-off: e.g., caching expensive but unpopular objects may not bring effective cost reductions. The design of the cost-aware function should thus permit to bias objects coming from links with different prices, but should still permit to differentiate between popular and unpopular objects. In other words, it would be useful to explicitly assign a weight between popularity and cost-awareness in the decisions. These observations lead to the following choice of function:

$$\beta(o) = M \cdot \pi_o^\kappa / \sum_{j \in \mathcal{L}} \pi_j^\kappa \qquad (3)$$

where π_o is the price of the link through which the border ICN router received the new object o and M is a constant that can be used to adjust the overall cache admission probability. Finally, the exponent $\kappa \in \mathbb{R}$ is used to tune the relative importance of popularity vs cost in the decision: indeed, the larger κ, the larger the skew toward costly objects, while for $\kappa < 1$ the importance of cost in the decision diminishes (note that the function degenerates into a uniform probability $M/|\mathcal{L}|$ when $\kappa = 0$).

We ensure that the average cache admission probability is equal in the cost-blind and cost-aware cases, choosing M in (3) such that $\mathbb{E}[\alpha(\cdot)\beta(\cdot)] = \mathbb{E}[\alpha(\cdot)]$. While this is a second order detail as far as the *design* is concerned, it is however important in order to clearly distinguish the benefits coming from cost-awareness and *fairly compare* cost-aware vs cost-blind schemes in Sec. 3.

2.4 Terms of comparison

We contrast our design, that we denote with CoA, against several terms of comparison: (i) cache-less systems, (ii) traditional ICN schemes where cost heterogeneity is not directly taken into account, (iii) ideal distributed decision policies with perfect knowledge of object popularity and (iv) optimal centralized solutions achieving provably minimum cost.

2.4.1 Cache-less system

As naive benchmark, we consider costs incurred by systems that do not employ any kind of caching. We point out that, other than providing an upper-bound of the costs incurred by the system, considering a common reference significantly simplifies the assessment of the relative improvement between more sophisticated strategies.

2.4.2 Cost-blind ICN

Following our design, a natural term of comparison for cost-blind ICN consists in considering state-of-the-art meta-caching policies that ignore the costs of object retrieval (i.e., equivalent to setting $\beta(\cdot) = 1$). The popularity-driven meta-caching component could use Leave a Copy Everywhere (LCE, equivalent to setting $\alpha(\cdot) = 1$), Leave a Copy Down [20] (LCD, accepting new items only when they have traveled $d = 1$ hop in the network, expressed with the Dirac delta function $\alpha(\cdot) = \delta(d - 1)$), Uniform probabilistic decisions (Unif) [6] (where $\alpha(\cdot) = \alpha_0 \in [0, 1]$), or decisions based on distance [27], graph properties [9], correlation between consecutive requests [22], etc.

As it emerges from [22, 30], uniform probabilistic decisions are expected to be simple yet effective, and are thus preferable. Note that, while in the case of homogeneous prices a lower α_0 translates into better caching results (as it reduces eviction, due to less likely acceptance of rare objects, at the price of a slower convergence in learning the object popularity) this does however not hold in the case of heterogeneous prices: intuitively, a slower convergence also translates into more frequent downloads of objects before they are accepted into the cache, reducing the caching capability of absorbing costs. To gather a conservative estimate of cost-awareness benefits, we perform a preliminary calibration to find the most favorable setting in the scenarios under investigation, and fix $\alpha_0 = 1/100$.

2.4.3 Ideal strategies

We additionally consider strategies that ideally have perfect knowledge of object popularity, and that either explicitly take into account, or deliberately disregard, the object retrieval cost. Specifically, the decision whether to cache or not a new object is assisted by considering the eviction candidate of the Least Recently Used (LRU) replacement policy: the new object is accepted only if it is more "valuable" than the eviction candidate, which is expected to increase the value of the overall cache content over time. We implement two notions of value, depending on whether they limitedly consider object popularity, or jointly consider popularity and link price.

The ideal cost-blind strategy (Ideal-Blind) strives to keep only the most popular objects, deterministically admitting a new object o only if its arrival rate λ_o is greater than the one of the LRU eviction candidate.

The ideal cost-aware strategy (Ideal-CoA), instead, jointly considers the arrival rate and the price of the link through which the object has to be fetched. The aim is clearly to cache only the objects that are expected to provide the largest savings, which happens by admitting only objects whose $\lambda_o \pi_o$ is larger than that of the LRU eviction candidate.

2.4.4 Global optimum

We finally find the minimal ISP cost by solving the optimization problem formalized in [5], where we minimize the cost incurred by an ISP by storing in the cache, a priori, objects o with the largest product of cost times popularity $\lambda_o \pi_o$. Since we use the optimum as a reference against our design, we deem its full formulation to be outside the scope of the paper, and refer the interested reader to [5] for more details.

3. BENEFITS OF COST-AWARE DESIGN

We now assess the benefits of our proposed cost-aware design against cost-blind and cost-optimum ICN strategies. On the one hand, comparison with cost-blind ICN schemes can be viewed as a direct measure of the return of investment following ICN deployment, and more precisely sizes the additional gain that can be attained by a cost-aware architecture. On the other hand, comparison with the optimal cost allows us to gauge the extent of possible improvements in our design.

With the exception of the global optimal solution, that we compute numerically, all strategies are implemented in ccnSim, an efficient and scalable [29] open-source ICN simulator available at [2]. In our assessment, we initially consider a simple scenario (Sec. 3.1), over which we cross-compare, at a glance, all the above strategies (Sec. 3.2), and additionally expose deficiencies of cost-blind strategies (Sec. 3.3). We instead defer the analysis of more complex scenarios to Sec. 4.

3.1 Evaluation scenario

Without loss of generality, we focus on a scenario similar to the one depicted in Fig. 1, where we only consider settlement-free and provider links, and additionally consider that different providers may have different pricing agreements.

Object popularity follows a Zipf distribution having skew parameter α, and we model request arrivals with a Poisson process of intensity λ_o for an object o having rank r_o, with $\lambda_o = \Lambda r_o^{-\alpha} / \sum_{o' \in \mathcal{C}} r_{o'}^{-\alpha}$, Λ being the aggregated request arrival rate.

We split the catalog $\mathcal{C}$ so that only disjoint portions are accessible behind each link. Specifically, we denote with $\mathcal{C}_i$ the set of objects that are accessible via link i and with s_i the corresponding fraction of objects[4]. By definition, we have that $\cup_i \mathcal{C}_i = \mathcal{C}$, that $\mathcal{C}_i \cap \mathcal{C}_j = \emptyset, \forall i \neq j$, and $s_i = |\mathcal{C}_i|/|\mathcal{C}|$ with $\sum_i s_i = 1$.

For the sake of simplicity, in the reminder of the paper we limitedly consider a random mapping between objects and links, tunable by varying the breakdown of objects behind each link, i.e., the catalog split vector $\vec{s} = (s_1, \ldots, s_N)$. An important point is worth stressing: clearly, even in case that partitions i, j contain the same number of objects (i.e., $s_i = s_j$), their aggregate request rates differ, as objects have skewed popularity (i.e., $\sum_{o \in \mathcal{C}_i} \lambda_o \neq \sum_{o \in \mathcal{C}_j} \lambda_o$). We cope with this imbalance of the aggregate link load resulting from a catalog split vector $\vec{s}$ by averaging results over multiple runs.

Without loss of generality, let us consider a scenario with three links having increasing price $\pi_3 \geq \pi_2 > \pi_1$. Specifically, one link models a settlement-free relationship ($\pi_1 = 0$), whereas the two other links represent a cheap ($\pi_2 = 1$) and an expensive link ($\pi = \pi_3 \geq \pi_2$, with π a free parameter). By a slight abuse of language, in the reminder of this paper we will refer to an "expensive object" as an object that has been gathered through an expensive link (despite there is no longer a notion of cost within the ISP boundaries after the object has been retrieved). This price diversity, coupled to catalog split settings $\vec{s} = (s_1, s_2, s_3)$, permits to gauge cost-awareness gain in rather diverse scenarios.

---

[4]While in the real Internet an object can be reachable through multiple links, we suppose that only the one at minimum cost is used, which yields a conservative estimate of CoA gains.

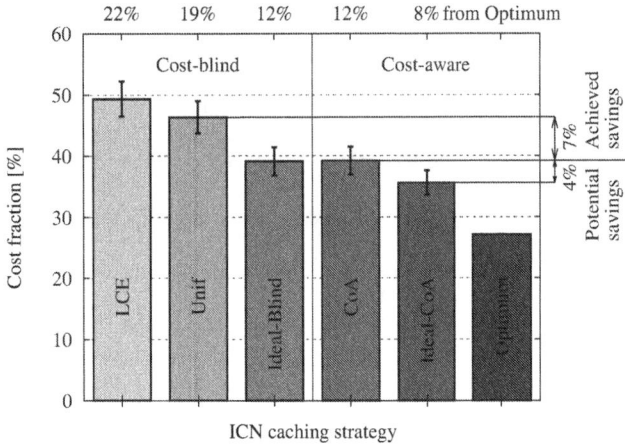

Figure 3: Benefits of cost-aware design. The cost fraction reported on the y-axis is calculated w.r.t. a cache-less system. Cost fraction difference from the global optimum is annotated on the top x-axis. Cost fraction difference of practical cost-aware policy (CoA) w.r.t. state of the art cost-blind policy (Ideal-Blind) and ideal cost-aware policy (Ideal-CoA) are annotated on the right.

Given our definition, it follows that a new object o is accepted in the cache with probability $\alpha(o)\beta(o)$. To ensure that the average cache admission probability is equal in the cost-blind and cost-aware cases, knowing the prices and the catalog split ratio, in (3) we fix $M = \sum_{j \in \mathcal{L}} \pi_j^\kappa / \sum_{j \in \mathcal{L}} s_j \pi_j^\kappa$. It follows that differences between the Unif and CoA strategies are solely due to the cost-aware bias in the meta-caching decision.

In the following we report the average results with 95% confidence intervals gathered from 20 runs for each setting; the duration of each run is sized to have statistically relevant results, and statistics are computed only after the initial transient period needed for the cache hit metric to reach a steady state.

3.2 Comparison at a glance

To evaluate the cost-effectiveness achieved by a caching strategy, we compute in each scenario a *cost fraction* as the ratio between the cost obtained by that strategy and the cost obtained by the cache-less strategy in the same scenario. Costs incurred by the ISP are evaluated in this steady state, where the same number of requests is handled by all different strategies. The cost is computed as the weighted sum of the link load ρ_i measured in the simulation, times the link price $\sum_{i \in \mathcal{L}} \rho_i \pi_i$. In case of a cache-less system, $\rho_i = \sum_{o \in \mathcal{C}_i} \lambda_o$ equals the aggregated arrival rate of the objects in $\mathcal{C}_i$, whereas in the case of ICN, ρ_i represents the aggregated miss stream. We express the *cost fraction* of a strategy X over the cache-less system as follows:

$$CF^X = \frac{\sum_{i \in \mathcal{L}} \rho_i^X \pi_i}{\sum_{i \in \mathcal{L}} \left(\sum_{o \in \mathcal{C}_i} \lambda_o \right) \pi_i} \quad (4)$$

with X being any of the strategies introduced earlier (i.e., LCE, Uniform, CoA, Ideal-Blind, Ideal-CoA, Optimum).

We start by considering a scenario with mild price variation $\vec{\pi} = (0, 1, 10)$, a uniform catalog split $\vec{s} = (1/3, 1/3, 1/3)$, a popularity skew $\alpha = 1$, and a cache to catalog ratio of $|c|/|\mathcal{C}| = 1\%$ (with $|\mathcal{C}| = 10^5$ and $|c| = 10^3$). Moreover, we initially set $\kappa = 1$. We instead assess gains in larger and more heterogeneous scenarios in Sec. 4.

Fig. 3 shows, at a glance, the cost fraction for cost-blind (left bars) and cost-aware (right bars) strategies. The figure is further annotated with the absolute distance (i.e., difference of cost fractions) for each strategy to the global optimum (top x-axis). Our strategy (CoA) can bring some sizable benefits, and these benefits appear even over the Ideal-Blind strategy. This means that, exploiting information already at hand, and that changes over relatively long timescales (i.e., the prices negotiated with different ISPs), can bring more important benefits with respect to information that is highly volatile and harder to infer (e.g., object popularity).

Additionally, consider the absolute distance from CoA to Uniform and Ideal-CoA, that is annotated in the right y-axis of Fig. 3: it turns out that (i) CoA brings a sizable improvement in terms of cost savings (7% of cost fraction reduction with respect to Uniform), and that (ii) there is still additional room for improvement (4% additional potential savings with respect to the Ideal-CoA scheme). Finally, notice that savings already achieved are larger than the additional potential saving, that are possibly tied to the popularity-driven component of the meta-caching policy of Fig. 2.

3.3 Root cause of cost saving

To understand the root cause of the performance gap, we start by showing a scatter plot of the cost fraction versus the cache hit ratio in Fig. 4-(a). In this figure, each point corresponds to a different simulation run: recall that, while the catalog is equally split over the three links, only the *number* of objects that can be attained behind each link is the same, but their *relative popularity* is not, hence the dispersion follows from the variability of aggregated demand in each sub-catalog.

We observe that, despite the low hit ratio, cost-aware policies result in a lower cost fraction: this confirms that cost reduction does not only come from cache hit maximization, but is mainly due to price discrimination. Note that the partition of objects among the links at different prices changes from a run to the other. The cost fraction is sensitive to this partition, and this explains why all the policies exhibit high cost fraction variance (y-axis). Additionally, since the objects that are behind the expensive link are more likely to be cached by cost aware policies, the hit ratio of those policies depends on the object partition among links and exhibits high variance (x-axis). On the contrary, cost-blind policies are insensitive to the object distribution and their hit ratio has small variance.

To further assess the impact of cost-aware caching on the network, in Fig. 4-(b) we measure the traffic load over the free, cheap and expensive links, i.e. the number of the objects downloaded on that link divided by the overall amount of user requests. Both CoA and Ideal-CoA achieve structurally similar configurations. Specifically, cost-aware strategies reduce the load on expensive and cheap links (cir-

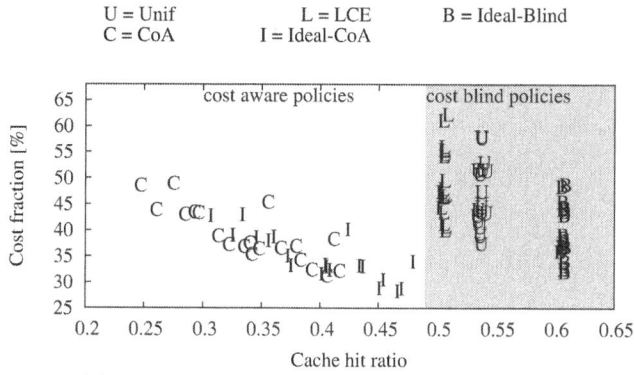

(a) Scatter plot of cost fraction versus hit ratio

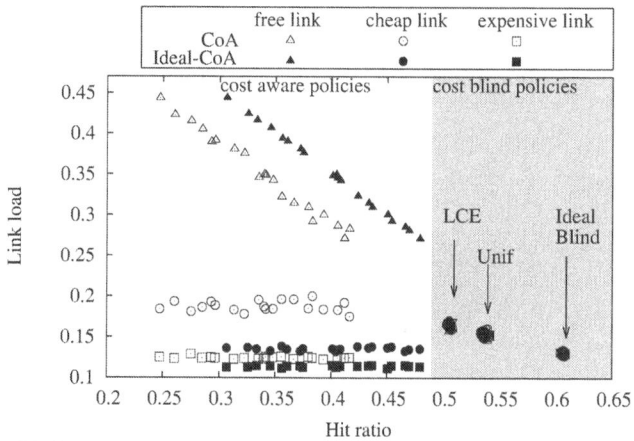

(b) Scatter plot of load over free, cheap and expensive links

Figure 4: Comparison of cost-aware vs cost-blind policies: (a) higher cache hit ratio does not necessarily imply lower cost and (b) cost-aware policies differentiate load on links with heterogeneous prices.

cles and squares in the figure), even if the average hit ratio on the network changes, at the expense of a load increase in the free link (triangles). Note that as the hit ratio decreases, the load on the free link increases: this means that all the additional miss stream includes only free objects. Finally, observe that Ideal-CoA and CoA induce a similar load on the free link, though Ideal-CoA has better hit ratio statistics in reason of perfect knowledge of object popularity.

While cost-aware policies differentiate link load based on link prices, cost-blind policies uniformly distribute the load, resulting in overlapping points in the scatter plot. Note that, while reasonable, this result is not straightforward and is due to the cache filtering effect: in other words, despite the load in a cache-less scenario would not be uniform due to the variability of the aggregated demand in each sub-catalog, however, the cache equalizes the miss-stream over these links. This is intuitive, since in a uniform scenario, links with higher demand (before caching) are those behind which the most popular objects are accessible (thus, they will be most affected by load reduction due to caching).

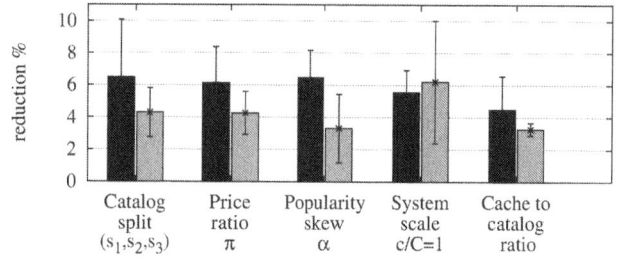

Figure 5: Robustness against external factors.

As final remark, it is worth pointing out that the price differentiation operated by cost-aware policies permit to cache only the objects that would result in a cost for the operator. This has two consequences: (i) it reduces cache efficiency in terms of hit ratio but, on the other hand, (ii) it limits ISP costs thanks to the diminished utilization of the costly links.

4. ROBUSTNESS OF COST-AWARE DESIGN

While the previous sections have assessed potential benefits of cost-aware ICN routers operation, for the CoA design to be of any practical interest, the consistency of these gains has to be confirmed in the general case – which is the aim of this section. Specifically, we extend our evaluation to cover (i) a wider range of evaluation scenarios (ii) CoA settings and (iii) practical implementation aspects. We anticipate that gains are consistent, and despite our evaluation is thorough (overall, we perform over 500 simulation runs, accounting for over $8 \cdot 10^9$ requests), we will report it in the most compact way for the sake of synthesis.

4.1 External factors

For what concern evaluation scenarios, there are many factors that are unknown at best, that will likely change in unpredictable manner, and that are by the way not under the control of either manufacturers or ISPs. We therefore evaluate the CoA gain under a wider range of settings in terms of (i) the achieved gain over Unif (ii) the achievable gain to attain Ideal-CoA savings.

Detailed parameters and results are reported in Fig. 5. Clearly, each parameter concurs in determining the absolute savings: e.g., the absolute cost savings may be marginal for very low skew α, or when most of the catalog is accessible only through the most costly link, or when the cache is too small, etc.

Yet, we see that the gains resulting from biasing the cache admission policy along the cost dimension are consistent over all the parameter variations: on average, CoA obtains a cost fraction higher by 4% with respect to the ideal case, gaining 6% over Unif. Note also that these are *absolute* cost fraction differences. While, for the sake of clarity in the exposition, in this paper we refer mostly to absolute cost fraction differences, it is worth stressing that the *relative* gain is more interesting from an economic point of view.

In *relative* terms, the distance between CoA and Ideal-CoA is $(CF^{\text{CoA}} - CF^{\text{Ideal-CoA}})/CF^{\text{CoA}} = 10\%$, while the distance between Unif and CoA is $(CF^{\text{Unif}} - CF^{\text{CoA}})/CF^{\text{Unif}} =$ 14%. These gain can be interpreted by considering an ISP in which an ICN caching system is already deployed, which is tuned in a cost-blind fashion to maximize hit-ratio. If the ISP decides to switch to CoA tuning, it will save about 14% of the current operational expenditure for content retrieval, without making any additional expense. Indeed, while the installation of the ICN infrastructure implies a capital expenditure (capex), our CoA mechanism consists in simple tuning and does not requires additional capex. Yet, CoA offer the ISP a consistent saving in the operational expenditure (opex), that becomes sizeable as it accumulates over the years. Otherwise stated, CoA is expected to yield a +14% gain in the revenue of an ISP having deployed a state-of-the art ICN infrastructure, which is very appealing especially at times of world-wise economic crisis.

4.2 Internal settings

As we have shown, for an efficient cost reduction, the worth of an item should jointly weight popularity and price. Fig. 6 shows the achievable gains for three representative catalog splits, namely: (i) an optimistic scenario where half of the catalog is accessible behind a peering link and the remaining is equally split, (ii) a uniform scenario, (iii) a pessimistic scenario where half of the catalog is accessible behind the most costly link and the remaining is equally split. First, notice from Fig. 6 that already for very small values of κ, price discrimination brings sizable gains over completely blind strategy (when $\kappa = 0.1$, items having price 10 have about 10% more chance to be cached than items having unitary price). Second, notice that κ effectively tunes between three regimes (namely, a mostly popularity-driven regime, a balanced one and a mostly cost-driven regime): as expected, gains are larger in the balanced regime (highlighted in gray in the picture). Finally, while largest gains are achieved by $\kappa \approx 1$, we also gather that performance smoothly varies on κ (so that its setting is not critical) and that ultimately $\kappa = 1$ offers a good performance and is thus a reasonable choice.

4.3 Implementation constraints

We have previously argued that limitations such as quantization of the cost information (due to the limited number of bits available in the packet header) can adversely impact the CoA gains. We set the link prices of the free, cheap and expensive link as $\pi_1 = 0, \pi_2 = z, \pi_3 = 10$ and we make z vary in $1, 2, \ldots, 10$. Effects are expected to be non trivial: for instance, when a single quantization bit is used (binary decision), objects of the cheap link are not cached (as if they were attainable through the free link) when $z < 5$, and are instead cached with the same probability of expensive objects when $z \geq 5$. Additionally, the magnitude of the impact, and not only the frequency of errors in the decision process, also depends on z. We thus represent the average cost fraction loss (with standard deviation) in Fig. 7 for dif-

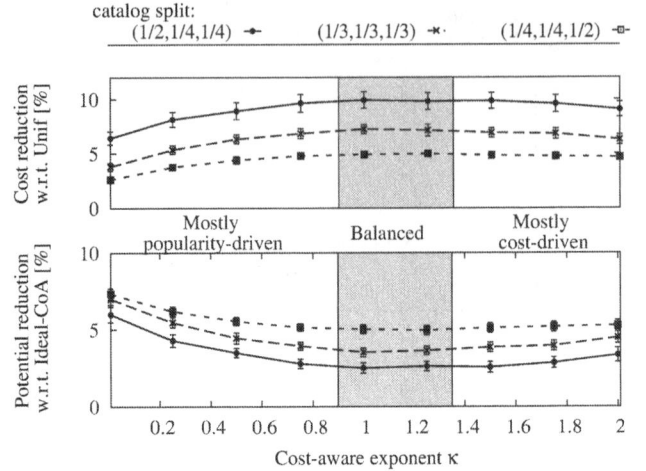

Figure 6: Robustness vs internal settings: impact of κ exponent for different catalog splits.

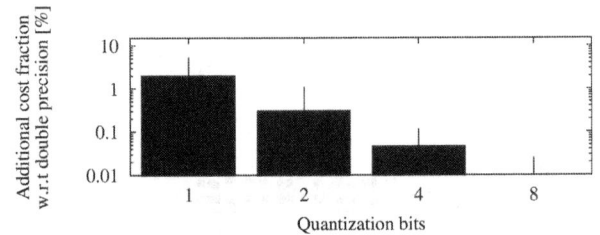

Figure 7: Robustness against implementation constraints: while price quantization affects accuracy of the decisions, the net effect is a negligible cost increase for the ISP.

ferent amount of quantization bits and z values w.r.t. the case when no quantization is applied: it can be seen that the performance degradation is less than 1% (0.1%) with 2 (4) quantization bits, which is an encouraging result. Yet, we point out that a more complete sensitivity analysis (larger number of links, where thus the CoA policy needs to discriminate prices at a possibly finer grain) is needed before a conservative estimate worth bringing up to standardization fora can be made.

5. RELATED WORK

We limit our discussion to recent literature, relevant to cost-aware solutions and ICN architectures. In terms of router design, we notice that ICN-capable routers are beginning to appear, with prototypes by Alcatel [35], Cisco [33] and Parc [3]. A first investigation on the possible architecture of an ICN router, with special attention towards computational issues related to the content store, appears in [6]. The work in [25] extends this analysis by presenting quantitative insights on the memory technologies that can be used to make wire-speed processing of ICN packets a reality. Both works focus on economic aspects, that however mostly relate to memory prices.

The design of these devices demands for specific hardware and software solutions to make them operate at wire speed, which will likely have remarkable effects on the pricing of the equipment, a capital expenditure with respect to the ISP's viewpoint. Yet, our focus in this work is more on the cost savings that caching can bring or in other words, an operational expenditure viewpoint. Closer to our work under this perspective are [4, 24, 26, 7]. In more details, [4] presents an engineering and economic model to evaluate the incentives of different network players (including regulators) to deploy (or support) distributed ICN storage. In [26, 17], authors study the economic incentives in caching and sharing content in an ICN interconnection scenario, with a game theoretic approach. The interaction of autonomous cache networks, at the Autonomous System (AS) level, is addressed in [24], which investigates conditions that lead to stable cache configurations, both with and without coordination between the ASes.

Finally, [7] proposes to take into account the "cost" of objects in the caching mechanism. Yet, the notion of cost is a general one, where cost is a proxy to express a combination of general metrics such as download latency, object size, congestion status of the link used to download the object or the price paid to use that link. Our work differs from [7] in two aspects. First, our notion of cost is more specifically aimed at estimating the realistic cost savings of an ISP in Internet. Second, [7] proposes a replacement algorithm based on complex computation that would be impossible at line speed. On the contrary, we propose a decision policy that is light-weight and easily implementable in an ICN-router.

6. CONCLUSIONS

In this paper, we tackled a fundamental question currently overlooked in the design of Information Centric Networks (ICNs): the reduction of operational costs as consequence of the reduced load on transit and provider links.

To achieve this goal, we designed a cost-aware ICN mechanism: following architectural principles that let our design be simple, flexible, interoperable and robust, we argue that cost-awareness should be embedded as a configurable block of the meta-caching function.

We performed a thorough analysis of the proposed scheme, comparing it with traditional, cost-blind mechanisms, as well as with numerical results that provide upper bounds to the cost reduction achievable in any network scenario. Our results show that, in the scenarios under investigation, exploiting information already at hand that changes over longer timescales (i.e., the prices negotiated with different ISPs), brings as much benefit as information that is much harder to get and more volatile (i.e., item popularity). Results show that not only the structural cache distribution, but also the raw performance, both in terms of cost as well as hit ratio, are very close to those achieved by ideal policies.

Overall our proposed solution is simple, scalable and robust, providing consistent performance improvements and cost savings, thus representing a promising framework to integrate in all future ICN architectures.

While this paper opens a new interesting direction, it however leaves some open questions. Indeed, as we limitedly focus on the economic implications of content retrieval on caching, we neglect aspects that deserve future attention. For instance, ISPs achieve cost reduction by penalizing delay for some contents and users: a more fine-grained assessment of this tradeoff is thus necessary. Additionally, this work limitedly considers caching of monolitic objects: in case of chunk-level caching and applications with quality of service constraints, such as video streaming, futher care should be put to ensure per-object coherence, to avoid video stuttering and quality degradation.

Acknowledgment

This work was carried out at LINCS *http://www.lincs.fr* and funded by the DIGITEO project Odessa-CCN.

7. REFERENCES

[1] http://trac.tools.ietf.org/group/irtf/trac/wiki/icnrg.

[2] http://www.enst.fr/~drossi/ccnSim.

[3] CCNX Community Meeting (CCNxCon 2013) Keynote . Palo Alto, CA, USA, Sep. 2013. Speaker: Glenn Edens - http://www.ccnx.org/events/ccnxcon2013/program/ Last accessed: May 2014.

[4] P. Agyapong and M. Sirbu. Economic incentives in information-centric networking: Implications for protocol design and public policy. In *IEEE Communications Magazine, vol. 50(12)*, pages 18–26, Dec. 2012.

[5] A. Araldo, M. Mangili, F. Martignon, and D. Rossi. Cost-aware caching: optimizing cache provisioning and object placement in ICN - http://www.enst.fr/~araldo/cost_aware_caching.pdf. Technical report, 2014.

[6] S. Arianfar, P. Nikander, and J. Ott. On content-centric router design and implications. In *ACM CoNEXT, Re-Architecting the Internet Workshop (ReArch)*, 2010.

[7] P. Cao and S. Irani. Cost-Aware WWW Proxy Caching Algorithms. In *Usenix symposium on internet technologies and systems*, 1997.

[8] G. Carofiglio, M. Gallo, and L. Muscariello. Bandwidth and Storage Sharing Performance in Information Centric Networking. In *ACM SIGCOMM, ICN Workshop*, 2011.

[9] W. Chai, D. He, I. Psaras, and G. Pavlou. Cache less for more in information-centric networks. In *IFIP Networking*. 2012.

[10] A. Dhamdhere and C. Dovrolis. The Internet is Flat: Modeling the Transition from a Transit Hierarchy to a Peering Mesh. In *ACM CoNEXT*, 2010.

[11] A. Y. Ding, J. Korhonen, T. Savolainen, M. Kojo, J. Ott, S. Tarkoma, and J. Crowcroft. Bridging the gap between internet standardization and networking research. *ACM SIGCOMM Computer Communication Review*, 44(1):56–62, 2013.

[12] S. K. Fayazbakhsh, Y. Lin, A. Tootoonchian, A. Ghodsi, T. Koponen, B. M. Maggs, K. Ng, V. Sekar, and S. Shenker. Less pain, most of the gain: Incrementally deployable icn. In *ACM SIGCOMM*, 2013.

[13] A. Ghodsi, S. Shenker, T. Koponen, A. Singla, B. Raghavan, and J. Wilcox. Information-centric networking: seeing the forest for the trees. In *ACM HotNets-X*, 2011.

[14] P. Gill, M. Schapira, and S. Goldberg. A survey of interdomain routing policies. *ACM SIGCOMM Computer Communications Review*, 44(1):28–35, 2014.

[15] T. Hau, D. Burghardt, and W. Brenner. Multihoming, content delivery networks, and the market for Internet connectivity. *Elsevier Telecommunications Policy*, 35(6):532–542, 2011.

[16] V. Jacobson, D. K. Smetters, N. H. Briggs, J. D. Thornton, M. F. Plass, and R. L. Braynard. Networking Named Content. In *ACM CoNEXT*, 2009.

[17] F. Kocak, G. Kesidis, T.-M. Pham, and S. Fdida. The effect of caching on a model of content and access provider revenues in information-centric networks. In *IEEE SocialCom*, 2013.

[18] T. Koponen, M. Chawla, B.-G. Chun, A. Ermolinskiy, K. H. Kim, S. Shenker, and I. Stoica. A data-oriented (and beyond) network architecture. *ACM SIGCOMM Computer Communication Review*, 37(4):181–192, 2007.

[19] J. Krämer, L. Wiewiorra, and C. Weinhardt. Net neutrality: A progress report. *Elsevier Telecommunications Policy*, 37(9):794–813, 2013.

[20] N. Laoutaris, S. Syntila, and I. Stavrakakis. Meta Algorithms for Hierarchical Web Caches. In *IEEE ICPCC*, 2004.

[21] D. Lee and J. Park. ISP vs. ISP + CDN : Can ISPs in Duopoly Profit by Introducing CDN Services? *ACM SIGMETRICS Performance Evaluation Review*, 40(2):46–48, 2012.

[22] V. Martina, M. Garetto, and E. Leonardi. A unified approach to the performance analysis of caching systems. In *IEEE INFOCOM*, 2014.

[23] W. Ockham. Summa totius logicae.

[24] V. Pacifici and G. Dan. Content-peering dynamics of autonomous caches in a content-centric network. In *IEEE INFOCOM*, 2013.

[25] D. Perino and M. Varvello. A Reality Check for Content Centric Networking. In *ACM SIGCOMM, ICN Workshop*, 2011.

[26] T.-M. Pham, S. Fdida, and P. Antoniadis. Pricing in Information-Centric Network Interconnection. In *IFIP Networking*, 2013.

[27] I. Psaras, W. Chai, and G. Pavlou. Probabilistic in-network caching for information-centric networks. In *ACM SIGCOMM, ICN Workshop*, 2012.

[28] D. Rossi and G. Rossini. On sizing ccn content stores by exploiting topological information. In *IEEE INFOCOM, NOMEN Worshop,*, 2012.

[29] G. Rossini and D. Rossi. ccnSim: a highly scalable CCN simulator. In *IEEE ICC*, 2013.

[30] G. Rossini and D. Rossi. Coupling caching and forwarding: Benefits, analysis, and implementation. Technical report, 2014.

[31] G. Rossini, D. Rossi, G. Garetto, and E. Leonardi. Multi-terabyte and multi-gbps information centric routers. In *IEEE INFOCOM*, 2014.

[32] S. Shakkottai and R. Srikant. Economics of Network Pricing With Multiple ISPs. *IEEE/ACM Transactions on Networking*, 14(6):1233–1245, 2006.

[33] W. So, A. Narayanan, D. Oran, and M. Stapp. Named Data Networking on a Router: Forwarding at 20Gbps and Beyond. In *ACM SIGCOMM*, 2013.

[34] S. Traverso, M. Ahmed, M. Garetto, P. Giaccone, E. Leonardi, and S. Niccolini. Temporal locality in today's content caching: why it matters and how to model it. *ACM SIGCOMM Computer Communication Review*, 43(5):5–12, 2013.

[35] M. Varvello, D. Perino, and J. Esteban. Caesar: A content router for high speed forwarding. In *ACM SIGCOMM, ICN Workshop*, 2012.

[36] G. Xylomenos, C. N. Ververidis, V. a. Siris, N. Fotiou, C. Tsilopoulos, X. Vasilakos, K. V. Katsaros, and G. C. Polyzos. A survey of information-centric networking research. *IEEE Communication Surveys and Tutorials*, 16(2):1024–1049, Jul. 2014.

[37] H. Yuan, T. Song, and P. Crowley. Scalable ndn forwarding: Concepts, issues and principles. In *IEEE ICCCN*, 2012.

Empirically Modeling How a Multicore Software ICN Router and an ICN Network Consume Power

Toru Hasegawa
Osaka University
Yamada-oka, Suita-shi,
Osaka, Japan
t-hasegawa@ist.osaka-u.ac.jp

Yuto Nakai
Osaka University
Yamada-oka, Suita-shi,
Osaka, Japan
y-nakai@ist.osaka-u.ac.jp

Kaito Ohsugi
Osaka University
Yamada-oka, Suita-shi,
Osaka, Japan
k-ohsugi@ist.osaka-u.ac.jp

Junji Takemasa
Osaka University
Yamada-oka, Suita-shi,
Osaka, Japan
j-takemasa@ist.osaka-u.ac.jp

Yuki Koizumi
Osaka University
Yamada-oka, Suita-shi,
Osaka, Japan
yuki@ist.osaka-u.ac.jp

Ioannis Psaras
University College London
WC1E 7JE, Torrington Place,
London, UK
i.psaras@ucl.ac.uk

ABSTRACT

ICN (Information Centric Networking) has received much attention due to its built-in functionalities such as caching and mobility-support. One of the important research challenges is to reduce the power consumed by ICN networks because ICN's packet forwarding and packet-level caching are power-hungry. As the first step to achieve power-efficient ICN networks, this paper develops a power consumption model of a multicore software ICN router while taking into account the power consumed by power-hungry computation. This paper makes the following three contributions: First, the model is one of the first realistic models which consider ICN packet forwarding and packet-level caching. Second, the model is represented as a concise set of equations with just a few parameters. Third, we apply the model to estimate power consumed by simple networks.

Categories and Subject Descriptors

C.2.1 [Computer-Communication Networks]: Network Architecture and Design

General Terms

Measurement, Performance, Design

Keywords

ICN (Information Centric Networking), NDN (Named Data Networking), Green Network, Power Consumption Model, Multicore Software Router

1. INTRODUCTION

ICN (Information Centric Networking) [1] has received much attention since it inherently provides attractive functionalities such as mobility support, caching and name-based routing. However, many issues should be resolved so that ICN networks are widely deployed. Among them, time-consuming packet forwarding and packet-level caching raise a couple of issues: forwarding performance [2] and power consumption.

Since name-based packet forwarding and packet-level caching are time-consuming, high performance ICN router implementations are a hot research topic and many studies focus on efficient prefix-matching and caching algorithms [3-6]. On the contrary, the study in [7] designs a protocol such that burdens of name-based longest prefix match (LPM) are mitigated by cooperating ICN routers.

Power reduction is a hot research topic as well, but many studies focus on traffic reduction due to caching, which may reduce power as a byproduct. A well-studied issue is optimizing cache amount allocations in a network [8, 9] assuming that memory devices for caching consume much power at the idle time. For example, Perino *et al.* assume that the DRAM (Dynamic Random Access Memory) devices used for CSs (Content Stores) consume 0.023 W/MBs at the idle time [3]. However, the power consumed by them is being reduced by voltage reduction and manufacturing technology improvement. Voglesng predicts that a decrease in power by bit consumed by DDR (Double-Data-Rate SDRAM) is 1.2 per generation of DDR [10]. The current generation is DDR3, and DDR4 and DDR5 are planned to be develop by 2018. A white paper of some vendor shows that power by the least power-efficient DDR3 device is 0.0000625 W/MBs [11]. Besides it is expected that non-volatile memory devices such as flash memory devices would be used for CSs in the future due to their improvement of reliability and access speed.

This power reduction tendency implies that reducing power consumed by time-consuming packet forwarding becomes important compared with power consumed by memory devices. Thus, in this paper, we address a tradeoff relation between power consumed by packet forwarding/packet level caching and traffic reduction due to caching in terms of power consumed by an ICN network. As the first step, we model how an ICN software router, especially its packet forwarding, consumes power. The targets of this paper are multicore software ICN routers because such routers used in access networks consume more power than routers in backbone networks [12, 13].

Our objectives are two-fold: The first objective is to understand how ICN packet forwarding and packet level caching consume power. This helps us obtain insight on designing power-efficient ICN routers and networks. The second one is to show the necessity of power consumption models of ICN routers so that researchers and engineers develop power-efficient techniques using these models.

The main contributions of this paper are three-fold: First, this is one of the first power consumption models which focus on power consumed by packet forwarding and packet-level caching. This allows us to identify insight on power-efficient parallel ICN packet processing at multicore software routers. Second, the model is represented as a concise set of equations with just a few parameters such as an interest packet rate and a cache hit rate so that the model is easily used in mathematical analysis and simulations for estimating power consumed by an ICN network. Third, we apply the model to estimate the power consumed by a small network. This validates the necessity of the proposed model by estimating the power consumed by ICN packet forwarding.

The rest of paper is organized as follows: Section 2 summarizes the related work. Section 3 proposes the reference architecture. Sections 4 and 5 empirically model how a multicore software router based on NDNx [14, 15] consumes power. Section 4 models the power consumed by the hardware platform and section 5 focuses on power consumed by NDNx packet forwarding. Section 6 applies the model to estimate power consumed by a small network. Section 7 concludes the paper.

2. RELATED WORK
Since name-based packet forwarding and packet-level caching are time-consuming, high-performance ICN router implementations are a hot research topic. Perino et al. [3] firstly address this issue and predict future name-based packet forwarding performance. So et al. [4, 5] design a high-performance forwarding algorithm and implement it on a commercial router chassis. Focusing on caching, Rossini et al. [6] design a caching algorithm to achieve high performance content access on multi-terabyte caching devices. Whereas these studies focus on individual routers, Fukushima et al. design a protocol which avoids redundant longest prefix matching due to neighboring routers' cooperation [7]. On the contrary, this paper focuses on power consumed by packet forwarding.

Many studies focus on the caching functionality because traffic reduction would contribute to power reduction in networks. Lee et al. [12, 13] investigate how much power is reduced by reducing hop counts to get contents. In their simulations, they use a power consumption model which only considers power consumed by lower layer packet forwarding devices. Choi et al. [8] show that the power consumed by memory devices used for caching and for the forwarding processes are not negligible. Imai et al. [9] propose a method of deciding capacities of ICN routers' memory devices so that the sum of power consumed by those is minimized.

The power consumption models of these studies consist of the following two analysis techniques: The first technique is analyzing the power consumed by devices. Many power consumption models focus on the power consumed by memory devices because they are power-hungry even at the idle time. On the contrary, this paper focusses on power consumed by packet forwarding, taking into account the memory power reduction tendency [10, 11]. The second technique is analytically calculating cache hit rates of all routers in an ICN network [16-18]. The cache hit rates are used to estimate the amount of packets forwarded by ICN routers and the power consumed by forwarding these packets. This paper also analytically calculates cache hit rates similarly to these studies.

Bolla et al. [19] empirically develop a power consumption model of a COTS (Commercial Off-The Shelf) multicore software router. Although this study has been a motivation for us, it only focuses on IP routers and does not consider ICN packet forwarding. Whereas this study formulates power as a 7 dimensional polynomial to model various power optimization techniques, this paper develops the model by avoiding effects from such optimizations.

3. REFERENCE ARCHITECTURE
3.1 Hardware Platform
We choose multicore software routers as our target hardware platforms because we predict that they are going to be used in access networks in the near future. First, full-fledged ICN routers which have all ICN functionalities including caching one would not be used in backbone networks, but only in access ones. This is because caching in backbone networks is not as effective as that in access ones [20]. Second, it is natural that ICN functionalities are not implemented by interface cards, but by service cards like *ISM (Internal Service Module)* cards of some vendor's routers. So et al. show that 20 Gbps throughput is feasible on such service cards on commercial routers [4] and the routers are a multicore software router which consists of a service card and multiple interface cards.

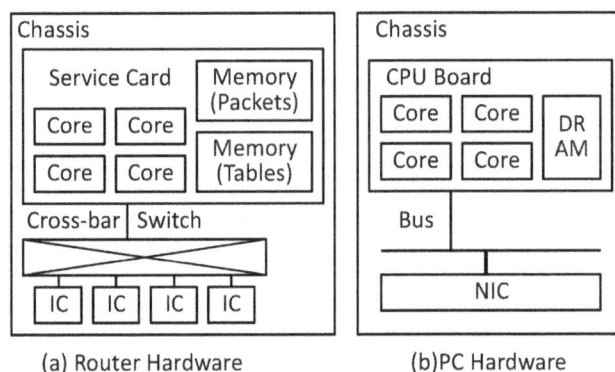

(a) Router Hardware   (b)PC Hardware

Figure 1. Multicore Software Router and PC Router.

Figure 1 (a) shows a reference multicore software router hardware platform. It consists of a service card and multiple ICs (Interface Cards) which are connected via a cross-bar switch. An ICN protocol is implemented as a program on the service card. Memory devices are used to store tables for name-prefix matching and packets themselves. What kinds of memory devices such as DRAM (DDR3) devices and SSD (Solid State Drive) devices are used is determined depending on requirements to the packet forwarding speed.

The service card is a multicore CPU board with memory devices and its architecture is similar to a PC (Personal Computer) which is shown in Fig 1 (b). We consider that a main difference between a commercial multicore software router and a PC is how devices are connected. For example, they are connected via a cross-bar switch and a bus in a commercial router and a PC, respectively. Thus assuming that these two hardware platforms similarly consume power [4], in this paper, we model power consumed by a PC instead of a commercial multicore software router.

Figure 1(b) shows a reference PC hardware platform. In this paper, we use the minimum configuration which consists of one CPU device with 4 CPU cores, one DDR3 memory device, a chassis and one NIC (Network Interface Card). The DDR3 memory device is used to store both tables and packets.

158

3.2 Software Architecture

We choose NDN/CCN [15] as the ICN protocol because it is widely used and its source code NDNx/CCNx[14] is available. However, since the current NDNx source code is single-threaded, how to extend it to be multi-threaded is an important issue. The two requirements need be considered to do so. First, mutual exclusion among CPU cores should be avoided. Second, none of CPU cores should be lightly loaded so that the number of active CPU cores is minimized. The second requirement comes from the observation that a CPU core fully consumes power even if it is lightly loaded. See section 4.3. In the rest of this section, after describing the hardware platform, we roughly sketch the algorithm because the objective is to show its feasibility.

3.2.1 Data Structures

In order to satisfy the first requirement, we re-design the tables of NDNx which record information used for packet forwarding and packet-level caching. The tables include the NPHT (Name Prefix Hash Table) and CS (Content Store). Each entry of the tables is identified by the name of the content. When incoming NDNx packets are processed by CPU cores in parallel, at least, the tables' entries of the same name should not be simultaneously accessed by multiple CPU cores. Thus we divide the tables to multiple groups of tables as shown in Fig. 2 so that each group of tables have entries of disjoint names with those of the other groups.

An intuitive way of grouping is to assign different name spaces to individual groups of tables similarly to [4]. No CPU core can access any entry which is not assigned to it because each entry of any table is identified by the name of incoming packet. We divide the name space of NDNx to M independent name spaces by hashing a root prefix of name, i.e., the first component of a hierarchical human-readable name, to M hash values. ($M = 4$ in Fig. 2) The names of the same hash value are assigned to the same group. Hashing root prefixes comes from the fact that entries of NPHT that have a parent-child relationship also have a link between them [2].

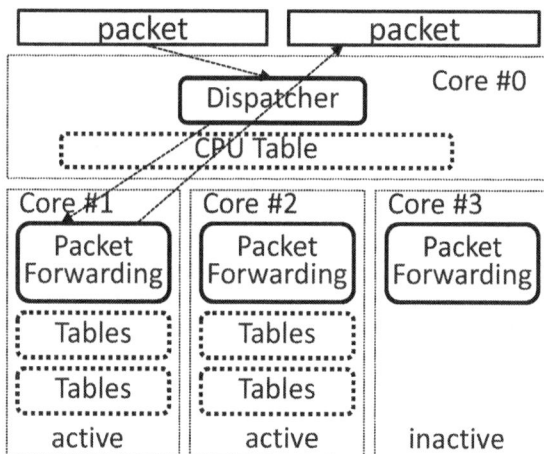

Figure 2. Parallel Processing of NDNx Packets.

3.2.2 Re-assignment Algorithm

In order to satisfy the second requirement, a dispatcher of dispatching incoming NDNx packets to CPU cores is designed as follows. As shown in Fig. 2, the dispatcher which is assigned to some core, e.g., Core #0, in Fig. 2, receives an NDNx packet and dispatches it to the CPU core, e.g., Core #1 in Fig.2. The dispatcher assigns each group of the tables to one CPU core and re-assigns the groups depending on the loads of the corresponding CPU cores. For example, when some CPU cores are lightly loaded, it re-assigns some groups assigned to it to other active CPU cores, so that the CPU core becomes inactive. On the contrary, when some CPU core is heavily loaded, some of their groups of tables are re-assigned to other CPU cores.

In order to do such re-assignments, we introduce a data structure (the *CPU Table* in Fig. 2) which manages pending incoming NDNx packets which are dispatched to individual groups, but are not processed. The dispatcher always monitor the numbers of pending packets and the loads of all CPU cores and re-assigns the groups so that that none of CPU cores is lightly loaded.

We omit the details of the re-assignment procedure. We only address the following three issues to design the algorithm: The first issue is how other processes than NDNx packet forwarding is assigned to CPU cores. We assume that one CPU core, i.e., Core #0 in the figure, is dedicated to them. Such processes include those of the dispatcher, forwarding IP packets encapsulating NDNx packets and routing protocols.

The second issue is the number of groups. Here, let M and N be the numbers of the groups and the CPU cores, respectively. M is any integer m such that $m \geq N - 1$ because one CPU core is dedicated to the dispatcher. We pick up N as m and thus M is N in the rest of the paper. We assume a simple re-assignment algorithm such that if the incoming packet rates to some CPU cores are heavy, some of the groups are re-assigned to in-active CPU cores. On the contrary, if the rates to some active CPU cores are light, the groups on it are re-assigned to active CPU cores. Since an active CPU core consumes the maximal power as described in section 4.3, the algorithm need not carefully re-assign groups of tables. The third issue is about caching hit rates when a CS is divided to smaller ones due to the above grouping and we address it in section 6.2.

4. POWER CONSUMPTION MODEL

We develop a power consumption model of multicore software NDNx router to satisfy the following requirements. The first requirement is that the model should reflect loads on a hardware platform. It means that the consumed power is a function of the loads. Such loads include a CPU core load, an access to a DRAM (DDR3) device and so forth. The second requirement is that the above loads on the hardware platform should be derived from loads of ICN packet forwarding. Sections 4 and 5 address the first and second requirements, respectively.

4.1 Formulation

We formulate the power consumed by the PC platform of the minimum configuration shown in Fig.1 (b). The power $P_{router}(cores, rate_{IP})$ [W] is defined in equation (1) and it is parameterized by the following two parameters: the number of active CPU cores, i.e., $cores$, and the IP packet forwarding rate, i.e., $rate_{IP}$ [packet/s].

$$P_{router}(cores, rate_{IP}) = P_{cpu}(cores) + P_{mem}(bytes)$$
$$P_{nic}(rate_{IP}) + P_{IDLE} \quad \text{[W]} \qquad (1)$$

- $P_{cpu}(cores)$ [W]: The power consumed by the CPU device. It is the function of the number of active CPU cores $cores$.

- $P_{mem}(bytes)$ [W]: The power consumed by accessing the DDR3 device. It is the function of the number of bytes which are accessed per second.
- $P_{nic}(rate_{IP})$ [W]: The power consumed by the NIC. It is the function of the IP packet forwarding rate $rate_{IP}$.
- P_{IDLE} [W]: The power consumed by the chassis when the router is idle. It includes the power of all devices.

In this section, we empirically measure the above four terms in order to model them. The measurement conditions are as follows: The PC is a PC server with Xeon E3-1220 processor (3.10 GHz*4 cores CPU and DDR3 16 GB memory device). One Intel Ethernet Converged Network Adapter X540-T2 (10 GbE NIC) and a Western Digital 2 T bytes SATA 3.5 inch HDD (Hard Disk Drive) are used. The operating system is Ubuntu 13.10. We use the power meter and the current transformer developed by Omron (ZN-CTX21 and ZN-CTS51-200As). The power is measured in the unit of *Joule/s*, i.e., *Watt*. We set the clock frequency of the CPU device at 1.6 GHz in order to avoid effects from the CPU clock frequency adaptation functions which modern CPU devices have. Each measurement under the same condition is performed twenty times and its measurement duration is ten minute long.

4.2 Power Consumed by Chassis

We measure the power consumed by the PC under the condition that all CPU cores are inactive (idle) and that the NIC is connected to a LAN switch, but any frame is neither sent nor received. The average and distribution are 36.06 [W] and $3.69 \cdot 10^{-6}$ and thus we determine P_{IDLE} to be 36.06 [W]. Besides we measure the average power of the NIC at the idle time $P_{NICIDLE}$ and its two-sided 95% confidence intervals are 13.42 and 13.90 [W].

4.3 Power Consumed by CPU Cores

The power consumed by the CPU device $P_{cpu}(cores)$ is determined by the number of active CPU cores *cores* as shown by the equation (2). This subsection shows that the power consumed by the CPU device is digitized by the number of active CPU cores.

$$P_{cpu}(cores) = \begin{cases} 5.98 \text{ [W]} & (cores = 1) \\ 8.20 \text{ [W]} & (cores = 2) \\ 11.50 \text{ [W]} & (cores = 3) \\ 14.90 \text{ [W]} & (cores = 4) \end{cases} \quad (2)$$

First, to show that power consumed by active CPU cores is digitized by their number, we measure the power consumed by one CPU core at various loads. We run a simple program which repeatedly performs the sequence of computations: arithmetic operations for 12.5 μs and, sleep for a fixed duration, arithmetic operations for 25.5 μs and sleep for a fixed duration. The CPU core is made inactive by using *nanosleep* command of Linux and the minimum sleeping duration is about 55 μs. This sequence emulates NDNx packet forwarding when a cache hit rate is 0, as described in Section 6. The 12.5 μs and 25.5 μs correspond to the duration when the NDNx router forwards one Interest packet to an upstream router and that when it forwards one Data packet to a downstream router, respectively. Thus we can regard the rate of the repetitions [sequence/s] as the input Interest packet rate [packet/s].

Figure 3 shows the measured power at various converted input Interest packet rates [packet/s] and the power that one active

CPU core consumes (the dotted line in Fig. 3). From the observation below, we conclude that an active CPU core consumes the maximum power. One CPU core consumes about 90% of the maximum power of one CPU core even if the input Interest packet rate, i.e., 6756.76 [packet/s], is just about 25.7% of the maximum rate which one CPU core provides. Please see the measured power at the rate of 6756.76 [packet/s].

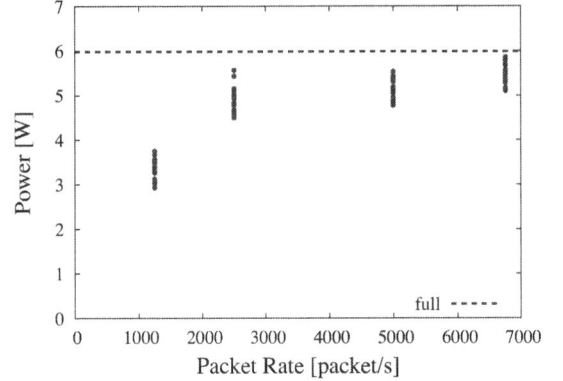

Figure 3. Power Consumed at Various Loads.

Second, we measure the power consumed by 1, 2, 3 and 4 CPU cores by running a program which calculates arithmetic operations. Figure 4 shows the measured power with a scattered graph. The averages for CPU cores are the constants in equation (2).

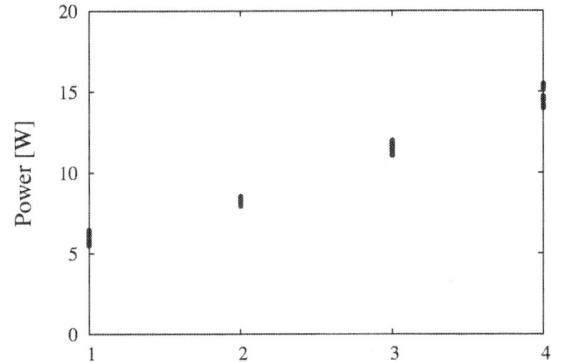

Figure 4. Power Consumed by Multiple CPU Cores.

4.4 Power Consumed by Memory Device

We formulate the power consumed by accessing data in the DDR3 device $P_{mem}(bytes)$ as a function of the number of accessed bytes per second *bytes* [byte/s] as follows:

$$P_{mem}(bytes) = P_{MEMIDLE} + P_{BYTE} \cdot bytes \text{ [W]}, \quad (3)$$

where $P_{MEMIDLE}$ is 1.10 [W] and P_{BYTE} is $0.44 \cdot 10^{-9}$ [Joule/byte]. The objectives of this subsection are to validate that the power consumed by accessing the DDR3 device is proportional to the rate of accessing it [21] and to decide the constants $P_{MEMIDLE}$ and P_{BYTE} in equation (3).

We run the program which repeatedly reads 8 byte data from the array allocated by the *malloc* function. We measure the following values at various sizes of the arrays: 32 MBs, 64 MBs, 256 MBs and 512 MBs.

- The power consumed by the PC hardware platform [W]: We derive the power consumed by accessing the DDR3 device by subtracting the power consumed by one active CPU core (5.98 W) from the measured power.

- The average number of accessed bytes in the DDR device per second (by using the *Intel® Performance Counter Monitor*).

Figure 5 shows the power consumed by the DDR3 device at various access rates [byte/s]. We decide the two constant $P_{MEMIDLE}$ and P_{BYTE} by using least squares approximation. We assume that the power consumed by reading and writing data is the same.

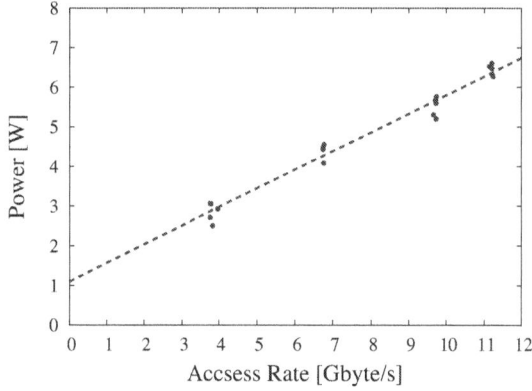

Figure 5. Power Consumed by DDR3 Device.

4.5 Power Consumed by NIC

We formulate the power consumed by the NIC is a function of the IP packet forwarding rate as

$$P_{nic}(rate_{IP}) = P_{PACKET} \cdot rate_{IP} \quad [W], \qquad (4)$$

where P_{PACKET} is $3.04 \cdot 10^{-6}$ [Joule/packet].

We measure the power consumed by the NIC at various rates in the following way: The three PCs are connected by 10 Gbps Ethernet links. One PC is used as an IP router and the other two are used as a client and server. The client sends UDP packets at various rates by running a simple program which switches between sending a UDP packet and sleeping. We measure the power consumed by the NIC by choosing 1500 bytes as the size of the IP packets.

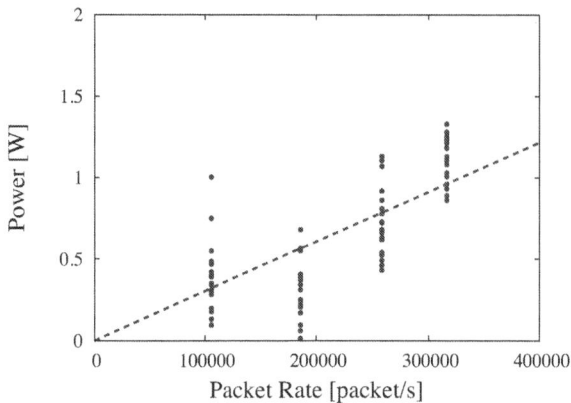

Figure 6. Power Consumed by NIC.

Figure 6 shows the power consumed by the NIC. The power is not exactly proportional to the forwarding rate; however, we assume that is proportional to the forwarding rate $rate_{IP}$. This is because its two-sided 95% confidence intervals are just 2.51 and 2.57 [W] and thus errors between the actual and estimated values

would be negligible. We decide the constant P_{PACKET} using least squares approximation.

5. PACKET FORWARDING ANALYSIS

This section addresses how the three parameters *cores*, *bytes* and $rate_{IP}$ of the PC hardware platform's model are defined. These three parameters are defined as functions of the average input Interest packet rate λ_{ICN}^{IN} [packet/s] and the average cache hit rate P_{CS}^{hit} as shown in the equations (5) to (8). This enables equation (1) to be easily used in mathematical analysis and simulations. This is because most studies on caching techniques estimate cache hit rates of all routers under assumed input Interest packet rates to edge routers.

$$cores(\lambda_{ICN}^{IN}, P_{CS}^{hit}) = \left\lceil \lambda_{ICN}^{IN} \cdot cl_{icn}(P_{CS}^{hit})/CL_{CORE} \right\rceil + 1 \quad (5)$$

$$cl_{icn}(P_{CS}^{hit}) = \sum_{f \in F_1} C_f + P_{CS}^{hit} \cdot \sum_{f \in F_2} C_f$$
$$+ (1 - P_{CS}^{hit}) \cdot \sum_{f \in F_3} C_f \quad [cycles]$$

$$= 17718 + P_{CS}^{hit} \cdot 4917 + (1 - P_{CS}^{hit}) \cdot 31069 \quad (6)$$

$$bytes(\lambda_{ICN}^{IN}, P_{CS}^{hit}) = \lambda_{ICN}^{IN} \cdot Chunk_{SIZE} \cdot R \quad [byte/s] \quad (7)$$

$$rate_{IP}(\lambda_{ICN}^{IN}, P_{CS}^{hit}) = \lambda_{ICN}^{IN} \cdot (2 - 1P_{CS}^{hit}) \quad (8)$$

The constant CL_{CORE} is the maximum CPU clock cycles of one CPU core per second. In this paper, CL_{CORE} is 1.6 G [cycle/s]. The constant R is 11.03 (See section 5.3) and $Chunk_{SIZE}$ is the average chunk size [bytes]. The first term, i.e., $\left[\lambda_{ICN}^{IN} \cdot cl_{icn}(P_{CS}^{hit})/CL_{CORE}\right]$, of equation (5) is the number of cores for the NDNx packet forwarding engine and the second term, i.e. 1, represents the CPU core which carries out all procedures other than NDNx packet forwarding. This corresponds to the core *Core #0* in Fig. 2.

5.1 IP Packet Forwarding Rate

This subsection describes how $rate_{IP}(\lambda_{ICN}^{IN}, P_{CS}^{hit})$ is calculated assuming that Interest and Data packets are encapsulated by UDP/IP packets. First, we explain how Interest and Data packets are forwarded. When the input Interest packet rate and the cache hit rate are λ_{ICN}^{IN} and P_{CS}^{hit}, respectively, Interest and Data packets are received and sent per second in the following way:

- λ_{ICN}^{IN} Interest packets are received from downstream routers,
- P_{CS}^{hit} Data packets are sent back to them
- $\lambda_{ICN}^{IN} \cdot (1 - P_{CS}^{hit})$ Interest packets are sent (forwarded) to upstream routers
- $\lambda_{ICN}^{IN} \cdot (1 - P_{CS}^{hit})$ Data packets are received from the upstream routers
- $\lambda_{ICN}^{IN} \cdot (1 - P_{CS}^{hit})$ Data packets are sent back to the downstream routers

Since each NDNx packet is encapsulated by an IP packet, $rate_{IP}(\lambda_{ICN}^{IN}, P_{CS}^{hit})$ is calculated as follows: $\lambda_{ICN}^{IN} \cdot (2 - 1P_{CS}^{hit})$ IP packets are sent and the same number of IP packets are received per second. It means that $\lambda_{ICN}^{IN} \cdot (2 - 1P_{CS}^{hit})$ IP packets are forwarded. Thus $rate_{IP}(\lambda_{ICN}^{IN}, P_{CS}^{hit})$ is $\lambda_{ICN}^{IN} \cdot (2 - 1P_{CS}^{hit})$. We note that in this paper we assume that one IP packet encapsulates one NDNx packet.

5.2 CPU Clock Cycles

The number of active CPU cores $cores(\lambda_{ICN}^{IN}, P_{CS}^{hit})$ is estimated based on the number of CPU clock cycles which the packet forwarding engine uses. It is obtained by ceiling the value which is obtained by dividing $\lambda_{ICN}^{IN} \cdot cl_{icn}(P_{CS}^{hit})$ by the CPU clock cycles of one CPU core per second.

$cl_{icn}(P_{CS}^{hit})$[cycles] is the average number of CPU clock cycles to perform all functions (in the NDNx source code) which are executed after receiving one Interest packet when the cache hit rate is P_{CS}^{hit}. Equation (6) describes how $cl_{icn}(P_{CS}^{hit})$ is calculated. C_f in equation (6) is the average number of CPU clock cycles to execute a block f. We call functions which are run sequentially as a block and classify all the functions in the NDNx source code into the following three groups of blocks so that the average number of CPU clock cycles is calculated from a cache hit rate of the router:

- The group of blocks F_1 : The block is always run when an Interest packet is received.
- The group of blocks F_2: The block is run only when an Interest packet hits a Data packet contained in the CS.
- The group of blocks F_3: The block is run only when an Interest packet does not hit any Data packet contained in the CS.

Thus the individual terms $\sum_{f \in F_1} C_f$, $\sum_{f \in F_2} C_f$ and $\sum_{f \in F_3} C_f$ are the total CPU clock number consumed by executing all the blocks in the group for processing one pair of an Interest and the corresponding Data packets. Since an Interest packet corresponds one-to-one with a Data packet, $\sum_{f \in F_1} C_f + P_{CS}^{hit} \cdot \sum_{f \in F_2} C_f + (1 - P_{CS}^{hit}) \cdot \sum_{f \in F_3} C_f$ calculates the average CPU clock cycle number with the cache hit rate P_{CS}^{hit} when one Interest packet is received. In section 5.4, we classify all the functions into the three groups. In section 5.5, we empirically measure individual bocks' CPU clock cycles.

5.3 Access Rate to DDR3 Device in Bytes

This subsection describes how $bytes(\lambda_{ICN}^{IN}, P_{CS}^{hit})$, i.e., the average number of accessed bytes in the DDR3 per second, is derived. Since it is difficult to precisely calculate how many bytes in the DDR3 device the blocks access at run time, we estimate it in the following way: First, we empirically measure how many bytes in the DDR3 device are accessed by observing a communicating NDNx router. We derive the ratio of the number of accessed (read or written) bytes in the DDR3 to that of bytes of contents which is retrieved. R in the equation (7) is this ratio. For example, if R is 10, when a 1 GBs of content is retrieved, the NDNx router is assumed to access 10 GBs in the DDR device.

Second, we assume that the above ratio is always the same for any NDNx packets. Here, since $\lambda_{ICN}^{IN} \cdot Chunk_{SIZE}$ is the average byte number of retrieved contents, equation (7) estimates the number of accessed bytes in the DDR3 device per second. We measure the average number of accessed bytes in the DDR3 device per second during the experiments in section 5.3. Each client retrieves between a 1 GBs and 4 GBs of contents from a server. We set the constant R as 11.03 in the equation (7) by averaging the measured values.

5.4 NDNx Source Code Analysis

In this subsection, we classify all the functions of the NDNx source code into the three groups of blocks and analyze packet flows among the blocks.

The blocks of group F_1 are the most darkly shaded in Fig. 7. For example, the block *Duplication Check* checks whether the nonce of the received Interest packet is the same as one of the previously received Interest packets or not. If this check is passed, the *PIT (Pending Interest Table)* is looked up to check the Interest packet is already stored in the PIT. If this check is true, the block *Name Prefix HTE Lookup&Insert* creates a NPHT entry and then the block *CS Lookup* checks whether the corresponding Data packet is stored at the CS or not. Otherwise, the blocks which are paled in Fig. 7, e.g., *Insert HTE Lookup&Insert, FIB lookup* and *PIT Insert*, are executed. Here, the probability of this check's being true is negligible because the number of outstanding Interest packets of which the corresponding are sent back from the upstream route is nearly 0. Thus the model assumes that the former blocks are always executed and the latter blocks are never executed.

The blocks of group F_2, which are executed when the Interest packet is hit, are medium shaded in Fig. 7. Since the Interest packet is hit at the CS, the block *Interest Consume* finds other pending Interest packets in the PIT related to the name such as Interest packets which are designated the lengths of names and do not exactly match the names but satisfy requirements for matching, and then sends back the Data packets to all the requesting downstream routers.

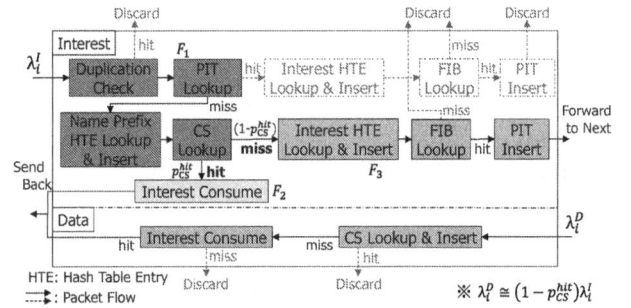

Figure 7. Flow of Blocks of NDNx Software.

The blocks of group F_3, which are executed when the Interest packet is not hit, are lightly shaded in Fig. 7. When the Interest packet does not hit any Data packets in the CS, it is forwarded to the upstream router. The three blocks are executed to forward such an Interest packet. Then the router receives the Data packet corresponding to the forwarded Interest packet, the router executes the two blocks to send back the Data packet after storing it at the CS.

We note that the blocks do not include functions for processing XML-based packets and their parameters. As the authors in [2] show, NDNx packet formats are compliant with XML and processing XML-based packets are 6 to 7 times heavier than the other procedures. We ignore these because future NDNx implementations may change XML-based formats to binary formats so that such packet format processing overhead would be negligible.

5.5 Clock Cycle Measurements

We measure CPU clock cycles of each block as follows: We connect three PCs via a Gigabit Ethernet switch. One PC acts as an NDNx router and two PCs act as a client and a server, respectively. At each server PC, 10 contents are stored and each size is 30 MBs. Four virtual machines are run in a client PC. At each virtual machine, one consumer is run and it requests two of contents at the server PC. Since four virtual machines are running, the client PC sends 8 Interest packets in parallel so that the CPU load of the router is high.

The parameters at the NDNx layer are chosen as follows: The length of content name is 20 characters. The size of CS is 400,000 chunks (about 16 GB) and the size of each content is 30 MBs. 10 contents are stored at each server. These parameters are chosen so that some blocks do not consume extremely large power. For example, the number of components of the name is set to 1. This is because the current implementation of block, *Name Prefix HTE Lookup&Insert* is extremely time-consuming when the component number is large and because the procedures used for name prefix filtering might be deleted in the future.

The NDNx software is run by adding RDTSC (Read Time-Stamp Counter), which reads a time stamp counter, a register incremented by CPU clock cycles in order to measure how many clock cycles each block consumes. Table 1 shows the average CPU clock cycles of individual blocks.

Table 1. The Numbers of Average CPU Clock Cycles

Group	Block f	Cycles
F_1	Duplication Check	2068
F_1	PIT Lookup	1029
F_1	Name Prefix HTE Lookup&Insert	4023
F_1	CS Lookup	10598
F_2	Interest Consume (Interest)	4917
F_3	Interest HTE Lookup&Insert	1684
F_3	FIB Lookup	807
F_3	PIT Insert	1232
F_3	CS Lookup&Insert	18176

6. CASE STUDY

This section addresses the following three issues in order to validate the power consumption model. The first issue is how cache hit rates of all routers are affected under the condition where the CS is divided to smaller CSs. The second issue is how our reassignment algorithm contributes to power reduction compared with the fixed dispatching such that groups of tables are assigned to the fixed CPU cores. The third issue is a good example of using our model. We discuss the issues after describing the scenarios used.

6.1 Scenarios

This section shows the conditions of estimations.

- The network topology is a three-level complete binary-tree of NDNx routers. The repository of contents is stored at the server directly connected to the root router.
- The number of contents G is 160,000. The size of contents is 10 MBs based on a recent study by Zhou *et al.* which estimates that there are currently $5 \cdot 10^8$ YouTube videos of average size 10 M bytes [22]. Each content is divided to chunks whose size is 1500 byte long.
- The number of CPU cores N of all level routers is 4. The number of groups of the tables M is 4. The total size of CSs of each router is 16 G bytes and that of each CS is 4 G bytes.
- The popularities of contents are defined in classes. Each class includes 4 contents. The popularities of classes is a Zipf distribution wherein $\alpha = 0.8$ [23].
- One client is connected to the 1st level router. The rate at which each client sends Interest packets is chosen so that the maximum number of CPU cores of the 3rd level router is less than 4. The Interest packet rate is 32,810 [packet/s]. This corresponds to 0.394 Gbps content retrieval.

6.2 Cache Hit Rate Calculation

We calculate the cache hit rates of all routers in the complete-binary tree topology based on the model which Che *et al.* [17] and Fricker *et al.* [18] propose. We assume that a content request process is an independent Poisson process with mean rate λ. We introduce classes to popularities of contents, so that contents of the same popularity distribution are handled by M independent caching algorithms based on LRU (Least Recently Used). Thus each class consists of M (=4) contents and their popularity is the same. The number of classes K is G/M where G is the number of all contents. The popularity of each class q_k is defined in the equation (9).

$$q_k = \frac{1/k^\alpha}{\sum_{n=1}^{K} 1/n^\alpha} \tag{9}$$

The CS of C contents is divided into M equal-sized CSs and the size of each CS is $C_m = C/M$ contents. Note that the CS corresponds to the sum of divided CSs of the proposed router in Section 4. Here, we assume that caching algorithms are independently executed under the IRM for CSs and thus that content requests independently arrive at individual CSs. This means that any content in the same class exclusively arrives at the same CS. Here, the number of contents which arrive at each CS is defined as $G_m = G/M = K$. Thus, the mean rate of all content requests λ_m, the popularity of the contents at k^{th} class $q_{m,k}$ and the mean rate of this content $\lambda_{m,k}$ of the divided CS m are defined in equations (10) to (12).

$$\lambda_m = \lambda/M \tag{10} \qquad q_{m,k} = \frac{1/k^\alpha}{\sum_{n=1}^{G_m} 1/n^\alpha} \tag{11}$$

$$\lambda_{m,k} = \lambda_m \cdot q_{m,k} \tag{12}$$

Since we assume the caching algorithms of individual CSs are independently executed, we can derive the cache hit rate of the content at the kth class $p_{m,k}$ by equation (13) and t_{m,C_m} is obtained by solving equations (14). (See the details in [18].)

$$p_{m,k} = 1 - e^{-\lambda_{m,k} \cdot t_{m,C_m}} \tag{13} \qquad C_m = \sum_{k=1}^{G_m} p_{m,k} \tag{14}$$

We can derive the expected value of cache hit rate of the divided CS p_m by equation (15) and finally derive the expected value of the CS p by equation (16).

$$p_m = \sum_{k=1}^{G_m} \frac{\lambda_{m,k}}{\lambda_m} p_{m,k} \tag{15} \qquad p = \sum_{m=1}^{M} \frac{\lambda_m}{\lambda} p_m \tag{16}$$

We assume (i) that the forwarding process of the kth class content of each caching algorithm toward an upstream router is also an independent Poisson process with the mean rate $\Phi_{m,k}$ and (ii) that the arrival process of content requests on an upstream router is the superposition of forwarding processes from downstream routers. $\Phi_{m,k}$ is obtained by solving equation (17).

$$\Phi_{m,k} = \lambda_{m,k} \cdot (1 - p_{m,k}) \tag{17}$$

From these two assumptions (i) and (ii), we can derive cache hit rates of the 2nd and 3rd level routers by recalculating based on equations (13) to (16).

6.3 Power Reduction Due To Reassignment

We compare the power consumed by routers both with and without our reassignment algorithm of groups of tables as follows.

We calculate the cache hit rates of the 1st, 2nd and 3rd routers based on section 6.2 and they are 0.188, 0.055, 0.043, respectively. We assume that CPU cores of all routers consume the maximum power when the reassignment algorithm is not used (without reassignment in Figures 8 and 9). Figure 8 and 9 show the power at the various Interest packet sending rates up to 32,810 [packet/s].

Figure 8 and 9 show the total power consumed by all routers and the power which is obtained by subtracting the power constantly consumed, i.e., the sum of all routers' P_{IDLE}. In other words, the latter power is the power proportional to loads. The reason why we show Fig. 9 is as follows. The loads of all routers are light due to the small network configuration. The power constantly consumed accounts for a large portion of the total tower. In other words, the power proportional to loads accounts for just a small portion. Thus the difference between the two, i.e., *with re-assignment* and *without re-assignment* in Fig.8 is small even if the power proportional to loads would account for a large portion in actual large-scale networks.

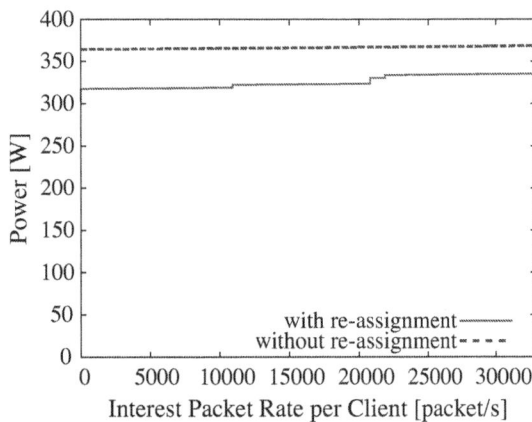

Figure 8. Total Power.

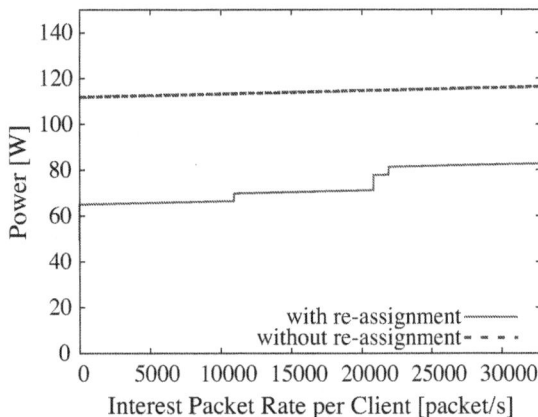

Figure 9. Power Obtained by Subtracting P_{IDLE}.

The observation from the figures is that the reassignment algorithm reduces power consumed by an NDNx network, especially at light loads. However, we note that estimations with the algorithm are the minimum values which would be obtained in ideal conditions.

6.4 Power Reduction Due To Caching

Caching reduces the number of forwarded NDNx packets as the prices for CPU clock cycles for packet level caching, i.e., those of

CS Lookup and *CS Lookup& Insert* blocks in Table 1. Thus the following question is raised. Whether does caching actually reduce the power consumed by an NDNx network? Thus we try to answer this question by comparing the power consumed by three configurations of networks: all routers, only the 1st level routers and none of routers provide the cache functionality. The three configurations called as *cnfg-all*, *cnfg-1st* and *cnfg-none*, respectively.

Table 2 show the power consumed in the three configurations. The second and third rows show the total power and the power proportional to loads. The difference in the row *(b)* somewhat remarkable compared with that in the row *(a)*. The power of *cnfg-all* is the largest among three configurations. At least, in this small network, the packet number reduction due to caching does not compensate for the prices for CPU clock cycles for packet level caching.

This observation is somewhat contradictory to the intuition that caching would reduce power consumptions. What we want to say from the observation is not that caching is not effective to reduce power, but that the precise power consumption model estimating the power consumed by packet forwarding is inevitable both to estimate power consumed by an NDNx network and to analyze tradeoffs between the reduction of forwarded packets and the increase of power due to packet level caching.

Table 2. Power Consumed by NDNx Network [W]

	cnfg-all	cnfg-1st	cnfg-none
(a)Total power	335.2	325.3	326.0
(b)Power proportional to load	82.9	73.0	73.7

6.5 Lessons Learned

The power consumption model which we develop and the case studies are pre-mature, but we obtain important lessons to achieve power-efficient ICN networks.

- The power consumed by ICN packet forwarding and packet level caching accounts for a large portion of the power consumed by an ICN network. Although this may be partly because the current ICN routers' designs are not mature, it is important to understand more precisely how ICN packet forwarding consumes power and to improve the forwarding algorithm. Our power consumption model focussing on packet forwarding would play an important role to do so.
- The proposed algorithm of re-assigning loads, e.g., the groups of tables, among CPU cores is such an example of algorithm. The algorithm is designed so that the number of active CPU cores is minimized. Multicore software ICN routers should be designed to consider efficiency in both forwarding performances and power consumed by packet forwarding.
- Caching itself does not reduce power due to the prices for CPU clock cycles for packet level caching in some environments. This shows that reducing the power is not trivial and it is an important research topic.
- Switching-off devices when their load is light is useful to reduce power. The proposed re-assignment algorithm is such an example. Another promising candidate is to switch-off NICs because the power at the idle time is high. For example, the power of the NIC in this paper is between 13.42 and 13.90 W and it is about three times larger than that of one CPU core. This observation implies that caching would play an important role to achieve traffic engineering techniques for switching-off redundant links [24].

- Although the model is hardware platform dependent, we consider that the models on the other hardware platforms are easily developed. First, our modelling technique is concise and it specifies the power as functions with a few parameters. Second, most assumptions on power consumptions are confirmed in section 4 and we believe that they would be true on other platforms. An example assumption is that power consumed by the DDR device is proportional to the access rate [byte/s].
- In addition, although the model focuses on a specific PC which is implemented in terms of current technology, we believe that the modelling method which the paper proposes is applicable to model multi-core software routers in the future due to the following reasons: First, the hardware platforms of multicore software routers and PCs of current technology are similar as described in section 3.1. Second, since most technologies of devices including memory devices are mature, it is expected that their performances and consumed energy are gradually improved.

Finally, we note that the current model does not precisely estimate power consumed by longest-prefix matching when the number of entries in the NPHT is large. This modelling is necessary to model backbone routers and thus we are on the way to extend the model so as to provide such modeling.

7. CONCLUSION

This paper develops a power consumption model of a multicore software ICN router focusing on power consumed by packet forwarding and packet-level caching. We develop the model from a PC hardware platform and the NDNx/CCNx source code assuming that commercial multicore software routers and PC-based routers similarly consume power. We obtain several lessons from developing the precise power consumption model. We believe that modeling power consumptions is as an important research topic in networking communities as in hardware/system communities wherein power consumption models of memory devices [10] and server systems [21] are developed.

8. ACKNOWLEDGMENTS

The research leading to these results has partially received funding from the EU-JAPAN initiative by the EC Seventh Framework Programme (FP7/2007-2013) Grant Agreement No. 608518 and NICT under Contract 167 (the GreenICN project).

9. REFERENCES

[1] Dannewitz, C., Imbrenda, C., Kutscher, D. and B. Ohlman. Survey of Information-Centric Networking. IEEE Communication magazine, Vol. 50, Issue 7, pp.26-36, July 2012.

[2] Yuan, H., Song, T. and Crowley P. Scalable NDN forwarding: Concepts, issues and principles. In Proceedings of IEEE ICCCN 2012, pp. 1–9, Aug. 2012.

[3] Perino, D. and Varvello, M. A Reality Check for Content Centric Networking. In Proceedings of ACM ICN'11, pp. 44-49, Aug. 2011.

[4] So, W., Narayanan, A., Oran, D. and Stapp, M. Named Data Networking on a Router: Forwarding at 20Gbps and Beyond. In Proceedings of ACM SIGGOMM 2013, pp. 495-496, Aug. 2013.

[5] So, W., Narayanan, A., Oran, D. Named Data Networking on a Router: Fast and DoS-resistant Forwarding with Hash Tables. In Proceedings of ACM/IEEE ANCS '13 pp.215-226, Oct. 2013.

[6] Rossini, G., Rossi1, D., Garetto, M. and Leonardi, E. Multi-Terabyte and Multi-Gbps Information Centric Routers. In Proceeding of IEEE Infocom 2014, pp.181-189, May 2014.

[7] Fukushima, M., Tagami, A. and Hasegawa, T. Efficient Lookup Scheme for Non-aggregatable Name Prefixes and Its Evaluation. IEICE Trans. on Communications, Vol. E96-B No.12, pp.2953-2963, Dec. 2013.

[8] Choi, N., Guan, K., Kilper, D. and Atkinson G. In-network caching effect on optimal energy consumption in content-centric networking. In Proceedings of 2012 IEEE ICC, pp. 2889–2894, June 2012.

[9] Imai, S., Leibnitz, K. and Murata M. Energy efficient data caching for content dissemination networks. Journal of High Speed Networks, vol. 19, pp. 215–235, Oct. 2013.

[10] Vogelsang, T. Understanding the Energy Consumption of Dynamic Random Access Memories. In Proceedings of 43rd IEEE/ACM MICRO, pp. 363-374, Dec. 2010.

[11] Hewlett-Packard Company. DDR3 memory technology: http://h20000.www2.hp.com/bc/docs/ support/SupportManual/c02126499/c02126499.pdf

[12] Lee, U., Rimac, I., Kilper D., and V. Hilt, V. Toward energy-efficient content dissemination. IEEE Network, vol. 25, pp. 14–19, Mar. 2011.

[13] Lee, U., Rimac, I., and Hilt, V. Greening the internet with content-centric networking. In Proceedings of the first International Conference on Energy-Efficient Computing and Networking, pp. 179-182, Apr. 2010.

[14] http://named-data.net/codebase/platform/

[15] Jacobson, V., Smetters, D., Thornton, J., Plass, M., Briggs, N. and Braynard, R. Networking named content. In Proceedings of ACM CoNEXT 2009, pp. 1–12, Dec. 2009.

[16] Psaras, I., Clegg, R., Landa, R., Chai, W. and Pavlou, G. Modelling and Evaluation of CCN-caching Trees. In Proceedings of Networking'11, pp.78-91, May 2011.

[17] Che, H., Tung, Y. and Wang, Z. Hierarchical Web caching systems: Modeling, design and experimental results. IEEE J. Selected Areas in Communications, vol. 20, pp. 1305–1314, Sept. 2002.

[18] Fricker, C., Robert, P. and Roberts, J. A Versatile and Accurate Approximation for LRU Cache Performance. In Proceedings of ITC'12, pp.1-8, Sept. 2012.

[19] Bolla, R., Bruschi, R. and Ranieri. Performance and Power Consumption Modeling for Green COTS Software Router. In Proceedings of COMSNETS 2009, pp. 1-8, Jan. 2009.

[20] Fayazbakhsh, S., Lin, Y., Tootoonchian, A., Ghodsi, A., Koponen, T., Maggs, B., Ng, K., Sekar, V. and Shenker, S. Less pain, most of the gain: incrementally deployable ICN. In Proceedings of ACM SIGCOMM 2013, pp. 147-158, August 2013.

[21] Kim, M., Ju, Y., Chae, J. and Park, M. A simple Model for Estimating Power Consumption of a Multicore System Server. International Journal of Multimedia and Ubiquitous Computing, Vol.9, No.2, pp. 153-160, 2014.

[22] Zhou, J., Li, Y., Adhikari, K. and Zhang, Z-L. Counting YouTube Videos via Random Prefix Sampling. In Proceedings of ACM IMC'11, pp.371-380, Nov. 2011.

[23] Fricker, C. Robert, P., Roberts, J. and Sbihi N. Impact of Traffic Mix on Caching Performance in a Content-Centric Network. In Proceedings of IEEE NOMEN 2012, pp. 310-315, March 2012.

[24] Xu, L. and Yagyu, T. Multiple-tree based Online Traffic Engineering for Energy Efficient Content Centric Networking. IEICE Technical Report, IA2013-78, vol.113, no.424, pp.61-66, Jan. 2014.

Interest Packets Retransmission in Lossy CCN Networks and its Impact on Network Performance

Amuda James Abu
ajabu@cse.ust.hk

Brahim Bensaou
brahim@cse.ust.hk

Jason Min Wang
jasonwangm@cse.ust.hk

The Department of Computer Science and Engineering
The Hong Kong University of Science and Technology

ABSTRACT

When both interest packets and data chunks can be dropped on the way, due to network impairments, deciding who, the CCN router or the end-system, sets the timeout duration and retransmits the interest packet after a timeout are two key issues that affect the performance of the network. More specifically, they impact directly the occupancy of the pending interest table (PIT). The standard does not address these issues clearly and the typical CCN implementations (like CCNx) address them naively leaving room for further improvements. In lossy networks, if the router does not retransmit pending interests (no-rtx) the average PIT entry lifetime increases dramatically. Conversely, if the CCN router retransmits pending interests (rtx) periodically, it is not clear how frequently it should do so. In this paper we investigate the performance of the two types of routers in lossy networks, in the presence of both caching and interest aggregation. The study aims at shedding some light on how much performance improvement is achieved by one type of routers over the other. We also introduce a new method for estimating the PIT entry timeout that is shown to perform better than the currently used default method in CCN.

Categories and Subject Descriptors

C.2.1 [**Network Architecture and Design**]: Network communications; C.2.3 [**Network Operations**]: Network management

Keywords

PIT lifetime, CCN, lossy networks, interest packet retransmission, network performance evaluation

1. INTRODUCTION

Content Centric Networking (CCN) [13] is one of the recently proposed architectures [2] for the future Internet aimed at reengineering the current Internet to support named-data communication. In CCN, contents (data) are divided into chunks and each chunk is singly identified using a hierarchical naming scheme. Communication in CCN is driven by the requesters of the data; more specifically, a receiver requests for chunks by sending interest packets, each containing the identifier of the requested chunk. This identifier is used in routing an interest packet towards the probable location of the chunk, then using the reverse path traversed by the interest packet, the data chunk is returned to the receiver when found. To improve the network performance, CCN recommends caching the data chunk at each intermediate node it traverses to possibly serve future requests for the same chunk.

The so-called Pending Interest Table (PIT) is one of the three fundamental data structures newly introduced in the CCN router design to enable a full functionality of CCN. An entry is created in the PIT for every interest packet forwarded upstream. The entry stores the incoming and outgoing interfaces for the interest packet. Having forwarded the interest upstream, the PIT entry manager waits for a period of time for the data to return. We refer in the sequel to this period of time as the PIT Entry Lifetime (PEL). In order to avoid transforming the PIT size into a bottleneck for the whole CCN, entries that are created are normally purged when either of the following events takes place: (i) the requested data is returned within the PEL and is forwarded downstream via the incoming interface(s) as indicated by the corresponding PIT entry; (ii) the PEL expires while the requested data has not arrived. To improve the performance of CCN, during the PEL of each PIT entry, subsequent interests that request for the same pending data are not forwarded but rather aggregated in the corresponding PIT entry, triggering an update of PEL [10].

According to the CCNx protocol technical documentation [10], *"A node MUST retransmit interest messages periodically for pending PIT entries"*. However there is no unanimous agreement on how often should this periodic retransmission be done. A common implementation is for a CCN node (router) to retransmit interest packet when it receives a new request for data chunk for which an entry exists in the PIT and the incoming interface through which the request is received also exists in the entry [22, 24]. The most obvious rationale to explain this approach is that a duplicate interest arriving on the same interface is probably a retransmitted interest that has timed out at the consumer. While this argument is fully justified for one-timers (unpopular content, requested by one user), it is however seldom the case in practice for popular content. We dub a router in which interest retransmission for active PIT entries an rtx node, and conversely we call a router in which such interest retransmission is disabled a no-rtx node. Clearly the overall impact of using rtx routers is a higher traffic load in the network than using no-rtx routers, especially in networks where packets can be lost due to network impairments such as congestion, channel error or link failure. However, keeping network traffic load moderate is desirable without compromising the efficiency of content delivery in CCN. Early works on comparative analysis of switch-based packet-retransmission (switch-rtx) and end-host-based packet-retransmission (endhost-rtx) in lossy networks report that switch-rtx is better than endhost-rtx if the number of connected switches is large [12] while endhost-rtx is better than switch-rtx in high speed networks [4]. However, with the special features of the recently proposed CCN such as aggregation, caching and multi-path routing, it is not clear whether such conclusions are still valid. A comparative performance study of rtx and no-rtx CCN routers is still needed to shed more light on how promising are rtx and no-rtx CCN routers. This is the focus of our paper and we aim to fill this gap within the Information Centric Networking (ICN) research community.

Our contributions in this paper are twofold. First, we present a comparative study of rtx and no-rtx CCN routers in scenarios with and without packet losses. Our findings show that a rtx router achieves little or no performance improvement over no-rtx routers, except in the number of total interest satisfied. We also show that an increasing packet loss rate negatively affects both rtx and no-rtx routers. Secondly, we propose an efficient method for managing the PIT entry lifetime to avoid long reaction delays in purging stale PIT entries. Our method is based on data chunk response delays over a window of samples. Simulation results show that our method improves the performance of both rtx and no-rtx routers including the total number of interests satisfied.

The remainder of this paper is organized as follows: we present in Section 2 background information on CCN with a special focus on the Pending Interest Table management. The problem description is given in Section 3 while Section 4 describes our method for estimating the PIT entry timer. Simulation analysis and results are given in Section 5. Section 6 discusses some related work and we finally conclude the paper in Section 7.

2. BACKGROUND

In this section, we give a brief overview of Content Centric Networking, while focusing our description on the PIT issues.

2.1 Overview of Content Centric Networking

A CCN client injects an interest packet into the network to request for a portion of a content. The entire interest packet is a header including among other fields, *Identifier and interest lifetime fields*. Each intermediate CCN node on the path traversed by the interest packet checks its Content Store, if a copy of the requested data is in the cache, the data is returned along the reverse path traversed by the interest packet. Otherwise, it checks the PIT if an entry has earlier been created for the requested named data chunk. If yes, the interest is aggregated in this PIT entry. Otherwise the interest is prepared for forwarding upstream by checking the Forwarding Information Based (FIB) and if at least one outgoing interface exists in the FIB for this interest, then

an entry is created in the PIT and the interest is forwarded. Otherwise, the interest is simply discarded.

If the requested data is not cached in any of the intermediate nodes, the interest packet will eventually arrive at the content producer/custodian (the original source) of the data. The producer forwards the corresponding data downstream. When delivering the data towards the requester, each intermediate node that receives the data chunk caches it in its content store to serve future requests for the same data, if the caching policy so permits.

2.2 Pending Interest Table

The Pending Interest Table in a CCN router does not only keep track of interests forwarded upstream towards a data source but also stores the interfaces (also called faces) on which the interests have been received. An entry is created in the PIT for each interest forwarded upstream and is deleted either when the requested data chunk is returned and forwarded downstream or when the PIT entry lifetime expires. Multiple requests for the same interest name are not forwarded but rather aggregated and all the faces on which all instances of the same interest have been received are stored. The stored faces are used to drive the forwarding of the returned data towards the requesters.

Specifically, a PIT entry contains an interest name, a list of incoming faces on which all interest instances for the same name have been received and a list of outgoing faces through which the interest has been forwarded. Each incoming face $j, j = 0, ..., N$ is associated with a lifetime t_j, with N being the number of faces stored in the PIT entry. The PEL is denoted as t_{PIT}. Time t_j is refreshed whenever a new interest for the same name is received on the same face j. Denote the interest for a data with name A received on face j by I_{Aj}. If t_j expires before the requested data chunk returns, then face j is removed from the PIT entry. If this continues all faces are eventually removed, provided the requested data has not returned. The removal of the last face from the entry triggers the removal of the entry from the PIT. Therefore the lifetime of a typical PIT entry for a given data chunk A is $t_{PITj} = \max_{i=1,...,N}\{t_i\}$ where t_{PITj} is the current time plus the lifetime of the interest arriving through face j.

2.3 CCN PIT entry timer

After waiting for a reasonable amount of time, each entry created in the CCN PIT must be purged if the requested data chunk fails to return before the PEL timer expires. As such, the timer estimation remains an important factor to consider as it affects the performance of the network. Too short a timer, leads to redundant unnecessary retransmissions of interests and as a result of data. Too long a timer, makes the network response to interest or data losses sluggish and thus reduces the network throughput. In the technical documentation of CCN protocol [10], no clear directive is given as to the default setting of the PIT entry lifetime. However, in the source code of CCN protocol (lines 4025–4045 and 4176–4274) [9], a node's PIT entry inherits its lifetime from the lifetime of interest packets that arrive at the node. As suggested in [10, 3] applications using CCN protocol should be the main entity that decides the value of interest lifetime. This value is chosen depending on the properties of the application (delay sensitive or insensitive). The PIT entry is set and refreshed as specified in [10] and described in Section 2.2.

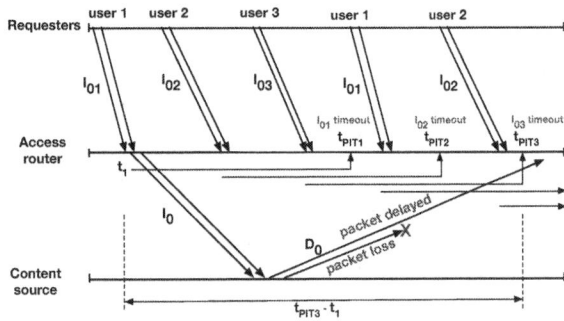

Figure 1: A scenario showing 3 CCN users sending interest packets for the same content at the rate of 2 interests per unit time to the content source via an access router, demonstrating how the PIT entry lifetime is updated in a CCN router when packets are lost or delayed

3. PROBLEM DESCRIPTION

3.1 System model

Consider the example of Figure 1 where the definitions of I_{Aj}, I_A and t_{PITj} are the same as defined in Section 2.2, D_A is the data requested by interest I_A. In Figure 1 note that there could be $m \geq 0$ intermediate nodes between the access router and the content source. With the current method used for setting and updating the PIT entry lifetime [10], the number of entries in the PIT and consequently the number of pending interests may increase dramatically, resulting in requesters waiting longer to download content, in lossy networks where both packet types or interests can be lost or delayed upstream. However enabling the periodic retransmission of interest packets by the intermediate node may eventually help retrieve the requested data chunk before the PEL expires, at the cost of increased network traffic load especially if interests are forwarded over all available output faces as suggested in CCN.

Focusing on the interest direction, assume all arriving interest packets with cache (content store) misses are processed by the PIT and there are always available outgoing interfaces in the FIB to forward interests upstream. Denote by μ the average rate of forwarding interests upstream and by τ, the average duration from the time one PIT entry is created until this PIT entry is purged. Furthermore, let the fraction of interests that are satisfied from the cache be h_{cs} and denote by h_{pit} the fraction of interests that are processed by the PIT but do not require forwarding upstream because of interest aggregation. Simply put, h_{cs} is typically the cache hit rate while h_{pit} is the PIT hit rate when looking for an entry that matches a given interest. Given the above notations, the average rate of forwarding interests upstream can be written as

$$\mu = (1 - h_{cs})(1 - h_{pit})\lambda$$

where λ is the average arrival rate of interest packet at a CCN node. Note that, due to aggregation, only the interests for which new PIT entries are created are forwarded upstream. Furthermore, a PIT entry that is created is purged on average after τ when the corresponding data has arrived (assuming no losses). Consequently the average rate at which entries are created in the PIT is also equal to μ,

and the average number of entries in the PIT, can be simply obtained by Little's theorem, as

$$\Gamma = \mu \times \tau = (1 - h_{cs})(1 - h_{pit})\lambda\tau. \qquad (1)$$

From (1), we can make a few observations: Γ can be kept small if we can devise a good caching mechanism to increase h_{cs} or increase h_{pit}. However due to limited router memory, high caching dynamics and the ubiquitous caching used in CCN, cache hit rates h_{cs} in intermediate nodes (not including the first hop caching node) is known to be very small [7, 19] especially for popular contents. Furthermore, the dominance of one-timer contents in most content distribution networks implies a very small value of h_{pit} [7], resulting in an increased value of Γ. In addition, the actual number of entries in the PIT depends on several factors such as the loss rate, λ and τ. The instantaneous number of entries in the PIT oscillates around Γ. Interest packets could have been dropped due to the fluctuation of the PIT occupancy before the mean stabilized at Γ. As such, given a PIT size, P, on a 90% quantile for example, we can avoid dropping interest packets by keeping the probability that the PIT is full very small.

3.2 PIT sizing problem

As new interests for data chunks arrive at a CCN router, entries are created in the PIT for all interest packets forwarded upstream. When the PIT is saturated, i.e., when new PIT entries cannot be created as the PIT memory is full, newly arrived interests at a router are not inserted into the PIT but discarded, which may degrade the performance of the network. To avoid such PIT congestion, several approaches are worth investigating; the most obvious being to conduct a PIT dimensioning study via queueing theory. A good PIT size is one that almost always (e.g., with probability 0.99) has room for new entries. This implies that the probability that the PIT is full when a new request arrives at a CCN router should be kept small. To achieve this a fully fledged queueing model has to be designed. As such, one needs to characterise accurately λ, τ, h_{cs} and h_{pit}, which in turn depend on several non-trivial unknowns and complicated factors such as the caching/replacement policy, the traffic spatial and temporal distribution, the routing, the filtering effect due to interest aggregation, and so on. The work in [21] provides a rough estimate of a typical PIT size but the analysis therein does not consider requests aggregation (i.e., assumes $h_{pit} = 0$) among others.

Heuristic approaches may be adopted to avoid the complication of the modelling. For example a router may apply cache replacement policies to the PIT as well, by removing the longest-lived entry from the PIT to accommodate the new one. Such approach needs further investigation.

3.3 Interest packet retransmission: Frequency and timer estimation

Now consider the case where requested data never returns due to packet loss or link failure along the path towards the data source[1]: in this case, $\tau \to PEL$, and the requesters retransmits interests after the expiration of a given timer. No recommended method for computing the timer has yet been proposed, but [22] for example adopts a TCP-like RTO

---

[1]Here we define a data source as either the data producer/custodian or the node that has a cached copy of the data in its Content Store.

while [3] uses the interest lifetime. To make a CCN requester proactive we follow the method used in [22].

A CCN node must periodically retransmit interest packets for data chunks it has not yet received. The frequency of the interest retransmission is not specified in [10] at the time of writing of this paper, and a candidate approach is to retransmit only when the node receives a retransmitted interest from an Interface that is already stored in the PIT entry for the same data name. A problem with this strategy is an increased traffic load in the network especially when the requested data chunk experiences some delay (queuing and/or propagation) and the FIB entries are associated with multiple output interfaces per entry. Another problem is the unnecessary retransmissions caused by the arrival of interests for popular contents, thus making a misbehaving/misconfigured CCN consumer stage a DoS attack of interest-request retransmissions. This is in contrast to one advantage of built-in DoS resilience (DoS-ed interests are not always forwarded) claimed for CCN.

In addition we consider an alternative strategy where an intermediate CCN node does not retransmit interest packet even when it receives retransmitted interests from the requester. It rather waits for a period of *PEL* for the requested data to arrive. If the requested data is not received before PEL expires the PIT entry is purged. As the requester always retransmits interests for the data chunks that it has not received within a timer, the intermediate node will eventually receive the retransmitted interests, create new PIT entries for these interests and forward them upstream. In contrast, with this strategy, the traffic load in the network is expected to be moderate.

How these two strategies perform comparatively in CCN is not yet reported, and in this paper we use a packet-level simulation to study the two strategies, highlighting their performance merits and demerits.

4. A DYNAMIC PIT ENTRY TIMER

Given the existence of caching in CCN, the rate at which entries are purged from the PIT depends on where the requests are being satisfied. It also depends on whether or not packets experience additional delay (queueing and processing), as well as the presence of multiple paths for forwarding interests. Thus a good value of the PIT entry lifetime should take into account the aforementioned factors. To this end, we consider an alternative approach for setting the PIT entry lifetime.

Denote the time from which a given node forwards an interest upstream to the time the node receives the requested data as the response delay RD. Ideally the PIT entry lifetime should commensurate with the maximum response delay observed for a content over all the requests sent for the same content from a router to all the nodes from which the content is retrieved (including in-network caching). In view of this, we propose to set the PEL based on the maximum response delay over all samples of data packets received in a given window of samples. See Figure 2. We avoid any fluctuation in the measured response delay due to in-network caching by taking the maximum from all the values observed. Although a router R_1 estimates RD for each of the returned data chunk, only the maximum of all the RDs is stored implying that a router keeps only the RD of the content producer if the content is a one-timer, or that of the farthest caching node if the content is popular. The entry lifetime for

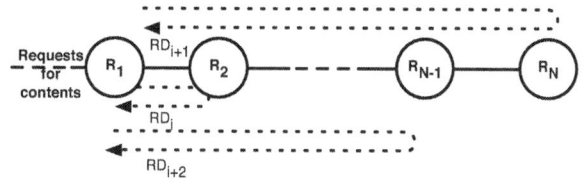

Figure 2: Estimating PIT entry lifetime from all requests for a given content

a given content C is set as follows: Initially $\tau^C = 1$s. After receiving the first data chunk for C, $\tau^C = RD_1$. For subsequent data chunk i for the same content C received within an interval of time γ, $\tau^C = RD_i$ if $\tau^C < RD_i$ where $i > 1$. We use $\gamma = 60$s in our experiments. To ensure the freshness of τ^C, we set $\tau^C = RD_{min} + (RD_{max} - RD_{min})\delta$ every 60s, $\delta = 0.5$. In the next interval, τ^C is compared with subsequent RD_i and updated accordingly. τ^C is discarded after an idle period of τ^C. The idle period for a given content is the period in which no request for the content is received. The values of γ and δ used in our experiment are the same as those used in [17] and [15], respectively. However, we make use of the values of γ and δ at the routers while the works in [17] and [15] use them at the end-hosts.

The resulting PIT entry lifetimes adapt well to the dynamics of the network upstream. For scalability reason, τ^C is maintained per content as opposed to per interest packet.

5. PERFORMANCE EVALUATION

We discuss in this section the simulation scenario under consideration in our study including simulation setup in ns-3. Simulation results showing the advantages and disadvantages of an interest-retransmission enabled/disabled CCN router in both lossy and lossless scenarios are presented.

5.1 Scenario description

We consider a parking-lot topology as shown in Figure 3. Access routers $R1$ and $R2$ receive requests from many users. Users' requests follow a Zipf probability distribution with Zipf's skewness parameter α. In the event that requests cannot be satisfied by in-network caches, all requests from access router $R1$ can only be satisfied by content producer $P1$ while all requests from $R2$ can only be satisfied by producer $P2$. To introduce traffic mixing and caching dynamics, we add CCN cross traffic sources and receivers. We believe that this topology is sufficient to capture the impact of caching and aggregation on the performance of the network. This is because the arrivals of traffic (interest packets) in one direction are capable of filling up the entries in the PIT. As such we do not consider complex topologies and bidirectional flows of interest packets.

We consider lossy scenarios where packets are dropped randomly on the link marked L_D in Figure 3. L_D actually represents multiple links connecting the content producers to the rest of the network. So randomly dropping packets on L_D does not necessarily mean that we drop a packet on the link directly connecting the content producer. For performance comparison we also consider lossless scenarios where no packet is dropped in the network. $R1$, $R2$, C_R1, C_R2 and C_R3 have relatively small cache sizes and thus requests are not satisfied by these nodes. Requests are forwarded us-

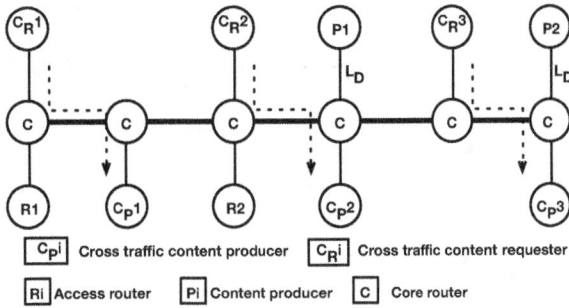

Figure 3: A parking-lot simulation model showing the access routers, content producers, cross traffic sources and receivers

ing the default CCN flooding and content request arrivals follow a Poisson process. All requests for the same content have the same interest lifetime. Consumers do not need to receive data for interest packets in flight before sending the next interest packets, but can retransmit interests for which data have not been received, after a timer expiration.

There are 2 groups of user requests and each group is associated with a content producer. For each group, including cross traffic, we use proWGen [5] to generate workloads for our experiments. Details are given in Section 5.2.

Performance metrics considered in this study include: the number of entries in the PIT (i.e., the number of pending interest entries in the PIT), the PIT entry actual lifetime, the fraction of requests satisfied by in-network caching including the content producer, the total number of interests satisfied, the data chunk response delay and the network traffic load.

5.2 Simulation setup

The scenario described in Section 5.1 was simulated in ns-3 network simulator using the ndn/ccn ns-3 modules [1]. We developed a custom application module that can use the workload generated by ProwGen in ns-3. Our algorithm for estimating PIT entry lifetime was also implemented in ndn/ccn ns-3.

All link delays are set to 20ms while the capacities of all thin links in Figure 3 are set to 200Mbps unless otherwise stated. Each thick link as shown in Figure 3 has a capacity of 500Mbps. Cross traffic sources and receivers run for the entire duration of the simulation. Each returned data chunk is 1500 bytes. For the characteristics of our workload, we use $\alpha = 0.96$, respectively 0.76, for user groups $R1$, respectively $R2$. For the cross traffic, α is in the range [0.6, 0.8]. The values of α used are within the values recommended in the literature. There are 60% one-timers and 40% unique contents. The mean file size for contents is 14KB. For both group, we generated 100,000 content requests (not at the chunk level). Note that the number of data chunks per content depends on the file size of the content. We enable in-network caching with LRU replacement policy using the default ubiquitous caching policy of CCN. We set the interest lifetime to 4s, the default value in CCNx.

We refer to a network with packet loss as a lossy scenario while a network without packet loss as lossless scenario. In each of the two scenarios considered in our simulations, we use rtx routers in one simulation set and no-rtx routers in another set. We observed similar results for access routers $R1$ and $R2$. Thus we report simulation results for $R1$ in the

following sections. The default values for the parameters that we vary in our experiments are the average request rate (5000 interest/s), the packet loss rate (0.01), and the cache size per router (500 chunks). Next, we present simulation results with 95-percent confidence intervals.

5.3 PIT occupancy and entry actual lifetime

Figure 4 shows the CDFs of the number of entries in the PIT for different loss rates using rtx and no-rtx. It can be observed in Figure 4a that most of the time the number of entries in the PIT remains at 900, 1100, 1750 and 2700 for 0.001, 0.01, 0.05 and 0.1 loss rates respectively. This large variation in the PIT size is a consequence of the entries staying longer than necessary in the PIT as corroborated by the PIT entries lifetime CDF shown in Figure 5a. More importantly, the figures clearly show that rtx does not offer much improvement over no-rtx. In contrast if we replace the PEL calculation algorithm with our approach, as shown in Figure 4b, about 99% of the time the number of PIT entries is less than 1000 in all the cases considered, regardless of the loss rate. This shows that using our method for estimating PEL prevents the size of the PIT from becoming a bottleneck in a CCN infrastructure as more packets are dropped.

Figure 5 shows the CDFs of the PIT entry actual lifetime for rtx and no-rtx using different packet loss rates. The actual lifetime is the time between the entry creation and its deletion (because of timeout or interest satisfaction by a data chunk). Specifically, the data in Figure 5a indicates that about 30%, 50%, 80% and 98% of the PIT entries stay longer than 200ms[2] in the PIT for 0.1, 0.05, 0.01 and 0.001 packet loss rates respectively. Note that about 10% of the entries stay more than 4s for 0.1 loss rate. These are entries that contain aggregated interests for the same name resulting in the PEL being refreshed for every aggregation. Similarly, rtx's improvement over no-rtx's remains insignificant. However, with our method for calculating the PEL, most of the entries' actual lifetimes are within the maximum response delay from the content source as shown in Figure 5b. Due to aggregation only a few entries stay beyond the maximum response delay.

We also present in Figure 7 the average number of entries in the PIT for different cache sizes and request rates. Figures 6a and 6b show the average number of entries in the PIT with varying average request rate in lossy (0.01 loss rate) and lossless scenarios. Both figures show that the average number of entries grows as we increase the average request rate. However, with our method for estimating the PEL it can be observed in Figure 6b that we can achieve a similar performance for lossy and lossless scenarios. Caching indeed plays a key role in CCN. Figures 7a and 7b further assert this as the average number of entries in the PIT decreases with increasing cache size. In lossy scenario rtx and no-rtx differ in performance with cache size up to 5000 chunks but converge at relatively large cache sizes (this represents the case where there is always room for caching data chunk, see Figure 7a). Similarly Figure 7b shows the same performance for lossy and lossless scenarios as well as for rtx and no-rtx routers.

5.4 Network traffic load

In this section we study the total traffic load injected into the network for different loss rates and average request rates

---

[2]200ms is the end-to-end RTT in our network.

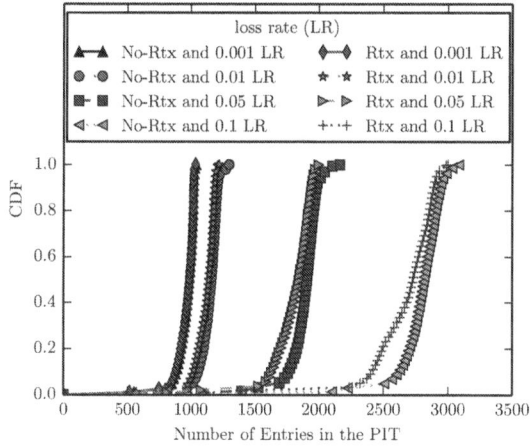

(a) Using a fixed 4s *PEL*

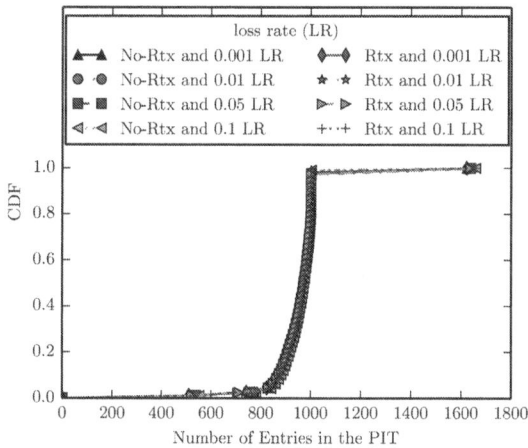

(b) Alternative method for estimating *PEL*

Figure 4: CDFs of the number of entries in the PIT

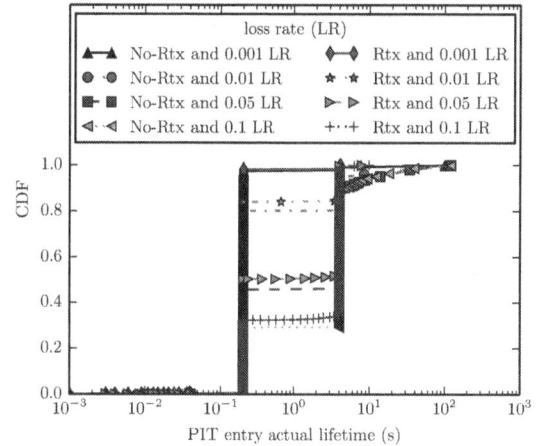

(a) Using a fixed 4s *PEL*

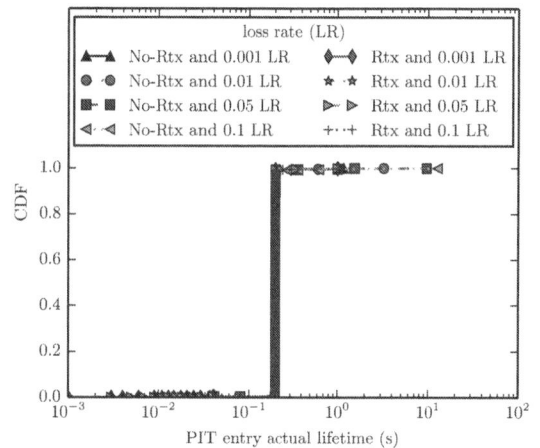

(b) Alternative method for estimating *PEL*

Figure 5: CDFs of the PIT entry actual lifetime (x-axes in log scale)

in Figure 8a and 8b respectively. Although both rtx and no-rtx increase the total network traffic load as we increase the packet loss rate, they differ in that rtx incurs about 3×10^4 additional traffic load. That is, not only rtx is shown in the previous section to not improve the PIT occupancy much, it also increases the traffic load. In Figure 8b both rtx and no-rtx show nearly similar performance up to 5000 interest/s average request rate, but diverge for rates greater than 5000 interest/s. Ideally such divergence should not be present when there is no packet loss. However, note that the retransmission timer estimated by the requester may expires prematurely triggering a retransmission for data chunks that are still in transit. The results described in Figures 8a and 8b show that no-rtx is better than rtx in terms of traffic load.

5.5 Interests satisfied

In Figure 9, we show the total number of interests satisfied for different packet loss rates using rtx and no-rtx routers. The total number of interests satisfied can be observed to decrease as we increase the loss rate. Despite the no-rtx method achieving less traffic load compared to rtx, the for-

mer suffers from a lower throughput (number of satisfied interests). Note that there is not much performance improvement achieved by rtx over the performance of no-rtx in the presence of little or no packet losses. The improvement becomes significant as the rate of packets drop increases. More importantly, using our method for calculating the *PEL* we can improve the performance of no-rtx making it nearly the same as rtx as shown in Figure 9b.

5.6 Data chunk response delay and hop count for satisfied interests

Figure 10 further demonstrates that rtx offers no much improvement over no-rtx in terms of data chunk response delay for different packet loss rates. Both rtx and no-rtx are affected by increasing loss rates. When using our method for estimating the *PEL* the performance of rtx and no-rtx becomes similar as shown in Figure 10b.

Figure 11 shows the fraction of requests for popular contents served by in-network caches including the content producer for different cache sizes. Similarly, rtx does not achieve

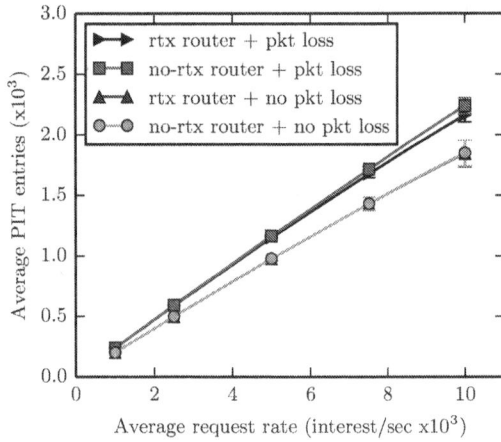

(a) Using a fixed 4s *PEL*

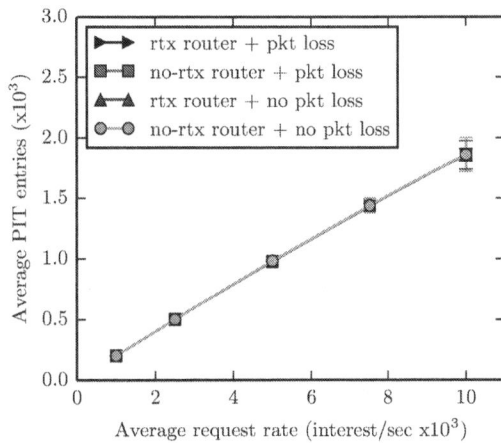

(b) Alternative method for estimating *PEL*

Figure 6: Average number of entries in the PIT with different average request rates

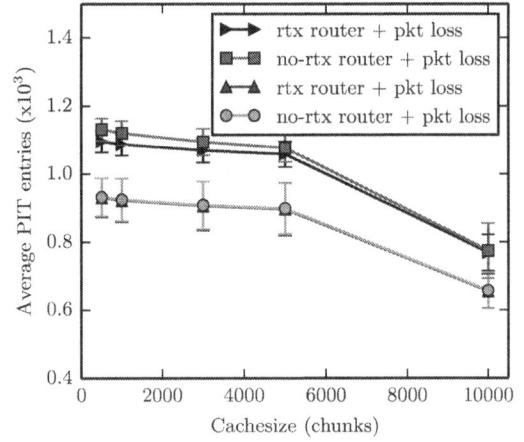

(a) Using a fixed 4s *PEL*

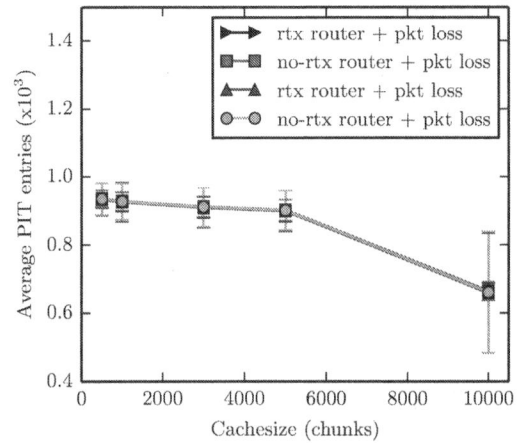

(b) Alternative method for estimating *PEL*

Figure 7: Average number of entries in the PIT with different cache sizes

much performance improvement over no-rtx in terms of bringing the contents closer to the requesters. A better performance can be observed with relatively large cache size than small cache size. Both rtx and no-rtx benefit from this. Using our method for calculating *PEL* achieves similar performance with using a fixed *PEL* as shown in Figures 11b .

5.7 Additional remarks

In addition to preventing the size of the PIT from becoming a bottleneck in CCN, our proposed method for PIT entry management does not require the exchange of control message(s) such as Interest NACKs between neighbour nodes to trigger the purging of a PIT entry if upstream nodes fail to deliver the requested data downstream. Similar to [8] we believe that this is desirable as exchanging control messages between neighbour nodes may require message prioritization and incur additional overhead. Besides, the method has the virtue of being very simple to implement. A potential distributed denial of service (DDoS) attack has been demon-

strated by Virgilio *et al* [18] where artificial interests with relatively large lifetimes are crafted by malicious users with the goal of occupying the available PIT memory in CCN routers. Our proposed method for estimating the PIT entry timer is capable of minimizing the impact of such PIT overloading as it is independent of the interest lifetime.

The performance study of rtx and no-rtx presented in this paper has been carried out using a parking-lot topology. Although the insights gained from the study are of great importance in understanding how rtx and no-rtx perform in CCN, there still remains many other aspects to consider such as other network topologies as well as the impact of different content sizes, transport strategies and distance between a CCN consumer and the content provider.

Our proposed method can help reduce the PIT occupancy for rtx and no-rtx in CCN by measuring the response delay for every data received per content. Yet there are other mechanisms that can achieve the same goal. One approach is to make one-timer content requests bypass both the content store and the PIT while popular content requests pass

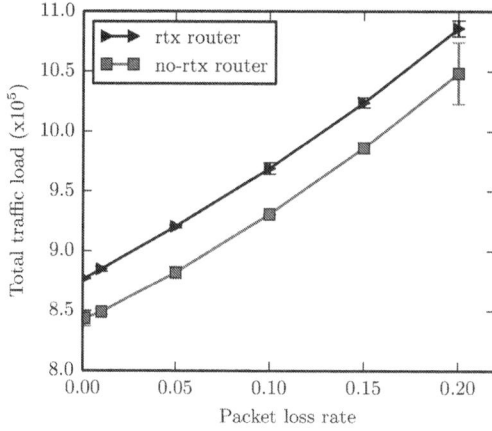

(a) Different packet loss rates

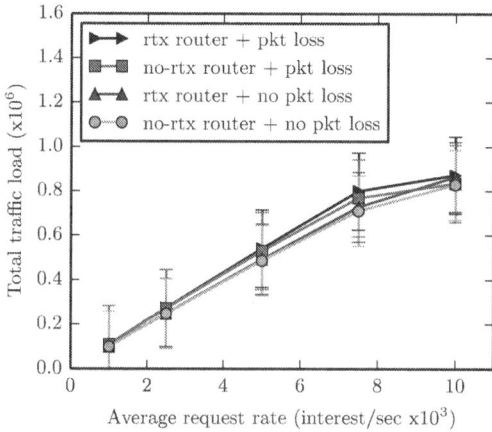

(b) Different average request rates

Figure 8: Total traffic load from $R1$

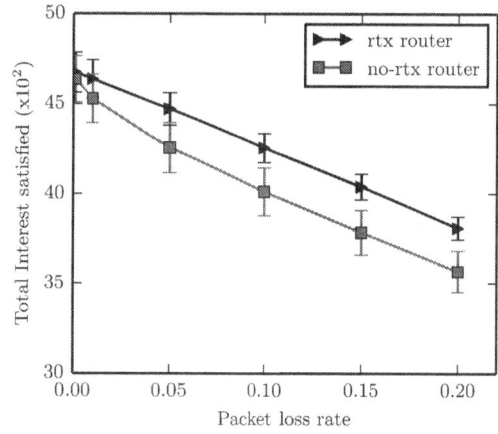

(a) Using a fixed 4s *PEL*

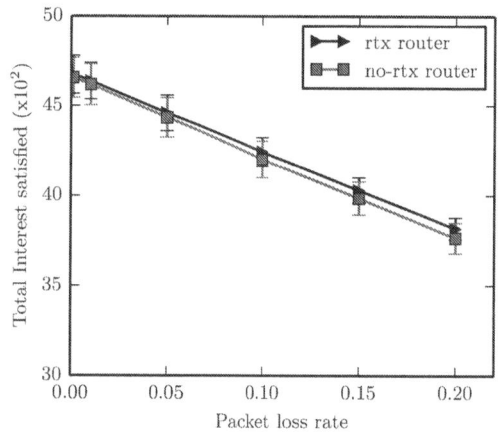

(b) Alternative method for estimating *PEL*

Figure 9: Total number of interests satisfied with different packet loss rates

through the content store and the PIT [16]. With the dominance of one-timer contents in most content distribution networks, the load on the PIT as well as the content store can be greatly reduced, thus reducing the PIT occupancy. Nevertheless this method requires the classification of traffic into one-timer and popular content which is a characteristic that changes in both time, space and may be different from one router to another (due to the well known filtering effect in CCN caused by Interest aggregation). Another interesting approach to explore is regulating the rate of interest packets transmission via flow control.

6. RELATED WORK

CCN has recently drawn a significant attention from the networking community. In particular, efforts have been directed towards exhaustive performance evaluation of CCN caching [19, 20] (Content Store), routing and forwarding (FIB and PIT), security (data integrity and confidentiality) and transport (congestion control) under different network conditions. For example, how to efficiently manage the PIT entry lifetime and the size of the PIT is still an ongoing research issue.

The work by You *et. al.* [23] proposes a new implementation of the PIT based on Bloom Filter to reduce the memory space required to implement the PIT. Evaluation results show that the proposed PIT architecture achieves a significant reduction of the memory space. A tree-like implementation of the PIT is also proposed in [11] to shrink the size of the PIT. Another proposed solution to reduce the size of the PIT employs the idea of traffic differentiation where non-shareable traffic (one-timer content) bypasses both the content store and the PIT while shareable traffic (always cached content) follows the conventional CCN processing [16]. None of these approaches has addressed the impact of the PIT entry lifetime on the PIT size (also known as the number of pending downloads in [18]). A more recent work by Virgilio *et. al.* [18] compares via simulation the existing PIT architectures (SimplePIT, HashedPIT and DiPIT) under heavy traffic load. The analysis results show that all three architectures are adversely affected, making thus the case for the need of a better PIT entry lifetime management.

The PIT entry lifetime determines when the entry can be purged in the event the data takes too long to return (queue-

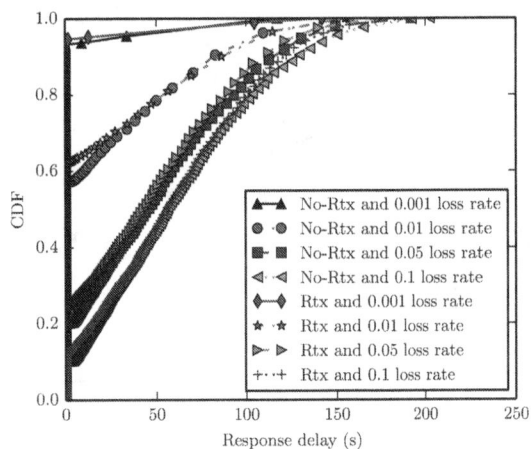

(a) Using a fixed 4s *PEL*

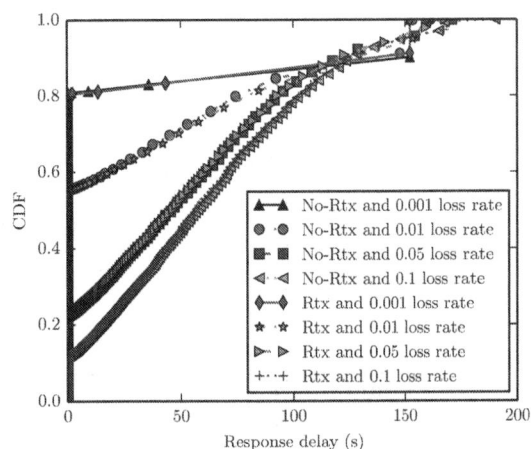

(b) Alternative method for estimating *PEL*

Figure 10: CDFs of the data chunk response delay

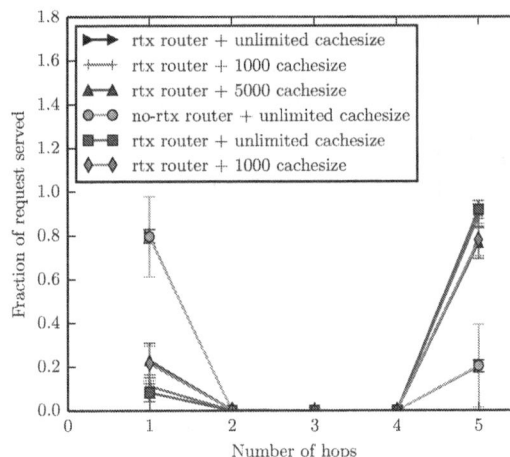

(a) A fixed 4s *PEL*

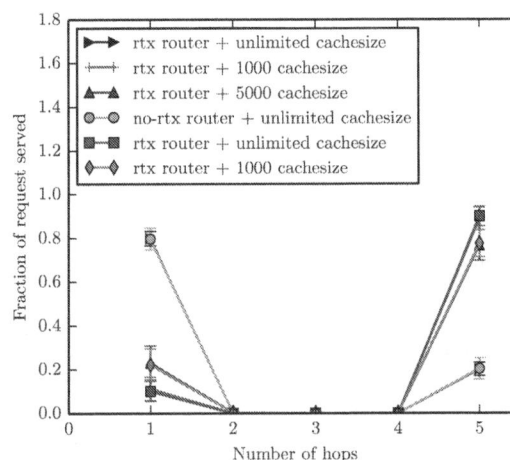

(b) Alternative method for estimating *PEL*

Figure 11: Fraction of requests satisfied by content sources including in network caches

ing delay) or never returns (packet loss) due to congestion in the network. In view of this, Yi *et. al.* [22] proposed a mechanism where intermediate nodes can send a NACK packet to downstream neighbour nodes if an interest cannot be satisfied. On receiving the NACK packet, the node either retransmits the request via another outgoing interface if one exists. Otherwise it purges the corresponding PIT entry. In addition to the drawbacks reported in [8], potential issues with this method are threefold: first upstream nodes's *PEL* may take a long time to expire or never expire when each of the intermediate nodes or the last hop node always receive multiple requests for the same yet-to-return data, resulting in the *PEL* being refreshed/extended [10]. Second, the NACK packet may itself be lost due to congestion. Third, consumers may no longer be interested in receiving an earlier requested data resulting in an inefficient usage of network resources.

Unlike existing works such as [18, 6] that use fixed value for the *PEL*, Kazi and Badr propose a novel method for estimating the *PEL* at routers and the interest packet timeout at receivers [14]. The estimates depend on the queue size

at the most congested node in the network, the processing and propagation delays and the network diameter. However, this approach assumes both interest and data traverse the full diameter of the network. This assumption is indeed not realistic as content sources may be in practice anywhere in the network, requiring actually a more robust and adaptive method to estimate the timer.

7. DISCUSSION AND CONCLUSION

This paper presented a performance study of CCN with rtx and no-rtx routers, shedding more light on how much performance improvement is achieved by one approach over the other.

Our findings suggest that interest retransmission at a CCN router does not appear to be a good design idea. While it has the virtue of speeding up the recovery of delayed or lost packets in the network, it turned out to increase the network traffic load without reducing the number of entries in the PIT. This may eventually result into the PIT memory becoming a performance bottleneck. Since CCN does not specify any method of retransmitting lost packets we have considered in this paper one approach that intuitively leads to a small additional overhead: an rtx router retransmits an interest only when it receives a retransmitted interest from an Interface that is already stored in the PIT entry for the same data name. Other frequencies of retransmission are expected to yield similar or worse results.

In addition, results from our study reveal that the default method used for setting the PIT entry timer is not a good design choice as it is oblivious of the network conditions such as packet loss and delay and can be subject to malicious attacks. Notably, it has the potential of bloating the PIT making it a performance bottleneck. To address this issue we introduced a novel adaptive method to estimate the PIT entry timer that relies on the data chunk response delays observed over a window of samples. Simulation results show that our approach outperforms the currently used method especially in lossy networks. Nevertheless, our proposed solution still needs additional performance analysis considering the impact of different factors such as the number of hops between a content requester and producer, different network topologies, and so on. We leave this as future work.

8. ACKNOWLEDGMENTS

This work was in part supported by HKPFS (PF11-02174) and UGC grant FS-GRF14EG24.

9. REFERENCES

[1] A. Afanasyev, I. Moiseenko, and L. Zhang. ndnSIM: NDN simulator for NS-3. Technical Report NDN-0005, NDN, October 2012.

[2] B. Ahlgren, C. Dannewitz, C. Imbrenda, D. Kutscher, and B. Ohlman. A survey of information-centric networking. *IEEE Comm. Mag.*, 50(7):26–36, 2012.

[3] S. Arianfar, P. Sarolahti, and J. Ott. Deadline-based resource management for information-centric networks. In *Proceedings of the 3rd ACM SIGCOMM workshop on ICN*, pages 49–54, 2013.

[4] A. Bhargava, J. F. Kurose, D. Towsley, and G. Vanleemput. Performance comparison of error control schemes in high-speed computer communication networks. *IEEE Journal on Selected Areas in Communications*, 6(9):1565–1575, Dec 1988.

[5] M. Busari and C. Williamson. Prowgen: a synthetic workload generation tool for simulation evaluation of web proxy caches. *Comp. Net.*, 38(6):779 – 794, 2002.

[6] G. Carofiglio, M. Gallo, and L. Muscariello. Icp: Design and evaluation of an interest control protocol for content-centric networking. In *Proceedings of the 2012 IEEE INFOCOM Workshops*, pages 304–309, Orlando, FL, Mar. 2012.

[7] G. Carofiglio, M. Gallo, and L. Muscariello. On the performance of bandwidth and storage sharing in information-centric networks. *Computer Networks*, 57(17):3743 – 3758, 2013.

[8] G. Carofiglio, M. Gallo, L. Muscariello, M. Papalini, and S. Wang. Optimal multipath congestion control and request forwarding in information-centric networks. In *Proceedings of the 21st IEEE ICNP*, Gottingen, Germany, Oct. 2013.

[9] CCNx. Source code for ccnx 0.8.2. `http://www.ccnx.org/software-download-information-request/download-releases/`, Accessed on 1st May 2014, Apr. 2014.

[10] CCNx Protocol. Technical documentation for ccnx 0.8.2. `http://www.ccnx.org/releases/ccnx-0.8.2/doc/technical/CCNxProtocol.html`, Accessed on 30th May 2014, July 2013.

[11] H. Dai, B. Liu, Y. Chen, and Y. Wang. On pending interest table in named data networking. In *Proceedings of the Eighth ACM/IEEE ANCS*, pages 211–222, New York, NY, USA, 2012.

[12] M. Irland and G. Pujolle. Comparison of two packet-retransmission techniques (corresp.). *IEEE Trans. Inf. Theory*, 26(1):92–97, Jan 1980.

[13] V. Jacobson, D. K. Smetters, J. D. Thornton, M. F. Plass, N. H. Briggs, and R. L. Braynard. Networking named content. In *Proceedings of CoNEXT '09*, pages 1–12, New York, NY, USA, 2009.

[14] A. Kazi and H. Badr. Some observations on the performance of ccn-flooding. In *Proceedings of ICNC*, pages 334–340, Honolulu, HI, Feb. 2014.

[15] A. Kuzmanovic and E. W. Knightly. TCP-LP: Low-priority service via end-point congestion control. *IEEE/ACM Trans. Netw.*, 14(4):739–752, Aug. 2006.

[16] R. Ravindran, G. Wang, X. Zhang, and A. Chakraborti. Supporting dual-mode forwarding in content-centric network. In *Proceedings of the 2012 IEEE ANTS*, pages 55–60, 2012.

[17] S. Shalunov, G. Hazel, J. Iyengar, and M. Kuehlewind. Low Extra Delay Background Transport (LEDBAT). IETF RFC 6817, Dec. 2012. `http://www.rfc-base.org/txt/rfc-6817.txt`.

[18] M. Virgilio, G. Marchetto, and R. Sisto. Pit overload analysis in content centric networks. In *Proceedings of the 3rd ACM SIGCOMM Workshop on ICN*, pages 67–72, New York, NY, USA, 2013.

[19] J. Wang and B. Bensaou. Progressive caching in ccn. In *Proceedings of the 2012 IEEE GLOBECOM*, pages 2727–2732, Anaheim, CA, Dec. 2012.

[20] J. M. Wang, J. Zhang, and B. Bensaou. Intra-as cooperative caching for content-centric networks. In *Proceedings of the 3rd ACM SIGCOMM Workshop on ICN*, pages 61–66, 2013.

[21] M. WÄd'hlisch, T. C. Schmidt, and M. Vahlenkamp. Backscatter from the data plane âĂŞ threats to stability and security in information-centric network infrastructure. *Computer Networks*, 57(16):3192–3206, 2013.

[22] C. Yi, A. Afanasyev, I. Moiseenko, L. Wang, B. Zhang, and L. Zhang. A case for stateful forwarding plane. *Computer Communications*, 36(7):779–791, 2013.

[23] W. You, B. Mathieu, P. Truong, J. Peltier, and G. Simon. Dipit: A distributed bloom-filter based pit table for ccn nodes. In *Proceedings of the 21st ICCCN*, pages 1–7, 2012.

[24] L. Zhang, A. Afanasyev, J. Burke, V. Jacobson, K. Claffy, P. Crowley, C. Papadopoulos, L. Wang, and B. Zhang. Named data networking. Technical Report NDN-0019, NDN project, Apr. 2014.

Consumer-Producer API
for Named Data Networking

Ilya Moiseenko
UCLA
iliamo@cs.ucla.edu

Lixia Zhang
UCLA
lixia@cs.ucla.edu

ABSTRACT

This paper presents a new network programming interface to NDN communication protocols and architectural modules. This new API is made of (1) a consumer context which associates a name prefix with consumer-specific data fetch parameters controlling Interest transmission and Data packet processing, and (2) a producer context which associates a name prefix with producer-specific data transfer parameters controlling Interests demultiplexing and Data packet production. Both API contexts are extensible to new functionalities once they are identified.

Categories and Subject Descriptors

C.2 [**COMPUTER-COMMUNICATION NETWORKS**]: Distributed Systems; D.2 [**SOFTWARE ENGINEERING**]: Software Libraries

Keywords

NDN; API; data producer and consumer

1. INTRODUCTION

As a new architecture, NDN requires a new API. Today's socket API cannot be reused for NDN communication because its foundational concept is point-to-point virtual channel that does not exist in NDN. The NDN architecture development has been following an application-driven approach by going through the cycles of design → experimenting with pilot applications → revision. Our experience with pilot NDN applications [1], [2], [3] has provided us with enough hints to sketch a new NDN API, then we can put it back to application development to verify and validate.

Unlike TCP/IP's point-to-point data delivery, where data transfer parameters are the properties of the channel between two endpoints, in NDN network, data transfer parameters are the properties of the namespace and the node that produces/consumes the data in that namespace. Note that producer and consumer applications of the same namespace do not directly talk to each other, thus they do not share the same set of data transfer parameters as the two endpoints do in TCP/IP networks.

ICN'14, September 24–26, 2014, Paris, France.
ACM 978-1-4503-3206-4/14/09.
http://dx.doi.org/10.1145/2660129.2660158.

Our proposed NDN API has two programming abstractions: consumer context and producer context. A context keeps all necessary state of ongoing data transfer related to a specific name prefix. A contexts allow the following operations:

$$setOption(option, value)$$
$$consume(name\,prefix),\,or$$
$$produce(name\,prefix,\,content)$$

Consumer context is an abstraction that assists application designer to perform unreliable or reliable retrieval of potentially multi-segment content of a given name prefix. The context can perform packet ordering, packet reassembly, as well as give access to raw Interest and Data packets. It also provides event notifications to enable application designers to closely monitor data delivery progress and various errors that may occur in the process.

Producer context is an abstraction that assists application designer to publish single or multi-segment content under a specified name prefix.

Both consumer and producer contexts allow application designers to plug in user-defined, content-based security actions to secure outgoing Interests or Data packets, and verify incoming packets.

2. CONSUMER CONTEXT

Consumer context associates a name prefix with a set of data fetching, transmission, and verification parameters, and integrates processing of Interest and Data packets on the consumer side. An application designer interacts with consumer context by calling API primitives listed in Table 1 and supplying callback functions to process events that may be triggered by the consumer context.

```
consumer(name prefix, type, sequencing) ➜ handle

consume (handle, name suffix)
stop (handle)
close (handle)
setcontextopt (handle, option name, value)
getcontextopt (handle, option name) ➜ value
```

Table 1: API primitives for consuming data.

The first thing an application designer must do is to initialize a consumer context with a desired name prefix and data transfer parameters. The name prefix is a meaningful application-specific name that is expected to bring Data packet(s) back. The required data transfer parameters specify what type of protocol machinery is to be used inside the consumer context. For example, specifying the pair *(UNRELIABLE, DATAGRAM)* instructs consumer context to send a single Interest and receive a single Data packet, whereas the pair *(RELIABLE, SEQUENCE)* results in consumer context to involve necessary machinery to send multiple Interest packets, perform Interest retransmission when needed, manage flow control window size, and reassemble received Data packets.

Any parameter of the consumer context can be obtained or modified using *get/setcontextopt()* API primitives. An application designer can specify what Interest selectors, what flow & congestion control parameters, what size of receive and send buffers to be used by the consumer context during the data transfer. In addition, callback functions can be passed as an argument to the *setcontextopt()* primitive to plug in user defined actions in packet processing pipeline. For example, when consumer context has reassembled enough content from incoming Data packets, it executes *Content-Callback* to return the content to the application. As another example, *VerificationCallback* accepts a Data packet to perform customized Data verification operations. Other callbacks can be activated to monitor events such as Interest timeouts, Data packet arrival, etc.

When all context parameters are set, an application designer can start data transfer using *consume()* primitive that accepts name suffix which augments name prefix of the consumer context. Name suffix, such as version component, provides the flexibility of fetching multiple data objects without having to recreate a consumer context for every object.

Data fetching in the consumer context can progress in non-blocking way. An application designer can terminate the transfer at any moment by calling the *stop()* primitive, which will reset the consumer context to its initial state.

When a consumer context is no longer needed, an application designer can release all its associated resources by executing *close()* primitive.

3. PRODUCER CONTEXT

Producer context associates a name prefix with a set of packet framing, caching, content-based security, and namespace registration parameters, and integrates processing of Interest and Data packets on the producer side. An application designer interacts with producer context by calling API primitives listed in Table 2 and supplying callback functions to process events that may be triggered by the producer context.

```
producer (name prefix) ➜ handle

produce (handle, name suffix, content)
setup (handle)
close (handle)
setcontextopt (handle, option name, value)
getcontextopt (handle, option name) ➜ value
```

Table 2: API primitives for producing data.

The application designer must first initialize a producer context with a desired name prefix and parameters for data publishing. The name prefix is to be used for publishing content under it, and demultiplexing incoming Interest packets.

Any parameter of the consumer context can be obtained and modified using *get/setcontextopt()* API primitives. An application designer can specify the size, freshness and security properties of Data packets. In addition, callback functions can be passed as an argument to the *setcontextopt()* primitive to plug in user defined actions in the packet processing pipeline.

Prior to publishing any content, *setup()* primitive must be called in order to set up Interest demultiplexing by name prefix, and to acquire a routable prefix using the built-in prefix discovery/registration

protocol (similar to [4]) in cases when Interest packets need to be routed to the producer.

An application designer can seamlessly transform any raw content (e.g. memory buffer) into Data packets with *produce()* primitive. The producer context will use its own parameters to package the content in a right number of Data segments (packets) that fully conform with naming and other packet conventions.

When a producer context is no longer needed, an application designer executes *close()* primitive.

4. USING NDN API CONTEXTS

We use NDN FileSync as a use case to illustrate the new API. NDN Filesync is a distributed peer-to-peer application to support file synchronization in a shared directory [3]. As one of the simple pilot NDN applications, it requires reliable data delivery service, but does not have an elaborate security model.

The application's Interest packets contain a name of the file to be downloaded from any other peer. When an Interest is received, the application parses the name to locate the file on the disk, then packages the file in Data packets. Sample data packet name: */broadcast/apps/filesync/class217/Reports/Report.pdf/<timestamp>*.

Pseudocode 1 Sharing a file

1: $h \leftarrow$ **producer**("/broadcast/apps/filesync")
2: **setcontextopt**(h, **packet_size**, *16KB*)
3: **setcontextopt**(h, **interest_callback**, *ProcessInterest*)
4: **setup**(h)

5: **function** PROCESSINTEREST(Interest **i**)
6:     *Name suffix* $\leftarrow$ extract file name from **i**.name to understand what file is needed
7:     *content* $\leftarrow$ read file from disk
8:     *Name suffix* $\leftarrow$ append current time stamp
9:     **produce**(h, *Name suffix*, *content*)
10: **end function**

Pseudocode 2 Downloading a file

1: $h \leftarrow$ **consumer**("/broadcast/apps/filesync", *RELIABLE, SEQUENCE*)
2: **setcontextopt**(h, **receive_buffer_size**, *10MB*)
3: **setcontextopt**(h, **content_callback**, *ProcessContent*)
4: **consume**(h, *"/class217/Reports/Report.pdf"*)

5: **function** PROCESSCONTENT(byte[] **content**)
6:     *file* $\leftarrow$ read **content**
7:     Save *file* on disk
8: **end function**

Interested readers can find other use cases, such as streaming live video (NDNvideo [1]) and building automation system (NDNlighting [2]), from the full version of this paper [5].

5. REFERENCES

[1] D. Kulinski and J. Burke, "NDN Video: Live and Prerecorded Streaming over NDN," NDN, Tech. Rep., 2012.
[2] J. Burke, A. Horn, A. Marianantoni, "Authenticated Lighting Control Using Named Data Networking," NDN, Tech. Rep., 2012. johnbernando@gmail.com
[3] J. Lindblom, M. Huang, J. Burke, L. Zhang, "FileSync/NDN: Peer-to-Peer File Sync over Named Data Networking," NDN, Tech. Rep., 2013.
[4] [Online]. Available: https://www.ccnx.org/releases/latest/doc/technical/Registration.html
[5] I. Moiseenko and L. Zhang, "Consumer-Producer API for Named Data Networking," NDN, Tech. Rep., February 2014. [Online]. Available: http://named-data.net/publications/techreports/tr17-consumer-producer-api/

Kite: A Mobility Support Scheme for NDN

Yu Zhang   Hongli Zhang
Harbin Institute of Technology
{yuzhang, zhanghongli}@hit.edu.cn

Lixia Zhang
UCLA
lixia@cs.ucla.edu

ABSTRACT

Named Data Networking (NDN) natively supports the mobility of data consumers through its data-centric design and stateful forwarding plane. However, the mobility support for data producers remains open in the original proposal. In this paper, we introduce Kite, a design of mobility support for NDN. Kite leverages the state of the Pending Interest Table (PIT) at each router to reach mobile nodes. We describe how Kite can support typical scenarios including group communications among mobiles.

Categories and Subject Descriptors

C.2 [**Computer Systems Organization**]: COMPUTER-COMMUNICATION NETWORKS; C.2.1 [**Network Architecture and Design**]: Packet-switching networks—*Internet*

Keywords

Mobility Support; Named Data Networking

1. INTRODUCTION

Named Data Networking (NDN, aka CCN) [3, 6] has two built-in features that are beneficial to mobility: its *data-centric* design and *stateful* forwarding plane. First, every packet, either Interest or Data, carriers a data name only, instead of any address. Second, the states of data requests, namely Interests packets in the Pending Interest Tables (PITs) of the forwarding plane, enable the reverse path forwarding of Data packets, which makes the location of data consumers transparent to the routing plane and data producers. Thus, NDN natively supports data delivery to mobile consumers, as described in the seminal paper of NDN [3]. However, the paper did not sketch out any specific design for supporting mobile producers.

Several recent efforts have focused on filling in this missing piece. CBIS [2] introduced custodians as intermediaries between names and endpoints. Both [1] and [5] proposed

ICN'14, September 24–26, 2014, Paris, France.
ACM 978-1-4503-3206-4/14/09.
http://dx.doi.org/10.1145/2660129.2660159 .

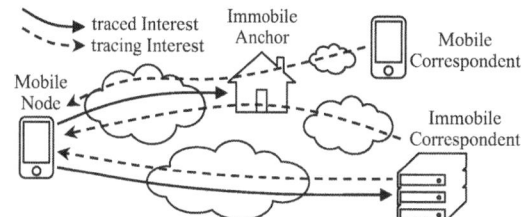

Figure 1: Framework of Kite

to let each mobile producer keep its location updated at a home agent. [4] lets a mobile node (MN) issue a special Interest to its previous location to set up a reverse path by creating FIB entries.

In this paper we present *Kite*, a mobility support scheme for NDN. The key idea of Kite is to fully exploit NDN's forwarding states in PITs (a hop-by-hop *trace*) to keep track of an Interest issuer on the move. This idea is analogous to flying a kite: a kite (like an application) will be reachable along a string (like a trace) from hands (like an anchor). A full description of the design is in an NDN technical report[7].

2. KITE

NDN forwards each Data following the trace left by an Interest. Kite allows each specially marked Interest to be forwarded in the same way, along the trace left by another Interest. We call an Interest which leaves a trace back to an MN a *traced Interest*, and an Interest that traverses the trace left by a traced Interest *tracing Interest*. As shown in Figure 1, a trace may be set up directly between an MN and a correspondent node (CN) or indirectly via an immobile anchor.

We introduce a new forwarding mechanism, *Interest trace forwarding*, into NDN's forwarding plane. For each *tracing Interest* I_{tg}, we add (1) a new `TraceName` field to indicate which traced Interest I_{td} to be traced, and (2) a new `TraceOnly` flag to indicate how to forward the tracing Interest: If the flag is unset, I_{tg} will be forwarded along both the routes in FIBs and trace in PITs; Otherwise I_{tg} will only follow the trace of I_{td} if a match of its trace name is found in the PIT. I_{tg} will be sent (fan out) via the incoming interfaces of matched I_{td} entry.

3. KITE PROTOCOL DESIGN

Generally speaking, we may categorize mobile applications into the following 4 scenarios. (1) An MN, e.g., a smart

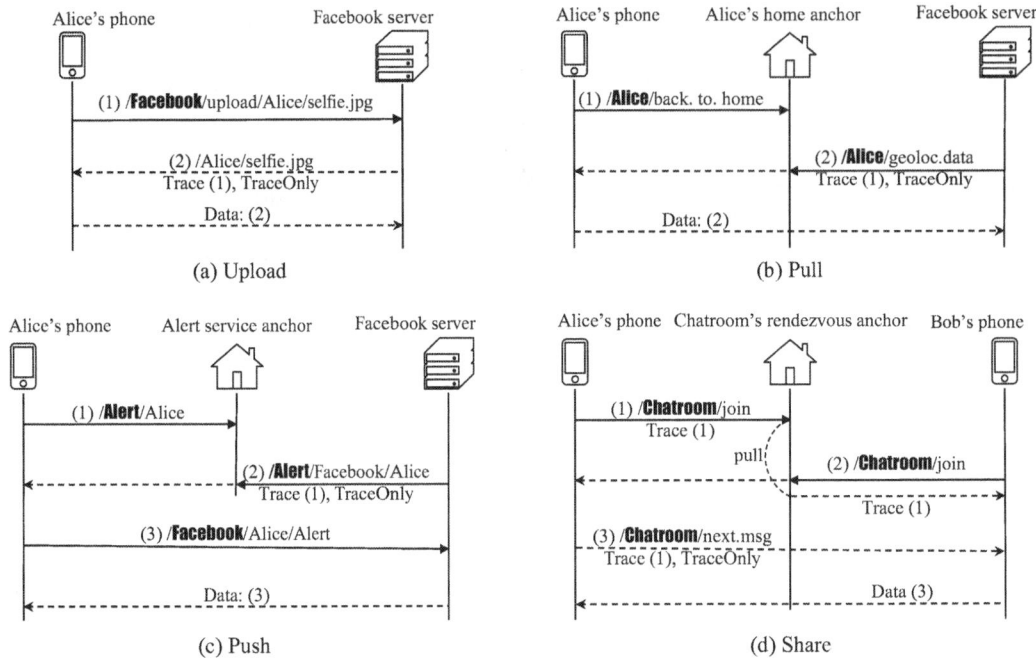

Figure 2: Message exchanges in mobile application protocols. Bold prefixes are in FIBs.

phone, *uploads* data to a stationary CN, e.g., a server; (2) a stationary CN *pulls* data from a mobile; (3) a stationary CN *pushes* data to a mobile; and (4) a group of mobiles *share* data among each other, such as chat via phones directly without a central server. In this case both producers and consumers are mobiles.

The upload scenario can be directly supported by Kite. For example, when Alice uploads her selfie from her phone to a Facebook server, an stationary consumer, the packet exchange is shown in Figure 2 (a). First, the phone sends Interest-1 to both notify the server of the data name to be uploaded, and set up a trace back to the mobile. The server then fetches the data with a tracing Interest-2, whose `TraceName` is derived from Interest-1. In the case of move-before-get, i.e., Alice moves before receiving Interest-2, the phone resends Interest-1, which will pull Interest-2 back to the phone.

Kite can support data pull and push scenarios by utilizing stationary anchors as shown in Figure 2 (b) and (c), respectively. An MN sends traced Interests which follow routes in FIBs to reach its anchor. Tracing Interests from stationary CNs first follow routes in FIBs to reach the anchors, then traverse the traces in PITs to MNs. With the `TraceOnly` flag set, the tracing Interest is only forwarded along traces after arriving at the anchor.

In the share scenario, Kite helps group members build a *bidirectional (shared) tree* rooted at a stationary anchor. As shown in Figure 2 (d), Alice and Bob each need to first send a join Interests-1 and -2, which meet at the anchor. Interest-2 will then trace Interest-1 to reach Alice, and Interest-1 reaches Bob. As a result, a bidirectional trace between Alice and Bob is set up. Afterward, Alice and Bob can express Interests to each other on the tree.

As a proof-of-concept of Kite, we implemented the protocols for the upload and share scenarios in ndnSIM and conducted a preliminary evaluation[7].

4. CONCLUSION

Kite contributes two new features to the mobility support of NDN. 1) *Locator-free*: There is no explicit locator for MNs which are implicitly addressed by the hop-by-hop states instead. 2) *Scenario-aware*: As traces are generated and utilized directly by application protocols, protocol developers are partially empowered to devise their own designs of mobility support tailored to their scenarios.

5. ACKNOWLEDGMENTS

This work is supported by National NSF of China (No. 61202457) and State Scholarship Fund from China Scholarship Council (No. 201206125041).

6. REFERENCES

[1] F. Hermans, E. Ngai, and P. Gunningberg. Global source mobility in the content-centric networking architecture. In *NoM '12*, 2012.

[2] V. Jacobson et al. Custodian-based information sharing. *IEEE Communications Magazine*, 50(7):38–43, 2012.

[3] V. Jacobson, D. K. Smetters, J. D. Thornton, M. F. Plass, N. H. Briggs, and R. L. Braynard. Networking named content. In *CoNEXT '09*, 2009.

[4] D.-h. Kim, J.-h. Kim, Y.-s. Kim, H.-s. Yoon, and I. Yeom. Mobility support in content centric networks. In *ICN '12*, 2012.

[5] J. Lee, S. Cho, and D. Kim. Device mobility management in content-centric networking. *IEEE Commun. Magazine*, 50(12):28–34, 2012.

[6] L. Zhang et al. Named data networking. *Tech. Rep. NDN-0019*, 2014.

[7] Y. Zhang, H. Zhang, and L. Zhang. Kite: A mobility support scheme for ndn. *Tech. Rep. NDN-0020*, 2014.

Poster – iSync: A High Performance and Scalable Data Synchronization Protocol for Named Data Networking[*]

Wenliang Fu[1], Hila Ben Abraham[2] and Patrick Crowley[2]
[1]School of Computer Science, Beijing Institute of Technology
[2]Computer Science and Engineering, Washington University in St. Louis
fuwenl@bit.edu.cn, {hila, pcrowley}@wustl.edu

ABSTRACT

This paper presents a high performance synchronization protocol for named data networking (NDN). The protocol, called iSync, uses a two-level invertible Bloom filter (IBF) structure to support efficient data reconciliation. Multiple differences can be found by subtracting a remote IBF from a local IBF, and therefore, from a single round of data exchange. We evaluated iSync's performance by comparing it to the default data synchronization protocol of CCNx. Experiments show that iSync is significantly faster for different network sizes and topologies, and it requires less overhead for synchronizing various file sizes.

Categories and Subject Descriptors

C.2.2 [**computer-communication networks**]: Network Protocols—*Applications*

Keywords

Named data network; high performance; data synchronization; invertible Bloom filters

1. INTRODUCTION

Data synchronization of multiple nodes is a fundamental operation in many Internet applications, such as cloud storage, group communication, and routing protocols. In named data networking (NDN) [1], keeping namespaces synchronized has recently emerged as a basic service required by many NDN applications, from Dropbox-style file sharing to supporting mobile and ad-hoc vehicular communication. NDN also uses a core synchronization protocol to support a key-based trust model which requires public key exchange.

The goal of a synchronization protocol is to keep a dataset (or a *collection*) up-to-date among distributed participants. In other words, a synchronization protocol must replicate a dataset's content among participating hosts. In NDN, a

[*]Hila Ben Abraham is the corresponding author of this work.

ICN'14, September 24–26, 2014, Paris, France.
ACM 978-1-4503-3206-4/14/09.
http://dx.doi.org/10.1145/2660129.2660161.

content item is represented by a namespace, so a synchronized NDN collection consists of the content names – a list of namespaces.

Data synchronization consists of three basic tasks: 1) understanding whether a set is up-to-date or out-of-date, 2) finding set differences, and 3) retrieving missing items.

This paper describes iSync, a high performance and scalable data synchronization protocol based on IBFs. iSync uses a two-level IBF structure to support efficient data reconciliation. The first level identifies collections which are out-of-date; the second level discovers the IDs of all the items that exist in a remote collection, but are missing in the local one. This feature allows the difference reconciliation process to efficiently skip collections that have no updates.

2. PROTOCOL DESIGN

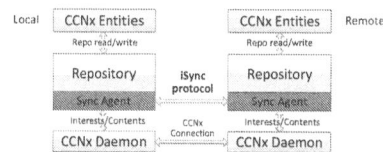

Figure 1: Data Synchronization Model.

As shown in Fig.1, iSync consists of two components: a repository and a sync agent. The repository offers an interface for CCNx entities (i.e., applications) to insert files and publish sync collections. The iSync protocol operates between any two nodes that publish the same collection. In the NDN architecture, a collection is defined by a namespace. All the content items to be synchronized under a published collection must be named using the collection's namespace in their prefix. Upon a content insertion, iSync automatically adds the new content to the local collections whose namespace matches the new item prefix.

The sync agent indexes the inserted files' names and updates a digest that reflects the current contents of each sync collection. It periodically broadcasts local digests, while receiving remote ones. By comparing local with remote digests, the sync agent can identify whether the collections (local and remote) are synchronized. Synchronization starts when a remote collection digest does not match the local collection digest. The set difference of a local and a remote node is found by repeatedly requesting, receiving, and subtracting remote IBF tables from local and global IBF tables. Multiple differences can be found from each subtraction, and therefore, from a single round of data exchange.

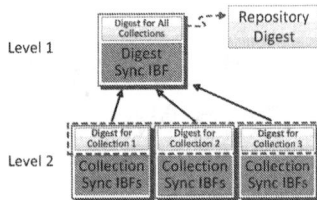

Figure 2: Hierarchical Data Structure.

Fig. 2 shows the hierarchical IBF design. The protocol utilizes a two-level IBF design, *Digest sync IBF* and *collection sync IBFs*, to perform the tasks mentioned above. While level one records the status of the entire repository, level two logs file insertions or deletions of each sync collection separately. An update changes a second level IBF by hashing the content name into the corresponding *collection sync IBF*. This hashing causes a change to the collection digest, and therefore invokes an update in the first level IBF, including the repository digest.

The original design of the IBF handles only fixed-length item names and does not support content lookup very well [2]. To address these limitations, iSync performs two tasks: mapping variable-length file names into fixed-length IDs, and recording what items have been inserted. The former is done by using a hash-indexed table to support bidirectional mapping between file names and IDs. During the entire synchronization process, file names are replaced by fixed-length file IDs. The latter utilizes a counting Bloom filter to support file insertions, deletions, and queries.

The iSync protocol utilizes IBFs to hold the set of name IDs for each sync collection. While it is very efficient to compute differences between two IBFs by subtracting them and decoding the resulting IBF, there is no guarantee that all the differences can be decoded. For a fixed-size IBF, the more updates it holds, the less likely it can be perfectly decoded. To ensure the decoding of all the differences, iSync implements a difference size control mechanism. Hosts that have declared the same sync collections periodically confirm the consistency of their data sets by exchanging their repository digests. This periodic operation guarantees bounded delay of file shares and limits the potential number of differences between the hosts.

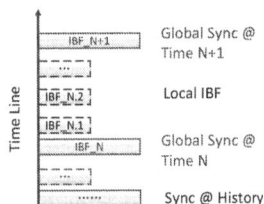

Figure 3: Local and Global IBFs for one Sync Collection.

For each collection, two types of IBFs are used: global and local. A change in a local collection is indexed into the current local IBF. When the number of differences exceeds a defined maximum, iSync creates a new local IBF to store future changes. A global IBF is the local IBF on the time of a sync cycle and is regarded as a public version of the collection data. To find all changes made in a sync cycle, iSync subtracts a remote global IBF from the host's global IBF.

If the subtraction fails to obtain the complete set difference, iSync uses the local IBFs between the two latest global IBFs to decode smaller set differences. The combination of those IBF types makes differences between two IBFs traceable. An application can tune the periodic sync time and the IBF size to support its specific requirements.

3. EVALUATION

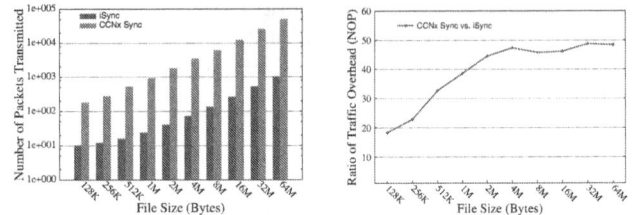

Figure 4: Traffic Overhead for Various File Sizes.

We synchronized files of different sizes (from 128 KB to 64 MB) and measured the traffic overhead by capturing the network traffic. Fig. 4 shows the number of packets transmitted by CCNx Sync [3] and iSync for different file sizes. In terms of the number of packets, iSync is about 18 and 48 times more efficient than CCNx Sync while sharing files of 128 KB and 64 MB respectively.

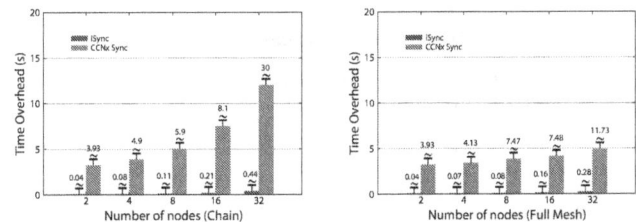

Figure 5: Average Synchronization Time of iSync and CCNx Sync.

We evaluated and compared the performance of the iSync and CCNx Sync protocols in multiple network topologies with a range of nodes scaling from 2 to 32. As shown in Fig. 5, iSync is significantly faster in both chain and full mesh topologies for a range of network sizes.

4. CONCLUSION

This paper presents a high performance synchronization protocol which utilizes the IBF to synchronize published collections between nodes. The protocol uses a two-level IBF design and can reconcile a number of differences in a single comparison. We found that on average, iSync is about 66 times faster than CCNx on a range of network sizes, while it uses 18 to 48 times fewer packets.

5. REFERENCES

[1] Lixia Zhang, Deborah Estrin, and et al. Named data networking project. *Relatório Técnico NDN-0001, Xerox Palo Alto Research Center-PARC*, 2010.

[2] Michael T Goodrich and Michael Mitzenmacher. Invertible bloom lookup tables. In *Communication, Control, and Computing (Allerton), 2011 49th Annual Allerton Conference on*, pages 792–799. IEEE, 2011.

[3] Content centric networking (CCNx) project website. http://www.ccnx.org.

Client Starvation: A Shortcoming of Client-driven Adaptive Streaming in Named Data Networking

Daniel Posch, Christian Kreuzberger, Benjamin Rainer and Hermann Hellwagner
Institute of Information Technology (ITEC)
Alpen-Adria-Universität (AAU) Klagenfurt, Austria
firstname.lastname@itec.aau.at

ABSTRACT

Information-centric Networking (ICN) as a potential Future Internet architecture has to efficiently support the consumption of multimedia content. Recent proposals consider the reuse of MPEG-DASH to provide adaptive streaming in ICN. Due to the fact that MPEG-DASH relies on pure client-driven adaptation, it encounters difficulties dealing with ICN's inherent caching and multi-path transmission. By conducting simulations using the concrete ICN approach Named Data Networking (NDN), we show that pure client-driven adaptation leads to shortcomings. Furthermore, we propose to use in-network adaptation based on scalable content for overcoming these shortcomings in NDN.

Categories and Subject Descriptors

C.2.1 [**Network Architecture and Design**]:
Network communications

General Terms

Design, Theory

Keywords

Information-centric Networking; Adaptive Streaming

1. INTRODUCTION

In today's Internet, multimedia content represents the biggest traffic source. This draws the attention of ICN research towards the question of how to realize effective audio-visual content dissemination. Due to its effectiveness in IP-based networks, the integration of MPEG-DASH (ISO/IEC 23009-1) in NDN has been investigated by recent research [3]. MPEG-DASH is able to consider consumer demands, e.g., heterogeneous end-devices, and responds well to fluctuating network conditions. It uses an elegant approach: Content is split into independent segments, which are encoded in various quality levels. Complexity is pushed to

the clients, which are responsible for selecting and fetching appropriate segments. The adaptation process considers only local parameters. ICN's specifics, e.g, network inherent caching and multipath delivery, are disregarded. This causes negative side-effects on other network participants. One example is *client starvation*, which is presented in this article. It describes the fact that requests for popular content overwhelm requests for less popular content, providing insufficient service for some clients.

2. EXPERIMENTAL SETUP

The objective of adaptive streaming is the enhancement of user-perceived quality, also referred to as Quality of Experience (QoE). As we consider only reliable ICN transport, the most influential QoE factors are [6]: (1) startup delay, (2) playout stalling time, (3) number of quality switches and (4) playback quality.

Using ns-3/ndnSIM [1], we set up a simulation with 100 MPEG-DASH clients, streaming 10 different videos over a bottleneck link (20, 25, 30 Mbit/s). The node was equipped with a 256 MB LRU content store. For each evaluated bottleneck-speed we perform 30 simulation runs and for each of the runs the video streamed by a client is randomly assigned based on the popularity distribution depicted in Table 1. Clients start streaming at varying times, following an exponential distribution.

The videos are encoded according to the Scalable Video Coding (SVC) extension of H.264/MPEG-4 AVC [4] using SNR-scalability. The encoder was configured to provide contents in six different quality layers, resulting in the following average bitrates: 1290, 1768, 2220, 2608, 2933 and 3197 kbit/s. We selected SVC-based encoding because ICN caches can be used more efficiently compared to non-scalable content encodings.

The clients use a buffer-based adaptation logic as described in [5]. Additionally a TCP-like congestion-control window (AIMD) was used to adapt a client's data request rate. We justify this step by the latest developments in the Future Internet community [2], which argues for a dual-stack deployment of ICN and TCP/IP.

Content consumed	by X Clients
Video 0 / Video 1	1 / 1
Video 2 / Video 3 / Video 4	2 / 2 / 2
Video 5 / Video 6 / Video 7	4 / 8 / 16
Video 8 / Video 9	32 / 33

Table 1: **Popularity distribution of the videos.**

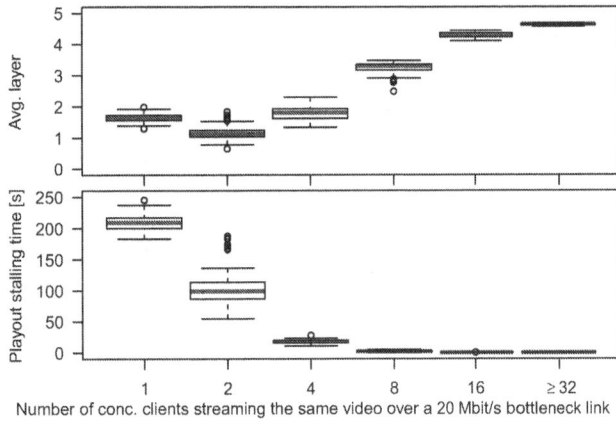

Figure 1: Average received layer and stalling time versus video popularity.

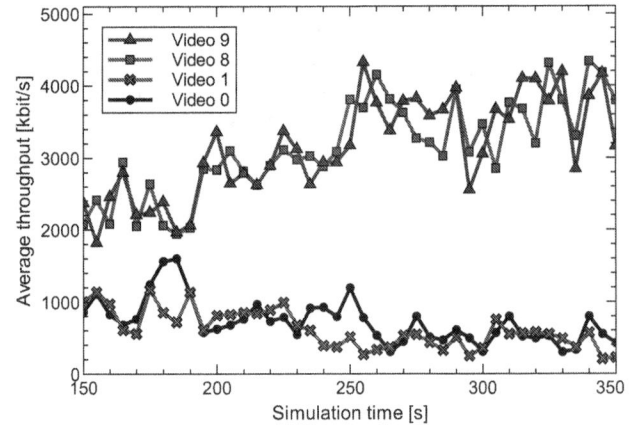

Figure 2: Average bandwidth share on the bottleneck link per video for a single simulation run.

3. RESULTS

Figure 1 depicts the results of the simulation with a bottleneck of 20 Mbit/s via box plots (we omit similar results for 25 and 30 Mbit/s due to space constraints). The X-axis represents the number of concurrent clients according to Table 1, while the Y-axis shows the playout stalling time and the average received layer. The box plots show that the more popular a video is, the better the received quality and the lower the number of stalls on average is. Exceptions are videos requested by only one client. They have a higher average quality than videos requested by two clients. Due to the high playout stalling time, videos requested by only one client receive more bandwidth towards the end of the simulation.

The higher quality levels of clients requesting popular videos can be partly explained by efficient cache utilization in ICN, however, the long playout stalling duration of some clients has another cause. In the case of congestion, ICN nodes discard packets due to buffer overflows. Therefore, requests stay unsatisfied, resulting in timeouts, and clients reduce their congestion window to avoid future congestion. However, if multiple clients request the same content, dropped requests are likely to be re-issued by other clients. This may result in delivery of data even if a previous request has been discarded. Consumers who stream the same video as many other clients, may not notice congestion. Therefore they will not reduce their congestion window, and continue to utilize a higher bandwidth share. Furthermore, cache hits increase the congestion window's size, and once cache misses are encountered, those clients demand a too large share of the available bandwidth. The simulations indicate that clients requesting unpopular content starve, as illustrated by the high stalling duration in Figure 1. We call this problem *client starvation*. In addition, Figure 2 shows that the average bandwidth share per video on the bottleneck link is higher for popular than for unpopular videos. For illustration purposes only a subset of the videos are depicted during 200 seconds of simulation time.

4. CONCLUSION AND FUTURE WORK

We outlined the problem of *client starvation*. This issue is mainly caused by the fact that the clients are not aware of how many other concurrent users are consuming the same video, nor do they know anything about the received video quality of other clients. Therefore client-driven adaptation can not solve *client starvation* satisfactorily. As this problem emerges within the network, we propose the usage of in-network adaptation (INA) to tackle the problem at its place of origin, which is part of our future research. We are going to investigate INA in ICN based on layered content encodings. This enables INA despite ICN's content-based security model, which prohibits content manipulation due to security constraints introduced by digital signatures.

5. ACKNOWLEDGMENTS

This work was partially funded by the Austrian Science Fund (FWF) under the CHIST-ERA project CONCERT (A Context-Adaptive Content Ecosystem Under Uncertainty), project number *I1402*.

6. REFERENCES

[1] A. Afanasyev, I. Moiseenko, and L. Zhang. ndnSIM: NDN Simulator for NS-3. Tech. Report NDN-005, 2012.

[2] S. Braun, M. Monti, M. Sifalakis, and C. Tschudin. CCN & TCP Co-Existence in the Future Internet: Should CCN be Compatible to TCP? In *IFIP/IEEE International Symposium on Integrated Network Management*, 2013.

[3] S. Lederer, C. Müller, B. Rainer, C. Timmerer, and H. Hellwagner. Adaptive Streaming over Content Centric Networks in Mobile Networks using Multiple Links. In *Proceedings of the IEEE International Conference on Communication (ICC)*, 2013.

[4] H. Schwarz, D. Marpe, and T. Wiegand. Overview of the Scalable Video Coding Extension of the H. 264/AVC Standard. *IEEE Transactions on Circuits and Systems for Video Technology*, 17(9):1103–1120, 2007.

[5] C. Sieber, T. Hoßfeld, T. Zinner, P. Tran-Gia, and C. Timmerer. Implementation and User-centric Comparison of a Novel Adaptation Logic for DASH with SVC. In *IFIP/IEEE Workshop QCMan*, 2013.

[6] L. Yitong, S. Yun, M. Yinian, L. Jing, L. Qi, and Y. Dacheng. A Study on Quality of Experience for Adaptive Streaming Service. In *IEEE International Conference on Communication (ICC)*, June 2013.

NaNET: Socket API and Protocol Stack for Process-to-Content Network Communication

Massimo Gallo, Lin Gu, Diego Perino, Matteo Varvello
Bell Labs, Alcatel-Lucent
first.last@alcatel-lucent.com

ABSTRACT

Inter-process communication (IPC) refers to the set of methods which enable data exchange among processes. When two processes are remote (connected via a network), IPC is realized through the socket and the networking protocol stack implemented at end-hosts. Today, most computer networks rely on the Internet NETworking socket domains (INET) and the Internet Protocol (IP) suite.

Information-centric networking (ICN) is a novel networking paradigm centered around named data rather than named hosts. ICN shifts the communication principle from process-to-process towards process-to-content (PCC) by mean of a novel name-based protocol suite. We propose Named NETworking, a new socket domain and protocol stack that realize PCC à la NDN [1] while remaining compatible with current protocols and standards. Finally we implement NaNET in the Unix operating system as a set of kernel modules.

Categories and Subject Descriptors

C.2.1 [**Network Architecture and Designs**]: Network communications; C.2.2 [**Network Protocols**]: Protocol architecture

General Terms

Design, Implementation.

Keywords

NDN, API, stack, protocols.

1. PCC AND NaNET

We call NaNET socket domain and protocol stack that enables PCC à la NDN. NaNET has two main design goals: backward compatibility, and ease of integration with existing operating systems. Accordingly, we rethink current API and protocol stack to support PCC as shown in Figure 1.

To realize an incremental shift from IPC to PCC, our rationale is to extend the Unix implementation of the BSD

ICN'14, September 24–26, 2014, Paris, France.
ACM 978-1-4503-3206-4/14/09.
http://dx.doi.org/10.1145/2660164.

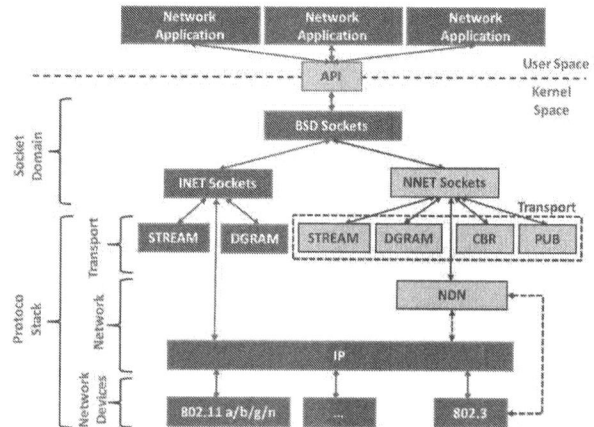

Figure 1: Comparison of TCP/IP and NaNET API and protocol stack.

sockets with a novel socket domain, and to deploy NDN as an overlay over existing technologies. Differently from [5], we propose a protocol stack composed of two layers, transport and network, which sits between socket API and an underlying technology that provides connectivity between two NDN nodes. NaNET supports Ethernet and IP to provide connectivity between two NDN nodes.

Similarly to [5], we identify two key processes involved in the *process-to-content* communication model (PCC) used by NDN: the *publisher* and the *consumer*. The publisher process makes content publicly and permanently available to the network by opening one or more sockets that simply wait for incoming requests. The consumer process requests content, based on the end-user interest. Such request targets the desired content (that can be cached in the middle of the network) instead of its publisher process.

In the following we briefly describe NaNET stack and consumer/publisher API.

1.1 Socket Addressing Scheme

NaNET uses the hierarchical naming scheme proposed by NDN to address content. To avoid conversion between application data unit (ADU) and transmission unit, we follow the application layer framing design principle by Clark et. al [4]. Accordingly, an ADU corresponds to a content segment and defines the granularity for which the application can support out-of-order packets and recovery from packet losses. The publisher process is in charge of defining the proper ADU size based on application constraints.

Consumer Operation	System Call
Open the socket	`socket(domain,type,protocol)`
Associates a content name or prefix to open a NaNET socket.	`bind(fd,*addr,addrlen)`
Allows to verify if the desired content exists, and to retrieve its meta-data	`connect(fd,*addr,addrlen)`
Set/Get the socket options. e.g., receiver timeout, transmission rate, etc...	`setsockopt(fd,level,optname,*optval,optlen)` `getsockopt(fd,level, optname,*optval,*optlen)`
Start process for named data retrieval. The major difference between these system calls lies in the fact that `recvfrom()` and `recvmsg()` can specify the name of the content to be received, while `recv()` and `read()` do not.	`recv(fd,*buf,len,flags)` `read(fd,*buf,len)` `recvfrom(fd,*buf,buflen,flags,*addr,*addrlen)` `recvmsg(fd,*msg,flags)`
Close the socket	`close(fd)`

Table 1: Consumer operations.

Publisher Operation	System Call
Open the socket	`socket(domain,type,protocol)`
Associates a content name or prefix to open a NaNET socket.	`bind(fd,*addr,addrlen)`
Set/Get the socket options. e.g., receiver timeout, transmission rate, etc...	`setsockopt(fd,level,optname,*optval,optlen)` `getsockopt(fd,level, optname,*optval,*optlen)`
Inform underlying network layer that this process can serve all content items whose names fall within a content prefix, triggering forwarding table update.	`listen(fd,backlog)`
Instruct a socket to wait for incoming Interests. Once an Interest is received, it returns the packet to the publisher process that is responsible to handle it.	`accept(fd,*addr,addrlen)`
Send data back to the requester spedifying the data name.	`sendto(fd,*buf,len,flags,*addr,addrlen)` `sendmsg(fd,*msg,flags)`
Close the socket	`close(fd)`

Table 2: Publisher operations.

1.2 Socket API

NaNET is designed to be easily integrated with the current Unix implementation of the BSD socket. Indeed NaNET API mimics current socket's API, though with different functionalities and implementations.

Similarly to [6], we make the NDN communication protocol available through the socket's API by introducing new NaNET address and protocol families, AF_NANET and PF_NANET.

Available Consumer/Publisher system calls and a brief description of their meaning are listed in Tab.1,2.

1.3 Transport Layer

Transport layer has different functionalities at the consumer and producer process.

The consumer's transport layer is responsible for transfer reliability, flow/congestion control, data encapsulation and decapsulation, data multiplexing and demultiplexing. We identify three transport protocols at the consumer:

DATAGRAM: It allows the consumer to directly request an ADU without the need of either flow or congestion control. DATAGRAM is the is unreliable and the consumer process is responsible of managing retransmissions if needed.
STREAM: It allows the consumer to retrieve a sequence of bytes using a congestion control mechanism like the ones proposed in [2, 3]. STREAM is reliable but packet losses recovery can be disabled.
CBR: It allows the consumer to request a "constant bit rate" for the delivery of a byte range. As STREAM, CBR is reliable by default but packet losses recovery can be disabled.

At the publisher only one transport protocol is available, **PUB**, which is is responsible for data encapsulation and decapsulation, and multiplexing and demultiplexing. Publisher's process simply listens for incoming requests to which it replies with the requested data, if available.

Transport layer functionalities described above naturally arise when moving from IPC to PCC. NDN also introduces additional functionalities dictated by security as signature generation (producer) and verification (consumer) are needed.

1.4 Network Layer

As for the IP network layer, packet forwarding is the main operation the NDN network layer is responsible of. However, packets are forwarded based on content names rather than IP addresses. When shifting from IP address to content names, several functionalities naturally arise, such as caching and multi-path. It follows that the network layer should implement additional operations to support such functionalities. Differently from IP, data fragmentation and re-assembly are delegated to underlying layers (possibly an additional messaging layer) which provides connectivity between two NDN nodes.

2. REFERENCES

[1] Named data networking. http://named-data.net/.
[2] G. Carofiglio, M. Gallo, L. Muscariello, and L. Papalini. Multipath congestion control in content-centric networks. In *Proc. of IEEE INFOCOM NOMEN workshop*, 2013.
[3] G. Carofiglio, M. Gallo, L. Muscariello, M. Papalini, and S. Wang. Optimal multipath congestion control and request forwarding in information-centric networks. In *Proc. of ICNP*, 2013.
[4] D. D. Clark and D. L. Tennenhouse. Architectural considerations for a new generation of protocols. In *Proc. of ACM SIGCOMM*, 1990.
[5] I. Moiseenko and L. Zhang Anand. Consumer-producer api for named data networking. *NDN Technical Report*, 2014.
[6] E. Nordstrom, D. Shue, P. Gopalan, R. Kiefer, M. Arye, S. Ko, J. Rexford, and M. J. Freedman. Serval: An end-host stack for service-centric networking. In *Proc. of USENIX NSDI*, 2012.

SAVANT: Aggregated Feedback and Accountability Framework for Named Data Networking

Diarmuid Ó Coileáin
CTVR, School of Computer Science and
Statistics,
Trinity College Dublin,
Dublin 2, Ireland.
collindi@tcd.ie

Donal O'Mahony
CTVR, School of Computer Science and
Statistics,
Trinity College Dublin,
Dublin 2, Ireland.
Donal.OMahony@cs.tcd.ie

ABSTRACT

Content providers (i.e., entities that own or are licensed to sell or distribute content e.g., BBC, Netflix) are looking for more efficient, secure, cheaper, accountable and scalable mechanisms for the delivery of content to end-users. The *Information Centric Networking* (ICN) paradigm offers solutions to some of these challenges by decoupling a user's trust in content from where it is obtained by enabling the content to *self-verify* (i.e., the user can establish integrity, trust and provenance in content received from trusted or untrusted infrastructure). However, there are still associated challenges with using ICN architectures related to content feedback and accountability. In this paper, we propose an ICN architecture extension for content feedback and accountability called the Savant framework, which we apply to the *Named Data Networking* (NDN) architecture.

Categories and Subject Descriptors

C.2.4 [**COMPUTER-COMMUNICATION NETWORKS**]: Distributed Systems–Distributed applications

General Terms

Management, Measurement, Design

Keywords

Information Centric Networking, Content Feedback and Accountability, Analytics

1. INTRODUCTION

Content feedback and accountability information enables a content provider and a content distributor (e.g. Content Distribution Network (CDN)) to track the content delivered to consumers. We define *feedback* as the information returned to a content provider so that future or in-progress operations can be monitored, supported, altered or corrected.

ICN'14, September 24–26, 2014, Paris, France.
ACM 978-1-4503-3206-4/14/09.
http://dx.doi.org/10.1145/2660129.2660165.

This information can help a content provider to determine what content is popular, the geographical location of users and what kind of performance clients are receiving from the network [1]. In comparison to feedback, we define *accountability* as the willingness of trusted or untrusted communicating entities to produce accurate and verifiable information about the content distribution process. The primary difference between a feedback architecture and an accountability architecture is that when there is a problem the latter has the tools to pinpoint (with non-repudiation) the responsible entity [5]. In the remainder of this paper we briefly outline Savant's framework for providing content feedback and accountability (depicted in Figure 1), which we apply to the NDN architecture.

2. THE SAVANT FRAMEWORK

The main components in the Savant architecture include content providers, content ingestion, accountability engine, NDN caches and NDN clients (collectively referred to as *NDN agents*), configuration manager and aggregator functions. The *content ingestion* process prepares content for distribution to many different users, devices and networks, performing tasks such as transcoding, resolution conversion, encryption and adding *metadata*. The *metadata* specified during ingestion identifies the content provider. This helps the NDN agent establish contact with the closest available *accountability engine* responsible for collecting information for that content provider.

The accountability engine is composed of geographically dispersed infrastructure located close to the end-user (similar to CDN infrastructure). It has primary responsibility for collecting, aggregating and validating published feedback and accountability information collected from NDN agents. Once two-way communication has been established between the NDN agent and accountability engine, the accountability engine will issue a continuous stream of NDN *Interests* for feedback and accountability information.

Both the accountability engine and NDN agents run a configuration manager and aggregator functions. At their simplest level, *aggregator functions* work to filter, summarise and publish feedback data containing specified attributes. Moreover, they determine what information is collected and the frequency of collection. Due to the nature of the NDN publish/subscribe architecture, only requested information is pulled for aggregation (i.e., there is no duplicate or unnecessary information requested for aggregation).

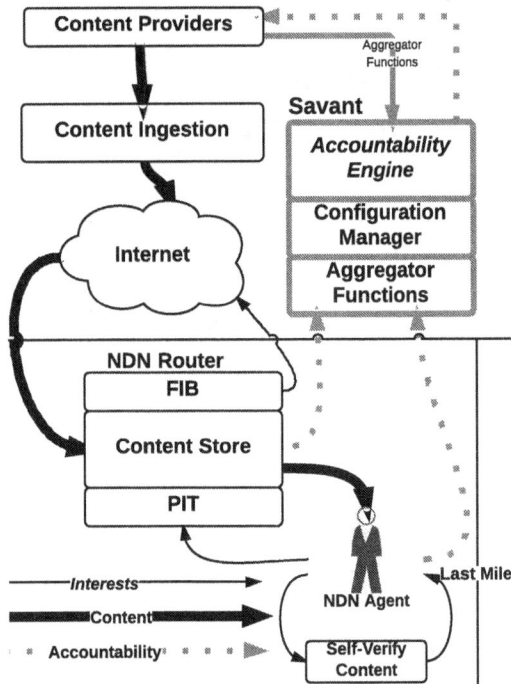

Figure 1: The NDN architecture with the Savant framework.

Finally, aggregator functions are installed (and uninstalled) on distributed accountability engines and NDN agents by their local *configuration manager*. The configuration manager also manages the publication of key/value pair attributes and aggregator function output for collection by accountability engine infrastructure.

2.1 Savant Accountability

A major challenge in distributing content from untrusted infrastructure is the inability to directly observe or trust the interactions between communicating peers [1]. However, NDN (and ICN architectures) offer natural support for accountability due to published content's ability to self-verify. This is underpinned by public/private key pairs, deterministic inputs and outputs (i.e., *Interest*/Data), hash functions and digital signatures [5][3]. The Savant framework provides the remaining tools for accountability such as log auditing and providing certified public/private key pairs to agents. To achieve this, we follow similar principles to those already described by PeerReview (which provides a secure record of accountability in distributed systems [3]) and Reliable Client Accounting (RCA) (a non-repudiable accounting system for hybrid CDN-P2P systems [1]). These systems use a hash chain of log entries in order to detect inconsistencies between the logs of communicating peers. This is achieved by getting both sending and receiving peer infrastructure to maintain tamper evident logs for all communication-taking place between peers [1][3].

3. IMPLEMENTATION

In 2011, a team at Conviva performed an analysis of data collected from over 1 million unique viewers, content providers, Internet service providers and CDNs in order to determine how video quality impacts end-user engagement [2]. In or-

der to prove the viability of the Savant architecture we attempted to partially replicate that experiment by gathering and comparing (with Conviva's analysis) a subset of these metrics for a small number of ICN users.

We achieved this objective using an implementation of the Savant framework in conjunction with small modifications to the NDN Video [4] software. First, both the NDN Video server and Savant Server run on independent Amazon Elastic Compute Cloud (EC2) micro-instance machines (i.e., Ubuntu-12.04.3-64 bit; memory: 613MB and disk: 8GB). Second, we published a video-on-demand (VoD) content file using the NDN Video software to the NDN Video Server. This machine acted as the data source for NDN clients requesting content from EC2. Third, we modified the NDN Video Client to publish accountability events as it receives and renders video content from the NDN Video Server. Fourth, this published feedback and accountability information is collected by the Savant Server (i.e., the accountability engine) by requesting chunks of published information from the NDN Clients. Finally, the Savant Server processes, aggregates and republishes/persists the data collected based on aggregator functions.

4. CONCLUSION

Based on this implementation and the Conviva's analysis of end-user engagement we were able to demonstrate the viability of an ICN architecture collecting real-time analytic information supporting the ICN content distribution process. For example, Savant consistently measured NDN Video's join-time at just over 10 seconds for VoD content. In comparison, Conviva measured 95% of users in their analysis having a join-time of less than 10 seconds for CDN content distribution [2]. These and similar comparisons focus attention on the importance of feedback and accountability metrics for ICN content providers, content distributors and end-users.

5. ACKNOWLEDGEMENTS

This research, a part of the Telecommunications Graduate Initiative, is funded by the Irish Higher Education Authority under the Programme for Research in Third-Level Institutes (PRTLI) and co-funded under the European Regional Development fund.

6. REFERENCES

[1] P. Aditya, M. Zhao, Y. Lin, A. Haeberlen, P. Druschel, B. Maggs, and B. Wishon. Reliable client accounting for p2p-infrastructure hybrids. In *Proc of NSDI'12*, pages 8–8, 2012.

[2] F. Dobrian, V. Sekar, A. Awan, I. Stoica, D. Joseph, A. Ganjam, J. Zhan, and H. Zhang. Understanding the impact of video quality on user engagement. In *Proc of the ACM SIGCOMM*, 2011.

[3] A. Haeberlen, P. Kouznetsov, and P. Druschel. Peerreview: Practical accountability for distributed systems. In *Proc of SOSP*, 2007.

[4] D. Kulinski and J. Burke. Ndn video: Live and prerecorded streaming over ndn. Technical report, Technical Report, The NDN Project Team, 2012.

[5] A. R. Yumerefendi and J. S. Chase. The role of accountability in dependable distributed systems. In *Proc of HotDep*, volume 5, pages 3–3, 2005.

Flash-Forward CCN: Flow-driven Forwarding Architecture for Content Centric Networks

Aytac Azgin, Ravishankar Ravindran, and Guoqiang Wang

Huawei Research Center, Santa Clara, CA, USA.

{aytac.azgin, ravi.ravindran, gq.wang}@huawei.com

ABSTRACT

Content-centric Networking (CCN) promises significant advantages over the current Internet architecture by replacing its host-centric design with a content-centric one, and enabling in-network caching and name-based forwarding. However, despite its advantages, wire-speed forwarding in CCN remains a challenge, as CCN uses stateful forwarding and requires lookups on packets carrying hierarchically structured and variable-length content names. As a result, storage and computing requirements to support name-based forwarding in CCN determines the forwarding capacity.

In this paper, to address the forwarding scalability concerns in CCN, we propose an overlay forwarding architecture that utilizes a flow-driven adaptive forwarding strategy and tradeoffs between flexibility and scalability. The proposed architecture exploits the correlations in user traffic to create active flow states in content routers to bypass the default CCN forwarding for future requests.

1. INTRODUCTION

Information-centric Networking (ICN) is a new networking paradigm that addresses the shortcomings of the current Internet architecture by shifting the focus from host-centric communication model to a content-centric one [1]. ICN uses a unique naming convention to name the content, which represents the main driving force for information dissemination. ICN architectures are uniquely defined by how they handle *naming* and *name resolution*. Our research focuses on the Content-centric Networking (CCN) architecture [2], which uses hierarchically structured names, and addresses one of its major challenges, scalable forwarding [3].

CCN relies on the pull model to acquire content, with client sending explicit requests (*i.e.*, Interest*s*) for the named content (*i.e.*, Data). Interests are forwarded using name-based forwarding, with each Content Router (CR) resolving content name to an outgoing interface by performing lookups on the forwarding information base (FIB) (if no match is found in the Content Store (CS)). As FIB size is expected to scale to hundreds of millions of entries, or more, in CCN, accessing FIB entries in a timely manner to support forwarding at line speeds of 100Gbps or higher becomes a critical concern. As FIB access requires the use of longest prefix matching (LPM), false positives limit the efficiency of LPM. Furthermore, since FIB is implemented on the high-latency off-chip memory, accessing those entries and making a forwarding decision can easily take hundreds (or thousands) of processing cycles [4]. The above problem is exacerbated if the router regularly receives packets leading to many false-positive triggered checks, for instance, in the case of end-to-end content flows that can generate hundreds or thousands of requests during the lifetime of a flow.

To efficiently address the scalable forwarding problem in CCN, we need approaches that are capable of switching an incoming packet over the matching outgoing interface after parsing the header, instead of performing lookups locally. In this paper, we present one such approach, which supports flow-based fast forwarding for CCN.

2. PROPOSED ARCHITECTURE

The proposed flow-driven forwarding solution limits the number of lookups performed on an end-to-end basis by enabling the bypassing of certain hops along the path to the content source. For that purpose, we make use of the previously made *local* forwarding decisions to speed up the processing of Interests. To support *hop-bypassing*, we include three additional fields in the Interest header (as shown in Figure 1), namely the Flow-State (FS) field, the Forwarding Segment Label (FSL) field, and the Flow-Hash (FH) field. FS indicates whether or not the Interest packet utilizes or takes advantage of flow state information, and if it is, the status for the flow.[1] FH is used to identify the flow as assigned by the Producer. Variable-sized FSL carries the related fast-forwarding information, *i.e.*, number of hops using Hop-Count (HC) field, and forwarding interface list, using a sequence of forwarding-component size (F-CS) and forwarding-interface value (F-IV) fields. F-CS represents the number of name components initially used by the local forwarder to find the outgoing interface towards the next hop, and F-IV identifies the outgoing interface value at the given hop. Note that, components included within the FSL are updated at each forwarding hop.[2]

---

[1] A bit-string of 00 indicates default *no-flow* state; 01 signals the need to set-up flow-states along the path; 11 indicates the presence of an active flow; and 10 signals the end of an active flow.

[2] For instance, HC is decremented at each hop, while the local forwarding parameters (F-CS and F-IV) are removed from the Interest before forwarding it to the next hop.

ICN'14, September 24–26, 2014, Paris, France.

ACM 978-1-4503-3206-4/14/09.

http://dx.doi.org/10.1145/2660129.2660163.

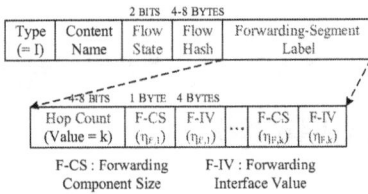

Figure 1: Proposed PDU format for the Interest.

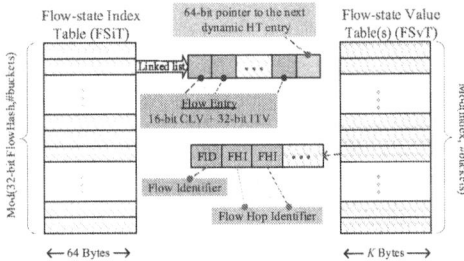

Figure 2: Structure of the flow state table.

To enable quick access to local flow states as opposed to directly accessing the FIB, we create a third database (in addition to Pending Interest Table (PIT) and FIB) referred to as the Flow State Table (FST) to contain all the active flow state information. The general structure for FST is shown in Figure 2, which uses compact array buckets to organize the flow table entries (as suggested in [4] for the FIB). FST is hierarchically structured to include two sub-tables: Flow-state Index Table (FSiT) and Flow-state Value Table (FSvT). FSiT is used to (i) check for the existence of entries, by locating with the initial 4-Byte portion of the FH, and matching Component-Length-Value (CLV) field [3], and, if the entry exists, (ii) locate the associated forwarding parameters using Index-Type-Value (ITV) field pointing to a matching entry in FSvT. Each FSvT entry consists of a Flow Identifier (FID) field (representing the last 4-Byte portion of FH and 2-Byte long outgoing interface metric), and multiple Flow Hop Identifier (FHI) fields (representing forwarding parameters for the future hops).[4] For each flow, forwarding parameters are stored within one of the available FSvT s (depending on the maximum allowed hop count).

To setup the flow states, Consumer sends the first Interest with FS set to 1, and FH equal 0. After the Interest is received by the Producer, Data delivery ensues along the reverse path, using CCN's breadcrumb approach. Data packet format is modified to enable flow table setup along the reverse path, by assigning the FH and setting the FS to 1. Each hop extracts the flow information from the Data to update its FST, while updating FSL within Data. After an FST is populated with active flow entries, forwarding lookup procedure follows the state flow diagram shown in Figure 3 (summarizing the steps after CS/PIT check, with no match).

To terminate an ongoing flow and clear the active flow-states at a CR, either (i) Consumer side sends an Interest with FS set to 2 [5], or (ii) Producer sends Data with FS set to

---

[3] CLV combines component and character length for the routable portion of content name extracted from the Data packet.

[4] FID is 6-Byte long, and FHI is 5-Byte long.

[5] If a flow's data is shared by multiple Consumers, then corresponding flow entries are placed into a pending state, and a timer

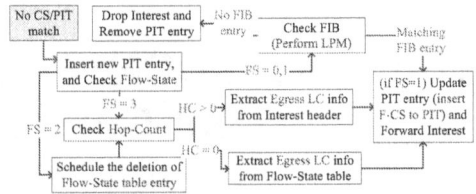

Figure 3: Modified forwarding lookup procedure at an FF-CCN router, based on FS/HC values.

2, requiring matching entries to be immediately flushed out from the routers along the reverse path to the Consumer.

3. PERFORMANCE ANALYSIS

We numerically analyzed the performance of our solution following the architecture considered in [4], which studied the performance of an optimized NDN forwarder implemented on an ISM-enabled ASR9000 router running on 2 multi-core 2GHz Xeon processors. We analyzed the overhead (consisting of parsing, hashing, PIT/CS lookup and/or insert or delete, and FIB lookup including reads from the high-latency off-chip memory) corresponding to Interest/Data processing, and approximated the ratio of FIB lookup, which can reach up to 60%.

We observe that by minimizing the need on FIB lookup or avoiding it whenever possible, which is possible with the proposed architecture, we can reduce the overall processing overhead for an Interest-Data pair by more than 44%, allowing a CCN router to almost double the number of packets it can process per second. Furthermore, with additional hardware support (i.e., on-chip Bloom filters to search for existing PIT/FIB entries), use of faster memory components to store the PIT entries, and overhead limited to memory access (which suggests that the majority of the overhead is due to FIB lookups), we observe 4-to-12 times performance (i.e., forwarding capacity) improvement. By also storing FST entries on faster memory components (due to smaller space requirements, e.g., same number of entries requires 70% less space with FST when compared to FIB), we can significantly reduce access time to flow entries (i.e., more than 5 times when compared to FIB access latency).

Lastly, we observe that significant energy savings are possible with the proposed architecture, with improvements proportional to active flow count, ratio of flow-based traffic, and line rate, to support green networking.

4. REFERENCES

[1] G. Xylomenos, C. Ververidis, V. Siris, N. Fotiou, C. Tsilopoulos, X. Vasilakos, K. Katsaros, and G. Polyzos, "A survey of information-centric networking research," 2013.

[2] V. Jacobson, D. K. Smetters, J. D. Thornton, M. F. Plass, N. H. Briggs, and R. L. Braynard, "Networking named content," in *ACM CoNEXT*, 2009.

[3] H. Yuan, T. Song, and P. Crowley, "Scalable ndn forwarding: Concepts, issues and principles," in *IEEE ICCCN*, 2012.

[4] S. Won, A. Narayanan, and D. Oran, "Named data networking on a router: Fast and DoS-resistant forwarding with hash tables," in *ACM/IEEE Symposium on Architectures for Networking and Communications Systems, ANCS'13*, 2013.

---

is started to initiate their purge, if no request is received during that period.

Demo Overview: Fully Decentralised Authentication Scheme for ICN in Disaster Scenarios (Demonstration on Mobile Terminals)

Jan Seedorf, Bilal Gill, and Dirk Kutscher
NEC Laboratories Europe
Heidelberg, Germany
jan.seedorf@neclab.eu,
bilal.gill@neclab.eu,
dirk.kutscher@neclab.eu

Benjamin Schiller and Dirk Kohlweyer
Technical University of Darmstadt
Darmstadt, Germany
schiller@cs.tu-darmstadt.de,
dirk@kohlweyer.net

ABSTRACT

Self-certifying names provide the property that any entity in a distributed system can verify the binding between a corresponding public key and the self-certifying name without relying on a trusted third party. However, self-certifying names lack a binding with a corresponding real-world identity. In this demonstration, we present the implementation of a concrete mechanism for using a Web-of-Trust in conjunction with self-certifying names to provide this missing binding. Our prototype runs on Android devices and demonstrates a decentralised message authentication scheme for any kind of content-oriented architecture. In the demonstration, we show how our proposed scheme performs—in terms of time needed to assess the trustworthiness of information retrieved—in a fully decentralised scenario: fragmented (mobile) networks. In such a scenario, connectivity to centralized authentication entities and Web-of-Trust key-servers is not available. Our scheme is hence executed solely on end-user terminals itself (which have limited processing capabilities).

1. INTRODUCTION

Self-certifying names provide the useful property that any entity in a distributed system can verify the binding between a corresponding public key and the self-certifying name without relying on a trusted third party [3]. This is normally achieved by basing the self-certifing name (in some way) on the pre-image resistant hash of the corresponding public key. Self-certifying names are very useful for addressing the security requirements in *Information Centric Networking (ICN)* architectures: Any source can append a public key and a digital signature (computed with the corersponding private key) to a data item which belongs to a self-certifying name, and any intermediate entity (e.g. an ICN-router/Cache) or any receiving entity (i.e. the issuer of an interest for the self-certifying name) can verify the signature with the received public key. The binding between public key and self-certifying name can be verified by anybody, without relying on a trusted third party or a *Public Key Infrastructure (PKI)*. There is thus no need to authenticate the identity of the host that caches an object; the approach does not follow today's *host-centric* security but is inline with ICN's

ICN'14, September 24–26, 2014, Paris, France.
ACM 978-1-4503-3206-4/14/09.
http://dx.doi.org/10.1145/2660129.2660130.

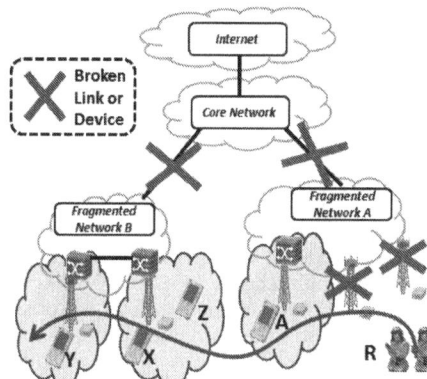

Figure 1: Mobile Network after Disaster with Fragmented Networks [5]

propagated *data-centric* security paradigm. Self-certifying names thus provide a decentralized form of data origin authentication and are very useful in ICN architectures. However, self-certifying names lack a binding with a so-called *Real-World Identity (RWI)* [4]: While the concept enables to verify that whoever signed some data was in possession of the private key associated with the self-certifying name, it does not provide any means to verify what real-world identity corresponds to the public/private key pair, i.e. who actually signed the data [4].

In this demonstration, we present our prototype implementation of a concrete mechanism we have proposed previously [5] for using a Web-of-Trust (WoT) in conjunction with self-certifying names to provide precisely this RWI-binding. We consider a decentralised scenario: fragmented (mobile) networks, where connectivity to centralized authentication entities and WoT keyservers is not available. Our approach enables a particular functionality in this scenario: The assessment of messages from previously unknown publishers. The demonstration will show a prototype running on Android devices.

2. DISASTER SCENARIO

Recently, ICN approaches are considered as a solution to enable communication after a disaster took place (e.g. a hurricane, earthquake, or tsunami) [6] [2]. In such a situation, it can be expected that parts of the communication infrastructure have broken down. The (formerly connected) network may be *fragmented* into several islands, e.g. due to failure of certain devices and communication links. Communication resources will be more limited than before the disaster, while at the same time it is important to efficiently distribute key disaster-related information (e.g. notifications from authorities, or critical rescue information to and among citizens) over the remaining functional parts of the communication infrastructure. One can assume that users (or rescue teams) can move among several of the fragmented network 'islands' over time, connecting each time to any functional network equipment in each 'visited' fragmented network. Given such a setting, decentralised authentication is challenging: In mobile networks, users are authenticated via central entities. Another challenge is the decentralised authentication of content retrieved from the network. Independent of the network being fixed or mobile, data origin authentication of content retrieved from the network is challenging when being 'offline', i.e. disconnected from servers of a security infrastructure such as a PKI [2].

Figure 1 [5] shows an example scenario of a mobile network after a disaster. Connectivity to the backbone or the Internet is broken, but certain parts of a mobile network infrastructure, e.g. base stations, are functional, forming small fragmented sub-networks. User A is in a different fragment than user X. Rescue teams (R) are moving across different network fragments, and may transport messages from one disconnected sub-network to another one in a DTN[1]-like routing/forwarding fashion.

3. HIGH-LEVEL OVERVIEW OF SCHEME

We have proposed a detailed scheme for decentralised message authentication in ICN in a previous publication [5]. Here we summarize our scheme on a very high level; we refer the reader to our previous publication [5] for a detailed description and analysis of our scheme. Our scheme is based on a *Web-of-Trust (WoT)*. In particular, a so-called 'WoT file' (which can be retrieved from a WoT keyserver before the disaster takes place) is being used by terminals. This file contains the verified certificate graph for the whole WoT in a compressed, machine-readable format. Terminals thus have the complete trust relationships within the WoT at their disposal, in the from of a 'WoT-graph' stored in a file.

The binding between self-certifying ICN names and a Web-of-Trust is achieved as follows (see [5] for a detailed naming scheme and message flow): The WoT key-ID is equivalent to the self-certifying name part used in the ICN naming scheme. This ties the self-certifying name with the ID of the correct public key in the WoT, and thus transitively with the RWI in the WoT (e.g. an email address of a user). When information is received as a response to a given request ('Interest' in CCNx jargon) for a certain name (which in ICN usually represents the publisher of the name in some form), a *distributed Breadth First Search (dBFS)* algorithm is executed on the WoT-graph to find *certificate chains* between the initiator of the request and the publisher of the content. Depending on a *trust metric* (see Section 4 for some examples) that is applied on the result of the *dBFS* algorithm, the information received is regarded as trustworthy or not by the initiator of the request.

4. DEMONSTRATION OUTLINE

The use case the demontration will show is *Assessing Warnings* (compare Fig. 1): A member of a mobile rescue team, R, is retrieving messages from citizens that publish warnings or other important information under a given name in a content-oriented architecture. R is disconnected from any central server or authentication infrastructure (i.e. R is 'offline'), so R needs to assess the trustworthiness of messages from unknown parties (e.g. X, Y), in order to decide whether to react immediately on a given message, or which messages to forward to authorities at the next encounter of

a new fragmented network. Note that the same use case occurs when R is not a member of a rescue team but an average user: Still assessment of information retrieved which has been published by potentially unknown parties is necessary. The demonstration will show how our scheme actually performs—for addressing the use case described above—in a completely decentralised fashion, i.e. running solely on terminals without any help from infrastructure nodes. It will exemplify how how the computation of several trust metrics scales with increasing WoT sizes, and how the scheme actually performs on common smartphones/tablets (depending on WoT-size and concrete trust metric, which both can be selected by the user of the demo).

To evaluate our approach on realistic large-scale WoT-files, we developed a methodology to synthesize WoT-graphs of arbitrary size that maintain several key graph theoretic properties as prevalent in the PGP Web-of-Trust. We implemented this WoT-model in the JAVA-based *Graph-Theoretic Analysis Framework GTNA* [1], such that WoT-graphs with arbitrary size can be generated that conform to degree distribution, path length distribution, and other key graph-theoretic properties as found in existing small-size PGP-graphs. Also, we implemented a *dBFS*-algorithm in *GTNA* for finding certificate chains on WoT-graphs. Furthermore, we implemented several trust metrics (a user-defined threshold for each metric decides whether a given WoT-node will be regarded as trustworthy or not): a) shortest certificate chain found, b) number of certificate chains found with maximum length, c) weighted certificate chain based on centrality-degree of intermediate nodes in the WoT-graph.

The demonstration will feature an Android-based terminal on which artificially-generated large-scale Web-of-Trust graphs will have been pre-loaded in the form of 'WoT files'. The terminal executes our implementation of the scheme on a given WoT-graph. In the demo, the user can choose among various trust metrics and parameters, as well as the WoT network size. Then, a publisher and retriever of information are randomly choosen from the WoT-graph; algorithm-execution, time, and other performance indicators are visualised to the user. The user can thus get a feeling of how the scheme actually performs (i.e. how much time it takes) on real devices depending on WoT-size and trust metric.

Acknowledgment: This work has been partially supported by the GreenICN project, a research project supported jointly by the European Commission under its 7th Framework Program (contract no. 608518) and the National Institute of Information and Communications Technology (NICT) in Japan (contract no. 167).

5. REFERENCES

[1] "Gtna - graph-theoretic network analyzer," website. [Online]. Available: https://www.p2p.tu-darmstadt.de/research/gtna/

[2] M. Arumaithurai, J. Seedorf, A. Tagami, K. Ramakrishnan, and N. B. Melazzi, "Using icn in disaster scenarios," Internet Engineering Task Force, Internet-Draft draft-seedorf-icn-disaster-02, June 2014, work in progress. [Online]. Available: http://tools.ietf.org/html/draft-seedorf-icn-disaster-02

[3] T. Aura, "Cryptographically generated addresses (cga)," in *Proc. of Information Security, 6th International Conference, ISC 2003*, ser. LNCS, Springer, Ed., no. 2851, October 2003, pp. 29–43.

[4] A. Ghodsi, T. Koponen, J. Rajahalme, P. Sarolahti, and S. Shenker, "Naming in content-oriented architectures," in *Proceedings of the ACM SIGCOMM Workshop on Information-centric Networking*, 2011, pp. 1–6.

[5] J. Seedorf, D. Kutscher, and F. Schneider, "Decentralised binding of self-certifying names to real-world identities for assessment of third-party messages in fragmented mobile networks," in *2nd Workshop on Name Oriented Mobility (NOM)*, 2014.

[6] G. Tyson, E. Bodanese, J. Bigham, and A. Mauthe, "Beyond content delivery: Can icns help emergency scenarios?" *IEEE Network (to appear)*, 2014.

---

[1]Delay Tolerant Networking

Demo Overview: Reliable Contents Retrieval in Fragmented ICNs for Disaster Scenario

Tomohiko Yagyu
NEC Corporation
Kawasaki, Japan
yagyu@cp.jp.nec.com

Shuya Maeda
NEC Solution Innovators Ltd.
Hiroshima, Japan
maeda-sxb@necst.nec.co.jp

ABSTRACT

Aftermath of disaster, e.g., earthquake, existing communication infrastructure such as cellular networks will be severely damaged. A large number of user terminals suffer disconnection from central servers. Due to the fault of BaseStations(BS) and cable cut between BS and Backhaul, network is fragmented into portions. Because of the novel capabilities such as name-based communication and in-network caching, Information Centric Networking (ICN) is one of the promising technologies to support reliable communication among such fragmented parts of network. This demo presents dynamic name-based routing and reliable contents retrieval among fragmented networks with NDN (Named Data Networking) architecture in the context of disaster situation.

Categories and Subject Descriptors

C.2 [Computer-Communication Networks]: Network Architecture and Design, Network Protocols

Keywords

Information Centric networking; Fragmented networks; Disaster recovery; DSDVN;

1. INTRODUCTION

Named Data Networking (NDN)[1] is one of the promising ICN architectures. Name based communication is useful not only in ordinary cases but also in disaster cases. Aftermath of disaster, existing communication infrastructure such as the Internet and cellular networks will be severly damaged. If DNS (Domain Name Syatem) becomes unavailable, users can't access URL or FQDN at all. With ICN, the victims can retrieve desired information without resolving server's IP address. However, current NDN architecture basically assumes well connected networks such like wired or densely populated wireless networks. PIT entry is short-lived, e.g., a few seconds, and message arrival is not guaranteed. In case of disaster, due to the fault of BaseStations(BS) and

ICN'14, September 24–26, 2014, Paris, France.
ACM 978-1-4503-3206-4/14/09.
http://dx.doi.org/10.1145/2660129.2660131.

cable cut between BS and Backhaul, network will be fragmented into portions. We call thus partitioned network the fragmented network. To achieve reliable content retrieval in fragmented networks, we designed routing protocol and retransmission mechanism suitable for fragmented networks. We implemented proposed solution on top of CCNx [2] for the proof of concept.

2. PROPOSED SOLUTION

In the disaster case, a large number of people take refuge in shelters. Even if each shelter has a local network, it may not have connection to other sites. Hundreds of people share limited precious resources in a shelter. The motivation of our soluiton is to realize efficient and reliable content retrieval by NDN protocol in fragmented networks without congestion and waste of resources. Our solution comprises of two technologies, i.e., dynamic routing and retransmission control. Our proposed routing protocol has two roles in the solution. One is to establish route to name prefixes, another is to detect the state of connectivity in the networks. Proposed retransmission control achieves reliable message transmission via intermittent links. Unlink original NDN, our scheme employs hop by hop retransmission rather than retransmission by end nodes. This relies on long-lived PIT. Thanks to the routing protocol, intermittence of the routes toward the target name can be informed to end nodes. Therefore it is possible for end nodes to adjust lifetime of *Interest* (and PIT entry) in accordance with the network conditions. Though current solution uses fixed long lifetime, we will develop dynamic lifetime adjustment mechanism in future.

2.1 Routing protocol

We developed dynamic name-based routing protocol for fragmented networks, namely DSDVN. DSDVN is based on the wellknown adhoc routing protocol DSDV[3]. DSDV is a distance-vector protocol for MANET. We chose the distance-vector protocol to support fragmented networks rather than link state protocol (e.g., OLSR[4]) or reactive protocol (e.g., AODV[5]). There are two reasons as follows.

1) DSDV doesn't need to flood messages throughout the network. In fragmented networks, it is very hard for all nodes in the network to receive same message due to the intermittent connections. Unlike TC message in OLSR or RREQ message in AODV, DSDV has to inform only direct neighbors of its routing information. This mechanism is suitable for the fragmented networks.

2) It is easy to manage control overhead. In the disaster cases, it is a critical problem to minimize control over-

head due to the resource (bandwidth, energy, etc) shortage. Distance vector protocol can reduce control overhead with simple way, i.e., making message interval longer. It is also easy to estimate overhead because no control messages are forwarded beyond one hop away.

DSDVN extends DSDV to convey name prefix information in the routing message. In the fragmented networks, connection between nodes are intermittent. DSDVN has a role to manage the state of links ,i.e., *connected* or *disconnected,* with the potential neighbors. This status is set to *Face* in CCNx and utilized to control retransmission described in the next section. With DSDVN, even if the nexthop becomes *disconnected*, the routes remain valid for a while untill the node learns new valid routes from connected neighbors.

2.2 Retransmission control

To achieve reliable contents retrieval via intermittent links, it is useful to retransmit messages in hop by hop manner. On the other hand, restransmission of messages should be minimized to avoid network congestion and reduce energy consumption. For the disaster application, lifetime of *Interest* sent by end users should be much longer than that in ordinary case, e.g., 1 hour. While end users suppress retransmission, intermediate routers should be responsible for forwarding messages. Routers retransmits *Interest* iff PIT entry exists and status of *Face* of nexthop node is *connected*. Figure 1 shows a message sequence with proposed retransmission mechanism. In the figure, an end user sends *Interest* to the adjacent router (router1). Suppose that FIB entry toward the publisher is populated by DS-DVN in advance. The end user waits for the content for a long time. When router1 receives *Interst* from the user, it creates PIT entry and forwards the *Interest* to the nexthop (router2), then starts retransmission timer for it. Because the nexthop node toward the publisher (router2) is disconnected with router1, router1 suspends retransmission of *Interest* even if PIT entry exists. When router2 is connected with router1, router1 resumes retransmission until *ContentObject* is received. When router2 received *Interest* from router1, it also creates PIT entry and starts retransmission timer. When router2 goes away from router1, router1 suspends retransmission again. When router2 moves close to the publisher (nexthop in FIB entry), router2 retransmits the *interest* and receives *ContentObject* from the publisher. Although router2 tries to forward *ContentObject* to router1 based on the PIT entry, it fails beacuse router1 is disconnected. As NDN principle, *ContentObject* is not retransmiited to avoid waste of resources. Router2 caches the content and removes PIT entry. When router2 is connected with router1 again, router1 retransmits *Interest* to router2. Then router2 replies *ContentObject* because it cached the content. Router1 forwards *ContentObject* to the user based on the PIT entry.

3. DEMO SETUP

This demo shows dynamic routing and content retrieval via *DataMule*. The fragmented network in demo is emulated with our wireless network emulator. Figure 2 shows the setup of this demonstration. There are six nodes in this scenario. *Gov.Office* has the repository and provides some contents for refugees in shelters. *Gov.Office* periodically advertises route information for the name-prefix *ccnx* : *//government* by DSDNV. The route information

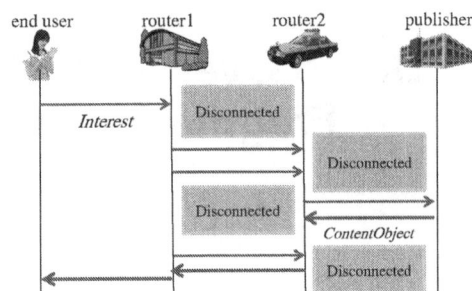

Figure 1: Message sequence

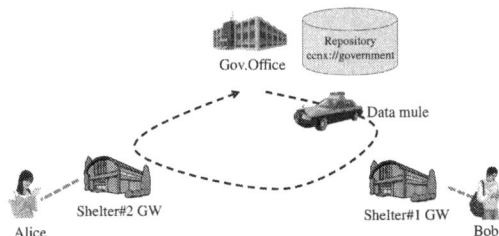

Figure 2: Demo Setup

is propagated to *DataMule* and *GWs*. There are two shelters in the region. *GWs* provide wireless access (e.g., WiFi) to persons,e.g., *Alice* and *Bob*, in the shelters. *Gov.Office* and *GWs* are fragmented due to the damage to the communication infrastructure. *DataMule* is a vehicle mounted ICN router on. *DataMule* conveys messages and contents between *Gov. Office* and persons in shelters. The demonstration shows that *Alice* and *Bob* can retreive map information from the repository in *Gov.Office* via *DataMule*.

4. CONCLUSIONS

In this demo we show our proposed solution which achieves reliable contents retrieval in fragmented ICNs. We designed routing protocol and retransmission mechanism suitable for fragmented network with intermittent connections. This approach enables victims in disaster area to retrieve desired information without frequent retransmission of *Interest*, namely less consuming battery in their terminals.

5. ACKNOWLEDGMENT

The work for this paper was partly performed in the FP7/ NICT EU-JAPAN GreenICN project.

6. REFERENCES

[1] V.Jacobson, D.Smetters, J.Thorton, M.Plass, N.Briggs, and R.Braynard, "Networking Named Content," in Proc. ACM CoNEXT 2009, Dec. 2009, pp.1-12.

[2] CCNx implementation, http://www.ccnx.org/

[3] C. Perkins and P. Bhagwat, Highly dynamic destination sequeneced distance vector routing (DSDV) for mobile comptuers, In proc. ACM SIGCOMM pp.234-244,1994.

[4] T. Clausen and P. Jacquet, Optimized Link State Routing (OLSR), IETF RFC 3626, 2003

[5] C. Perkins, E. Belding-Royer and S. Das, Ad hoc On-Demand Distance Vector (AODV) Routing, IETF RFC 3561, 2003

Demonstrating a Unified ICN Development and Evaluation Framework

Alina Quereilhac
alina.quereilhac@inria.fr

Damien Saucez
damien.saucez@inria.fr

Priya Mahadevan
priya.mahadevan@parc.com

Thierry Turletti
thierry.turletti@inria.fr

Walid Dabbous
walid.dabbous@inria.fr

ABSTRACT

Information-Centric Networking solutions target world-wide deployment in the Internet. It is hence necessary to dispose of a development and evaluation environment which enables both controllable and realistic experimentation to thoroughly understand how ICN solutions would behave in real life deployment. In this demonstration, we present an ICN development and evaluation framework that combines emulation and live prototyping environments to provide ICN designers and implementers the means to build "beyond-prototype" ICN solutions. We will demonstrate the benefits of such integrated approach by showing how complete experimental studies can be carried out with minimum manual intervention and experiment set-up overhead, in both emulation and live environments.

Categories and Subject Descriptors

C.4 [**Computer-Communication Networks**]: Performance of Systems

Keywords

ICN evaluation, emulation, NEPI, PlanetLab, ns-3/DCE

1. THE NEED FOR EMULATION AND LIVE EVALUATION IN ICN

Simulators and models are at the basis of ICN design and allow to rapidly estimate the impact of new algorithms and strategies. Nevertheless, ICN aims at being deployed in real networks and targets large-scale adoption. In this sense, live deployment offers a rapid feedback on the workability of ICN solutions as it permits to confront hypothesis with the reality. However, since it relies on the usage of real resources, the scalability of live deployment is bounded by physical resource availability. Furthermore, it is also more difficult to debug and isolate faults in real environments due to their uncontrolled nature. Conversely, emulators, offering a less realistic but controllable environment, permit to

ICN'14, Sept 24-26 2014, Paris, France.
ACM 978-1-4503-3206-4/14/09.
http://dx.doi.org/10.1145/2660129.2660132.

observe the behavior of ICN in larger-scale scenarios or under specific conditions which might be difficult to produce in live environments.

Emulation and live deployment are complementary techniques, as they permit to evaluate a same ICN solution from different angles. However, while it exists a plethora of simulators, emulators, and testbeds to evaluate ICN networking models [2, 9, 3, 5, 10, 4], using any of theses approaches in a same study or software development process is non trivial since it requires to manually re-map experiments from one environment to another. We advocate that, for the success of ICN, the community must dispose of a framework to easily use both emulation and real deployment in an integrated and interchangeable way.

Ideally, such framework should reduce to its minimum the burden caused by manual experiment setup (e.g., installing software, configuring the emulator or machines in the testbed), and simplify the transition from emulation to live deployment and vice versa. Furthermore, it should allow easy modeling of a wide range of experiment scenarios, provide a simple way of debugging experiments through adequate instrumentation, and facilitate gathering statistically meaningful data.

2. A FRAMEWORK FOR ICN DEVELOPMENT AND EVALUATION

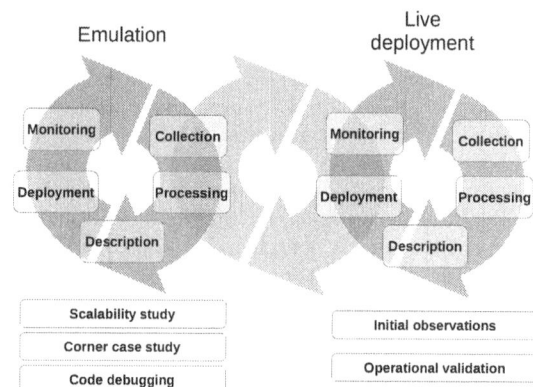

Figure 1: **Iterations between Emulation and Live deployment as means of developing ICN software.**

The past 30 years of research in the field of the Internet have shown that moving from a lab prototype to a deployable implementation is far from being trivial and requires substantial implementation efforts (coding, testing, and debugging). Emulation and live deployment play complementary roles in the development and evaluation of ICN solutions. Interchanging live deployment and emulation is hence a way to take the best of the two worlds. Both approaches can be combined in a same iterative development process, which can be employed to produce robust ICN software from a lab prototype, as depicted in Fig. 1.

With the objective of simplifying the adoption of such development process, we propose a framework for ICN development featuring adequate abstractions to automate the five fundamental steps of experimentation, independently of the target evaluation environment. These steps are: a) scenario *description*, b) experiment *deployment*, c) experiment *monitoring*, and d) result *collection* and e) *processing*.

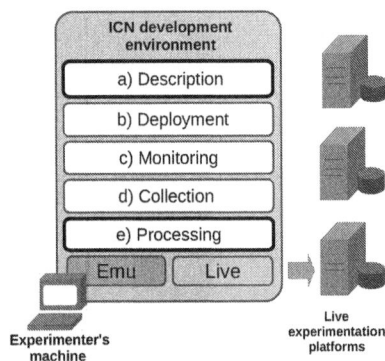

Figure 2: Components of the ICN development and evaluation environment, combining emulation and live evaluation in a unified framework.

Our framework extends the *Network Experimentation Programming Interface* (NEPI) [7, 1] and leverages on, but is not limited to, the ns-3 simulator tool and its direct code execution emulation extension (DCE) [2, 8], and the live deployment Planetlab testbed [4]. We use DCE as it allows to run real application binaries in ns-3, which means that the exact same code can be used in both the emulation environment as well as in live deployment experiments. Fig. 2 summarizes the architecture of our framework.

From the five experimentation steps, only a) and e) require user intervention, while b), c) and d) are resolved by the framework. Based on a scenario description provided by the user, our framework automates experiment deployment, monitoring and data collection. Statistically meaningful data can be gathered by requesting the framework to automatically repeat steps b) through e) a fixed number of times, or until a criteria specified by the user is met (e.g., convergence of a given metric estimator).

3. DEMONSTRATION

In this demonstration we focus on how to implement experiments using our framework. To this end, we first show how to describe experiments independently of the execution environment, using a graph abstraction. We then show how to use NEPI resource modeling primitives to translate an abstract experiment description into an executable scenario for a concrete target environment. We additionally explore the primitives used to deploy and monitor experiments, and

to collect data generated during experiment execution. Furthermore, since one of the usual questions that arises when performing experimental studies is the number of experiment runs to carry out, we show how the framework can be used to automatically re-run an experiment until it determines that the number of runs is sufficient to cover the variability of the studied system. Finally, we show how, thanks to the ability to execute the same application binaries on PlanetLab and DCE environments alike, results generated for a same scenario in either environment have exactly the same format, and thus the obtained data can be processed using the same data processing functions defined by the user. This feature renders comparability of results between emulated and live scenarios feasible.

The demonstration is articulated around three variations of the same content retrieval scenario using CCNx [6]. The first two variants show how, thanks to our framework, it is possible to execute the same scenario in two different environments (i.e., live and emulated), performing only simple changes in the experiment description. The third variant shows how, with almost no extra effort, a scenario can be scaled in size or its topology modified.

All the material presented in this demonstration is available at http://nepi.inria.fr/.

4. REFERENCES

[1] Nepi: Network experiment programming interface. http://nepi.inria.fr.

[2] The ns-3 network simulator. http://www.nsnam.org/.

[3] A. Afanasyev, I. Moiseenko, and L. Zhang. ndnSIM: NDN simulator for NS-3. Technical Report NDN-0005, NDN, October 2012.

[4] B. Chun, D. Culler, T. Roscoe, A. Bavier, L. Peterson, M. Wawrzoniak, and M. Bowman. Planetlab: an overlay testbed for broad-coverage services. In *SIGCOMM '03*, volume 33, pages 3–12, New York, NY, USA, July 2003. ACM Press.

[5] N. Handigol, B. Heller, V. Jeyakumar, B. Lantz, and N. McKeown. Reproducible network experiments using container-based emulation. In *CoNEXT*, pages 253–264, New York, NY, USA, 2012. ACM.

[6] V. Jacobson, D. K. Smetters, J. D. Thornton, M. F. Plass, N. H. Briggs, and R. L. Braynard. Networking named content. CT, pages 1–12, New York, NY, USA, 2009. ACM.

[7] A. Quereilhac, C. Freire, M. Lacage, T. Turletti, and W. Dabbous. Nepi: An integration framework for network experimentation. SoftCOM, pages 1–5, 2011.

[8] H. Tazaki, F. Uarbani, E. Mancini, M. Lacage, D. Camara, T. Turletti, and W. Dabbous. Direct code execution: Revisiting library os architecture for reproducible network experiments. CoNEXT, pages 217–228, New York, NY, USA, 2013. ACM.

[9] A. Varga and R. Hornig. An overview of the omnet++ simulation environment. Simutools, pages 60:1–60:10, ICST, Brussels, Belgium, 2008.

[10] B. White, J. Lepreau, L. Stoller, R. Ricci, S. Guruprasad, M. Newbold, M. Hibler, C. Barb, and A. Joglekar. An integrated experimental environment for distributed systems and networks. In *OSDI*, pages 255–270, Boston, MA, Dec. 2002.

CCN Simulators: Analysis and Cross-Comparison

Michele Tortelli*, Dario Rossi†, Gennaro Boggia*, Luigi Alfredo Grieco*
*Politecnico di Bari, Bari, Italy - first.last@poliba.it
†Telecom ParisTech, Paris, France - first.last@telecom-paristech.fr

ABSTRACT

This demo focuses on the cross-comparison of CCN simulators available as open source software. The aim is to start a quantitative evaluation of the accuracy, coherence, as well as scalability of software tools available for CCN, in order to understand their boundaries and check if they achieve consistent results. The demo process consists of showing results produced by the tracing systems of each simulator using an interactive parallel coordinate graph, which allows different metrics to be shown at the same time. Both the consistency of simulation results and the differences between several combinations of forwarding strategies, cache replacements policies, and network settings can be verified by users that can interact by proposing and reproducing their own scenario in more than one simulator.

Categories and Subject Descriptors

D.2.4 [**Software Engineering**]: Software/Program Verification—*validation*; D.2.8 [**Software Engineering**]: Metrics—*performance measures*.

Keywords

Information Centric Networks; Open-Source Software; Simulation; Performance Evaluation;

1. INTRODUCTION

The relevance that Information Centric Networking (ICN) has gained inside the research community over the last years is confirmed by the number of architectural proposals that go under its umbrella, which are surveyed in [4], as well as by the number of tools (i.e., prototypes, emulators, simulators) released as open source software, which are surveyed in a technical report available at [1].

This demo is motivated by the main findings presented in [1], which complements the qualitative description of the different ICN architectures done in [4]. In particular, in [1] the authors highlight that half of the ICN software tools

are related to a specific architecture, that is Content Centric Networking (CCN) [3], while the other half is divided between 5 different architectures. Furthermore, CCN is the only architecture that presents a complete software ecosystem, including prototypes, emulators and simulators, which represent the majority among them, while most of the ICN tool set is composed by prototypes. This means that, at this stage, the comparison of different strategies within the CCN architecture, combined with a cross-comparison of simulators that are specifically designed for that, is feasible (multiple tools are available) and relevant (increasing attention is dedicated to CCN). A cross-comparison of two or more ICN architectures, instead, would be far more complex and resource expensive, both because of the absence of a software tool that embraces more than a single architecture, and because of the need to set up and run real experiments.

The predominance of simulators as the main software tool for CCN is justified by the fact that, despite the relevance that real experiments have in the standardization process of a new architecture, they guarantee a good compromise between cost and complexity. But even considering only simulators for CCN, only a few common set of features and algorithms is shared between all of them [1]. Therefore, a comparison of different strategies would often require the use of different simulators, whose results need to be validated through a rigorous cross-comparison. Indeed, starting from the implementation of the same scenario in different simulators, the accuracy and the consistency of results can be validated, thus allowing users to choose a specific simulator according to their needs and scenario of interest. Furthermore, the cross-comparison of software tools in terms of accuracy and consistency finds its motivation also in the literature, where, not rarely, discrepancies are found across multiple tools when reproducing the same scenario [2, 5].

The goal of this demo is to provide users a tool to verify the consistency of results produced by different simulators (e.g., by simulating the same scenario in more than one simulator), as well as to compare the performance of different combinations of forwarding strategies, cache replacement policies, cache decision policies, and other parameters. In practice, using an interactive parallel coordinate graphs, which let us show different metrics at the same time, users can: (i) use the mouse to scroll through results obtained using a predefined set of simulations, thus highlighting and showing up statistics of the ones they are interested in; (ii) propose different and new scenarios that will be simulated in real time using a connection with a remote server, on which

ICN'14, September 24–26, 2014, Paris, France.
ACM 978-1-4503-3206-4/14/09.
http://dx.doi.org/10.1145/2660129.2660133.

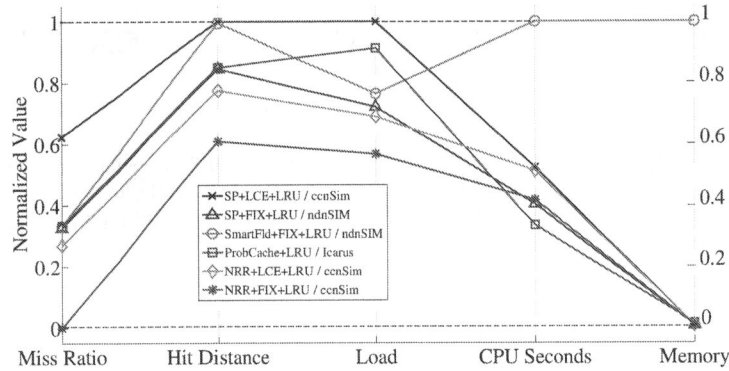

Figure 1: Comparison of the three CCN simulators through different strategies.

all the simulators are installed, thus adding new lines to the interactive parallel coordinate graph.

2. DEMO SOFTWARE

In this section a more detailed description of the demo software is presented, introducing the available simulators, the monitored metrics and the interactive way they are presented to the users.

2.1 Simulators and Parameter Set

After having surveyed the open source software tools for ICN, the authors in [1] provide a brief overview of the CCN simulators, showing their main features in terms of available cache replacement strategies, cache decision policies, forwarding strategies, application levels, and so on. Following their description, three CCN simulators have been chosen to be included inside the demo software. In particular, these simulators are *ndnSIM*, *ccnSim*, *Icarus* (a detailed description is reported in [1]).

During the demo, users can perform simulations by combining different parameters chosen from the main ones reported in Tab. 1; furthermore, they can propose their own scenario by changing other settings, like the simulated network, the content catalog cardinality, the cache to catalog ratio, and so on.

Table 1: Tuneable Features of available CCN Simulators

	Cache Replacement	Decision policy	Forwarding strategy
ndnSIM	LRU,LFU FIFO,RND	LCE,FIX	SP FLD variants BestRoute
ccnSim	LRU,LFU FIFO,RND	LCE,FIX LCD,BTW ProbCache	SP FLD variants NRR
Icarus	LRU,LFU FIFO,RND	LCE,FIX LCD,BTW ProbCache,HR	SP HR variants

LCE = Leave Copy Everywhere, FIX=Fixed probability
LCD=Leave Copy Down, BTW=Betweness
HR=HashRouting, FLD=Flooding
SP=ShortestPath, NRR=Nearest Replica Routing

2.2 Metric Definition and Representation

The performance metrics that the demo software is set to gather from each simulator are representative of the performance of the simulated CCN strategy (i.e., the combination of cache replacement, cache decision policy, and forwarding

strategy), as well as of the performance of the simulators themselves. In particular, they include: mean *miss ratio*, calculated as 1-*hit ratio*, mean *hit distance*, expressed in number of hops needed to satisfy an Interest packet, and *network load*, expressed in terms of total number of packets (both Interest and Data) generated inside the network. To quantify the performance of each simulator, instead, two metrics are shown: the *CPU seconds* and the *Memory usage*.

The aforementioned metrics will be shown during the demo using an interactive parallel graph, an example of which is reported in Fig. 1. Here the collected metrics are reported after having them normalied with the respective maximum observed values. It is worth to specify that the miss ratio is calculated as 1-*normalized hit ratio* (so the most performing strategy could provide a zero miss ratio). Furthermore, a zero memory consumption for some strategies reported in Fig. Fig. 1 is due to the normalization with the far greater memory consumption value of ndnSIM in that scenario.

This kind of graph permits to have a view of all the metrics at the same time, and its interactivity relates to the possibility that users have to simulate new scenarios, and/or to highlight particular curves using the mouse, in order to read the corresponding scenario and have information about the main settings related to that scenario.

Acknowledgements

This work has been carried out at LINCS *http://www.lincs.fr*

3. REFERENCES

[1] http://telematics.poliba.it/images/file/tortelli/icn-2014.pdf.

[2] S. Jansen and A. McGregor. Performance, validation and testing with the network simulation cradle. In *IEEE MASCOTS*, 2006.

[3] V. Jacobson et al. Networking Named Content. In *ACM CoNEXT*, 2009.

[4] G. Xylomenos et al. A survey of information-centric networking research. *Communication Surveys and Tutorials, IEEE*, 16(2), 2014.

[5] A. Stetsko, M. Stehlik, and V. Matyas. Calibrating And Comparing Simulators for Wireless Sensor Networks. In *IEEE MASS*, 2011.

A High Speed Information-Centric Network in a Mobile Backhaul Setting

Diego Perino*, Massimo Gallo*, Roger Boislaigue*, Leonardo Linguaglossa‡
Matteo Varvello*, Giovanna Carofiglio*, Luca Muscariello±, Zied Ben Houidi*
* Bell Labs, Alcatel-Lucent, first.last@alcatel-lucent.com, ‡ INRIA, first.last@inria.com
± Orange, first.last@orange.com

ABSTRACT

We demonstrate a high speed Information-Centric Network in a mobile backhaul setting. Specifically, we show the feasibility of an information aware data plane and we highlight the significant benefits it provides in terms of both user experience and network provider cost in the backhaul setting. Our setup consists of high-speed ICN devices employed in a down-scaled realistic representation of a mobile backhaul topology, fed with traffic workloads characterized from Orange's mobile network.

Categories and Subject Descriptors

C.2.1 [**Network Architecture and Designs**]: Network communications; C.2.6 [**Internetworking**]: Routers

General Terms

Design, Implementation, Experiments

Keywords

ICN, forwarding, router, architecture,protocols.

1. INTRODUCTION

Internet traffic and especially its mobile variant are rapidly increasing. As an example, mobile traffic is growing at the incredible rate of about 66% every year in the timeframe 2012-2017. On the one hand, this growth is driven by the radical terminal evolution; on the other hand, it is due to a shift of Internet usage from *host-centric* to *information-centric*. The Internet is not used anymore as a medium to connect machines or hosts, but rather to connect people with content they are interested in.

Since such radical shift in Internet usage was not followed by an architectural change, inefficiencies quickly arose. Many of them are especially noticeable in the mobile network segment. They translate into difficulties in dynamic content-to-location mapping, mobility management, multicasting, multipath and multi-homing.

ICN'14, September 24–26, 2014, Paris, France.
ACM 978-1-4503-3206-4/14/09.
http://dx.doi.org/10.1145/2660129.2660134.

Application layer solutions and bandwidth over provisioning have been so far the ways to mask such inefficiencies.

From a technical perspective, realizing efficient data delivery without capacity over-dimensioning demands for a flexible and adaptive traffic control coupled with in-network caching. However, due to the host centric nature of today's network architecture, there is a lack of mechanisms that natively perform dynamic and flexible information aware traffic control. This situation is even worse in mobile backhauls whereby, for mobility management reasons, the traffic is tunneled between backhaul ingress/egress nodes (*i.e.*, eNodeB and Service Gateway).

We believe that Information-centric Networking (ICN) provides a natural answer to such needs by rethinking network data delivery around content/information. ICN introduces a connection-less name-based transport model, enables in-network caching and multi-point to multi-point communication.

In this demonstration, we build a high-speed prototype of an information aware data plane spanning an entire network, including content consumers and content producers. To provide evidence of the ICN benefits in a realistic use case, our setting is based on a down-scaled mobile backhaul topology, and traffic workloads characterized from Orange's mobile network.

2. INFORMATION AWARE DATA PLANE

This section describes the information aware data plane we implemented for this demonstration. Specifically: i) we enrich the original ICN data plane defined in [2] with forwarding, traffic control and caching mechanisms described in the following sections; ii) we propose a design to realize an ICN data plane at high-speed. Our solution remains compatible with current Internet architecture and can be integrated in existing network equipment.

2.1 Request Routing and Forwarding

ICN nodes forward user requests by name and in a hop-by-hop fashion towards a permanent copy of the requested content item. To this goal, every node has a name-based forwarding table, the FIB, that associates one or more potential next hops towards a set of content items. We developed a dynamic forwarding algorithm [1] that selects a next forwarding hop while achieving optimal throughput and minimum network cost. ICN nodes also keep track of received requests in order to return content chunks to the user following the reverse request path. This functionality is achieved via a pending request table, also called PIT.

2.2 Pull Based Connection-less Transport

Data transfer is triggered by user requests addressed to chunks of the requested content item, *i.e.*, pull based model. Rate and congestion control are performed at the end user by mean of a connection-less, yet stateful transport protocol. The receiver process maintains a pipeline of requests whose size is controlled by a window-based *AIMD* mechanism. For the demonstration, we implement the congestion control mechanism we proposed in [1] which realizes remote active queue management, based on the estimate of round trip delay per route. This protocol optimally allocates bandwidth resources among users in a fair and efficient fashion [1].

2.3 In Network Caching

In an ICN network, requests for the same data are served in network with no need to fetch any bytes from the original server/repository. Also, packet losses can be recovered in network, with no need for the sender to identify and retransmit the lost packet.

ICN's content-awareness enables a novel usage of buffers at the network nodes. In ICN, buffers are used to absorb input/output rate unbalance, as in today's IP networks, but also to cache in-transit data. Storage resources can also be added to a router augmenting its caching capabilities. We call content store, or CS, the data structure enabling caching at an ICN node.

2.4 System Design

To integrate ICN mechanisms within today's Internet architecture, we deploy ICN as an overlay over IP.

Several network devices currently employed in the Internet architecture are based on programmable elements, e.g., network processors. It is thus possible to integrate ICN mechanisms, name-based forwarding and caching, via simple firmware upgrades with no need to install ad-hoc hardware. We implement the required data structures, namely PIT, FIB and CS, and associated lookup algorithms following the design guidelines proposed in our previous work [3, 5, 4]. In addition, we implement the dynamic request forwarding scheme presented in [1].

End-host mechanisms like rate or congestion control can be implemented either at proxies co-located with network elements, or at the application layer directly at the end user. In this demonstration, we implement the multipath congestion-control algorithm described in [1] as an application over UDP/IP.

3. DEMONSTRATION

The demonstration platform consists of: i) a content router testbed, with a set of hardware nodes running the ICN data plane described above; ii) custom application layer data retrieval/server implementations running on general purpose servers.

For the demonstration, we realize the network topology shown in Figure 1, which is a representative down-scaled model of a mobile backhaul topology. To this end, we use hardware traffic shapers and L2 tunneling between physical boards. ICN content requests are generated by a generic data retrieval application that uses the end-host congestion controller described above. The workload we use for our demonstration follow a traffic profile characterized from Orange mobile network traces.

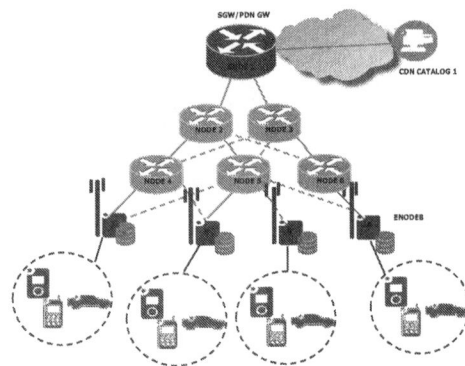

Figure 1: Down-scaled backhaul model topology used in the demonstration.

With the above described demonstration setup, we show the advantages of adopting an ICN data plane in this scenario, by enabling and disabling ICN functionalities. We compare our solution with the technology currently deployed in the mobile backhaul, characterized by IP tunnels between ingress/egress nodes (*i.e.*, 3GPP standard), in terms of both user experience and network provider costs.

4. CONCLUSION

In this demonstration we have focused on a high speed Information-Centric Network in a mobile backhaul setting. The demonstration shows that the introduction of an ICN data plane is feasible and scalable Also ICN significantly reduces the content delivery time which improves end-user experience. Last but not least, ICN largely reduces the traffic load on the mobile backhaul with relevant bandwidth, and hence cost, savings.

ACKNOWLEDGMENTS

This work has been partially carried out in the framework of the common research laboratory between INRIA and Bell Labs, Alcatel-Lucent.

5. REFERENCES

[1] G. Carofiglio, M. Gallo, L. Muscariello, M. Papalini, and S. Wang. Optimal multipath congestion control and request forwarding in information-centric networks. In *proc. of ICNP*, 2013.

[2] V. Jacobson, D. K. Smetters, J. D. Thronton, M. F. Plass, N. H. Briggs, and R. L. Braynard. Network Named Content. In *proc. of ACM CoNext*, Rome, Italy, Dec. 2009.

[3] D. Perino and M. Varvello. A reality check for content centric networking. In *proc. of ACM Sigcomm ICN workshop*, Toronto, Canada, Aug. 2011.

[4] D. Perino, M. Varvello, L. Linguaglossa, R. Laufer, and R. Boislaigue. Caesar: A content router for high-speed forwarding on content names. In *proc. of ACM/IEEE ANCS*, Los Angeles, CA, USA, 2014.

[5] M. Varvello, D. Perino, and L. Linguaglossa. On the design and implementation of a wire-speed pending interest table. In *proc. of IEEE Infocom NOMEN workshop*, Turin, Italy, Aug. 2013.

Analyzing Cacheability in the Access Network with HACkSAw

Claudio Imbrenda
Orange Labs
claudio.imbrenda@orange.com

Luca Muscariello
Orange Labs
luca.muscariello@orange.com

Dario Rossi
Telecom ParisTech
dario.rossi@enst.fr

ABSTRACT

Web traffic is growing, and the need for accurate traces of HTTP traffic is therefore also rising, both for operators and researchers, as accurate HTTP traffic traces allow to analyse and characterize the traffic and the clients, and to analyse the performance of the network and the perceived quality of service for the final users. Since most ICN proposals also advocate for pervasive caching, it's imperative to measure the cacheability of traffic to assess the impact and/or the potential benefits of such solutions. This demonstration will show a both a tool to collect HTTP traces that is both fast and accurate and that overcomes the limitations of existing tools, and a set of important statistics that can be computed in post processing, like aggregate/demultiplexed cacheability figures.

Categories and Subject Descriptors

C.2.3 [**COMPUTER-COMMUNICATION NETWORKS**]: Network Operations—*Network monitoring*

Keywords

Cacheability; caching; high performance; http analysis; live traffic monitoring

1. INTRODUCTION AND MOTIVATION

Web content is nowadays skyrocketing, causing significant additional infrastructure costs to network operators, therefore, an accurate characterization of the traffic and the users is a fundamental prerequisite for strategic decisions. Moreover, most ICN proposals advocate for pervasive caching; a correct measure of cacheability and traffic reduction is therefore fundamental to assess the impact and/or the potential benefits of such solutions.

Characterization of web traffic usually means logging the IDs of the requested objects along with a timestamp; some further details can be collected almost effortlessly, like the content type and in some cases the size of the object. The methodology of collection varies, and the accuracy of the results also varies consequently.

The next step is analysis or post processing of the logs, in order to extract the required statistics. Cacheability and traffic reduction, as

ICN'14, September 24–26, 2014, Paris, France.
ACM 978-1-4503-3206-4/14/09.
http://dx.doi.org/10.1145/2660129.2660135 .

introduced in [1, 4], are very important metrics, as pointed before. In order to quickly and accurately calculate those values, a log is needed containing all the requested objects, the time of the request and the real amount of traffic generated.

There are already some tools that perform HTTP traffic analysis [3, 6, 7, 9], only some of which are publicly available. The performace and the accuracy of the publicly available tools is in general not satisfactory for some kinds of traffic analysis, especially in relation to cacheability.

Tstat [5] performs a packet-level analysis of HTTP connections, this allows it to operate quickly and with a reduced memory footprint, but on the other hand it misses many details. In most cases the Content-Length field of the object is missed because it didn't appear in the first packet of the reply.

Bro is an intrusion detection system, meant to protect a single host, and not to be executed at line speed in an operational network; it is however used in the research community to generate traces of HTTP traffic [2, 8].

Table 1 shows a comparison of HACkSAw with the other publicly available tools performed on the same hardware and on the same 1-hour packet-level trace; 0-length replies are those replies to HTTP requests where the length of the content is either zero or missing, and CPU is the cumulative runtime of all threads. It

Tool	Detected Requests	CPU [sec]	Memory [GB]	0-length replies
Tstat	2 531 210	445	0.3	1 128 109
bro	2 559 056	8033	4.2	424 355
HACkSAw	2 426 391	368	5.8	328 465

Table 1: Performance of bro, Tstat and HACkSAw.

can be seen that bro is too slow and tstat is inaccurate. In both cases both bro and Tstat only report the Content-Length field from the HTTP headers. There are many cases in which such header is unavailable; in cases where the chunked HTTP Transfer-Encoding was used, for example, the total size of the object is not known in advance. HACkSAw manages to be both fast and accurate thanks to its simple, yet effective, implementation; some key features include:

- the full TCP stream is reconstructed, therefore the full HTTP headers are available and the real size of the downloaded object is available.

- no per-packet pattern matching is performed to identify HTTP requests, the payload is skipped, thus significantly lowering the CPU consumption

- multithreading; can scale up almost linearly with more processors

While our tool does require a significant amount of memory, it was successfully used uninterruptedly over a period of one month to collect statistics on a real access network (see [4]).

Only clear-text connections can be analysed, as obviously no dissection of SSL traffic is possible. Although the amount of HTTPS traffic is rising with time, especially since popular websites like Facebook or YouTube started to push in that direction, and therefore potentially rendering this approach useless in the long run, we measured in our observations that, currently, only approximately 15% of the total HTTP traffic is HTTPS.

2. STATISTICS

In addition to the usual statistics collected by other tools, like for example the client ID, the object ID, the hostname or the User-Agent string, HACkSAw also collects many statistics that other tools neglect, like the time between the HTTP request and the HTTP reply or the first byte of content; the indication whether cookies or ETAG headers were used, the size of the headers, and the byte-range in case of range(partial) request.

The results collected by the tool allow to easily compute aggregate statistics as shown in [4]; those aggregate statistics are calculated with a simple post-processing of the output log of the tool, which is in plain text. The relevant statistics that can be calculated easily are:

- Request cacheability (the share of HTTP requests that can potentially be cached in a given timeframe)

- Traffic reduction (the percentage of actual traffic potentially saved assuming all cacheable items are pre-fetched during off-peak hours)

- Virtual cache size (the minimum cache size needed to cache all cacheable content, assuming perfect "oracle" replacement strategy)

- Average number of HTTP requests per connection (many connections perform more than one HTTP request, as per HTTP/1.1)

- Share of requests with cookies and/or ETAG (ETAG headers potentially indicate different content for the same URL; the presence of cookies generally hinders cacheability)

- download completion of requests (for each request, the percentage of bytes of the object actually downloaded by the client; values under 100% thus indicate that the object was not downloaded completely)

- average actual throughput and average latency of requests (time between the first and the last byte of content, and between start of the HTTP request and the first byte of content, respectively)

3. DEMONSTRATION

The tool will be run live on the conference network, as it is as close to the actual access network as we can get; relevant statistics will be computed from the anonymized output of the tool and shown almost live, with a small delay to allow for processing.

Some of the statistics that will be shown (apart from the classical ones like total traffic, number of HTTP requests, etc), are those presented above in section 2.

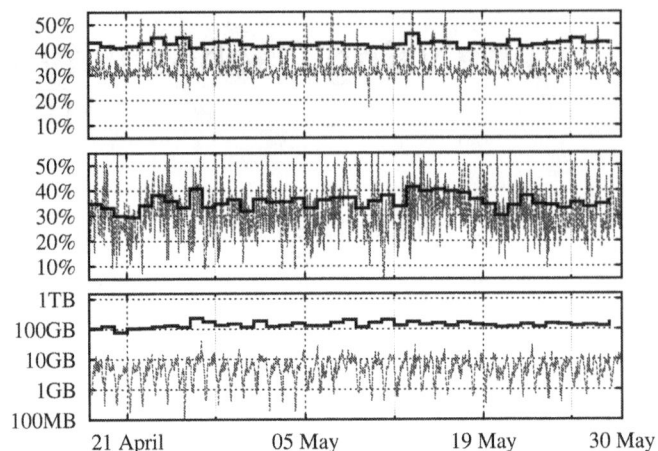

Figure 1: Timeseries of Requests cacheability (top), Traffic reduction (middle) and Virtual cache size (bottom); 1 day aggregate (thick black line) and 1 hour aggregate (thin blue line) calculated on the data gathered in [4].

All statistics will be computed over different timescales, from 1 hour to 1 day; figure 1 shows an example of some of the presentation of the statistics that will be shown in the demo.

4. REFERENCES

[1] B. Ager, F. Schneider, J. Kim, and A. Feldmann. Revisiting Cacheability in Times of User Generated Content. In *Proc. of IEEE INFOCOM*, 2010.

[2] B. Ager, F. Schneider, J. Kim, and A. Feldmann. Revisiting cacheability in times of user generated content. In *INFOCOM IEEE Conference on Computer Communications Workshops , 2010*, pages 1–6, March 2010.

[3] A. Finamore, M. Mellia, M. Meo, M. Munafo, and D. Rossi. Experiences of internet traffic monitoring with tstat. *IEEE Network Magazine*, May 2011.

[4] C. Imbrenda, L. Muscariello, and D. Rossi. Analyzing cacheable traffic in isp access networks for micro cdn applications via content-centric networking. In *Proc. of ACM ICN*, 2014.

[5] M. Mellia and al. http://tstat.tlc.polito.it.

[6] V. Paxson. http://www.bro.org.

[7] B. Ramanan, L. Drabeck, M. Haner, N. Nithi, T. Klein, and C. Sawkar. Cacheability analysis of HTTP traffic in an operational LTE network. In *In Proc. of WTS*, 2013.

[8] F. Schneider, B. Ager, G. Maier, A. Feldmann, and S. Uhlig. Pitfalls in HTTP Traffic Measurements and Analysis. In *Proc. of PAM*, 2012.

[9] S. Woo, E. Jeong, S. Park, J. Lee, S. Ihm, and K. Park. Comparison of caching strategies in modern cellular backhaul networks. In *Proc. of ACM MobiSys*, 2013.

Demo Overview: HTTP Live Streaming over NetInf Transport

Bengt Ahlgren
SICS
bengta@sics.se

Arndt Jonasson
SICS
arndt@sics.se

Börje Ohlman
Ericsson
borje.ohlman@ericsson.com

ABSTRACT

We modified a commercial Android TV app to use NetInf ICN transport. It was straightforward to adapt the standard HTTP Live Streaming to NetInf naming and network service. We demonstrate that NetInf's in-network caching and request aggregation result in efficient live TV distribution.

Categories and Subject Descriptors

C.2.1 [**Computer-Communication Networks**]: Network Architecture and Design

Keywords

Information-centric networking; NetInf; Live streaming; HLS; In-network caching

1. INTRODUCTION

Information-centric networking (ICN) [1] is an approach for designing the network of the future based on *named data objects* (NDOs) as the main abstraction. Clients request NDOs by name and publishers make NDOs available. The location of an NDO is secondary – any node holding a copy can satisfy a request for it, enabling ubiquitous in-network caching as part of the normal network service. The ICN approach was largely motivated by large scale media distribution which is dominating the Internet traffic volume, both playback of stored content and broadcast of live content.

We demonstrate live video streaming with NetInf ICN transport [2, 5] to a modified commercial TV app on Android devices. The standard HTTP Live Streaming (HLS) [6] format was adapted to the NetInf network service. The adaptation was straightforward, but required extending the NetInf implementation with support for dynamic data. The demo shows that NetInf's in-network caching and request aggregation provide efficient multicast distribution to many clients, off-loading the server and reducing network load.

ICN'14, September 24–26, 2014, Paris, France.
ACM 978-1-4503-3206-4/14/09.
http://dx.doi.org/10.1145/2660129.2660136.


```
ni://example.com/sha-256;wFNeS-K3n_2T
KRMFQ2v4iTFOSj-uwF7P_Lt98xrZ5Ro
```

Figure 1: Example 'ni' name for the named data object "Hello world!".

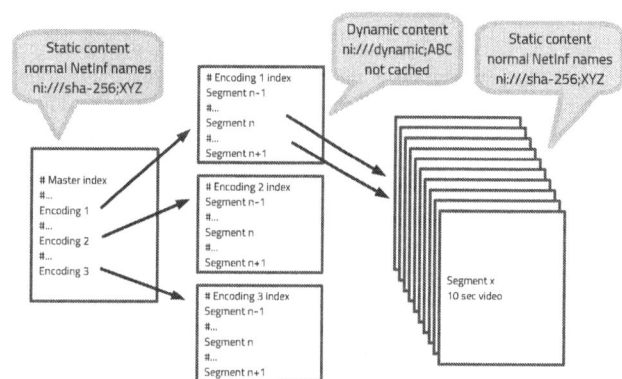

Figure 2: Live HLS video mapping to NetInf transport.

2. THE NETINF PROTOCOL

Network of Information (NetInf) [2] is an ICN architecture mainly developed in the SAIL EU FP7 project [4]. The project designed the 'ni' naming scheme for NetInf which has become IETF RFC 6920 [3]. The URI-encoded 'ni' names contain the content hash, or message digest, of the NDO, as shown in Figure 1. *Name-data integrity*, that is, verification of that the NDO received is the NDO requested, a crucial function of any information-centric network, is directly provided by the content hash.

The NetInf protocol has three major functions: `GET`, `PUBLISH` and `SEARCH`. Clients request NDOs by sending `GET` messages which are forwarded hop-by-hop by NetInf routers towards publishers. Any intermediate node that has a requested NDO, ultimately the publisher, responds with the corresponding `GET-RESP` message supplying the NDO. `PUBLISH` is used to make NDOs available, and `SEARCH` can be used to find out what NDOs are available. NetInf also has a name resolution-based model, complementing the hop-by-hop forwarding, which is not used in this demo.

3. MAPPING HLS TO NETINF

Figure 2 illustrates the three kinds of files defined by HTTP Live Streaming (HLS) and how they are mapped to NetInf. A master index file (left in the figure) lists the available video encodings, including information on bit rates. The content of the master index file is static and can therefore be named with standard hash-based

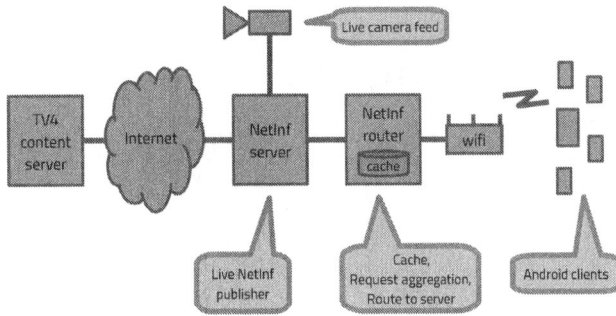

Figure 3: Setup of NetInf live streaming demo.

'ni' names. The content of the file, however, has to be modified for NetInf transport by listing the 'ni' names of the encoding-specific segment index files (middle in the figure).

When a new video segment (right in the figure) has finished recording for the live stream, the segment index files must be updated. The three most current video segments are typically listed. We have chosen to define a new name type for NDOs with dynamic content to handle this, since 'ni' names based on content hashes do not support dynamic data. The alternative would be to create new names for the segment index files after each update, but that in turn requires that the master index file has to be modified, resulting in other problems. The new name type has to use publisher signatures in order to provide name-data integrity. This is however not yet implemented in the demo. Similar to the master index file, the content of the segment index files are changed to list the video segment files by their 'ni' names.

The segment index file regularly has to be re-requested by the clients so that the clients learn the names of new video segment files. These video segment files do not change after they are recorded, and therefore regular hash-based 'ni' names work well. When a client learns the name of a new video segment file, it requests and plays back that segment.

Finally, we have turned off in-network caching for the segment index files. Otherwise the clients would never get the updates and learn the names of new video segments. It would, however, be beneficial with time-limited caching so that the distribution of these files to many clients becomes more scalable.

4. THE DEMO SETUP

Figure 3 illustrates the setup of the demo. There are two possible sources for the video: the public servers for the live and stored TV content of the Swedish TV4 channel, and our own video camera. The 'NetInf server' in the figure publishes either of these video streams in real time in the NetInf system.

A set of Android clients are illustrated at the right hand side of the figure. These run a modified version of the TV4 app that can use the NetInf network service for retrieving the HLS-encoded video streams. There is a NetInf router in between that cache NDOs, except the segment index files. The router implements aggregation of requests, which means that simultaneous requests for the same NDO from multiple clients, which is likely to happen for live streaming, result in a single request being sent upstreams to the server.

The clients and the router forward GET requests towards the server with default next-hop forwarding. There is a clear need for a more advanced scheme in larger setups.

An Android NetInf implementation from Ericsson is run on the clients, and the open source NetInf Python implementation devel-

oped as part of the SAIL EU project[1] is run on the server and router with Ubuntu Linux. The NetInf Python implementation has been extended with request aggregation and simple names for dynamic NDOs.

5. RESULTS AND CONCLUSIONS

We have adapted a commercial HTTP Live Streaming system to use NetInf ICN transport. The implemented system demonstrator shows the feasibility and performance of live video streaming to several clients. The caching and request aggregation of the NetInf transport result in efficient multicast to many clients. The caching removes the need for synchronisation between the clients, in contrast to the synchronous nature of IP multicast.

It was straightforward to adapt HTTP Live Streaming to use NetInf ICN transport. A naming scheme for the dynamic segment index files had to be designed and implemented for the demo.

6. ACKNOWLEDGEMENTS

This work has been supported by the EFRAIM project funded by Vinnova in the challenge-driven innovation programme, and by EIT ICT Labs. Many colleagues have considerably contributed to this work, especially Linus Sunde at Ericsson Research and Anders Lindgren at SICS. We also thank Swedish TV4, partner in EFRAIM, for making their Android app available for our experiments.

7. REFERENCES

[1] B. Ahlgren, C. Dannewitz, C. Imbrenda, D. Kutscher, and B. Ohlman. A survey of information-centric networking. *IEEE Communications Magazine*, 50(7):26–36, July 2012.

[2] C. Dannewitz, D. Kutscher, B. Ohlman, S. Farrell, B. Ahlgren, and H. Karl. Network of information (NetInf) – an information-centric networking architecture. *Computer Communications*, 36(7):721–735, Apr. 2013.

[3] S. Farrell, D. Kutscher, C. Dannewitz, B. Ohlman, A. Keranen, and P. Hallam-Baker. Naming Things with Hashes. RFC 6920 (Proposed Standard), Apr. 2013.

[4] B. Kauffmann, J.-F. Peltier, et al. D.B.3 (D-3.3) final NetInf architecture. Deliverable D-3.3, version 1.1, SAIL EU FP7 Project 257448, Jan. 2013. FP7-ICT-2009-5-257448/D.B.3.

[5] D. Kutscher, S. Farrell, and E. Davies. The NetInf Protocol. Internet-Draft draft-kutscher-icnrg-netinf-proto-01, Internet Engineering Task Force, Feb. 2013. Work in progress.

[6] R. Pantos and W. May. HTTP live streaming. Internet-Draft draft-pantos-http-live-streaming-12, IETF Secretariat, Oct. 2013. Work in Progress.

---

[1]See http://www.netinf.org, and http://sourceforge.net/projects/netinf/.

Multi-party Conference over Virtual Service Edge Router (VSER) Platform

Asit Chakraborti†, Vinodkumar Rajaraman‡, Shuai Zhao§, Aytac Azgin†, Ravishankar Ravindran†, and Guoqiang Wang†

†Huawei Research Center, Santa Clara, CA, USA.
{asit.chakraborti, aytac.azgin, ravi.ravindran, gq.wang}@huawei.com

‡Infinite Computer Solutions, Chennai, India. vinodkumarr@infinite.com
§University of Missouri-Kansas City, MO, USA. shuai.zhao@mail.umkc.edu

ABSTRACT

Realizing large scale multi-party conference is a challenge today when realtime and high bandwidth multimedia components are involved due to lack of scalability of server and bandwidth resources. We demonstrate a scalable conference design over the Virtual Service Edge Router (VSER) platform which is an ICN edge service router with the capability of hosting arbitrary realtime and non-realtime services as virtual machines (VM). The platform services are orchestrated through a programmable framework and takes advantage of scalable forwarding plane for content distribution.

1. INTRODUCTION

Scalability challenges of IP based multi-party conference solutions when bandwidth consuming media streams such as video are involved has been shown in many studies, e.g. [2]. In server based solutions, the server is the bottleneck; while P2P based solution suffer from the per-participant processing and uplink bottleneck constraint. Studying different commercial systems, [2] observes server based systems offer better performance compared to P2P architectures and scale to a maximum of 20 active participants, albeit with poor overall QoE. ICN (CCN [1] in our case) can address bandwidth scaling through network-level content abstraction over per-participant namespace, thereby enabling large scale multicast of user's media. The service scaling is addressed by the Virtual Service Edge Router (VSER) platform comprising of distributed CCN-based service edge routers managed by a service orchestrator based on NFV and SDN frameworks. A problem from applying CCN directly to realtime conference is the lack of knowledge of a producer's latest content name by the consuming participants. Chronos [4] addresses this through a serverless digest synchronizing mechanism that suffers from multiple simultaneous updates and failure recovery issues; also this proposal doesn't naturally support

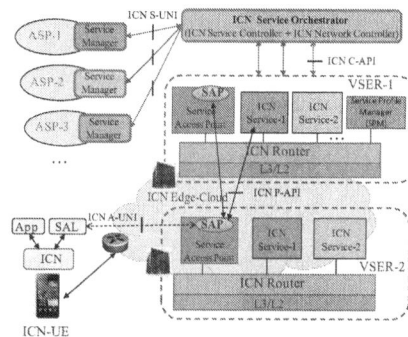

Figure 1: VSER platform architecture.

realtime audio or video sessions.

We propose a *Push* based solution on the VSER platform. To aid multi-party conference, service instances are realized that help synchronize content *fingerprints* (*i.e.* unique name component suffixes of the *content*-ID) among participants, where a participant maps to one of these service instances over VSER. Once the fingerprint is learnt, the content is *Pulled* by the consumer through the CCN forwarding plane. While this approach scales to many participants for text-based chat with generous QoE requirements, the synchronization latency is too high for participants generating realtime audio or video stream. We adapt our scheme on such streams by enabling periodic notifications over multiple encoded audio-video frames, and taking advantage of Interest pipelining to retrieve them. Recovery from user entity's (UE) transient or long term failures, discussed in [3], is also easy to handle in this model as only two entities, *i.e.* the UE and the service instance are involved during the recovery.

Service provisioning and name-based routing between these VMs are controlled by conference-specific service and network controllers. In general, the VSER platform can host any service ranging from content distribution, conferencing, or an IoT application controlled by respective service controller application.

2. CONFERENCE OVER VSER PLATFORM

The VSER platform is envisioned as a service hosting CCN edge router to enable service contextualization (*e.g.* mobility, user preference adaptation) and customization (*e.g.* geography preference, service scaling) through Open-APIs to consumers and application service providers (ASP). The

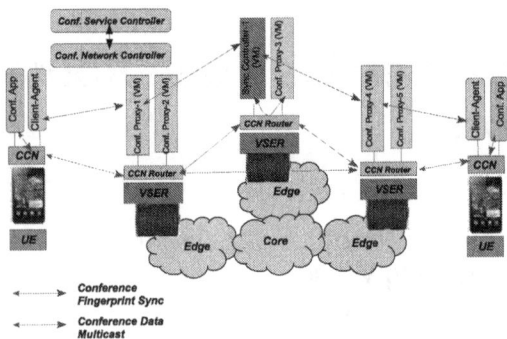

Figure 2: VSER based conference architecture.

VSER platform shown in Fig. 1 is discussed in [3]. The key components of the architecture are the service access layer (SAL) on the UE that aids service discovery and service context expression; service access point (SAP) per VSER node to help UE applications connect to services, and help device or service context adaptation; global service profile manager (SPM) manages the database of active services; VSER forwarding plane is based on CCN; and the ICN service orchestration layer with service and network controller components to conduct service provisioning and dynamic name-based routing based on factors affecting the service.

The conference solution proposed in [3] is shown in Fig. 2. Here participants are connected to distributed VSER nodes and serviced by two service components (realized as VMs): *Conference Proxy* (*cPrx*) and the *Sync Controller* (*sCon*). To aid chat application sync its fingerprints, *client-agent* in the UE helps push them to the serving *cPrx*. *sCon* and *cPrxs* forms a hub-and-spoke topology to support faster synchronization and recovery from transient failures. The provisioning of *cPrx* and *sCon* is managed by a *conference service controller*, and routing between client-agent and *cPrx*, among *sCon* and *cPrx* instances, and the UEs is managed by the *conference network controller*. We evaluated the scalability performance of the architecture in [3] using simulations. The results on convergence time for the multi-party *video* conference for varying number of participants is shown in Fig. 4(a). Here the participants are equally distributed among the *cPrx* instances. The two plots correspond to the convergence among consumers local to the producer hosted by the same *cPrx* and those hosted by remote *cPrxs*.

3. CONFERENCE DEMO

The demo is realized on two Dell PowerEdge M1000e chassis, each with a high end blade (12 cores, 128GB) for CCN forwarding and two lower end blades to host the VMs. The forwarding engine follows the CCNx1.0 protocol specification [1]. The demo set-up shown in Fig. 3, begins by the user (ASP) providing conference provisioning parameters such as conference service namespace, chat room name, and the maximum number of users to the conference controller interface that is normalized to the number of conference service functions (*cPrx* and *sCon* (VMs)) to be provisioned in the VSERs. The provisioning event is notified to the conference network controller that in turn programs VSER's FIB to inter-connect *cPrx* and *sCon* functions. The UE then discovers the provisioned chat rooms through the SAL by querying the SAP. This information is notified to the ap-

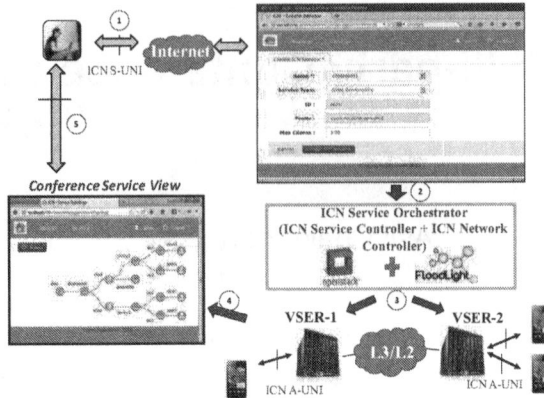

Figure 3: VSER platform based conference demo.

plication which joins a chat room through a user initiated action. The join action results in learning the control namespace, the list of active participants and their corresponding participant-specific content namespace to allow participant interaction. The smart clients interact through rich text, audio, and video.

Extended OpenStack and Floodlight realize the ICN conference service and network controller. A conference application controller over the network controller has a real-time view of conference topology such as the mapping of *cPrx* and *sCon* VMs to the VSERs, and participant list corresponding to each *cPrx* instance. Similar parallel views exist when multiple simultaneous conference sessions are provisioned. The prototype is evaluated by emulating up to 48 participants. Fig. 4(b) shows relative invariance of convergence time for varying number of active chat participants distributed over two VSER nodes hosting a *sCon* and two *cPrx* instances.

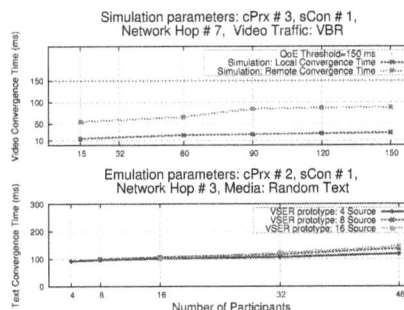

Figure 4: VSER convergence performance: (a)simulation, (b)emulation

4. REFERENCES

[1] CCNx1.0 protocol specification, http://www.ietf.org/mail-archive/web/icnrg/current/pdfZyEQRE5tFS.pdf.

[2] Y. Lu, Y. Zhao, F. Kuipers, and P. Van Mieghem. Measurement study of multi-party video conferencing. In *IFIP Networking*, 2010.

[3] R. Ravindran, X. Liu, A. Chakraborti, X. Zhang, and G. Wang. Towards software defined icn based edge-cloud services. In *CloudNet*, 2013.

[4] Z. Zhu, C. Bian, A. Afanasyev, V. Jacobson, and L. Zhang. Chronos: Serverless multi-user chat over ndn. Technical report, NDN-0008, 2012.

Scalable Control Panel for Media Streaming in NDN

Kai Lei, LongYu Yu

School of Electronics and Computer Engineering (SECE),
Peking University, Shenzhen 518055, P.R. China

leik@pkusz.edu.cn

1201213683@sz.pku.edu.cn

Jun Wei

Samsung Research America, Silicon Valley

jun01.wei@samsung.com

ABSTRACT

An NDN-based scalable control panel for a media streaming system was designed and implemented in this paper. The system is developed based on a previous IP-based P2P media streaming system named Hippo [1], which contains a group of control servers to manipulate P2P functionalities, such as the tracker, etc. System scalability becomes one of the most difficult problems when the user size of P2P system grows very large. We took the advantages from the same principle of SNC [2] to design the NDN-Hippo's control layer. As for implementation, we took a two-step approach: First porting the control layer of Hippo to NDN-based system, then porting media traffic layer later. By separating control and media layers, our demo demonstrates that not only some management functions of tracker can be smartly and instinctively achieved in NDN, but also the scalability of NDN version of Hippo has been greatly improved.

Categories and Subject Descriptors

C.2.1 [Network Architecture and Design]: Network communications.

Keywords

P2P; NDN; SNC; Media Streaming

1. INTRODUCTION

Hippo [1], an IP based P2P VOD streaming system, was developed by The Center for Internet Research Engineering (CIRE) at Peking University. Like many other P2P systems, Hippo's control relies heavily on a tracker system. It is difficult to scale the tracker system when the user size of Hippo grows large. We ported Hippo to NDN with a scalable control layer described in SNC [2]. As for implementation, we took a two-step approach: First porting the control layer of Hippo to NDN-based system, then porting media traffic layer later.

In this demo, it presents the architecture of the new NDN control layer for NDN-Hippo, which is based on SNC. It shows that NDN-based control system is easier to manage than that of its IP-

based counterpart. The server failover of NDN-Hippo requires no additional specific design compared to IP-Hippo. The media traffic part of the system has not finished yet, but it would not impact our demonstration since these two layers work independently.

2. SYSTEM ARCHITECTURE

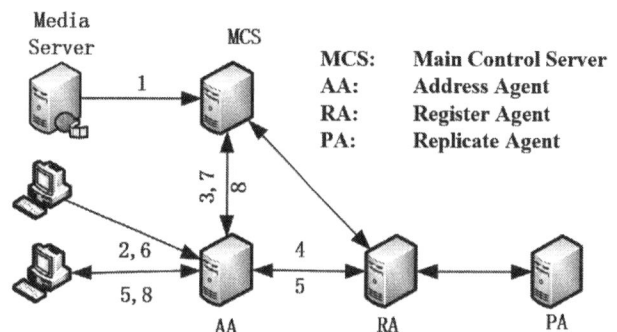

Figure 1: The architecture of the system

The Hippo media system is separated into two layers, one is the control layer and the other is the media layer. The control layer is responsible for system operation like user and server management, while the media layer is mainly responsible for streaming data sharing, transportation and distribution. This kind of architecture has two benefits. First, it separates the mass of media data and the small quantity of light-weighted control data. Second, it separates the control and the data function.

The control layer notifies the median layer with available data source information, having replaced the tracker of IP-based Hippo. Similar to many other P2P media systems, Hippo relies on a centralized server, which brings problems like single point of failure or traffic over concentration. It often gets into large scalability problems.

We reference SNC and modify the design of NDN-Hippo to suit for Hippo's need. Similar to SNC, when a new user joins, NDN provides the nearest server from the server pool. This select is implemented by a suppress mechanism, which can inform the other nodes to stop when the nearest node receives the interest.

The Hippo's control system architecture is shown in [1], including the following four components:

1. The Main Control Server (MCS) is the main node that initializes the server pool. Other server nodes ask it for a unique ID in the system. It also takes the

responsibility for controlling the distribution of media address information.

2. The RA (Register Agent) is the node that clients register, and it allocates the group ID for clients, generating a code for client authentication.

3. The PA (Replicate Agent) is in charge of backup the state of other nodes, preparing for recovery whenever other nodes fail-over.

4. The AA (Address Agent) provides service with the name follow SNC. It accepts the request of client, and provides verification and returns the relevant data.

In addition, there is a Hippo control server named Media Server responses for activate the MCS.

These four kinds of nodes except the Media Server are not running at beginning. They all are installed in every node of the server pool, and only run after someone calls them. The agent running firstly is the MCS. It must be called by Media Server, and will serve the other agent.

From that time, the other agents can join the cluster. MCS will request replicate service, so the nearest node will run the PA. And users will request the data it need, which will firstly select a node to be AA. After that AA will select a RA to register. These 3 nodes need to ask MCS for an ID before they run their service. The system works as follows:

Register: 1) The Media Server assigns a nearest server as the MCS, which signifies the server pool is created. 2) One client registers in the server cluster by sending an interest to it. 3) The node who receives the interest joins the server pool by sending an interest to MCS to apply an ID. 4) Then it requests the RA to process the registering. 5) After request, RA produces an access code and returns back to the client, the client can use it to request media service.

Request Data: 6) Then the client can send an interest to request the data with the access code. 7) The AA which receives the interest authenticates the access code, and requests data from MCS. The AA can be ever server in this cluster. 8) Then returns the data back to client.

3. DEMONSTRATION

In this demo, we demonstrate 1) the NDN-based Hippo control system allows users to select the nearest control server; 2) the failover of Hippo server is automatically supported; 3) the Hippo registration work flow in NDN. We build a simple test system as shown in Figure 2. The implementation uses CCNx.

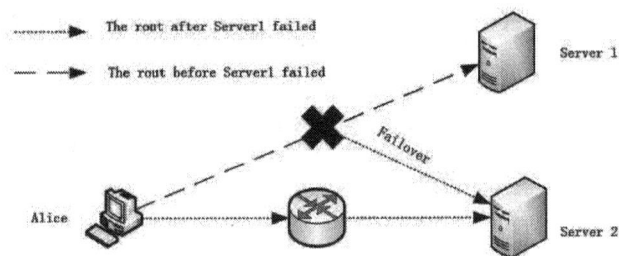

Figure 2: The Network Topology

3.1 Server selection from server pool

Similar to SNC, we implement suppression mechanism in Hippo control system. With suppression, each server delays its response by a delayed timer before returning a suppression interest message. Upon receiving suppression message, a server suppresses its pending response.

With carefully designed suppression mechanism, usually a server that is nearby responds first to a user's registration request. This process is demonstrated in our implementation of Hippo NDN-based control layer.

3.2 Server failover

The server failover in Hippo is handled by heartbeat mechanism. It becomes difficult to manage when introducing server cluster for large size of Hippo users.

The NDN-based Hippo tracker server cluster supports failover automatically without addition effort. There is no need to maintain heartbeat with tracker server. Upon failure of a server, the second nearest server from the server cluster will be automatically pick up and serve.

In our system in [2], the four different servers act a little differently upon failure. MCS and RA need to save data in the Replicate server, so that if they failed, other nodes can request the back-up and take place of them. Detail design is similar to SNC. The failover for AA is straightforward. The client only needs to send interest as normal and there will be another tracker server from the cluster pops up and automatically handles the request.

3.3 Registration process

The register function and the server-less distribution are the important features of this system. To validate the set-up, we put some information in the system. Then we can register in and access the data from different node in this system.

4. REFERENCES

[1] Kai LEI, Lihua Li, Cheng Peng, Longyu Yu, "HIPPO: an Adaptive, Scalable, Hierarchical P2P Live Streaming System", CSETIS 2014, Guilin, China, Mar.2014.

[2] Debessay Fesehaye, Jun Wei, "SNC: Scalable NDN-Based Conferencing Architecture", IEEE CCNC, Las Vegas, NV, Jan 10-13, 2014

Matryoshka: Design of NDN Multiplayer Online Game

Zhehao Wang
REMAP, University of California,
Los Angeles
102 East Melnitz Hall
Los Angeles, CA 90095
zhehao.mail@gmail.com

Zening Qu
REMAP, University of California,
Los Angeles
102 East Melnitz Hall
Los Angeles, CA 90095
quzening@gmail.com

Jeff Burke
REMAP, University of California,
Los Angeles
102 East Melnitz Hall
Los Angeles, CA 90095
jburke@remap.ucla.edu

ABSTRACT

Massive multiplayer online games (MOG) have become increasingly popular over the past decade. Peer-to-peer structures were explored for commercial online games. However, maintaining security and availability while scaling users has driven most multiplayer online games towards a client-server or client-superpeer architecture.

Client-server multiplayer games face certain problems: a small number of points of failure and traffic centralizing at several servers. Users of popular games complain about the decrease in quality of service, largely caused by these two factors. In order to tackle the problems of traditional client-server online games, this demo presents Matryoshka, a pure peer-to-peer multiplayer online game using the named data networking[1] (NDN) future internet architecture.

NDN has several major strengths over IP; among them are natural multicast support, content-based security and mobility support. By utilizing the strength of multicast and content caching, we believe that a pure peer-to-peer MOG design in NDN can avoid challenges and limitations found in IP.

Synchronization in a serverless distributed environment is a key problem for pure peer-to-peer structure. Namespace synchronization in just such a situation has been studied for other serverless NDN applications like chat and file sharing. The ChronoSync[2] model is proposed for both use cases. Other cases like vehicular network also study synchronization in a physical environment.

The challenges faced by an online game are different, which we explore in this project. In this case, the environment is a virtual world. Each player has an area of interest, and it only needs to know things in this virtual area instead of everything happening in the game, and this we define as 'locality in the game world'. In addition,

ICN'14, September 24–26, 2014, Paris, France.
Copyright © 2014 ACM 978-1-4503-3206-4/14/09...$15.00.
http://dx.doi.org/10.1145/2660129.2660139

players whose areas of interest intersect with each other should reach consistent conclusions about things in the intersected area, which introduces the synchronization problem.

NDN's content caching and natural multicast support feature may facilitate the distribution of game synchronization data. We utilize these features by statically and recursively partitioning the whole virtual environment into octants, thus providing a shared namespace for every peer running the game. Then, all the peers that care about the same region can share the data brought by synchronization interests towards the same nodes in the octree. Figure 1 presents the octree partition of the game world.

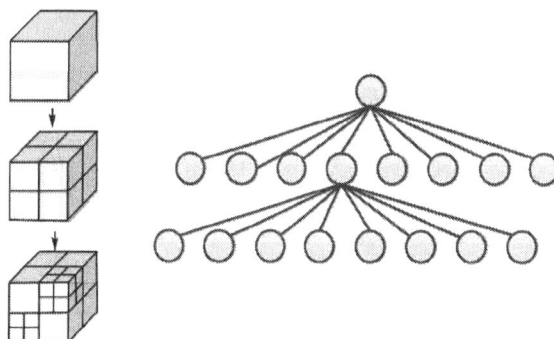

Figure 1 Octree partition of the game world

Then, we apply a two-step synchronization to deal with the two questions which each peer addresses the network: "which players are in my vicinity" (*discovery*) and "what are those players doing" (*update*). Below we explain this mechanism and present the namespace design.

For the first question, peers who care about the same octant synchronize their name dataset belonging to the octant. To do this, discovery interests containing the octant indices and a digest of the octant's set of object names are expressed periodically to all peers in a "broadcast" namespace. Peers receiving the discovery interest respond with their own set of object names, if they have different digests for the octant.

The namespace for discovery is given in Figure 2. The top-level game name component separates the game into several sub-worlds, and only players in the same sub-world need to discover each other. Below the sub-world are octant indices, which indicate the octant's absolute location in the game world. For each interest, we append a digest component, which contains the hash of the set of object name strings in that octant. Every peer should have the same hash for octants belonging to their intersection, when steady state is reached.

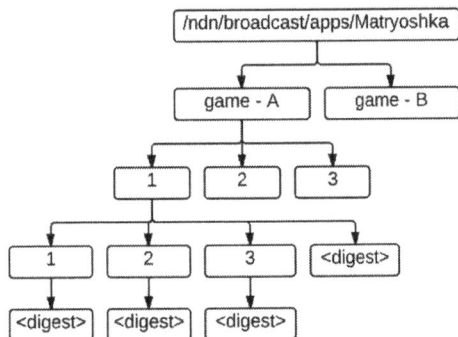

Figure 2. Broadcast discovery namespace

Using the object names returned in response to the discovery interest, update interests are expressed by each peer on an ongoing basis for the virtual location of the players and several non-player characters (NPC) that remain in their area of interest. The requesting peer decides whether the resulting objects should be recorded and rendered in the local game instance.

Figure 3 demonstrates the update namespace. Each physical peer running the game is represented by a globally unique process name. In each process, a variety of objects—e.g., player and NPCs as well as other elements of the game—are hosted. For each object, interests are expressed for its position and actions using the namespace as shown. Position and action names follow NDN versioning conventions, enabling interest selectors to be used to ensure the latest version is received by the requesting peer.

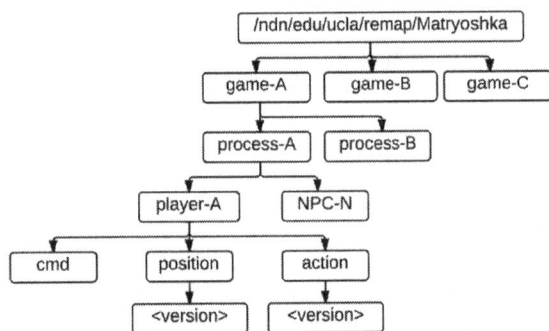

Figure 3. Position and action update namespace

Our approach also explores techniques for progressive discovery, an optimization for leveraging the usage of larger octants, as well as dynamic adjustment of the area of interest for a player.

Representing a player's spherical areas of interest with only leaf octants can cause the amount of discovery interests to be large, thus increasing synchronization traffic. Progressive discovery aims to allow peers to issue interest packets corresponding to larger octants, so that we can approximate spherical areas of interest with fewer interests. In this case, a peer may receive synchronization interests for large octants, about which it may have incomplete knowledge. Our approach balances the impact of unanswered interests vs. incomplete responses by having answering peers wait to reply with a delay proportional to the completeness of their knowledge of the requested octant. Further, the requesting peer adjusts the area of interest based on response performance. For example, when the latency in discovery interests getting answered is large (suggesting few peers with knowledge), or the number of objects in a player's area of interest exceeds a preconfigured threshold (resulting in a lot of traffic), the game application automatically shrinks the area of interest.

The demo application *Matryoshka*, a game environment implementing the design outlined above, was built using Unity3D game engine, and ndn-dot-net, a C# adaptation of NDN Common Client Library. The demo will show the game code running on a small number of peers, and with a visualization of the network traffic going on in the two namespaces as players navigate the game world on each peer.

For the demo, player characters and NPCs are instantiated by each peer, and each peer can navigate around the common world using their player character. Player and NPC discovery, and position update under several preferences and scenarios will be demonstrated. Challenging scenarios to handle with static octree partitioning, such as having players that are close to the border between two sub-regions of the highest subdivision hierarchy, will be shown in addition to easier to handle situations.

Categories and Subject Descriptors
C.2.4 [**Distributed Systems**]: Distributed Application

Keywords
Massive multiplayer online game; named data networking; synchronization

REFERENCES
[1] V. Jacobson, D. K. Smetters, J. D. Thornton, M. F. Plass, N. H. Briggs, R. L. Braynard. 2009. Networking Named Content. CoNEXT 2009, Rome, Dec. 2009. DOI=http://doi.acm.org/10.1145/1658939.1658941.

[2] Z. Zhu, A. Afanasyev. 2013. Let's ChronoSync: Decentralized dataset state synchronization in Named Data Networking. ICNP 2013, Oct. 2013. DOI=http://dx.doi.org/10.1109/ICNP.2013.6733578.

Authur Index